Pearson's Commitment to Diversity, Equity, and Inclusion

Pearson is dedicated to creating bias-free content that reflects the diversity of all learners. We embrace the many dimensions of diversity, including but not limited to race, ethnicity, gender, socioeconomic status, ability, age, sexual orientation, and religious or political beliefs.

Education is a powerful force for equity and change in our world. It has the potential to deliver opportunities that improve lives and enable economic mobility. As we work with authors to create content for every product and service, we acknowledge our responsibility to demonstrate inclusivity and incorporate diverse scholarship so that everyone can achieve their potential through learning. As the world's leading learning company, we have a duty to help drive change and live up to our purpose to help more people create a better life for themselves and to create a better world.

Our ambition is to purposefully contribute to a world where:

- Everyone has an equitable and lifelong opportunity to succeed through learning.

- Our educational products and services are inclusive and represent the rich diversity of learners.

- Our educational content accurately reflects the histories and experiences of the learners we serve.

- Our educational content prompts deeper discussions with learners and motivates them to expand their own learning (and worldview).

While we work hard to present unbiased content, we want to hear from you about any concerns or needs with this Pearson product so that we can investigate and address them.

- Please contact us with concerns about any potential bias at https://www.pearson.com/report-bias.html.

Contents at a Glance

Contents

Chapter 9   Working with math functions   189

Chapter 12   Building inferential statistical formulas   259

Chapter 19 Using Excel's business modeling tools   417

Chapter 20 Solving complex problems with Solver   439

Acknowledgments

Substitute damn every time you're inclined to write very; your editor will delete it and the writing will be just as it should be.

—*Mark Twain*

I didn't follow Mark Twain's advice in this book (the word *very* appears throughout), but if my writing still appears "just as it should be," then it's because of the keen minds and sharp linguistic eyes of the editors at Pearson Education. Near the front of the book, you'll find a long list of the hard-working professionals whose fingers made it into this particular paper pie. However, there are a few folks I worked with directly, so I'd like to single them out for extra credit. A big, heaping helping of thanks goes out to executive editor Loretta Yates, development and copy editor Rick Kughen, and technical editor Bob Umlas.

About the author

Paul McFedries is an Excel expert and full-time technical writer. Paul has been authoring computer books since 1991 and has more than 100 books to his credit, which combined have sold more than 4 million copies worldwide. His titles include the Que Publishing books *My Office 2016*, *Windows 10 In Depth* (with coauthor Brian Knittel), and *PCs for Grownups*, as well as the Sams Publishing book *Windows 7 Unleashed*. Please drop by Paul's personal website at paulmcfedries.com or follow Paul on Twitter (twitter.com/paulmcf) and Facebook (facebook.com/PaulMcFedries).

For companion files, you can visit the book's page at paulmcfedries.com, https://paulmcfedries.com/books/book.php?title=excel-365-formulas-and-functions, or at the Microsoft Press Store, MicrosoftPressStore.com/Excel365FormulasFunctions/downloads.

Introduction

The old 80/20 rule for software—that 80 percent of a program's users use only 20 percent of a program's features—doesn't apply to Microsoft Excel. Instead, this program probably operates under what could be called the 95/5 rule: Ninety-five percent of Excel users use a mere 5% of the program's power. On the other hand, most people *know* that they could be getting more out of Excel if they could only get a leg up on building formulas and using functions. Unfortunately, this side of Excel appears complex and intimidating to the uninitiated, shrouded as it is in the mysteries of mathematics, finance, and impenetrable spreadsheet jargon.

If this sounds like the situation you find yourself in, and if you're a businessperson who *needs* to use Excel as an everyday part of your job, you've come to the right book. In *Microsoft Excel Formulas and Functions (Office 2021 and Microsoft 365)*, I demystify the building of worksheet formulas and present the most useful of Excel's many functions in an accessible, jargon-free way. This book not only takes you through Excel's intermediate and advanced formula-building features, but it also tells you *why* these features are useful to you and shows you *how* to use them in everyday situations and real-world models. This book does all this with no-nonsense, step-by-step tutorials and lots of practical, useful examples aimed directly at business users.

Even if you've never been able to get Excel to do much beyond storing data and adding a couple of numbers, you'll find this book to your liking. I show you how to build useful, powerful formulas from the ground up, so no experience with Excel formulas and functions is necessary.

What's in the book

This book isn't meant to be read from cover to cover, although you're certainly free to do just that if the mood strikes you. Instead, most of the chapters are set up as self-contained units that you can dip into at will to extract whatever nuggets of information you need. However, if you're relatively new to Excel formulas and functions, I suggest starting with Chapter 1, "Building basic formulas," and Chapter 4, "Understanding functions," to ensure that you have a thorough grounding in the fundamentals.

The book is divided into four main parts. To give you the big picture before diving in, here's a summary of what you'll find in each part:

- **Part I, "Mastering Excel formulas"**—The three chapters in Part I tell you just about everything you need to know about building formulas in Excel. This part discusses operators, expressions, advanced formula features, and formula-troubleshooting techniques.

- **Part II, "Harnessing the power of functions"**—Functions take your formulas to the next level, and you learn all about them in Part II. After you see how to use functions in your formulas, you examine seven main function categories—text, logical, information, lookup, date, time, and math. In each case, I tell you how to use the functions and give you lots of practical examples that show you how you can use the functions in everyday business situations.

- **Part III, "Building business formulas"**—This part is crammed with business goodies related to performing financial wizardry with Excel. You learn how to implement many standard business formulas in Excel, and you get in-depth looks at Excel's descriptive and inferential statistical tools, powerful regression-analysis techniques to track trends and make forecasts, and techniques and functions for amortizing loans, analyzing investments, and using discounting for business-case and cash-flow analysis.

- **Part IV, "Building business models"**—The four chapters in Part IV are all business, as they examine various facets of building useful and robust business models. You learn how to analyze data with Excel tables and PivotTables, how to use what-if analysis and Excel's Goal Seek and scenarios features, and how to use the amazing Solver feature to solve complex problems.

This book's special features

Microsoft Excel Formulas and Functions (Office 2021 and Microsoft 365) is designed to give you the information you need without making you wade through ponderous explanations and interminable technical background. To make your life easier, this book includes various features and conventions that help you get the most out of the book and Excel itself:

- **Steps:** Throughout the book, each Excel task is summarized in step-by-step procedures.

- **Things you type:** Whenever I suggest that you type something, what you type appears in a **bold** font.

- **Commands:** I use the following style for Excel menu commands: **File** > **Open**. This means that you pull down the File menu and select the Open command.

- **Dialog box controls:** The names of dialog box controls and other onscreen elements appear in bold text: Select the **OK** button.

- **Functions:** Excel worksheet functions appear in capital letters: SUM. When I list the arguments you can use with a function, they appear in italic to indicate that they're placeholders you replace with actual values; also, optional arguments appear surrounded by square brackets: CELL(*info_type* [, *reference*]).

This book also uses the following boxes to draw your attention to important (or merely interesting) information.

Note   The Note box presents asides that offer more information about the topic under discussion. These tidbits provide extra insights that give you a better understanding of the task at hand.

Tip   The Tip box tells you about Excel methods that are easier, faster, or more efficient than the standard methods.

Caution   The all-important Caution box tells you about potential accidents waiting to happen. There are always ways to mess things up when you're working with computers. These boxes help you avoid at least some of the pitfalls.

About the companion content

To make it easier for you to learn Excel formulas and functions, all the sample content used in the book is available online. To download the sample workbooks, look for the download link on the book's page:

MicrosoftPressStore.com/Excel365FormulasFunctions/downloads

Alternatively, visit the book's page at paulmcfedries.com and click the Examples.zip link to download the files:

https://paulmcfedries.com/books/book.php?title=excel-365-formulas-and-functions

Support and feedback

The following sections provide information on errata, book support, feedback, and contact information.

Errata, updates, and book support

We've made every effort to ensure the accuracy of this book and its companion content. You can access updates to this book—in the form of a list of submitted errata and their related corrections—at the following page:

MicrosoftPressStore.com/Excel365FormulasFunctions/errata

If you discover an error that is not already listed, please submit it to us at the same page.

For additional book support and information, please visit *MicrosoftPressStore.com/ Support.*

Please note that product support for Microsoft software and hardware is not offered through the previous addresses. For help with Microsoft software or hardware, go to *http://support.microsoft.com.*

Stay in touch

Let's keep the conversation going! We're on Twitter:

http://twitter.com/MicrosoftPress

PART 1

Mastering Excel Formulas

CHAPTER 1

Building basic formulas

In this chapter, you will:

- Learn the basics of building formulas in Excel.

- Understand operator precedence and how it affects your formula results.

- Learn how to control worksheet calculations.

- Learn how to copy and move formulas.

- Learn how to work with range names in formulas.

- Build formulas that contain links to cells or ranges in other worksheets and workbooks.

A worksheet is merely a lifeless collection of numbers and text until you define a relationship among the various entries. You do this by creating *formulas* that perform calculations and produce results. This chapter takes you through some formula basics, including constructing simple arithmetic and text formulas; understanding the all-important topic of operator precedence; copying and moving worksheet formulas; and making formulas easier to build and read by taking advantage of range names.

Understanding formula basics

Most worksheets are created to provide answers to specific questions: What is the company's profit? Are expenses over or under budget and by how much? What is the future value of an investment? How big will an employee's bonus be this year? You can answer these questions, and an infinite number of others, by using Excel formulas.

All Excel formulas have the same general structure: an equal sign (=) followed by one or more *operands*—which can be values, cell references, ranges, range names, or function names—separated by one or more *operators*—which are symbols that combine the operands in some way, such as the plus sign (+) and the greater-than sign (>).

Note Excel doesn't object if you use spaces between operators and operands in your formulas. This is actually a good practice to get into because separating the elements of a formula in this way can make them much easier to read. Note, too, that Excel accepts line breaks in formulas. This is handy if you have a very long formula because it enables you to "break up" the formula so that it appears on multiple lines. To create a line break within a formula, press Alt+Enter.

Formula limits in Excel 365

It's a good idea to know the limits Excel sets on various aspects of formulas and worksheet models, even though it's unlikely that you'll ever bump up against these limits. Formula limits that were expanded in Excel 2007 remain the same in Excel 365. So, in the unlikely event that you're coming to Excel 365 from Excel 2003 or earlier, Table 1-1 shows you the updated limits.

TABLE 1-1 Formula-related limits in Excel 365

Object	Excel 365 Maximum	Excel 2003 Maximum
Columns	16,384	1,024
Rows	1,048,576	65,536
Formula length (characters)	8,192	1,024
Function arguments	255	30
Formula nesting levels	64	7
Array references (rows or columns)	Unlimited	65,335
PivotTable columns	16,384	255
PivotTable rows	1,048,576	65,536
PivotTable fields	16,384	255
Unique PivotField items	1,048,576	32,768

Formula nesting levels refers to the number of expressions that are nested within other expressions using parentheses; see "Controlling the order of precedence," later in this chapter.

Entering and editing formulas

Entering a new formula into a worksheet appears to be a straightforward process:

1. Select the cell in which you want to enter the formula.

2. Type an equal sign (=) to tell Excel that you're entering a formula.

3. Type the formula's operands and operators.

4. Select Enter to confirm the formula.

However, Excel has three different *input modes* that determine how it interprets certain keystrokes and mouse actions:

- When you type the equal sign to begin the formula, Excel goes into *Enter mode*, which is the mode you use to enter text (such as the formula's operands and operators).

- If you select any keyboard navigation key (such as Page Up, Page Down, or any arrow key), or if you select any other cell in the worksheet, Excel enters *Point mode*. This is the mode you use to select a cell or range as a formula operand. When you're in Point mode, you can use any of the standard range-selection techniques. Note that Excel returns to Enter mode as soon as you type an operator or any character.

- If you press F2, Excel enters *Edit mode*, which is the mode you use to make changes to the formula. For example, when you're in Edit mode, you can use the left and right arrow keys to move the cursor to another part of the formula for deleting or inserting characters. You can also enter Edit mode by selecting anywhere within the formula. Press F2 to return to Enter mode.

> **Tip** You can tell which mode Excel is currently in by looking at the status bar at the bottom of the Excel window. On the left side, you'll see Enter, Point, or Edit.

After you've entered a formula, you might need to return to it to make changes. Excel gives you three ways to enter Edit mode and make changes to a formula in the selected cell:

- Press the F2 key.

- Double-click the cell.

- Use the formula bar (the large text box that appears just above the column headers) to position the cursor anywhere inside the formula text.

Excel divides formulas into four groups: arithmetic, comparison, text, and reference. Each group has its own set of operators, and you use each group in different ways. In the next few sections, I show you how to use each type of formula.

Using arithmetic formulas

Arithmetic formulas are by far the most common type of formula. They combine numbers, cell addresses, and function results with mathematical operators to perform calculations. Table 1-2 summarizes the mathematical operators used in arithmetic formulas.

TABLE 1-2 The arithmetic operators

Operator	Name	Example	Result
+	Addition	=10+5	15
–	Subtraction	=10-5	5
–	Negation	=-10	–10
*	Multiplication	=10*5	50
/	Division	=10/5	2
%	Percentage	=10%	0.1
^	Exponentiation	=10^5	100000

Most of these operators are straightforward, but the exponentiation operator might require further explanation. The formula =x^y means that the value **x** is raised to the power **y**. For example, the formula =3^2 produces the result **9** (that is, **3*3=9**). Similarly, the formula =2^4 produces **16** (that is, **2*2*2*2=16**).

Using comparison formulas

A *comparison formula* is a statement that compares two or more numbers, text strings, cell contents, or function results. If the statement is true, the result of the formula is given the logical value **TRUE** (which is equivalent to any nonzero value). If the statement is false, the formula returns the logical value **FALSE** (which is equivalent to zero). Table 1-3 summarizes the operators you can use in comparison formulas.

TABLE 1-3 Comparison formula operators

Operator	Name	Example	Result
=	Equal to	=10=5	**FALSE**
>	Greater than	=10>5	**TRUE**
<	Less than	=10<5	**FALSE**
>=	Greater than or equal to	="a">="b"	**FALSE**
<=	Less than or equal to	="a"<="b"	**TRUE**
<>	Not equal to	="a"<>"b"	**TRUE**

Comparison formulas have many uses. For example, you can determine whether to pay a salesperson a bonus by using a comparison formula to compare actual sales with a predetermined quota. If the sales are greater than the quota, the rep is awarded the bonus. You also can monitor credit collection. For example, if the amount a customer owes is more than 150 days past due, you might send the invoice to a collection agency.

Using text formulas

The two types of formulas that I discussed in the previous sections—arithmetic formulas and comparison formulas—calculate or make comparisons and return values. A *text formula*, on the other hand, is a formula that returns text. Text formulas use the ampersand (**&**) operator to work with text cells, text strings enclosed in quotation marks, and text function results.

One way to use text formulas is to concatenate text strings. For example, if you enter the formula **="soft"&"ware"** into a cell, Excel displays **software**. Note that the quotation marks and the ampersand aren't shown in the result. You also can use **&** to combine cells that contain text. For example, if A1 contains the text **Ben** and A2 contains **Jerry**, entering the formula **=A1&" and "&A2** returns **Ben and Jerry**.

Using reference formulas

The reference operators combine two cell references or ranges to create a single joint reference. Table 1-4 summarizes the operators you can use in reference formulas.

TABLE 1-4 Reference formula operators

Operator	Name	Description
: (colon)	Range	Produces a range from two cell references (for example, A1:C5).
(space)	Intersection	Produces a range that is the intersection of two ranges (for example, A1:C5 B2:E8).
, (comma)	Union	Produces a range that is the union of two ranges (for example, A1:C5,B2:E8).

Understanding operator precedence

You'll often use simple formulas that contain just two values and a single operator. In practice, however, most formulas you use will have a number of values and operators. In more complex expressions, the order in which the calculations are performed becomes crucial. For example, consider the formula **=3+5^2**. If you calculate from left to right, the answer you get is 64 (3+5 equals 8, and 8^2 equals 64). However, if you perform the exponentiation first and then the addition, the result is 28 (5^2 equals 25, and 3+25 equals 28). As this example shows, a single formula can produce multiple answers, depending on the order in which you perform the calculations.

To control this problem, Excel evaluates a formula according to a predefined *order of precedence*. This order of precedence enables Excel to calculate a formula unambiguously by determining which part of the formula it calculates first, which part second, and so on.

The order of precedence

Excel's order of precedence is determined by the various formula operators outlined earlier. Table 1-5 summarizes the complete order of precedence used by Excel.

TABLE 1-5 The Excel order of precedence

Operator	Operation	Order of Precedence
:	Range	1st
<space>	Intersection	2nd
,	Union	3rd
–	Negation	4th
%	Percentage	5th
^	Exponentiation	6th
* and /	Multiplication and division	7th
+ and –	Addition and subtraction	8th
&	Concatenation	9th
= < > <= >= <>	Comparison	10th

From this table, you can see that Excel performs exponentiation before addition. Therefore, the correct answer for the formula =3+5^2, given previously, is 28. Also, notice that some operators in Table 1-5 have the same order of precedence (for example, multiplication and division). This means that it usually doesn't matter in which order these operators are evaluated. For example, consider the formula =5*10/2. If you perform the multiplication first, the answer you get is 25 (5*10 equals 50, and 50/2 equals 25). If you perform the division first, you also get an answer of 25 (10/2 equals 5, and 5*5 equals 25). By convention, Excel evaluates operators with the same order of precedence from left to right, so you should assume that's how your formulas will be evaluated.

Controlling the order of precedence

Sometimes you want to override the order of precedence. For example, suppose that you want to create a formula that calculates the pre-tax cost of an item. If you bought something for $10.65, including 7 percent sales tax, and you want to find the cost of the item minus the tax, you use the formula =10.65/1.07, which gives you the correct answer, $9.95. In general, the formula is the total cost divided by 1 plus the tax rate.

Figure 1-1 shows how you might implement such a formula. Cell B5 displays the Total Cost variable, and cell B6 displays the Tax Rate variable. Given these parameters, your first instinct might be to use the formula =B5/1+B6 to calculate the original cost. This formula is shown (as text) in cell E9, and the result is given in cell D9. As you can see, this answer is incorrect. What happened? Well, according to the rules of precedence, Excel performs division before addition, so the value in B5 first is divided by 1 and then is added to the value in B6. To get the correct answer, you must override the order of precedence so that the addition 1+B6 is performed first. You do this by surrounding that part of the formula with parentheses, as shown in cell E10. When this is done, you get the correct answer (cell D10).

Tip In Figure 1-1, how did I convince Excel to show the formulas in cells E9 and E10 as text? I used Excel's FORMULATEXT function (see "Displaying a cell's formula by using FORMULATEXT," later in this chapter).

D8			✕ ✓ ƒx	=B4 / 1 + B5		
	A	B	C	D	E	
1	Calculating the Pre-Tax Cost of an Item					
2						
3	Variables:					
4	Total Cost	$10.65				
5	Tax Rate	7%				
6			Pre-Tax Cost Calculation:			
7				Result	Formula in D	
8			Without controlling precedence →	$10.72	=B4 / 1 + B5	
9			Controlling precedence →	$9.95	=B4 / (1 + B5)	
10						

FIGURE 1-1 Use parentheses to control the order of precedence in your formulas.

In general, you can use parentheses to control the order that Excel uses to calculate formulas. Terms inside parentheses are always calculated first; terms outside parentheses are calculated sequentially (according to the order of precedence).

Tip Another good use for parentheses is raising a number to a fractional power. For example, if you want to take the *n*th root of a number, you use the following general formula:

```
=number ^ (1 / n)
```

For example, to take the cube root of the value in cell A1, use this:

```
=A1 ^ (1 / 3)
```

To gain even more control over your formulas, you can place parentheses inside one another; this is called *nesting* parentheses. Excel always evaluates the innermost set of parentheses first. Here are a few sample formulas:

Formula	1st Step	2nd Step	3rd Step	Result
3^(15/5)*2-5	3^3*2-5	27*2-5	54-5	49
3^((15/5)*2-5)	3^(3*2-5)	3^(6-5)	3^1	3
3^(15/(5*2-5))	3^(15/(10-5))	3^(15/5)	3^3	27

Notice that the order of precedence rules also hold within parentheses. For example, in the expression **(5*2-5)**, the term 5*2 is calculated before 5 is subtracted.

Using parentheses to determine the order of calculations enables you to gain full control over your Excel formulas. This way, you can make sure that the answer given by a formula is the one you want.

> **Caution** One of the most common mistakes when using parentheses in formulas is to forget to close a parenthetic term with a close parenthesis character—). In such a case, Excel generates an error message (and offers a solution to the problem). To make sure that you've closed each parenthetic term, count all the open and close parentheses. If these totals don't match, you know you've left out a parenthesis.

Controlling worksheet calculation

Excel always calculates a formula when you confirm its entry, and the program normally recalculates existing formulas automatically whenever their data changes. This behavior is fine for small worksheets, but it can slow you down if you have a complex model that takes several seconds or even several minutes to recalculate. To turn off this automatic recalculation, Excel gives you two ways to get started:

- Select **Formulas** > **Calculation Options**.

- Select **File** > **Options** > **Formulas**.

Either way, you're presented with three calculation options:

- **Automatic:** This is the default calculation mode, and it means that Excel recalculates formulas as soon as you enter them and as soon as the data for a formula changes.

- **Automatic Except for Data Tables:** In this calculation mode, Excel recalculates all formulas automatically, except for those associated with data tables (which I discuss in Chapter 19, "Using Excel's business modeling tools"). This is a good choice if your worksheet includes one or more massive data tables that are slowing down the recalculation.

- **Manual:** Select this mode to force Excel not to recalculate any formulas until either you manually recalculate or you save the workbook. If you're in the Excel Options dialog box, you can tell Excel not to recalculate when you save the workbook by deselecting the **Recalculate Workbook Before Saving** check box.

With manual calculation turned on, you see "Calculate" in the status bar whenever your worksheet data changes and your formula results need to be updated. When you want to recalculate, first display the Formulas tab. In the Calculation group, you have three choices:

- Select **Calculate Now** (or press F9) to recalculate every open worksheet.

- Select **Calculate Sheet** (or press Shift+F9) to recalculate only the active worksheet.

- Click the word "Calculate" in the status bar. (This is the same as choosing **Calculate Now**.)

> **Tip** If you want Excel to recalculate every formula—even those that are unchanged—in all open worksheets, press Ctrl+Alt+Shift+F9.

If you want to recalculate only part of your worksheet while manual calculation is turned on, you have two options:

- To recalculate a single formula, select the cell containing the formula, place the cursor inside the formula bar, and then confirm the cell (by pressing Enter or by selecting the Formula bar's **Enter** button).

- To recalculate a range, select the range; select **Home** > **Find & Select** > **Replace** (or select Ctrl+H); enter an equal sign (=) in both the **Find What** and **Replace With** boxes; finally, select **Replace All**. Excel "replaces" the equal sign in each formula with another equal sign. This doesn't actually change any formula, but it forces Excel to recalculate each formula.

> **Tip** Excel supports *multithreaded* calculation where, for each processor—or, more likely, each processor core—Excel sets up a *thread*, which is a separate process of execution. Excel can then use each available thread to process multiple calculations concurrently. For a worksheet with multiple independent formulas, this can dramatically speed calculations. Multithreaded calculation is turned on by default, but to make sure, select **File** > **Options** > **Advanced**, and then in the **Formulas** section, ensure that the **Enable Multi-Threaded Calculation** check box is selected.

Copying and moving formulas

You copy and move ranges that contain formulas the same way you copy and move regular ranges, but the results aren't always straightforward.

For example, Figure 1-2 shows a list of expense data for a company. The formula in cell C11 uses SUM(**C6:C10**) to total the January expenses. The idea behind this worksheet is to calculate a new expense budget number for 2022 as a percentage increase of the actual 2021 total. Cell C3 displays the INCREASE variable. (In this case, the increase being used is 3 percent.) The formula that calculates the 2022 BUDGET number (cell C13 for the month of January) multiplies the 2021 TOTAL by the INCREASE (that is, =**C11** * **C3**).

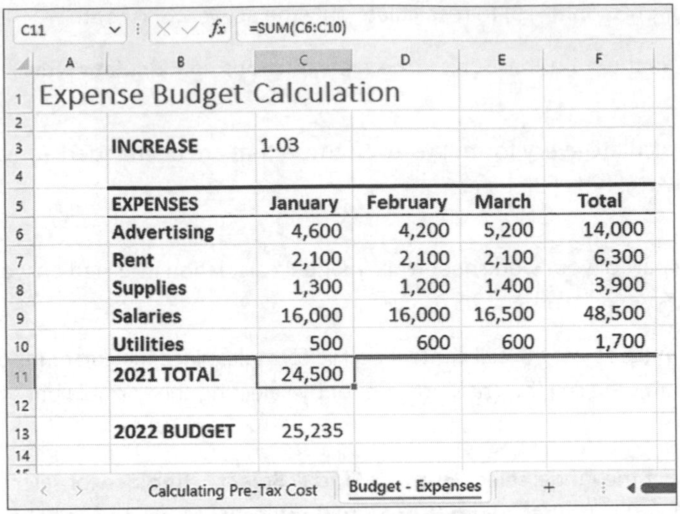

FIGURE 1-2 Here is a budget expenses worksheet with two calculations for the January numbers: the total (cell C11) and a percentage increase for next year (cell C13).

The next step is to calculate the 2021 TOTAL expenses and the 2022 BUDGET figure for February. You could just type each new formula, but you can copy a cell much more quickly. Figure 1-3 shows the results when you copy the contents of cell C11 into cell D11. As you can see, the formula in D11 is =SUM(**D6:D10**), which means that Excel adjusted the range in the formula's function so that only the February expenses are totaled. How did Excel know to do this? To answer this question, you need to know about Excel's relative reference format, which I discuss in the next section.

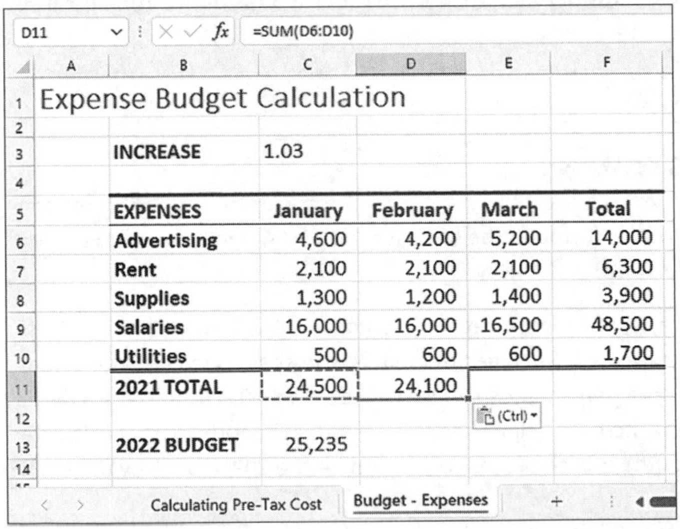

FIGURE 1-3 When you copy the January 2021 TOTAL formula to February, Excel automatically adjusts the range reference.

Understanding relative reference format

When you use a cell reference in a formula, Excel looks at the cell address relative to the location of the formula. For example, suppose that you have the formula =A1 * 2 in cell A3. To Excel, this formula says, "Multiply the contents of the cell two rows above this one by 2." This is called the *relative reference format*, and it's the default format for Excel. This means that if you copy this formula to cell A4, the relative reference is still "Multiply the contents of the cell two rows above this one by 2," but the formula changes to =A2 * 2 because A2 is two rows above A4.

Figure 1-4 shows why this format is useful. You had only to copy the formula in cell C11 to cell D11 and, thanks to relative referencing, everything came out perfectly. To get the expense total for March, you'd just have to paste the same formula into cell E11. You'll find that this way of handling copy operations will save you incredible amounts of time when you're building worksheet models.

However, you need to exercise some care when copying or moving formulas. Let's see what happens if you return to the budget expense worksheet and try copying the 2022 BUDGET formula in cell C13 to cell D13. Figure 1-4 shows that the result is 0!

What happened? The formula bar shows the problem: The new formula is =D11 * D3. Cell D11 is the February 2021 TOTAL, and that's fine, but instead of the INCREASE cell (C3), the formula refers to a blank cell (D3). Excel treats blank cells as 0, so the formula result is 0. The problem is the relative reference format. When the formula was copied, Excel assumed that the new formula should refer to cell D3. To see how you can correct this problem, you need to learn about another format, the *absolute reference format*, which I discuss in the next section.

D13			fx	=D11 * D3		
	A	B	C	D	E	F
1	Expense Budget Calculation					
2						
3		INCREASE	1.03			
4						
5		EXPENSES	January	February	March	Total
6		Advertising	4,600	4,200	5,200	14,000
7		Rent	2,100	2,100	2,100	6,300
8		Supplies	1,300	1,200	1,400	3,900
9		Salaries	16,000	16,000	16,500	48,500
10		Utilities	500	600	600	1,700
11		2021 TOTAL	24,500	24,100		
12						
13		2022 BUDGET	25,235	0 (Ctrl) ▾		
14						

Calculating Pre-Tax Cost | Budget - Expenses | +

FIGURE 1-4 Copying the January 2022 BUDGET formula to February creates a problem.

> **Note** The relative reference format problem doesn't occur when you move a formula. When you move a formula, Excel assumes that you want to keep the same cell references.

Understanding absolute reference format

When you refer to a cell in a formula using the absolute reference format, Excel uses the physical address of the cell. You tell the program that you want to use an absolute reference by placing dollar signs ($) before the row and column of the cell address. To return to the example in the preceding section, Excel interprets the formula =$A$1 * 2 as "Multiply the contents of cell A1 by 2." No matter where you copy or move this formula, the cell reference doesn't change. The cell address is said to be *anchored*.

To fix the budget expense worksheet, you need to anchor the **INCREASE** variable. To do this, you first change the January 2022 BUDGET formula in cell C13 to read =C11 * $C$3. After making this change, copying the formula to the February 2022 BUDGET column gives the new formula =D11 * $C$3, which produces the correct result.

> **Caution** Most range names refer to absolute cell references. This means that when you copy a formula that uses a range name, the copied formula will use the same range name as the original. This might produce errors in your worksheet.

You also should know that you can enter a cell reference using a mixed-reference format. In this format, you anchor either the cell's row (by placing the dollar sign in front of the row address only—for example, B$6) or its column (by placing the dollar sign in front of the column address only—for example, $B6).

> **Tip** You can quickly change the reference format of a cell address by using the F4 key. When editing a formula, place the cursor to the left of the cell address (or between the row and column values) and then keep pressing F4. Excel cycles through the various formats. When you see the format you want, press Enter. If you want to apply the new reference format to multiple cell addresses, select the addresses, select F4 until you get the format you want, and press Enter.

Copying a formula without adjusting relative references

If you need to copy a formula but don't want the formula's relative references to change, follow these steps:

1. Select the cell that contains the formula you want to copy.

2. Place the cursor inside the formula bar.

3. Use the mouse or keyboard to select the entire formula.

4. Copy the selected formula.

5. Select Esc to deactivate the formula bar.

6. Select the cell in which you want the copy of the formula to appear.

7. Paste the formula.

> **Note** Here are two other methods you can use to copy a formula without adjusting its relative cell references:
>
> - To copy a formula from the cell above, select the lower cell and press Ctrl+' (apostrophe).
> - Activate the formula bar and type an apostrophe (') at the beginning of the formula (that is, to the left of the equal sign) to convert it to text. Press Enter to confirm the edit, copy the cell, and then paste it in the desired location. Then delete the apostrophe from both the source and destination cells to convert them back to formulas.

Displaying worksheet formulas

By default, Excel displays in a cell the results of the cell's formula instead of the formula itself. If you need to see a formula, you can select the formula's cell and look at the formula bar. However, sometimes you'll want to see all the formulas in a worksheet (such as when you're troubleshooting your work).

Displaying all worksheet formulas

To display all the formulas in a worksheet, select **Formulas** > **Show Formulas**.

> **Tip** You can also select Ctrl+` (backquote) to toggle a worksheet between values and formulas.

Displaying a cell's formula by using FORMULATEXT

In some cases, rather than showing all the formulas in a sheet, you might prefer to show the formulas in only a cell or two. For example, if you're presenting a worksheet to other people, that sheet might have some formulas you want to show, but it might also have one or more proprietary formulas that you don't want your audience to see. In such a case, you can display individual cell formulas by using the **FORMULATEXT** function:

FORMULATEXT(*cell*)

cell	The address of the cell that contains the formula you want to show

For example, the following formula displays the formula text from cell D9:

=FORMULATEXT(D9)

Converting a formula to a value

If a cell contains a formula where the value will never change, you can convert the formula to that value. This speeds large worksheet recalculations and frees memory for your worksheet because values use much less memory than formulas do. For example, you might have formulas in part of your worksheet that use values from a previous fiscal year. Because these numbers aren't likely to change, you can safely convert the formulas to their values. To do this, follow these steps:

1. Select the cell containing the formula you want to convert.

2. Press F2 to activate in-cell editing. (You can also usually double-click the cell to open it for editing. If this doesn't work for you, select **File** > **Options** > **Advanced**, and then select the **Allow Editing Directly In Cells** check box.)

3. Press F9. The formula changes to its value.

4. Press Enter or select the **Enter** button. Excel changes the cell to the value.

You'll often need to use the result of a formula in several places. If a formula is in cell C5, for example, you can display its result in other cells by entering =**C5** in each of the cells. This is the best method if you think the formula result might change because, if it does, Excel updates the other cells automatically. However, if you're sure that the result won't change, you can copy only the value of the formula into the other cells. Use the following procedure to do this:

1. Select the cell that contains the formula.

2. Copy the cell.

3. Select the cell or cells to which you want to copy the value.

4. Select **Home**, open the **Paste** list, and then select **Paste Values**. Excel pastes the cell's value to each cell you selected.

Another method is to copy the cell, paste it into the destination, open the **Paste Options** list, and then select **Values Only**.

> **Caution** If your worksheet is set to manual calculation (select **Formulas** > **Calculations Options** > **Manual**), make sure that you update your formulas (by pressing F9) before copying the values of your formulas.

Working with range names in formulas

You probably use range names often in your formulas. After all, a cell that contains the formula =**Sales** - **Expenses** is much more comprehensible than one that contains the more cryptic formula =**F12** - **F3**. The next few sections show you some techniques that make it easier to use range names in formulas.

Pasting a name into a formula

One way to enter a range name in a formula is to type the name in the formula bar. But what if you can't remember the name? Or what if the name is long, and you've got a deadline looming? For these kinds of situations, Excel has several features that enable you to select the name you want from a list and paste it right into the formula. Start your formula, and when you get to the spot where you want the name to appear, use any of the following techniques:

- Select **Formulas** > **Use in Formula** and then select the name in the list that appears (see Figure 1-5).

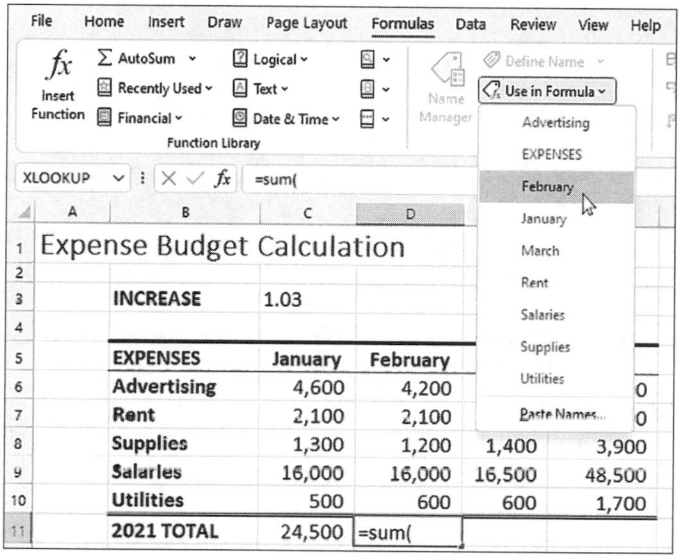

FIGURE 1-5 Open the Use in Formula drop-down menu and then select the range name you want to insert into your formula.

- Select **Formulas** > **Use in Formula** > **Paste Names** (or select F3) to display the Paste Name dialog box, select the range name you want to use, and then select **OK**.

- Type the first letter or two of the range name to display a list of names and functions that start with those letters, select the name you want, and then select Tab.

Applying names to formulas

If you've been using ranges in your formulas and you name those ranges later, Excel doesn't automatically apply the new names to the formulas. Instead of substituting the appropriate names by hand, you can get Excel to do the hard work for you. Follow these steps to apply the new range names to your existing formulas:

1. Select the range in which you want to apply the names or select a single cell if you want to apply the names to the entire worksheet.

2. Select **Formulas** > **Define Name** > **Apply Names**. Excel displays the Apply Names dialog box, shown in Figure 1-6.

3. In the **Apply Names** list, choose the name or names you want to be applied from this list.

4. Select the **Ignore Relative/Absolute** check box to ignore relative and absolute references when applying names. (See the next section for more information on this option.)

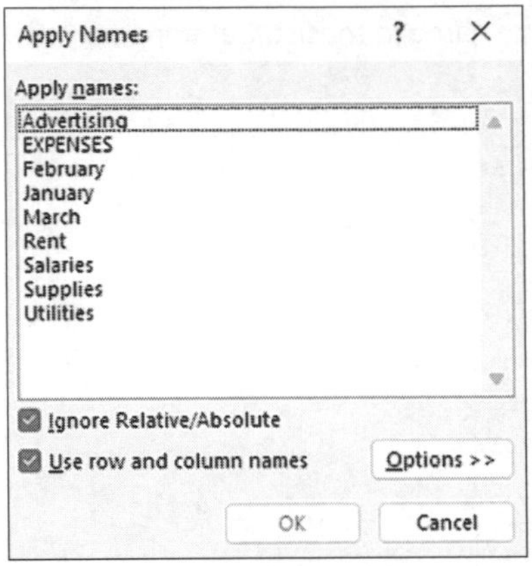

FIGURE 1-6 Use the Apply Names dialog box to select the names you want to apply to your formula ranges.

5. Select the **Use Row And Column Names** check box to tell Excel whether to use the work-sheet's row and column names when applying names. If you select this check box, you also can select the **Options** button to see more choices. (See the section "Using row and column names when applying names," later in this chapter, for details.)

6. Select **OK** to apply the names.

Ignoring relative and absolute references when applying names

If you deselect the **Ignore Relative/Absolute** option in the **Apply Names** dialog box, Excel replaces relative range references only with names that refer to relative references, and it replaces absolute range references only with names that refer to absolute references. If you leave this option selected, Excel ignores relative and absolute reference formats when applying names to a formula.

For example, suppose you have a formula such as =SUM(A1:A10) and a range named Sales that refers to $A$1:$A$10. With the **Ignore Relative/Absolute** option deselected, Excel won't apply the name Sales to the range in the formula; Sales refers to an absolute range, and the formula contains a relative range. Unless you think you'll be moving your formulas around, you should leave the **Ignore Relative/ Absolute** option selected.

Using row and column names when applying names

For extra clarity in your formulas, leave the **Use Row And Column Names** check box selected in the **Apply Names** dialog box. This option tells Excel to rename all cell references that can be described as the intersection of a named row and a named column. In Figure 1-7, for example, the range C6:C10 is named January, and the range C7:E7 is named Rent. This means that cell C7—the intersection of these two ranges—can be referenced as January Rent.

As shown in Figure 1-7, the Total for the Advertising row (cell F6) currently contains the formula =C6 + D6 + E6. If you applied range names to this worksheet and selected the Use Row And Column Names option, you'd think this formula would be changed to this:

```
=January Advertising + February Advertising + March Advertising
```

F6				f_x	=C6 + D6 + E6		
	A	B	C	D	E	F	
1	Expense Budget Calculation						
2							
3		INCREASE	1.03				
4							
5		EXPENSES	January	February	March	Total	
6		Advertising	4,600	4,200	5,200	14,000	
7		Rent	2,100	2,100	2,100		
8		Supplies	1,300	1,200	1,400		
9		Salaries	16,000	16,000	16,500		
10		Utilities	500	600	600		

FIGURE 1-7 Before range names are applied to the formulas, cell F6 (Total Advertising) contains the formula =C6 + D6 + E6.

However, if you try this, you'll get a slightly different formula, as shown in Figure 1-8.

F6				f_x	=January + February + March		
	A	B	C	D	E	F	
1	Expense Budget Calculation						
2							
3		INCREASE	1.03				
4							
5		EXPENSES	January	February	March	Total	
6		Advertising	4,600	4,200	5,200	14,000	
7		Rent	2,100	2,100	2,100	6,300	
8		Supplies	1,300	1,200	1,400	3,900	
9		Salaries	16,000	16,000	16,500	48,500	
10		Utilities	500	600	600	1,700	

FIGURE 1-8 After range names are applied, the Total Advertising cell contains the formula =January + February + March.

That is because when Excel is applying names, it omits the row name if the formula is in the same row. (It also omits the column name if the formula is in the same column.) In cell F6, for example, Excel omits Advertising in each term because F6 is in the Advertising row.

> **Note** Notice that applying names not only modified the formula in cell F6, it also filled in the rest of the formulas in the Total column. That happened because Excel created a dynamic array for the entire column. To learn more about dynamic arrays, see Chapter 2, "Creating advanced formulas."

Omitting row headings isn't a problem in a small model, but it can be confusing in a large worksheet, where you might not be able to see the names of the rows. Therefore, if you're applying names to a large worksheet, you'll probably prefer to include the row names when applying names.

Selecting the **Options** button in the Apply Names dialog box displays the expanded dialog box shown in Figure 1-9. This includes extra options that enable you to include column (and row) headings:

- **Omit Column Name If Same Column:** Clear this check box to include column names when applying names.

- **Omit Row Name If Same Row:** Clear this check box to include row names.

- **Name Order:** Use these options (**Row Column** or **Column Row**) to select the order of names in the reference.

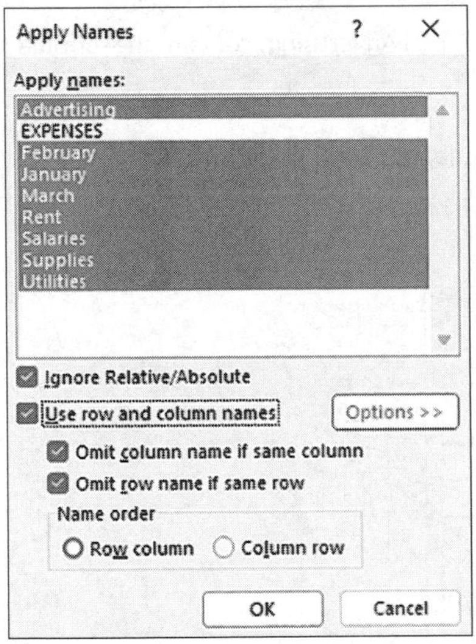

FIGURE 1-9 The expanded Apply Names dialog box

Naming formulas

You can define names for often-used formulas. The formula doesn't physically have to appear in a cell. This not only saves memory but often makes your worksheets easier to read. Follow these steps to name a formula:

1. Select **Formulas** > **Define Name** to display the **New Name** dialog box.

2. Enter the name you want to use for the formula in the Name text box.

3. In the **Refers To** box, enter the formula exactly as you would if you were entering it in a worksheet.

4. Select **OK**.

Now you can enter the formula name in your worksheet cells (instead of the formula itself). For example, the following is the formula for the volume of a sphere (**r** is the radius of the sphere):

$4\pi r^3/3$

So, assuming that you have a cell named Radius somewhere in the workbook, you could create a formula named, say, SphereVolume. Then you could make the following entry in the Refers To box of the New Name dialog box (where **PI** is the Excel worksheet function that returns the value of pi):

```
=4 * PI() * Radius ^ 3 / 3
```

Working with links in formulas

If you have data in one workbook that you want to use in another, you can set up a link between the two workbooks. This action enables your formulas to use references to cells or ranges in the other workbook. When the other data changes, Excel automatically updates the link.

For example, Figure 1-10 shows two linked workbooks. The Budget Summary sheet in the Chapter01 workbook includes data from the Details worksheet in the Chapter01a workbook. Specifically, the formula shown for cell B2 in the Budget Summary sheet contains an external reference to cell R7 in the Details worksheet. If the value in R7 changes, Excel immediately updates the Chapter01 workbook.

> **Note** The workbook that contains the external reference is called the *dependent* workbook (or the *client* workbook). The workbook that contains the original data is called the *source* workbook (or the *server* workbook).

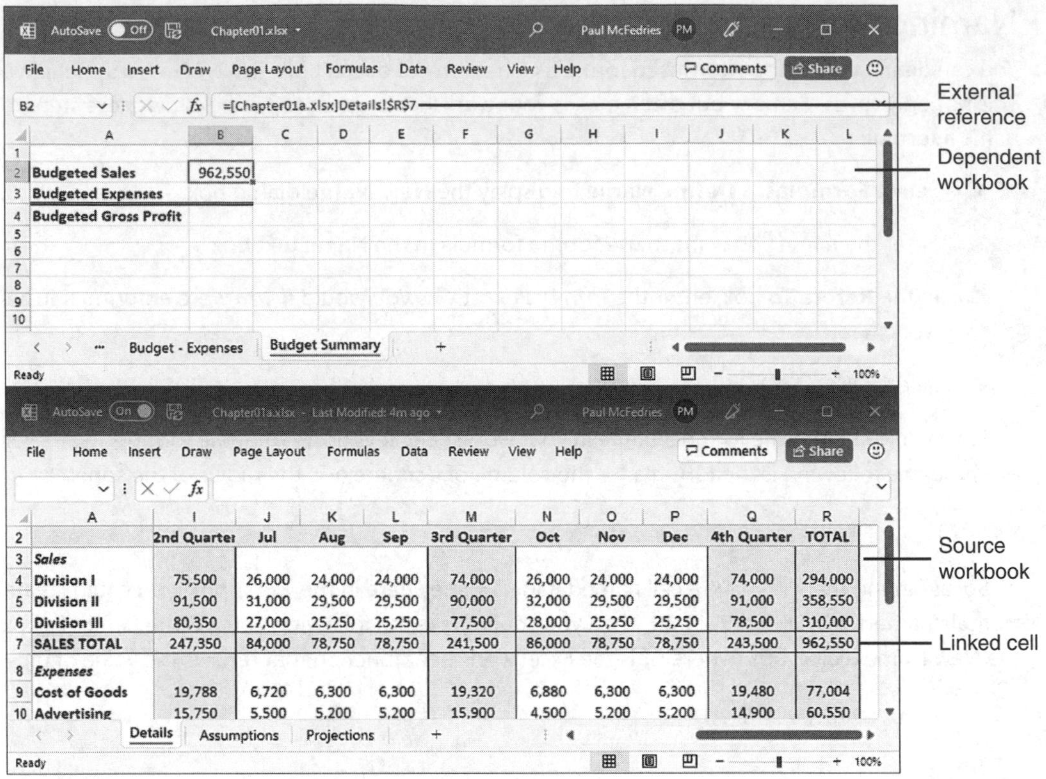

FIGURE 1-10 These two workbooks are linked because the formula in cell B2 of the Chapter01 workbook references cell R7 in the Chapter01a workbook.

Understanding external references

There's no big mystery behind external reference links. You set up links by including an external reference to a cell or range in another workbook (or in another worksheet from the same workbook). To get the external reference in the example shown in Figure 1-10, I entered an equal sign in cell B2 of the Budget Summary worksheet, and then I selected cell R7 in the Details worksheet.

You just need to be comfortable with the structure of an external reference. Here's the syntax:

```
'path[workbookname]sheetname'!reference
```

path	The drive and directory in which the workbook is located, which can be a local path or a network path; alternatively, enter the URL if the workbook is on OneDrive. You need to include the path only when the workbook is closed.
workbookname	The name of the workbook, including an extension. Always enclose the workbook name in square brackets ([ ]). You can omit *workbookname* if you're referencing a cell or range in another sheet of the same workbook.
Sheetname	The name of the worksheet's tab. You can omit *sheetname* if *reference* is a defined name in the same workbook.
Reference	A cell or range reference, or a defined name.

For example, if you close the Chapter01a workbook, Excel automatically changes the external reference shown in Figure 1-10 to this (depending on the actual path of the file):

```
='C:\Users\Paul\Documents\[Chapter01a.xlsx]Details'!$R$7
```

> **Note** You need the single quotation marks around the path, workbook name, and sheet name only if the workbook is closed or if the path, workbook, or sheet name contains spaces. If in doubt, include the single quotation marks anyway; Excel happily ignores them if they're not required.

Updating links

The purpose of a link is to avoid duplicating formulas and data in multiple worksheets. If one workbook contains the information you need, you can use a link to reference the data without re-creating it in another workbook.

To be useful, however, the data in the dependent workbook should always reflect what actually is in the source workbook. You can make sure of this by updating the link, as explained here:

- If both the source and the dependent workbooks are open, Excel automatically updates the link whenever the data in the source file changes.

- If the source workbook is open when you open the dependent workbook, Excel automatically updates the links again.

- If the source workbook is closed when you open the dependent workbook, Excel displays a security warning in the information bar, which tells you that automatic updating of links has been disabled. In this case, select **Enable Content**.

> **Tip** If you always trust the links in your workbooks (that is, if you never deal with third-party workbooks or any other workbooks from sources you don't completely trust), you can configure Excel to always update links automatically. To begin, select **File** > **Options** > **Trust Center** > **Trust Center Settings**. In the Trust Center dialog box, select **External Content** and then select the **Enable Automatic Update For All Workbook Links** option. Select **OK** and then select **OK** again.

- If you didn't update a link when you opened the dependent document, you can update it any time by choosing **Data** > **Edit Links**. In the Edit Links dialog box that appears (see Figure 1-11), select the link and then select **Update Values**.

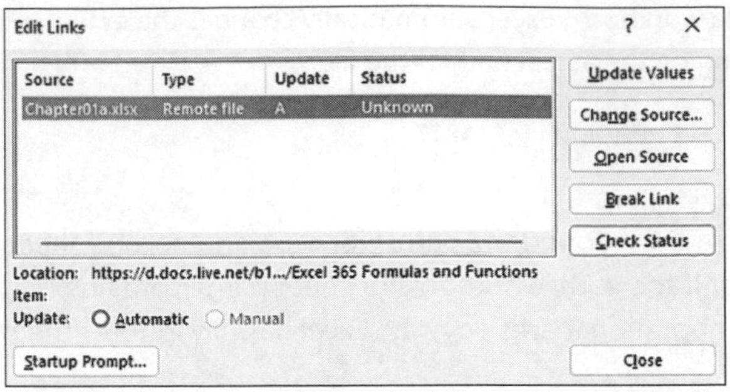

FIGURE 1-11 Use the Edit Links dialog box to update the linked data in the source workbook.

Changing the link source

If the name of the source document changes, you'll need to edit the link to keep the data up to date. You can edit the external reference directly, or you can change the source by following these steps:

1. With the dependent workbook active, select **Data** > **Edit Links** to display the **Edit Links** dialog box.

2. Select the link you want to work with.

3. Select **Change Source**. Excel displays the **Change Source** dialog box.

4. Find and then select the new source document and then select **OK** to return to the **Edit Links** dialog box.

5. Select **Close** to return to the workbook.

CHAPTER 2

Creating advanced formulas

In this chapter, you will:

- Learn how to create powerful, flexible formulas with arrays.

- Understand how iteration works and how you can use it to create approximate formula solutions.

- Consolidate data from multiple worksheets into a single summary sheet.

- Learn how to keep your data models accurate by applying data-validation rules to formula input cells.

- See how to make formula inputs easier for users by adding check boxes, lists, and other dialog box controls to your worksheets.

Excel is a versatile program with many uses, from acting as a checkbook to a flat-file database-management system, to an equation solver, to a glorified calculator. For most business users, however, Excel's forte is building models that enable quantification of particular aspects of the business. The skeleton of the business model is made up of the chunks of data entered, imported, or copied into the worksheets. But the lifeblood of the model and the animating force behind it is the collection of formulas for summarizing data, answering questions, and making predictions.

You saw in Chapter 1, "Building basic formulas," that, armed with the humble equal sign and Excel's operators and operands, you can cobble together useful, robust formulas. But Excel has many other tricks up its digital sleeve, and these techniques enable you to create muscular formulas that can take your business models to the next level.

Working with arrays

When you work with a range of cells, it might appear as though you're working with a single thing. In reality, however, Excel treats the range as a number of discrete units.

This is in contrast with the subject of this section: the array. An *array* is a group of cells or values that Excel treats as a unit. In a range configured as an array, Excel no longer treats the cells individually. Instead, it works with all the cells at once, which means you can apply a formula to every cell in the range by using just a single operation.

You create arrays either by running a function that returns an array result (such as **RANDARRAY** or **DOCUMENTS**) or by entering an *array formula*, which is a single formula that either uses an array as an argument or enters its results in multiple cells. (See the section "Functions that use or return arrays," later in this chapter.)

Using array formulas

In this section, I introduce you to the old way of using array formulas in Excel. Starting with Excel 2019, so-called *dynamic* arrays are supported, which are much easier to use and understand. I get to dynamic arrays in the next section, but it pays to take a few minutes now to get to know the old way. Why? Because you might still come across old-fashioned array formulas in other users' worksheets, so you need to know what you're dealing with. And understanding the old way of doing array formulas will help you appreciate the relative ease and simplicity of the new way.

Here's a straightforward example that illustrates how array formulas work. In the Expenses worksheet shown in Figure 2-1, the 2022 BUDGET totals are calculated using a separate formula for each month, as shown here:

> **Note** You can work with all the examples in this chapter by downloading Chapter02.xslx from either of the companion content sites mentioned in the Introduction.

Total	Formula
January 2022 BUDGET	=C11*$C$3
February 2022 BUDGET	=D11*$C$3
March 2022 BUDGET	=E11*$C$3

	A	B	C	D	E	F
1	Expense Budget Calculation					
2						
3		INCREASE	1.03			
4						
5		EXPENSES	January	February	March	
6		Advertising	4,600	4,200	5,200	
7		Rent	2,100	2,100	2,100	
8		Supplies	1,300	1,200	1,400	
9		Salaries	16,000	16,000	16,500	
10		Utilities	500	600	600	
11		2021 TOTAL	24,500	24,100	25,800	
12						
13		2022 BUDGET	25,235	24,823	26,574	
14						

Cell reference box: C13, formula bar: =C11 * $C$3

FIGURE 2-1 This worksheet uses three formulas to calculate the 2022 BUDGET figures.

You can replace all three formulas with a single array formula by following these steps:

1. Select the range you want to use for the array formula. In the 2022 BUDGET example, you'd select C13:E13.

2. Enter the formula and, in the places where you would normally enter a cell reference, specify a range reference that includes the cells you want to use. *Do not*—I repeat, *do not*—press Enter when you're done. In the example, you'd enter =C11:E11*$C$3.

3. To enter the formula as an array, press Ctrl+Shift+Enter.

The 2022 BUDGET cells (C13, D13, and E13) now contain the same formula:

{=C11:E11*$C$3}

In other words, you were able to enter a formula into three different cells by using just a single operation. This can save you significant amounts of time when you would otherwise have to enter the same formula into many different cells.

Notice that the formula is surrounded by braces ({ }). This identifies the formula as an array formula. (When you enter array formulas, you never need to enter these braces yourself; Excel adds them automatically when you press Ctrl+Shift+Enter.)

> **Note**   Because Excel treats an array as a unit, you can't move or delete part of an array. If you need to work with an array, you must select the whole thing. If you want to reduce an array's size, select the formula, select the formula bar, and then press Ctrl+Enter to change the entry to a normal formula. You can then select the smaller range and reenter the array formula.
>
> Note that you can select an array quickly by selecting one of its cells and pressing Ctrl+/.

Building dynamic array formulas

Building an array formula, as I described in the previous section, suffers from three problems:

- You must select the array formula range in advance. That's fine for just three cells, as in the previous section's example, but it's a pain in the neck if you're dealing with dozens or even hundreds of cells.

- When it's time to accept the formula, you must remember to press Ctrl+Shift+Enter instead of just Enter.

- The resulting formula is surrounded by braces ({ }), which can confuse things because people new to arrays often think they need to enter those braces manually.

These conundrums might be why Microsoft decided to change how array formulas work starting in Excel 2019. In particular, although the steps in the previous section still work, as an alternative, you can now use the following steps to build an array formula:

1. Select the first cell in the range you want to use for the array formula. In the 2022 BUDGET example, you'd select C13.

2. Make sure the other cells in the range you want to use for the array formula are empty. In the 2022 BUDGET example, delete the existing formulas from cells D13 and E13.

3. Enter the formula and specify a range reference that includes the cells you want to use in the places where you would normally enter a cell reference. In the example, you'd enter =C11:E11*$C$3.

4. Press Enter.

In these steps, you see that Excel solves the problems I outlined at the beginning of this section as follows:

■ You have to select only the first cell in the array formula's results range. Excel automatically fills in—or *spills*—the results to the rest of the range based on the parameters in your formula, which is why this new type of array is called a *dynamic array*. It's also why you need to clear out the rest of the array results range; a dynamic array will only spill into blank cells.

> **Note** If the dynamic array formula's results range isn't blank, Excel generates a #SPILL! Error. Delete or move the data that's blocking the spill, and Excel automatically displays the correct results.

■ You can now accept the array formula by pressing Enter instead of Ctrl+Shift+Enter.

■ The resulting dynamic array formula is no longer surrounded by braces. In the example, the 2022 BUDGET cells (C13, D13, and E13) now contain this formula:

=C11:E11*$C$3

> **Caution** Dynamic array formulas and array spilling are welcome new modifications to arrays, but they only work with Excel 2019 or later. If your workbook will be viewed or used by someone using an earlier version of Excel, then you need to enter your array formula the old way.

Understanding array formulas

To understand how Excel processes an array, you need to keep in mind that Excel always sets up a correspondence between the array cells and the cells of whatever range you entered into the array formula. In the 2022 BUDGET example, the array consists of cells C13, D13, and E13, and the range used in the formula consists of cells C11, D11, and E11. Excel sets up correspondences between array cell C13 and input cell C11, between D13 and D11, and between E13 and E11. To calculate the value of cell C13 (the January 2022 BUDGET), for example, Excel just grabs the input value from cell C11 and substitutes that in the formula. Figure 2-2 shows a diagram of this process.

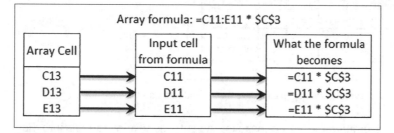

FIGURE 2-2 When processing an array formula, Excel sets up a correspondence between the array cells and the range used in the formula.

Array formulas can be confusing, but keeping these correspondences in mind can help you figure out what's going on.

Array formulas that operate on multiple ranges

In the preceding example, the array formula operated on a single range, but array formulas also can operate on multiple ranges. For example, consider the Invoice Template worksheet shown in Figure 2-3. The totals in the Extension column (cells F12 through F16) are generated by a series of formulas that multiply the item's price by the quantity ordered:

Cell	Formula
F12	=B12ᴬE12
F13	=B13*E13
F14	=B14*E14
F15	=B15*E15
F16	=B16*E16

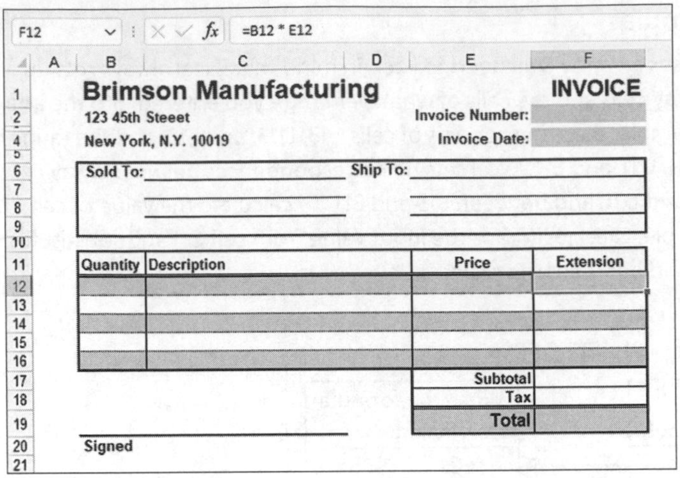

FIGURE 2-3 This worksheet uses several formulas to calculate the extended totals for each line.

You can replace all these formulas by making the following entry as an array formula into the selected range F12:F16:

```
=B12:B16*E12:E16
```

Again, you've created the array formula by replacing each cell reference with the corresponding range (and by pressing Ctrl+Shift+Enter).

If you want to use a dynamic array, instead, delete the formulas from the range F13:F16, and then enter the following formula in cell F12 and select Enter:

```
=B12:B16*E12:E16
```

> **Note** You don't have to enter array formulas in multiple cells. For example, if you don't need the Extended totals in the Invoice Template worksheet, you can still calculate the Subtotal by making the following entry an array formula in cell F17:
>
> ```
> =SUM(B12:B16*E12:E16)
> ```

Using array constants

In the array formulas you've seen so far, the array arguments have been cell ranges. You also can use constant values as array arguments. This procedure enables you to input values into a formula without having them clutter your worksheet.

To enter an array constant in a formula, observe the following guidelines while entering the values right in the formula:

- Enclose the values in braces ({}).

- If you want Excel to treat the values as a row, enter a comma after each value (except the last value).

- If you want Excel to treat the values as a column, enter a semicolon after each value (except the last value).

For example, the following array constant is the equivalent of entering the individual values in a column on your worksheet:

{1;2;3;4}

Similarly, the following array constant is equivalent to entering the values in a worksheet range of three columns and two rows:

{1,2,3;4,5,6}

As a practical example, Figure 2-4 shows two different array formulas. The one on the left (used in the range E4:E7) calculates various loan payments, given the different interest rates in the range C5:C8. The array formula on the right (used in the range F4:F7) does the same thing, but the interest rate values are entered as an array constant directly in the formula.

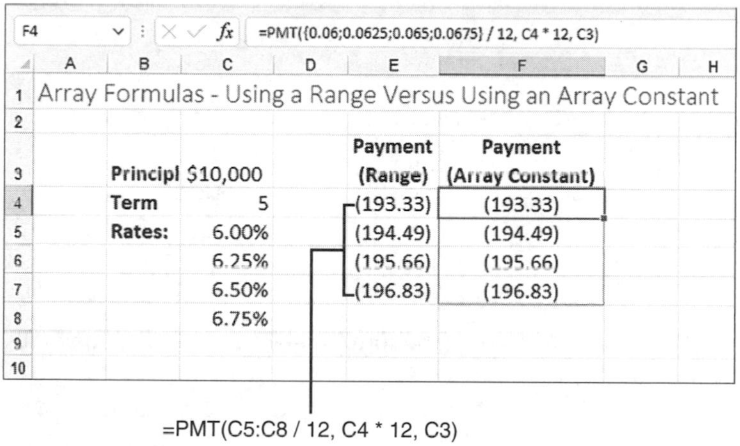

=PMT(C5:C8 / 12, C4 * 12, C3)

FIGURE 2-4 Using array constants in your array formulas means you don't have to clutter your worksheet with the input values.

Functions that use or return arrays

Many of Excel's worksheet functions either require an array argument or return an array result (or both). Table 2-1 lists several of these functions and explains how each one uses arrays. (See Part II, "Harnessing the power of functions," for explanations of these functions.)

TABLE 2-1 Some Excel functions that use arrays

Function	Uses Array Argument?	Returns Array Result?
COLUMN	No	Yes, if the argument is a range
COLUMNS	Yes	No
GROWTH	Yes	Yes
HLOOKUP	Yes	No
INDEX	Yes	Yes
LINEST	No	Yes
LOGEST	No	Yes
LOOKUP	Yes	No
MATCH	Yes	No
MDETERM	Yes	No
MINVERSE	No	Yes
MMULT	No	Yes
ROW	No	Yes, if the argument is a range
ROWS	Yes	No
SUMPRODUCT	Yes	No
TRANSPOSE	Yes	Yes
TREND	Yes	Yes
VLOOKUP	Yes	No
XLOOKUP	Yes	Yes

> **Note** When you use functions that return arrays, be sure to select an empty range that's large enough to hold the resulting array.

Excel also includes several dynamic array functions that you include as part of a single cell's formula and produce results that spill into multiple cells. Table 2-2 lists the dynamic array functions in Excel.

TABLE 2-2 Dynamic array functions in Excel

Function	Uses Array Argument?	Returns Array Result?
FILTER	No	Yes
RANDARRAY	No	Yes
SEQUENCE	No	Yes
SINGLE	Yes	Yes
SORT	Yes	Yes

Function	Uses Array Argument?	Returns Array Result?
SORTBY	Yes	Yes
UNIQUE	Yes	Yes

Note When you use functions that return dynamic arrays, be sure to enter the formula only in the first cell of the results range. Also, be sure that the rest of the results range is empty.

Arrays become truly powerful weapons in your Excel arsenal when you combine them with worksheet functions such as IF and SUM. I'll provide you with many examples of array formulas as I introduce you to Excel's worksheet functions throughout Part II.

Using iteration and circular references

A common business problem involves calculating a profit-sharing plan contribution as a percentage of a company's net profits. This isn't a simple multiplication problem because the net profit is determined partly by the profit-sharing figure. For example, suppose that a company has revenue of $1,000,000 and expenses of $900,000, which leaves a gross profit of $100,000. The company also sets aside 10 percent of net profits for profit sharing. The net profit is calculated with the following formula:

```
Net Profit - Gross Profit - Profit Sharing Contribution
```

This is called a *circular reference formula* because there are terms on the left and right sides of the equal sign that depend on each other. Specifically, Profit Sharing Contribution is derived with the following formula:

```
Profit Sharing Contribution = (Net Profit) * 0.1
```

One way to solve such a formula is to guess at an answer and see how close you come. For example, because profit sharing should be 10 percent of net profits, a good first guess might be 10 percent of *gross* profits, or $10,000. If you plug this number into the formula, you end up with a net profit of $90,000. However, this isn't right because 10 percent of $90,000 is $9,000. Therefore, the profit-sharing guess is off by $1,000.

So, you can try again. This time, use $9,000 as the profit-sharing number. Plugging this new value into the formula gives a net profit of $91,000. This number translates into a profit-sharing contribution of $9,100—which is off by only $100.

If you continue this process, your profit-sharing guesses will get closer to (that is, they will *converge* on) the calculated value. When the guesses are close enough (for example, within $1), you can stop and pat yourself on the back for finding the solution. This technique is called *iteration*.

Of course, you didn't spend your (or your company's) hard-earned money on a computer so that you could do this sort of thing by hand. Excel makes iterative calculations a breeze, as you see in the following procedure:

1. Set up your worksheet and enter your circular reference formula. Figure 2-5 shows a worksheet for the profit-sharing example just discussed. If Excel displays a dialog box telling you that it can't resolve circular references, select **OK** and then select **Formulas** > **Remove Arrows** (see Chapter 3, "Troubleshooting formulas").

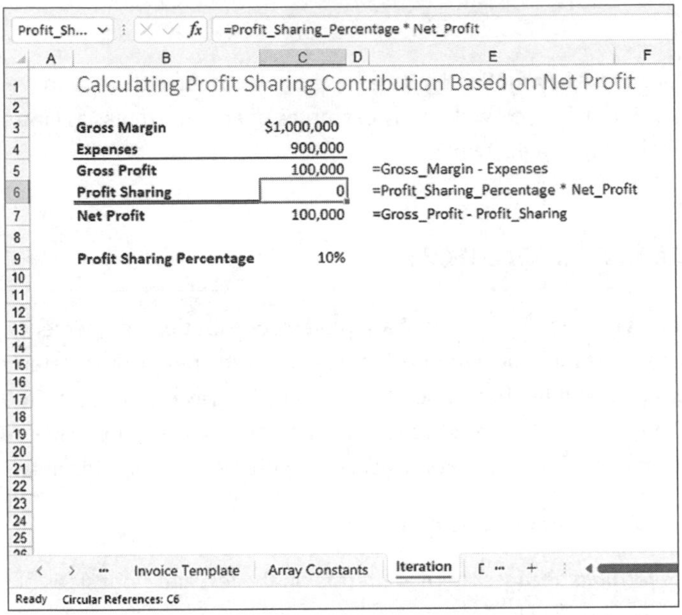

FIGURE 2-5 This worksheet has a circular reference formula.

2. Select **File** > **Options** > **Formulas** to display Excel formula options.

3. Select the **Enable Iterative Calculation** check box.

4. Use the **Maximum Iterations** spin box to enter the number of iterations you need. In most cases, the default figure of 100 is more than enough.

5. Use the **Maximum Change** text box to enter how accurate you want your results to be. The smaller the number, the longer the iteration takes and the more accurate the calculation will be. Again, the default value of 0.001 is a reasonable compromise in most situations.

6. Select **OK**. Excel begins the iteration and stops when it has found a solution (see Figure 2-6).

Profit_Sh... ⌄	:	✗ ✓	*fx*	=Profit_Sharing_Percentage * Net_Profit		

▲	A	B	C	D	E	F
1		Calculating Profit Sharing Contribution Based on Net Profit				
2						
3		**Gross Margin**	$1,000,000			
4		**Expenses**	900,000			
5		**Gross Profit**	100,000	=Gross_Margin - Expenses		
6		**Profit Sharing**	9,091	=Profit_Sharing_Percentage * Net_Profit		
7		**Net Profit**	90,909	=Gross_Profit - Profit_Sharing		
8						
9		**Profit Sharing Percentage**	10%			
10						

FIGURE 2-6 This is the solution to the iterative profit-sharing problem.

> **Tip** If you want to watch the progress of the iteration, select the Manual option button in the Calculation Options section of the Formulas tab and enter **1** in the Maximum Iterations spin box. When you return to your worksheet, each time you press F9, Excel performs a single pass of the iteration.

Consolidating multisheet data

Many businesses create worksheets for specific tasks and then distribute them to various departments. The most common example is budgeting. Accounting might create a generic "budget" template that each department or division in the company must fill out and return. Similarly, you often see worksheets distributed for inventory requirements, sales forecasting, survey data, experimental results, and more.

Creating these worksheets, distributing them, and filling them in are all straightforward operations. However, the tricky part comes when the sheets are returned to the originating department, and all the new data must be combined into a summary report showing companywide totals. This task is called *consolidating* the data, and it's often no picnic, especially for large, multisheet workbooks. However, as you'll soon see, Excel has some powerful features that can take the drudgery out of consolidation.

Excel can consolidate your data using one of the following two methods:

- **Consolidating by position:** With this method, Excel consolidates the data from several worksheets, using the same range coordinates on each sheet. You can use this method if the worksheets you're consolidating have an identical layout.

- **Consolidating by category:** This method tells Excel to consolidate the data by looking for identical row and column labels in each sheet. For example, if one worksheet lists monthly Gizmo sales in row 1 and another lists monthly Gizmo sales in row 5, you can consolidate this information as long as both sheets have a "Gizmo" label at the beginning of these rows.

In both cases, you specify one or more *source ranges* (the ranges that contain the data you want to consolidate) and a *destination range* (the range where the consolidated data will appear). The next couple of sections take you through the details for both consolidation methods.

Consolidating by position

If the sheets you're working with have the same layout, consolidating by position is the easiest way to go. For example, check out the three worksheets—Division I, Division II, and Division III—shown in Figure 2-7. As you can see, each sheet uses the same row and column labels, so they're perfect candidates for consolidation by position.

Begin by creating a new worksheet that has the same layout as the sheets you're consolidating. Figure 2-8 shows a new Consolidate By Position worksheet that I'll use to consolidate the three budget sheets. (The zeroes you see in this worksheet are the results of the sheet's formulas, which will update automatically when the consolidation is complete.)

Let's look at how to go about consolidating the sales data in the three budget worksheets shown in Figure 2-7. We're dealing with three source ranges:

```
'[Division I'!B4:M6
'[Division II'!B4:M6
'[Division III'!B4:M6
```

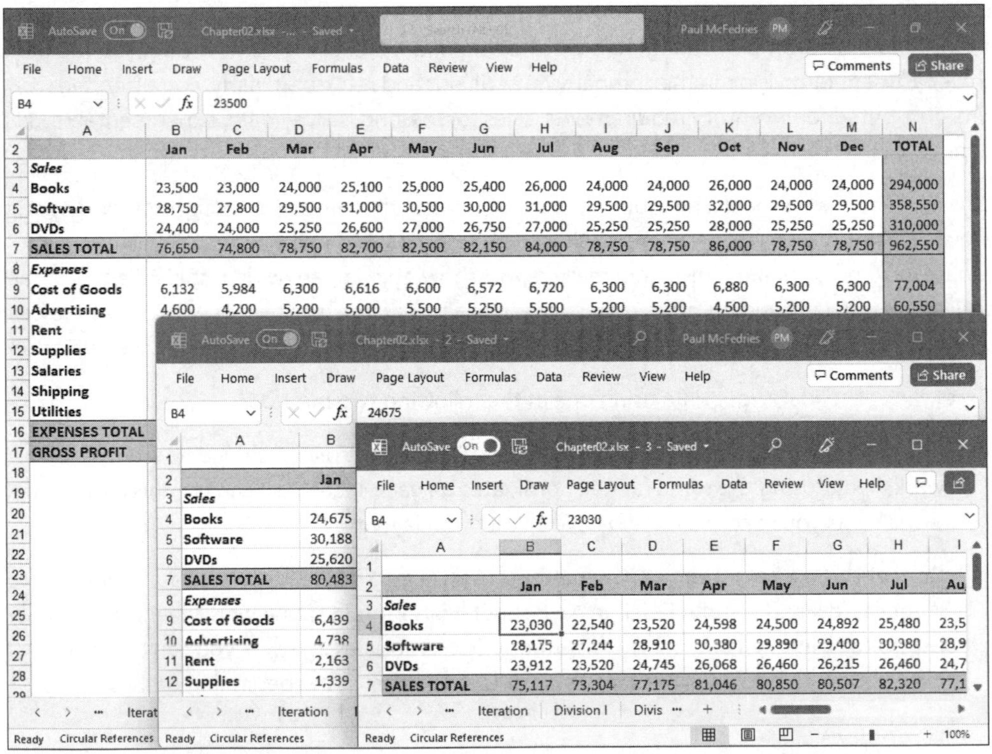

FIGURE 2-7 When your worksheets are laid out identically, use consolidation by position.

	A	B	C	D	E	F	G	H	I	J	K	L	M	N
1														
2		Jan	Feb	Mar	Apr	May	Jun	Jul	Aug	Sep	Oct	Nov	Dec	TOTAL
3	Sales													
4	Books													0
5	Software													0
6	CD-ROMs													0
7	SALES TOTAL													0
8	Expenses													
9	Cost of Goods	0	0	0	0	0	0	0	0	0	0	0	0	0
10	Advertising													0
11	Rent													0
12	Supplies													0
13	Salaries													0
14	Shipping													0
15	Utilities													0
16	EXPENSES TOTAL	0	0	0	0	0	0	0	0	0	0	0	0	0
17	GROSS PROFIT	0	0	0	0	0	0	0	0	0	0	0	0	0
18														

Consolidate By Position | Division A | Division B | ... | +

FIGURE 2-8 When consolidating by position, create a separate consolidation worksheet that uses the same layout as the sheets you're consolidating.

With the consolidation sheet active, follow these steps to consolidate by position:

1. Select the upper-left corner of the destination range. In the Consolidate By Position worksheet, the cell to select is B4.

2. Select **Data** > **Consolidate**. Excel displays the **Consolidate** dialog box.

3. In the **Function** drop-down menu, select the operation to use during the consolidation. You'll use Sum most of the time, but Excel has 10 other operations to choose from, including **Count**, **Average**, **Max**, and **Min**.

4. In the **Reference** text box, enter a reference for one of the source ranges. Use one of the following methods:

   - Enter the range coordinates by hand. If the source range is in another workbook, be sure to include the workbook name enclosed in square brackets. If the workbook is in a different drive or folder, include the full path to the workbook as well.

   - If the sheet is open, select it and then select the range.

   - If the workbook isn't open, select **Browse**, select the file in the Browse dialog box, and then select **OK**. Excel adds the workbook path to the Reference box. Enter the sheet name and the range coordinates.

5. Select **Add**. Excel adds the range to the **All References** box (see Figure 2-9).

6. Repeat steps 4 and 5 to add all the source ranges.

7. If you want the consolidated data to change whenever you make changes to the source data, leave the **Create Links To Source Data** check box selected.

8. Select **OK**. Excel gathers the data, consolidates it, and then adds it to the destination range (see Figure 2-10).

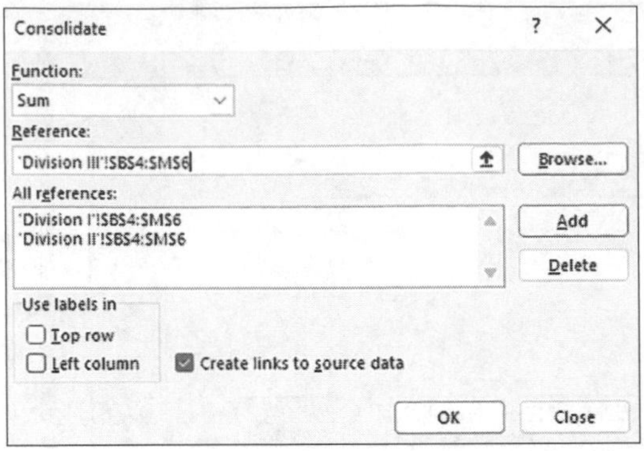

FIGURE 2-9 The Consolidate dialog box, with several source ranges added

If you chose not to create links to the source data in step 7, Excel just fills the destination range with the consolidation totals. However, if you did create links, Excel does three things:

■ Adds link formulas to the destination range for each cell in the source ranges you selected.

■ Consolidates the data by adding **SUM** functions (or whichever operation you selected in the **Function** list) that total the results of the link formulas.

■ Outlines the consolidation worksheet and hides the link formulas, as you can see in Figure 2-10.

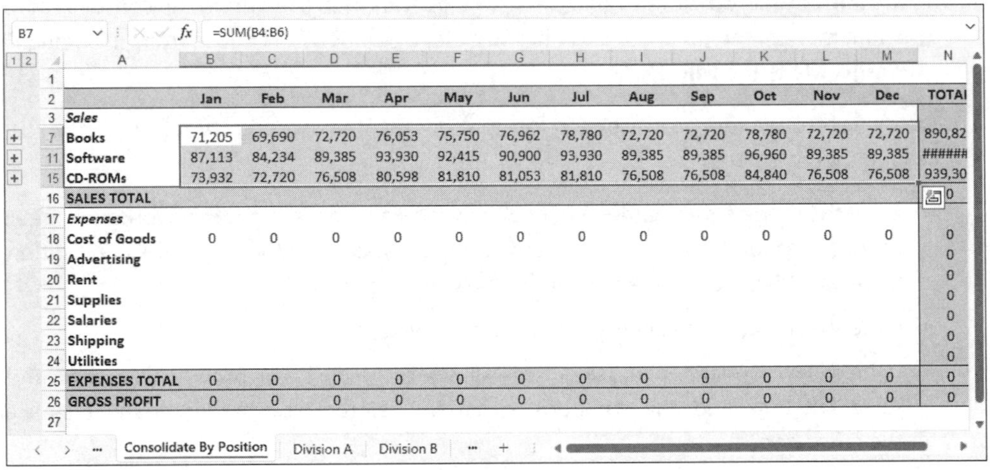

	A	Jan	Feb	Mar	Apr	May	Jun	Jul	Aug	Sep	Oct	Nov	Dec	TOTAl
3	*Sales*													
7	**Books**	71,205	69,690	72,720	76,053	75,750	76,962	78,780	72,720	72,720	78,780	72,720	72,720	890,82
11	**Software**	87,113	84,234	89,385	93,930	92,415	90,900	93,930	89,385	89,385	96,960	89,385	89,385	######
15	**CD-ROMs**	73,932	72,720	76,508	80,598	81,810	81,053	81,810	76,508	76,508	84,840	76,508	76,508	939,30
16	**SALES TOTAL**													0
17	*Expenses*													
18	**Cost of Goods**	0	0	0	0	0	0	0	0	0	0	0	0	0
19	**Advertising**													0
20	**Rent**													0
21	**Supplies**													0
22	**Salaries**													0
23	**Shipping**													0
24	**Utilities**													0
25	**EXPENSES TOTAL**	0	0	0	0	0	0	0	0	0	0	0	0	0
26	**GROSS PROFIT**	0	0	0	0	0	0	0	0	0	0	0	0	0

FIGURE 2-10 Here is a worksheet with the consolidated sales budgets.

If you display the Level 1 data, you'll see the linked formulas. For example, Figure 2-11 shows the detail for the consolidated sales number for Books in January (cell B7). Cells B4, B5, and B6 contain formulas that link to the corresponding cells in the three budget worksheets (for example, `'Division I'!$B$4`).

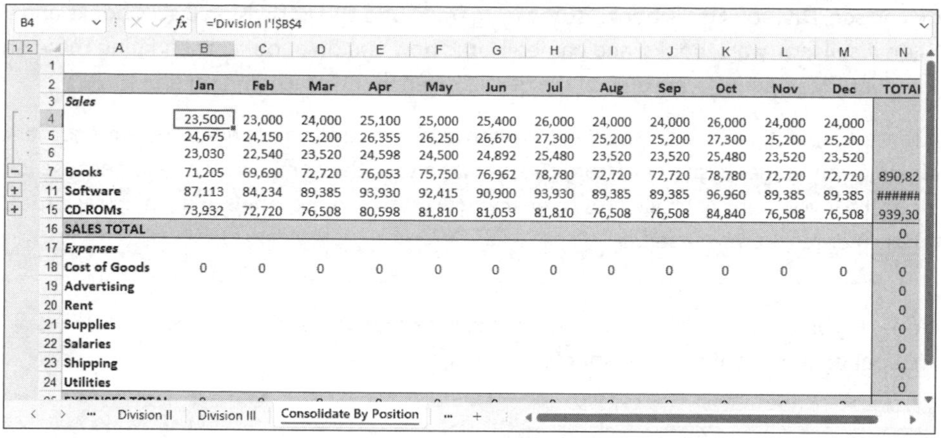

B4   ✕ ✓ *fx*   ='Division I'!$B$4

	A	B	C	D	E	F	G	H	I	J	K	L	M	N
2		Jan	Feb	Mar	Apr	May	Jun	Jul	Aug	Sep	Oct	Nov	Dec	TOTAL
3	*Sales*													
4		23,500	23,000	24,000	25,100	25,000	25,400	26,000	24,000	24,000	26,000	24,000	24,000	
5		24,675	24,150	25,200	26,355	26,250	26,670	27,300	25,200	25,200	27,300	25,200	25,200	
6		23,030	22,540	23,520	24,598	24,500	24,892	25,480	23,520	23,520	25,480	23,520	23,520	
7	Books	71,205	69,690	72,720	76,053	75,750	76,962	78,780	72,720	72,720	78,780	72,720	72,720	890,82
11	Software	87,113	84,234	89,385	93,930	92,415	90,900	93,930	89,385	89,385	96,960	89,385	89,385	######
15	CD-ROMs	73,932	72,720	76,508	80,598	81,810	81,053	81,810	76,508	76,508	84,840	76,508	76,508	939,30
16	SALES TOTAL													0
17	*Expenses*													
18	Cost of Goods	0	0	0	0	0	0	0	0	0	0	0	0	0
19	Advertising													0
20	Rent													0
21	Supplies													0
22	Salaries													0
23	Shipping													0
24	Utilities													0

‹ › ⋯   Division II   Division III   **Consolidate By Position**   ⋯ +

FIGURE 2-11 The detail (linked formulas) for the consolidated data

Consolidating by category

If you want to consolidate data from worksheets that don't use the same layout, you need to tell Excel to consolidate the data *by category*. In this case, Excel examines each of your source ranges and consolidates data that uses the same row or column labels. For example, take a look at the Sales rows in the three worksheets shown in Figure 2-12.

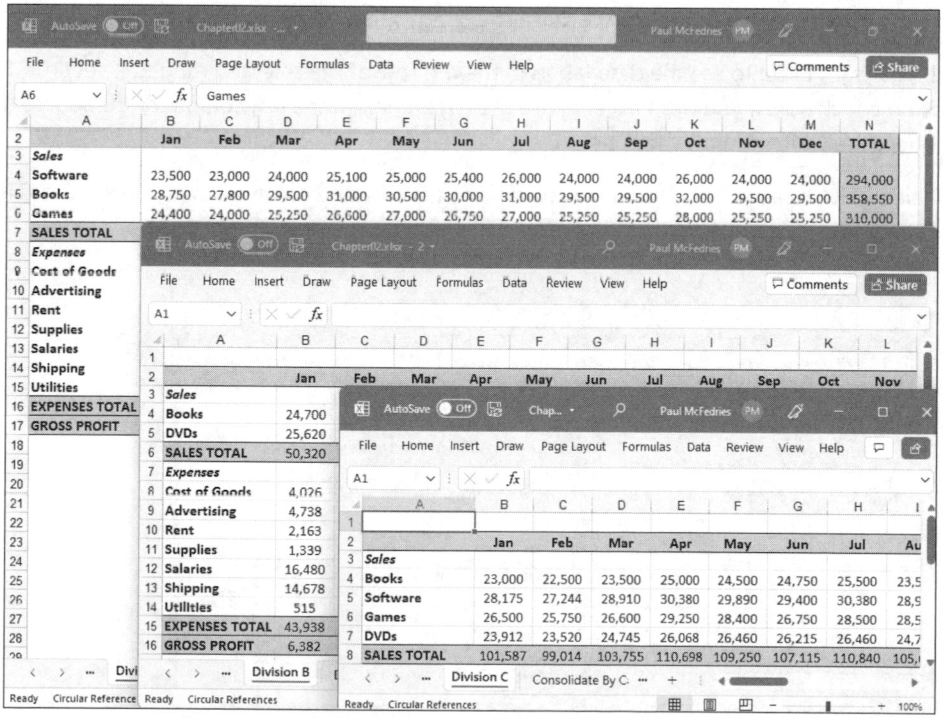

FIGURE 2-12 Each division sells a different mix of products, so we need to consolidate by category.

As you can see, Division C sells books, software, games, and DVDs; Division B sells books and DVDs; and Division A sells software, books, and games. Here's how you go about consolidating these numbers. (Note that I'm skipping over some of the details given in the preceding section.)

1. Create or select a new worksheet for the consolidation and select the upper-left corner of the destination range. It isn't necessary to enter labels for the consolidated data because Excel does it for you automatically. However, if you want to see the labels in a particular order, it's okay to enter them yourself.

> **Caution** If you enter the labels yourself, make sure that you spell the labels exactly as they're spelled in the source worksheets.

2. Select **Data** > **Consolidate** to display the Consolidate dialog box.
3. In the **Function** drop-down menu, select the operation to use during the consolidation.
4. In the **Reference** text box, enter a reference for one of the source ranges. In this case, make sure you include in each range the row and column labels for the data.
5. Select **Add** to add the range to the **All References** box.
6. Repeat steps 4 and 5 to add all the source ranges.
7. If you want the consolidated data to change whenever you make changes to the source data, leave the **Create Links To Source Data** check box selected.
8. If you want Excel to use the data labels in the top row of the selected ranges, select the **Top Row** check box. If you want Excel to use the data labels in the left column of the source ranges, select the **Left Column** check box.
9. Select **OK**. Excel gathers the data according to the row and column labels, consolidates it, and then adds it to the destination range (see Figure 2-13).

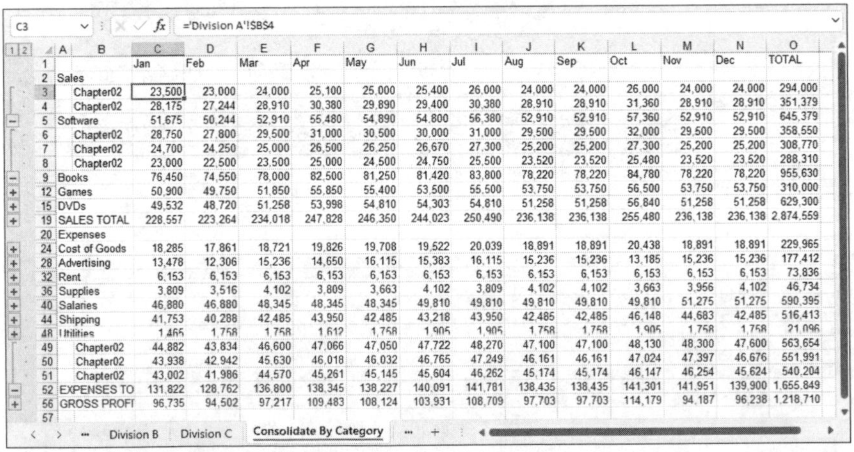

	A / B	C	D	E	F	G	H	I	J	K	L	M	N	O
1		Jan	Feb	Mar	Apr	May	Jun	Jul	Aug	Sep	Oct	Nov	Dec	TOTAL
2	Sales													
3	Chapter02	23,500	23,000	24,000	25,100	25,000	25,400	26,000	24,000	24,000	26,000	24,000	24,000	294,000
4	Chapter02	28,175	27,244	28,910	30,380	29,890	29,400	30,380	28,910	28,910	31,360	28,910	28,910	351,379
5	Software	51,675	50,244	52,910	55,480	54,890	54,800	56,380	52,910	52,910	57,360	52,910	52,910	645,379
6	Chapter02	28,750	27,800	29,500	31,000	30,500	30,000	31,000	29,500	29,500	32,000	29,500	29,500	358,550
7	Chapter02	24,700	24,250	25,000	26,500	26,250	26,670	27,300	25,200	25,200	27,300	25,200	25,200	308,770
8	Chapter02	23,000	22,500	23,500	25,000	24,500	24,750	25,500	23,520	23,520	25,480	23,520	23,520	288,310
9	Books	76,450	74,550	78,000	82,500	81,250	81,420	83,800	78,220	78,220	84,780	78,220	78,220	955,630
12	Games	50,900	49,750	51,850	55,850	55,400	53,500	55,500	53,750	53,750	56,500	53,750	53,750	310,000
15	DVDs	49,532	48,720	51,258	53,998	54,810	54,303	54,810	51,258	51,258	56,840	51,258	51,258	629,300
19	SALES TOTAL	228,557	223,264	234,018	247,828	246,350	244,023	250,490	236,138	236,138	255,480	236,138	236,138	2,874,559
20	Expenses													
24	Cost of Goods	18,285	17,861	18,721	19,826	19,708	19,522	20,039	18,891	18,891	20,438	18,891	18,891	229,965
28	Advertising	13,478	12,306	15,236	14,650	16,115	15,383	16,115	15,236	15,236	13,185	15,236	15,236	177,412
32	Rent	6,153	6,153	6,153	6,153	6,153	6,153	6,153	6,153	6,153	6,153	6,153	6,153	73,836
36	Supplies	3,809	3,516	4,102	3,809	3,663	4,102	3,809	4,102	4,102	3,663	3,956	4,102	46,734
40	Salaries	46,880	46,880	48,345	48,345	48,345	49,810	49,810	49,810	49,810	49,810	51,275	51,275	590,395
44	Shipping	41,753	40,288	42,485	43,950	42,485	43,218	43,950	42,485	42,485	46,148	44,683	42,485	516,413
48	Utilities	1,465	1,758	1,758	1,612	1,758	1,905	1,905	1,758	1,758	1,905	1,758	1,758	21,096
49	Chapter02	44,882	43,834	46,600	47,066	47,050	47,722	48,270	47,100	47,100	48,130	48,300	47,600	563,654
50	Chapter02	43,938	42,942	45,630	46,018	46,032	46,765	47,249	46,161	46,161	47,024	47,397	46,676	551,991
51	Chapter02	43,002	41,986	44,570	45,261	45,145	45,604	46,262	45,174	45,174	46,147	46,254	45,624	540,204
52	EXPENSES TO	131,822	128,762	136,800	138,345	138,227	140,091	141,781	138,435	138,435	141,301	141,951	139,900	1,655,849
56	GROSS PROFI	96,735	94,502	97,217	109,483	108,124	103,931	108,709	97,703	97,703	114,179	94,187	96,238	1,218,710
57														

FIGURE 2-13 Here, the sales numbers are consolidated by category.

Applying data validation rules to cells

It's an unfortunate fact of spreadsheet life that formulas are only as good as the data they're given. It's the GIGO effect, as programmers say: garbage in, garbage out. In worksheet terms, *garbage in* means entering erroneous or improper data into a formula's input cells. For basic data entry errors (for example, entering the wrong date or transposing a number's digits), there's not a lot you can do other than exhorting yourself or the people who use your worksheets to enter data carefully. Fortunately, you have a bit more control when it comes to preventing improper data entry. By *improper*, I mean data that falls in either of the following categories:

- **Data that is the wrong type:** For example, typing a text string in a cell that requires a number

- **Data that falls outside of an allowable range:** For example, typing **200** in a cell that requires a number between 1 and 100

You can prevent these kinds of improper entries, to a certain extent, by adding comments that provide details on what is allowable inside a particular cell. However, this requires other people to both read *and* act on the comment text. Another solution is to use custom numeric formatting to "format" a cell with an error message if the wrong type of data is entered. This is useful, but it works only for certain kinds of input errors.

The best solution for preventing data entry errors is to use Excel's data-validation feature. With data validation, you create *rules* that specify exactly what kind of data can be entered and in what range that data can fall. You can also specify pop-up input messages that appear when a cell is selected, as well as error messages that appear when data is entered improperly.

You can also ask Excel to "circle" any cells that contain data-validation errors (which is handy when you import data into a list that contains data-validation rules). You do this by choosing **Data** > **Data Validation** > **Circle Invalid Data**.

Follow these steps to define the settings for a data-validation rule:

1. Select the cell or range to which you want to apply the data-validation rule.

2. Select **Data** > **Data Validation**. Excel displays the **Data Validation** dialog box.

3. In the **Settings** tab, use the **Allow** list to select one of the following validation types:

   - **Any Value:** Allows any value in the range. (That is, it removes any previously applied validation rule. If you're removing an existing rule, be sure to also clear the input message if you created one, as shown later in step 7.)

   - **Whole Number:** Allows only whole numbers (integers). Use the **Data** list to select a comparison operator (between, equal to, less than, and so on), and then enter the specific criteria. (For example, if you select the **Between** option, you must enter **Minimum** and **Maximum** values, as shown in Figure 2-14.)

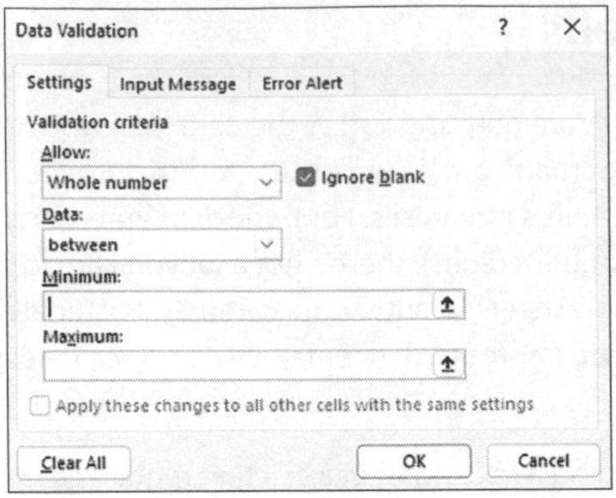

FIGURE 2-14 Use the Data Validation dialog box to set up a data-validation rule for a cell or range.

- **Decimal:** Allows decimal numbers or whole numbers. Use the **Data** list to select a comparison operator, and then enter the specific numeric criteria.

- **List:** Allows only values specified in a list. Use the **Source** box to specify either a range on the same sheet or a range name on any sheet that contains the list of allowable values. (Precede the range or range name with an equal sign.) Alternatively, you can enter the allowable values directly into the **Source** box (separated by commas). If you want the user to be able to select from the allowable values using a drop-down list, leave the **In-Cell Dropdown** check box selected.

- **Date:** Allows only dates. (If the user includes a time value, the entry is invalid.) Use the **Data** list to select a comparison operator, and then enter the specific date criteria (such as a **Start Date** and an **End Date**).

- **Time:** Allows only times. (If the user includes a date value, the entry is invalid.) Use the **Data** list to select a comparison operator, and then enter the specific time criteria (such as a **Start Time** and an **End Time**).

- **Text Length:** Allows only alphanumeric strings of a specified length. Use the **Data** list to select a comparison operator, and then enter the specific length criteria (such as **Minimum** and **Maximum** lengths).

- **Custom:** Use this option to enter a formula that specifies the validation criteria. You can either enter the formula directly into the **Formula** box (be sure to precede the formula with an equal sign), or enter a reference to a cell that contains the formula. For example, if you're restricting cell A2 and you want to be sure the entered value is not the same as what's in cell A1, enter the formula =A2<>A1.

4. To allow blank entries, either in the cell itself or in other cells specified as part of the validation settings, leave the **Ignore Blank** check box selected. If you deselect this check box, Excel treats blank entries as zero and applies the validation rule accordingly.

5. If the range had an existing validation rule that also applied to other cells, you can apply the new rule to those other cells by selecting the **Apply These Changes To All Other Cells With The Same Settings** check box.

6. Select the **Input Message** tab.

7. If you want a pop-up box to appear when the user selects the restricted cell or any cell within the restricted range, leave the **Show Input Message When Cell Is Selected** check box selected. Use the **Title** and **Input Message** boxes to specify the message that appears. For example, you could use the message to give the user information on the type and range of allowable values.

8. Select the **Error Alert** tab.

9. If you want a dialog box to appear when the user enters invalid data, leave the **Show Error Alert After Invalid Data Is Entered** check box selected. In the **Style** list, select the error style you want: **Stop**, **Warning**, or **Information**. Use the **Title** and **Error Message** boxes to specify the message that appears.

> **Caution** Only the Stop style can prevent the user from ignoring the error and entering the invalid data anyway.

10. Click **OK** to apply the data-validation rule.

Using dialog box controls on a worksheet

In the previous section, you saw how using List for the type of validation enabled you to supply yourself or the customer with an in-cell drop-down list of allowable choices. This is good data entry practice because it reduces the uncertainty about the allowable values.

One of Excel's slickest features is that it enables you to extend this idea and place not only lists but also other dialog box controls, such as spin boxes and check boxes, directly on a worksheet. You can then link the values returned by these controls to a cell to create an elegant method for entering data.

Displaying the Developer tab

Before working with dialog box controls, you need to display the Ribbon's Developer tab:

1. Right-click any part of the ribbon and then select Customize The Ribbon. The Excel Options dialog box appears, with the Customize Ribbon tab displayed.

2. In the Customize The Ribbon list, select the **Developer** check box.

3. Select **OK**.

Using the form controls

You add the dialog box controls by choosing **Developer** > **Insert** and then selecting tools from the **Form Controls** list, shown in Figure 2-15. Note that only some of the controls are available for worksheet duty. I will discuss the controls in detail a bit later in this section.

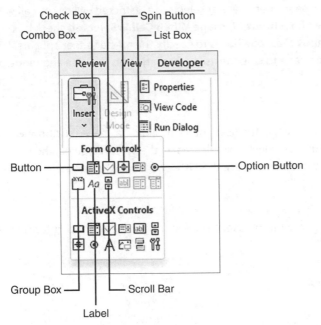

FIGURE 2-15 Use the controls in the Form Controls list to draw dialog box controls on a worksheet.

Adding a control to a worksheet

You add controls to a worksheet using the same steps you use to create any graphics object. Here's the basic procedure:

1. Select **Developer** > **Insert** and then select the form control you want to create. The mouse pointer changes to a crosshair.

2. Move the pointer onto the worksheet at the location where you want the control to appear.

3. Drag to create the control.

Excel assigns a default caption to each group box, check box, and option button. To edit this caption, you have two ways to get started:

■ Right-click the control and select **Edit Text**.

■ Hold down Ctrl and click the control to select it. Then select inside the control.

Edit the text accordingly; when you're done, select outside the control. To reselect a control, hold down Ctrl and click the control.

Linking a control to a cell value

To use the dialog box controls for inputting data, you need to associate each control with a worksheet cell. The following steps walk you through the procedure:

1. Select the control you want to work with. (Again, remember to hold down the Ctrl key before you select the control.)

2. Right-click the control and then select **Format Control** (or select Ctrl+1) to display the **Format Control** dialog box.

3. Select the **Control** tab and then use the **Cell Link** box to enter the cell's reference.

4. Select **OK** to return to the worksheet.

Tip Another way to link a control to a cell is to select the control and enter a formula in the formula bar in the form =`cell`. Here, `cell` is a reference to the cell you want to use. For example, to link a control to cell A1, you enter the formula =`A1`.

Note When working with option buttons, you have to enter the linked cell for only one of the buttons in a group. Excel automatically adds the reference to the rest.

Understanding the worksheet controls

To get the most out of worksheet controls, you need to know the specifics of how each control works and how you can use each one for data entry. To that end, the next few sections take you through detailed accounts of various controls.

Group boxes

Group boxes don't do much on their own. You use one to create a grouping of two or more option buttons. The user can then select only one option from the group. For this to work, you must proceed as follows:

1. Select **Developer** > **Insert** > **Group Box** in the **Form Controls** list.

2. Drag to draw the group box on the worksheet.

3. Select **Developer** > **Insert** > **Option Button** in the **Form Controls** list.

4. Drag within the group box to create an option button.

5. Repeat steps 3 and 4 as many times as needed to create the other option buttons.

Remember, it's important that you create the group box first and then draw option buttons within the group box.

> **Note** If you have one (and only one) option button outside a grouping, you can still include it in a group box. (If you have multiple option buttons outside a group box, this technique won't work.) To do this, first, hold down Ctrl and click the option button to select it. Release Ctrl, and then move the option button to within the group box.

Option buttons

Option buttons are controls that usually appear in groups of two or more, and the user can select only one of the options. As I said in the previous section, option buttons work in tandem with group boxes, in which the user can select only one of the option buttons within a group box.

> **Note** All the option buttons that don't lie within a group box are treated as a de facto group. (That is, Excel allows you to select only one of these nongroup options at a time.) This means that a group box isn't strictly necessary when using option buttons on a worksheet. Most people do use them because they give the user visual clues about which options are related.

By default, Excel draws each option button in the unselected state. Therefore, you should specify in advance which of the option buttons is selected by default:

1. Hold down Ctrl and select the option button you want to display as selected.

2. Right-click the control and then select **Format Control** (or press Ctrl+1) to display the Format Control dialog box.

3. In the **Control** tab, select the **Checked** option.

4. Select **OK**.

On the worksheet, selecting an option button changes the value stored in the linked cell. The value stored depends on the option button, where the first button added to the group box has the value **1**, the second button has the value **2**, and so on. The advantage of this is that it enables you to translate a text option into a numeric value. For example, Figure 2-16 shows a worksheet in which the option buttons give the user three freight choices: **Surface Mail**, **Air Mail**, and **Courier**. The value of the chosen option is stored in the linked cell, which is E4. For example, if **Air Mail** is selected, the value **2** is stored in E4. For example, in a production model, the worksheet would use this value to look up the corresponding freight charges and adjust an invoice accordingly. (To learn how to look up values in a worksheet, see Chapter 7, "Working with lookup functions.")

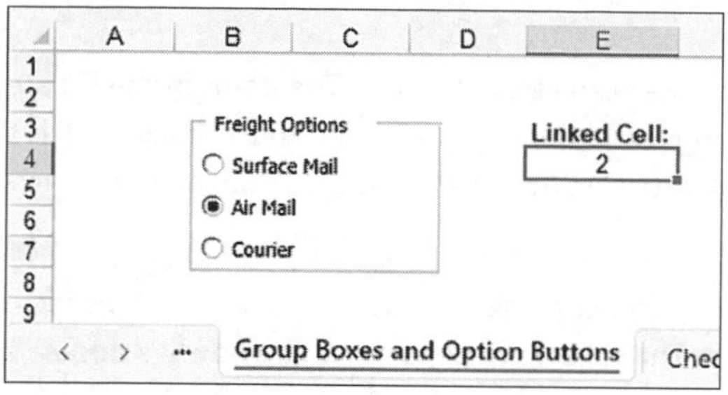

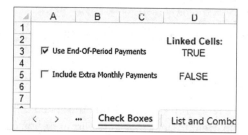

FIGURE 2-16 For option buttons, the value stored in the linked cell is based on the order in which the buttons were added to the group box.

Check boxes

Check boxes enable you to include options that the user can toggle on or off. As with option buttons, Excel draws each check box in the unchecked state. If you prefer to have a check box start in the checked state, use the Format Control dialog box to select the control's **Checked** option, as described in the previous section.

On the worksheet, a selected check box stores the value TRUE in its linked cell; if the check box is deselected, it stores the value FALSE (see Figure 2-17). This is handy because it enables you to add a bit of logic to your formulas. That is, you can test whether a check box is selected and adjust a formula accordingly. Figure 2-17 shows a couple of examples:

- **Use End-Of-Period Payments:** This check box could be used to specify whether a formula that determines the monthly payments on a loan assumes that those payments are made at the end of each period (TRUE) or at the beginning of each period (FALSE).

- **Include Extra Monthly Payments:** This check box could be used to determine whether a model that builds a loan amortization schedule formula includes an extra principal repayment each month.

FIGURE 2-17 For check boxes, the value stored in the linked cell is TRUE when the check box is selected and FALSE when it is not selected.

In both cases, and in most formulas that take into account check box results, you would use the IF worksheet function to read the current value of the linked cell and branch accordingly. To learn how to use the IF worksheet function, see Chapter 6, "Working with logical and information functions."

List boxes and combo boxes

A list box control creates a list box from which the user can select an item. The items in the list are defined by the values in a specified worksheet range, and the value returned to the linked cell is the number of the chosen item. A combo box is similar to a list box; however, the control shows only one item at a time until it's dropped down.

List boxes and combo boxes are different from other controls because you also have to specify a range that contains the items to appear in the list. The following steps show you how it's done:

1. Enter the list items in a range. (The items must be listed in a single row or a single column.)

2. Add the list box control to the sheet (if you haven't done so already), and then select it.

3. Right-click the control and then select **Format Control** (or press Ctrl+1) to display the Format Control dialog box.

4. Select the Control tab and then use the **Input Range** box to enter a reference to the range of items.

5. Select **OK** to return to the worksheet.

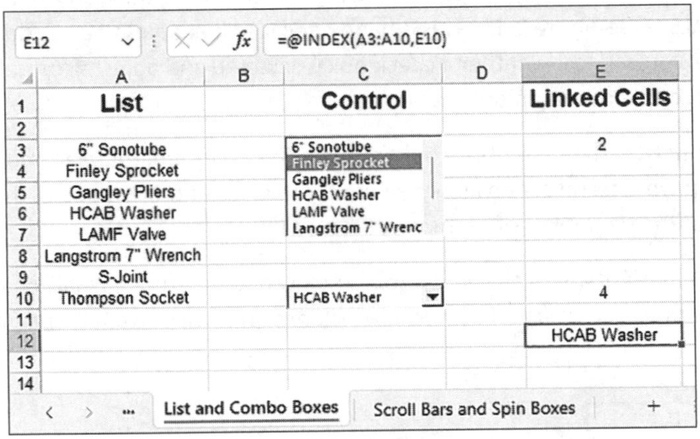

FIGURE 2-18 For list boxes and combo boxes, the value stored in the linked cell is the number of the selected list item. To get the item text, use the INDEX() function.

Figure 2-18 shows a worksheet with a list box and a drop-down list.

The list used by both controls in this example is in the range A3:A10. Notice that the linked cells display the number of the list selection, not the selection itself. To get the selected list item, you can use the INDEX function with the following syntax:

```
INDEX(list_range, list_selection)
```

list_range	The range used in the list box or drop-down list.
list_selection	The number of the item selected in the list.

For example, to find the item that's currently selected in the combo box in Figure 2-18, you use the following formula (as shown in cell E12):

```
=INDEX(A3:A10,E10)
```

To learn more about the INDEX function, see Chapter 7.

Scroll bars and spin boxes

The Scroll Bar tool creates a control that resembles a window scroll bar. You use this type of scroll bar to select a number from a range of values. Selecting the arrows or dragging the scroll box changes the value of the control. This value is what gets returned to the linked cell. Note that you can create either a horizontal scroll bar or a vertical scroll bar.

In the Format Control dialog box for a scroll bar, the **Control** tab includes the following options:

- **Current Value:** The initial value of the scroll bar.

- **Minimum Value:** The value of the scroll bar when the scroll box is at its leftmost position (for a horizontal scroll bar) or its topmost position (for a vertical scroll bar).

- **Maximum Value:** The value of the scroll bar when the scroll box is at its rightmost position (for a horizontal scroll bar) or its bottommost position (for a vertical scroll bar).

- **Incremental Change:** The amount that the scroll bar's value changes when the user clicks a scroll arrow.

- **Page Change:** The amount that the scroll bar's value changes when the user clicks between the scroll box and a scroll arrow.

The Spin Box tool creates a control that is similar to a scroll bar; that is, you can use a spin box to select a number between a maximum value and a minimum value by selecting the arrows. The number is returned to the linked cell. Spin box options are identical to those of scroll bars, except that you can't set a **Page Change** value.

Figure 2-19 shows an example of a scroll bar and an example of a spin box. Note that the numbers above the scroll bar giving the minimum and maximum values are extra labels I added by hand. Doing this is usually a good idea because it gives the user the numeric limits of the control.

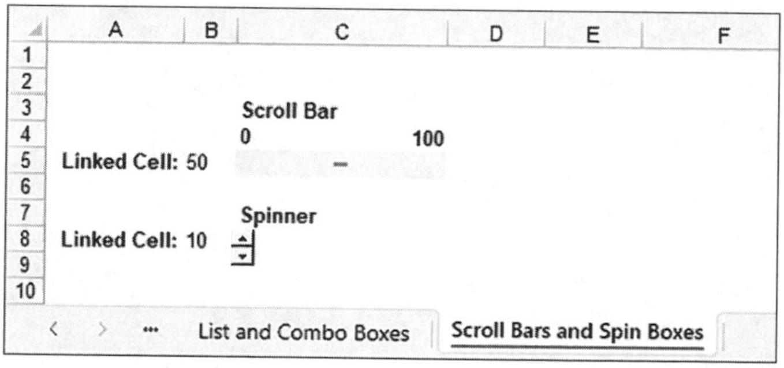

FIGURE 2-19 For scroll bars and spin boxes, the value stored in the linked cell is the current numeric value of the control.

CHAPTER 3

Troubleshooting formulas

In this chapter, you will:

- Decipher the formula error values that Excel displays

- Learn how to fix a few other common formula error types

- Handle formula errors gracefully with the IFERROR function

- Diagnose formula problems using Excel's Formula Error Checker

- Learn how to use Excel's worksheet auditing tools

Despite your best efforts, the odd error might appear in your formulas from time to time. Such errors can be mathematical (for example, dividing by zero), or Excel might simply be incapable of interpreting the formula. In the latter case, problems can be caught while you're entering the formula. For example, if you try to enter a formula that has unbalanced parentheses, Excel doesn't accept the entry, and it displays an error message. Other errors are more insidious. For example, your formula might *appear* to be working—that is, it might return a value—but the result might be incorrect because the data is flawed or because your formula has referenced the wrong cell or range.

Whatever the error and cause, formula woes need to be worked out because you or someone else in your company likely depends on your models to produce accurate results. Don't fall into the trap of thinking that *your* spreadsheets are problem-free. A recent University of Hawaii study found that 50 percent of spreadsheets contained errors that led to "significant miscalculations." And the more complex the model, the greater the chance that errors can creep in. A KPMG study from a few years ago found that a staggering 90 percent of spreadsheets used for tax calculations contained errors.

The good news is that fixing formula flaws need not be drudgery. With a bit of know-how and Excel's top-notch troubleshooting tools, sniffing out and repairing model maladies isn't hard. This chapter tells you everything you need to know.

> **Tip** If you try to enter an incorrect formula, Excel won't let you do anything else until you either fix the problem or cancel the operation (which means you lose your formula). If the formula is complex, you might not be able to see the problem right away. Instead of deleting all your work, place an apostrophe (') at the beginning of the formula to convert it to text. This way, you can save your work while you try to figure out the problem.

Understanding Excel's error values

When you enter or edit a formula or change one of the formula's input values, Excel might show an error value as the formula result. Excel has eleven different error values: **#CALC!**, **#DIV/0!**, **#FIELD!**, **#N/A**, **#NAME?**, **#NULL!**, **#NUM!**, **#REF!**, **#SPILL!**, **#UNKNOWN!**, and **#VALUE!**. The next few sections give you a detailed look at these error values and offer suggestions for dealing with them.

#CALC!

The new **#CALC!** error appears when Excel's calculation engine comes across a formula or expression that it doesn't support. Examples include one of the following:

- An array nested inside another array

- An array that includes one or more range references

- An array that contains no items

#DIV/0!

The **#DIV/0!** error almost always means that the cell's formula is trying to divide by zero, a mathematical no-no. The cause is usually a reference to a cell that either is blank or contains the value **0**. Check the cell's precedents (the cells that are directly or indirectly referenced in the formula; see "Auditing a worksheet," later in this chapter) to look for possible culprits. You'll also see **#DIV/0!** if you enter an inappropriate argument in some functions. **MOD**, for example, returns **#DIV/0!** if the second argument is **0**.

That Excel treats blank cells as the value **0** can pose problems in a worksheet that requires the user to fill in the data. If your formula requires division by one of the temporarily blank cells, it will show **#DIV/0!** as the result, possibly confusing the user. You can get around this by telling Excel not to perform the calculation if the cell used as the divisor is **0**. This is done with the **IF** worksheet function, which I discuss in detail in Chapter 6, "Working with logical and information functions." (For an even better way to deal with potential formula errors, **see** "Handling formula errors with **IFERROR**," later in this chapter.) For example, consider the following formula, which uses named cells to calculate gross margin:

```
=GrossProfit / Sales
```

To prevent the **#DIV/0!** error from appearing if the Sales cell is blank (or 0), you'd modify the formula as follows:

```
=IF(Sales = 0, "", GrossProfit / Sales)
```

If the value of the Sales cell is **0**, the formula returns the empty string; otherwise, it performs the calculation.

#FIELD!

The **#FIELD!** error value tells you that your formula is referencing an invalid linked data type. This can happen in three ways:

- Your formula includes a data-type reference to a field that isn't found in a linked data type. For example, if cell A1 contains a Stocks data type and your formula references **A1.[52-week high]**, you'll get a **#FIELD!** error because the **52-week high** field doesn't exist. In this example, you can solve the problem by removing the dash: **A1.[52 week high]**.

- Your formula includes a data-type reference (for example, **A1.Price** for a Stocks data type) to a cell that doesn't use a linked data type.

- Your formula includes a data-type reference (for example, **A1.Description** for a Stocks data type) to a cell that doesn't have any data for the referenced field.

#N/A

The **#N/A** error value is short for *not available*, and it means that the formula couldn't return a legitimate result. You usually see **#N/A** when you use an inappropriate argument (or when you omit a required argument) in a function. **HLOOKUP** and **VLOOKUP**, for example (see Chapter 7, "Working with lookup functions"), return **#N/A** if the lookup value is smaller than the first value in the lookup range.

To solve the problem, first check the formula's input cells to see whether any of them are displaying the **#N/A** error. If so, that's why your formula is returning the same error; the problem actually lies in the input cell. When you've found where the error originates, examine the formula's operands to look for inappropriate data types. In particular, check the arguments used in each function to ensure that they make sense for the function and that no required arguments are missing.

> **Note** It's common in spreadsheet work to purposely generate an **#N/A!** error to show that a particular cell value isn't currently available. For example, you might be waiting for budget figures from one or more divisions or for the final numbers from month- or year-end. In such a case, you enter **=NA()** into the cell. You fix this "problem" by replacing the **NA** function with the appropriate data when it arrives.

#NAME?

The **#NAME?** error appears when Excel doesn't recognize a name you used in a formula or when it interprets text within the formula as an undefined name. This means that the **#NAME?** error pops up in a wide variety of circumstances:

- You spelled a range name incorrectly.

- You used a range name that you haven't yet defined.

- You spelled a function name incorrectly.

- You used a function that's part of an uninstalled add-in.

- You used a string value without surrounding it with quotation marks.

- You entered a range reference and accidentally omitted the colon.

- You entered a reference to a range on another worksheet and didn't enclose the sheet name in single quotation marks.

> **Tip** When entering function names and defined names, use all lowercase letters. If Excel recognizes a name, it converts the function to all uppercase and the defined name to its original case. If no conversion occurs, you know that you misspelled the name, you haven't defined it yet, or you're using a function from an add-in that isn't loaded.

Remember that you also can use these commands to enter functions and names safely:

- **Formulas** > **Insert Function** (or press Shift+F3)

- **Formulas** > **Use In Formula**

- **Formulas** > **Use In Formula** > **Paste Names** (or press F3)

These are mostly syntax errors, so fixing them means double-checking your formula and correcting range name or function name misspellings or inserting missing quotation marks or colons. Also, be sure to define any range names you use and to install the appropriate add-in modules for functions you use.

Avoiding #NAME? errors when deleting range names

If you've used a range name in a formula and then you delete that name, Excel generates the #NAME? error. Wouldn't it be better if Excel just converted the name to its appropriate cell reference in each formula? Possibly, but there is an advantage to Excel's seemingly inconvenient approach. By generating an error, Excel enables you to catch range names that you delete by accident. Because Excel leaves the names in the formula, you can recover by redefining the original range name.

Redefining the original range name becomes problematic if you can't remember the appropriate range coordinates. This is why it's always a good idea to paste a list of range names and their references into each of your workbooks (select **Formulas** > **Use In Formula** > **Paste Names** > **Paste List**).

If you don't need this safety net, you can force Excel to convert deleted range names into their cell references. Here are the steps to follow:

1. Select **File** > **Options** to display the **Excel Options** dialog box.

2. Select **Advanced**.

3. In the **Lotus Compatibility Settings For** section, use the list to select the worksheet you want to use.

4. Select the **Transition Formula Entry** check box.

5. Select **OK**.

Excel now treats your formula entries the same way Lotus 1-2-3 did way back in days of yore. Specifically, in formulas that use a deleted range name, the name automatically gets converted to its appropriate range reference. As an added bonus, Excel also performs the following automatic conversions:

- If you enter a range reference in a formula, the reference gets converted to a range name (provided that a name exists, of course).

- If you define a name for a range, Excel converts any existing range references into the new name.

> **Caution**   The treatment of formulas in the Lotus 1-2-3 manner only applies to formulas that you create *after* you select the **Transition Formula Entry** check box.

#NULL!

Excel displays the #NULL! error in a very specific case: when you use the intersection operator (a space) on two ranges that have no cells in common. For example, because the ranges A1:B2 and C3:D4 have no common cells, the following formula returns the #NULL! error:

```
=SUM(A1:B2 C3:D4)
```

Check your range coordinates to ensure that they're accurate. Also, check to see if one of the ranges has been moved, causing the two ranges in your formula to no longer intersect.

#NUM!

The #NUM! error means there's a problem with a number in a formula. This almost always means that you entered an invalid argument in a math or trig function. For example, perhaps you entered a negative number as the argument for the SQRT or LOG function. Check the formula's input cells—particularly those that are used as arguments for mathematical functions—to make sure the values are appropriate.

The #NUM! error also appears if you're using iteration (or a function that uses iteration; see Chapter 2, "Creating advanced formulas"), and Excel can't calculate a result. There could be no solution to the problem, or you might need to adjust the iteration parameters.

#REF!

The **#REF!** error means that a formula contains an invalid cell reference, which is usually caused by one of the following actions:

- You deleted a cell to which the formula refers. You need to add the cell back in or adjust the formula reference.

- You cut a cell and then pasted it into a cell used by the formula. You need to undo the cut and then paste the cell elsewhere. (Note that it's okay to *copy* a cell and paste it onto a cell used by the formula.)

- Your formula references a nonexistent cell address, such as B0. This can happen if you cut or copy a formula that uses relative references and paste it in such a way that the invalid cell address is created. For example, suppose that your formula references cell B1. If you cut or copy the cell containing the formula and paste it one row higher, the reference to B1 becomes invalid because Excel can't move the cell reference up one row.

#SPILL!

You see the **#SPILL!** error when a dynamic array formula or function that needs to spill data into one or more adjacent cells encounters a non-empty cell in the spill range. (See Chapter 2 to learn more about spill ranges.) You have two ways to handle a **#SPILL!** error:

- Move the formula that needs the spill range to a new location where the spill range is empty.

- Move the existing data out of the spill range.

In both cases, Excel removes the **#SPILL!** error and spills the formula result in the new spill range.

#UNKNOWN!

If you see the **#UNKNOWN!** error, it means your formula or expression is referencing a data type that isn't supported in your version of Excel. This most often means that the reference is to a data type that was added to a later version of Excel, so the only way to resolve the error is to upgrade to a version of Excel that supports the data type.

#VALUE!

When Excel generates a **#VALUE!** error, it means you've used an inappropriate argument in a function. This is most often caused by using the wrong data type. For example, you might have entered or referenced a string value instead of a numeric value. Similarly, you might have used a range reference in a function argument that requires a single cell or value. Excel also generates this error if you use a value that's larger or smaller than Excel can handle. In all these cases, you solve the problem by double-checking your function arguments to find and edit the inappropriate arguments.

Note Excel can work with values between –1E–307 and 1E+307.

Fixing other formula errors

Not all formula errors generate one of Excel's 11 error values. Instead, you might see a warning dialog box from Excel (for example, if you try to enter a function without including a required argument). Or, you might not see any indication that something is wrong. To help you in these situations, the following sections cover some of the most common formula errors.

Missing or mismatched parentheses

If you miss a parenthesis when typing a formula or place a parenthesis in the wrong location, Excel usually displays a dialog box like the one shown in Figure 3-1 when you attempt to confirm the formula. If the edited formula is what you want, select **Yes** to have Excel enter the corrected formula automatically; if the edited formula is incorrect, select **No** and edit the formula by hand.

Note You can work with all the examples in this chapter by downloading Chapter03.xslx from either of the companion content sites mentioned in the Introduction.

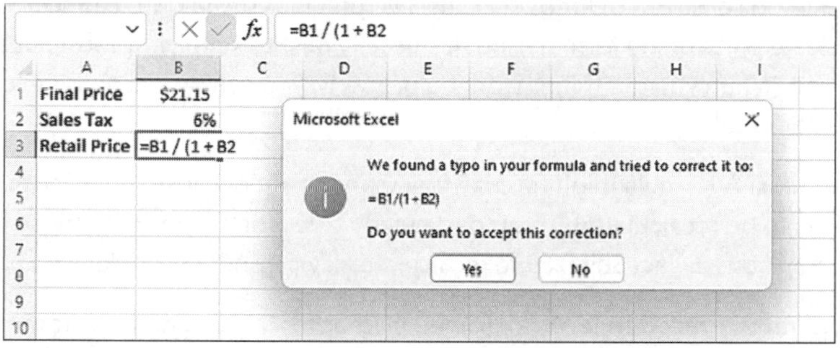

FIGURE 3-1 If you miss a parenthesis, Excel attempts to fix the problem and displays this dialog box to ask if you want to accept the correction.

Caution Excel doesn't always fix missing parentheses correctly. It tends to add the missing parenthesis to the end of the formula, which is often not what you want. Therefore, always check Excel's proposed solution carefully before accepting it.

To help you avoid missing or mismatched parentheses, Excel provides two visual clues in the formula itself when you're editing it:

- The first clue occurs when you type a close parenthesis character—**)**. Excel temporarily bolds both the close parenthesis and its corresponding open parenthesis—**(**. If you type what you think is the last close parenthesis, but Excel doesn't bold the first open parenthesis, your parentheses are unbalanced.

- The second clue occurs when you use the left and right arrow keys to navigate a formula. When you cross over a parenthesis, Excel bolds the other parenthesis in the pair.

Erroneous formula results

If a formula produces no warnings or error values, the result might still be in error. If the result of a formula is incorrect, here are a few techniques that can help you understand and fix the problem:

- **Calculate complex formulas one term at a time.** In the formula bar, select the expression you want to calculate and then press F9. Excel converts the expression into its value. Make sure that you press the Esc key when you're done to avoid entering the formula with just the calculated values.

- **Evaluate the formula.** You can step through the various parts of a formula, a technique that I describe later in this chapter (see "Evaluating formulas").

- **Break up long or complex formulas.** One of the most problematic aspects of formula troubleshooting is making sense out of long formulas. The previous techniques can help (by enabling you to evaluate parts of the formula), but it's usually best to keep your formulas as short as you can at first. When you get things working properly, you can often combine formulas for a more efficient model.

- **Recalculate all formulas.** A formula might display the wrong result because other formulas on which it depends need to be recalculated. This is particularly true if one or more of those formulas use custom VBA functions. Select Shift+F9 to recalculate all worksheet formulas.

- **Pay attention to operator precedence.** As explained in Chapter 1, "Building basic formulas," Excel's operator precedence means that certain operations are performed before others. An erroneous formula result could, therefore, be caused by Excel's precedence order. To control precedence, use parentheses.

- **Watch out for nonblank "blank" cells.** A cell might appear to be blank but actually contain data or even a formula. For example, some users "clear" a cell by selecting the spacebar, and Excel then treats the cell as nonblank. Similarly, some formulas return an empty string instead of a value. (For example, see the `IF` function formula earlier in this chapter for avoiding the `#DIV/0!` error.)

- **Watch unseen values.** In a large model, your formula could be using cells that you can't see because they're offscreen or on another sheet. Excel's **Watch Window** enables you to keep an eye on the current value of one or more cells. To learn about the Watch Window, see "Watching cell values," later in this chapter.

Fixing circular references

A *circular reference* occurs when a formula refers to its own cell. This can happen in one of two ways:

- **Directly:** The formula explicitly references its own cell. For example, a circular reference would result if the following formula were entered into cell A1:

  =A1+A2

- **Indirectly:** The formula references a cell or function that, in turn, references the formula's cell. For example, suppose that cell A1 contains the following formula:

  =A5*10

- A circular reference would result if cell A5 referred to cell A1, as in this example:

  =SUM(A1:D1)

When Excel detects a circular reference, it displays the dialog box shown in Figure 3-2. Here's the formula in cell B3:

=B1 / (1 + B2)

Here's the formula in cell B1:

=B3 * (1 + B2)

These formulas refer to each other's cells, creating a circular reference.

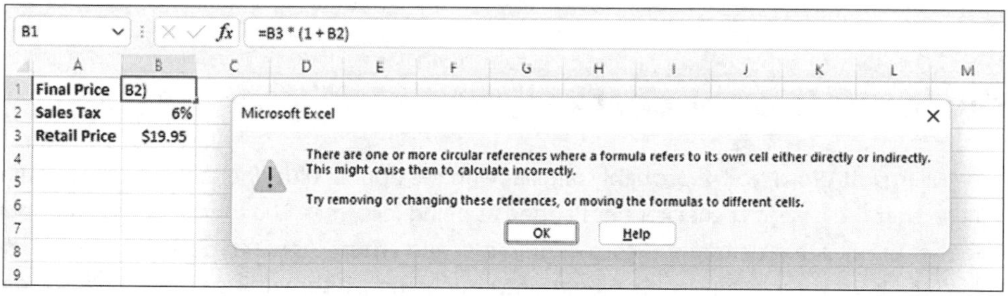

FIGURE 3-2 If you attempt to enter a formula that contains a circular reference, Excel displays this dialog box.

When you select **OK**, Excel displays *tracer* arrows that connect the cells involved in the circular reference. (Tracers are discussed in detail later in this chapter; see "Auditing a worksheet.") Knowing which cells are involved enables you to correct the formula in one of them to solve the problem.

Handling formula errors with IFERROR

Earlier, you saw how to use the `IF` function to avoid a `#DIV/0!` error by testing the value of the formula divisor to see if it equals 0. This works fine if you can anticipate the specific type of error the user might make. However, in many instances, you can't know the exact nature of the error in advance. For example, the simple formula `=GrossProfit/Sales` would generate a `#DIV/0!` error if `Sales` equals `0`. However, it would generate a `#NAME?` error if the name `GrossProfit` or the name `Sales` no longer exists, or it would generate a `#REF!` error if the cells associated with one or both of `GrossProfit` and `Sales` were deleted.

If you want to handle errors gracefully in your worksheets, it's often best to assume that *any* error can occur. Fortunately, that doesn't mean you have to construct complex tests using deeply nested `IF` functions that check for every error type (`#DIV/0!`, `#N/A`, and so on). Instead, Excel enables you to use a simple test for *any* error by offering the `IFERROR` function:

```
IFERROR(value, value_if_error)
```

value	The expression that might generate an error
value_if_error	The value to return if *value* returns an error

If the *value* expression doesn't generate an error, `IFERROR` returns the expression result; otherwise, it returns *value_if_error* (which might be the null string or an error message). Here's an example:

```
=IFERROR(GrossProfit / Sales, "")
```

> **Note** If you want to handle the specific case of the #N/A error, use the IFNA(*value, value_if_na*) function. Here, *value* is the expression that you're testing for the #N/A error, and *value_if_na* is the value to return if *value* returns the #N/A error.

Using the formula error checker

If you use Microsoft Word, you're probably familiar with the double blue line that appears under words and phrases that the grammar checker has flagged as being incorrect. The grammar checker operates by using a set of rules that determines correct grammar and syntax. As you type, the grammar checker operates in the background, constantly monitoring your writing. If something you write goes against one of the grammar checker's rules, the wavy line appears to let you know there's a problem.

Excel has a similar feature: the formula error checker. Like the grammar checker, the formula error checker uses a set of rules to determine correctness, and it operates in the background to monitor your formulas. If it detects something amiss, it displays an *error indicator*—a green triangle—in the upper-left corner of the cell containing the formula, as shown in Figure 3-3.

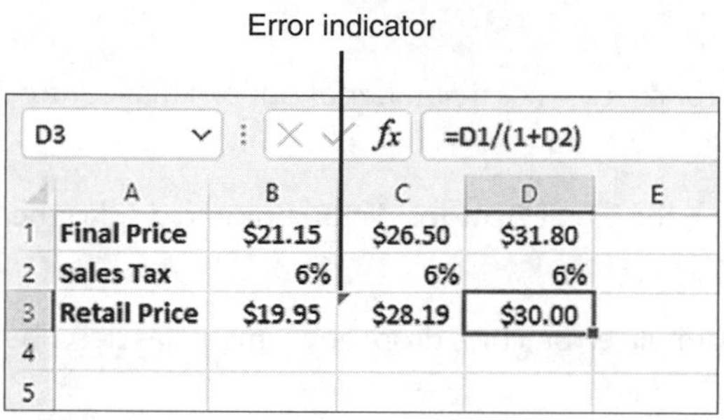

Error indicator

FIGURE 3-3 If Excel's formula error checker detects a problem, it displays a green triangle in the upper-left corner of the formula's cell.

Choosing an error action

When you select the cell with the formula error, Excel displays a formula error icon beside the cell. If you hover your mouse pointer over the icon, a pop-up message describes the error, as shown in Figure 3-4. The formula error icon drop-down menu contains the following actions:

- **Corrective Action:** This is a command (the name of which depends on the type of error) that Excel believes either will fix the problem or help you troubleshoot the error. For example, in Figure 3-4, Excel is reporting that the formula in cell C3 differs from its neighboring formulas. (In the formula bar, the expression in the parentheses should be **1+C2** instead of **1–C2**.) In this case, the corrective action command in the formula error icon is **Copy Formula From Left**. Or, if Excel can't suggest a solution, it might show the command Show Calculation Steps, which runs the Evaluate Formula feature. See "Evaluating formulas," later in this chapter.

- **Help On This Error:** Select this option to get information on the error via the Excel Help system.

- **Ignore Error:** Select this option to leave the formula as is.

- **Edit In Formula Bar:** Select this option to display the formula in **Edit** mode in the formula bar. You can then fix the problem by editing the formula.

- **Error-Checking Options:** Select this option to display the **Formulas** tab of the **Excel Options** dialog box (discussed next).

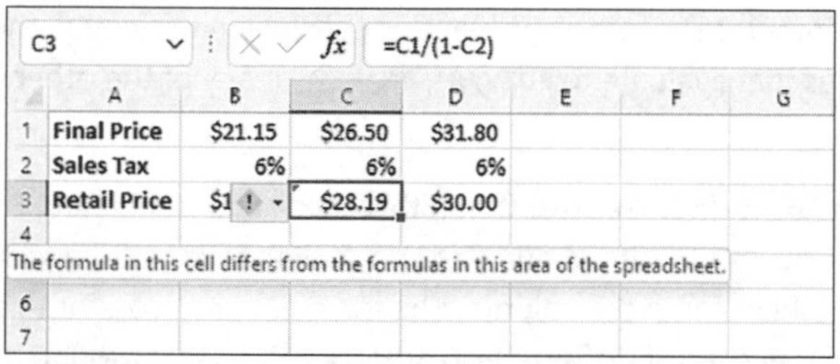

FIGURE 3-4 Select the cell containing the error and then move the mouse pointer over the formula error icon to see a description of the error.

Setting error checker options

Like Word's grammar checker, Excel's formula error checker has a number of options that control how it works and which errors it flags. To see these options, you have two choices:

- Select **File** > **Options** > **Formulas** to open the **Excel Options** dialog box and display the **Formulas** tab.

- Select **Error-Checking Options** in the formula error icon's drop-down menu (as described in the previous section).

Either way, the options appear in the **Error Checking** and **Error Checking Rules** sections in the **Formulas** tab, as shown in Figure 3-5.

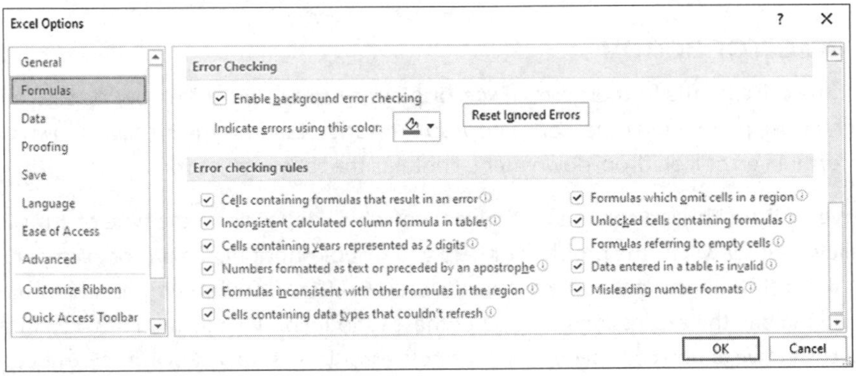

FIGURE 3-5 In the Formulas tab, the Error Checking and Error Checking Rules sections contain the options that govern the workings of the formula error checker.

Here's a rundown of the available options:

- **Enable Background Error Checking:** This check box toggles the formula error checker's background operation on and off. If you turn off the background checking, you can run a check at any time by choosing **Formulas** > **Error Checking**.

- **Indicate Errors Using This Color:** Use this color palette to select the color of the error indicator.

- **Reset Ignored Errors:** If you've ignored one or more errors, you can redisplay the error indicators by selecting this button.

- **Cells Containing Formulas That Result In An Error:** When this check box is selected, the formula error checker flags formulas that evaluate to #DIV/0!, #NAME?, or any of the other error values discussed earlier.

- **Inconsistent Calculated Column Formula In Tables:** When this check box is selected, Excel examines the formulas in a table's calculated column and flags any cell that contains a formula with a different structure than the other cells in the column. The formula error icon for this error includes the command **Restore To Calculated Column Formula**, which enables you to update the formula so that it's consistent with the rest of the column.

- **Cells Containing Years Represented As 2 Digits:** When this check box is selected, the formula error checker flags formulas that contain date text strings in which the year contains only two digits (a possibly ambiguous situation because the string could refer to a date in either the 1900s or the 2000s). In such a case, the list of options supplied in the formula error icon contains two commands—**Convert XX To 19XX** and **Convert XX To 20XX**—that enable you to convert the two-digit year to a four-digit year.

- **Numbers Formatted As Text Or Preceded By An Apostrophe:** When this check box is selected, the formula error checker flags cells that contain a number that is either formatted as text or preceded by an apostrophe. In such a case, the list of options supplied in the formula error icon contains the **Convert To Number** command to convert the text to its numeric equivalent.

- **Formulas Inconsistent With Other Formulas In The Region:** When this check box is selected, the formula error checker flags formulas that are structured differently from similar formulas in the surrounding area. In such a case, the list of options supplied in the formula error icon contains a command such as **Copy Formula From Left** to make the formula consistent with the surrounding cells.

- **Formulas Which Omit Cells In A Region:** When this check box is selected, the formula error checker flags formulas that omit cells that are adjacent to a range referenced in the formula. For example, suppose that the formula is =AVERAGE(C4:C21), where C4:C21 is a range of numeric values. If cell C3 also contains a numeric value, the formula error checker flags the formula to alert you to the possibility that you missed including cell C3 in the formula. Figure 3-6 shows this example. In such a case, the list of options supplied in the formula error icon will contain the command **Update Formula To Include Cells** to adjust the formula automatically

C23		fx =AVERAGE(C4:C21)		
A	B	C	D	E
1				
2	Sales Rep	2017 Sales	2018 Sales	
3	Nancy Freehafer	$996,336	$960,492	
4	Andrew Cencini	$606,731	$577,983	
5	Jan Kotas	$622,781	$967,580	
6	Mariya Sergienko	$765,327	$771,399	
7	Steven Thorpe	$863,589	$827,213	
8	Michael Neipper	$795,518	$669,394	
9	Robert Zare	$722,740	$626,945	
10	Laura Giussani	$992,059	$574,472	
11	Anne Hellung-Larsen	$659,380	$827,932	
12	Maria Anders	$509,623	$569,609	
13	Thomas Hardy	$987,777	$558,601	
14	Hanna Moos	$685,091	$692,182	
15	Victoria Ashworth	$540,484	$693,762	
16	Patricio Simpson	$650,733	$823,034	
17	Elizabeth Brown	$509,863	$511,569	
18	Ann Devon	$503,699	$975,455	
19	Paolo Accorti	$630,263	$599,514	
20	Carlos Hernández	$779,722	$596,353	
21	Yoshi Latimer	$592,802	$652,171	
22	TOTAL	$13,414,518	$13,475,660	
23	AVERAGE	$690,000		
24				
25				

The formula in this cell refers to a range that has additional numbers adjacent to it.

FIGURE 3-6 The formula error checker can flag formulas that omit cells that are adjacent to a range referenced by the formula. In this case, the formula in C23 should include cell C3.

- **Unlocked Cells Containing Formulas:** When this check box is selected, the formula error checker flags formulas that reside in unlocked cells. This isn't an error so much as a warning that other people could tamper with the formula even after you have protected the sheet. In such a case, the list of options supplied in the formula error icon will contain the command **Lock Cell** to lock the cell and prevent users from changing the formula after you protect the sheet.

- **Formulas Referring To Empty Cells:** When this check box is selected, the formula error checker flags formulas that reference empty cells. In such a case, the list of options supplied in the formula error icon will contain the command **Trace Empty Cell** to enable you to find the empty cell. (At this point, you can either enter data into the cell or adjust the formula so that it doesn't reference the cell.)

- **Data Entered In A Table Is Invalid:** When this check box is selected, the formula error checker flags cells that violate a table's data-validation rules. This can happen if you set up a data-validation rule with only a Warning or Information style, in which case the user can still opt to enter the invalid data. In such cases, the formula error checker will flag the cells that contain invalid data. The formula error icon list includes the **Display Type Information** command, which shows the data-validation rule that the cell data violates.

- **Misleading Number Formats:** When this check box is selected, the formula error checker flags cells that have a numeric, date, or time format that Excel deems incompatible with the formula result. For example, Excel displays this error if a formula applies a mathematical operation to a currency value, but the formula's cell is formatted as a date or time. The formula error icon list includes the **Update Format** command, which changes the cell data format to fit the formula result.

Auditing a worksheet

As you've seen, some formula errors result from referencing other cells that contain errors or inappropriate values. The first step in troubleshooting these formula problems is to determine which cell (or group of cells) is causing an error. This is straightforward if the formula references only a single cell, but it gets progressively more difficult as the number of references increases. (Another complicating factor is the use of range names because it won't be obvious which range each name is referencing.)

To determine which cells are wreaking havoc on your formulas, you can use Excel's auditing features to visualize and trace a formula's input values and error sources.

Understanding auditing

Excel's formula-auditing features operate by creating *tracers*—arrows that literally point out the cells involved in a formula. You can use tracers to find three kinds of cells:

- **Precedents:** These are cells that are directly or indirectly referenced in a formula. For example, suppose that cell B4 contains the formula =**B2**; then B2 is a direct precedent of B4. Now suppose that cell B2 contains the formula =A2/2; this makes A2 a direct precedent of B2, but it's also an *indirect* precedent of cell B4.

- **Dependents:** These are cells that are directly or indirectly referenced by a formula in another cell. In the preceding example, cell B2 is a direct dependent of A2, and B4 is an indirect dependent of A2.

- **Errors:** These are cells that contain an error value and are directly or indirectly referenced in a formula (and therefore cause the same error to appear in the formula).

Figure 3-7 shows a worksheet with three examples of tracer arrows:

- Cell B4 contains the formula =B2, and B2 contains =A2/2. The arrows (they're blue onscreen) point out the precedents (direct and indirect) of B4.

- Cell D4 contains the formula =D2, and D2 contains =D1/0. The latter produces the #DIV/0! error. Therefore, the same error appears in cell D4. The arrow (it's red onscreen) is pointing out the source of the error.

- Cell G4 contains the formula =Sheet5!A1. Excel displays the dashed arrow with the worksheet icon whenever the precedent or dependent exists on a different worksheet.

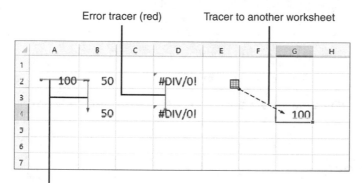

FIGURE 3-7 This worksheet demonstrates the three types of tracer arrows.

Tracing cell precedents

To trace cell precedents, follow these steps:

1. Select the cell that contains the formula whose precedents you want to trace.

2. Select **Formulas** > **Trace Precedents**. Excel adds a tracer arrow to each direct precedent.

3. Keep repeating step 2 to see more levels of precedents.

> **Tip** You also can trace precedents by pressing Ctrl+], or by double-clicking the cell, provided that you turn off in-cell editing. You do this by choosing **File** > **Options** > **Advanced** and then deselecting the **Allow Editing Directly In Cells** check box. Now when you double-click a cell, Excel selects the formula's precedents.

Tracing cell dependents

Here are the steps to follow to trace cell dependents:

1. Select the cell whose dependents you want to trace.

2. Select **Formulas** > **Trace Dependents**. Excel adds a tracer arrow to each direct dependent.

3. Keep repeating step 2 to see more levels of dependents.

> **Tip** You also can trace dependents by pressing Ctrl+[.

Tracing cell errors

To trace cell errors, follow these steps:

1. Select the cell that contains the error you want to trace.

2. Select **Formulas** > **Error Checking** > **Trace Error**. Excel adds a tracer arrow to each cell that produced the error.

Removing tracer arrows

To remove the tracer arrows, you have three choices:

- To remove all the tracer arrows, select **Formulas** > **Remove Arrows**.

- To remove precedent arrows one level at a time, select **Formulas**, open the **Remove Arrows** drop-down menu, and select **Remove Precedent Arrows**.

- To remove dependent arrows one level at a time, select **Formulas**, open the **Remove Arrows** drop-down menu, and select **Remove Dependent Arrows**.

Evaluating formulas

Earlier, you learned that you could troubleshoot a wonky formula by evaluating parts of it. You do this by selecting the part of the formula you want to evaluate and then selecting F9. This works fine, but it can be tedious in a long or complex formula, and there's always a danger that you might accidentally confirm a partially evaluated formula and lose your work.

A better solution is to use Excel's Evaluate Formula feature. It does the same thing as the F9 technique, but it's easier and safer. Here's how it works:

1. Select the cell that contains the formula you want to evaluate.

2. Select **Formulas** > **Evaluate Formula**. Excel displays the **Evaluate Formula** dialog box.

3. The current term in the formula is underlined in the **Evaluation** box. At each step, you select from one or more of the following buttons:

   - **Evaluate:** Display the current value of the underlined term.

   - **Step In:** Display the first dependent of the underlined term. If that dependent also has a dependent, select this button again to see it (see Figure 3-8).

   - **Step Out:** Hide a dependent and evaluate its precedent.

4. Repeat step 3 until you've completed your evaluation.

5. Select **Close**.

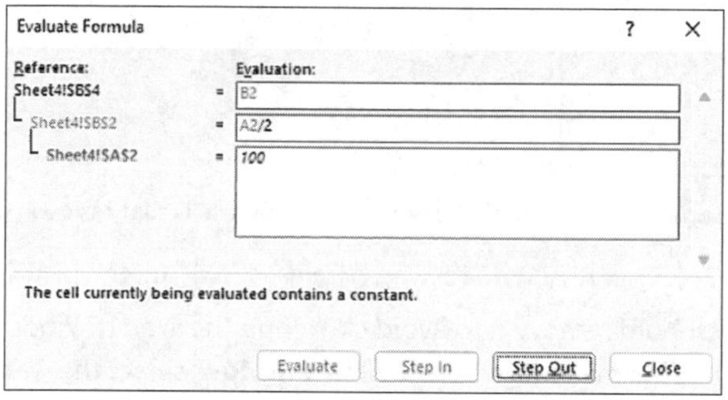

FIGURE 3-8 With the Evaluate Formula feature, you can "step into" the formula to display its dependent cells.

Watching cell values

In the precedent tracer example shown in Figure 3-7, the formula in cell G4 refers to a cell in another worksheet, which is represented in the trace by a worksheet icon. In other words, you can't see the formula cell and the precedent cell simultaneously. This could also happen if the precedent existed on another workbook or even elsewhere on the same sheet if you're working with a large model.

This is a problem because there's no easy way to determine the current contents or value of the unseen precedent. If you're having a problem, troubleshooting requires that you track down the far-off precedent to see if it might be the culprit. That's bad enough with a single unseen cell, but what if your formula refers to 5 or 10 such cells? And what if those cells are scattered in different worksheets and workbooks?

This level of hassle—not uncommon in the spreadsheet world—was undoubtedly the inspiration behind an elegant solution: the Watch Window. This window enables you to keep tabs on both the value and the formula in any cell in any worksheet in any open workbook. Here's how you set up a watch:

1. Switch to the workbook that contains the cell or cells you want to watch.

2. Select **Formulas** > **Watch Window**. Excel displays the **Watch Window**.

3. Select **Add Watch**. Excel displays the **Add Watch** dialog box.

4. Either select the cell you want to watch or type in a reference formula for the cell (for example, **=A1**). Note that you can select a range to add multiple cells to the Watch Window.

5. Select **Add**. Excel adds the cell or cells to the **Watch Window**, as shown in Figure 3-9.

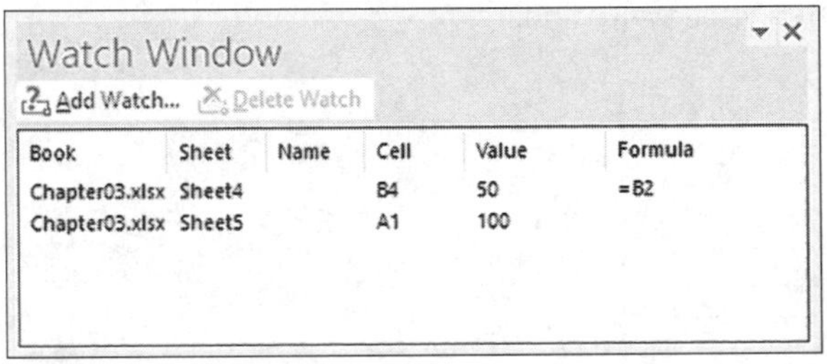

FIGURE 3-9 Use the Watch Window to keep an eye on the values and formulas of unseen cells that reside in other worksheets or workbooks.

When you no longer need a watch, you should remove it to avoid cluttering the Watch Window. To remove a watch, select **Formulas** > **Watch Window** to open the **Watch Window**, select the watch, and then select **Delete Watch**.

PART 2

Harnessing the Power of Functions

CHAPTER 4

Understanding functions

In this chapter, you will:

- Gain an understanding of Excel's worksheet functions

- Decipher the structure of a typical Excel function

- Learn how to type a function into a formula

- Learn how to add a function to a formula by using Excel's Insert Function feature

- Load Excel's powerful and useful Analysis ToolPak

The formulas that you can construct based on the information presented in Part I, "Mastering Excel formulas," can range from simple additions and subtractions to powerful iteration-based solutions for otherwise difficult problems. Formulas that combine Excel's operators with basic operands such as numeric and string values are the bread and butter of any spreadsheet.

But to get to the real meat of a spreadsheet model, you need to expand your formula repertoire to include Excel's worksheet functions. Dozens of these functions exist, and they're essential to making your worksheet easier to work with and more powerful. Excel has various function categories, including the following:

- Database and table

- Date and time

- Financial

- Information

- Logical

- Lookup and reference

- Math and trigonometry

- Statistical

- Text

This chapter gives you a short introduction to Excel's built-in worksheet functions. You'll find out what the functions are, what they can do, and how to use them. The next five chapters give you detailed descriptions of the functions in the preceding list of categories. (The exceptions are the statistical category, which I cover in Chapter 11, "Building descriptive statistical formulas," the financial category, which I cover in Chapters 14, 15, and 16, and the database and table category, which I cover in Chapter 17, "Analyzing data with tables.")

> **Note** You can even create your own custom functions when Excel's built-in functions aren't up to the task you need to complete. You build these functions by using the Visual Basic for Applications (VBA) macro language, and it's easier than you think. See the book *Excel 365 VBA and Macros* (Microsoft Press, 2019).

About Excel's functions

Functions are formulas that Excel has predefined. They're designed to take you beyond the basic arithmetic and text formulas you've seen so far. They do this in three ways:

- Functions make simple but cumbersome formulas easier to use. For example, suppose that you want to add a list of 100 numbers in a column, starting at cell A1 and finishing at cell A100. It's unlikely that you have the time or patience to enter 100 separate additions in a cell (that is, the formula =A1+A2+...+A100). Luckily, there's an alternative: the SUM function. With this function, you'd just enter =SUM(A1:A100).

- Functions enable you to include in your worksheets complex mathematical expressions that otherwise would be difficult or impossible to construct using simple arithmetic operators. For example, determining a mortgage payment given the principal, interest, and term is a complicated matter at best, but you can do it with Excel's PMT function just by entering a few arguments.

- Functions enable you to include data in your applications that you couldn't access otherwise. For example, the INFO function can tell you how much memory is available on your system, what operating system you're using, what version number it is, and more. Similarly, the powerful IF function enables you to test the contents of a cell—for example, to see whether it contains a particular value or an error—and then perform an action accordingly, depending on the result.

As you can see, functions are a powerful addition to your worksheet-building arsenal. With proper use of these tools, there is no practical limit to the kinds of models you can create.

The structure of a function

Every function has the same basic form:

```
FUNCTION(argument1, argument2, ...)
```

The *FUNCTION* part is the function's name, which always appears in uppercase letters (such as SUM or PMT). Note, however, that you don't need to type the function name using uppercase letters. Whatever case you use, Excel automatically converts the name to all uppercase. In fact, it's good practice to enter function names using only lowercase letters. That way, if Excel doesn't convert the function name to uppercase, you know that it doesn't recognize the name, which means you probably misspelled it.

The items that appear within the parentheses and are separated by commas are the function *arguments*. The arguments are the function's inputs—the data the function uses to perform its calculations. With respect to arguments, functions come in two flavors:

- **No arguments:** Many functions don't require arguments. For example, the NOW function returns the current date and time, and it doesn't require arguments.

- **One or more arguments:** Most functions accept at least one argument, and some accept as many as nine or ten arguments. These arguments fall into two categories: required and optional. Required arguments are the arguments you *must* include when you use the function; otherwise, the formula will generate an error. You use the optional arguments only if your formula needs them.

Let's look at an example. The FV function determines the future value of a regular investment, based on three required arguments and two optional ones:

FV(*rate*, *nper*, *pmt*[, *pv*][, *type*])

rate	The fixed rate of interest over the term of the investment.
nper	The number of deposits over the term of the investment.
pmt	The amount deposited each period.
pv	The present value of the investment. The default value is **0**.
type	When the deposits are due (**0** for the beginning of the period; **1** for the end of the period, which is the default).

This is called the function *syntax*. Three conventions are at work here and throughout the rest of this book:

- *Italic type* indicates a placeholder. That is, when you use the function, you replace the placeholder with an actual value.

- Arguments surrounded by square brackets are optional.

- All other arguments are required.

> **Caution** Be careful how you use commas in functions that have optional arguments. If you omit the last optional argument, you must leave out the comma that precedes the argument. For example, if you omit just the *type* argument from **FV**, you write the function like so:
>
> ```
> FV(rate, nper, pmt, pv)
> ```
>
> However, if you omit an optional argument within the syntax, you need to include all the commas to avoid ambiguity about which value refers to which argument. For example, if you omit the *pv* argument from **FV**, you write the function like this:
>
> ```
> FV(rate, nper, pmt, , type)
> ```

For each argument placeholder, you substitute an appropriate value. For example, in the **FV** function, you substitute *rate* with a decimal value between 0 and 1, *nper* with an integer, and *pmt* with a dollar amount. Arguments can take any of the following forms:

- Literal alphanumeric values

- Expressions

- Cell or range references

- Range names

- Arrays

- The result of another function

The function operates by processing the inputs and then returning a result. For example, the **FV** function returns the total value of the investment at the end of the term. Figure 4-1 shows a simple future-value calculator that uses this function. (In case you're wondering, I entered the Payment value in cell B4 as negative because Excel always treats any money you have to pay as a negative number.)

> **Note** You can work with all the examples in this chapter by downloading Chapter04.xslx from either of the companion content sites mentioned in the Introduction.

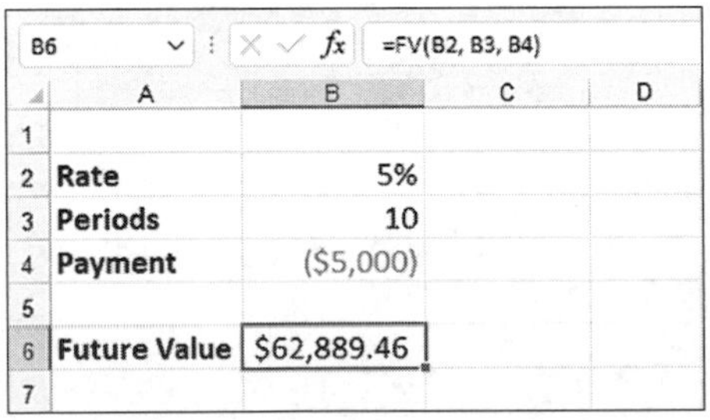

FIGURE 4-1 This example of the FV function uses the values in cells B2, B3, and B4 as inputs for calculating the future value of an investment.

Typing a function into a formula

You always use a function as part of a cell formula. So, even if you're using the function by itself, you still need to precede it with an equal sign (=). Whether you use a function on its own or as part of a larger formula, here are a few rules and guidelines to follow:

- You can enter the function name in either uppercase or lowercase letters. Excel always converts function names to uppercase.

- Always enclose function arguments in parentheses.

- Always separate multiple arguments with commas. (You might want to add a space after each comma to make a function more readable. Excel ignores the extra spaces.)

- You can use a function as an argument for another function. This is called *nesting* functions. For example, the function `AVERAGE(SUM(A1:A10), SUM(B1:B15))` sums two columns of numbers and returns the average of the two sums.

Excel offers the AutoComplete feature for function names that shows you a list of functions that begin with the characters you've typed in a formula. As you can see in Figure 4-2, when you begin typing a name in Excel, the program displays a list of the functions that start with the letters you've typed and displays a description of the currently selected function. Select the function you want to use and then select Tab to include it in the formula (or double-click the function)

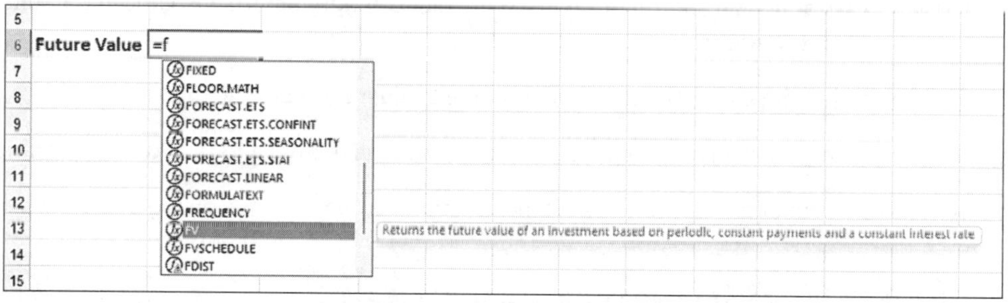

FIGURE 4-2 When you begin typing a name in Excel, the program displays a list of functions with names that begin with the typed characters.

After selecting the function from the AutoComplete list (or when entering a function name followed by the open parenthesis), Excel displays a pop-up banner that shows the function syntax. The current argument is displayed in bold type. In the example shown in Figure 4-3, the *nper* argument is shown in bold, so the next value (or cell reference, or whatever) entered will apply to that argument. When you enter a comma, Excel bolds the next argument in the list.

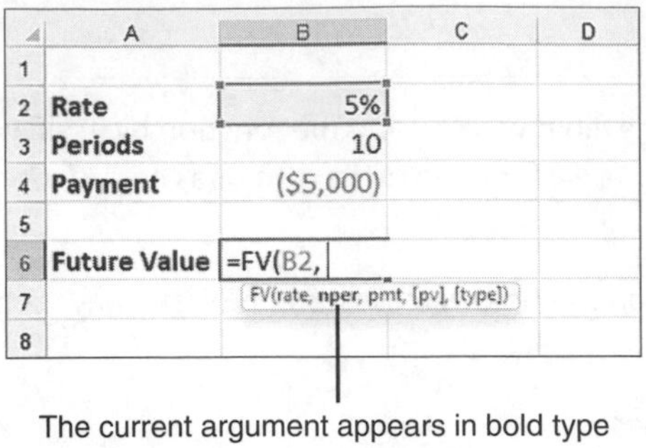

The current argument appears in bold type

FIGURE 4-3 After you type the function name and the left parenthesis, Excel displays the function syntax, with the current argument shown in bold type.

Using the Insert Function feature

Although you'll usually enter your functions by hand, sometimes you might prefer to get a helping hand from Excel, such as in these circumstances:

- You're not sure which function to use.

- You want to see the syntax of a function before you use it.

- You want to examine similar functions in a particular category before you choose the function that best suits your needs.

- You want to see the effect that different argument values have on the function result.

For these situations, Excel offers two tools: the Insert Function feature and the Function Wizard.

You use the Insert Function feature to select the function you want from a dialog box. Here's how it works:

1. Select the cell in which you want to use the function.

2. Enter the formula up to the point where you want to insert the function.

3. Choose one of the following:

   - If the function you want is one you inserted recently, it might appear on the list of recent functions in the **Name** box. Open the **Name** box drop-down menu (see Figure 4-4); if you see the name of the function you want, select it and skip to step 7.

   - To pick any function, select **Formulas** > **Insert Function**. (You can also select the **Insert Function** button in the formula bar—see Figure 4-4—or select Shift+F3.) In this case, the **Insert Function** dialog box appears, as shown in Figure 4-4.

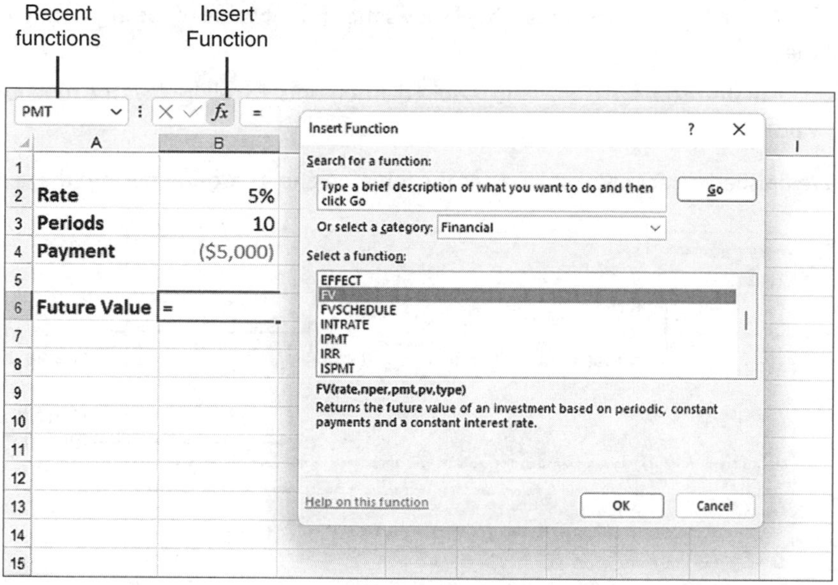

FIGURE 4-4 Select Formulas > Insert Function or select the Insert Function button to display the Insert Function dialog box.

4. (Optional) In the **Or Select A Category** list in the **Insert Function** dialog box, select the type of function you need. If you're not sure, select **All**.

5. In the **Select A Function** list, select the function you want to use. (Note that once you're in the **Select A Function** list, selecting a letter moves the selection down to the first function that begins with that letter.)

6. Select **OK**. Excel displays the **Function Arguments** dialog box.

> **Tip** To skip the first six steps and go directly to the **Function Arguments** dialog box, enter the name of the function and the open parenthesis, and then either select the **Insert Function** button or select Ctrl+A. Alternatively, select the equal sign (=) key and select the function from the list of recent functions in the **Name** box. To skip the **Function Arguments** dialog box altogether, enter the name of the function in the cell and select Ctrl+Shift+A.

7. For each required argument and each optional argument you want to use, enter a value, an expression, or a cell reference in the appropriate text box. Here are some notes to bear in mind when you're working in this dialog box (see Figure 4-5):

    -   The names of the required arguments are shown in bold type.

    -   When you move the cursor to an argument text box, Excel displays a description of the argument.

- After you fill in an argument text box, Excel shows the current value of the argument to the right of the box.

- After you fill in the text boxes for all the required arguments, Excel displays the function's current value.

8. When you're finished, select **OK**. Excel pastes the function and its arguments into the cell.

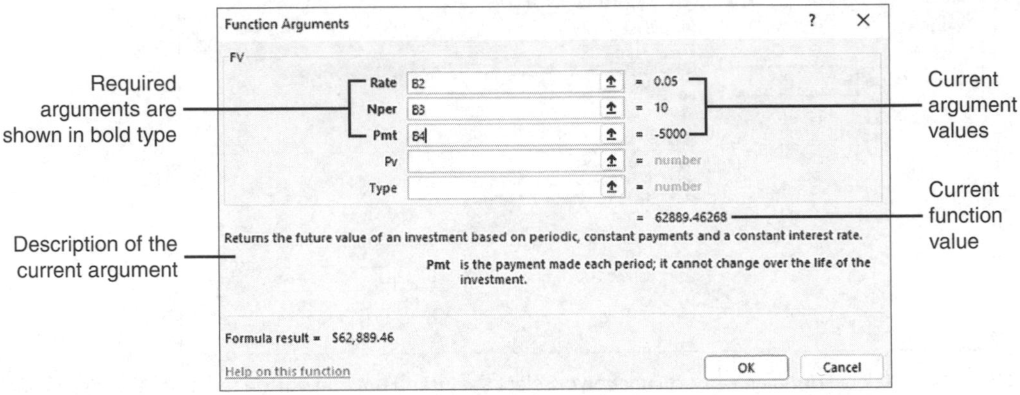

FIGURE 4-5 Use the Function Arguments dialog box to enter values for a function's arguments.

Loading the Analysis ToolPak

Excel's Analysis ToolPak is a large collection of powerful statistical tools. Some of these tools use advanced statistical techniques and were designed with only a limited number of technical users in mind. However, many of them have general applications and can be amazingly useful. I discuss these tools in several chapters later in the book. (In particular, see Chapters 11, 12, and 13.)

In early versions of Excel (that is, prior to Excel 2007), the Analysis ToolPak included dozens of powerful functions. In Excel 2007 and later, however, all those functions are now part of the Excel function library, so you can use them without loading the Analysis ToolPak.

If you need to use the Analysis ToolPak features, you must load the add-in that makes them available to Excel. The following procedure takes you through the steps:

1. Select **File** > **Options** to open the **Excel Options** dialog box.

2. Select **Add-Ins**.

3. In the **Manage** list, select **Excel Add-Ins** and then select **Go**. Excel displays the **Add-Ins** dialog box.

4. Select the **Analysis ToolPak** check box, as shown in Figure 4-6.

5. Select **OK**.

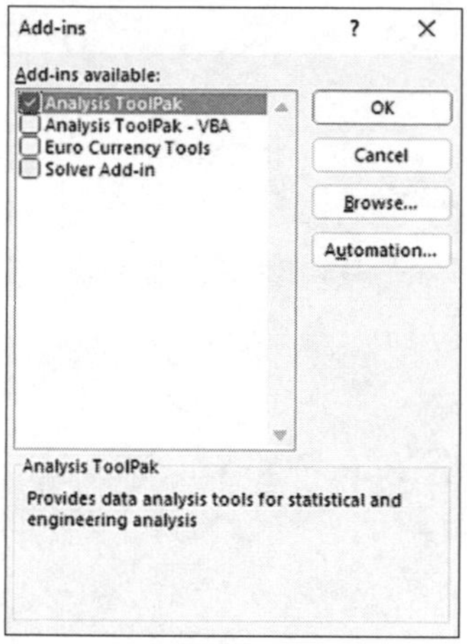

FIGURE 4-6 Select the Analysis ToolPak check box to load this add-in into Excel.

CHAPTER 5

Working with text functions

In this chapter, you will:

- Get an overview of Excel's extensive collection of text-related functions

- Work with characters and ANSI codes

- Manipulate strings by converting, formatting, cleaning, joining, and extracting text

- Perform case-sensitive and case-insensitive searches for substrings within larger strings

- Substitute one substring for another

In Excel, *text* is any collection of alphanumeric characters that isn't a numeric value, a date or time value, or a formula. Words, names, and labels are all obviously text values, but so are cell values preceded by an apostrophe (') or formatted as text. *Text values* are also called *strings*, and I use both terms interchangeably in this chapter.

In Chapter 1, "Building basic formulas," you learned about building text formulas in Excel—not that there was much to learn. Text formulas consist only of the concatenation operator (**&**) used to combine two or more strings into a larger string.

Excel's text functions enable you to take text formulas to a more useful level by giving you numerous ways to manipulate strings. With these functions, you can convert numbers to strings, change lowercase letters to uppercase (and vice versa), compare two strings, and more.

Excel's text functions

Table 5-1 summarizes Excel's text functions, and the rest of this chapter gives you details about and examples of how to use most of them.

TABLE 5-1 Excel's text functions

Function	Description
ARRAYTOTEXT (*array*[, *format*])	Returns the text representation of *array*.
BAHTTEXT (*number*)	Converts *number* to baht (Thai) text.
CHAR (*number*)	Returns the character that corresponds to the ANSI code given by *number*.

Function	Description
CLEAN(*text*)	Removes all nonprintable characters from *text*.
CODE(*text*)	Returns the ANSI code for the first character in *text*.
CONCAT(*text1*[, *text2*],...)	Joins the specified strings into a single string.
DOLLAR(*number*[, *decimals*])	Converts *number* to a string that uses the Currency format.
EXACT(*text1*, *text2*)	Compares two strings to see whether they are identical.
FIND(*find*, *within*[, *start*])	Returns the character position of the text *find* within the text *within*. **FIND** is case sensitive.
FIXED(*number*[, *decimals*] [, *no_commas*])	Converts *number* to a string that uses the Number format.
LAMBDA([*parameter1*] [, *parameter2*],... *calculation*)	Defines a custom function that returns the result of the *calculation* using the optional parameters as inputs (see Chapter 9).
LEFT(*text*[, *number*])	Returns the leftmost *number* of characters from *text*.
LEN(*text*)	Returns the length of *text*.
LET(*name*, *value*, *calculation*)	Assigns *value* to the variable *name* and uses that variable as an input to the calculation, the result of which is returned by the function (see Chapter 9).
LOWER(*text*)	Converts *text* to lowercase.
MID(*text*, *start*, *number*)	Returns *number* characters from *text*, starting at *start*.
NUMBERVALUE(*text*, *decimal*, *group*)	Converts *text* to a number by interpreting the decimal symbol within *text* as the *decimal* separator and the *group* symbol as the group separator.
PROPER(*text*)	Converts *text* to proper case (first letter of each word capitalized).
REPLACE(*old*, *start*, *chars*, *new*)	Replaces the *old* string with the *new* string.
REPT(*text*, *number*)	Repeats the *text* string *number* times.
RIGHT(*text*[, *number*])	Returns the rightmost *number* characters from *text*.
SEARCH(*find*, *within*[, *start_num*])	Returns the character position of the text *find* within the text *within*. **SEARCH** is not case sensitive.
SUBSTITUTE(*text*, *old*, *new*[, *num*])	In *text*, substitutes the *new* string for the *old* string; optionally substitutes only the instance specified by *num*.
T(*value*)	Converts *value* to text.
TEXT(*value*, *format*)	Formats *value* and converts it to text.
TEXTJOIN(*delimiter*, *ignore_empty*, *text1*, *text2*,...)	Joins the text strings, separating each with the *delimiter* character.
TRIM(*text*)	Removes excess spaces from *text*.
UNICHAR(*number*)	Returns the character that corresponds to the UNICODE value given by *number*.
UNICODE(*text*)	Returns the UNICODE value for the first character in *text*.
UPPER(*text*)	Converts *text* to uppercase.
VALUE(*text*)	Converts *text* to a number.
VALUETOTEXT(*value*)	Returns the text representation of *value*.

Working with characters and codes

Every character you can display on your screen has its own underlying numeric code. For example, the code for the uppercase letter *A* is 65, whereas the code for the ampersand (&) is 38. These codes apply not only to the alphanumeric characters accessible via your keyboard but also to extra characters. The collection of these characters is called the *ANSI character set*, and the numbers assigned to each character are called the *ANSI codes*.

For example, the ANSI code for the copyright character (©) is 169. To display this character, press Alt+0169, using your keyboard's numeric keypad to enter the digits.

> **Note** When entering digits, remember to always include the leading zero for codes higher than 127.

The ANSI codes run from 1 to 255, although the first 31 codes are nonprinting codes that define characters such as carriage returns and line feeds.

The CHAR function

Excel enables you to determine the character represented by an ANSI code using the **CHAR** function:

CHAR(*number*)

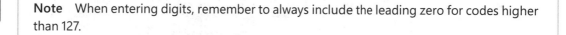

| *number* | The ANSI code, which must be a number between 1 and 255 |

For example, the following formula displays the copyright symbol (ANSI code 169):

=CHAR(169)

> **Note** If you are working with UNICODE values instead of ANSI values, use the **UNICHAR** function instead of the **CHAR** function.

Generating the ANSI character set

Figure 5-1 shows a worksheet that displays the entire ANSI character set, excluding the first 31 nonprinting characters (and note that ANSI code 32 represents the space character). In each case, the character is displayed by applying the **CHAR** function to the value in the cell to the left.

> **Note** The actual character displayed by an ANSI code depends on the font applied to the cell. The characters shown in Figure 5-1 are the ones you see with normal text fonts, such as Arial. However, if you apply a font such as Symbol or Wingdings to the worksheet, you see a different set of characters.

Note You can work with all the examples in this chapter by downloading Chapter05.xlsx from either of the companion content sites mentioned in the Introduction.

L14 =CHAR(K14)

Code	CHAR()	Code	CHAR()	Code	CHAR()	Code	CHAR()	Code	CHAR()	Code	CHAR()	Code	CHAR()	Code	CHAR()	Code	CHAR()
32		57	9	82	R	107	k	132	„	157		182	¶	207	Ï	232	è
33	!	58	:	83	S	108	l	133	…	158	ž	183	·	208	Ð	233	é
34	"	59	;	84	T	109	m	134	†	159	Ÿ	184		209	Ñ	234	ê
35	#	60	<	85	U	110	n	135	‡	160		185	¹	210	Ò	235	ë
36	$	61	=	86	V	111	o	136	ˆ	161	¡	186	º	211	Ó	236	ì
37	%	62	>	87	W	112	p	137	‰	162	¢	187	»	212	Ô	237	í
38	&	63	?	88	X	113	q	138	Š	163	£	188	¼	213	Õ	238	î
39	'	64	@	89	Y	114	r	139	‹	164	¤	189	½	214	Ö	239	ï
40	(	65	A	90	Z	115	s	140	Œ	165	¥	190	¾	215	×	240	ð
41	)	66	B	91	[	116	t	141		166	¦	191	¿	216	Ø	241	ñ
42	*	67	C	92	\	117	u	142	ž	167	§	192	À	217	Ù	242	ò
43	+	68	D	93	]	118	v	143		168	¨	193	Á	218	Ú	243	ó
44	,	69	E	94	^	119	w	144		169	©	194	Â	219	Û	244	ô
45	-	70	F	95	_	120	x	145	'	170	ª	195	Ã	220	Ü	245	õ
46	.	71	G	96	`	121	y	146	'	171	«	196	Ä	221	Ý	246	ö
47	/	72	H	97	a	122	z	147	"	172	¬	197	Å	222	Þ	247	÷
48	0	73	I	98	b	123	{	148	"	173		198	Æ	223	ß	248	ø
49	1	74	J	99	c	124	|	149	•	174	®	199	Ç	224	à	249	ù
50	2	75	K	100	d	125	}	150	–	175	¯	200	È	225	á	250	ú
51	3	76	L	101	e	126	~	151	—	176	°	201	É	226	â	251	û
52	4	77	M	102	f	127		152	˜	177	±	202	Ê	227	ã	252	ü
53	5	78	N	103	g	128	€	153	™	178	²	203	Ë	228	ä	253	ý
54	6	79	O	104	h	129		154	š	179	³	204	Ì	229	å	254	þ
55	7	80	P	105	i	130	‚	155	›	180	´	205	Í	230	æ	255	ÿ
56	8	81	Q	106	j	131	ƒ	156	œ	181	µ	206	Î	231	ç		

FIGURE 5-1 This worksheet uses the CHAR function to display each printing member of the ANSI character set.

To build the character set shown in Figure 5-1, I entered the ANSI code and the **CHAR** function at the top of each column, and then I filled down to generate the rest of the column. A less tedious method (albeit one with a less useful display) is to take advantage of the **ROW** function, which returns the row number of the current cell. Assuming that you want to start your table in row 2, you can generate any ANSI character by using the following formula:

```
=CHAR(ROW + 30)
```

Generating a series of letters

Excel's fill handle and the **Home** > **Fill** > **Series** command are great for generating a series of numbers or dates, but they don't do the job when you need a series of letters (such as *a*, *b*, *c*, and so on). However, you can use the **CHAR** function in an array formula to generate such a series.

To generate a column of the letters beginning with *a* (which corresponds to ANSI code 97), enter the following formula where you want the series to begin:

```
=CHAR(ROW(A97))
```

To generate a row of the letters beginning with *a*, enter the following formula where you want the series to begin:

```
=CHAR(COLUMN(CS1))
```

Now extend the series by dragging the fill handle down (for a column) or right (for a row).

For uppercase letters (where *A* corresponds to ANSI 65), begin with the following formulas and use the fill handle to extend the series:

```
=CHAR(ROW(A65))
=CHAR(COLUMN(BM1))
```

The CODE function

The **CODE** function is the opposite of **CHAR**. That is, given a text character, **CODE** returns its ANSI code value:

```
CODE(text)
```

text	A character or text string. Note that if you enter a multicharacter string, **CODE** returns the ANSI code of the first character in the string.

For example, the following formulas both return **83**, the ANSI code of the uppercase letter *S*:

```
CODE("S")
CODE("Spacely Sprockets")
```

> **Note** If you need to determine a character's UNICODE value instead of its ANSI value, use the **UNICODE** function instead of the **CODE** function.

Generating a series of letters starting from any letter

Earlier in this section, you learned how to combine **CHAR** and **ROW** in a formula to generate a series of letters beginning with the letter *a* or *A*. What if you prefer a different starting letter? You can do that by changing the initial value that's plugged in to the **CHAR** function before the offsets are calculated. I used **97** in the previous example to begin the series with the letter *a*, but you could use **98** to start with *b*, **99** to start with *c*, and so on.

Instead of looking up the ANSI code of the character you prefer, however, use the **CODE** function to have Excel do it for you:

```
=CHAR(CODE("letter") + ROW(range) - ROW(first_cell))
```

Here, replace *letter* with the letter with which you want to start the series. For example, the following formula begins the series with uppercase *N*:

```
=CHAR(CODE("N") + ROW(A1:A13) - ROW(A1))
```

> **Tip** If you're using a version of Excel prior to 2019, when working with the formulas in this section, remember to enter them as array formulas in the range specified in the first **ROW** function (for example, A1:A13).

Converting text

Excel's forte is number crunching, and it often seems to give short shrift to strings, particularly when it comes to displaying strings in a worksheet. For example, appending a numeric value to a string results in the number being displayed without any formatting, even if the original cell had a numeric format applied to it. Similarly, strings imported from a database or text file can have the wrong case or no formatting. However, as you'll see in the next few sections, Excel offers a number of worksheet functions that enable you to convert strings to a more suitable text format or to convert between text and numeric values.

The **LOWER** function

The **LOWER** function converts a specified string to all-lowercase letters:

```
LOWER(text)
```

text	The string you want to convert to lowercase

For example, the following formula converts the text in cell B10 to lowercase:

```
=LOWER(B10)
```

The **LOWER** function is often used to convert imported data, particularly data imported from a main-frame computer, which often arrives in all-uppercase characters.

The **UPPER** function

The **UPPER** function converts a specified string to all-uppercase letters:

```
UPPER(text)
```

text	The string you want to convert to uppercase

For example, the following formula converts the text in cells A5 and B5 to uppercase and concatenates the results with a space between them:

```
=UPPER(A5) & " " & UPPER(B5)
```

The PROPER function

The PROPER function converts a specified string to proper case, which means the first letter of each word appears in uppercase and the rest of the letters appear in lowercase:

```
PROPER(text)
```

text	The string you want to convert to proper case

For example, the following formula (entered as an array of ten vertical cells in Excel 2016 or earlier) converts the text in the range A1:A10 to proper case:

```
=PROPER(A1:A10)
```

The NUMBERVALUE function

The NUMBERVALUE function converts a text value to a number by specifying the symbol used for the decimal and groups:

```
NUMBERVALUE(text[, decimal_separator][, group_separator])
```

text	The text representation of the number
decimal_separator	The symbol used within text to separate the integer portion from the fractional portion
group_separator	The symbol used within text to separate the numeric groupings, such as thousands and millions

This function is useful if you're faced with a worksheet that contains numbers that use nonstandard symbols for the decimal and group separators. For example, suppose cell C6 contains 12,34, where the comma (,) is being used as a decimal separator (which is common in many European locales). To convert this value to a number that uses a period (assuming that's your local decimal separator symbol), you'd use the following formula:

```
=NUMBERVALUE(C6, ",")
```

As another example, suppose cell E5 contains the value 2~345'67, where tilde (~) is the group (thousands, in this case) separator and apostrophe (') is the decimal separator. Then the following formula converts this value to a number:

```
=NUMBERVALUE(E5, "'", "~")
```

The **ARRAYTOTEXT** function

The **ARRAYTOTEXT** function returns a range of values as a text representation:

ARRAYTOTEXT(*array*[, *format*])

array	The range to return as text
format	The format of the returned text: **0** (the default) returns the text as a concise list with each item separated by a comma and a space; **1** returns the text using a strict array format, with rows separated by semi-colons and text values enclosed in quotation marks.

The *format* argument's concise (0) and strict (1) values are a bit confusing, so let's look at a simple example. Suppose you have the values **123**, **Primrose Lane**, and **Indianapolis** in cells A1, B1, and C1, respectively, and the values **987**, **Blue Jay Way,** and **Toronto** in cells A2, B2, and C2, respectively. The formula =**ARRAYTOTEXT(A1:C2, 0)** returns the following text:

123, Primrose Lane, Indianapolis, 987, Blue Jay Way, Toronto

However, the formula =**ARRAYTOTEXT(A1:C2, 1)** returns the following text:

{123,"Primrose Lane","Indianapolis";987,"Blue Jay Way","Toronto"}

Note the curly braces that now appear around the text, which indicate that the the result is an array; also note the semi-colon (;) between **"Indianapolis"** and **987**, which indicates the array is starting a new row.

The **VALUETOTEXT** function

The **VALUETOTEXT** function returns a text representation of a value:

VALUETOTEXT(*value*[, *format*])

value	The value to return as text (which could be a range of values).
format	The format of the returned text: **0** (the default) returns the text as a concise list with each item separated by a comma and a space; **1** returns the text using a strict array format, with rows separated by semi-colons and text values enclosed in quotation marks.

Perhaps the most common use of **VALUETOTEXT** is to convert a cell value that uses one of Excel's advanced data types—such as Geography or Stocks—into a text representation. For example, suppose cell A1 contains **Indianapolis** formatted as the Geography data type. To get just the name "Indianapolis" from that entry, you'd normally use the following:

A1.Name

Following is a (perhaps?) more straightforward way to use **VALUETOTEXT**:

```
VALUETOTEXT(A1)
```

If you use **VALUETOTEXT(A1, 1)**, then Excel returns the name surrounded by double quotation marks.

Formatting text

You learned in Chapter 1 that you can enhance the results of your formulas by using built-in or custom numeric formats to control things such as commas, decimal places, currency symbols, and more. That's fine for cell results, but what if you want to incorporate a result within a string? For example, consider the following text formula:

```
="The expense total for this quarter in 2022 is " & F11
```

No matter how you've formatted the result in F11, the number appears in the string using Excel's General number format. For example, if cell F11 contains **$74,400**, the previous formula will appear in the cell as follows:

```
The expense total for this quarter in 2022 is 74400
```

You need some way to format the number within the string. The next three sections show you some Excel functions that let you do just that.

The **DOLLAR** function

The **DOLLAR** function converts a numeric value into a string value that uses the Currency format:

```
DOLLAR(number [,decimals])
```

number	The number you want to convert
decimals	The number of decimals to display (the default is **2**)

To fix the string example from the previous section, you need to apply the **DOLLAR** function to cell F13:

```
="The expense total for this quarter in 2022 is " & DOLLAR(F13, 0)
```

In this case, the number is formatted with no decimal places. Figure 5-2 shows a variation of this formula in action in cell B16. (For comparison, cell B15 contains a similar formula that doesn't use the DOLLAR function.)

B16 | fx ="The expense total for this quarter in 2022 is " & DOLLAR(F13,0)

	A	B	C	D	E	F	G	H	I
1	**Expense Budget Calculation - 1st Quarter**								
2									
3		**INCREASE**	1.03						
4									
5		**EXPENSES**	**January**	**February**	**March**	**Total**			
6		Advertising	$4,600	$4,200	$5,200	$14,000			
7		Rent	$2,100	$2,100	$2,100	$6,300			
8		Supplies	$1,300	$1,200	$1,400	$3,900			
9		Salaries	$16,000	$16,000	$16,500	$48,500			
10		Utilities	$500	$600	$600	$1,700			
11		2021 TOTAL	$24,500	$24,100	$25,800	$74,400			
12									
13		2022 BUDGET	$25,235	$24,823	$26,574	$76,632			
14									
15		The expense total for this quarter in 2021 is 74400							
16		The expense total for this quarter in 2022 is $76,632							
17									

FIGURE 5-2 Use the DOLLAR function to display a number as a string with the Currency format.

The **FIXED** function

For some kinds of numbers, you can control the number of decimals and whether commas are inserted as the thousands separator by using the **FIXED** function:

FIXED(*number* [,*decimals*] [,*no_commas*])

number	The number you want to convert to a string.
decimals	The number of decimals to display. (The default is **2**.)
no_commas	A logical value that determines whether commas are inserted into the string. Use **TRUE** to suppress commas; use **FALSE** to include commas. (This is the default.)

For example, the following formula uses the **SUM** function to take a sum of a range and applies the **FIXED** function to the result so that it's displayed as a string with commas and no decimal places:

="Total show attendance: " & FIXED(SUM(A1:A8), 0, FALSE) & " people."

The **TEXT** function

DOLLAR and **FIXED** are useful functions in specific circumstances. However, if you want total control over the way a number is formatted within a string, or if you want to include dates and times within strings, the powerful **TEXT** function is what you need:

TEXT(*number*, *format*)

number	The number, date, or time you want to convert
format	The numeric or date/time format you want to apply to *number*

The power of the **TEXT** function lies in its *format* argument, which is a custom format that specifies exactly how you want the number to appear.

Table 5-2 lists the special symbols you use to define a numeric format.

TABLE 5-2 Numeric formatting symbols

Symbol	Description
General	Displays the number with the General format.
#	Holds a place for a digit and displays the digit exactly as typed. Displays nothing if no number is entered.
0	Holds a place for a digit and displays the digit exactly as typed. Displays 0 if no number is entered.
?	Holds a place for a digit and displays the digit exactly as typed. Displays a space if no number is entered.
. (period)	Sets the location of the decimal point.
, (comma)	Sets the location of the thousands separator. Marks only the location of the first thousand.
%	Multiplies the number by 100 (for display only) and adds the percent (%) character.
E+ e+ E- e-	Displays the number in scientific format. **E-** and **e-** place a minus sign in the exponent; **E+** and **e+** place a plus sign in the exponent.
/ (slash)	Sets the location of the fraction separator.
$ ( ) : – + <space>	Displays the character.
*	Repeats whatever character immediately follows the asterisk until the cell is full. Doesn't replace other symbols or numbers.
_ (underscore)	Inserts a blank space the width of whatever character follows the underscore.
\ (backslash)	Inserts the character that follows the backslash.
"text"	Inserts the text that appears within the quotation marks.
@	Holds a place for text.

Table 5-3 lists the date and time formatting symbols.

TABLE 5-3 Date and time formatting symbols

Symbol	Description
Date Formats	
d	Day number without a leading zero (**1—31**)
dd	Day number with a leading zero (**01—31**)
ddd	Three-letter day abbreviation (**Mon**, for example)
dddd	Full day name (**Monday**, for example)
m	Month number without a leading zero (**1—12**)
mm	Month number with a leading zero (**01—12**)
mmm	Three-letter month abbreviation (**Aug**, for example)

Symbol	Description
mmmm	Full month name (**August**, for example)
yy	Two-digit year (**00—99**)
yyyy	Full year (**1900—9999**)
Time Formats	
h	Hour without a leading zero (**0—24**)
hh	Hour with a leading zero (**00—24**)
m	Minute without a leading zero (**0—59**)
mm	Minute with a leading zero (**00—59**)
s	Second without a leading zero (**0—59**)
ss	Second with a leading zero (**00—59**)
AM/PM, am/pm, A/P	12-hour clock time
/ : . —	Symbols used to separate parts of dates or times

For example, the following formula uses the **AVERAGE** function to take an average over the range A1:A31, and then it uses the **TEXT** function to apply the custom format **#,##0.00°F** to the result:

```
="The average temperature was " & TEXT(AVERAGE(A1:A31), "#,##0.00°F")
```

Note To insert the degree symbol (°), type **Alt+0176** using your keyboard's numeric keypad.

Displaying when a workbook was last updated

Many people like to annotate their workbooks by setting Excel in manual calculation mode and entering a **NOW** function into a cell (which returns the current date and time). The **NOW** function doesn't update unless you save or recalculate the sheet, so you always know when the sheet was last updated.

Instead of just entering **NOW** by itself, you might find it better to preface the date with an explanatory string, such as **This workbook last updated:**. To do this, you can enter the following formula:

```
="This workbook last updated: " & NOW
```

Unfortunately, your output will look something like this:

```
This workbook last updated: 42238.51001
```

The number **42238.51001** is Excel's internal representation of a date and time. (The number to the left of the decimal is the date, and the number to the right of the decimal is the time.) To get a properly formatted date and time, use the **TEXT** function. For example, to format the results of the **NOW** function in the MM/DD/YY HH:MM format, use the following formula:

```
="This workbook last updated: " & TEXT(NOW, "mm/dd/yy hh:mm")
```

Manipulating text

This section takes you into the real heart of Excel's text-manipulation tricks. All the functions you'll learn about over the next few pages will be useful, but you'll see that by combining two or more of these functions into a single formula, you can bring out the amazing versatility of Excel's text-manipulation prowess.

Removing unwanted characters from a string

Characters imported from databases and text files often come with all kinds of string baggage in the form of extra characters that you don't need. These could be extra spaces in the string, or they could be line feeds, carriage returns, and other nonprintable characters embedded in the string. To fix these problems, Excel offers a couple of functions: **TRIM** and **CLEAN**.

The TRIM function

You use the **TRIM** function to remove excess spaces within a string:

TRIM(*text*)

text	The string from which you want the excess spaces removed

Here, *excess* means all spaces before and after the string, as well as two or more consecutive spaces within the string. In the latter case, **TRIM** removes all but one of the consecutive spaces.

Figure 5-3 shows the **TRIM** function at work. Each string in the range A2:A7 contains a number of excess spaces before, within, or after the name. The **TRIM** functions appear in column C. To help confirm the **TRIM** function's operation, I use the **LEN** text function in columns B and D. **LEN** returns the number of characters in a specified string, using the following syntax:

LEN(*text*)

text	The string for which you want to know the number of characters

	A	B	C	D	E
	C2	⌄ : ✕ ✓ *fx*	=TRIM(A2)		
1	**Original String**	**Length**	**Trimmed String**	**Length**	
2	Maria Anders	16	Maria Anders	12	
3	Ana Trujillo	17	Ana Trujillo	12	
4	Antonio Moreno	23	Antonio Moreno	14	
5	Thomas Hardy	17	Thomas Hardy	12	
6	Angus Glen Dunlop	26	Angus Glen Dunlop	17	
7	Christina Berglund	22	Christina Berglund	18	

FIGURE 5-3 Use the TRIM function to remove extra spaces from a string.

The CLEAN function

You use the CLEAN function to remove nonprintable characters from a string:

CLEAN(*text*)

text	The string from which you want the nonprintable characters removed

Recall that the nonprintable characters are the codes 1 through 31 of the ANSI character set. The CLEAN function is most often used to remove line feeds (ANSI 10) or carriage returns (ANSI 13) from multiline data. Figure 5-4 shows an example.

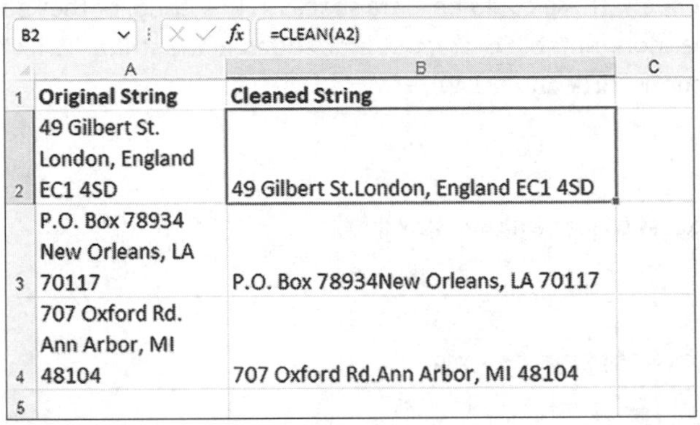

FIGURE 5-4 Use the CLEAN function to remove nonprintable characters such as line feeds from a string.

The TEXTJOIN function: Concatenating text with a delimiter

In Chapter 1, I mentioned Excel's concatenation operator (&), which you use to join two or more strings into a single text value. This operator works well, but things can get unwieldy fast when you need to separate the joined strings with one or more characters. For example, suppose you have four columns of contact data: a title, first name, initial, and last name for each person. When concatenating these values, you'll want a space between each one, so combining all four columns into a single text value requires a formula such as the following:

=A2 & " " & B2 & " " & C2 & " " & D2

That's a bit of a mess, and things just get worse if any contact has blank data (such as no title or no initial). To better handle this kind of string concatenation, Excel now offers the TEXTJOIN function:

TEXTJOIN(*delimiter, ignore_empty, text1, text 2, …*)

delimiter	The character you want to insert between each string
ignore_empty	A Boolean value; use TRUE to not include empty cells in the join (this is the default); use FALSE to include empty cells
text1, text 2, …	The strings you want to join

Figure 5-5 shows an example.

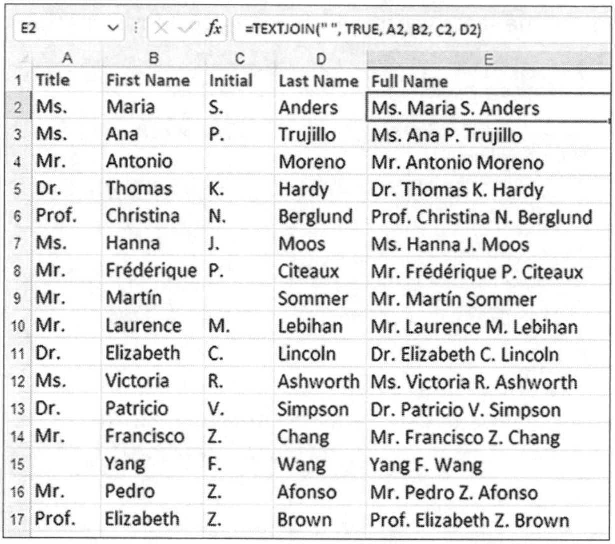

	A	B	C	D	E
1	Title	First Name	Initial	Last Name	Full Name
2	Ms.	Maria	S.	Anders	Ms. Maria S. Anders
3	Ms.	Ana	P.	Trujillo	Ms. Ana P. Trujillo
4	Mr.	Antonio		Moreno	Mr. Antonio Moreno
5	Dr.	Thomas	K.	Hardy	Dr. Thomas K. Hardy
6	Prof.	Christina	N.	Berglund	Prof. Christina N. Berglund
7	Ms.	Hanna	J.	Moos	Ms. Hanna J. Moos
8	Mr.	Frédérique	P.	Citeaux	Mr. Frédérique P. Citeaux
9	Mr.	Martín		Sommer	Mr. Martín Sommer
10	Mr.	Laurence	M.	Lebihan	Mr. Laurence M. Lebihan
11	Dr.	Elizabeth	C.	Lincoln	Dr. Elizabeth C. Lincoln
12	Ms.	Victoria	R.	Ashworth	Ms. Victoria R. Ashworth
13	Dr.	Patricio	V.	Simpson	Dr. Patricio V. Simpson
14	Mr.	Francisco	Z.	Chang	Mr. Francisco Z. Chang
15		Yang	F.	Wang	Yang F. Wang
16	Mr.	Pedro	Z.	Afonso	Mr. Pedro Z. Afonso
17	Prof.	Elizabeth	Z.	Brown	Prof. Elizabeth Z. Brown

E2 = `=TEXTJOIN(" ", TRUE, A2, B2, C2, D2)`

FIGURE 5-5 Use the TEXTJOIN function to concatenate multiple strings with a delimiter character between them.

The REPT function: Repeating a character or string

The **REPT** function repeats a character or string a specified number of times:

REPT(*text*, *number*)

text	The character or string you want to repeat
number	The number of times to repeat *text*

Padding a cell

The **REPT** function is sometimes used to pad a cell with characters. For example, you can use it to add leading or trailing dots in a cell. Here's a formula that creates trailing dots after a string:

="Advertising" & REPT(".", 20 - LEN("Advertising"))

This formula writes the string *Advertising* and then uses **REPT** to repeat the dot character according to the following expression: **20 - LEN("Advertising")**. This expression ensures that a constant number of characters are written to the cell. Because *Advertising* is 11 characters, the expression result is **9**, which means that nine dots are added to the right of the string. If the string were *Rent* (four characters) instead, 16 dots would be added as padding. Figure 5-6 shows how this technique creates a *dot follower* effect.

A2	⌄	⦂	× ✓ *fx*	="Advertising" & REPT(".", 20 - LEN("Advertising"))			

	A	B	C	D	E
1	**EXPENSES**				
2	Advertising.........				
3	Rent...............				
4	Supplies............				
5	Salaries............				
6	Utilities..........				

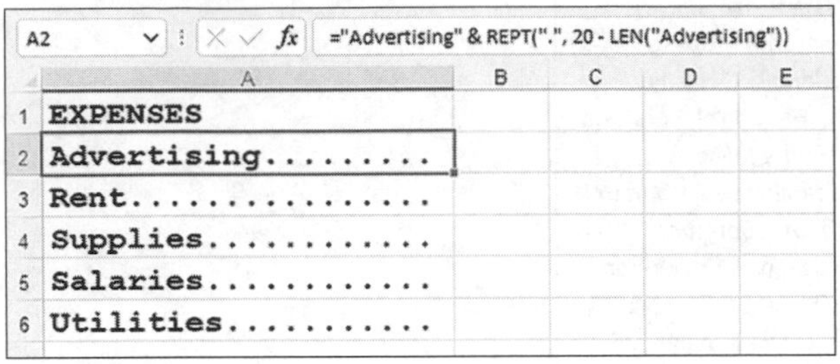

FIGURE 5-6 Use the REPT function to pad a cell with characters, such as the dot followers shown here.

Building text charts

A more common use for the **REPT** function is to build text-based charts. In this case, you use a numeric result in a cell as the **REPT** function's **number** argument, and the repeated character then charts the result.

A simple example is a basic histogram, which shows the frequency of a sample over an interval. Figure 5-7 shows a text histogram in which the intervals are listed in column A and the frequencies are listed in column B. The **REPT** function creates the histogram in column C by repeating the vertical bar (|) according to each frequency, as in this sample formula:

```
=REPT("|", B4)
```

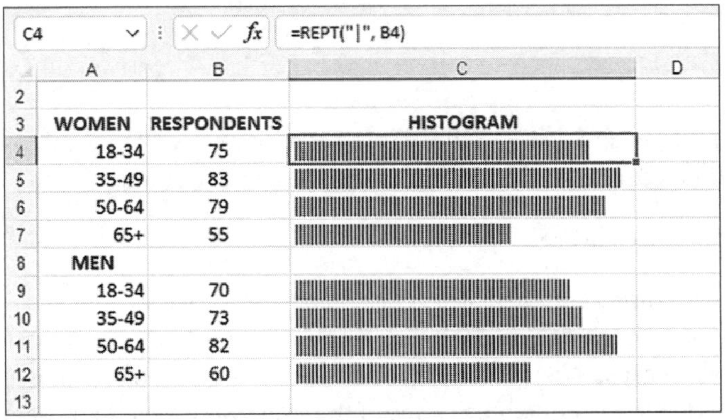

C4	⌄	⦂	× ✓ *fx*	=REPT("|", B4)	

	A	B	C	D
2				
3	**WOMEN**	**RESPONDENTS**	**HISTOGRAM**	
4	18-34	75	‖‖‖‖‖‖‖‖‖‖‖‖‖‖‖‖‖‖‖‖‖‖‖‖‖‖	
5	35-49	83	‖‖‖‖‖‖‖‖‖‖‖‖‖‖‖‖‖‖‖‖‖‖‖‖‖‖‖	
6	50-64	79	‖‖‖‖‖‖‖‖‖‖‖‖‖‖‖‖‖‖‖‖‖‖‖‖‖‖	
7	65+	55	‖‖‖‖‖‖‖‖‖‖‖‖‖‖‖‖‖‖	
8	**MEN**			
9	18-34	70	‖‖‖‖‖‖‖‖‖‖‖‖‖‖‖‖‖‖‖‖‖‖‖	
10	35-49	73	‖‖‖‖‖‖‖‖‖‖‖‖‖‖‖‖‖‖‖‖‖‖‖‖	
11	50-64	82	‖‖‖‖‖‖‖‖‖‖‖‖‖‖‖‖‖‖‖‖‖‖‖‖‖‖‖	
12	65+	60	‖‖‖‖‖‖‖‖‖‖‖‖‖‖‖‖‖‖‖‖	
13				

FIGURE 5-7 Use the REPT function to create a text-based histogram.

With a simple trick, you can turn the histogram into a text-based bar chart, as shown in Figure 5-8. The trick here is to format the chart cells with the Webdings font. In this font, the letter *g* is represented by a block character, and repeating that character produces a solid bar.

Tip To get the repeat value, I multiplied the percentages in column B by 100 to get a whole number. To keep the bars relatively short, I divided the result by 5.

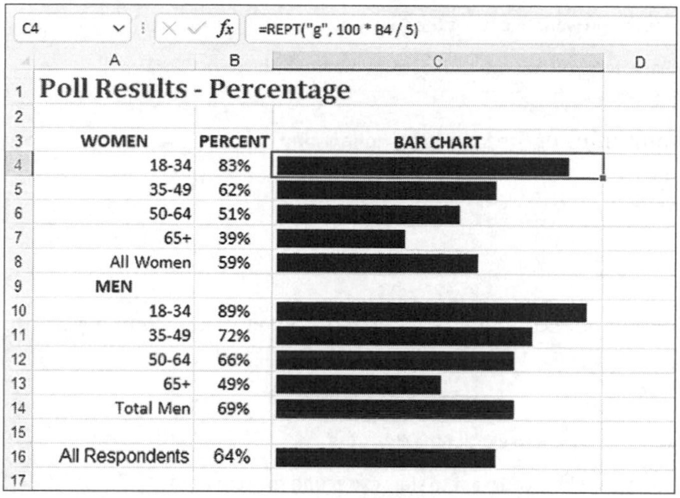

FIGURE 5-8 Use the REPT function to create a text-based bar chart.

Excel offers a feature called data bars (**Home** > **Conditional Formatting** > **DataBars**) that enables you to easily add histogram-like analysis to your worksheets without formulas.

Extracting a substring

String values often contain smaller strings, or *substrings*, that you need to work with. In a column of full names, for example, you might want to deal with only the last names so that you can sort the data. Similarly, you might want to extract the first few letters of a company name to include in an account number for that company.

Excel gives you three functions for extracting substrings, as described in the next three sections.

The LEFT function

The **LEFT** function returns a specified number of characters, starting from the left of a string:

```
LEFT(text [,num_chars])
```

text	The string from which you want to extract the substring
num_chars	The number of characters you want to extract from the left (the default is **1**)

For example, the following formula returns the substring **Karen**:

```
=LEFT("Karen Elizabeth McHammond", 5)
```

The RIGHT function

The **RIGHT** function returns a specified number of characters, starting from the right of a string:

RIGHT(*text* [,*num_chars*])

text	The string from which you want to extract the substring
num_chars	The number of characters you want to extract from the right (the default is **1**)

For example, the following formula returns the substring **McHammond**:

=RIGHT("Karen Elizabeth McHammond", 9)

The MID function

The **MID** function returns a specified number of characters starting from any point within a string:

MID(*text*, *start_num*, *num_chars*)

text	The string from which you want to extract the substring
start_num	The character position at which you want to start extracting the substring
num_chars	The number of characters you want to extract

For example, the following formula returns the substring **Elizabeth**:

=MID("Karen Elizabeth McHammond", 7, 9)

Converting text to sentence case

Microsoft Word's Change Case command has a *sentence case* option that converts a string to all-lowercase letters, except for the first letter, which is converted to uppercase (just as the letters would appear in a normal sentence). You saw earlier that Excel has **LOWER**, **UPPER**, and **PROPER** functions, but it has nothing that can produce sentence cases directly. However, it's possible to construct a formula that does this by using the **LOWER** and **UPPER** functions combined with the **LEFT** and **RIGHT** functions.

You begin by extracting the leftmost letter and converting it to uppercase (assuming here that the string is in cell A1):

UPPER(LEFT(A1))

Then you extract everything to the right of the first letter and convert it to lowercase:

LOWER(RIGHT(A1, LEN(A1) - 1))

Finally, you concatenate these two expressions into the complete formula:

```
=UPPER(LEFT(A1)) & LOWER(RIGHT(A1, LEN(A1) - 1))
```

Figure 5-9 shows a worksheet that puts this formula through its paces.

A2	✓	fx	=UPPER(LEFT(A1)) & LOWER(RIGHT(A1, LEN(A1) - 1))
			A
1	IT WAS THE BEST OF TIMES, IT WAS THE WORST OF TIMES.
2	It was the best of times, it was the worst of times.
3	
4	iT wAs A dArK aNd StOrMy NiGhT.
5	It was a dark and stormy night.
6	
7	Alice Was Beginning To Get Very Tired Of Sitting By Her Sister On The Bank, And Of Having Nothing To Do.
8	Alice was beginning to get very tired of sitting by her sister on the bank, and of having nothing to do.
9	

FIGURE 5-9 The LEFT and RIGHT functions combine with the UPPER and LOWER functions to produce a formula that converts text to sentence case.

A date-conversion formula

If you import mainframe or server data into your worksheets, or if you import online service data such as stock market quotes, you'll often end up with date formats that Excel can't handle. One common example is the YYYYMMDD format (for example, **20220823**).

To convert this value into a date that Excel can work with, you can use the **LEFT**, **MID**, and **RIGHT** functions. If the unrecognized date is in cell A1, **LEFT(A1, 4)** extracts the year, **MID(A1,5,2)** extracts the month, and **RIGHT(A1,2)** extracts the day. Plugging these functions into a **DATE** function gives Excel a date it can handle:

```
=DATE(LEFT(A1, 4), MID(A1, 5, 2), RIGHT(A1, 2))
```

To learn more about the **DATE** function, see Chapter 8, "Working with date and time functions."

Case study: Generating account numbers, part I

Many companies generate supplier or customer account numbers by combining part of an account's name with a numeric value. Excel's text functions make it easy to generate such account numbers automatically.

To begin, let's extract the first three letters of the company name and convert them to uppercase for easier reading (assuming here that the name is in cell A2):

```
UPPER(LEFT(A2, 3))
```

Next, generate the numeric portion of the account number by grabbing the row number: ROW(A2). However, it's best to keep all account numbers a uniform length, so use the TEXT function to pad the row number with zeros:

```
TEXT(ROW(A2), "0000")
```

Here's the complete formula, and Figure 5-10 shows some examples:

```
=UPPER(LEFT(A2, 3)) & TEXT(ROW(A2), "0000")
```

	A	B	C	D
	B2 ⌄ : × ✓ *fx* =UPPER(LEFT(A2, 3)) & TEXT(ROW(A2), "0000")			
1	**Company Name**	**Account Number**		
2	Exotic Liquids	EXO0002		
3	New Orleans Cajun Delights	NEW0003		
4	Grandma Kelly's Homestead	GRA0004		
5	Tokyo Traders	TOK0005		
6	Cooperativa de Quesos 'Las Cabras'	COO0006		
7	Mayumi's	MAY0007		
8	Pavlova, Ltd.	PAV0008		
9	Specialty Biscuits, Ltd.	SPE0009		
10	Bigfoot Breweries	BIG0010		

FIGURE 5-10 This worksheet uses the UPPER, LEFT, and TEXT functions to automatically generate account numbers from company names.

Searching for substrings

You can take Excel's text functions up a notch or two by searching for substrings within some given text. For example, in a string that includes a person's first and last names, you can find out where the space falls between the names and then use that fact to extract either the first name or the last name.

The FIND and SEARCH functions

Searching for substrings is handled by the FIND and SEARCH functions:

```
FIND(find_text, within_text [,start_num])
SEARCH(find_text, within_text [,start_num])
```

find_text	The substring you want to look for
within_text	The string in which you want to look
start_num	The character position at which you want to start looking (the default is **1**)

Here are some notes to bear in mind when using these functions:

- These functions return the character position of the first instance (after the *start_num* character position) of *find_text* in *within_text*.

- Use **SEARCH** for non-case-sensitive searches. For example, **SEARCH("e", "Expenses")** returns **1**.

- Use **FIND** for case-sensitive searches. For example, **FIND("e", "Expenses")** returns **4**.

- These functions return the **#VALUE!** error if *find_text* is not in *within_text*.

- In the *find_text* argument of **SEARCH**, use a question mark (?) to match any single character.

- In the *find_text* argument of **SEARCH**, use an asterisk (*) to match any number of characters.

- To include the character ? or * in a **SEARCH** operation, precede each instance in the *find_text* argument with a tilde (~). If you want to search for a tilde character, use two tildes (~~).

Extracting a first name or last name

If you have a range of cells containing people's first and last names, it can often be advantageous to extract these names from each string. For example, you might want to store the first and last names in separate ranges for later importing into a database table. Or perhaps you need to construct a new range using a *Last Name, First Name* structure for sorting the names.

The solution is to use the **SEARCH** function (or the **FIND** function) to find the space that separates the first and last names and then use either the **LEFT** function to extract the first name or the **RIGHT** function to extract the last name. (Although, remember that Excel offers the Flash Fill feature, which is usually easier for tasks such as extracting names.)

For the first name, you use the following formula (assuming that the full name is in cell A2):

```
=LEFT(A2, SEARCH(" ", A2) - 1)
```

Notice that the formula subtracts **1** from the **SEARCH(" ", A2)** result to avoid including the space in the extracted substring. You can use this formula in more general circumstances to extract the first word of any multiword string.

For the last name, you need to build a similar formula using the **RIGHT** function:

```
=RIGHT(A2, LEN(A2) - SEARCH(" ", A2))
```

To extract the correct number of letters, the formula takes the length of the original string and subtracts the position of the space. You can use this formula in more general circumstances to extract the second word in any two-word string.

Figure 5-11 shows a worksheet that puts both formulas to work.

| D2 | | | f_x | =TEXTJOIN(", ", TRUE, RIGHT(A2, LEN(A2) - SEARCH(" ", A2)), LEFT(A2, SEARCH(" ", A2) - 1)) | | | | |

	A	B	C	D	E	F	G	H
1	**Full Name**	**First Name**	**Last Name**	**Last Name, First Name**				
2	Charlotte Cooper	Charlotte	Cooper	Cooper, Charlotte				
3	Shelley Burke	Shelley	Burke	Burke, Shelley				
4	Regina Murphy	Regina	Murphy	Murphy, Regina				
5	Yoshi Nagase	Yoshi	Nagase	Nagase, Yoshi				
6	Mayumi Ohno	Mayumi	Ohno	Ohno, Mayumi				
7	Ian Devling	Ian	Devling	Devling, Ian				
8	Peter Wilson	Peter	Wilson	Wilson, Peter				
9	Lars Peterson	Lars	Peterson	Peterson, Lars				
10	Carlos Diaz	Carlos	Diaz	Diaz, Carlos				
11	Petra Winkler	Petra	Winkler	Winkler, Petra				
12	Martin Bein	Martin	Bein	Bein, Martin				

FIGURE 5-11 Use the LEFT and SEARCH functions to extract the first name; use the RIGHT and SEARCH functions to extract the last name.

> **Caution** These formulas cause an error in any string that contains only a single word. To allow for this, use the **IFERROR** function:
>
> `=IFERROR(LEFT(A2, FIND(" ", A2) - 1), A2)`
>
> This way, if the cell contains a space, all is well, and the formula runs normally. If the cell does not contain a space, the **FIND** function returns an error. Therefore, the **IFERROR** function returns just the cell text instead of returning the formula result.

Extracting first name, last name, and middle initial

If the full name you have to work with includes the person's middle initial, the formula for extracting the first name remains the same. However, you need to adjust the formula for finding the last name. There are a couple of ways to go about this, but the method I'm showing you utilizes a useful **FIND** and **SEARCH** trick. Specifically, if you want to find the *second* instance of a substring, start the search one character position after the *first* instance of the substring. Here's an example of a string:

`Karen E. McHammond`

Assuming that this string is in A2, the formula **=SEARCH(" ", A2)** returns **6**, the position of the first space. If you want to find the position of the second space, instead set the **SEARCH** function's **start_num** argument to **7**—or, more generally, to the location of the first space, plus 1:

`=SEARCH(" ", A2, FIND(" ",A2) + 1)`

You can then apply this result within the **RIGHT** function to extract the last name:

`=RIGHT(A2, LEN(A2) - SEARCH(" ", A2, SEARCH(" ", A2) +1))`

To extract the middle initial, search for the period (.) and use **MID** to extract the letter before it:

```
=MID(A2, SEARCH(".", A2) - 1, 1)
```

Figure 5-12 shows a worksheet that demonstrates these techniques.

D2		× ✓ fx	=RIGHT(A2, LEN(A2) - SEARCH(" ", A2, SEARCH(" ", A2) + 1))		
	A	B	C	D	E
1	**Full Name**	**First Name**	**Middle Initial**	**Last Name**	
2	Charlotte P. Cooper	Charlotte	P	Cooper	
3	Shelley R. Burke	Shelley	R	Burke	
4	Regina O. Murphy	Regina	O	Murphy	
5	Yoshi H. Nagase	Yoshi	H	Nagase	
6	Mayumi U. Ohno	Mayumi	U	Ohno	
7	Ian F. Devling	Ian	F	Devling	
8	Peter W. Wilson	Peter	W	Wilson	
9	Lars X. Peterson	Lars	X	Peterson	
10	Carlos B. Diaz	Carlos	B	Diaz	
11	Petra Q. Winkler	Petra	Q	Winkler	

FIGURE 5-12 Apply SEARCH after the first instance of a substring to find the second instance of the substring.

Determining the column letter

Excel's **COLUMN** function returns the column number of a specified cell. For example, for a cell in column A, **COLUMN** returns **1**. This is handy, as you saw earlier in this chapter ("Generating a series of letters starting from any letter"), but in some cases, you might prefer to know the actual column letter.

This is a tricky proposition because the letters run from *A* to *Z*, then *AA* to *AZ*, and so on. However, Excel's **CELL** function (see Chapter 6, "Working with logical and information functions") can return (among other things) the address of a specified cell in absolute format—for example, **$A$2** or **$AB$10**. To get the column letter, you need to extract the substring between the two dollar signs. It's clear to begin with that the substring will always start at the second character position, so we can begin with the following formula:

```
=MID(CELL("Address", A2), 2, num_chars)
```

The *num_chars* value will be either **1**, **2**, or **3**, depending on the column. Notice, however, that the position of the second dollar sign will either be **3**, **4**, or **5**, depending on the column. In other words, the length of the substring will always be two less than the position of the second dollar sign. So, the following expression will give the *num_chars* value:

```
SEARCH("$", CELL("address",A2), 3) - 2
```

Here, then, is the full formula:

```
=MID(CELL("Address", A2), 2, SEARCH("$", CELL("address", A2), 3) - 2)
```

Getting the column letter of the current cell requires a slightly shorter formula:

```
=MID(CELL("Address"), 2, SEARCH("$", CELL("address"), 3) - 2)
```

Substituting one substring for another

The Office programs (and indeed most Windows programs) come with a Replace command that enables you to search for some text and then replace it with some other string. Excel's collection of worksheet functions also comes with such a feature, in the guise of the **REPLACE** and **SUBSTITUTE** functions.

The **REPLACE** function

Here's the syntax of the **REPLACE** function:

REPLACE(*old_text*, *start_num*, *num_chars*, *new_text*)

old_text	The original string that contains the substring you want to replace
start_num	The character position at which you want to start replacing
num_chars	The number of characters to replace
new_text	The substring you want to use as the replacement

The tricky parts of this function are the *start_num* and *num_chars* arguments. How do you know where to start and how much to replace? This isn't hard if you know the original string in which the replacement will take place and if you know the replacement string. For example, consider the following string:

Expense Budget for 2021

To replace **2021** with **2022** in the preceding example, and assuming that the string is in cell A1, the following formula does the job:

=REPLACE(A1, 20, 4, "2022")

However, it's a pain to have to calculate by hand the *start_num* and *num_chars* arguments. And in more general situations, you might not even know these values. Therefore, you need to calculate them:

- To determine the *start_num* value, use the **FIND** or **SEARCH** function to locate the substring you want to replace.

- To determine the *num_chars* value, use the **LEN** function to get the length of the replacement text.

The revised formula then looks something like this (assuming that the original string is in A1 and the replacement string is in A2):

=REPLACE(A1, FIND("2021", A1), LEN("2021"), A2)

The SUBSTITUTE function

The extra steps required make the **REPLACE** function unwieldy, so most people use the more straight-forward **SUBSTITUTE** function:

SUBSTITUTE(*text, old_text, new_text* [,*instance_num*])

text	The original string that contains the substring you want to replace.
old_text	The substring you want to replace.
new_text	The substring you want to use as the replacement.
instance_num	The instance you want to be replaced. (The default is all instances.)

The following simpler formula does the same thing as the example in the previous section:

=SUBSTITUTE(A1, "2021", "2022")

Removing a character from a string

Earlier, you learned about the **CLEAN** function, which removes nonprintable characters from a string, as well as the **TRIM** function, which removes excess spaces from a string. A common text scenario involves removing all instances of a particular character from a string. For example, you might want to remove spaces from a string or an apostrophe from a name.

Here's a generic formula that does this:

=SUBSTITUTE(*text, character*, "")

Here, replace *text* with the original string and *character* with the character you want to remove. For example, the following formula removes all the spaces from the string in cell A1:

=SUBSTITUTE(A1, " ", "")

> **Note** One surprising use of the **SUBSTITUTE** function is to count the number of characters that appear in a string. The trick here is that if you remove a particular character from a string, the difference in length between the original string and the resulting string is the same as the number of times the character appeared in the original string. For example, the string **expenses** has eight characters. If you remove all the **e**'s, the resulting string is **xpnss**, which has five characters. The difference is 3, which is how many **e**'s there were in the original string.
>
> To calculate this in a formula, use the **LEN** function and subtract the length of a string with the character removed from the length of the original string. Here's the formula that counts the number of **e**'s for a string in cell A1:
>
> =LEN(A1) - LEN(SUBSTITUTE(A1, "e", ""))

Removing two different characters from a string

It's possible to nest one **SUBSTITUTE** function inside another to remove two different characters from a string. For example, first consider the following expression, which uses **SUBSTITUTE** to remove periods from a string:

```
SUBSTITUTE(A1, ".", "")
```

Because this expression returns a string, you can use that result as the **text** argument in another **SUBSTITUTE** function. Here, then, is a formula that removes both periods and spaces from a string in cell A1:

```
=SUBSTITUTE(SUBSTITUTE(A1, ".", ""), " ", "")
```

Case study: Generating account numbers, part II

The formula I showed you earlier for automatically generating account numbers from an account name produces valid numbers only if the first three letters of the name are letters. If you have names that contain characters other than letters, you need to remove those characters before generating the account number. For example, if you have an account name such as J. D. BigBelly, you need to remove periods and spaces before generating the account name. You can do this by adding the expression from the previous section to the formula for generating an account name from earlier in this chapter. Specifically, you replace the cell address in **LEFT** with the nested **SUBSTITUTE** functions, as shown in Figure 5-13. Notice that the formula still works on account names that begin with three letters.

FIGURE 5-13 This worksheet uses nested SUBSTITUTE functions to remove periods and spaces from account names before generating the account numbers.

Removing line feeds

Earlier in this chapter, you learned about the **CLEAN** function, which removes nonprintable characters from a string. In the example, I used **CLEAN** to remove the line feeds from a multiline cell entry. However, you might have noticed a small problem with the result: There was no space between the end of one line and the beginning of the next line (refer to Figure 5-4).

If all you're worried about is line feeds, use the following **SUBSTITUTE** formula instead of the **CLEAN** function:

```
=SUBSTITUTE(A2, CHAR(10), " ")
```

This formula replaces the line feed character (ANSI code 10) with a space, resulting in a proper string, as shown in Figure 5-14.

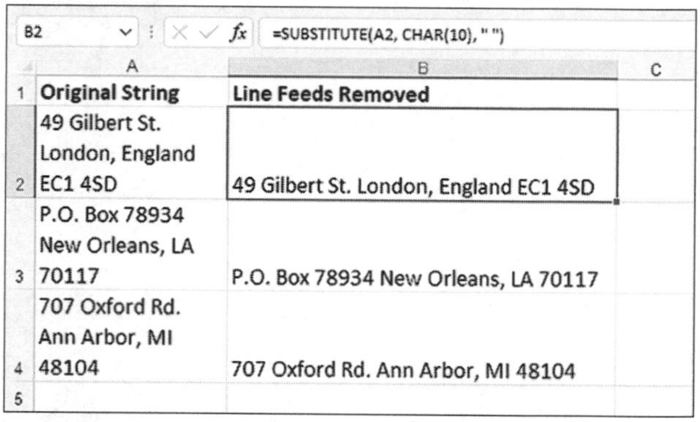

	A	B	C
	B2 ∨ : × ✓ fx =SUBSTITUTE(A2, CHAR(10), " ")		
1	**Original String**	**Line Feeds Removed**	
2	49 Gilbert St. London, England EC1 4SD	49 Gilbert St. London, England EC1 4SD	
3	P.O. Box 78934 New Orleans, LA 70117	P.O. Box 78934 New Orleans, LA 70117	
4	707 Oxford Rd. Ann Arbor, MI 48104	707 Oxford Rd. Ann Arbor, MI 48104	
5			

FIGURE 5-14 This worksheet uses SUBSTITUTE to replace each line feed character with a space.

CHAPTER 6

Working with logical and information functions

In this chapter, you will:

- Add logical tests to your formulas with the IF function

- Perform multiple logical tests with nested IF functions and the AND and OR functions

- Create powerful formulas that combine logical tests with arrays

- Interrogate Excel using the information functions

- Count blanks, errors, and similar values with Excel's IS functions

In Chapter 4, "Understanding functions," I mentioned that one of the advantages of using Excel's worksheet functions is that they enable you to build formulas that perform actions that are simply not possible with the standard operators and operands.

This idea becomes readily apparent when you learn about functions that can add intelligence and knowledge—the two cornerstones of good business analysis—to your worksheet models. You get these via Excel's logical and information functions, which I describe in detail in this chapter.

Adding intelligence with logical functions

In the computer world, we *very* loosely define something as *intelligent* if it can perform tests on its environment and act in accordance with the results of those tests. However, computers are binary beasts, so "acting in accordance with the results of a test" means that the machine can do only one of two things. Still, even with this limited range of options, you'll be amazed at how much intelligence you can bring to your worksheets. Your formulas will actually be able to test the values in cells and ranges and then return results based on those tests.

This is all done with Excel's logical functions, which are designed to create decision-making formulas. For example, you can test cell contents to see whether they're numbers or labels, or you can test formula results for errors. Table 6-1 summarizes Excel's logical functions.

TABLE 6-1 Excel's logical functions

Function	Description
AND(*logical1*[,*logical2*],...)	Returns **TRUE** if all the arguments are true.
FALSE	Returns **FALSE**.
IF(*logical_test,value_if_true* [,*value_if_false*])	Performs a logical test and returns a value based on the result.
IFERROR(*value, value_if_error*)	Returns **v***alue_if_error* if *value* is an error; otherwise, returns *value*.
IFNA(*value, value_if_na*)	Returns *value_if_na* if *value* returns the #N/A error.
IFS(*logical_test1, value_if_true1,*[*logical_test2, value_if_true2, ...*])	Performs one or more logical tests and returns a value from the first test that returns **TRUE**.
NOT(*logical*)	Reverses the logical value of the argument.
OR(*logical1*[,*logical2*],...)	Returns **TRUE** if any argument is true.
SWITCH(*expression, value1, result1,*[,*value2,result2*],...)	Compares the result of *expression* with a series of values and returns the result associated with the first matching value.
TRUE	Returns **TRUE**.
XOR(*logical1*[,*logical2*],...)	Returns **TRUE** if an odd number of the arguments are **TRUE**; returns **FALSE** if an even number of the arguments are **TRUE**.

To learn about the **IFERROR** and **IFNA** functions, see Chapter 3, "Troubleshooting formulas."

Using the IF function

I'm not exaggerating even the slightest when I tell you that the royal road to becoming an accomplished Excel formula builder involves mastering the **IF** function. If you become comfortable wielding this function, a whole new world of formula prowess and convenience opens up to you. Yes, **IF** is *that* powerful.

To help you master this crucial Excel feature, I'm going to spend a lot of time on it in this chapter. I give you copious examples that show you how to use it in real-world situations.

IF: The simplest case

Let's start with the simplest version of the **IF** function:

IF(*logical_test, value_if_true*)

logical_test	A logical expression—that is, an expression that returns **TRUE** or **FALSE** (or their equivalent numeric values: **0** for **FALSE** and any other number for **TRUE**)
value_if_true	The value returned by the function if *logical_test* evaluates to **TRUE**

For example, consider the following formula:

```
=IF(A1 >= 1000, "It's big!")
```

The logical expression **A1 >= 1000** is used as the test. Let's say you enter this formula in cell B1. If the logical expression proves to be true (that is, if the value in cell A1 is greater than or equal to 1,000), the function returns the string **It's big!**, and that's the value you see in cell B1. (If A1 is less than 1,000, you see the value **FALSE** in cell B1 instead.)

Another common use for the simple **IF** test is to flag values that meet a specific condition. For example, suppose you have a worksheet that shows the percentage increase or decrease in the sales of a long list of products. It would be useful to be able to flag just those products that had a sales decrease. A basic formula for doing this would look something like this:

```
=IF(cell < 0, flag)
```

Here, *cell* is the cell you want to test, and *flag* is some text that you use to point out a negative value. Here's an example:

```
=IF(B2 < 0, "<<<<<")
```

A slightly more sophisticated version of this formula would vary the flag, depending on the negative value. That is, the larger the negative number, the more less-than signs (in this case) the formula would display. This can be done using the **REPT** function, which I discussed in Chapter 5, "Working with text functions":

```
REPT("<", B2 * -100)
```

This expression multiplies the percentage value by -100 and then uses the result as the number of times the less-than sign is repeated. Here's the revised **IF** formula:

```
=IF(B2 < 0, REPT("<", B2 * -100))
```

Figure 6-1 shows how it works in practice.

> **Note**   You can work with all the examples in this chapter by downloading Chapter06.xslx from either of the companion content sites mentioned in the Introduction.

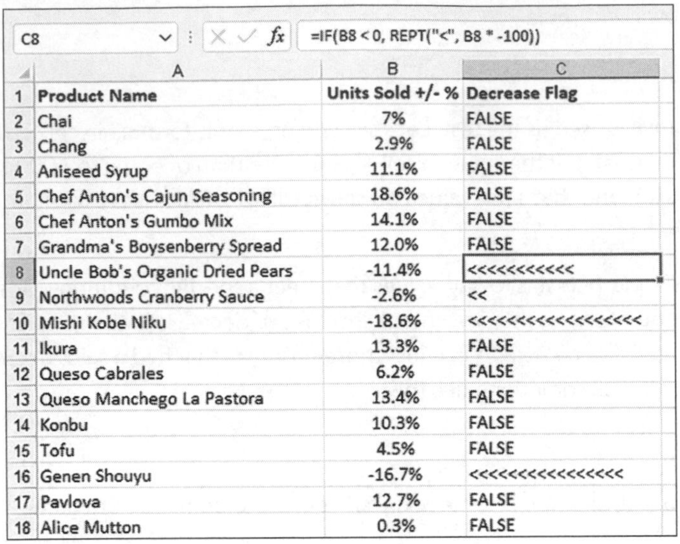

C8	=IF(B8 < 0, REPT("<", B8 * -100))	
A	**B**	**C**
Product Name	**Units Sold +/- %**	**Decrease Flag**
Chai	7%	FALSE
Chang	2.9%	FALSE
Aniseed Syrup	11.1%	FALSE
Chef Anton's Cajun Seasoning	18.6%	FALSE
Chef Anton's Gumbo Mix	14.1%	FALSE
Grandma's Boysenberry Spread	12.0%	FALSE
Uncle Bob's Organic Dried Pears	-11.4%	<<<<<<<<<<<
Northwoods Cranberry Sauce	-2.6%	<<
Mishi Kobe Niku	-18.6%	<<<<<<<<<<<<<<<<<<
Ikura	13.3%	FALSE
Queso Cabrales	6.2%	FALSE
Queso Manchego La Pastora	13.4%	FALSE
Konbu	10.3%	FALSE
Tofu	4.5%	FALSE
Genen Shouyu	-16.7%	<<<<<<<<<<<<<<<<
Pavlova	12.7%	FALSE
Alice Mutton	0.3%	FALSE

FIGURE 6-1 This worksheet uses the IF function to test for negative values and then uses REPT to display a flag for those values.

Handling a FALSE result

As you can see in Figure 6-1, if the result of the **IF** condition calculates to **FALSE**, the function returns **FALSE** as its result. That's not inherently bad, but the worksheet would look tidier (and, hence, be more useful) if the formula returned, say, the null string ("") instead.

To do this, you need to use the full **IF** function syntax:

```
IF(logical_test, value_if_true, value_if_false)
```

logical_test	A logical expression
value_if_true	The value returned by the function if *logical_test* evaluates to **TRUE**
value_if_false	The value returned by the function if *logical_test* evaluates to **FALSE**

For example, consider the following formula:

```
=IF(A1 >= 1000, "It's big!", "It's not big!")
```

This time, if cell A1 contains a value that's less than 1,000, the formula returns the string **`It's not big!`**.

For the negative value flag example, use the following revised version of the formula to return no value if the cell contains a non-negative number:

```
=IF(B2 < 0, REPT("<", B2 * -100), "")
```

As you can see in Figure 6-2, the resulting worksheet looks much tidier than the first version.

C2	: × ✓ fx	=IF(B2 < 0, REPT("<", B2 * -100), "")	

	A	B	C
1	Product Name	Units Sold +/- %	Decrease Flag
2	Chai	7%	
3	Chang	2.9%	
4	Aniseed Syrup	11.1%	
5	Chef Anton's Cajun Seasoning	18.6%	
6	Chef Anton's Gumbo Mix	14.1%	
7	Grandma's Boysenberry Spread	12.0%	
8	Uncle Bob's Organic Dried Pears	-11.4%	<<<<<<<<<<<
9	Northwoods Cranberry Sauce	-2.6%	<<
10	Mishi Kobe Niku	-18.6%	<<<<<<<<<<<<<<<<<<
11	Ikura	13.3%	
12	Queso Cabrales	6.2%	
13	Queso Manchego La Pastora	13.4%	
14	Konbu	10.3%	
15	Tofu	4.5%	
16	Genen Shouyu	-16.7%	<<<<<<<<<<<<<<<<
17	Pavlova	12.7%	
18	Alice Mutton	0.3%	

FIGURE 6-2 This worksheet uses the full IF syntax to return no value if the cell being tested contains a non-negative number.

Avoiding division by zero

As you saw in Chapter 3, Excel displays the **#DIV/0!** error if a formula tries to divide a quantity by zero. To avoid this error, you can use **IF** to test the divisor and ensure that it's nonzero before performing division.

For example, the basic equation for calculating gross margin is (Sales — Expenses)/Sales. To make sure that Sales isn't zero, use the following formula (assuming that you have cells named Sales and Expenses that contain the appropriate values):

```
=IF(Sales <> 0, (Sales - Expenses)/Sales, "Sales are zero!")
```

If the logical expression **Sales <> 0** is true, that means Sales is nonzero, so the gross margin calculation can proceed. If **Sales <> 0** is false, the Sales value is **0**, so the message **Sales are zero!** is displayed instead.

Performing multiple logical tests

The capability to perform a logical test on a cell is a powerful weapon indeed. You'll find endless uses for the basic **IF** function in your everyday worksheets. The problem, however, is that the everyday world often presents us with situations that are more complicated than can be handled in a basic **IF** function's logical expression. It's often the case that you have to test two or more conditions before you can make a decision.

To handle these more complex scenarios, Excel offers several techniques for performing two or more logical tests: nested **IF** functions, the **IFS** function, the **AND** function, and the **OR** function. You'll learn about these techniques over the next few sections.

Nested IF functions

When building models using **IF**, it's common to come upon a *second* fork in the road when evaluating either the *value_if_true* or *value_if_false* argument.

For example, consider the variation of our formula that outputs a description based on the value in cell A1:

```
=IF(A1 >= 1000, "Big!", "Not big")
```

What if you want to return a different string for values greater than, say, 10,000? In other words, if the condition **A1 >= 1000** proves to be true, you want to run another test that checks to see whether **A1 >= 10000**. You can handle this scenario by nesting a *second* **IF** function inside the first as the *value_if_true* argument:

```
=IF(A1 >= 1000, IF(A1 >= 10000, "Really big!!", "Big!"), "Not big")
```

If **A1 >= 1000** returns **TRUE**, the formula evaluates the nested **IF**, which returns **Really big!!** if **A1 >= 10000** is **TRUE** and returns **Big!** if it's **FALSE**; if **A1 >= 1000** returns **FALSE**, the formula returns **Not big**.

Note, too, that you can nest the **IF** function in the *value_if_false* argument. For example, if you want to return the description **Small** for a cell value less than 100, you use this version of the formula:

```
=IF(A1 >= 1000, "Big!", IF(A1 < 100, "Small", "Not big"))
```

Calculating tiered bonuses

A good time to use nested **IF** functions arises when you need to calculate a *tiered* payment or charge. That is, if a certain value is **X**, you want one result; if the value is **Y**, you want a second result; and if the value is **Z**, you want a third result.

For example, suppose you want to calculate tiered bonuses for a sales team as follows:

- If the salesperson did not meet the sales target, no bonus is given.

- If the salesperson exceeds the sales target by less than 10 percent, a bonus of $1,000 is awarded.

- If the salesperson exceeds the sales target by 10 percent or more, a bonus of $10,000 is awarded.

Assuming that cell D2 contains the percentage that each salesperson's actual sales were above or below his target sales, here's a formula that handles these rules:

```
=IF(D2 < 0, "", IF(D2 < 0.1, 1000, 10000))
```

If the value in D2 is negative, nothing is returned; if the value in D2 is less than 10 percent, the formula returns **1000**; if the value in D2 is greater than or equal to 10 percent, the formula returns **10000**. Figure 6-3 shows this formula in action.

E2		⌄	:	×	✓	fx	=IF(D2 < 0, "", IF(D2 < 0.1, 1000, 10000))		

◢	A	B	C	D	E	F
1	Salesperson	Target Sales	Actual Sales	Pct +/-	Bonus	
2	Nancy Davolio	$ 250,000	$ 259,875	4.0%	$ 1,000	
3	Andrew Fuller	$ 275,000	$ 293,827	6.8%	$ 1,000	
4	Janet Leverling	$ 300,000	$ 347,119	15.7%	$ 10,000	
5	Margaret Peacock	$ 200,000	$ 189,345	-5.3%		
6	Steven Buchanan	$ 200,000	$ 209,283	4.6%	$ 1,000	
7	Michael Suyama	$ 225,000	$ 222,384	-1.2%		
8	Robert King	$ 300,000	$ 299,550	-0.2%		
9	Laura Callahan	$ 225,000	$ 239,990	6.7%	$ 1,000	
10	Anne Dodsworth	$ 225,000	$ 256,919	14.2%	$ 10,000	

FIGURE 6-3 This worksheet uses nested IF functions to calculate a tiered bonus payment.

The IFS function

Nesting one **IF** function inside another is a handy way to perform a couple of logical tests, but the method quickly becomes unwieldly and difficult to decipher when the nesting goes three or more **IF** functions deep. If your data analysis requires more than two logical tests, then you can make your worksheet model easier to read by turning to the **IFS** function:

IFS(logical_test1, value_if_true1, [logical_test2, value_if_true2,…])

logical_test1, logical_test2,…	Logical expressions—that is, expressions that return **TRUE** or **FALSE** (or their equivalent numeric values: **0** for FALSE and any other number for **TRUE**)
value_if_true1, value_if_true2,…	Value returned by the function if the corresponding logical test is the first to evaluate to **TRUE**

The **IFS** function consists of a series of logical tests, each with an associated return value. **IFS** performs each logical test in turn and, when it comes across the first logical test to return **TRUE**, it returns that logical test's associated value.

For example, consider the following formula:

=IFS(A1 >= 10000, "Really big!!", A1 >= 1000, "Big!", A1 < 1000, "Not big")

There are three logical expressions here: **A1 >= 10000**, **A1 >= 1000**, and **A1 < 1000**. The first of these that calculates to **TRUE** gets its associated value ("**Really big!!**", "**Big!**", or "**Not big**", respectively) returned by the function.

What if none of the logical tests return **TRUE**? In that case, **IFS** returns the **#NA** error. To avoid this, you can set up a default return value by setting the last logical "test" to **TRUE** and then specifying the value you want to use as the default. Here's an example:

=IFS(A1 >= 10000, "Really big!!", A1 >= 1000, "Big!", TRUE, "Not big")

Here's how you'd use **IFS** to calculate the tiered bonuses that I introduced in the previous section:

=IFS(D2 < 0, "", D2 < 0.1, 1000, D2 >= 0.1, 10000)

The AND function

It's often necessary to perform an action if and only if two conditions are true. For example, you might want to pay a salesperson a bonus if and only if dollar sales exceeded the budget *and* unit sales exceeded the budget. No bonus is paid if either the dollar sales or the unit sales fell below budget (or if they both fell below budget). In Boolean logic, this is called an *And* condition because one expression *and* another must be true for a positive result.

In Excel, And conditions are handled, appropriately enough, by the **AND** logical function:

AND(*logical1* [, *logical2*,...])

| logical1 | The first logical condition to test |
| logical2, ... | The second logical condition to test |

You can enter up to 255 logical conditions.

The **AND** result is calculated as follows:

- If *all* the arguments return **TRUE** (or any nonzero number), **AND** returns **TRUE**.

- If one or more of the arguments return **FALSE** (or **0**), **AND** returns **FALSE**.

You can use the **AND** function anywhere you would use a logical formula, but it's most often pressed into service as the logical condition in an **IF** function. In other words, if all the logical conditions in the **AND** function are **TRUE**, **IF** returns its *value_if_true* result; if one or more of the logical conditions in the **AND** function are **FALSE**, **IF** returns its *value_if_false* result.

For example, suppose you want to pay out a bonus only if a salesperson exceeds his budget for both dollar sales and unit sales. Assuming that the difference between the actual and budgeted dollar amounts is in cell B2 and the difference between the actual and budgeted unit amounts is in cell C2, here's an example of a formula that determines whether a bonus is paid:

=IF(AND(B2 > 0, C2 > 0), "1000", "No bonus")

If the value in B2 is greater than 0 and the value in C2 is greater than 0, the formula returns **1000**; otherwise, it returns **No bonus**.

Slotting values into categories

A good use for the **AND** function is to slot items into categories that consist of a range of values. For example, suppose you have a set of poll or survey results, and you want to categorize these results based on the following age ranges: 18–34, 35–49, 50–64, and 65+. Assuming that each respondent's age is in cell B9, the following **AND** function can serve as the logical test for entry into the 18–34 category:

AND(B9 >= 18, B9 <= 34)

If the response is in C9, the following formula will display it if the respondent is in the 18–34 age group:

```
=IF(AND(B9 >= 18, B9 <= 34), C9, "")
```

Figure 6-4 tries this on some data. Here are the formulas used for the other age groups:

```
35-49: =IF(AND(B9 >= 35, B9 <= 49), C9, "")
50-64: =IF(AND(B9 >= 50, B9 <= 64), C9, "")
65+: =IF(B9 >= 65, C9, "")
```

D9			f_x	=IF(AND(B9 >= 18, B9 <= 34), C9, "")			
	A	B	C	D	E	F	G
1	Poll Results — Question #1						
2		Key: 1 = Strongly Disagree					
3		2 = Disagree					
4		3 = Neutral					
5		4 = Agree					
6		5 = Strongly Agree					
7							
8	Subject ID	Age	Response	18-34	35-49	50-64	65+
9	1	19	4	4			
10	2	23	5	5			
11	3	38	3		3		
12	4	44	4		4		
13	5	51	2			2	
14	6	20	4	4			
15	7	65	1				1
16	8	49	4		4		
17	9	60	3			3	
18	10	69	2				2

FIGURE 6-4 This worksheet uses the AND function as the logical condition for an IF function to slot poll results into age groups.

The OR function

Similar to an And condition is the situation when you need to take an action if one thing *or* another is true. For example, you might want to pay a salesperson a bonus if she exceeded the dollar sales budget *or* if she exceeded the unit sales budget. In Boolean logic, this is called an *Or* condition.

You won't be surprised to hear that Or conditions are handled in Excel by the **OR** function:

```
OR(logical1 [,logical2,...])
```

logical1	The first logical condition to test
logical2,...	The second logical condition to test

You can enter up to 255 logical conditions.

The **OR** result is calculated as follows:

- If one or more of the arguments return **TRUE** (or any nonzero number), **OR** returns **TRUE**.

- If *all* of the arguments return **FALSE** (or **0**), **OR** returns **FALSE**.

As with **AND**, you use **OR** wherever a logical expression is called for, most often within an **IF** function. This means that if one or more of the logical conditions in the **OR** function are **TRUE**, **IF** returns its *value_if_true* result; if all the logical conditions in the **OR** function are **FALSE**, **IF** returns its *value_if_false* result.

For example, suppose you want to pay out a bonus only if a salesperson exceeds her budget for either dollar sales or unit sales (or both). Assuming that the difference between the actual and budgeted dollar amounts is in cell B2 and the difference between the actual and budgeted unit amounts is in cell C2, here's an example of a formula that determines whether a bonus is paid:

```
=IF(OR(B2 > 0, C2 > 0), "1000", "No bonus")
```

If the value in B2 is greater than 0 or the value in C2 is greater than 0, the formula returns **1000**; otherwise, it returns **No bonus**.

> **Note** The **OR** function returns **TRUE** when one or more of its arguments are **TRUE**. However, in some cases, you want an expression to return **TRUE** only when just *one* of the arguments is **TRUE**. In that case, use the **XOR** function, which returns **TRUE** when one and only one of its arguments evaluates to **TRUE**.

Applying conditional formatting with formulas

The powerful conditional formatting features available in Excel enable you to highlight cells, create top and bottom rules, and apply three types of formatting: data bars, color scales, and icon sets. Excel comes with another conditional formatting component that makes this feature even more powerful: You can apply conditional formatting based on the results of a formula. In particular, you can set up a logical formula as the conditional formatting criteria. If that formula returns **TRUE**, Excel applies the formatting to the cells; if the formula returns **FALSE**, instead, Excel doesn't apply the formatting. In most cases, you use an **IF** function, often combined with another logical function such as **AND** or **OR**.

Before I get to an example, here are the basic steps to follow to set up formula-based conditional formatting:

1. Select the cells to which you want the conditional formatting applied.

2. Select **Home** > **Conditional Formatting** > **New Rule**. Excel displays the New Formatting Rule dialog box.

3. Select **Use A Formula To Determine Which Cells To Format**.

4. In the **Format Values Where This Formula Is True** range box, type your logical formula.

5. Select **Format** to open the Format Cells dialog box.

6. Use the **Number**, **Font**, **Border**, and **Fill** tabs to specify the formatting you want to apply and then select **OK**.

7. Select OK.

For example, suppose you have a range or table of items, and you want to highlight those items that have the maximum and minimum values in a particular column. You could set up separate top and bottom rules, but you can make things easier and more flexible by instead using a logical formula.

How you go about this in a conditional formatting rule is a bit tricky, but it can be extremely powerful when you know the trick. First, you can use the MAX worksheet function to determine the maximum value in a range. For example, if the range is D2:D10, then the following function returns the maximum:

MAX($D$2:$D$10)

However, a conditional formatting formula works only if it returns TRUE or FALSE, so you need to create a comparison formula:

=MAX($D$2:$D$10)=$D2

There are two things to note here: First, you compare the range to the first value in the range; second, the cell address uses the mixed-reference format $D2, which tells Excel to keep the column (D) fixed, while varying the row number.

Next, you can use the MIN function to determine the minimum, so you create a similar comparison formula:

=MIN($D$2:$D$10)=$D2

Finally, you want to check each cell in the column to see if it's the maximum or the minimum, so you need to combine these expressions by using the OR function, like so:

=OR(MAX($D$2:$D$10)=$D2, MIN($D$2:$D$10)=$D2)

Figure 6-5 shows a range of sales results (A2:E10) that are conditionally formatted using the preceding formula. This shows which reps had the maximum and minimum percentage differences between target sales and actual sales (column D).

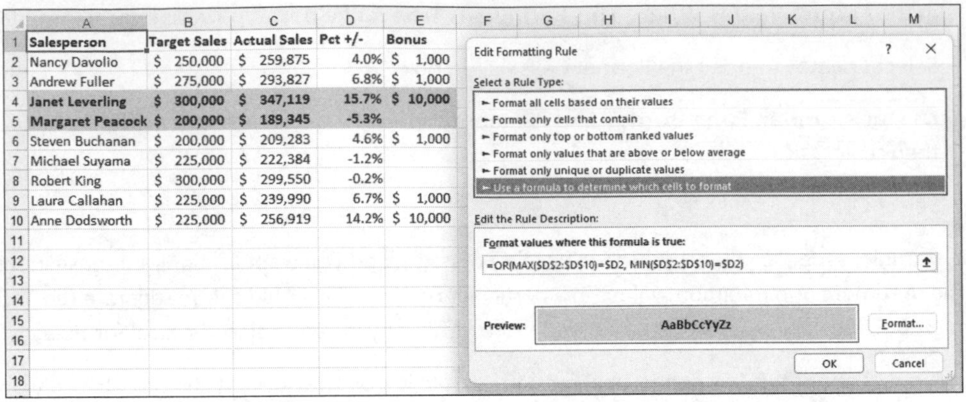

FIGURE 6-5 The range of sales rep data is conditionally formatted using a logical formula.

Combining logical functions with arrays

When you combine the array formulas you learned about in Chapter 2, "Creating advanced formulas," with **IF**, you can perform some remarkably sophisticated operations. Arrays enable you to do things such as apply the **IF** logical condition across a range and sum only those cells in a range that meet the **IF** condition.

Applying a condition across a range

Using **AND** as the logical condition in an **IF** function is useful for perhaps three or four expressions. After that, it just gets too unwieldy to enter all those logical expressions. If you're essentially running the same logical test on a number of different cells, a better solution is to apply **AND** to a range and enter the formula as an array.

For example, suppose that you want to sum the cells in the range B3:B7 but only if all those cells contain values greater than 0. Here's an array formula to do this:

```
=IF(AND(B3:B7 > 0), SUM(B3:B7), "")
```

> **Note** Recall from Chapter 2 that if you're using Excel 2016 or earlier, type the formula and then select Ctrl+Shift+Enter to enter it as an array formula; if you're using Excel 2019 or later, type the formula and just select Enter.

This is useful in a worksheet in which you might not have all the numbers yet, and you don't want a total entered until the data is complete. Figure 6-6 shows an example. The array formula in B8 is the same as the previous one. The array formula in B16 returns nothing because cell B14 is blank.

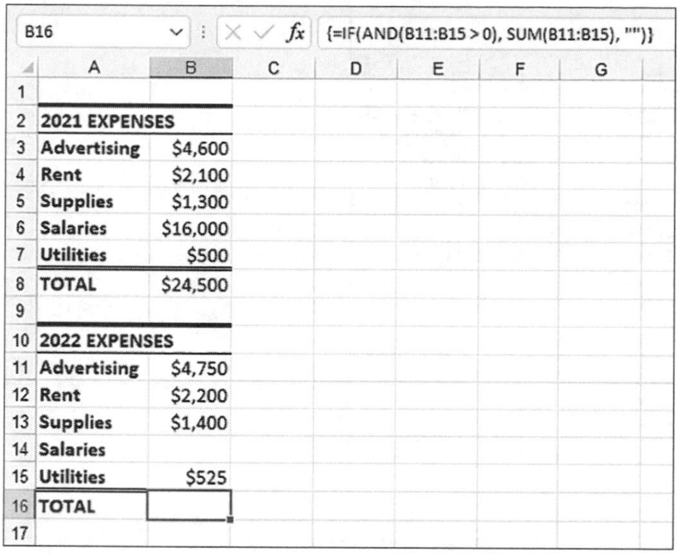

FIGURE 6-6 This worksheet uses IF, AND, and SUM in two array formulas (B8 and B16) to total a range only if all the cells have nonzero values.

> **Note** The example files for this chapter use static arrays rather than Excel 2019's new dynamic arrays (see Chapter 2). This is to ensure that the example workbooks remain compatible with older versions of Excel.

Operating only on cells that meet a condition

In the previous section, you saw how to use an array formula to perform an action only if a certain condition is met across a range of cells. A related scenario arises when you want to perform an action on a range, but only on cells that meet a certain condition. For example, you might want to sum only values that are positive.

To do this, you need to move the operation outside the **IF** function. For example, here's an array formula that sums only values in the range B3:B7 that contain positive values:

```
=SUM(IF(B3:B7 > 0, B3:B7, 0))
```

The **IF** function returns an array of values based on the condition (the cell value if it's positive; **0** otherwise), and the **SUM** function adds those returned values.

For example, suppose you have a series of investments that mature in various years. It would be nice to set up a table that lists these years and tells you the total value of the investments that mature in each year. Figure 6-7 shows a worksheet set up to do just that.

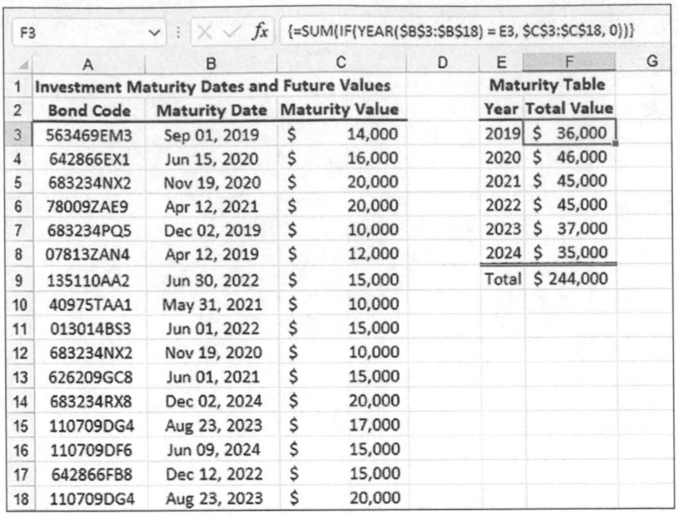

F3 {=SUM(IF(YEAR($B$3:$B$18) = E3, $C$3:$C$18, 0))}

	A	B	C	D	E	F	G
1	Investment Maturity Dates and Future Values				Maturity Table		
2	Bond Code	Maturity Date	Maturity Value		Year	Total Value	
3	563469EM3	Sep 01, 2019	$ 14,000		2019	$ 36,000	
4	642866EX1	Jun 15, 2020	$ 16,000		2020	$ 46,000	
5	683234NX2	Nov 19, 2020	$ 20,000		2021	$ 45,000	
6	78009ZAE9	Apr 12, 2021	$ 20,000		2022	$ 45,000	
7	683234PQ5	Dec 02, 2019	$ 10,000		2023	$ 37,000	
8	07813ZAN4	Apr 12, 2019	$ 12,000		2024	$ 35,000	
9	135110AA2	Jun 30, 2022	$ 15,000		Total	$ 244,000	
10	40975TAA1	May 31, 2021	$ 10,000				
11	013014BS3	Jun 01, 2022	$ 15,000				
12	683234NX2	Nov 19, 2020	$ 10,000				
13	626209GC8	Jun 01, 2021	$ 15,000				
14	683234RX8	Dec 02, 2024	$ 20,000				
15	110709DG4	Aug 23, 2023	$ 17,000				
16	110709DF6	Jun 09, 2024	$ 15,000				
17	642866FB8	Dec 12, 2022	$ 15,000				
18	110709DG4	Aug 23, 2023	$ 20,000				

FIGURE 6-7 This worksheet uses array formulas to sum the yearly maturity values of various investments.

The investment maturity dates are in column B, the investment values at maturity are shown in column C, and the various maturity years are in column E. To calculate the maturity total for 2019, for example, the following array formula is used:

```
=SUM(IF(YEAR($B$3:$B$18) = E3, $C$3:$C$18, 0))
```

The **IF** function compares the year value in cell E3 (2019) with the year component of the maturity dates in range B3:B18. For cells in which these are equal, **IF** returns the corresponding value in column C; otherwise, it returns **0**. The **SUM** function then adds these returned values.

> **Note** In Figure 6-7, notice that, with the exception of the reference to cell E3, I used absolute references so the formula can be filled down to the other years.

Determining whether a value appears in a list

Many spreadsheet applications require you to look up a value in a list. For example, you might have a table of customer discounts in which the percentage discount is based on the number of units ordered. For each customer order, you need to look up the appropriate discount, based on the total units in the order. Similarly, a teacher might convert a raw test score into a letter grade by referring to a table of conversions.

You'll see some sophisticated tools for looking up values in Chapter 7, "Working with lookup functions." However, array formulas combined with logical functions also offer some tricks for looking up values.

For example, suppose that you want to know whether a certain value exists in an array. You can use the following general formula, entered into a single cell as an array:

```
=OR(value = range)
```

Here, *value* is the value you want to search for, and *range* is the range of cells in which to search. For example, Figure 6-8 shows a list of customers with overdue accounts. You enter the account number of the customer in cell B1, and cell B2 tells you whether the number appears in the list.

Here's the array formula in cell B2:

```
=OR(B1 = B6:B29)
```

The array formula checks each value in the range B6:B29 to see whether it equals the value in cell B1. If any one of those comparisons is true, **OR** returns **TRUE**, which means the value is in the list.

> **Tip** As a similar example, here's an array formula that returns **TRUE** if a particular account number is *not* in the list:
>
> ```
> =AND(B1 <> B6:B29)
> ```
>
> The formula checks each value in B6:B29 to see whether it does not equal the value in B1. If all those comparisons are true, **AND** returns **TRUE**, which means the value is not in the list.

B2 fx {=OR(B1 = B6:B29)}

	A	B	C	D	E	F	G
1	**Account Number:**	09-2111					
2	**In the List?**	TRUE	**First Row:**	14			
3	**How Many Times?**	2	**Last Row:**	22			
4							
5	**Account Name**	**Account Number**	**Invoice Number**	**Invoice Amount**	**Due Date**	**Date Paid**	**Days Overdue**
6	Emily's Sports Palace	08-2255	117316	$ 1,584.20	26-Apr-19		55
7	Refco Office Solutions	14-5741	117317	$ 303.65	27-Apr-19		54
8	Brimson Furniture	10-0009	117321	$ 2,144.55	3-May-19		48
9	Katy's Paper Products	12-1212	117322	$ 234.69	4-May-19		47
10	Door Stoppers Ltd.	01-0045	117324	$ 101.01	10-May-19		41
11	Voyatzis Designs	14-1882	117325	$ 1,985.25	10-May-19		41
12	Brimson Furniture	10-0009	117327	$ 1,847.25	16-May-19		35
13	Door Stoppers Ltd.	01-0045	117328	$ 58.50	17-May-19		34
14	O'Donoghue Inc.	09-2111	117329	$ 1,234.56	18-May-19		33
15	Refco Office Solutions	14-5741	117330	$ 456.78	18-May-19		33
16	Renaud & Son	07-0025	117331	$ 565.77	23-May-19		30
17	Simpson's Ltd.	16-6658	117332	$ 898.54	22-May-19		31
18	Door Stoppers Ltd.	01-0045	117333	$ 1,685.74	26-May-19		27
19	Renaud & Son	07-0025	117335	$ 3,005.14	28-May-19		25
20	Rooter Office Solvents	07-4441	117336	$ 78.85	30-May-19		23
21	Emily's Sports Palace	08-2255	117337	$ 4,347.21	2-Jun-19		20
22	O'Donoghue Inc.	09-2111	117338	$ 2,144.55	2-Jun-19		20
23	Brimson Furniture	10-0009	117339	$ 1,234.69	3-Jun-19		19

FIGURE 6-8 This worksheet uses the OR function in an array formula to determine whether a value appears in a list.

Counting occurrences in a range

Now you know how to find out whether a value appears in a list, but what if you need to know how many times the value appears? The following formula does the job:

```
=SUM(IF(value = range, 1, 0))
```

Again, *value* is the value you want to look up, and *range* is the range for searching. In this array formula, the IF function compares *value* with every cell in *range*. The values that match return 1, and those that don't return 0. The SUM function adds these returned values, and the final total is the number of occurrences of *value*. Here's a formula that does this for our list of overdue invoices:

```
=SUM(IF(B1 = B6:B29, 1, 0))
```

Figure 6-9 shows this formula in action (see cell B3).

B3		fx	{=SUM(IF(B1 = B6:B29, 1, 0))}				

	A	B	C	D	E	F	G
1	Account Number:	09-2111					
2	In the List?	TRUE	First Row:	14			
3	How Many Times?	2	Last Row:	22			
4							
5	Account Name	Account Number	Invoice Number	Invoice Amount	Due Date	Date Paid	Days Overdue
6	Emily's Sports Palace	08-2255	117316	$ 1,584.20	26-Apr-19		55
7	Refco Office Solutions	14-5741	117317	$ 303.65	27-Apr-19		54
8	Brimson Furniture	10-0009	117321	$ 2,144.55	3-May-19		48
9	Katy's Paper Products	12-1212	117322	$ 234.69	4-May-19		47
10	Door Stoppers Ltd.	01-0045	117324	$ 101.01	10-May-19		41
11	Voyatzis Designs	14-1882	117325	$ 1,985.25	10-May-19		41
12	Brimson Furniture	10-0009	117327	$ 1,847.25	16-May-19		35
13	Door Stoppers Ltd.	01-0045	117328	$ 58.50	17-May-19		34
14	O'Donoghue Inc.	09-2111	117329	$ 1,234.56	18-May-19		33
15	Refco Office Solutions	14-5741	117330	$ 456.78	18-May-19		33
16	Renaud & Son	07-0025	117331	$ 565.77	23-May-19		30
17	Simpson's Ltd.	16-6658	117332	$ 898.54	22-May-19		31
18	Door Stoppers Ltd.	01-0045	117333	$ 1,685.74	26-May-19		27
19	Renaud & Son	07-0025	117335	$ 3,005.14	28-May-19		25
20	Rooter Office Solvents	07-4441	117336	$ 78.85	30-May-19		23
21	Emily's Sports Palace	08-2255	117337	$ 4,347.21	2-Jun-19		20
22	O'Donoghue Inc.	09-2111	117338	$ 2,144.55	2-Jun-19		20
23	Brimson Furniture	10-0009	117339	$ 1,234.69	3-Jun-19		19

FIGURE 6-9 This worksheet uses SUM and IF in an array formula to count the number of occurrences of a value in a list.

Note The generic array formula =SUM(IF(*condition*, 1, 0)) is useful in any context where you need to count the number of occurrences in which *condition* returns **TRUE**. The *condition* argument is normally a logical formula that compares a single value with each cell in a range of values. However, it's also possible to compare two ranges, as long as they're the same shape. (That is, they have the same number of rows and columns.) For example, suppose that you want to compare the values in two ranges named **Range1** and **Range2** to see if any of the values are different. Here's an array formula that does this:

=SUM(IF(Range1 <> Range2, 1, 0))

This formula compares the first cell in **Range1** with the first cell in **Range2**, the second cell in **Range1** with the second cell in **Range2**, and so on. Each time the values don't match, the comparison returns **1**; otherwise, it returns **0**. The sum of these comparisons is the number of different values between the two ranges.

Determining where a value appears in a list

What if you want to know not just whether a value appears in a list but *where* it appears in the list? You can do this by getting the **IF** function to return the row number for a positive result:

IF(*value* = *range*, ROW(*range*), "")

Whenever *value* equals one of the cells in *range*, the **IF** function uses **ROW** to return the row number; otherwise, it returns the empty string.

To return that row number, use either the **MIN** function or the **MAX** function, which returns the minimum or maximum, respectively, in a collection of values. The trick here is that both functions ignore null values, so applying this to the array that results from the previous **IF** expression tells where the matching values are:

- To get the first instance of the value, use the **MIN** function in an array formula, like so:

    =MIN(IF(*value* = *range*, ROW(*range*), ""))

- To get the last instance of the value, use the **MAX** function in an array formula, as shown here:

    =MAX(IF(*value* = *range*, ROW(*range*), ""))

Here are the formulas you would use to find the first and last occurrences in the previous list of overdue invoices:

=MIN(IF(B1 = B6:B29, ROW(B6:B29), ""))
=MAX(IF(B1 = B6:B29, ROW(B6:B29), ""))

Figure 6-10 shows the results (with the row of the first occurrence in cell D2 and the row of the last occurrence in cell D3).

D2		✓ : × ✓ f_x	{=MIN(IF(B1 = B6:B29, ROW(B6:B29), ""))}			

⊿	A	B	C	D	E	F	G
1	Account Number:	09-2111					
2	In the List?	TRUE	First Row:	14			
3	How Many Times?	2	Last Row:	22			
4							
5	Account Name	Account Number	Invoice Number	Invoice Amount	Due Date	Date Paid	Days Overdue
6	Emily's Sports Palace	08-2255	117316	$ 1,584.20	26-Apr-19		55
7	Refco Office Solutions	14-5741	117317	$ 303.65	27-Apr-19		54
8	Brimson Furniture	10-0009	117321	$ 2,144.55	3-May-19		48
9	Katy's Paper Products	12-1212	117322	$ 234.69	4-May-19		47
10	Door Stoppers Ltd.	01-0045	117324	$ 101.01	10-May-19		41
11	Voyatzis Designs	14-1882	117325	$ 1,985.25	10-May-19		41
12	Brimson Furniture	10-0009	117327	$ 1,847.25	16-May-19		35
13	Door Stoppers Ltd.	01-0045	117328	$ 58.50	17-May-19		34
14	O'Donoghue Inc.	09-2111	117329	$ 1,234.56	18-May-19		33
15	Refco Office Solutions	14-5741	117330	$ 456.78	18-May-19		33
16	Renaud & Son	07-0025	117331	$ 565.77	23-May-19		30
17	Simpson's Ltd.	16-6658	117332	$ 898.54	22-May-19		31
18	Door Stoppers Ltd.	01-0045	117333	$ 1,685.74	26-May-19		27
19	Renaud & Son	07-0025	117335	$ 3,005.14	28-May-19		25
20	Rooter Office Solvents	07-4441	117336	$ 78.85	30-May-19		23
21	Emily's Sports Palace	08-2255	117337	$ 4,347.21	2-Jun-19		20
22	O'Donoghue Inc.	09-2111	117338	$ 2,144.55	2-Jun-19		20
23	Brimson Furniture	10-0009	117339	$ 1,234.69	3-Jun-19		19

FIGURE 6-10 This worksheet uses MIN, MAX, ROW, and IF in array formulas to return the row numbers of the first (cell D2) and last (cell D3) occurrences of a value in a list.

> **Tip** It's also possible to determine the address of the cell that contains the first or last occurrence of a value in a list. To do this, use the **ADDRESS** function, which returns an absolute address, given a row and column number:
>
> ```
> =ADDRESS(MIN(IF(B1 = B6:B29, ROW(B6:B29), "")), COLUMN(B6:B29))
> =ADDRESS(MAX(IF(B1 = B6:B29, ROW(B6:B29), "")), COLUMN(B6:B29))
> ```

Case study: Building an accounts receivable aging worksheet

If you use Excel to store accounts receivable data, it's a good idea to set up an aging worksheet that shows past-due invoices, calculates the number of days past due, and groups the invoices into past-due categories (1–30 days, 31–60 days, and so on).

Figure 6-11 shows a simple implementation of an accounts receivable database. For each invoice, the due date (column D) is calculated by adding 30 to the invoice date (column C). Column E subtracts the due date (column D) from the current date (in cell B1) to calculate the number of days each invoice is past due.

| D4 | | | f_x | =C4 + 30 | | | | | | |

	A	B	C	D	E	F	G	H	I	J	K
1	Date:	21-Jun-22									
2							Past Due (Days):				
3	Account Number	Invoice Number	Invoice Date	Due Date	Past Due	Amount Due	1-30	31-60	61-90	91-120	Over 120
4	07-0001	1000	21-Apr-22	Saturday May 21, 2022	31	$2,433.25		$2,433.25			
5	07-0001	1025	10-May-22	Thursday Jun 9, 2022	12	$2,151.20	$ 2,151.20				
6	07-0001	1031	17-May-22	Thursday Jun 16, 2022	5	$1,758.54	$ 1,758.54				
7	07-0002	1006	3-Mar-22	Saturday Apr 2, 2022	80	$ 898.47			$ 898.47		
8	07-0002	1035	17-May-22	Thursday Jun 16, 2022	5	$1,021.02	$ 1,021.02				
9	07-0004	1002	21-Apr-22	Saturday May 21, 2022	31	$3,558.94		$3,558.94			
10	07-0005	1008	22-Feb-22	Thursday Mar 24, 2022	89	$1,177.53			$1,177.53		
11	07-0005	1018	7-May-22	Monday Jun 6, 2022	15	$1,568.31	$ 1,568.31				
12	08-0001	1039	19-Jan-22	Friday Feb 18, 2022	123	$2,958.73					$2,958.73
13	08-0001	1001	21-Apr-22	Saturday May 21, 2022	31	$3,659.85		$3,659.85			
14	08-0001	1024	10-May-22	Thursday Jun 9, 2022	12	$ 565.00	$ 565.00				

FIGURE 6-11 This is a simple accounts receivable database.

Calculating a smarter due date

You might have noticed a problem with the due dates in Figure 6-11: Several of the dates, including the date in cell D4, fall on weekends. The problem here is that the due date calculation just adds 30 to the invoice date. To avoid weekend due dates, you need to test whether the invoice date plus 30 falls on a Saturday or Sunday. The WEEKDAY function helps because it returns 7 if the date is a Saturday and 1 if the date is a Sunday.

So, to check for a Saturday, you could use the following formula:

```
=IF(WEEKDAY(C4 + 30) = 7, C4 + 32, C4 + 30)
```

Here, I'm assuming that the invoice date resides in cell C4. If WEEKDAY(C4 + 30) returns 7, the date is a Saturday, so you add 32 to C4 instead (to make the due date the following Monday). Otherwise, you just add 30 days as usual.

Checking for a Sunday is similar:

```
=IF(WEEKDAY(C4 + 30) = 1, C4 + 31, C4 + 30)
```

The problem, though, is that you need to combine these two tests into a single formula. To do that, you can nest one IF function inside another. Here's how it works:

```
=IF(WEEKDAY(C4+30) = 7, C4+32, IF(WEEKDAY(C4+30) = 1, C4+31, C4+30))
```

The main IF checks whether the date is a Saturday. If it is, you add 32 days to C4; otherwise, the formula runs the second IF, which checks for Sunday. Figure 6-12 shows the revised aging sheet with the nonweekend due dates in column D.

For calculating due dates based on workdays (that is, excluding weekends and holidays), Excel has a function named WORKDAY that handles this calculation with ease; see "A workday alternative: The WORKDAY function," in Chapter 8, "Working with date and time functions."

| D4 | | | f_x | =IF(WEEKDAY(C4 + 30) = 7, C4 + 32, IF(WEEKDAY(C4 + 30) = 1, C4 + 31, C4 + 30)) | | | | | | |

	A	B	C	D	E	F	G	H	I	J	K
1	Date:	21-Jun-22									
2							Past Due (Days):				
3	Account Number	Invoice Number	Invoice Date	Due Date	Past Due	Amount Due	1-30	31-60	61-90	91-120	Over 120
4	07-0001	1000	21-Apr-22	Monday May 23, 2022	29	$2,433.25	$ 2,433.25				
5	07-0001	1025	10-May-22	Thursday Jun 9, 2022	12	$2,151.20	$ 2,151.20				
6	07-0001	1031	17-May-22	Thursday Jun 16, 2022	5	$1,758.54	$ 1,758.54				
7	07-0002	1006	3-Mar-22	Monday Apr 4, 2022	78	$ 898.47			$ 898.47		
8	07-0002	1035	17-May-22	Thursday Jun 16, 2022	5	$1,021.02	$ 1,021.02				
9	07-0004	1002	21-Apr-22	Monday May 23, 2022	29	$3,558.94	$ 3,558.94				
10	07-0005	1008	22-Feb-22	Thursday Mar 24, 2022	89	$1,177.53			$1,177.53		
11	07-0005	1018	7-May-22	Monday Jun 6, 2022	15	$1,568.31	$ 1,568.31				
12	08-0001	1039	19-Jan-22	Friday Feb 18, 2022	123	$2,958.73					$2,958.73
13	08-0001	1001	21-Apr-22	Monday May 23, 2022	29	$3,659.85	$ 3,659.85				
14	08-0001	1024	10-May-22	Thursday Jun 9, 2022	12	$ 565.00	$ 565.00				

FIGURE 6-12 The revised worksheet uses the IF and WEEKDAY functions to ensure that due dates don't fall on weekends.

Aging overdue invoices

For cash-flow purposes, you also need to correlate the invoice amounts with the number of days past due. Ideally, you'd like to see a list of invoice amounts that are between 1 and 30 days past due, between 31 and 60 days past due, and so on. Figure 6-13 shows one way to set up accounts receivable aging.

The worksheet in Figures 6-11 through 6-13 uses ledger shading for easier reading. To learn how to apply ledger shading automatically, see "Creating ledger shading," in Chapter 9, "Working with math functions."

| I7 | | | f_x | =IF(AND(E7 >= 61, E7 <= 90), F7, "") | | | | | | |

	A	B	C	D	E	F	G	H	I	J	K
1	Date:	21-Jun-22									
2							Past Due (Days):				
3	Account Number	Invoice Number	Invoice Date	Due Date	Past Due	Amount Due	1-30	31-60	61-90	91-120	Over 120
4	07-0001	1000	21-Apr-22	Monday May 23, 2022	29	$2,433.25	$ 2,433.25				
5	07-0001	1025	10-May-22	Thursday Jun 9, 2022	12	$2,151.20	$ 2,151.20				
6	07-0001	1031	17-May-22	Thursday Jun 16, 2022	5	$1,758.54	$ 1,758.54				
7	07-0002	1006	3-Mar-22	Monday Apr 4, 2022	78	$ 898.47			$ 898.47		
8	07-0002	1035	17-May-22	Thursday Jun 16, 2022	5	$1,021.02	$ 1,021.02				
9	07-0004	1002	21-Apr-22	Monday May 23, 2022	29	$3,558.94	$ 3,558.94				
10	07-0005	1008	22-Feb-22	Thursday Mar 24, 2022	89	$1,177.53			$1,177.53		
11	07-0005	1018	7-May-22	Monday Jun 6, 2022	15	$1,568.31	$ 1,568.31				
12	08-0001	1039	19-Jan-22	Friday Feb 18, 2022	123	$2,958.73					$2,958.73
13	08-0001	1001	21-Apr-22	Monday May 23, 2022	29	$3,659.85	$ 3,659.85				
14	08-0001	1024	10-May-22	Thursday Jun 9, 2022	12	$ 565.00	$ 565.00				

FIGURE 6-13 You can use IF and AND to categorize past-due invoices for aging purposes.

The aging worksheet calculates the number of days past due by subtracting the due date from the date shown in cell B1. If you calculate days past due using only workdays (weekends and holidays excluded), a better choice is the **NETWORKDAYS** function, covered in "**NETWORKDAYS**: Calculating the number of workdays between two dates," in Chapter 8.

For the invoice amounts shown in column G (1–30 days), the sheet uses the following formula (which appears in G4):

```
=IF(E4 <= 30, F4, "")
```

If the number of days the invoice is past due (cell E4) is less than or equal to 30, the formula displays the amount (from cell F4); otherwise, it displays a blank.

The amounts in column H (31–60 days) are a little trickier. Here, you need to check whether the number of days past due is greater than or equal to 31 days *and* less than or equal to 60 days. To accomplish this, you can press the **AND** function into service:

```
=IF(AND(E4 >= 31, E4 <= 60), F4, "")
```

The **AND** function checks two logical expressions: **E4> = 31** and **E4 <= 60**. If both are true, **AND** returns **TRUE**, and the **IF** function displays the invoice amount. If one of the logical expressions isn't true (or if they're both not true), **AND** returns **FALSE**, and the **IF** function returns a blank. Similar formulas appear in column I (61–90 days) and column J (91–120 days). Column K (Over 120) looks for past-due values that are greater than 120.

Getting data with information functions

Excel's information functions return data concerning cells, worksheets, and formula results. Table 6-2 lists all the information functions.

TABLE 6-2 Excel's information functions

Function	Description
CELL(*info_type*[,*reference*])	Returns information about various cell attributes, including formatting, contents, and location.
ERROR.TYPE(*error_val*)	Returns a number corresponding to an error type.
INFO(*type_text*)	Returns information about the operating system and environment.
ISBLANK(*value*)	Returns **TRUE** if *value* is blank.
ISERR(*value*)	Returns **TRUE** if *value* is any error value except **#N/A**.
ISERROR(*value*)	Returns **TRUE** if *value* is any error value.
ISEVEN(*number*)	Returns **TRUE** if *number* is even.
ISFORMULA(*reference*)	Returns **TRUE** if the cell specified by *reference* contains a formula.
ISLOGICAL(*value*)	Returns **TRUE** if *value* is a logical value.
ISNA(*value*)	Returns **TRUE** if *value* is the **#N/A** error value.
ISNONTEXT(*value*)	Returns **TRUE** if *value* is not text.
ISNUMBER(*value*)	Returns **TRUE** if *value* is a number.
ISODD(*number*)	Returns **TRUE** if *number* is odd.
ISOMITTED(*argument*)	Returns **TRUE** if the *argument* parameter is missing from a LAMBDA function (see Chapter 9).
ISREF(*value*)	Returns **TRUE** if *value* is a reference.
ISTEXT(*value*)	Returns **TRUE** if *value* is text.

Function	Description
N(*value*)	Returns *value* converted to a number (a serial number if *value* is a date, 1 if *value* is **TRUE**, 0 if *value* is any other non-numeric).
NA	Returns the error value #N/A.
SHEET(*value*)	Returns the sheet number of the sheet referenced by *value*.
SHEETS(reference)	Returns the number of sheets in *reference*.
TYPE(*value*)	Returns a number that indicates the data type of *value*: **1** for a number, **2** for text, **4** for a logical value, **8** for a formula, **16** for an error, or **64** for an array.

The rest of this chapter takes you through the details of several of these functions.

The CELL function

CELL is *one* of the most useful information functions. Its job is to return information about a particular cell:

CELL(*info_type*, [*reference*])

info_type	A string that specifies the type of information you want.
reference	The cell you want to use. (The default is the cell that contains the **CELL** function.) If *reference* is a range, **CELL** applies to the cell in the upper-left corner of the range.

Table 6-3 lists the various possibilities for the *info_type* argument.

TABLE 6-3 The CELL function's info_type argument

Info_Type Value	What CELL Returns
address	The absolute address, as text, of the *reference* cell.
col	The column number of *reference*.
color	Returns **1** if *reference* has a custom cell format that displays negative values in a color; returns **0** otherwise.
contents	The contents of *reference*.
filename	The full path and file name of the file that contains *reference*, as text. Returns the null string ("") if the workbook that contains *reference* hasn't been saved for the first time.
format	A string that corresponds to the built-in Excel numeric format applied to *reference*. Here are the possible return values:

Built-In Format	CELL Returns
General	G
0	F0
#,##0	,0
0.00	F2
#,##0.00	,2
$#,##0_);($#,##0)	C0

Info_Type Value	What CELL Returns	
	`$#,##0_);[Red]($#,##0)`	C0-
	`$#,##0.00_);($#,##0.00)`	C2
	`$#,##0.00_);[Red]($#,##0.00)`	C2-
	`0%`	P0
	`0.00%`	P2
	`0.00E+00`	S2
	`# ?/?` or `# ??/??`	G
	d-mmm-yy or **dd-mmm-yy**	D1
	d-mmm or **dd-mmm**	D2
	mmm-yy	D3
	m/d/yy or **m/d/yy** `h:mm` or **mm/dd/yy**	D4
	mm/dd	D5
	`h:mm:ss` AM/PM	D6
	`h:mm` AM/PM	D7
	`h:mm:ss`	D8
	`h:mm`	D9
parentheses	Returns **1** if *reference* has a custom cell format that uses parentheses for positive or all values; returns **0** otherwise.	
prefix	A character that represents the text alignment used by *reference*. Here are the possible return values:	

Alignment	CELL Returns
Left	'
Center	^
Right	"
Fill	\

protect	Returns **0** if *reference* isn't locked; **1** otherwise.	
row	The row number of *reference*.	
type	A letter that represents the type of data in the *reference*. Here are the possible return values:	

Data Type	CELL Returns
Text	L
Blank	B
All others	V

width	The column width of *reference*, rounded to the nearest integer, where one unit equals the width of one character in the default font size.

Figure 6-14 shows how the **CELL** function works.

C6	✓ : ✗ ✓ fx	=@CELL("address",C4)		
	A	B	C	D	E

	A	B	C	D	E
1					
2					
3			**Cell #1**	**Cell #2**	**Cell #3**
4			50	a cell	1/1/2022
5		**Function:**			
6		=CELL("address",cell)	$C$4	$D$4	$E$4
7		=CELL("col",cell)	3	4	5
8		=CELL("contents",cell)	50	a cell	44562
9		=CELL("format",cell)	F0	G	D4
10		=CELL("prefix",cell)	'	^	"
11		=CELL("row",cell)	4	4	4
12		=CELL("type",cell)	v	l	v
13		=CELL("width",cell)	8	8	11
14					

FIGURE 6-14 These are examples of the CELL function.

The ERROR.TYPE function

The **ERROR.TYPE** function returns a value that corresponds to a specific Excel error value:

ERROR.TYPE(*error_val*)

error_val	A reference to a cell containing a formula that you want to check for the error value. Here are the possible return values:

***ERROR_VAL* Value**	**ERROR.TYPE Returns**
#NULL!	1
#DIV/0!	2
#VALUE!	3
#REF!	4
#NAME?	5
#NUM!	6
#N/A!	7
#GETTING_DATA	8
#SPILL!	9
#UNKNOWN!	12
#FIELD!	13
#CALC!	14
All others	#N/A

You most often use the **ERROR.TYPE** function to intercept an error and then display a more useful or friendly message. You do this by using the **IF** function to see if **ERROR.TYPE** returns a value less than or equal to **7**; if so, the cell in question contains an error value. Because the **ERROR.TYPE** returns value ranges from **1** to **14**, you can apply the return value to the **CHOOSE** function to display the error message.

For the details of the **CHOOSE** function, see "The **CHOOSE** function," in Chapter 7.

Here's a formula that does all that. (I've split the formula so that different parts appear on different lines to make it easier for you to see what's going on.)

```
=IF(ISERROR(D8), IF(ERROR.TYPE(D8) <= 14,
    ***ERROR IN " & CELL("address",D8) & ": " &
    CHOOSE(ERROR.TYPE(D8),"The ranges do not intersect",
    "The divisor is 0",
    "Wrong data type in function argument",
    "Invalid cell reference",
    "Unrecognized range or function name",
    "Number error in formula",
    "Inappropriate function argument",
    "Waiting for query data",
    "Non-empty spill range",
    "",
    "",
    "Unknown data type",
    "Referenced field is not found",
    "Calculation error")), "")
```

Figure 6-15 shows this formula in an example. (Note that the formula displays **#N/A** when there is no error; this is the return value of **ERROR.TYPE** when there is no error.)

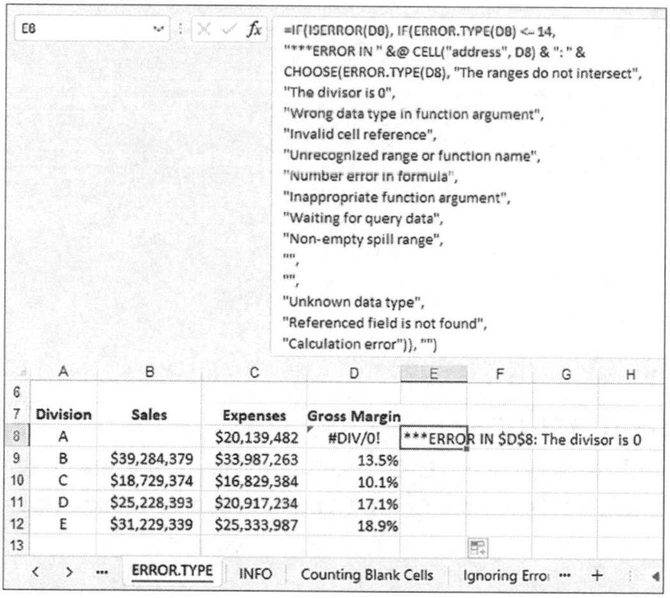

FIGURE 6-15 This formula uses IF and ERROR.TYPE to return a more descriptive error message to the user.

The INFO function

The **INFO** function is seldom used, but it's handy when you need it because it gives you information about the current operating environment:

INFO(*type_text*)

type_text	A string that specifies the type of information you want.

Table 6-4 lists the possible values for the *type_text* argument.

TABLE 6-4 The INFO function's type_text argument

TYPE_TEXT Value	What INFO Returns
`directory`	The full pathname of the current folder. (That is, the folder that will appear the next time you display the Open or Save As dialog box.)
`numfile`	The number of worksheets in all the open workbooks, including hidden ones.
`origin`	The address of the upper-left cell that is visible in the current worksheet. In Figure 6-16, for example, cell A2 is the visible cell in the upper-left corner. The absolute address begins with **$A:** for Lotus 1-2-3 release 3.x compatibility.
`osversion`	A string containing the current operating system version.
`recalc`	A string containing the current recalculation mode: **Automatic** or **Manual**.
`release`	A string containing the version of Microsoft Excel.
`system`	A string containing a code representing the current operating environment: **pcdos** for Windows or **mac** for Macintosh.

Figure 6-16 shows the **INFO** function at work.

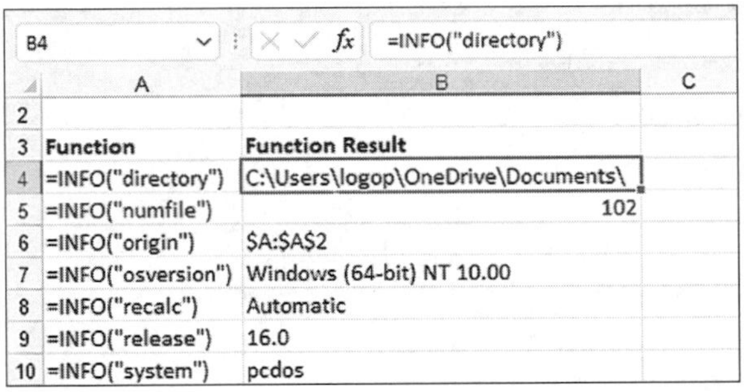

FIGURE 6-16 The INFO function is in action here.

The SHEET and SHEETS functions

Excel includes two information functions—**SHEET** and **SHEETS**—that return information about the worksheets in a workbook. You use the **SHEET** function to return a sheet number using the following syntax:

SHEET([*value*])

value	An optional value that specifies a sheet. If you omit *value*, Excel references the current sheet.

For example, the formula =**SHEET** returns the number of the sheet that contains the formula, where 1 is the first sheet in the workbook, 2 is the second sheet, and so on. Note that Excel counts all sheet types, including worksheets and chart sheets.

If a worksheet has the name **Budget**, then the formula =**SHEET("Budget")** returns its sheet number. Alternatively, you can use a cell reference within that sheet, such as **SHEET(Budget!A1)**.

You use the **SHEETS** function (which takes no arguments) to return the total number of worksheets in the current workbook.

The IS functions

Excel's so-called **IS** functions are Boolean functions that return either **TRUE** or **FALSE**, depending on the argument they're evaluating:

```
ISBLANK(value)
ISERR(value)
ISERROR(value)
ISEVEN(number)
ISFORMULA(reference)
ISLOGICAL(value)
ISNA(value)
ISNONTEXT(value)
ISNUMBER(value)
ISODD(number)
ISREF(value)
ISTEXT(value)
```

value	A cell reference, function return value, or formula result
reference	A cell reference
number	A numeric value

The operation of these functions is straightforward, so rather than run through the specifics of all 11 functions, in the next few sections I show you some interesting and useful techniques that make use of these functions.

Counting the number of blanks in a range

When putting together the data for a worksheet model, it's common to pull the data from various sources. Unfortunately, this often means that the data arrives at different times, and you end up with an incomplete model. If you're working with a big list, you might want to keep a running total of the number of pieces of data you're still missing.

This is the perfect opportunity to break out the **ISBLANK** function and plug it into the array formula for counting that you learned earlier:

```
=SUM(IF(ISBLANK(range), 1, 0))
```

The **IF** function runs through the *range*, looking for blank cells. Each time it comes across a blank cell, it returns **1**; otherwise, it returns **0**. The **SUM** function adds the results to give the total number of blank cells. Figure 6-17 shows an example (see cell G1).

> **Tip** Using an array formula to count blank cells is fine, but it's not the easiest way to go about it. In most cases, you're better off just using the **COUNTBLANK(***range***)** function, which counts the number of blank cells that occur in the range specified by the *range* argument.

`{=SUM(IF(ISBLANK(G3:G79), 1, 0))}`

	C	D	E	F	G
			Missing Values for 'Units In Stock':		10
	Supplier	**Category**	**Quantity Per Unit**	**Unit Price**	**Units In Stock**
	Exotic Liquids	Beverages	10 boxes x 20 bags	$18.00	39
	Exotic Liquids	Beverages	24 - 12 oz bottles	$19.00	17
	Exotic Liquids	Condiments	12 - 550 ml bottles	$10.00	13
Seasoning	New Orleans Cajun Delights	Condiments	48 - 6 oz jars	$22.00	
Mix	New Orleans Cajun Delights	Condiments	36 boxes	$21.35	
erry Spread	Grandma Kelly's Homestead	Condiments	12 - 8 oz jars	$25.00	120
Dried Pears	Grandma Kelly's Homestead	Produce	12 - 1 lb pkgs.	$30.00	15
ry Sauce	Grandma Kelly's Homestead	Condiments	12 - 12 oz jars	$40.00	6
	Tokyo Traders	Meat/Poultry	18 - 500 g pkgs.	$97.00	29
	Tokyo Traders	Seafood	12 - 200 ml jars	$31.00	31
	Cooperativa de Quesos 'Las Cabras'	Dairy Products	1 kg pkg.	$21.00	22
Pastora	Cooperativa de Quesos 'Las Cabras'	Dairy Products	10 - 500 g pkgs.	$38.00	
	Mayumi's	Seafood	2 kg box	$6.00	24
	Mayumi's	Produce	40 - 100 g pkgs.	$23.25	35
	Mayumi's	Condiments	24 - 250 ml bottles	$15.50	
	Pavlova, Ltd.	Confections	32 - 500 g boxes	$17.45	29

FIGURE 6-17 As shown in cell G1, you can plug ISBLANK into the array counting formula to count the number of blank cells in a range.

Checking a range for non-numeric values

A similar idea is to check a range on which you'll be performing a mathematical operation to see if it holds any cells that contain non-numeric values. In this case, you plug the **ISNUMBER** function into the array counting formula and then return **0** for each **TRUE** result and **1** for each **FALSE** result. Here's the general formula:

`=SUM(IF(ISNUMBER(range), 0, 1))`

Counting the number of errors in a range

For the final counting example, it's often nice to know not only whether a range contains an error value but also how many such values it contains. You can do this easily with the **ISERROR** function and the array counting formula:

`=SUM(IF(ISERROR(range), 1, 0))`

Ignoring errors when working with a range

Sometimes you have to work with ranges that contain error values. For example, suppose that you have a column of gross margin results (which require division), but one or more of the cells are showing the **#DIV/0!** error because you're missing data. You could wait until the missing data is added to the model, but it's often necessary to perform preliminary calculations. For example, you might want to take the average of the results that you *do* have.

To do this efficiently, you need some way of bypassing the error values. Again, this is possible by using the **ISERROR** function plugged into an array formula. For example, here's a general formula for taking an average across a range while ignoring any error values:

```
=AVERAGE(IF(ISERROR(range), "", range))
```

Figure 6-18 provides an example.

	A	B	C	D	E	F	G
					fx	{=AVERAGE(IF(ISERROR(D3:D12), "", D3:D12))}	
1							
2	Division	Sales	Expenses	Gross Margin			
3	A	$20,139,482		#DIV/0!			
4	B	$39,284,379	$33,987,263	15.6%			
5	C	$18,729,374	$16,829,384	11.3%			
6	D	$25,228,393	$20,917,234	20.6%			
7	E	$31,229,339	$25,333,987	23.3%			
8	F	$27,392,837		#DIV/0!			
9	G	$33,987,228	$27,829,384	22.1%			
10	H	$30,828,374	$25,398,883	21.4%			
11	I	$19,029,384		#DIV/0!			
12	J	$22,009,876	$19,023,098	15.7%			
13			AVERAGE:	18.6%			
14							

FIGURE 6-18 As shown in cell D13, you can use ISERROR in an array formula to run an operation on a range while ignoring any errors in the range.

CHAPTER 7

Working with lookup functions

In this chapter, you will

- Get an overview of Excel's lookup functions

- Understand how lookup tables work

- Taking lookup to the next level with XLOOKUP

- Look up a value using the CHOOSE function

- Look up a value using a table

- Perform advanced lookup operations

Getting the meaning of a word in the dictionary is always a two-step process: First, you look up the word itself, and then you read its definition. Same with an encyclopedia: First look up the topic, and then read the article.

This idea of looking something up to retrieve some related information is at the heart of many spreadsheet operations. For example, you saw in Chapter 2, "Creating advanced formulas," that you can add option buttons and list boxes to a worksheet. Unfortunately, these controls return only the number of the item the user has chosen. To find out the item's actual value, you need to use the returned number to look up the value in a table.

Taking a look at Excel's lookup functions

In many worksheet formulas, the value of one argument often depends on the value of another. Here are some examples:

- In a formula that calculates an invoice total, the customer's discount might depend on the number of units purchased.

- In a formula that charges interest on overdue accounts, the interest percentage might depend on each invoice's number of overdue days.

- In a formula that calculates employee bonuses as a percentage of salary, the percentage might depend on how much the employee improved on the given budget.

The usual way to handle these kinds of problems is to look up the appropriate value. This chapter introduces you to a number of functions that enable you to perform lookup operations in your worksheet models. Table 7-1 lists Excel's lookup functions.

TABLE 7-1 Excel's lookup functions

Function	Description
CHOOSE(*num*,*value1*[,*value2*,...])	Uses *num* to select one of the list of arguments given by *value1*, *value2*, and so on.
FIELDVALUE(*value*,*field_name*)	Extracts data from a table. (See Chapter 17, "Analyzing data with tables.")
GETPIVOTDATA(*data*,*table*,*field1*, *item1*,...)	Extracts data from a PivotTable. (See Chapter 18, "Analyzing data with PivotTables.")
HLOOKUP(*value*,*table*,*row*[,*range*])	Searches for *value* in *table* and returns the value in the specified *row*.
INDEX(*ref*,*row*[,*col*][,*area*])	Looks in *ref* and returns the value of the cell at the intersection of *row* and, optionally, *col*.
LOOKUP(*lookup_value*, *array*)	Looks up a value in a range or array.
MATCH(*value*,*range*[,*match_type*])	Searches *range* for *value* and, if found, returns the relative position of *value* in *range*.
RTD(*progID*, **server**, *topic1*[,*topic2*,...])	Retrieves data in real time from an automation server (not covered in this book).
VLOOKUP(*value*,*table*,*col*[,*range*])	Searches for *value* in *table* and returns the value in the specified *col*.
XLOOKUP(*value*,*lookup_range*,*return_range*)	Searches for *value* in *lookup_range* and returns the corresponding item from *return_range*.
XMATCH(*value*, *range*[,*match_mode*] [,*search_mode*])	Searches *range* for *value* and, if found, returns the relative position of *value* in *range*.

Understanding lookup tables

The *lookup table*—a rectangular range of data with a special structure that I describe later—is the key to performing lookup operations in Excel. The most straightforward lookup table structure is one that consists of two columns (or two rows):

- **Lookup column:** This column contains the values that you look up. For example, if you were constructing a lookup table for a dictionary, this column would contain the words.

- **Data column:** This column contains the data associated with each lookup value. In the dictionary example, this column would contain the definitions.

In most lookup operations, you supply a value that the function locates in the designated lookup column. It then retrieves the corresponding value in the data column.

As you'll see in this chapter, there are many variations on the lookup table theme. The lookup table can be one of these:

- **A single column (or a single row):** In this case, the lookup operation consists of finding the *n*th value in the column.

- **A range with multiple data columns:** For instance, in the dictionary example, you might have a second column for each word's part of speech (noun, verb, and so on), and perhaps a third column for its pronunciation. In this case, the lookup operation must also specify which of the data columns contains the value required.

- **An array:** In this case, the table doesn't exist on a worksheet but is either an array of literal values or the result of a function that returns an array. The lookup operation finds a particular position within the array and returns the data value at that position.

The CHOOSE function

The simplest of the lookup functions is **CHOOSE**, which enables you to select a value from a list. Specifically, given an integer *n*, **CHOOSE** returns the *n*th item from the list. Here's the function's syntax:

```
CHOOSE(num, value1[, value2,...])
```

num	Determines which of the values in the list is returned. If *num* is **1**, *value1* is returned; if *num* is **2**, *value2* is returned, and so on. *num* must be an integer (or a formula or function that returns an integer) between 1 and 254.
value1, value2...	The list of up to 254 values from which **CHOOSE** selects the return value. The values can be numbers, strings, references, names, formulas, or functions.

For example, consider the following formula:

```
=CHOOSE(2,"Surface Mail", "Air Mail", "Courier")
```

The *num* argument is **2**, so **CHOOSE** returns the second value in the list, which is the string value **Air Mail**.

> **Note** If you use range references as the list of values, **CHOOSE** returns the entire range as the result. For example, consider the following:
>
> ```
> CHOOSE(1, A1:D1, A2:D2, A3:D3)
> ```
>
> This function returns the range A1:D1. This enables you to perform conditional operations on a set of ranges, where the *condition* is the lookup value used by **CHOOSE**. For example, the following formula returns the sum of the range A1:D1:
>
> ```
> =SUM(CHOOSE(1, A1:D1, A2:D2, A3:D3))
> ```

Determining the name of the day of the week

As you'll see in Chapter 8, "Working with date and time functions," Excel's **WEEKDAY** function returns a number that corresponds to the day of the week, where Sunday is **1**, Monday is **2**, and so on.

What if you want to know the actual day (not the number) of the week? If you need only to display the day of the week, you can format the cell as **dddd**. If you need to use the day of the week as a string value in a formula, you need a way to convert the **WEEKDAY** result into the appropriate string. Fortunately, the **CHOOSE** function makes this process easy. For example, suppose that cell B5 contains a date. You can find the day of the week it represents with the following formula:

```
=CHOOSE(WEEKDAY(B5), "Sun", "Mon", "Tue", "Wed", "Thu", "Fri", "Sat")
```

I've used abbreviated day names to save space, but you're free to use any form of the day names that suits your purposes.

> **Note** Here's a similar formula for returning the name of the month, given the integer month number returned by the **MONTH** function:
>
> ```
> =CHOOSE(MONTH(date), "Jan", "Feb", "Mar", "Apr", "May", "Jun", "Jul", "Aug",
> "Sep", "Oct", "Nov", "Dec")
> ```

Determining the month of the fiscal year

For many businesses, the fiscal year does not coincide with the calendar year. For example, the fiscal year might run from April 1 to March 31. In this case, month 1 of the fiscal year is April, month 2 is May, and so on. It's often handy to be able to determine the fiscal month, given the calendar month.

To see how you'd set this up, first consider the following table, which compares the calendar month and the fiscal month for a fiscal year beginning April 1.

Month	Calendar Month	Fiscal Month
January	1	10
February	2	11
March	3	12
April	4	1
May	5	2
June	6	3
July	7	4
August	8	5
September	9	6
October	10	7
November	11	8
December	12	9

You need to use the calendar month as the lookup value and the fiscal months as the data values. Here's the result:

```
=CHOOSE(CalendarMonth, 10, 11, 12, 1, 2, 3, 4, 5, 6, 7, 8, 9)
```

Figure 7-1 shows an example.

> **Note** You can work with all the examples in this chapter by downloading Chapter07.xslx from either of the companion content sites mentioned in the Introduction.

FIGURE 7-1 This worksheet uses the CHOOSE function to determine the fiscal month (B3), given the start of the fiscal year (shown in B1) and the current date (B2).

Calculating weighted questionnaire results

One common use for **CHOOSE** is to calculate weighted questionnaire responses. For example, suppose you've created a survey in which the respondents have to enter a value between 1 and 5 for each question. Some questions and answers are more important than others, so each question is assigned a set of weights. You use these weighted responses for your data. How do you assign the weights? The easiest way is to set up a **CHOOSE** function for each question. For instance, suppose that question 1 uses the following weights for answers 1 through 5: 1.5, 2.3, 1.0, 1.8, and 0.5. If so, the following formula can be used to derive the weighted response:

```
=CHOOSE(Answer1, 1.5, 2.3, 1.0, 1.8, 0.5)
```

Assume that the answer for question 1 is in a cell named Answer1.

Integrating CHOOSE and worksheet option buttons

The **CHOOSE** function is ideal for lookup situations in which you have a small number of data values, and you have a formula or function that generates sequential integer values beginning with 1. A good example of this is the use of the worksheet option buttons I mentioned at the beginning of this chapter (and that I discuss in detail in Chapter 2). The option buttons in a group return integer values in the linked cell: **1** if the first option is selected, **2** if the second option is selected, and so on. Therefore, you can use the value in the linked cell as the lookup value in the **CHOOSE** function. Figure 7-2 shows a worksheet that does this.

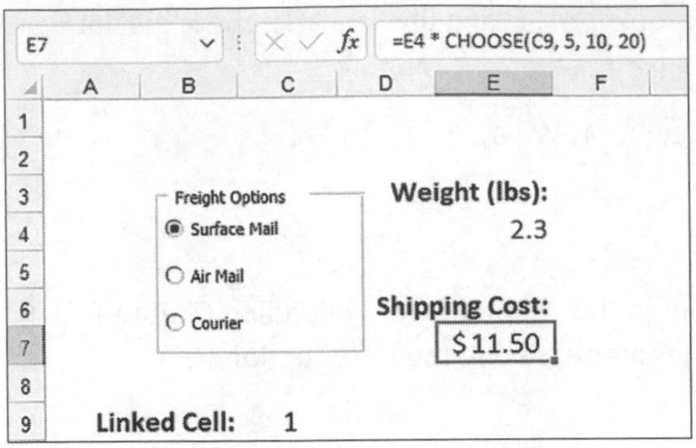

FIGURE 7-2 This worksheet uses the CHOOSE function to calculate the shipping cost based on the option selected in the Freight Options group.

The Freight Options group presents three option buttons: **Surface Mail**, **Air Mail**, and **Courier**. The number of the currently selected option is shown in the linked cell, C9. A weight, in pounds, is entered into cell E4. Given the linked cell and the weight, cell E7 calculates the shipping cost by multiplying the weight by a constant selected by using CHOOSE:

```
=E4 * CHOOSE(C9, 5, 10, 20)
```

Looking up values in ranges or tables

As you've seen, the CHOOSE function is a handy addition to your formula toolkit, and it's a function you'll turn to quite often if you build a lot of worksheet models. However, CHOOSE does have its drawbacks:

- The lookup values must be positive integers.

- The maximum number of data values is 254.

- Only one set of data values is allowed per function.

You'll trip over these limitations eventually, and you'll wonder if Excel has more flexible lookup capabilities. Can it use a wider variety of lookup values (negative numbers, non-integers, strings, and so on)? Can it accommodate multiple data sets that each can have any number of values (subject, of course, to the worksheet's inherent size limitations)? The answer to both questions is "yes"; in fact, Excel has three functions that meet these criteria: VLOOKUP, HLOOKUP, and XLOOKUP.

The big news in Excel lookups is the addition of the XLOOKUP function to Excel 365 back in 2019. Make no mistake: XLOOKUP is the future of lookups and should be the function you turn to whenever you need to look up a value in a table or range. So why do I spend quite a bit of time teaching you how to use the old VLOOKUP and HLOOKUP functions in the next few sections? Two reasons:

- When reviewing other users' worksheets, you might come across formulas that use VLOOKUP or HLOOKUP, so you need to know how they work.

- **XLOOKUP** is compatible with Excel for Microsoft 365 and Excel 2021, so if you'll be sharing a workbook with people who use Excel 2019 or earlier, then any formulas that rely on **XLOOKUP** will fail, so you'll need to use either **VLOOKUP** or **HLOOKUP** instead.

The **VLOOKUP** function

The **VLOOKUP** function works by looking in the first column of a table for the value you specify. (The *V* in **VLOOKUP** stands for *vertical*.) It then looks across a specified number of columns and returns whatever value it finds there.

Here's the full syntax for **VLOOKUP**:

VLOOKUP(`lookup_value`, `table_array`, `col_index_num`[, `range_lookup`])

lookup_value	This is the value you want to find in the first column of *table_array*. You can enter a number, string, or reference.
table_array	This is the table to use for the lookup. You can use a range reference or a range name.
col_index_num	If **VLOOKUP** finds a match, *col_index_num* is the column number in *table_array* that contains the data you want returned (the first column—that is, the lookup column—is **1**, the second column is **2**, and so on).
range_lookup	This is a Boolean value that determines how Excel searches for *lookup_value* in the first column: **TRUE**—**VLOOKUP** searches for the first exact match for *lookup_value*. If no exact match is found, the function looks for the largest value that is less than *lookup_value* (this is the default). **FALSE**—**VLOOKUP** searches only for the first exact match for *lookup_value*.

Here are some notes to keep in mind when you work with **VLOOKUP**:

- If *range_lookup* is **TRUE** or omitted, you must sort the values in the first column in ascending order.

- If the first column of the table is text, you can use the standard wildcard characters in the *lookup_value* argument. (Use **?** to substitute for individual characters; use * to substitute for multiple characters.)

- If *lookup_value* is less than any value in the lookup column, **VLOOKUP** returns the **#N/A** error value.

- If **VLOOKUP** doesn't find a match in the lookup column, and if you specified **FALSE** for **range_lookup**, it returns **#N/A**.

- If *col_index_num* is less than 1, **VLOOKUP** returns **#VALUE!**; if *col_index_num* is greater than the number of columns in *table_array*, **VLOOKUP** returns **#REF!**.

> **Tip** By far, the biggest source of inaccurate lookups (for both **VLOOKUP** and **HLOOKUP**) is assuming that Excel will look for an exact match for the *lookup_value* argument. If an exact match is what you want (and it almost always is), then be sure to enter **FALSE** for the optional *range_lookup* argument.

The HLOOKUP function

The **HLOOKUP** function is similar to **VLOOKUP** except that it searches for the lookup value in the first row of a table. (The *H* in **HLOOKUP** stands for *horizontal*.) If successful, this function then looks down the specified number of rows and returns the value it finds there. Here's the syntax for **HLOOKUP**:

```
HLOOKUP(lookup_value, table_array, row_index_num[, range_lookup])
```

lookup_value	This is the value you want to find in the first row of *table_array*. You can enter a number, string, or reference.
table_array	This is the table to use for the lookup. You can use a range reference or a name.
row_index_num	If **HLOOKUP** finds a match, *row_index_num* is the row number in *table_array* that contains the data you want returned. (The first row—that is, the lookup row—is **1**, the second row is **2**, and so on.)
range_lookup	This is a Boolean value that determines how Excel searches for *lookup_value* in the first row:
	TRUE—**HLOOKUP** searches for the first exact match for *lookup_value*. If no exact match is found, the function looks for the largest value that is less than *lookup_value*. (This is the default.)
	FALSE—**HLOOKUP** searches only for the first exact match for *lookup_value*.

Returning a customer discount rate with a range lookup

The most common use for **VLOOKUP** and **HLOOKUP** is to look for a match that falls within a range of values. This section and the next one take you through a few examples of this range-lookup technique.

In business-to-business transactions, the cost of an item is often calculated as a percentage of the retail price. For example, a publisher might sell books to a bookstore at half the suggested list price. The percentage that the seller takes off the list price for the buyer is called the *discount*. Often, the size of the discount depends on the number of units ordered. For example, ordering 1–3 items might result in a 20 percent discount, ordering 4–24 items might result in a 40 percent discount, and so on.

Figure 7-3 shows a worksheet that uses **VLOOKUP** to determine the discount a customer gets on an order, based on the number of units purchased.

D4		f_x	=VLOOKUP(A4, $H$5:$I$11, 2)					
	A	B	C	D	E	F	G	H	I

Units Ordered	Part	List Price	Discount	Net Price	Total		Discount Schedule	
							Units	Discount
20	D-178	$17.95	40%	$10.77	$215.40		0	20%
10	B-047	$6.95	40%	$4.17	$41.70		4	40%
1000	C-098	$2.95	50%	$1.48	$1,475.00		24	42%
50	B-111	$19.95	44%	$11.17	$558.60		49	44%
2	D-017	$27.95	20%	$22.36	$44.72		99	46%
25	D-178	$17.95	42%	$10.41	$260.28		249	48%
100	A-182	$9.95	46%	$5.37	$537.30		499	50%
250	B-047	$6.95	48%	$3.61	$903.50			

FIGURE 7-3 This worksheet uses VLOOKUP to look up a customer's discount in a discount schedule.

For example, cell D4 uses the following formula:

```
=VLOOKUP(A4, $H$5:$I$11, 2)
```

The *range_lookup* argument is omitted, which means **VLOOKUP** searches for the largest value that is less than or equal to the lookup value; in this case, this is the value in cell A4. Cell A4 contains the number of units purchased (20, in this case), and the range $H$5:$I$11 is the discount schedule table. **VLOOKUP** searches down the first column (H5:H11) for the largest value that is less than or equal to 20. The first such cell is H6, because the value in H7 (24) is larger than 20. **VLOOKUP** therefore moves to the second column (because you specified *col_index_num* to be **2**) of the table (cell I6) and grabs the value there (40%).

> **Tip** As I mentioned earlier in this section, both **VLOOKUP** and **HLOOKUP** return #N/A if no match is found in the lookup range, and you specified **FALSE** for the **range_lookup**. If you would prefer to return a friendlier or more useful message, use the **IFNA** function to test whether the lookup will fail. Here's the general idea:
>
> ```
> =IFNA(LookupExpression, "LookupValue not found")
> ```
>
> Here, *LookupExpression* is the **VLOOKUP** or **HLOOKUP** function, and *LookupValue* is the same as the *lookup_value* argument used in **VLOOKUP** or **HLOOKUP**. If **IFNA** detects an #N/A error, the formula returns the "*LookupValue not found*" string; otherwise, it runs the lookup normally.

Returning a tax rate with a range lookup

Tax rates are perfect candidates for a range lookup because a given rate applies to any income that is greater than some minimum amount and less than or equal to some maximum amount. For example, a rate of 22 percent might be applied to annual incomes over $38,700 and less than or equal to $82,500. Figure 7-4 shows a worksheet that uses **VLOOKUP** to return the marginal tax rate, given a specified income.

The lookup table is C8:G14, and the lookup value is cell B17, which contains the annual income. **VLOOKUP** finds in column C the largest income that is less than or equal to the value in B17, which is $50,000. In this case, the matching value is $38,700 in cell C10. **VLOOKUP** then looks in the fourth column to get the marginal rate in column F, which, in this case, is 22 percent.

B17   ✓ : × ✓ *fx*   =VLOOKUP(B16, C8:G14, 4)

	A	B	C	D	E	F	G
1	Tax Rate Schedule						
2							
3			If TAXABLE INCOME		The TAX Is		
4							
5				THEN			
6			Is Over	But Not Over	This Amount	Plus This %	Of the Excess Over
7	SCHEDULE X —						
8	Single		$0	$9,875	$0.00	10%	$0.00
9			$9,875	$40,125	$987.50	12%	$9,875
10			$40,125	$85,525	$4,617.50	22%	$40,125
11			$85,525	$163,300	$14,605.50	24%	$85,525
12			$163,300	$207,350	$33,271.50	32%	$163,300
13			$207,350	$518,400	$47,367.50	35%	$207,350
14			$518,400	--	$156,235.00	37%	$518,400
15							
16	Income:	$50,000					
17	Tax Rate:	22%					
18	Total Tax:	$6,790.00					

FIGURE 7-4 This worksheet uses VLOOKUP to look up a marginal income tax rate.

The worksheet in Figure 7-4 also includes a Total Tax calculation in cell B18. In the U.S. tax system, total tax is calculated by adding the base amount (column E in the tax table) plus the tax rate (column F) multiplied by the excess over the bracket minimum (column G). This involves looking up both the base amount and the bracket minimum amount, so here's the resulting formula:

```
=VLOOKUP(B16, C8:G14, 3) + B17 * (B16 - VLOOKUP(B16, C8:G14, 5))
```

Finding exact matches

In many situations, a range lookup isn't what you want. This is particularly true in lookup tables containing a set of unique lookup values representing discrete values instead of ranges. For example, if you need to look up a customer account number, a part code, or an employee ID, you want to be sure that your formula matches the value exactly. You can perform exact-match lookups with **VLOOKUP** and **HLOOKUP** by including the *range_lookup* argument with the value **FALSE**. The next couple of sections demonstrate this technique.

Looking up a customer account number

A table of customer account numbers and names is a good example of a lookup table that contains discrete lookup values. In such a case, you want to use **VLOOKUP** or **HLOOKUP** to find an exact match for an account number you specify and then return the corresponding account name. Figure 7-5 shows a simple data-entry screen that automatically adds a customer name after the user enters the account number in cell B2.

The function that accomplishes this is in cell B4:

```
=VLOOKUP(B2, D3:E15, 2, FALSE)
```

The value in B2 is looked up in column D, and because the *range_lookup* argument is set to **FALSE**, **VLOOKUP** searches for an exact match. If it finds one, it returns the text from column E.

	B4	✓ : ✗ ✓ fx	=VLOOKUP(B2, D3:E15, 2, FALSE)		
	A	B	C	D	E
1					
2	Enter Account Number:	**10-0009**		Account Number	Account Name
3				10-0009	Around the Horn
4	Account Name is:	Around the Horn		02-0200	Consolidated Holdings
5				01-0045	Eastern Connection
6				08-2255	Great Lakes Food Market
7				12-1212	Island Trading
8				12-3456	Laughing Bacchus Wine Cellars
9				09-2111	Old World Delicatessen
10				14-1882	Queen Cozinha
11				14-5741	QUICK-Stop
12				07-0025	Rattlesnake Canyon Grocery
13				07-4441	Seven Seas Imports
14				16-6658	Simon's Bistro
15				14-1882	Split Rail Beer & Ale

FIGURE 7-5 This simple data-entry worksheet uses the exact-match version of VLOOKUP to look up an account's name based on the entered account number.

Combining exact-match lookups with in-cell drop-down lists

In Chapter 2, you learned how to use data validation to set up an in-cell drop-down list. Whatever value the user selects from the list is the value that's stored in the cell. This technique becomes even more powerful when you combine it with exact-match lookups that use the current list selection as the lookup value.

Figure 7-6 shows an example. Cell C9 contains a drop-down menu that uses as its source the header values in row 1 (C1:N1). The formula in cell C10 uses **HLOOKUP** to perform an exact-match lookup using the currently selected list value from C9:

```
=HLOOKUP(C9, C1:N7, 7, FALSE)
```

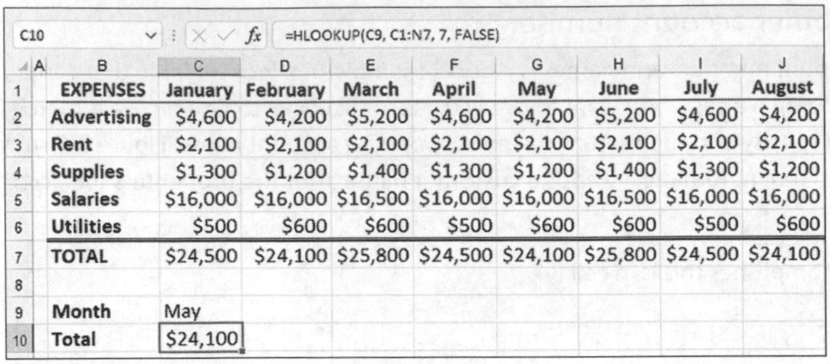

C10 =HLOOKUP(C9, C1:N7, 7, FALSE)

	A	B	C	D	E	F	G	H	I	J
1		EXPENSES	January	February	March	April	May	June	July	August
2		Advertising	$4,600	$4,200	$5,200	$4,600	$4,200	$5,200	$4,600	$4,200
3		Rent	$2,100	$2,100	$2,100	$2,100	$2,100	$2,100	$2,100	$2,100
4		Supplies	$1,300	$1,200	$1,400	$1,300	$1,200	$1,400	$1,300	$1,200
5		Salaries	$16,000	$16,000	$16,500	$16,000	$16,000	$16,500	$16,000	$16,000
6		Utilities	$500	$600	$600	$500	$600	$600	$500	$600
7		TOTAL	$24,500	$24,100	$25,800	$24,500	$24,100	$25,800	$24,500	$24,100
8										
9		Month	May							
10		Total	$24,100							

FIGURE 7-6 An HLOOKUP formula in C10 performs an exact-match lookup in row 1 based on the current selection in the in-cell drop-down menu in C9.

Advanced lookup operations

The basic lookup procedure will satisfy most of your needs by looking up a value in a column or row and then returning an offset value. However, a few operations require a more sophisticated approach. The rest of this chapter examines these more advanced lookups, most of which use two more lookup functions: `MATCH` and `INDEX`.

The MATCH and INDEX functions

The `MATCH` function looks through a row or column of cells for a value. If `MATCH` finds the value, it returns the relative position of the match in the row or column. Here's the syntax:

```
MATCH(lookup_value, lookup_array[, match_type])
```

lookup_value	The value you want to find. You can use a number, string, reference, or logical value.
lookup_array	The row or column of cells you want to use for the lookup.
match_type	How you want Excel to match the *lookup_value* with the entries in the *lookup_array*. You have three choices: **0** finds the first value that exactly matches *lookup_value*. The *lookup_array* can be in any order. **1** finds the largest value that's less than or equal to *lookup_value*. (This is the default value.) The *lookup_array* must be in ascending order. **-1** finds the smallest value that is greater than or equal to *lookup_value*. The *lookup_array* must be in descending order.

> **Tip** You can use the usual wildcard characters within the *lookup_value* argument (provided that *match_type* is **0** and *lookup_value* is text). You can use the question mark (?) for single characters and the asterisk (*) for multiple characters.

Normally, you don't use the MATCH function by itself; you combine it with the INDEX function. INDEX returns the value of a cell at the intersection of a row and column inside a reference. Here's the syntax for INDEX:

INDEX(*reference*, *row_num*[, *column_num*][, *area_num*])

Reference	A reference to one or more cell ranges.
row_num	The number of the row in *reference* from which to return a value.
column_num	The number of the column in *reference* from which to return a value. You can omit *column_num* if *reference* is a single column.
area_num	If you entered more than one range for *reference*, *area_num* is the range you want to use. The first range you entered is **1** (this is the default), the second is **2**, and so on.

The idea is that you use MATCH to get *row_num* or *column_num* (depending on how your table is laid out) and then use INDEX to return the value you need.

To give you the flavor of using these two functions, I duplicated my earlier effort of looking up a customer name, given the account number. Figure 7-7 shows the result.

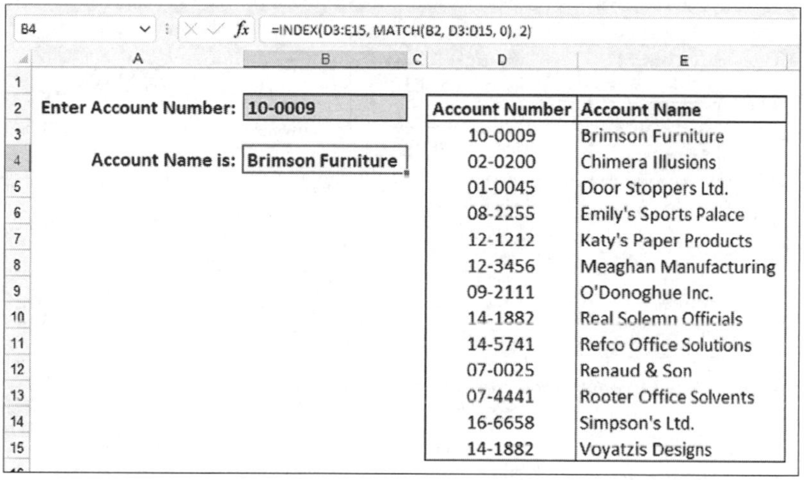

FIGURE 7-7 This worksheet uses INDEX and MATCH to look up an account's name, based on the entered account number.

In particular, notice the new formula in cell B4:

=INDEX(D3:E15, MATCH(B2, D3:D15, 0), 2)

The MATCH function looks up the value in cell B2 in the range D3:D15. That value is then used as the *row_num* argument for the INDEX function. That value is **1** in the example, so the INDEX function reduces to this:

=INDEX(D3:E15, 1, 2)

This returns the value in the first row and the second column of the range D3:E15.

Looking up a value using worksheet list boxes

If you use a worksheet list box or combo box as explained in Chapter 2, the linked cell contains the number of the selected item, not the item itself. Figure 7-8 shows a worksheet with a list box and a combo box. The list used by both controls is the range A3:A10. Notice that the linked cells (E3 and E10) display the number of the list selection, not the selection itself.

To get the selected list item, you can use the **INDEX** function with the following modified syntax:

INDEX(*list_range*, *list_selection*)

| *list_range* | The range used in the list box or combo box |
| *list_selection* | The number of the item selected in the list |

For example, to find the item selected from the list box in Figure 7-8, you use the following formula:

=INDEX(A3:A10, E3)

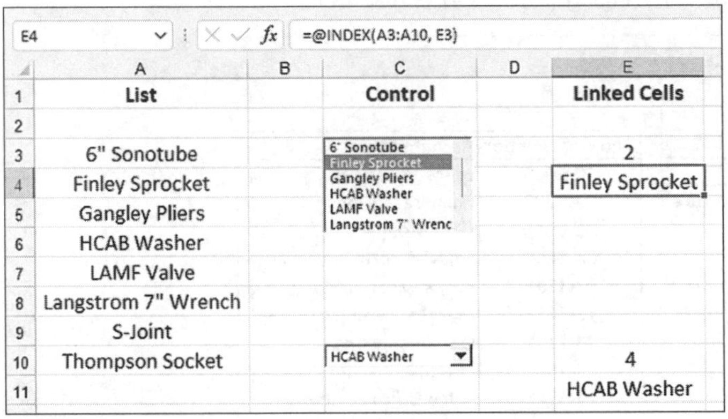

FIGURE 7-8 This worksheet uses INDEX to get the selected item from a list box and a combo box.

Using any column as the lookup column

One of the major disadvantages of the **VLOOKUP** function is that you must use the lookup table's leftmost column as the lookup column. (**HLOOKUP** suffers from a similar problem: The lookup table's topmost row must be used as the lookup row.) This isn't a problem if you remember to structure your lookup table accordingly, but that might not be possible in some cases, particularly if you inherit the data from someone else.

Fortunately, you can use the **MATCH** and **INDEX** combination to use *any* table column as the lookup column. For example, consider the parts database shown in Figure 7-9.

B2			fx	=INDEX(C6:C13, MATCH(B1, H6:H13, 0))						

	A	B	C	D	E	F	G	H
1	**Part Number**	D-178						
2	Quantity	57						
3								
4	**Parts Database**							
5	**Division**	**Description**	**Quantity**	**Cost**	**Total Cost**	**Retail**	**Gross Margin**	**Number**
6	4	Gangley Pliers	57	$10.47	$ 596.79	$17.95	71.4%	D-178
7	3	HCAB Washer	856	$ 0.12	$ 102.72	$ 0.25	108.3%	A-201
8	3	Finley Sprocket	357	$ 1.57	$ 560.49	$ 2.95	87.9%	C-098
9	2	6" Sonotube	86	$15.24	$1,310.64	$19.95	30.9%	B-111
10	4	Langstrom 7" Wrench	75	$18.69	$1,401.75	$27.95	49.5%	D-017
11	3	Thompson Socket	298	$ 3.11	$ 926.78	$ 5.95	91.3%	C-321
12	1	S-Joint	155	$ 6.85	$1,061.75	$ 9.95	45.3%	A-182
13	2	LAMF Valve	482	$ 4.01	$1,932.82	$ 6.95	73.3%	B-047

FIGURE 7-9 In this lookup table, the lookup values are in column H, and the value you want to find is in column C.

Column H contains the unique part numbers, so that's what you want to use as the lookup column. The data you need is the quantity in column C. To accomplish this, you first find the part number (as given by the value in B1) in column H using **MATCH**:

```
MATCH(B1, H6:H13, 0)
```

When you know which row contains the part, you plug this result into an **INDEX** function that operates only on the column that contains the data you want (column C):

```
=INDEX(C6:C13, MATCH(B1, H6:H13, 0))
```

Creating row-and-column lookups

So far, all the lookups you've seen have been one-dimensional, meaning that they searched for a lookup value in a single column or row. However, in many situations, you need a two-dimensional approach. This means that you need to look up a value in a column *and* a value in a row and then return the data value at the intersection of the two. I call this a *row-and-column lookup*.

You do this by using *two* **MATCH** functions: one to calculate the **INDEX** function's *row_num* argument, and the other to calculate the **INDEX** function's *column_num* argument. Figure 7-10 shows an example.

| B3 | : × ✓ f_x | =INDEX(A7:H14, MATCH(B1, H7:H14, 0), MATCH(B2, A6:H6, 0)) |

	A	B	C	D	E	F	G	H
1	Part Number	D-178						
2	Field Name	Cost						
3	Value	10.47						
4								
5	Parts Database							
6	Division	Description	Quantity	Cost	Total Cost	Retail	Gross Margin	Number
7	4	Gangley Pliers	57	$10.47	$ 596.79	$17.95	71.4%	D-178
8	3	HCAB Washer	856	$ 0.12	$ 102.72	$ 0.25	108.3%	A-201
9	3	Finley Sprocket	357	$ 1.57	$ 560.49	$ 2.95	87.9%	C-098
10	2	6" Sonotube	86	$15.24	$1,310.64	$19.95	30.9%	B-111
11	4	Langstrom 7" Wrench	75	$18.69	$1,401.75	$27.95	49.5%	D-017
12	3	Thompson Socket	298	$ 3.11	$ 926.78	$ 5.95	91.3%	C-321
13	1	S-Joint	155	$ 6.85	$1,061.75	$ 9.95	45.3%	A-182
14	2	LAMF Valve	482	$ 4.01	$1,932.82	$ 6.95	73.3%	B-047

FIGURE 7-10 To perform a two-dimensional row-and-column lookup, use MATCH functions to calculate both the row and the column values for the INDEX function.

The idea here is to use both the part numbers (column H) and the field names (row 6) to return specific values from the parts database.

The part number is entered into cell B1, and getting the corresponding row in the parts table is no different from what you did in the previous section:

```
MATCH(B1, H7:H14, 0)
```

The field name is entered into cell B2. Getting the corresponding column number requires the following **MATCH** expression:

```
MATCH(B2, A6:H6, 0)
```

These provide the **INDEX** function's *row_num* and *column_num* arguments (see cell B3):

```
=INDEX(A7:H14, MATCH(B1, H7:H14, 0), MATCH(B2, A6:H6, 0))
```

Creating multiple-column lookups

Sometimes it's not enough to look up a value in a single column. For example, in a list of employee names, you might need to look up both the first name and the last name if they're in separate fields. One way to handle this is to create a new field that concatenates all the lookup values into a single item. However, it's possible to do this without going to the trouble of creating a new concatenated field.

The secret is to perform the concatenation within the **MATCH** function, as in this generic expression:

```
MATCH(value1 & value2, array1 & array2, match_type)
```

Here, *value1* and *value2* are the lookup values you want to work with, and *array1* and *array2* are the lookup columns. You can then plug the results into an array formula that uses **INDEX** to get the needed data:

```
=INDEX(reference, MATCH(value1 & value2, array1 & array2, match_type))
```

For example, Figure 7-11 shows a database of employees, with separate fields for the first name, last name, title, and more.

B3		: × ✓ fx	{=INDEX(C6:C14, MATCH(B1 & B2, A6:A14 & B6:B14, 0))}			
▲	A	B	C	D	E	F
1	**First Name**	Nancy				
2	**Last Name**	Davolio				
3	**Title**	Account Manager				
4						
5	**First Name**	**Last Name**	**Title**	**Title Of Courtesy**	**Birth Date**	**Hire Date**
6	Nancy	Davolio	Account Manager	Ms.	8-Dec-48	1-May-02
7	Andrew	Fuller	Vice President, Sales	Dr.	19-Feb-52	14-Aug-02
8	Janet	Leverling	Account Manager	Ms.	30-Aug-63	1-Apr-02
9	Margaret	Peacock	Account Manager	Mrs.	19-Sep-37	3-May-03
10	Steven	Buchanan	Sales Manager	Mr.	4-Mar-55	17-Oct-03
11	Michael	Suyama	Account Manager	Mr.	2-Jul-63	17-Oct-03
12	Robert	King	Account Manager	Mr.	29-May-60	2-Jan-04
13	Laura	Callahan	Inside Sales Coordinator	Ms.	9-Jan-58	5-Mar-04
14	Anne	Dodsworth	Account Manager	Ms.	27-Jan-66	15-Nov-04

FIGURE 7-11 To perform a two-column lookup, use MATCH to find a row based on the concatenated values of two or more columns.

The lookup values are in B1 (first name) and B2 (last name), and the lookup columns are A6:A14 (the First Name field) and B6:B14 (the Last Name field). Here's the MATCH function that looks up the required column:

```
MATCH(B1 & B2, A6:A14 & B6:B14, 0)
```

We want the specified employee's title, so the INDEX function looks in C6:C14 (the Title field). Here's the array formula in cell B3:

```
=INDEX(C6:C14, MATCH(B1 & B2, A6:A14 & B6:B14, 0))
```

Modern lookups with XLOOKUP

Okay, I've spent quite a bit of time showing you how to perform lookups in Excel, so you might be more than a little shocked that I'm now going to tell you to pretty much forget everything you've learned! Why? Because Microsoft has introduced a new lookup function called XLOOKUP that can do everything that VLOOKUP, HLOOKUP, MATCH, and INDEX can do, plus more!

Before getting to the specifics of XLOOKUP, let's check out the main drawbacks of the lookup functions you've seen so far:

- Formulas that use VLOOKUP or HLOOKUP are difficult to understand because first, you have to find the lookup range (the *table_array* argument) and then use the offset value (the *col_index_num* or *row_index_num* argument) to count the number of columns or rows to see where the result comes from. They redefine the word *cumbersome*!

- The **VLOOKUP** *col_index_num* argument (as well as the **HLOOKUP** *row_index_num* argument) are hard-coded integers that don't adjust if you insert or delete a column (or row) in your range or table.

- If you forget to set the optional *range_lookup* argument to **FALSE**, **VLOOKUP** or **HLOOKUP** might return inaccurate results because they default to non-exact matches.

- **VLOOKUP** can only look up values to the right, and **HLOOKUP** can only look up values down.

- Advanced lookups require convoluted and hard-to-fathom formulas that combine the **MATCH** and **INDEX** functions.

All of these problems vanish when you switch to the **XLOOKUP** function, as you see in the examples that follow.

The **XLOOKUP** function

Like the older **VLOOKUP** and **HLOOKUP** functions, the **XLOOKUP** function searches for a lookup value. The key differences are that with **XLOOKUP**, you specify the range or array to use for the lookup (rather than being forced to use the first column or row). Also, you specify the range or array from which the result is returned (rather than using the cumbersome column or row offset in a larger range). Here's the syntax for **XLOOKUP**:

```
XLOOKUP(lookup_value, lookup_array, return_array[, if_not_found] [, match_mode]
[, search_mode])
```

lookup_value	The value you want to find in *lookup_array*. You can enter a number, string, or reference.
lookup_array	The range or array to use for the lookup. You can use a range reference or a name.
return_array	The range or array from which the corresponding item is returned. You can use a range reference or a name. The number or rows and columns in *return_array* must match the number of rows and columns in *lookup_array*.
if_not_found	The value to return if **XLOOKUP** doesn't find *lookup_value* in *lookup_array*.
match_mode	An optional integer value that determines how Excel searches for *lookup_value* in *lookup_array*:
	0—**XLOOKUP** searches for the first exact match for *lookup_value*. If no exact match is found, the function returns **#N/A**. (This is the default.)
	-1—**XLOOKUP** searches for the first exact match for *lookup_value*. If no exact match is found, the function looks for the largest value that is less than *lookup_value*.
	1—**XLOOKUP** searches for the first exact match for *lookup_value*. If no exact match is found, the function looks for the smallest value that is greater than *lookup_value*.
	2—**XLOOKUP** searches using wildcard characters: **?** for any single character and ***** for any number of characters. (You can precede ? and * with a tilde (~) to search for those characters.)
search_mode	An optional integer value that determines how Excel performs the search for *lookup_value*:
	1—**XLOOKUP** starts the search at the first item. (This is the default.)
	-1—**XLOOKUP** starts the search at the last item.
	2—**XLOOKUP** runs a binary search when *lookup_array* is sorted in ascending order.
	-2—**XLOOKUP** runs a binary search when *lookup_array* is sorted in descending order.

Note that **XLOOKUP** can do both vertical and horizontal lookups (the "X" implies that the function is, in this sense, "directionally neutral"). That is, if *lookup_array* and *return_array* are columns, **XLOOKUP** does a vertical lookup; if *lookup_array* and *return_array* are rows, **XLOOKUP** does a horizontal lookup.

Looking up a customer account number with XLOOKUP

To demonstrate how much more straightforward **XLOOKUP** is compared to **VLOOKUP** and **HLOOKUP**, let's return to the lookup table I discussed earlier in the "Looking up a customer account number" section. In the earlier example, I used **VLOOKUP** to find an exact match for a specified account number and return the corresponding account name. Here's the **VLOOKUP** function that accomplished that task:

```
=VLOOKUP(B2, D3:E15, 2, FALSE)
```

Figure 7-12 shows the same worksheet, but this time with the following **XLOOKUP** function performing the same task:

```
=XLOOKUP(B2, D3:D15, E3:E15)
```

This function tells Excel to take the value in B2, look it up in the range D3:D15, and then return the corresponding item from the range E3:E15. What could be simpler?

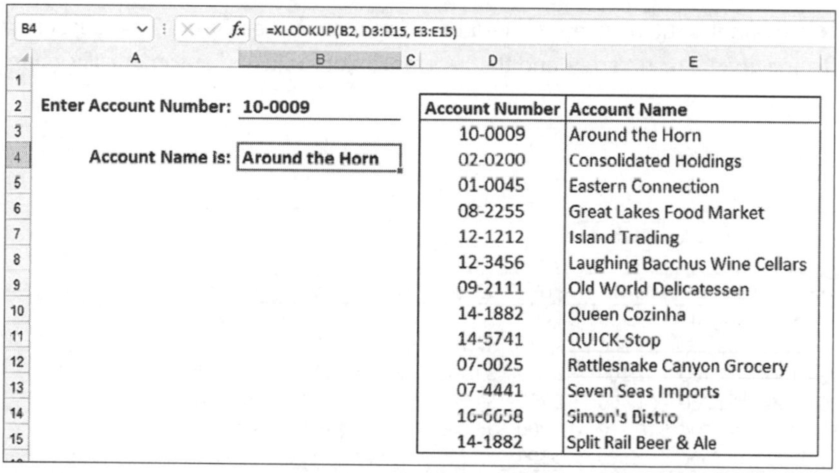

FIGURE 7-12 Using XLOOKUP to look up an account's name based on the entered account number.

Combining exact-match lookups with in-cell drop-down lists with XLOOKUP

Now I'll demonstrate the brittleness of **VLOOKUP** and **HLOOKUP** and show how **XLOOKUP** solves that problem. Let's return to the Expenses worksheet where I used an in-cell drop-down list to select a month, then looked up the expense total for that month (see "Combining exact-match lookups with in-cell drop-down lists"). Here's the **HLOOKUP** function used in the earlier example (see Figure 7-6):

```
=HLOOKUP(C9, C1:N7, 7, FALSE)
```

However, now let's see what happens when I insert a new row (**Cost of Goods**) into the Expenses range. As you can see in Figure 7-13, **HLOOKUP** now returns an incorrect result. Why? Because **HLOOKUP** uses a hard-coded row offset of **7** and that value didn't get adjusted automatically after I inserted the new row.

C11		fx	=HLOOKUP(C10, C1:N8, 7, FALSE)							
	A	B	C	D	E	F	G	H	I	J
1		EXPENSES	January	February	March	April	May	June	July	August
2		Advertising	$4,600	$4,200	$5,200	$4,600	$4,200	$5,200	$4,600	$4,200
3		Cost of Goods	$5,800	$5,300	$5,900	$6,000	$4,700	$5,600	$5,300	$5,500
4		Rent	$2,100	$2,100	$2,100	$2,100	$2,100	$2,100	$2,100	$2,100
5		Supplies	$1,300	$1,200	$1,400	$1,300	$1,200	$1,400	$1,300	$1,200
6		Salaries	$16,000	$16,000	$16,500	$16,000	$16,000	$16,500	$16,000	$16,000
7		Utilities	$500	$600	$600	$500	$600	$600	$500	$600
8		TOTAL	$30,300	$29,400	$31,700	$30,500	$28,800	$31,400	$29,800	$29,600
9										
10		Month	May							
11		Total	$600							
12										

FIGURE 7-13 After inserting the new Cost of Goods row, the HLOOKUP formula in C11 retuns an incorrect result.

By contrast, **XLOOKUP** handles the new row without breaking a sweat (see Figure 7-14) because it uses a range reference to specify the result array, and that reference gets adjusted automatically when you insert (or delete) a row:

```
=XLOOKUP(C9, C1:N1, C8:N8)
```

C11		fx	=XLOOKUP(C10, C1:N1, C8:N8)							
	A	B	C	D	E	F	G	H	I	J
1		EXPENSES	January	February	March	April	May	June	July	August
2		Advertising	$4,600	$4,200	$5,200	$4,600	$4,200	$5,200	$4,600	$4,200
3		Cost of Goods	$5,800	$5,300	$5,900	$6,000	$4,700	$5,600	$5,300	$5,500
4		Rent	$2,100	$2,100	$2,100	$2,100	$2,100	$2,100	$2,100	$2,100
5		Supplies	$1,300	$1,200	$1,400	$1,300	$1,200	$1,400	$1,300	$1,200
6		Salaries	$16,000	$16,000	$16,500	$16,000	$16,000	$16,500	$16,000	$16,000
7		Utilities	$500	$600	$600	$500	$600	$600	$500	$600
8		TOTAL	$30,300	$29,400	$31,700	$30,500	$28,800	$31,400	$29,800	$29,600
9										
10		Month	May							
11		Total	$28,800							
12										

FIGURE 7-14 XLOOKUP returns the correct result.

Using any column as the lookup column with XLOOKUP

With Excel's old lookup functions, to use any column (or row) as the lookup column, you bypass **VLOOKUP** and **HLOOKUP** (which only search the first column or row, respectively) and bring in the **MATCH** and **INDEX** functions. In an earlier section (see "Using any column as the lookup column"), I showed you how to look up a quantity given a part number using the following formula:

```
=INDEX(C6:C13, MATCH(B1, H6:H13, 0))
```

Unless you're very familiar with how **MATCH** and **INDEX** work, this formula will be as clear as mud. Here's the corresponding (and much more comprehensible) **XLOOKUP** version, which I've demonstrated in Figure 7-15:

```
=XLOOKUP(B1, H6:H13, C6:C13)
```

B2			✓	f_x	=XLOOKUP(B1, H6:H13, C6:C13)				
	A	B	C	D	E	F	G	H
1	**Part Number**	D-178						
2	**Quantity**	57						
3								
4	**Parts Database**							
5	**Division**	**Description**	**Quantity**	**Cost**	**Total Cost**	**Retail**	**Gross Margin**	**Number**
6	4	Gangley Pliers	57	$10.47	$ 596.79	$17.95	71.4%	D-178
7	3	HCAB Washer	856	$ 0.12	$ 102.72	$ 0.25	108.3%	A-201
8	3	Finley Sprocket	357	$ 1.57	$ 560.49	$ 2.95	87.9%	C-098
9	2	6" Sonotube	86	$15.24	$1,310.64	$19.95	30.9%	B-111
10	4	Langstrom 7" Wrench	75	$18.69	$1,401.75	$27.95	49.5%	D-017
11	3	Thompson Socket	298	$ 3.11	$ 926.78	$ 5.95	91.3%	C-321
12	1	S-Joint	155	$ 6.85	$1,061.75	$ 9.95	45.3%	A-182
13	2	LAMF Valve	482	$ 4.01	$1,932.82	$ 6.95	73.3%	B-047

FIGURE 7-15 In this lookup table, the lookup values are in column H, and the value you want to find is in column C.

Creating multiple-column lookups with XLOOKUP

As a final **XLOOKUP** example, let's see how this versatile function handles the problem of multiple-column lookups that I described earlier (see "Creating multiple-column lookups"). The solution in the earlier section used the following close-to-indecipherable array formula:

```
=INDEX(C6:C14, MATCH(B1 & B2, A6:A14 & B6:B14, 0))
```

To convert this formula to one that uses **XLOOKUP**, we can first note that it's possible to nest one **XLOOKUP** function inside another. In the case of looking up an employee's title given a first name and a last name, we can use one **XLOOKUP** function to look up the first name, then use that result as the *lookup_value* argument of a second **XLOOKUP** function. Here's the result, which is demonstrated in Figure 7-16:

```
=XLOOKUP(XLOOKUP(B1, A6:A14, B6:B14), B6:B14, C6:C14)
```

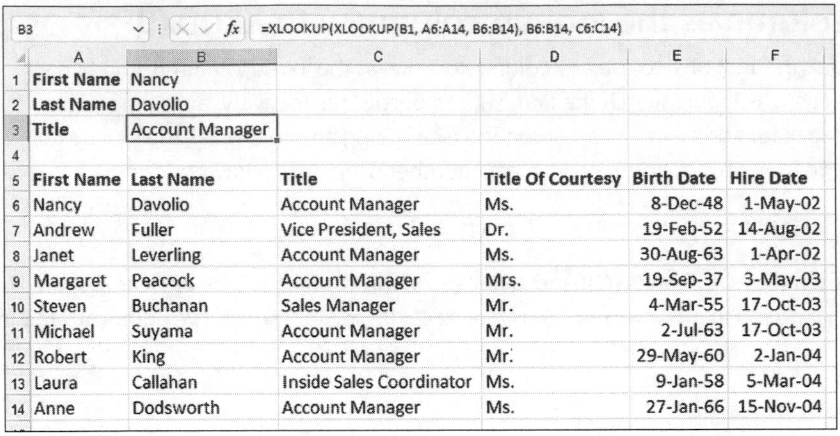

| B3 | | : × ✓ *fx* | =XLOOKUP(XLOOKUP(B1, A6:A14, B6:B14), B6:B14, C6:C14) | | | |

⊿	A	B	C	D	E	F
1	**First Name**	Nancy				
2	**Last Name**	Davolio				
3	**Title**	Account Manager				
4						
5	**First Name**	**Last Name**	**Title**	**Title Of Courtesy**	**Birth Date**	**Hire Date**
6	Nancy	Davolio	Account Manager	Ms.	8-Dec-48	1-May-02
7	Andrew	Fuller	Vice President, Sales	Dr.	19-Feb-52	14-Aug-02
8	Janet	Leverling	Account Manager	Ms.	30-Aug-63	1-Apr-02
9	Margaret	Peacock	Account Manager	Mrs.	19-Sep-37	3-May-03
10	Steven	Buchanan	Sales Manager	Mr.	4-Mar-55	17-Oct-03
11	Michael	Suyama	Account Manager	Mr.	2-Jul-63	17-Oct-03
12	Robert	King	Account Manager	Mr.	29-May-60	2-Jan-04
13	Laura	Callahan	Inside Sales Coordinator	Ms.	9-Jan-58	5-Mar-04
14	Anne	Dodsworth	Account Manager	Ms.	27-Jan-66	15-Nov-04

FIGURE 7-16 To perform a two-column lookup, nest one XLOOKUP function inside another.

An alternative solution is an array formula that uses a single **XLOOKUP** function to match both columns at once:

```
=XLOOKUP(B1 & B2, A6:A14 & B6:B14, C6:C14)
```

CHAPTER 8

Working with date and time functions

In this chapter, you will:

- Learn how Excel deals with dates and times

- Take a tour of Excel's extensive library of date-related worksheet functions

- Try out many of Excel's time-related worksheet functions

Excel's date and time functions enable you to convert dates and times to serial numbers and perform mathematical operations on those numbers. This capability is useful for such things as accounts receivable aging, project scheduling, time-management applications, and much more. This chapter introduces you to Excel's date and time functions and puts them through their paces with many practical examples.

How Excel deals with dates and times

Excel uses *serial numbers* to represent specific dates and times. To get a date serial number, Excel uses December 31, 1899, as an arbitrary starting point and then counts the number of days that have passed since then. For example, the date serial number for January 1, 1900, is 1; for January 2, 1900, it's 2; and so on. Table 8-1 displays some examples of date serial numbers.

TABLE 8-1 Examples of date serial numbers

Serial Number	Date
366	December 31, 1900
16229	June 6, 1944
44926	December 31, 2022

To get a time serial number, Excel expresses time as a decimal fraction of the 24-hour day to get a number between 0 and 1. The starting point, midnight, is given the value **0**, so noon—halfway through the day—has a serial number of **0.5**. Table 8-2 displays some examples of time serial numbers.

TABLE 8-2 Examples of time serial numbers

Serial Number	Time
0.25	6:00:00 a.m.
0.375	9:00:00 a.m.
0.70833	5:00:00 p.m.
.99999	11:59:59 p.m.

You can combine the two types of serial numbers. For example, 44926.5 represents noon on December 31, 2022.

The advantage of using serial numbers in this way is that it makes calculations involving dates and times very easy. A date or time is really just a number, so any mathematical operation you can perform on a number can also be performed on a date. This is invaluable for worksheets that track delivery times, monitor accounts receivable or accounts payable aging, calculate invoice discount dates, and so on.

Entering dates and times

Although it's true that serial numbers make it easier for the computer to manipulate dates and times, it's not the best format for humans to comprehend. For example, the number 25404.95555 is meaningless, but the moment it represents (July 20, 1969, at 10:56 PM EDT) is one of the great moments in history (the *Apollo 11* moon landing). Fortunately, Excel takes care of the conversion between these formats so that you never have to worry about it. If you live in the United States, you can enter a date or time by using any of the formats shown in Table 8-3. (Other locales use different formats, so you'll need to use the format defined for your location.)

TABLE 8-3 Excel date and time formats for the United States

Format	Example
m/d/yyyy	8/23/2022
d-mmm-yy	23-Aug-22
d-mmm	23-Aug (Excel assumes the current year.)
mmm-yy	Aug-22 (Excel assumes the first day of the month.)
h:mm:ss AM/PM	10:35:10 p.m.
h:mm AM/PM	10:35 p.m.
h:mm:ss	22:35:10
h:mm	22:35
m/d/y h:mm	8/23/22 22:35

> **Tip** Here are a couple of shortcuts that will let you enter dates and times quickly. To enter the current date in a cell, press Ctrl+; (semicolon). To enter the current time, press Ctrl+: (colon).

Table 8-3 shows Excel's built-in formats, but these aren't set in stone. You're free to mix and match these formats as long as you observe the following rules:

- You can use either the forward slash (**/**) or the hyphen (**-**) as a date separator. Always use a colon (**:**) as a time separator.

- You can combine any date and time formats, as long as you separate them with a space.

- You can enter date and time values using either uppercase or lowercase letters. Excel automatically adjusts the capitalization to its standard format.

- To display times using the 12-hour clock, include either **am** (or just **a**) or **pm** (or just **p**). If you leave these off, Excel uses the 24-hour clock.

Excel and two-digit years

Entering two-digit years (such as **22** for 2022 and **99** for 1999) is problematic in Excel. To see why, you need to know that Excel interprets the two-digit years 00 through 49 as the years 2000 through 2049, and it interprets 50 through 99 as the years 1950 through 1999. Therefore, you could throw a monkey wrench into your calculations by using a date such as 8/23/50 to mean August 23, 2050 because Excel treats it as August 23, 1950.

The easiest solution to both problems is to always use four-digit years to avoid ambiguity. Alternatively, you can put off the problem by changing how Excel and Windows interpret two-digit years. Here are the steps to follow in Windows 11, Windows 10, Windows 8, and Windows 7:

1. Open Control Panel:

   - **Windows 11 and Windows 10**—In the taskbar's **Search** box, enter **control** and select **Control Panel**.
   - **Windows 8**—Press Windows +X and then select **Control Panel**.
   - **Windows 7**—Select **Start** > **Control Panel**.

2. In Windows 11 or 10, select the **Change Date, Time, or Number Formats** link and skip to step 4; in Windows 8 or 7, select **Clock, Language, and Region**.

3. Select the **Change Date, Time, or Number Formats** link. The **Region** dialog box appears.

4. In the **Formats** tab, select **Additional Settings**. The **Customize Format** dialog box appears.

5. Select the **Date** tab.

6. Use the **When a Two-Digit Year Is Entered, Interpret It As a Year Between** spinner to adjust the maximum year in which a two-digit year is interpreted as a twenty-first-century date. For example, if you never use dates prior to 1960, you could change the spin box value to 2059, which means Excel interprets two-digit years as dates between 1960 and 2059 (see Figure 8-1).

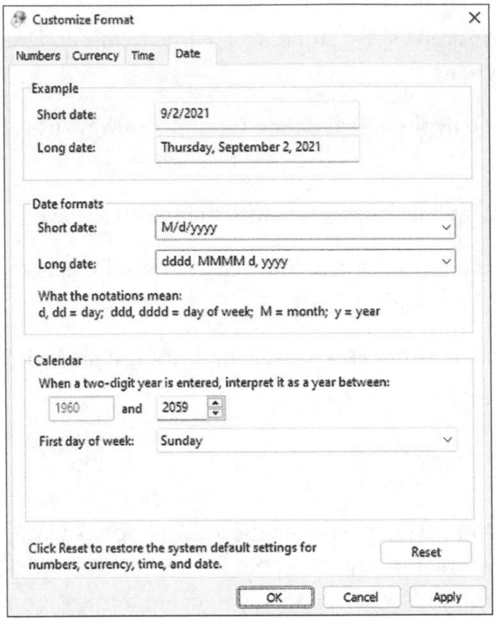

FIGURE 8-1 Use the Date tab to adjust how Windows (and, therefore, Excel) interprets two-digit years.

7. Select **OK** to return to the Region dialog box.

8. Select **OK** to put the new setting into effect.

Using Excel's date functions

Excel's date functions work with or return date serial numbers. All of Excel's date-related functions are listed in Table 8-4. (For the *date* arguments, you can use any valid Excel date.)

TABLE 8-4 Excel's date functions

Function	Description
DATE(*year, month, day*)	Returns the serial number of a date, in which *year* is a number from 1900 to 9999, *month* is a number representing the month of the year, and *day* is a number representing the day of the month.
DATEVALUE(*date_text*)	Converts a date from text to a serial number.
DAY(*date*)	Extracts the day component from the date given by *date*.
DAYS(*end_date, start_date*)	Returns the number of days between *start_date* and *end_date*.
DAYS360(*start_date, end_date* [,*method*])	Returns the number of days between *start_date* and *end_date*, based on a 360-day year.

Function	Description
EDATE(*start_date, months*)	Returns the serial number of a date that is the specified number of *months* before or after *start_date*.
EOMONTH(*start_date, months*)	Returns the serial number of the last day of the month that is the specified number of *months* before or after *start_date*.
ISOWEEKNUM(*date*)	Returns a number that corresponds to the ISO week number for *date*.
MONTH(*date*)	Extracts the month component from the date given by *date* (January = **1**).
NETWORKDAYS(*start_date, end_date* [, *holidays*])	Returns the number of working days between *start_date* and *end_date*; doesn't include weekends and any dates specified by *holidays*.
NETWORKDAYS.INTL(*start_date, end_date* [, *weekend, holidays*])	Returns the number of working days between *start_date* and *end_date*; same as **NETWORKDAYS**, but also enables you to specify when weekends occur.
TODAY	Returns the serial number of the current date.
WEEKDAY(*date* [, *return_type*])	Converts a serial number to a day of the week (Sunday = **1**).
WEEKNUM(*date* [, *return_type*])	Returns a number that corresponds to where the week that includes *date* falls numerically during the year.
WORKDAY(*start_date, days* [, *holidays*])	Returns the serial number of the day that is *days* working days from *start_date*; weekends and *holidays* are excluded.
WORKDAY.INTL(*start_date, days* [, *weekend, holidays*])	Returns the serial number of the day that is *days* working days from *start_date*; same as **WORKDAY**, but also enables you to specify when weekends occur.
YEAR(*date*)	Extracts the year component from the date given by *date*.
YEARFRAC(*start_date, end_date, basis*)	Converts the number of days between *start_date* and *end_date* into a fraction of a year.

Returning a date

If you need a date for an expression operand or a function argument, you can enter it by hand if you have a specific date in mind. Much of the time, however, you need more flexibility, such as always entering the current date or building a date from day, month, and year components. Excel offers three functions that can help: **TODAY**, **DATE**, and **DATEVALUE**. (The NOW function returns both the current date and the current time; see "NOW: Returning the current time," later in this chapter.)

TODAY: Returning the current date

When you need to use the current date in a formula, a function, or an expression, use the **TODAY** function, which doesn't take arguments:

TODAY()

This function returns the serial number of the current date, with midnight as the assumed time. For example, if today's date is December 31, 2022, the **TODAY** function returns the following serial number (although by default, what you see in the cell is the date in m/d/yyyy format):

44926

Note that **TODAY** is a dynamic function that doesn't always return the same value. Each time you edit the formula, enter another formula, recalculate the worksheet, or reopen the workbook, **TODAY** updates its value to return the current system date.

DATE: Returning any date

A date consists of three components: the year, month, and day. It often happens that a worksheet generates one or more of these components, and you need some way of building a proper date out of them. You can do that by using Excel's **DATE** function:

DATE(*year*, *month*, *day*)

year	The year component of the date (a number between 1900 and 9999)
month	The month component of the date
day	The day component of the date

> ⚠ **Caution** Excel's date inconsistencies rear up again with the **DATE** function. That's because if you enter a two-digit year (or even a three-digit year), Excel converts the number into a year value by adding 1900. So, entering **22** as the *year* argument gives you 1922, not 2022. To avoid problems, *always* use a four-digit year when entering the **DATE** function's *year* argument.

For example, the following expression returns Christmas Day in 2022:

DATE(2022, 12, 25)

Note, too, that **DATE** adjusts for wrong month and day values. For example, the following expression returns January 1, 2023:

DATE(2022, 12, 32)

Here, **DATE** adds the extra day to return the date of the next day. (There are 31 days in December.) Similarly, the following expression returns January 25, 2023:

DATE(2022, 13, 25)

DATEVALUE: Converting a string to a date

If you have a date value in string form, you can convert it to a date serial number by using the **DATEVALUE** function:

DATEVALUE(*date_text*)

date_text	The string containing the date

For example, the following expression returns the date serial number for the string August 23, 2022:

```
DATEVALUE("August 23, 2022")
```

Returning parts of a date

The three components of a date—year, month, and day—can also be extracted individually from a given date. This might not seem all that interesting at first, but many useful techniques arise from working with a date's component parts. A date's components are extracted using Excel's **YEAR**, **MONTH**, and **DAY** functions.

The YEAR function

The **YEAR** function returns a four-digit number that corresponds to the year component of a specified date:

YEAR(*date*)

date	The date (or a string representation of the date) you want to work with

For example, if today is August 23, 2022, the following expression will return **2022**:

YEAR(**TODAY**())

The MONTH function

The **MONTH** function returns a number between 1 and 12 that corresponds to the month component of a specified date:

MONTH(*date*)

date	The date (or a string representation of the date) you want to work with

For example, the following expression returns **8**:

MONTH("August 23, 2022")

The DAY function

The **DAY** function returns a number between 1 and 31 that corresponds to the day component of a specified date:

DAY(*date*)

date	The date (or a string representation of the date) you want to work with

For example, the following expression returns **23**:

```
DAY("8/23/2022")
```

The WEEKDAY function

The **WEEKDAY** function returns a number that corresponds to the day of the week upon which a specified date falls:

```
WEEKDAY(date [, return_type])
```

date	The date (or a string representation of the date) you want to work with.
return_type	An integer that determines how the value returned by **WEEKDAY** corresponds to the days of the week: **1:** The return values are **1** (Sunday) through **7** (Saturday); this is the default. **2:** The return values are **1** (Monday) through **7** (Sunday). **3:** The return values are **0** (Monday) through **6** (Sunday).

For example, the following expression returns **6** because August 23, 2022, is a Friday:

```
WEEKDAY("8/23/2022")
```

The WEEKNUM function

The **WEEKNUM** function returns a number that corresponds to where the week that includes a specified date falls numerically during the year:

```
WEEKNUM(date [, return_type])
```

date	The date (or a string representation of the date) you want to work with.
return_type	An integer that determines how **WEEKNUM** interprets the start of the week: **1:** The week begins on Sunday; this is the default. **2:** The week begins on Monday.

For example, the following expression returns **35** because August 23, 2022, falls in the 35th week of 2022:

```
WEEKNUM("August 23, 2022")
```

> **Tip** You might need to return a week number that corresponds to ISO (International Standards Organization) 8601, the international standard for representing dates and times. The ISO 8601 week-numbering year always begins on the week with the year's first Thursday, so there will be dates at the beginning of the year and the end of the year where the ISO week number differs from the calendar week number. To always return the ISO week number, use Excel's **ISOWEEKNUM**(*date*) function.

Returning a date *X* years, months, or days from now

You can take advantage of the fact that, as I mentioned earlier, **DATE** automatically adjusts wrong month and day values by applying formulas to one or more of the **DATE** function's arguments. The most common use for this is returning a date that occurs *X* number of years, months, or days from now (or from any date).

For example, suppose that you want to know which day of the week the 4th of July falls on next year. Here's a formula that figures it out:

```
=WEEKDAY(DATE(YEAR(TODAY())) + 1, 7, 4)
```

As another example, if you want to work with whatever date is 6 months from today, you'd use the following expression:

```
DATE(YEAR(TODAY()), MONTH(TODAY()) + 6, DAY(TODAY()))
```

Given this technique, you've probably figured out that you can return a date that is *X* days from now (or whenever) by adding to the day component of the **DATE** function. For example, here's an expression that returns a date 30 days from now:

```
DATE(YEAR(TODAY()), MONTH(TODAY()), DAY(TODAY() + 30))
```

This is overkill, however, because date addition and subtraction work at the day level in Excel. That is, if you simply add or subtract a number to or from a date, Excel adds or subtracts that number of days. For example, to return a date 30 days from now, you need only use the following expression:

```
TODAY() + 30
```

A workday alternative: The **WORKDAY** function

Adding days to or subtracting days from a date is straightforward, but the basic calculation includes *all* days: workdays, weekends, and holidays. In many cases, you might need to ignore weekends and holidays and return a date that's a specified number of workdays from some original date.

You can do this by using the **WORKDAY** function, which returns a date that is a specified number of working days from some starting date:

```
WORKDAY(start_date, days [, holidays])
```

start_date	The original date (or a string representation of the date).
days	The number of workdays before or after start_date. Use a positive number to return a later date; use a negative number to return an earlier date. Noninteger values are truncated (that is, the decimal part is ignored).
holidays	A list of dates to exclude from the calculation. This can be a range of dates or an array constant—that is, a series of date serial numbers or date strings, separated by commas and surrounded by braces (**{}**).

For example, the following expression returns a date that is 30 workdays from today:

```
WORKDAY(TODAY(), 30)
```

Here's another expression that returns the date that is 30 workdays from December 1, 2022, excluding December 25, 2022, and January 1, 2023:

```
=WORKDAY("12/1/2022", 30, {"12/25/2022","1/1/2023"})
```

> **Tip** It's possible to calculate the various holidays that occur within a year and place the dates within a range for use as the WORKDAY function's **holidays** argument. See "Calculating holiday dates," later in this chapter.

By default, WORKDAY doesn't include weekends, which it defines as Saturdays and Sundays. If your weekends fall on different days, you need to use the WORKDAY.INTL function, which adds a *weekend* argument:

```
WORKDAY.INTL(start_date, days [weekend, holidays])
```

The *weekend* argument can take one of two forms:

- A string of seven digits, each of which is either 0 or 1. The digits correspond to the days of the week from Monday through Sunday, where 0 means the day is a workday, and 1 means the day is a weekend day. So, for example, the string "1100000" designates Monday and Tuesday as weekend days, while the string "0010001" designates Wednesday and Sunday as weekend days.

- A numeric code that represents a predefined set of weekend days. Table 8-5 lists the codes you can use.

TABLE 8-5 Codes to use for the **WORKDAY.INTL** function's *weekend* argument

Code	Weekend Days
1 (this is the default)	Saturday, Sunday
2	Sunday, Monday
3	Monday, Tuesday
4	Tuesday, Wednesday
5	Wednesday, Thursday
6	Thursday, Friday
7	Friday, Saturday
11	Sunday only
12	Monday only
13	Tuesday only
14	Wednesday only
15	Thursday only
16	Friday only
17	Saturday only

Adding X months: A problem

You should be aware that adding X months to a specified date's month component won't always return the result you expect. The problem is that the months have a varying number of days. So, if you add a certain number of months to a date that falls on or near the end of a month, and the future month does not have the same number of days, Excel adjusts the day component accordingly.

For example, suppose that A1 contains the date 1/31/2023, and consider the following formula:

```
=DATE(YEAR(A1), MONTH(A1) + 3, DAY(A1))
```

You might expect this formula to return the last date in April as the result. Unfortunately, adding three months returns the wrong date, 4/31/2023 (there are only 30 days in April), which Excel automatically converts to 5/1/2023.

You can avoid this problem by using two functions: **EDATE** and **EOMONTH**.

The **EDATE** function

The **EDATE** function returns a date that's the specified number of months before or after a starting date:

```
EDATE(start_date, months)
```

start_date	The original date (or a string representation of the date).
months	The number of months before or after *start_date*. Use a positive number to return a later date; use a negative number to return an earlier date. Noninteger values are truncated. (That is, the decimal part is ignored.)

The nice thing about the **EDATE** function is that it performs a "smart" calculation when working with dates at or near the end of the month: If the day component of the returned date doesn't exist (for example, April 31), **EDATE** returns the last day of the month (April 30).

The **EDATE** function is useful for calculating the coupon payment dates for bond issues. Given the bond's maturity date, you calculate the bond's first payment as follows (assuming the bond was issued this year and the maturity date is in a cell named **MaturityDate**):

```
=DATE(YEAR(TODAY()), MONTH(MaturityDate), DAY(MaturityDate))
```

If this result is in cell A1, the following formula will return the date of the next coupon payment:

```
=EDATE(A1, 6)
```

The **EOMONTH** function

The **EOMONTH** function returns the date of the last day of the month that's the specified number of months before or after a starting date:

```
EOMONTH(start_date, months)
```

start_date	The original date (or a string representation of the date).
months	The number of months before or after *start_date*. Use a positive number to return a later date; use a negative number to return an earlier date. Noninteger values are truncated. (That is, the decimal part is ignored.)

For example, the following formula returns the last day of the month three months from now:

```
=EOMONTH(TODAY(), 3)
```

Returning the last day of any month

The EOMONTH function returns the last date of some month in the future or the past. However, what if you have a date, and you want to know the last day of the month in which that date appears?

You can calculate this by using yet another trick involving the DATE function's capability to adjust wrong values for date components. You want a formula that returns the last day of a particular month. You can't specify the *day* argument in the DATE function directly because the months can have 28, 29, 30, or 31 days. Instead, you can take advantage of an apparently trivial fact: The last day of any month is always the day *before* the first day of the next month. The number before 1 is 0, so you can plug in **0** to the DATE function as the *day* argument:

```
=DATE(YEAR(MyDate), MONTH(MyDate) + 1, 0)
```

Here, assume that MyDate is the date you want to work with.

Determining a person's birthday, given the birth date

If you know a person's birth date, determining that person's birthday is straightforward: Just keep the month and day the same and substitute the current year for the year of birth. To accomplish this in a formula, you could use the following:

```
=DATE(YEAR(NOW()), MONTH(Birthdate), DAY(Birthdate))
```

Here, I'm assuming the person's date of birth is in a cell named Birthdate. The YEAR(NOW()) component extracts the current year, and MONTH(Birthdate) and DAY(Birthdate) extract the month and day, respectively, from the person's date of birth. Combine these into the DATE function, and you have the birthday.

Returning the date of the *n*th occurrence of a weekday in a month

It's a common date task to have to figure out the *n*th weekday in a given month. For example, you might need to schedule a budget meeting for the first Monday of each month, or you might want to plan the annual company picnic for the third Sunday in June. These are tricky calculations, to be sure, but Excel's date functions are up to the task.

As with many other complex formulas, the best place to start is with what you know for sure. In this case, you always know for sure the date of the first day of whatever month you're dealing with. For example, Labor Day always occurs on the first Monday in September, so you could begin with

September 1 and know that the date you seek is some number of days after that. The formula begins like this:

```
=DATE(Year, Month, 1) + days
```

Here, *Year* is the year in which you want the date to fall, and *Month* is the number of the month you want to work with. The *days* value is what you need to calculate.

To simplify things for now, let's assume that you're trying to find a date that's the first occurrence of a particular weekday in a month (such as Labor Day, the first Monday in September).

Using the first of the month as your starting point, you need to ask whether the weekday you're working with is less than the weekday of the first of the month. (By "less than," I mean that the WEEKDAY value of the day of the week you're working with is numerically smaller than the WEEKDAY value of the first of the month.) In the Labor Day example, September 1, 2022, falls on a Sunday (WEEKDAY equals **1**), so the Monday (WEEKDAY equals **2**) is greater.

The result of this comparison determines how many days you add to the 1st to get the date you seek:

- If the day of the week you're working with is less than the first of the month, the date you seek is the first plus the result of the following expression:

```
7 - WEEKDAY(DATE(Year, Month, 1)) + Weekday
```

- Here, *Weekday* is the WEEKDAY value of the day of the week you're working with. Here's the expression for the Labor Day example:

```
7 - WEEKDAY(DATE(2022, 9, 1)) + 2
```

- If the day of the week you're working with is greater than or equal to the first of the month, the date you seek is the first plus the result of the following expression:

```
Weekday - WEEKDAY(DATE(Year, Month, 1))
```

- Again, *Weekday* is the WEEKDAY value of the day of the week you're working with. Here's the expression for the Labor Day example:

```
2 - WEEKDAY(DATE(2022, 9, 1))
```

A basic **IF** function can handle these conditions. Here, then, is the generic formula for calculating the first occurrence of a *Weekday* in a given *Year* and *Month:*

```
=DATE(Year, Month, 1) +
    IF(Weekday < WEEKDAY(DATE(Year, Month, 1)),
    7 - WEEKDAY(DATE(Year, Month, 1)) + Weekday,
    Weekday - WEEKDAY(DATE(Year, Month, 1)))
```

Here's the formula for calculating the date of Labor Day in 2022:

```
=DATE(2022, 9, 1) +
    IF(2 < WEEKDAY(DATE(2022, 9, 1)),
    7 - WEEKDAY(DATE(2022, 9, 1)) + 2,
    2 - WEEKDAY(DATE(2022, 9, 1)))
```

Generalizing this formula for the *n*th occurrence of a weekday is straightforward: The second occurrence comes one week after the first, the third occurrence comes two weeks after the first, and so on. Here's a generic expression to calculate the extra number of days to add (where *n* is an integer that represents the *n*th occurrence):

```
(n - 1) * 7
```

Here, then, in generic form, is the final formula for calculating the *n*th occurrence of a *Weekday* in a given *Year* and *Month*:

```
=DATE(Year, Month, 1) +
    IF(Weekday < WEEKDAY(DATE(Year, Month, 1)),
    7 - WEEKDAY(DATE(Year, Month, 1)) + Weekday,
    Weekday - WEEKDAY(DATE(Year, Month, 1))) +
    (n - 1) * 7
```

For example, the following formula calculates the date of the third Sunday (**WEEKDAY** equals **1**) in June for 2022:

```
=DATE(2022, 6, 1) +

    IF(1 < WEEKDAY(DATE(2022, 6, 1)),
    7 - WEEKDAY(DATE(2022, 6, 1)) + 1,
    1 - WEEKDAY(DATE(2022, 6, 1))) +
    (3 - 1) * 7
```

Figure 8-2 shows a worksheet used for calculating the *n*th occurrence of a weekday.

The input cells are as follows:

- **B1:** The number of the occurrence.

- **B2:** The number of the weekday. (The formula in C2 shows the name of the entered weekday.)

- **B3:** The number of the month. (The formula in C3 shows the name of the entered month.)

- **B4:** The year.

> **Note** You can work with all the examples in this chapter by downloading Chapter08.xslx from either of the companion content sites mentioned in the Introduction.

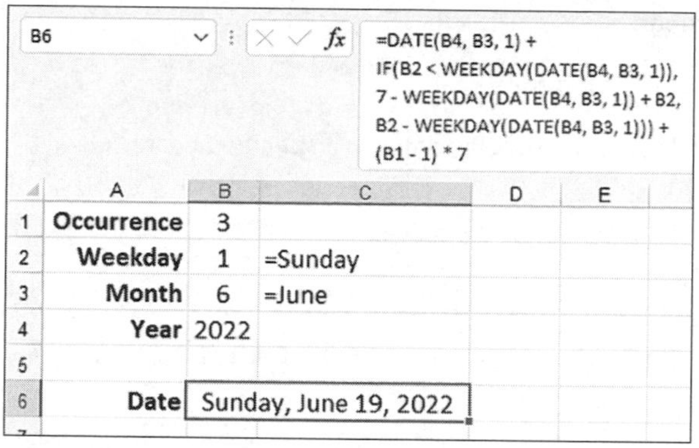

FIGURE 8-2 This worksheet calculates the *n*th occurrence of a specified weekday in a given year and month.

The date calculation appears in cell B6. Here's the formula:

```
=DATE(B4, B3, 1) +
    IF(B2 < WEEKDAY(DATE(B4, B3, 1)),
    7 - WEEKDAY(DATE(B4, B3, 1)) + B2,
    B2 - WEEKDAY(DATE(B4, B3, 1))) +
    (B1 - 1) * 7
```

Calculating holiday dates

Given the formula from the previous section, it becomes a relative breeze to calculate the dates for most floating holidays (that is, holidays that occur on the *n*th weekday of a month instead of on a specific date each year, as do holidays such as Christmas, Independence Day, and Canada Day).

Here are the standard statutory floating holidays in the United States:

- **Martin Luther King Jr. Day:** Third Monday in January
- **Presidents Day:** Third Monday in February
- **Memorial Day:** Last Monday in May
- **Labor Day:** First Monday in September
- **Columbus Day:** Second Monday in October
- **Thanksgiving Day:** Fourth Thursday in November

Here's the list for Canada:

- **Victoria Day:** Monday on or before May 24
- **Good Friday:** Friday before Easter Sunday

- **Labor Day:** First Monday in September

- **Thanksgiving Day:** Second Monday in October

Figure 8-3 shows a worksheet used to calculate the holiday dates in a specified year.

F4		× ✓ fx	=DATE($B$1, D4, 1) + IF(C4 < WEEKDAY(DATE($B$1, D4, 1)), 7 - WEEKDAY(DATE($B$1, D4, 1)) + C4, C4 - WEEKDAY(DATE($B$1, D4, 1))) + (B4 - 1) * 7

	A	B	C	D	E	F
1	Year:	2022				
2	Holidays (U.S.)	Occurrence or Day	Weekday	Month	When It Occurs	Date
3	New Year's Day	1		1	January 1	Sat Jan 1, 2022
4	Martin Luther King, Jr. Day	3	2	1	3rd Monday in January	Mon Jan 17, 2022
5	President's Day	3	2	2	3rd Monday in February	Mon Feb 21, 2022
6	Memorial Day	1	2	6	Last Monday in May (subtract 7 days from 1st Monday in June)	Mon May 30, 2022
7	Independence Day	4		7	July 4	Mon Jul 4, 2022
8	Labor Day	1	2	9	1st Monday in September	Mon Sep 5, 2022
9	Columbus Day	2	2	10	2nd Monday in October	Mon Oct 10, 2022
10	Veterans Day	11		11	November 11	Fri Nov 11, 2022
11	Thanksgiving Day	4	5	11	4th Thursday in November	Thu Nov 24, 2022
12	Christmas Day	25		12	December 25	Sun Dec 25, 2022
13						
14	Holidays (Canada)	Occurrence or Day	Weekday	Month	When It Occurs	Date
15	New Year's Day	1		1	January 1	Sat Jan 1, 2022
16	Good Friday				Friday before Easter Sunday	Fri Apr 15, 2022
17	Victoria Day	2	2	5	2nd Monday in May	Mon May 9, 2022
18	Canada Day	1		7	July 1	Fri Jul 1, 2022
19	Civic Holiday	1		8	August 1	Mon Aug 1, 2022

FIGURE 8-3 This worksheet calculates the dates of numerous holidays in a given year.

Column A holds the name of the holiday; column B holds the occurrence within the month or, for fixed holidays, the actual date within the month; column C holds the days of the week; and column D holds the number of the month.

Most of the values in column E are calculated. For the floating holidays, for example, several CHOOSE functions are used to construct the description. Here's an example for Martin Luther King, Jr. Day:

```
=B5 & CHOOSE(B5, "st", "nd", "rd", "th", "th") & " " & CHOOSE(C5,

    "Sunday", "Monday", "Tuesday", "Wednesday", "Thursday", "Friday",
    "Saturday") & " in " & CHOOSE(D5, "January", "February", "March",
    "April", "May", "June", "July", "August", "September", "October",
    "November", "December")
```

Finally, column F contains the formulas for calculating the date of each holiday based on the year entered in cell B1.

> **Note** Two exceptions exist in column F. The first is the formula for Memorial Day (cell F6), which occurs on the last Monday in May. To derive this date, you first calculate the first Monday in June and then subtract 7 days.
>
> The second exception is the formula for Good Friday (cell F16). This occurs two days before Easter Sunday, which is a floating holiday, but its date is based on the phase of the moon, of all things. (Officially, Easter Sunday falls on the first Sunday after the first ecclesiastical full moon after the spring equinox.) There are no simple formulas for calculating when Easter Sunday occurs in a given year. The formula in the Holidays worksheet is a complex bit of business that uses the **FLOOR** function, so I discuss it when I discuss that function in Chapter 9, "Working with math functions."

Calculating the Julian date

Excel has built-in functions that convert a given date into a numerical day of the week (the **WEEKDAY** function) and that return the numerical ranking of the week in which a given date falls (the **WEEKNUM** function). However, Excel doesn't have a function that calculates the Julian date for a given date—the numerical ranking of the date for the year in which it falls. For example, the Julian date of January 1 is 1, January 2 is 2, and February 1 is 32.

If you need to use Julian dates in your business, here's a formula that will do the job:

```
=MyDate - DATE(YEAR(MyDate) - 1, 12, 31)
```

This formula assumes that the date you want to work with is in a cell named **MyDate**. The expression **DATE(YEAR(MyDate) - 1, 12, 31)** returns the date serial number for December 31 of the preceding year. Subtracting this number from **MyDate** gives you the Julian number.

Calculating the difference between two dates

Earlier in this chapter, you saw that Excel enables you to subtract one date from another. Here's an example:

```
=Date1 - Date2
```

Here, **Date1** and **Date2** can be date values or date strings. When you create such a formula, Excel returns a value equal to the number of days between the two dates. This date-difference formula returns a positive number if **Date1** is larger than **Date2**; it returns a negative number if **Date1** is less than **Date2**. Calculating the difference between two dates is useful in many business scenarios, including receivables aging, interest calculations, benefits payments, and more.

Besides the basic date-difference formula, you can use the date functions from earlier in this chapter to perform date-difference calculations. Also, Excel boasts a number of worksheet functions that enable you to perform more sophisticated operations to determine the difference between two dates. The rest of this section runs through a number of these date-difference formulas and functions.

Calculating a person's age

If you have a person's birth date entered into a cell named Birthdate and you need to calculate how old the person is, you might think that the following formula would do the job:

```
=YEAR(TODAY()) - YEAR(Birthdate)
```

This works, but only if the person's birthday has already passed this year. If he hasn't had a birthday yet, this formula reports the age as being one year greater than it really is.

To solve this problem, you need to take into account whether the person's birthday has passed. To see how to do this, check out the following logical expression:

```
=DATE(YEAR(NOW()), MONTH(Birthdate), DAY(Birthdate)) > TODAY()
```

This expression asks whether the person's birthday for this year (which uses the formula from earlier in this chapter—see "Determining a person's birthday, given the birth date") is greater than today's date. If it is, the expression returns logical **TRUE**, which is equivalent to **1**; if it isn't, the expression returns logical **FALSE**, which is equivalent to **0**. In other words, you can get the person's true age by subtracting the result of the logical expression from the original formula, like so:

```
=YEAR(NOW()) - YEAR(Birthdate) - (DATE(YEAR(NOW()), MONTH(Birthdate),
    DAY(Birthdate)) > NOW())
```

DAYS: Returning the number of days between two dates

If all you're interested in is the number of days between two dates, then the easiest way to perform such a calculation is to use Excel's **DAYS** function:

```
DAYS(end_date, start_date)
```

end_date	The ending date
start_date	The starting date

For example, the following formula returns the number of days that have elapsed since the start of the current year:

```
=DAYS(TODAY(), DATE(YEAR(TODAY(), 1, 1))
```

NETWORKDAYS: Calculating the number of workdays between two dates

If you calculate the difference in days between two dates, Excel includes weekends and holidays. In many business situations, you need to know the number of workdays between two dates. For example, when calculating the number of days an invoice is past due, it's often best to exclude weekends and holidays.

This is readily done using the **NETWORKDAYS** function (read the name as *net workdays*), which returns the number of working days between two dates:

```
NETWORKDAYS(start_date, end_date [, holidays])
```

start_date	The starting date (or a string representation of the date).
end_date	The ending date (or a string representation of the date).
Holidays	A list of dates to exclude from the calculation. This can be a range of dates or an array constant—that is, a series of date serial numbers or date strings, separated by commas and surrounded by braces (**{}**).

For example, here's an expression that returns the number of workdays between December 1, 2022, and January 10, 2023, excluding December 25, 2022, and January 1, 2023:

```
=NETWORKDAYS("12/1/2022", "1/10/2023", {"12/25/2022","1/1/2023"})
```

Figure 8-4 shows an update to the accounts receivable worksheet that uses **NETWORKDAYS** to calculate the number of workdays that each invoice is past due.

				Past	Amount	Past Due (Days):	
Account Number	Invoice Number	Invoice Date	Due Date	Due	Due	1-30	31-60
07-0001	1000	January 11, 2022	Thursday Feb 10, 2022	47	$2,433.25		$2,433.25
07-0001	1025	January 29, 2022	Monday Feb 28, 2022	35	$2,151.20		$2,151.20
07-0001	1031	February 5, 2022	Monday Mar 7, 2022	30	$1,758.54	$1,758.54	
07-0002	1006	November 23, 2021	Thursday Dec 23, 2021	82	$898.47		
07-0002	1035	February 5, 2022	Monday Mar 7, 2022	30	$1,021.02	$1,021.02	
07-0004	1002	January 11, 2022	Thursday Feb 10, 2022	47	$3,558.94		$3,558.94
07 0005	1008	November 13, 2021	Monday Dec 13, 2021	90	$1,177.53		
07-0005	1018	January 28, 2022	Monday Feb 28, 2022	35	$1,568.31		$1,568.31
08-0001	1039	October 12, 2021	Thursday Nov 11, 2021	112	$2,958.73		
08-0001	1001	January 11, 2022	Thursday Feb 10, 2022	47	$3,659.85		$3,659.85
08-0001	1024	January 29, 2022	Monday Feb 28, 2022	35	$565.00		$565.00

(Cell E4: =NETWORKDAYS(D4,$B$1); Date: 15-Apr-22)

FIGURE 8-4 This worksheet calculates the number of workdays that each invoice is past due by using the NETWORKDAYS function.

NETWORKDAYS doesn't include weekends in its calculations. By default, the function defines the weekend days as Saturdays and Sundays, but if you need to use different weekend days, use the **NETWORKDAYS.INTL** function, which adds a *weekend* argument:

```
WORKDAY.INTL(start_date, days [weekend, holidays])
```

The *weekend* argument can either be a string of seven digits or a numeric code. See "The WEEKDAY function" earlier in this chapter, for the details on the *weekend* argument.

DAYS360: Calculating date differences using a 360-day year

Many accounting systems operate using the principle of a 360-day year, which divides the year into 12 periods of uniform (30-day) lengths. Finding the number of days between dates in such a system isn't possible with the standard addition and subtraction of dates. However, Excel makes such calculations easy with its **DAYS360** function, which returns the number of days between a starting date and an ending date, based on a 360-day year:

DAYS360(*start_date*, *end_date* [, *method*])

start_date	The starting date (or a string representation of the date).
end_date	The ending date (or a string representation of the date).
Method	A Boolean value that determines how **DAYS360** performs certain calculations:
	FALSE: If *start_date* is the 31st of the month, it is changed to the 30th of the same month. If *end_date* is the 31st of the month and *start_date* is less than the 30th of any month, the *end_date* is changed to the 1st of the next month. This is the North American method, and it's the default.
	TRUE: Any *start_date* or *end_date* value that falls on the 31st of a month is changed to the 30th of the same month. This is the European method.

For example, the following expression returns the value **1**:

DAYS360("3/30/2022", "4/1/2022")

YEARFRAC: Returning the fraction of a year between two dates

Business worksheet models often need to know the fraction of a year that has elapsed between one date and another. For example, if an employee leaves after three months, you might need to pay out a quarter of a year's worth of benefits. This calculation can be complicated by the fact that your company might use a 360-day accounting year. However, the **YEARFRAC** function can help you. This function converts the number of days between a start date and an end date into a fraction of a year:

YEARFRAC(*start_date*, *end_date* [, *basis*])

start_date	The starting date (or a string representation of the date).
end_date	The ending date (or a string representation of the date).
Basis	An integer that determines how **YEARFRAC** performs certain calculations:
	0: Uses a 360-day year divided into 12 30-day months. This is the North American method, and it's the default.
	1: Uses the actual number of days in the year and the actual number of days in each month.
	2: Uses a 360-day year and the actual number of days in each month.
	3: Uses a 365-day year and the actual number of days in each month.
	4: Any *start_date* or *end_date* value that falls on the 31st of a month is changed to the 30th of the same month. This is the European method.

For example, the following expression returns the value **0.25**:

YEARFRAC("3/15/2022", "6/15/2022")

Using Excel's time functions

Working with time values in Excel is not greatly different from working with date values, although there are some exceptions, as you'll see in this section. Here you'll work mostly with Excel's time functions, which work with or return time serial numbers. All of Excel's time-related functions are listed in Table 8-6. (For the *time* arguments, you can use any valid Excel time.)

TABLE 8-6 Excel's time functions function description

HOUR(*time*)	Extracts the minute component from the time given by *time*.
MINUTE(*time*)	Extracts the seconds component from the time given by *time*.
NOW	Returns the serial number of the current date and time.
SECOND(*time*)	Extracts the hour component from the time given by *time*.
TIME(*hour*, *minute*, *second*)	Returns the serial number of a time, in which *hour* is a number between 0 and 23, and *minute* and *second* are numbers between 0 and 59.
TIMEVALUE(*time_text*)	Converts a time from text to a serial number.

Returning a time

If you need a time value to use in an expression or a function, either you can enter it by hand if you have a specific date that you want to work with, or you can take advantage of the flexibility of three Excel functions: **NOW**, **TIME**, and **TIMEVALUE**.

NOW: Returning the current time

When you need to use the current time in a formula, a function, or an expression, use the **NOW** function, which doesn't take any arguments:

```
NOW()
```

This function returns the serial number of the current time, with the current date as the assumed date. For example, if it's noon and today's date is December 31, 2022, the **NOW** function returns the following serial number (although in the cell you see this displayed using the m/d/yyyy h:mm format):

```
44926.5
```

If you just want the time component of the serial number, subtract **TODAY** from **NOW**:

```
NOW() - TODAY()
```

Just like the **TODAY** function, remember that **NOW** is a dynamic function that doesn't keep its initial value (that is, the time at which you entered the function). Each time you edit the formula, enter another formula, recalculate the worksheet, or reopen the workbook, **NOW** uptimes its value to return the current system time.

TIME: Returning any time

A time consists of three components: the hour, minute, and second. It often happens that a worksheet generates one or more of these components, and you need some way of building a proper time out of them. You can do that by using Excel's **TIME** function:

TIME(*hour, minute, second*)

hour	The hour component of the time (a number between 0 and 23)
minute	The minute component of the time (a number between 0 and 59)
second	The second component of the time (a number between 0 and 59)

For example, the following expression returns the time 2:45:30 p.m.:

TIME(14, 45, 30)

Like the **DATE** function, **TIME** adjusts for wrong hour, month, and second values. For example, the following expression returns 3:00:30 p.m.:

TIME(14, 60, 30)

Here, **TIME** takes the extra minute and adds 1 to the hour value.

TIMEVALUE: Converting a string to a time

If you have a time value in string form, you can convert it to a time serial number by using the **TIMEVALUE** function:

TIMEVALUE(*time_text*)

time_text	The string containing the time

For example, the following expression returns the time serial number for the string **2:45:00 PM**:

TIMEVALUE("2:45:00 PM")

Returning parts of a time

The three components of a time—hour, minute, and second—can also be extracted individually from a given time, using Excel's **HOUR**, **MINUTE**, and **SECOND** functions.

The HOUR function

The **HOUR** function returns a number between 0 and 23 that corresponds to the hour component of a specified time:

HOUR(*time*)

time	The time (or a string representation of the time) you want to work with

For example, the following expression returns **12**:

```
HOUR(0.5)
```

The MINUTE function

The **MINUTE** function returns a number between 0 and 59 that corresponds to the minute component of a specified time:

```
MINUTE(time)
```

time	The time (or a string representation of the time) you want to work with

For example, if it's currently 3:15 PM, the following expression returns **15**:

```
MINUTE(NOW())
```

The SECOND function

The **SECOND** function returns a number between 0 and 59 that corresponds to the second component of a specified time:

```
SECOND(time)
```

time	The time (or a string representation of the time) you want to work with

For example, the following expression returns **30**:

```
SECOND("2:45:30 PM")
```

Returning a time X hours, minutes, or seconds from now

As I mentioned earlier, **TIME** automatically adjusts wrong hour, minute, and second values. You can take advantage of this by applying formulas to one or more of the **TIME** function's arguments. The most common use for this is to return a time that occurs X number of hours, minutes, or seconds from now (or from any time).

For example, the following expression returns the time 12 hours from now:

```
TIME(HOUR(NOW()) + 12, MINUTE(NOW()), SECOND(NOW()))
```

Unlike the **DATE** function, the **TIME** function doesn't enable you to simply add an hour, a minute, or a second to a specified time. For example, consider the following expression:

```
NOW() + 1
```

All this does is add one day to the current date and time.

If you want to add hours, minutes, and seconds to a time, you need to express the added time as a fraction of a day. For example, because there are 24 hours in a day, 1 hour is represented by the expression **1/24**. Similarly, because there are 60 minutes in an hour, 1 minute is represented by the expression **1/24/60**. Finally, because there are 60 seconds in a minute, 1 second is represented by the expression **1/24/60/60**. Table 8-7 shows you how to use these expressions to add *n* hours, minutes, and seconds.

TABLE 8-7 Adding hours, minutes, and seconds

Operation	Expression	Example	Example Expression
Add *n* hours	*n**(1/24)	Add 6 hours	NOW()+6*(1/24)
Add *n* minutes	*n**(1/24/60)	Add 15 minutes	NOW()+15*(1/24/60)
Add *n* seconds	*n**(1/24/60/60)	Add 30 seconds	NOW()+30*(1/24/60/60)

Summing time values

When working with time values in Excel, you need to be aware that there are two subtly different interpretations for the phrase "adding one time to another":

- **Adding time values to get a future time:** As you saw in the previous section, adding hours, minutes, or seconds to a time returns a value that represents a future time. For example, if the current time is 11:00 PM (23:00), adding 2 hours returns the time 1:00 AM.

- **Adding time values to get a total time:** In this interpretation, time values are summed to get a total number of hours, minutes, and seconds. This is useful if you want to know how many hours an employee worked in a week or how many hours to bill a client. In this case, for example, if the current total is 23 hours, adding 2 hours brings the total to 25 hours.

The problem is that adding time values to get a future time is Excel's default interpretation for added time values. So, if cell A1 contains 23:00 and cell A2 contains 2:00, the following formula returns **1:00:00 AM**:

```
=A1 + A2
```

The time value 25:00:00 is stored internally, but Excel adjusts the display so that you see the "correct" value **1:00:00 AM**. If you want to see 25:00:00 instead, apply the following custom format to the cell:

```
[h]:mm:ss
```

Calculating the difference between two times

Excel treats time serial numbers as decimal expansions (numbers between 0 and 1) that represent fractions of a day. Because they're just numbers, there's nothing to stop you from subtracting one from another to determine the difference between them:

```
EndTime - StartTime
```

This expression works just fine, as long as *EndTime* is greater than *StartTime*. (I used the names *EndTime* and *StartTime* purposefully so you'd remember to always subtract the later time from the earlier time.)

However, there's one scenario in which this expression fails: If *EndTime* occurs after midnight the next day, there's a good chance that it will be less than *StartTime*. For example, if a person works from 11:00 PM to 7:00 AM, the expression `7:00 AM - 11:00 PM` results in an illegal negative time value. (Excel displays the result as a series of # symbols that fill the cell.)

To ensure that you get the correct positive result in this situation, use the following generic expression:

```
IF(EndTime < StartTime, 1 + EndTime - StartTime, EndTime - StartTime)
```

The `IF` function checks to see whether *EndTime* is less than *StartTime*. If it is, 1 is added to the value *EndTime* - *StartTime* to get the correct result; otherwise, just *EndTime* - *StartTime* is returned.

Case study: Building an employee timesheet

In this case study, you put your new knowledge of time functions and calculations to good use building a timesheet that tracks the number of hours an employee works each week, takes into account hours worked on weekends and holidays, and calculates the total number of hours and the weekly pay. Figure 8-5 shows the completed timesheet.

H9			f_x	=IF(OR(WEEKDAY(A9) = 7, WEEKDAY(A9) = 1), F9, 0)					
	A	B	C	D	E	F	G	H	I
2	Employee Name:			Kyra Ferry					
3	Maximum Hours Before Overtime:			40:00					
4	Hourly Wage:			$14.50					
5	Overtime Pay Rate:			1.5					
6	Holiday Pay Rate:			2					
8	Date	Work Start Time	Lunch Start Time	Lunch End Time	Work End Time	Total Hours Worked	Non-Weekend, Non-Holiday Hours	Overtime Hours	Holiday Hours
9	Monday Sep 5, 2022	9:00 AM	12:00 PM	1:00 PM	6:00 PM	8:00	0:00	0:00	8:00
10	Tuesday Sep 6, 2022	8:00 AM	12:30 PM	1:45 PM	6:00 PM	8:45	8:45	0:00	0:00
11	Wednesday Sep 7, 2022	11:00 PM	3:00 AM	4:00 AM	9:00 AM	9:00	9:00	0:00	0:00
12	Thursday Sep 8, 2022	10:30 PM	2:00 AM	3:00 AM	5:00 AM	5:30	5:30	0:00	0:00
13	Friday Sep 9, 2022	7:00 PM	11:30 PM	12:30 AM	4:00 AM	8:00	8:00	0:00	0:00
14	Saturday Sep 10, 2022	12:00 PM	3:00 PM	3:30 PM	6:00 PM	5:30	0:00	5:30	0:00
15	Sunday Sep 11, 2022	12:00 PM			4:00 PM	4:00	0:00	4:00	0:00
17	**TOTAL WEEKLY HOURS**				**WEEKLY PAY**				
18	Total Hours	48:45			Regular Pay	$453.13			
19	Weekly Regular Hours	31:15			Overtime Pay	$206.63			
20	Weekly Overtime Hours	9:30			Holiday Pay	$232.00			
21	Weekly Holiday Hours	8:00			Total Pay	$891.75			

FIGURE 8-5 This employee timesheet tracks the daily hours, takes weekends and holidays into account, and calculates the employee's total working hours and pay.

Before starting, you need to understand three terms used in this case study:

- **Regular hours:** These are hours worked for regular pay.
- **Overtime hours:** These are hours worked beyond the maximum number of regular hours, as well as any hours worked on the weekend.
- **Holiday hours:** These are hours worked on a statutory holiday.

Entering the timesheet data

Let's begin at the top of the timesheet, where the following data is required:

- **Employee Name:** You'll create a separate sheet for each employee, so enter the person's name here. You might also want to augment this with the date the person started or other data about the employee.
- **Maximum Hours Before Overtime:** This is the number of regular hours an employee has to work in a week before overtime hours take effect. Enter the number using the hh:mm format. Cell D3 uses the [h]:mm custom format, to ensure that Excel displays the actual value.
- **Hourly Wage:** This is the amount the employee earns per regular hour of work.
- **Overtime Pay Rate:** This is the factor by which the employee's hourly rate is increased for overtime hours. For example, enter **1.5** if the employee earns time and a half for overtime.
- **Holiday Pay Rate:** This is the factor by which the employee's hourly rate is increased for holiday hours. For example, enter **2** if the employee earns double time for holidays.

Calculating the daily hours worked

Figure 8-6 shows the portion of the timesheet used to record the employee's daily hours worked. For each day, you enter five items:

- **Date:** Enter the date the employee worked. This is formatted to show the day of the week, which is useful for confirming overtime hours worked on weekends.
- **Work Start Time:** Enter the time of day the employee began working.
- **Lunch Start Time:** Enter the time of day the employee stopped for lunch.
- **Lunch End Time:** Enter the time of day the employee resumed working after lunch.
- **Work End Time:** Enter the time of day the employee stopped working.

F9 =IF(E9 < B9, 1 + E9 - B9, E9 - B9) - IF(D9 < C9, 1 + D9 - C9, D9 - C9)

	A	B	C	D	E	F	G	H	I
2		Employee Name:		Kyra Ferry					
3		Maximum Hours Before Overtime:		40:00					
4		Hourly Wage:		$14.50					
5		Overtime Pay Rate:		1.5					
6		Holiday Pay Rate:		2					
8	Date	Work Start Time	Lunch Start Time	Lunch End Time	Work End Time	Total Hours Worked	Non-Weekend, Non-Holiday Hours	Overtime Hours	Holiday Hours
9	Monday Sep 5, 2022	9:00 AM	12:00 PM	1:00 PM	6:00 PM	8:00	0:00	0:00	8:00
10	Tuesday Sep 6, 2022	8:00 AM	12:30 PM	1:45 PM	6:00 PM	8:45	8:45	0:00	0:00
11	Wednesday Sep 7, 2022	11:00 PM	3:00 AM	4:00 AM	9:00 AM	9:00	9:00	0:00	0:00
12	Thursday Sep 8, 2022	10:30 PM	2:00 AM	3:00 AM	5:00 AM	5:30	5:30	0:00	0:00
13	Friday Sep 9, 2022	7:00 PM	11:30 PM	12:30 AM	4:00 AM	8:00	8:00	0:00	0:00
14	Saturday Sep 10, 2022	12:00 PM	3:00 PM	3:30 PM	6:00 PM	5:30	0:00	5:30	0:00
15	Sunday Sep 11, 2022	12:00 PM			4:00 PM	4:00	0:00	4:00	0:00

FIGURE 8-6 The section of the employee timesheet in which you enter the hours worked and in which the total daily hours are calculated.

The first calculation occurs in Total Hours Worked (column F). The idea here is to sum the number of hours the employee worked in a given day. The first part of the calculation uses the time-difference formula from the previous section to derive the number of hours between the Work Start Time (column B) and the Work End Time (column F). Here's the expression for the first entry (row 9):

```
IF(E9 < B9, 1 + E9 - B9, E9 - B9)
```

However, you also have to subtract the time the employee took for lunch, which is the difference between Lunch Start Time (column C) and Lunch End Time (column D). Here's the expression for the first entry (row 9):

```
IF(D9 < C9, 1 + D9 - C9, D9 - C9)
```

Let's skip over to the Weekend Hours calculation (column H). The idea behind this column is that if the employee worked on the weekend, all the hours worked should be booked as overtime hours. So, the formula checks to see whether the date is a Saturday or a Sunday:

```
=IF(OR(WEEKDAY(A9) = 7, WEEKDAY(A9) = 1), F9, 0)
```

If the OR function returns TRUE, the date is on the weekend, so the value from the Total Hours Worked column (F9, in the example) is entered into the Weekend Hours column; otherwise, 0 is returned.

Next up is the Holiday Hours calculation (column I). Here, you want to see if the date is a statutory holiday. If it is, all of the hours worked that day should be booked as holiday hours. To that end, the formula checks to see if the date is part of the range of holiday dates calculated earlier in this chapter:

```
=SUM(IF(A9 = Holidays!F4:F13, 1, 0)) * F9
```

This is an array formula that compares the date with the dates in the holiday range (Holidays!F4:F13). If a match occurs, the SUM function returns 1; otherwise, it returns 0.

This result is multiplied by the value in the Total Hours Worked column (F9, in the example). So, if the date is a holiday, the hours for that day are entered as holiday hours.

Finally, the value in the Non-Weekend, Non-Holiday Hours column (G) is calculated by subtracting Weekend Hours and Holiday Hours from Total Hours Worked:

```
=F9 - H9 - I9
```

Calculating the weekly hours worked

Next up is the Total Weekly Hours section (refer to Figure 8-5), which adds the various types of hours the employee worked during the week.

The Total Hours value is a straight sum of the values in the Total Hours Worked column (F):

```
=SUM(F9:F15)
```

To derive the Weekly Regular Hours value, the calculation has to check to see if the total in the Non-Weekend, Non-Holiday Hours column (G) exceeds the number in the Maximum Hours Before Overtime cell (D3):

```
=IF(SUM(G9:G15) > D3, D3, SUM(G9:G15))
```

If this is true, the value in D3 is entered as the Regular Hours value; otherwise, the sum is entered.

Calculating the Weekly Overtime Hours value is a two-step process: First, you have to check to see if the sum in the Non-Weekend, Non-Holiday Hours column (G) exceeds the number in the Maximum Hours Before Overtime cell (D3). If so, the number of overtime hours is the difference between them; otherwise, it's 0:

```
IF(SUM(G9:G15) > D3, SUM(G9:G15) - D3, "0:00")
```

Second, you need to add the sum of the Overtime Hours column (H):

```
=IF(SUM(G9:G15) > D3, SUM(G9:G15) - D3, "0:00") + SUM(H9:H15)
```

Finally, the Weekly Holiday Hours value is a straight sum of the values in the Holiday Hours column (I):

```
=SUM(I9:I15)
```

Calculating the weekly pay

The final section of the timesheet is the Weekly Pay calculation. The dollar amounts for Regular Pay, Overtime Pay, and Holiday Pay are calculated as follows:

```
Regular Pay = Weekly Regular Hours * Hourly Wage * 24
Overtime Pay = Weekly Overtime Hours * Hourly Wage * Overtime Pay Rate * 24
Holiday Pay = Weekly Holiday Hours * Hourly Wage * Holiday Pay Rate * 24
```

Note that you need to multiply by 24 to convert the time value to a real number. Finally, the Total Pay is the sum of these values.

CHAPTER 9

Working with math functions

In this chapter, you will:

- Discover Excel's extensive collection of math worksheet functions
- Understand when and how to use Excel's worksheet functions for rounding numbers
- Examine Excel's worksheet functions related to summing values
- Get to know the powerful and useful MOD function
- Learn various ways to generate random numbers
- Programming with LET and LAMBDA

Excel's mathematical underpinnings are revealed in the long list of math-related functions that come with the program. Functions exist for basic mathematical operations such as absolute values, lowest and greatest common denominators, square roots, and sums. Plenty of high-end operations are also available for matrix multiplication, multinomials, and sums of squares. Not all of Excel's math functions are useful in a business context, but a surprising number of them are. For example, operations such as rounding and generating random numbers have business uses. This chapter introduces you to these and many other math-related worksheet functions.

Excel's math and trig functions

Table 9-1 lists the Excel math functions, but this chapter doesn't cover the entire list. Instead, I focus only on those functions that I think you'll find useful for your business formulas. Remember, too, that Excel comes with lots of statistical functions, many of which I cover in Chapter 11, "Building descriptive statistical formulas," and Chapter 12, "Building inferential statistical formulas."

TABLE 9-1 Excel's math functions

Function	Description
ABS(*number*)	Returns the absolute value of *number*.
AGGREGATE(*function_num,options, ref1*[,*ref2*,...])	Applies the function given by *function_num* (such as 1 for AVERAGE) to the specified range or table.
ARABIC(*string*)	Converts the Roman numeral specified by *string* into its Arabic equivalent.

Function	Description
BASE(*number*, *radix* [,*min_length*])	Converts *number* to the base given by *radix* (for example, set *radix* to 2 for binary).
BYCOL(*array*,*function*)	Returns an array created by applying a LAMBDA *function* to each column in *array*.
BYROW(*array*,*function*)	Returns an array created by applying a LAMBDA *function* to each row in *array*.
CEILING.MATH(*number* [, *significance*,*mode*])	Rounds *number* up to the nearest integer.
COMBIN(*number*,*number_chosen*)	Returns the number of unique ways that *number* objects can be combined in groups of *number_chosen*.
COMBINA(*number*,*number_chosen*)	Returns the number of non-unique ways that *number* objects can be combined in groups of *number_chosen*.
DECIMAL(*number*,*radix*)	Converts *number* to decimal from the base given by *radix*.
EVEN(*number*)	Rounds *number* up to the nearest even integer.
EXP(*number*)	Returns *e* raised to the power of *number*.
FACT(*number*)	Returns the factorial of *number*.
FACTDOUBLE(*number*)	Returns the double factorial of *number*.
FLOOR.MATH(*number*[, *significance*, *mode*])	Rounds *number* down to the nearest integer.
GCD(*number1*[,*number2*, ...])	Returns the greatest common divisor of the specified numbers.
INT(*number*)	Rounds *number* down to the nearest integer.
LCM(*number1*[,*number2*, ...])	Returns the least common multiple of the specified numbers.
LN(*number*)	Returns the natural logarithm of *number*.
LOG(*number*[,*base*])	Returns the logarithm of *number* in the specified *base*.
LOG10(*number*)	Returns the base-10 logarithm of *number*.
MAKEARRAY(*rows*,*columns*,*function*)	Creates an array with the specified number of *rows* and *columns* by applying a LAMBDA *function*.
MAP(*array(s)*,*function*)	Returns an array created by applying a LAMBDA *function* to each value in the *array(s)*.
MDETERM(*array*)	Returns the matrix determinant of *array*.
MINVERSE(*array*)	Returns the matrix inverse of *array*.
MMULT(*array1*, *array2*)	Returns the matrix product of *array1* and *array2*.
MOD(*number*,*divisor*)	Returns the remainder of *number* after dividing by *divisor*.
MROUND(*number*,*multiple*)	Rounds *number* to the desired *multiple*.
MULTINOMIAL(*number1*[,*number2*])	Returns the multinomial of the specified numbers.
MUNIT(*dimension*)	Returns the unit matrix for the specified *dimension* (for example, dimension 3 returns a 3×3-unit matrix).
ODD(*number*)	Rounds *number* up to the nearest odd integer.
PI	Returns the value pi.
POWER(*number*,*power*)	Raises *number* to the specified *power*.

Function	Description
PRODUCT(*number1*[,*number2*, . . .])	Multiplies the specified numbers.
QUOTIENT(*numerator*,*denominator*)	Returns the integer portion of the result obtained by dividing *numerator* by *denominator* (that is, the remainder is discarded from the result).
RAND	Returns a random number between 0 and 1.
RANDARRAY(*rows*,*columns*)	Returns an array of random numbers that has the specified number of *rows* and *columns*.
RANDBETWEEN(*bottom*,*top*)	Returns a random number between *bottom* and *top*.
REDUCE([*initial_value*],*array*,*function*)	Returns the accumulated value of applying a LAMBDA *function* to each value in *array*.
ROMAN(*number*[,*form*])	Converts the Arabic *number* to its Roman numeral equivalent (as text).
ROUND(*number*,*num_digits*)	Rounds *number* to a specified number of digits.
ROUNDDOWN(*number*,*num_digits*)	Rounds *number* down, toward 0.
ROUNDUP(*number*,*num_digits*)	Rounds *number* up, away from 0.
SCAN([*initial_value*],*array*,*function*)	Returns an array created by applying a LAMBDA *function* to each value in *array*.
SEQUENCE(*rows*,*columns*,*start*,*step*)	Returns a sequence of numbers, beginning with *start*, increasing by *step*, and arranged by the specified number of *rows* and *columns*.
SERIESSUM(*x*,*n*,*m*,*coefficients*)	Returns the sum of a power series.
SIGN(*number*)	Returns the sign of *number* (**1** = positive, **0** = zero, **−1** = negative).
SQRT(*number*)	Returns the positive square root of *number*.
SQRTPI(*number*)	Returns the positive square root of the result of the expression *number* * *pi*.
SUBTOTAL(*function_num*,*ref1*[,*ref2*, . . .])	Returns a subtotal from a list.
SUM(*number1*[,*number2*,...])	Adds the arguments.
SUMIF(*range*,*criteria* [,*sum_range*])	Adds only those cells in *range* that meet the *criteria*.
SUMIFS(*sum_range*,*criteria_range*, *criteria*,...)	Adds only those cells in each *sum_range* that correspond to the items in each *criteria_range* that satisfy each *criteria*.
SUMPRODUCT(*array1*, *array2*[,*array3*,...])	Multiplies the corresponding elements in the specified arrays and then sums the resulting products.
SUMSQ(*number1*[,*number2*,...])	Returns the sum of the squares of the arguments.
SUMX2MY2(*array_x*,*array_y*)	Squares the elements in the specified arrays and then sums the differences between the corresponding squares.
SUMX2PY2(*array_x*,*array_y*)	Squares the elements in the specified arrays and then sums the corresponding squares.
SUMXMY2(*array_x*,*array_y*)	Squares the differences between the corresponding elements in the specified arrays and then sums the squares.
TRUNC(*number*[,*num_digits*])	Truncates *number* to an integer.

Although I don't discuss the details of Excel's trig functions in this book, Table 9-2 lists all of them. Here are some notes to keep in mind when you use these functions:

- In each function syntax, *number* is an angle expressed in radians.

- If you have an angle in degrees, convert it to radians by multiplying it by **PI/180**. Alternatively, use the **RADIANS**(*angle*) function to convert *angle* from degrees to radians.

- A trig function returns a value in radians. If you need to convert a result to degrees, multiply it by **180/PI**. Alternatively, use the **DEGREES**(*angle*) function, which converts *angle* from radians to degrees.

TABLE 9-2 Excel's trigonometric functions

Function	Description
ACOS(*number*)	Returns a value in radians between 0 and pi that represents the arccosine of *number* (which must be between −1 and 1).
ACOSH(*number*)	Returns a value in radians that represents the inverse hyperbolic cosine of *number* (which must be greater than or equal to 1).
ACOT(*number*)	Returns a value in radians between 0 and pi that represents the arccotangent of *number*.
ACOTH(*number*)	Returns a value in radians that represents the inverse hyperbolic arccotangent of *number*.
ASIN(*number*)	Returns a value in radians between −pi/2 and pi/2 that represents the arcsine of *number* (which must be between −1 and 1).
ASINH(*number*)	Returns a value in radians that represents the inverse hyperbolic sine of *number*.
ATAN(*number*)	Returns a value in radians between −pi/2 and pi/2 that represents the arctangent of *number*.
ATAN2(*x_num*, *y_num*)	Returns a value in radians between (but not including) −pi and pi that represents the arctangent of the coordinates given by *x_num* and *y_num*.
ATANH(*number*)	Returns a value in radians that represents the inverse hyperbolic tangent of *number* (which must be between −1 and 1).
COS(number)	Returns a value in radians that represents the cosine of *number*.
COSH(*number*)	Returns a value in radians that represents the hyperbolic cosine of *number*.
COT(number)	Returns a value in radians that represents the cotangent of *number*.
COTH(*number*)	Returns a value in radians that represents the hyperbolic cotangent of *number*.
CSC(*number*)	Returns a value in radians that represents the cosecant of *number*.
CSCH(*number*)	Returns a value in radians that represents the hyperbolic cosecant of *number*.
DEGREES(*angle*)	Converts *angle* from radians to degrees.
RADIANS(*angle*)	Converts *angle* from degrees to radians.
SEC(*number*)	Returns a value in radians that represents the secant of *number*.
SECH(*number*)	Returns a value in radians that represents the hyperbolic secant of *number*.
SIN(*number*)	Returns a value in radians that represents the sine of *number*.
SINH(*number*)	Returns a value in radians that represents the hyperbolic sine of *number*.
TAN(*number*)	Returns a value in radians that represents the tangent of *number*.
TANH(*number*)	Returns a value in radians that represents the hyperbolic tangent of *number*.

Understanding Excel's rounding functions

Excel's rounding functions are useful in many situations, such as setting price points, adjusting billable time to, say, the nearest 15 minutes, and ensuring that you're dealing with integer values for discrete numbers, such as inventory counts.

The problem is that Excel has so many rounding functions that it's difficult to know which one to use in a given situation. To help you, this section looks at the details of—and differences between—Excel's 10 rounding functions: ROUND, MROUND, ROUNDUP, ROUNDDOWN, CEILING.MATH, FLOOR.MATH, EVEN, ODD, INT, and TRUNC.

The ROUND function

The rounding function you'll use most often is ROUND:

ROUND(*number*, *num_digits*)

number	The number you want to round
num_digits	An integer that specifies the number of digits you want *number* rounded to, as explained here:

	num_digits	Description
	> 0	Rounds *number* to *num_digits* decimal places
	0	Rounds *number* to the nearest integer
	< 0	Rounds *number* to *num_digits* to the left of the decimal point

Table 9-3 demonstrates the effect of the *num_digits* argument on the results of the ROUND function. Here, *number* is 1234.5678.

TABLE 9-3 Effect of the num_digits argument on the ROUND function result

num_digits	Result of ROUND(1234.5678, *num_digits*)
3	1234.568
2	1234.57
1	1234.6
0	1235
-1	1230
-2	1200
-3	1000

The MROUND function

MROUND is a function that rounds a number to a specified multiple:

MROUND(*number*, *multiple*)

number	The number you want to round
multiple	The multiple to which you want *number* rounded

Table 9-4 demonstrates MROUND with a few examples. Note that if *number* and *multiple* have different signs, MROUND produces the #NUM! error.

TABLE 9-4 Examples of the MROUND function

number	multiple	MROUND Result
5	2	6
11	5	10
13	5	15
5	5	5
7.31	0.5	7.5
–11	–5	–10
–11	5	#NUM!

The ROUNDDOWN and ROUNDUP functions

The ROUNDDOWN and ROUNDUP functions are similar to ROUND, except that they always round in a single direction: ROUNDDOWN always rounds a number toward 0, and ROUNDUP always rounds away from 0. Here is the syntax for each of these functions:

```
ROUNDDOWN(number, num_digits)
ROUNDUP(number, num_digits)
```

number	The number you want to round	
num_digits	An integer that specifies the number of digits you want *number* rounded to, as explained here:	
	num_digits	Description
	> 0	Rounds *number* down or up to *num_digits* decimal places
	0	Rounds *number* down or up to the nearest integer
	< 0	Rounds *number* down or up to *num_digits* to the left of the decimal point

Table 9-5 demonstrates ROUNDDOWN and ROUNDUP with a few examples.

TABLE 9-5 Examples of the ROUNDDOWN and ROUNDUP functions

number	num_digits	ROUNDDOWN	ROUNDUP
1.1	0	1	2
1.678	2	1.67	1.68
1234	–2	1200	1300
–1.1	0	–1	–2
–1234	–2	–1200	–1300

The CEILING.MATH and FLOOR.MATH functions

The **CEILING.MATH** and **FLOOR.MATH** functions are an amalgam of the features found in **MROUND**, **ROUNDDOWN**, and **ROUNDUP**. Here is the syntax of each one:

```
CEILING.MATH(number[, significance, mode])
FLOOR.MATH(number[, significance, mode])
```

number	The number you want to round
significance	The multiple to which you want *number* rounded; the default value is 1
mode	Determines whether Excel rounds negative numbers toward or away from zero

Both functions round the value given by *number* to a multiple of the value given by *significance*, but they differ in how they perform this rounding:

- **CEILING.MATH** rounds positive numbers *away from* 0 and negative numbers *toward* 0. For example, **CEILING.MATH(1.56, 0.1)** returns **1.6**, and **CEILING.MATH(-2.33, 0.5)** returns **-2**. If you prefer to round negative numbers *away* from 0, add the *mode* parameter with any nonzero value.

- **FLOOR.MATH** rounds positive numbers *toward* 0 and negative numbers *away from* 0. For example, **FLOOR.MATH(1.56, 0.1)** returns **1.5**, and **FLOOR.MATH(-2.33, -.5)** returns **-2.35**. If you prefer to round negative numbers *toward* 0, add the *mode* parameter with any nonzero value.

Calculating Easter dates

If you live or work in the United States, you'll rarely have to calculate for business purposes when Easter Sunday falls because there's no statutory holiday associated with Easter. However, if Good Friday or Easter Monday is a statutory holiday where you live (as Good Friday is in Canada and Easter Monday is in Britain), or if you're responsible for businesses in such jurisdictions, it can be handy to calculate when Easter falls in a given year.

Unfortunately, there's no straightforward way of calculating Easter. The official formula is that Easter falls on the first Sunday after the first ecclesiastical full moon after the spring equinox. Mathematicians have tried for centuries to come up with a formula, and although some have succeeded (most notably the famous mathematician Carl Friedrich Gauss), the resulting algorithms have been hideously complex.

Here's a relatively simple worksheet formula that employs the **FLOOR.MATH** function and that works for the years 1900 to 2078:

```
=FLOOR.MATH(DATE(B1, 5, DAY(MINUTE(B1 / 38) / 2 + 56)), 7) - 34
```

This formula assumes that the current year is in cell B1.

The EVEN and ODD functions

The **EVEN** and **ODD** functions round a single numeric argument:

```
EVEN(number)
ODD(number)
```

number	The number you want to round

Both functions round the value given by *number* away from 0, as follows:

- **EVEN** rounds to the next even number. For example, **EVEN(14.2)** returns **16**, and **EVEN(-23)** returns **-24**.

- **ODD** rounds to the next odd number. For example, **ODD(58.1)** returns **59**, and **ODD(-6)** returns **-7**.

The INT and TRUNC functions

The **INT** and **TRUNC** functions are similar in that you can use both of them to convert a value to its integer portion:

```
INT(number)
TRUNC(number[, num_digits])
```

number	The *number* you want to round
num_digits	An integer that specifies the number of digits you want *number* rounded to, as explained here:
> 0	Truncates all but *num_digits* decimal places
0	Truncates all decimal places (the default)
< 0	Converts *num_digits* to the left of the decimal point into zeros

For example, **INT(6.75)** returns **6**, and **TRUNC(3.6)** returns **3**. However, these functions have two major differences that you should keep in mind:

- For negative values, **INT** returns the next number away from 0. For example, **INT(-3.42)** returns **-4**. If you just want to lop off the decimal part, you need to use **TRUNC** instead.

- You can use the **TRUNC** function's second argument (*num_digits*) to specify the number of decimal places to leave on. For example, **TRUNC(123.456, 2)** returns **123.45**, and **TRUNC(123.456, -2)** returns **100**.

Using rounding to prevent calculation errors

Most of us are comfortable dealing with numbers in decimal—or base-10—format (the odd hexadecimal-loving computer geek notwithstanding). Computers, however, prefer to work in the simpler confines of the binary—or base-2—system. So when you plug a value into a cell or formula, Excel converts it from decimal to its binary equivalent, makes its calculations, and then converts the binary result back into decimal format.

This procedure is fine for integers because every decimal integer value has an exact binary equivalent. However, many noninteger values don't have exact equivalents in the binary world. Excel can only approximate such numbers, and that approximation can lead to errors in formulas. For example, try entering the following formula into any worksheet cell:

```
=0.01 = (2.02 - 2.01)
```

This formula compares the value **0.01** with the expression **2.02** - **2.01**. These should be equal, of course, but when you enter the formula, Excel returns a **FALSE** result. What gives?

The problem is that, in converting the expression **2.02** - **2.01** into binary and back again, Excel picks up a stray digit. To see it, enter the formula =**2.02** - **2.01** in a cell and then format it to show 16 decimal places. You should see the following surprising result:

```
0.0100000000000002
```

That wanton **2** in the 16th decimal place is what threw off the original calculation. To fix the problem, use the **TRUNC** function (or possibly the **ROUND** function, depending on the situation) to lop off the extra digits to the right of the decimal point. For example, the following formula produces a **TRUE** result:

```
=0.01 = TRUNC(2.02 - 2.01, 2)
```

Setting price points

One common worksheet task is to calculate a list price for a product based on the result of a formula that factors in production costs and profit margin. If the product will be sold at retail, you'll likely want the decimal (cents) portion of the price to be .95, .99, or some other standard value. You can use the **INT** function to help with this "rounding."

For example, the simplest case is to always round up the decimal part to .95. Here's a formula that does this:

```
=INT(RawPrice) + 0.95
```

Assuming that *RawPrice* is the result of the formula that factors in costs and profit, the formula adds 0.95 to the integer portion. (Note, too, that if the decimal portion of *RawPrice* is greater than .95, the formula rounds down to .95.)

Another case is to round up to .50 for decimal portions less than or equal to 0.5 and to round up to .95 for decimal portions greater than 0.5. Here's a formula that handles this scenario:

```
=INT(RawPrice) + IF(RawPrice - INT(RawPrice) <= 0.5, .50, .95)
```

Again, the integer portion is stripped from the *RawPrice*. Also, the **IF** function checks to see whether the decimal portion is less than or equal to 0.5. If it is, the value **.50** is returned; otherwise, the value **.95** is returned. This result is added to the integer portion.

Case study: Rounding billable time

An ideal use of MROUND is to round billable time to some multiple number of minutes. For example, it's common to round billable time to the nearest 15 minutes. You can do this with MROUND by using the following generic form of the function:

```
MROUND(BillableTime, 0:15)
```

Here, *BillableTime* is the time value you want to round. For example, the following expression returns the time value **2:15**:

```
MROUND(TIMEVALUE("2:10"), "0:15")
```

Using MROUND to round billable time has one significant flaw: Many (perhaps even most) people who bill their time prefer to round up to the nearest 15 minutes (or whatever). If the minute component of the MROUND function's *number* argument is less than half the *multiple* argument, MROUND rounds *down* to the nearest multiple.

To fix this problem, use the CEILING.MATH function instead because it always rounds away from 0. Note, however, that CEILING.MATH will only work in this scenario if you express your times using the TIME function. Here's the generic expression to use for rounding up to the next 15-minute multiple:

```
CEILING.MATH(TIME(BillableHours,BillableMinutes,BillableSeconds,) TIME(0,15,0))
```

Here, *BillableHours*, *BillableMinutes*, and *BillableSeconds* are the components of the time value you want to round. For example, the following expression rounds the time value 2:05 up to the time value **2:15**:

```
CEILING.MATH(TIME(2, 5, 0), TIME(0, 15, 0))
```

Summing values

Summing values—whether it's a range of cells, function results, literal numeric values, or expression results—is perhaps the most common spreadsheet operation. Excel enables you to add values by using the addition operator (+), but it's often more convenient to sum a number of values by using the SUM function, which you'll learn more about in the next section.

The SUM function

Here's the syntax of the SUM function:

```
SUM(number1[, number2, ...])
```

number1, *number2*, . . .	The values you want to add

You can enter up to 255 arguments into the SUM function. Note, too, that you can enter the SUM quickly by selecting the AutoSum command that appears in both the Home tab and the Formulas tab (or by selecting Alt+=).

For example, the following formula returns the sum of the values in three separate ranges:

```
=SUM(A2:A13, C2:C13, E2:E13)
```

> **Tip** If you need more than 255 arguments for the SUM function, group multiple arguments together using parentheses. For example, SUM(A1, B1, C1, D1) uses four arguments, but Excel sees SUM((A1, B1), (C1, D1)) as using just two arguments.

The SUMIF function

The SUMIF function is similar to SUM, except that it sums only those cells in a range that meet a specified condition:

```
SUMIF(range, criteria[, sum_range])
```

range	The range of cells to use for the criteria.
criteria	The criteria, entered as text, that determines which cells to sum. Excel applies the criteria to *range*.
sum_range	The range from which the sum values are taken. Excel sums only those cells in *sum_range* that correspond to the cells in *range* and meet the criteria. If you omit *sum_range*, Excel uses *range* for the sum.

For example, the following formula sums only those values in the range A2:A30 that are greater than 0:

```
=SUMIF(A2:A30, "> 0")
```

Summing only the positive or negative values in a range

If you have a range of numbers that contains both positive and negative values, what do you do if you need a total of only the negative values? Or only the positive ones? You could enter the individual cells into a SUM function, but there's an easier way: use SUMIF:

```
=SUMIF(range , "< 0")
```

Here, *range* is a range reference or named range. Similarly, you use the following formula to sum only the positive values in *range*:

```
=SUMIF(range , "> 0")
```

The SUMIFS function

The SUMIFS function sums cells in one or more ranges that meet one or more criteria:

```
SUMIFS(sum_range, range1, criteria1[, range2, criteria2, ...])
```

sum_range	The range from which the sum values are taken. Excel sums only those cells in *sum_range* that correspond to the cells that meet the criteria.
range1	The first range of cells to use for the sum criteria.
criteria1	The first criteria, entered as text, that determines which cells to sum. Excel applies the criteria to *range1*.
range2	The second range of cells to use for the sum criteria.
criteria2	The second criteria, entered as text, that determines which cells to sum. Excel applies the criteria to *range2*.

You can enter up to 127 range/criteria pairs. For example, the following formula sums only those values in the range B3:B100 where the corresponding cell in the range C3:C100 is greater than 10 and where the corresponding cell in the range D3:D100 equals 0:

```
=SUMIFS(B3:B100, C3:C100, "> 10", D3:D100, "= 0")
```

Calculating cumulative totals

Many worksheets need to calculate cumulative totals. Most budget worksheets, for example, show cumulative totals for sales and expenses over the course of the fiscal year. Similarly, loan amortizations often show the cumulative interest and principal paid over the life of the loan.

Calculating these cumulative totals is straightforward. For example, see the worksheet shown in Figure 9-1. Column F tracks the cumulative interest on the loan, and cell F7 contains the following SUM formula:

```
=SUM($D$7:D7)
```

> **Note** You can work with all the examples in this chapter by downloading Chapter09.xslx from either of the companion content sites mentioned in the Introduction.

FIGURE 9-1 The SUM formulas in column F calculate the cumulative interest paid on a loan.

This formula just sums cell D7, which is no great feat. However, when you fill the range F7:F54 with this formula, the left part of the SUM range ($D$7) remains anchored; the right side (D7) is relative and, therefore, changes. So, for example, the corresponding formula in cell F10 would be this:

```
=SUM($D$7:D10)
```

In case you're wondering, column G tracks the percentage of the total principal that has been paid off so far. Here's the formula used in cell G7:

```
=SUM($E$7:E7) / $B$4 * -1
```

The SUM($E$7:E7) part calculates the cumulative principal paid. To get the percentage, divide by the total principal (cell B4). The whole thing is multiplied by –1 to return a positive percentage.

The MOD function

The MOD function calculates the remainder (or *modulus*) that results after dividing one number into another. Here's the syntax for this more-useful-than-you-think function:

```
MOD(number, divisor)
```

number	The dividend (that is, the number to be divided)
divisor	The number by which you want to divide *number*

For example, MOD(24, 10) equals 4 (that is, 24÷10 = 2, with remainder 4).

The MOD function is well suited to values that are both sequential and cyclical. For example, the days of the week (as given by the WEEKDAY function) run from 1 (Sunday) through 7 (Saturday) and then start over (the next Sunday is back to 1). So, the following formula always returns an integer that corresponds to a day of the week:

```
=MOD(number, 7) + 1
```

If *number* is any integer, the MOD function returns integer values from 0 to 6, so adding 1 gives values from 1 to 7.

You can set up similar formulas using months (1 to 12), seconds or minutes (0 to 59), fiscal quarters (1 to 4), and more.

A better formula for time differences

In Chapter 8, "Working with date and time functions," I told you that subtracting an earlier time from a later time is problematic if the earlier time is before midnight and the later time is after midnight. Here's the expression I showed you to overcome this problem:

```
IF(EndTime < StartTime, 1 + EndTime - StartTime, EndTime - StartTime)
```

However, time values are sequential and cyclical: They're real numbers that run from **0** to **1** and then start over at midnight. Therefore, you can use **MOD** to greatly simplify the formula for calculating the difference between two times:

```
=MOD(EndTime - StartTime, 1)
```

This works for any value of *EndTime* and *StartTime*, as long as *EndTime* is later than *StartTime*.

Summing every *n*th row

Depending on the structure of your worksheet, you might need to sum only every *n*th row, where *n* is some integer. For example, you might want to sum only every 5th or 10th cell to get a sampling of the data.

You can accomplish this by applying the **MOD** function to the result of the **ROW** function, as in this array formula:

```
=SUM(IF(MOD(ROW(Range), n) = 1, Range, 0))
```

For each cell in *Range*, **MOD(ROW(***Range***)**, *n***)** returns **1** for every *n*th value. In that case, the value of the cell is added to the sum; otherwise, 0 is added. In other words, this sums the values in the first row of *Range*, the *n* + first row of *Range*, and so on. If instead, you want the second row of *Range*, the *n* + second row of *Range*, and so on, compare the **MOD** result with **2**, like so:

```
=SUM(IF(MOD(ROW(Range), n) = 2, Range, 0))
```

Special case no. 1: Summing only odd rows

If you want to sum only the odd rows in a worksheet, use this straightforward variation on the formula:

```
=SUM(IF(MOD(ROW(Range), 2) = 1, Range, 0))
```

Special case no. 2: Summing only even rows

To sum only the even rows, you need to sum those cells where **MOD(ROW(***Range***)**, **2)** returns **0**:

```
=SUM(IF(MOD(ROW(Range), 2) = 0, Range, 0))
```

Determining whether a year is a leap year

If you need to determine whether a given year is a leap year, the **MOD** function can help. Leap years (with some exceptions) are years divisible by 4. So, a year is (usually) a leap year if the following formula returns **0**:

```
=MOD(year, 4)
```

In this case, *year* is a four-digit year number. This formula works for the years 1901 to 2099, which should take care of most people's needs. The formula doesn't work for 1900 and 2100 because, despite being divisible by 4, these years aren't leap years. The general rule is that a year is a leap year if it's divisible by 4 and it's not divisible by 100, *unless* it's also divisible by 400. Therefore, because 1900 and 2100 are divisible by 100 and not by 400, they aren't leap years. The year 2000, however, is a leap year. If you want a formula that takes the full rule into account, use the following one:

```
=(MOD(year, 4) = 0) - (MOD(year, 100) = 0) + (MOD(year, 400) = 0)
```

The three parts of the formula that compare a **MOD** result to **0** return **1** or **0**. Therefore, the result of this formula always is **0** for leap years and nonzero for all other years.

Creating ledger shading

Ledger shading is formatting in which rows alternate cell shading between a light color and a slightly darker color (for example, white and light gray). This type of shading is often used in checkbook registers and account ledgers, but it's also useful in any worksheet that presents data in rows because it makes differentiating each row from its neighbors easier. Figure 9-2 shows an example.

	Rec	Date	Num	Payee/Description	Category	Debit	Credit	✓	Balance
2	1	4/1/2022		Starting Balance			5,000.00	✓	5,000.00
3	2	4/3/2022		Withdrawal	Auto - Fuel	(20.00)			4,980.00
4	3	4/10/2022		Al's Auto Repair	Auto - Repair	(1,245.00)			3,735.00
5	4	4/13/2022			Salary		1,834.69		5,569.69
6									
7									
8									
9									

FIGURE 9-2 This worksheet uses ledger shading for a checkbook register.

However, ledger shading isn't easy to work with by hand:

- If you have a large range to format, applying shading can take some time.

- If you insert or delete a row, you have to reapply the formatting.

To avoid these headaches, you can use a trick that combines the **MOD** function and Excel's conditional formatting. Here's how you do it:

1. Select the area you want to format with ledger shading.

2. Select **Home** > **Conditional Formatting** > **New Rule** to display the New Formatting Rule dialog box.

3. Select **Use A Formula To Determine Which Cells To Format**.

4. In the text box, enter the following formula:

   ```
   =MOD(ROW(), 2)
   ```

5. Select **Format** to display the Format Cells dialog box.

6. Select the **Fill** tab, select the color you want to use for the nonwhite ledger cells, and then select **OK** to return to the **New Formatting Rule** dialog box (see Figure 9-3).

7. Select **OK**.

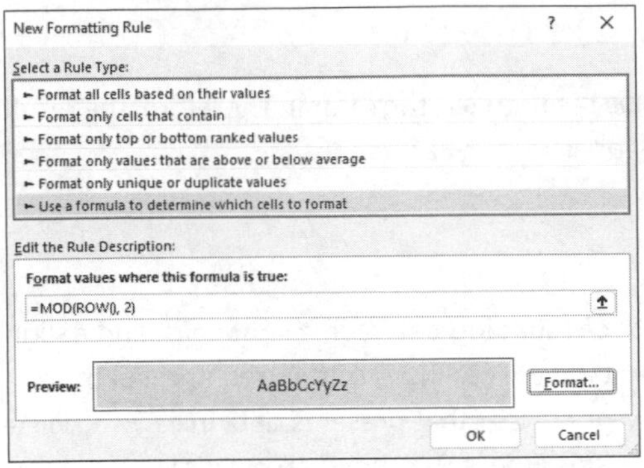

FIGURE 9-3 This MOD formula applies the cell shading to every second row (1, 3, 5, and so on).

The formula =MOD(ROW(), 2) returns **1** for odd-numbered rows and **0** for even-numbered rows. Because **1** is equivalent to **TRUE**, Excel applies the conditional formatting to the odd-numbered rows and leaves the even-numbered rows as they are.

> **Tip** If you prefer to alternate shading on columns instead of on rows, use the following formula in the **New Formatting Rule** dialog box:
>
> =MOD(COLUMN(), 2)
>
> If you prefer to have the even rows shaded and the odd rows unshaded, use the following formula in the **New Formatting Rule** dialog box:
>
> =MOD(ROW() + 1, 2)

Generating random numbers

If you're using a worksheet to set up a simulation, you need realistic data on which to do your testing. You could make up the numbers, but it's possible that you might unintentionally skew the data. A better approach is to generate the numbers randomly, using the worksheet functions **RAND** and **RANDBETWEEN**.

> **Tip** Excel's Analysis ToolPak also comes with a tool for generating random numbers. See Chapter 4, "Using functions."

The RAND function

The **RAND** function returns a random number that is greater than or equal to 0 and less than 1. **RAND** is often useful by itself. (For example, it's perfect for generating random time values.) However, you'll most often use it in an expression to generate random numbers between two values.

In the simplest case, if you want to generate random numbers greater than or equal to 0 and less than **n**, use the following expression:

```
RAND() * n
```

For example, the following formula generates a random number between 0 and 30:

```
=RAND() * 30
```

The more complex case is when you want random numbers greater than or equal to some number *m* and less than some number *n*. Here's the expression to use for this case:

```
RAND() * (n - m) + m
```

For example, the following formula produces a random number greater than or equal to 100 and less than 200:

```
=RAND() * (200 - 100) + 100
```

> **Caution**   **RAND** is a volatile function, meaning that its value changes each time you recalculate or reopen the worksheet or edit any cell on the worksheet. To enter a static random number in a cell, type **=RAND()**, press F9 to evaluate the function and return a random number, and then press Enter to place the random number into the cell as a numeric literal.

Generating random *n*-digit numbers

It's often useful to create random numbers with a specific number of digits. For example, you might want to generate a random six-digit account number for new customers, or you might need a random eight-digit number for a temporary file name.

The procedure for this is to start with the general formula from the previous section and apply the **INT** function to ensure an integer result:

```
INT(RAND() * (n - m) + m)
```

In this case, however, you set *n* equal to 10^n, and you set *m* equal to 10^{n-1}:

```
INT(RAND() * (10ⁿ - 10ⁿ⁻¹) + 10ⁿ⁻¹)
```

For example, if you need a random eight-digit number, use this formula:

```
INT(RAND() * (100000000 - 10000000) + 10000000)
```

This generates random numbers greater than or equal to 10,000,000 and less than or equal to 99,999,999.

Generating a random letter

You normally use **RAND** to generate a random number, but it's also useful for text values. For example, suppose that you need to generate a random letter of the alphabet. There are 26 letters in the alphabet, so you start with an expression that generates random integers greater than or equal to **1** and less than or equal to **26**:

```
INT(RAND() * 26 + 1)
```

If you want a random uppercase letter (A to Z), note that these letters have character codes that run from ANSI 65 to ANSI 90, so you take the preceding formula, add 64, and plug in the result to the **CHAR** function:

```
=CHAR(INT(RAND() * 26) + 65)
```

If you want a random lowercase letter (a to z) instead, note that these letters have character codes that run from ANSI 97 to ANSI 122, so you take the preceding formula, add 96, and plug the result into the **CHAR** function:

```
=CHAR(INT(RAND() * 26) + 97)
```

Sorting values randomly

If you have a set of values on a worksheet, you might need to sort them in random order. For example, if you want to perform an operation on a subset of data, sorting the table randomly removes any numeric biases that might be inherent if the data was sorted in any way.

Follow these steps to sort a data table randomly:

1. Assuming that the data is arranged in rows, select a range in the column immediately to the left or right of the table. Make sure that the selected range has the same number of rows as the table.

2. Enter =**RAND()** and then press Ctrl+Enter to add the **RAND** formula to every selected cell.

3. Select **Formulas** > **Calculation Options** > **Manual**.

4. Select the range that includes the data and the column of **RAND** values.

5. Select **Data** > **Sort** to display the **Sort** dialog box.

6. In the **Sort By** list, select the column that contains the **RAND** values.

7. Select **OK**.

8. Select **Formulas** > **Calculation Options** > **Automatic** and delete the **RAND** formulas from the table.

This procedure tells Excel to sort the selected range according to the random values, thus sorting the data table randomly. Figure 9-4 shows an example. The data values are in column A, the **RAND** values are in column B, and the range A2:B26 was sorted on column B.

B2		f_x =RAND()		
	A	B	C	D
1	**Data Values**	**RAND Values**		
2	24	0.044239354		
3	22	0.200288795		
4	20	0.5683119		
5	6	0.658148847		
6	3	0.673498673		
7	25	0.480440191		
8	9	0.963209469		
9	7	0.00149682		
10	16	0.300202047		
11	10	0.950951717		
12	11	0.528776596		
13	23	0.343005541		
14	14	0.865940199		
15	17	0.1143168		
16	13	0.931786068		
17	2	0.014122898		
18	18	0.141632938		
19	19	0.102198049		
20	15	0.808550566		
21	12	0.360595819		
22	1	0.978656822		
23	5	0.806258137		
24	8	0.1313765		
25	21	0.557702347		
26	4	0.707467089		

FIGURE 9-4 To randomly sort data values, add a column of =RAND() formulas and then sort the entire range on the random values.

The **RANDBETWEEN** function

Excel's **RANDBETWEEN** function can simplify working with certain sets of random numbers. **RANDBETWEEN** lets you specify a lower bound and an upper bound, and it returns a random integer between them:

RANDBETWEEN(*bottom*, *top*)

bottom	The smallest possible random integer. (That is, Excel generates a random number that is greater than or equal to *bottom*.)
top	The largest possible random integer. (That is, Excel generates a random number that is less than or equal to *top*.)

For example, the following formula returns a random integer between 0 and 59:

=RANDBETWEEN(0, 59)

The **RANDARRAY** function

The **RAND** function returns a single random value, but sometimes you need a set—that is, a range with a specified number of rows and columns—of random values to test a worksheet model. One way to generate such a set is to enter =**RAND** in one cell, and then use that cell's fill handle to generate the range of random values you need. That works, but it's a bit of a hassle, especially because you must use two separate fill operations: one for the rows and another for the columns.

Fortunately, Excel 2019 offers a much simpler method: the new **RANDARRAY** function, which generates an array of random numbers greater than or equal to 0 and less than 1:

RANDARRAY([*rows*][, *columns*])

rows	The number of rows you want in the array. If you omit this argument, Excel generates a single row.
columns	The number of columns you want in the array. If you omit this argument, Excel generates a single column.

For example, the following formula generates an array of random values that contains six rows and four columns:

=RANDARRAY(6,4)

> **Caution** **RANDARRAY** generates a dynamic array (see Chapter 2, "Creating advanced formulas") that spills right and down into the range defined by the function's *rows* and *columns* parameters. If this results range isn't blank, Excel generates a #SPILL! error, which means you need to delete or move the data that's blocking the spill.

Creating increasing random numbers with the SEQUENCE function

A special case for a set of random numbers is one where the values increase as you run through the set. One possible solution would be to enter =RAND() in the initial cell, add RAND() to that value in the next cell, and then fill this formula into the full set you want. For example, if you enter =RAND() in cell A1 and you want a vertical set, here are the formulas in cells A2, A3, and A4:

```
=A1 + RAND()
=A2 + RAND()
=A3 + RAND()
```

For more flexibility, you can take advantage of the **SEQUENCE** function, which generates a range of increasing numbers:

SEQUENCE(*rows* [, *columns*] [, *start*] [, *step*])

rows	The number of rows you want in the array.
columns	The number of columns you want in the array. If you omit this argument, Excel generates a single column.
start	The first value in the array. If you omit this argument, Excel starts the array at 1.
step	The amount by which each new value in the array is incremented. If you omit this argument, Excel uses a *step* value of 1.

For example, the following formula generates an array of increasing values that contains five rows and three columns, starting at 100 and incrementing by 10:

=RANDARRAY(5, 3, 100, 10)

> **Caution** SEQUENCE generates a dynamic array (see Chapter 2) that spills right and down into the range defined by the function's *rows* and *columns* parameters. If this results range isn't blank, Excel generates a `#SPILL!` error, which means you need to delete or move the data that's blocking the spill.

To generate a set of increasing random numbers, use the RAND function (or an expression that includes the RAND function) for both the *start* and *step* parameters:

```
=SEQUENCE(10, 5, RAND(), RAND())
```

Programming with Excel's formula language

When you build formulas using Excel's operators, operands, and worksheet functions, are you programming? It might not seem like it because coding in a language such as JavaScript or Visual Basic for Applications (VBA) feels completely different than entering a formula into a cell. However, what if you define programming broadly as, say, "implementing an algorithm." Ah, then things become a tad more interesting, don't they? Surely, almost any formula you can think of is, when you break it down, a sequence of instructions designed to solve a problem. That, by definition, is the implementation of an algorithm.

Excel has data types, predefined functions, and branching statements (via functions such as IF), all of which are core components of any programming language. What Excel's formula language hasn't had are two other core programming constructions: variables and custom functions. Sure, you could simulate the latter with custom VBA functions, but few Excel users want to learn VBA.

Happily, the latest version of Excel introduces two new worksheet functions that fill these gaps: The LET function enables you to create formula variables and the LAMBDA function enables you to create custom functions. The rest of this chapter takes you through these new functions and shows you how to use them to take your Excel "programming" to a higher level.

> **Note** As this book went to press, the **LET** and **LAMBDA** functions (as well as functions that use **LAMBDA**, such as **REDUCE**, **MAP**, and **SCAN**) were available only to folks in the Office Insiders program. These functions will eventually be released to all Excel users, but they might not be available to you when you read this.

Using LET to create formula variables

One common problem you'll come across numerous times in your formula-building career is having to repeat a calculation two or more times in the same formula. I provided a good example of this back in Chapter 8 when I took you through the formula for calculating the nth occurrence of a weekday in a given year and month. Figure 9-5 shows the following formula at work:

```
=DATE(B4, B3, 1) +
IF(B2 < WEEKDAY(DATE(B4, B3, 1)),
```

```
7 - WEEKDAY(DATE(B4, B3, 1)) + B2,
 B2 - WEEKDAY(DATE(B4, B3, 1)) +
(B1 - 1) * 7)
```

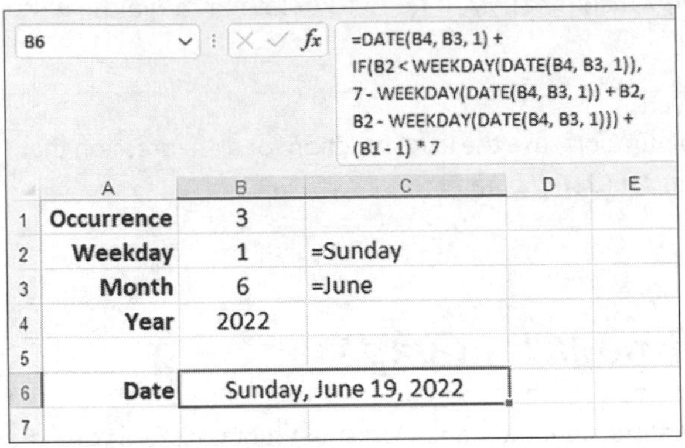

FIGURE 9-5 A formula that calculates the nth occurrence of a weekday in a given year and month.

Notice that this formula uses the expression **DATE(B4, B3, 1)** four times and the expression **WEEKDAY(DATE(B4, B3, 1))** three times. This not only makes the formula harder to read, but it also burdens Excel with having to repeat the same calculations multiple times. Fortunately, you can both simplify such formulas and reduce their calculation cost by using the **LET** function to turn repeated expressions into variables.

Here's a simplified version of the **LET** syntax:

```
LET(name, name_value, calculation)
```

name	The name of the variable. Note that the name must start with a letter and is *not* enclosed in quotation marks.
name_value	The value you want to assign to the *name* variable. The value can be a literal, a cell or range reference, an expression, or a function. If you create multiple variables, as I describe a bit later in this section, a *name_value* expression can include a previously-defined variable name.
calculation	An expression that uses one or more instances of the *name* variable. The **LET** function returns the result of this expression.

> ⚠ **Caution** If you use a range reference for the *name_value* argument, LET generates a dynamic array (see Chapter 2) that spills into the corresponding results range. If the results range contains data, Excel shows a `#SPILL!` error. To resolve this error, delete or move whatever data is blocking the spill.

Here's a trivial example:

```
=LET(x, 10, x * 2)
```

This formula assigns the value 10 to the variable named **x**, then returns the result of **x * 2**, which is 20.

> 📝 **Note** The variables you create within a LET function can only be used within that LET function—either as part of the calculation or as part of a variable value expression. In programming parlance, LET variables are said to be *scoped* to their LET function.

For more complex cases, you can create and assign multiple variables—up to 126—within a single **LET** function. In the syntax, place all your variable names and values first, then the *calculation* argument last. Here's an example:

```
=LET(height, 4, base, 3, SQRT(height ∧ 2 + base ∧2))
```

This formula defines two variables named **height** and **base** and returns the square root of the sum of their squares. Assuming **height** and **base** are the lengths of adjacent sides of a right-angled triangle, this **LET** function returns the length of the triangle's hypotenuse (via the Pythagorean Theorem), which is 5, in this example.

We can now use LET to solve our earlier problem concerning the repeated expressions **DATE(B4, B3, 1)** and **WEEKDAY(DATE(B4, B3, 1))** in the formula for calculating the nth occurrence of a weekday in a given year and month. Figure 9-6 shows the following formula at work:

```
=LET(firstDayOfMonth, DATE(B4, B3, 1), dayOfWeek, WEEKDAY(firstDayOfMonth),
firstDayOfMonth +
IF(B2 < dayOfWeek,
7 - dayOfWeek + B2,
 B2 - dayOfWeek +
(B1 - 1) * 7)
```

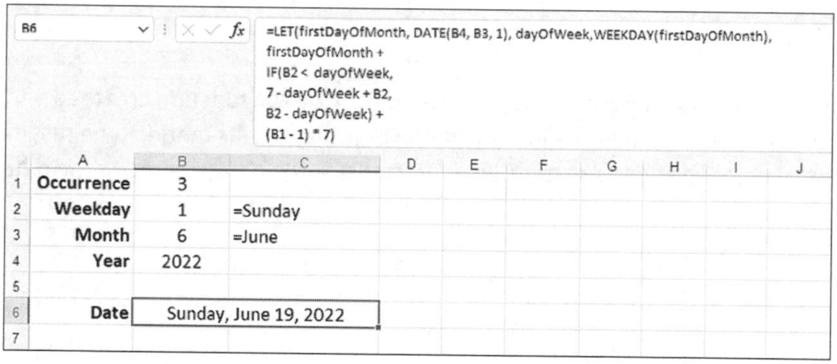

FIGURE 9-6 Using LET to simplify the formula that calculates the nth occurrence of a weekday in a given year and month.

This simpler formula defines the variable **firstDayOfMonth** as the expression **DATE(B4, B3, 1)** and the variable **dayOfWeek** as the expression **WEEKDAY(firstDayOfMonth)**, and then uses those variables in the calculation.

Using LAMBDA to create custom functions

Excel's hundreds of worksheet functions enable you to solve an amazing variety of problems and to analyze a wide array of business data. As powerful as Excel's built-in functions are, they can't solve every problem or perform every type of analysis you might need. In the past, when you came across a situation where Excel's worksheet functions weren't up to the task, the solution was to code a custom function using VBA. As long as the workbook that contains the VBA code was open, you could call the function by name in your formulas as often as you need it.

That's a viable solution if you know VBA, if you're up for learning VBA, or if you're willing and able to outsource the coding to a third party who knows VBA. That's a lot of ifs! Wouldn't life be simpler and easier if you could just create custom functions using the Excel formula language that you already know?

Well, I'm happy to report that now you can! Using the powerful **LAMBDA** function, you can create custom functions that are as complex as you need them to be *and* you build those functions using the same language that you use to build regular Excel formulas.

Here's the LAMBDA syntax:

```
LAMBDA([parameter1, parameter2,...], calculation)
```

parameter1, etc.	On or more optional inputs to the custom function. Note that each parameter name must start with a letter and is not enclosed in quotation marks.
calculation	An expression that may use one or more instances of the parameters. The **LAMBDA** function returns the result of this expression.

The parameters are the **LAMBDA** function equivalents to the arguments used with Excel's worksheet functions. When you call the **LAMBDA** function, you include a value for each parameter, and the value can be a literal, a cell or range reference, an expression, a worksheet function, or another **LAMBDA** function.

> ⚠ **Caution**   If you use a range reference for a parameter, your LAMBDA function creates a dynamic array (see Chapter 2) that spills into the corresponding results range. If the results range isn't empty, Excel generates a #SPILL! error. To fix the error, delete or move the data that's blocking the spill.

Here's a trivial example:

```
=LAMBDA(x,  x * 2)
```

This function takes a single parameter named **x** and returns the result of the expression **x * 2**. If you name this function **DoubleMe**, then the following cell entry returns the value **20**:

```
=DoubleMe(10)
```

The key to using **LAMBDA** custom functions is that you don't enter them directly into the worksheet. Instead, you assign them a name by following these steps:

1. Select **Formulas** > **Define Name** to display the New Name dialog box.

2. In the **Name** text box, enter the name you want to use for the custom function.

3. In the **Refers To** box, type an equal sign (=), followed by the **LAMBDA** function that defines your custom function. Figure 9-7 shows an example.

4. Select **OK**.

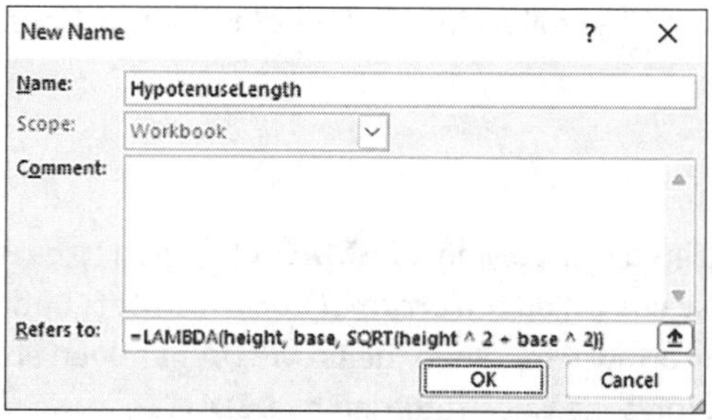

FIGURE 9-7 You use the New Name dialog box to assign a name to your custom LAMBDA function.

In Figure 9-7, I'm defining a custom function named **HypotenuseLength** that uses the following **LAMBDA** function:

```
=LAMBDA(height, base, SQRT(height ^ 2 + base ^ 2))
```

This custom function uses two parameters named **height** and **base** and returns the square root of the sum of their squares. Assuming **height** and **base** are the lengths of adjacent sides of a right-angled triangle, the **LAMBDA** calculation returns the length of the triangle's hypotenuse (via the Pythagorean Theorem).

Once you've named your custom function, you can use it in any formula in the same workbook (assuming you've given your custom function workbook scope). For example, Figure 9-8 shows the **HypotenuseLength** custom function used in a worksheet. Note that because I used ranges for the **height** and **base** parameters (A2:A7 and B2:B7, respectively), Excel spills the results of the custom function as a dynamic array into the corresponding range (C2:C7).

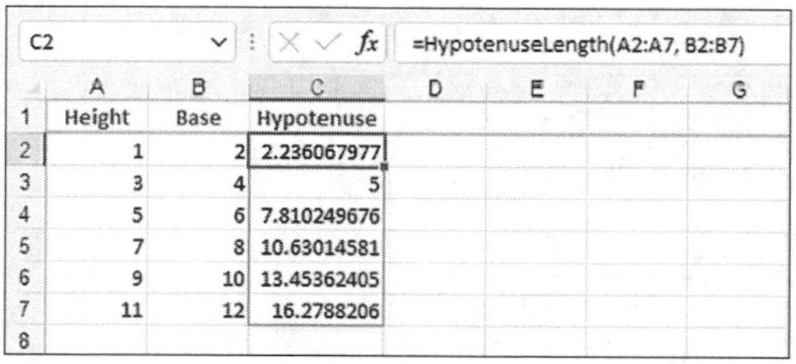

FIGURE 9-8 The custom function from Figure 9-7 used in a worksheet.

Using a LAMBDA to process an array

The latest version of Excel also includes several new functions that enable you to use a **LAMBDA** function to process an array or range of values. The sections that follow look at four of these functions: **REDUCE**, **MAP**, **BYCOL**, and **BYROW**.

REDUCE

The **REDUCE** function returns a numeric value calculated by applying a **LAMBDA** function to each item in an array. Along the way, **REDUCE** keeps track of a value called the *accumulator*, which gets updated with each application of the **LAMBDA** function to an array item. When the **LAMBDA** has been applied to all the array items, the final value of the accumulator is the value returned by **REDUCE**.

Here's the **REDUCE** syntax:

REDUCE([*initial_value*], *array*, LAMBDA(*accumulator*, *currentItem*))

initial_value	The optional starting value for the accumulator. The default value is 0.
Array	The array or range you want to reduce.
Accumulator	A **LAMBDA** variable that stores the current value of the accumulator.
currentItem	A **LAMBDA** variable that represents the current item in the array.

Figure 9-9 shows a range (B2:F10) of historical sales results for several sales reps.

| F13 | ▼ : × ✓ *fx* | =REDUCE(1, B2:F10, LAMBDA(accumulator,currentItem, IF(currentItem > 300000, accumulator + currentItem * 5%, accumulator))) | | | | | | | | | |

▲	A	B	C	D	E	F	G	H	I	J	K
1	**Salesperson**	**2018**	**2019**	**2020**	**2021**	**2022**					
2	Nancy Davolio	$ 259,875	$ 267,671	$ 254,287	$ 254,287	$ 239,030					
3	Andrew Fuller	$ 293,827	$ 293,827	$ 276,197	$ 278,959	$ 284,538					
4	Janet Leverling	$ 347,119	$ 364,474	$ 338,961	$ 359,299	$ 362,892					
5	Margaret Peacock	$ 189,345	$ 195,025	$ 200,876	$ 218,954	$ 221,144					
6	Steven Buchanan	$ 209,283	$ 223,932	$ 210,496	$ 231,546	$ 247,754					
7	Michael Suyama	$ 222,384	$ 217,936	$ 217,936	$ 233,191	$ 249,515					
8	Robert King	$ 299,550	$ 305,541	$ 317,762	$ 340,006	$ 336,605					
9	Laura Callahan	$ 239,990	$ 256,789	$ 282,468	$ 310,715	$ 301,393					
10	Anne Dodsworth	$ 256,919	$ 256,919	$ 246,642	$ 241,709	$ 258,629					
11											
12		Total number of sales results over $300,000:				11					
13		Total of all bonuses (5% of each sales result over $300,000):				$ 184,239					
14											

FIGURE 9-9 The REDUCE function in action.

One way to use **REDUCE** is as a counter, where when you apply the **LAMBDA** to each array item, if the item meets a specified criterion, you increment the accumulator. That's what's happening in cell F12, which uses the following formula:

```
=REDUCE(0, B2:F10, LAMBDA(accumulator,currentItem, IF(currentItem > 300000,
accumulator + 1, accumulator)))
```

If any item in the range B2:F10 is greater than 300,000, the accumulator is incremented; otherwise, the accumulator is unchanged.

Suppose the company pays a 5 percent bonus to any rep who generates sales over $300,000. What is the total of all the bonuses paid out? The following formula (which appears in cell F13) returns the answer:

```
=REDUCE(1, B2:F10, LAMBDA(accumulator,currentItem, IF(currentItem > 300000,
accumulator + currentItem * 5%, accumulator)))
```

In this case, if any item in the range B2:F10 is greater than 300,000, 5 percent of the current item is added to the accumulator; otherwise, the accumulator is unchanged.

MAP

The **MAP** function creates a new array, the items in which are derived by applying a **LAMBDA** function to each value in one or more existing arrays.

Here's the **MAP** syntax:

```
MAP(array(s), lambda)
```

array(s)	One or more arrays or ranges you want to map.
lambda	A **LAMBDA** function that applies a calculation to each item in the array(s). Your **LAMBDA** function requires one variable to represent each array.

The simplest case is when you map a single array. For example, Figure 9-10 shows the range (B2:F10) of historical sales results for several reps.

H2	⌄ : × ✓ fx	=MAP(F2:F10, LAMBDA(sales, sales * 1.06))						
	A	B	C	D	E	F	G	H
1	Salesperson	2018	2019	2020	2021	2022	Bonus?	2023 Target
2	Nancy Davolio	$ 259,875	$ 267,671	$ 254,287	$ 254,287	$ 239,030	No	$ 253,372
3	Andrew Fuller	$ 293,827	$ 293,827	$ 276,197	$ 278,959	$ 284,538	Yes	$ 301,610
4	Janet Leverling	$ 347,119	$ 364,474	$ 338,961	$ 359,299	$ 362,892	Yes	$ 384,666
5	Margaret Peacock	$ 189,345	$ 195,025	$ 200,876	$ 218,954	$ 221,144	Yes	$ 234,413
6	Steven Buchanan	$ 209,283	$ 223,932	$ 210,496	$ 231,546	$ 247,754	Yes	$ 262,619
7	Michael Suyama	$ 222,384	$ 217,936	$ 217,936	$ 233,191	$ 249,515	Yes	$ 264,486
8	Robert King	$ 299,550	$ 305,541	$ 317,762	$ 340,006	$ 336,605	No	$ 356,801
9	Laura Callahan	$ 239,990	$ 256,789	$ 282,468	$ 310,715	$ 301,393	No	$ 319,477
10	Anne Dodsworth	$ 256,919	$ 256,919	$ 246,642	$ 241,709	$ 258,629	Yes	$ 274,147
11								

FIGURE 9-10 The MAP function in action.

Suppose you want to populate a new column (H2:H10) named 2023 Target that adds 6 percent to each value in the 2022 column (F2:F10). Here's a **MAP** formula that does the job:

```
=MAP(F2:F10, LAMBDA(sales, sales * 1.06))
```

The **LAMBDA** function's **sales** variable represents each item in the range F2:F10. The **LAMBDA** calculation multplies **sales** by 1.06 and the resulting dynamic array is spilled into the range H2:H10.

As another example, suppose you want to know which reps are getting a bonus, the criterion for which is that sales in the current year (2022) exceeded those of last year (2021). That's what's happening in the range G2:G10, which is a dynamic array generated by the following formula:

```
=MAP(E2:E10, F2:F10, LAMBDA(last year, currentYear, IF(currentYear > last year,
"Yes", "No")))
```

This **MAP** function works on two arrays: 2021 sales (E2:E10) and 2022 sales (F2:F10). In the **LAMBDA** function, the **lastYear** variable represents the items in the first array, and the **currentYear** variable represents the items in the second array. In the **LAMBDA** calculation, an **IF** function compares **currentYear** with **lastYear**: if the former is greater, **Yes** is returned to indicate a bonus will be paid; otherwise, **No** is returned.

BYCOL

The **BYCOL** function creates a new array, the items in which are derived by applying a **LAMBDA** function to each column in a specified range or array. The resulting array is a single row, with one item for each column in the original array.

Here's the **BYCOL** syntax:

```
BYCOL(array, lambda)
```

array	The array or range you want to work with.
lambda	A **LAMBDA** function that applies a calculation to each column in the *array*.

For example, Figure 9-11 shows the range (B2:F10) of historical sales results for several reps.

B12		:	× ✓ fx	=BYCOL(B2:F10, LAMBDA(col, MAX(col)))		

	A	B	C	D	E	F
1	**Salesperson**	**2018**	**2019**	**2020**	**2021**	**2022**
2	Nancy Davolio	$ 259,875	$ 267,671	$ 254,287	$ 254,287	$ 239,030
3	Andrew Fuller	$ 293,827	$ 293,827	$ 276,197	$ 278,959	$ 284,538
4	Janet Leverling	$ 347,119	$ 364,474	$ 338,961	$ 359,299	$ 362,892
5	Margaret Peacock	$ 189,345	$ 195,025	$ 200,876	$ 218,954	$ 221,144
6	Steven Buchanan	$ 209,283	$ 223,932	$ 210,496	$ 231,546	$ 247,754
7	Michael Suyama	$ 222,384	$ 217,936	$ 217,936	$ 233,191	$ 249,515
8	Robert King	$ 299,550	$ 305,541	$ 317,762	$ 340,006	$ 336,605
9	Laura Callahan	$ 239,990	$ 256,789	$ 282,468	$ 310,715	$ 301,393
10	Anne Dodsworth	$ 256,919	$ 256,919	$ 246,642	$ 241,709	$ 258,629
11						
12	**Highest sales:**	$ 347,119	$ 364,474	$ 338,961	$ 359,299	$ 362,892
13						

FIGURE 9-11 The BYCOL function in action.

Suppose you want to create an array that consists of the maximum sales values for each year. Here's a **BYCOL** formula that does the job:

```
=BYCOL(B2:F10, LAMBDA(col, MAX(col)))
```

The **BYCOL** function takes the range B2:F10 as the *array* argument. In the **LAMBDA** function, the **col** variable represents each column in the range, and the calculation uses **MAX** to return the maximum value from each column, with the results generated as a dynamic array spilled into the range B12:F12.

BYROW

The **BYROW** function creates a new array, the items in which are derived by applying a **LAMBDA** function to each row in a specified range or array. The resulting array is a single column, with one item for each row in the original array.

Here's the **BYROW** syntax:

```
BYROW(array, lambda)
```

array	The array or range you want to work with.
lambda	A **LAMBDA** function that applies a calculation to each row in the *array*.

For example, Figure 9-12 shows the range (B2:F10) of historical sales results for several reps.

	A	B	C	D	E	F	G
G2			f_x	=BYROW(B2:F10, LAMBDA(row, MAX(row)))			

	A	B	C	D	E	F	G
1	Salesperson	2018	2019	2020	2021	2022	Best Year
2	Nancy Davolio	$ 259,875	$ 267,671	$ 254,287	$ 254,287	$ 239,030	267671
3	Andrew Fuller	$ 293,827	$ 293,827	$ 276,197	$ 278,959	$ 284,538	293827
4	Janet Leverling	$ 347,119	$ 364,474	$ 338,961	$ 359,299	$ 362,892	364474
5	Margaret Peacock	$ 189,345	$ 195,025	$ 200,876	$ 218,954	$ 221,144	221144
6	Steven Buchanan	$ 209,283	$ 223,932	$ 210,496	$ 231,546	$ 247,754	247754
7	Michael Suyama	$ 222,384	$ 217,936	$ 217,936	$ 233,191	$ 249,515	249515
8	Robert King	$ 299,550	$ 305,541	$ 317,762	$ 340,006	$ 336,605	340006
9	Laura Callahan	$ 239,990	$ 256,789	$ 282,468	$ 310,715	$ 301,393	310715
10	Anne Dodsworth	$ 256,919	$ 256,919	$ 246,642	$ 241,709	$ 258,629	258629
11							

FIGURE 9-12 The BYROW function in action.

Suppose you want to create an array that consists of the maximum sales values for each rep. Here's a **BYROW** formula that does the job:

```
=BYROW(B2:F10, LAMBDA(row, MAX(row)))
```

The **BYROW** function takes the range B2:F10 as the *array* argument. In the **LAMBDA** function, the **row** variable represents each row in the range, and the calculation uses **MAX** to return the maximum value from each row, with the results generated as a dynamic array spilled into the range G2:G10.

PART 3

Building Business Formulas

CHAPTER 10

Implementing basic business formulas

In this chapter, you will:

- Learn useful formulas for price markup and discounts, as well as the break-even point.

- Discover powerful financial formulas for analyzing sales, costs, margins, and fixed assets.

- Try out several formulas for analyzing and managing inventory.

- Learn how to analyze a company's liquidity by examining its accounts receivable, accounts payables, working capital, and more.

Is it possible to run a business without Excel? It might be, but I doubt there are many businesses—and very few *successful* businesses—that don't have Excel running on a computer or three somewhere. That's because Excel was built with business in mind, so it's bristling with tools that enable you to analyze and organize a company's data. I get to many of these powerful tools later in the book, but Excel's real usefulness in the day-to-day hurly-burly of business is that it enables you to quickly build all the basic formulas used by a business. Whether you need to calculate a discounted price, a break-even point, a product's gross margin, or your company's working capital (to mention just a few of the business formulas I explain in this chapter), Excel is up to the task.

Pricing formulas

Setting the price for a product or service is a crucial aspect of financial management. Set the price too high, and sales might suffer; set the price too low, and you might forgo revenue that customers would have been otherwise willing to pay. The main formulas govern three aspects of pricing: markups, discounts, and the break-even point.

Price markups

A product's *markup* is the dollar amount added to the production cost to obtain the selling price. Here are some useful formulas associated with price markups.

Selling price

The selling price is the price at which the item will be sold. Given the item's cost price and a markup rate as a percentage, you calculate the selling price using the following formula:

```
=Cost Price * (100% + Markup Rate)
```

For example, if a product's cost price is $30.00 and the markup rate is 70 percent, then the selling price is $30.00 * (100% + 70%), or $51.00 (see Figure 10-1).

B4		f_x	=B2 * (100% + B3)	
	A		B	C
1	**Selling Price**			
2	Cost Price		$30.00	
3	Markup Rate		70%	
4	Selling Price		$51.00	
5				

FIGURE 10-1 This formula calculates the selling price given the cost price and a markup rate.

Markup amount

The markup amount is the amount by which the cost of the item is increased to get the selling price. Given the item's cost price and a markup rate as a percentage, you calculate the markup amount using the following formula:

```
=Cost Price * Markup Rate
```

For example, if a product's cost price is $30.00 and the markup rate is 70 percent, then the markup amount is $30.00 * 70%, or $21.00 (see Figure 10-2).

B9		f_x	=B7 * B8
	A		B
6	**Markup Amount**		
7	Cost Price		$30.00
8	Markup Rate		70%
9	Markup Amount		$21.00
10			

FIGURE 10-2 This formula calculates the markup amount given the cost price and a markup rate.

Markup rate

The markup rate is the percentage by which the cost of the item is increased to get the selling price. Given the item's cost price and selling price, you calculate the markup rate using the following formula:

```
= (Selling Price - Cost Price) / Cost Price
```

For example, if a product's selling price is $51.00 and its cost price is $30.00, then the markup rate is ($51.00 – $30.00) / $30.00, or 70 percent (see Figure 10-3).

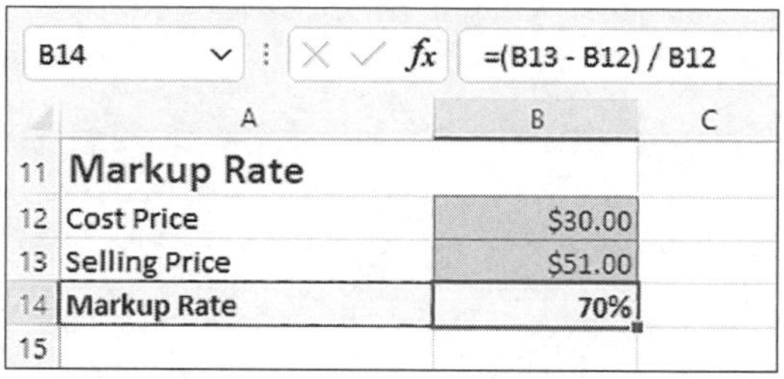

FIGURE 10-3 This formula calculates the markup rate given the cost price and the selling price.

Cost price

The cost price is the original price of a marked-up item. Given the item's selling price and a markup rate as a percentage, you calculate the cost price using the following formula:

```
=Selling Price / (100% + Markup Rate)
```

For example, if a product's selling price is $51.00 and the markup rate is 70 percent, then the cost price is $51.00 / (100% + 70%), or $30.00 (see Figure 10-4).

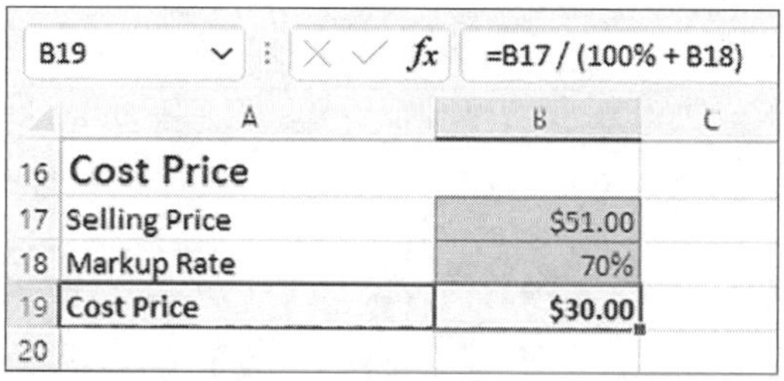

FIGURE 10-4 This formula calculates the cost price given the selling price and a markup rate.

Price discounts

The default price of a retail item is the *manufacturer's suggested retail price* (MSRP; often shortened to just *retail*), also known as the *list price* (or just *list*) or the *catalog price*. If you've heard the phrase "Retail is for suckers," it means that the retail price is just a suggestion, and many products can be purchased for a lower price. That lower price is the *net price* (also called the *discounted price*), which is obtained by applying a *discount rate* to the retail price. There are several formulas associated with price discounts:

Net price

The net price is the reduced price of the item. Given the item's list price and a discount rate as a percentage, you calculate the net price using the following formula:

```
=List Price * (100% - Discount Rate)
```

For example, if a product's list price is $89.99 and the discount rate is 30 percent, then the net price is $89.99 * (100% – 30%), or $62.99 (see Figure 10-5).

B4	✓ : × ✓ fx	=B2 * (100% - B3)

	A	B	C
1	**Net Price**		
2	List Price	$89.99	
3	Discount Rate	30%	
4	Net Price	$62.99	
5			

FIGURE 10-5 This formula calculates the net price given the list price and a discount rate.

Discount amount

The amount by which the price of the item is reduced. Given the item's list price and a discount rate as a percentage, you calculate the discount amount using the following formula:

```
=List Price * Discount Rate
```

For example, if a product's list price is $89.99 and the discount rate is 30 percent, then the discount amount is $89.99 * 30%, or $27.00 (see Figure 10-6).

B9	✓ : × ✓ fx	=B7 * B8

	A	B	C
6	**Discount Amount**		
7	List Price	$89.99	
8	Discount Rate	30%	
9	Discount Amount	$27.00	
10			

FIGURE 10-6 This formula calculates the discount amount given the list price and a discount rate.

Discount rate

The discount rate is the percentage by which the price of the item is reduced. Given the item's list price and net price, you calculate the discount rate using the following formula:

```
=100% - (Net Price / List Price)
```

> **Note** Technically, you don't need the parentheses in this formula because Excel always performs division before subtraction. However, I've added them here to make the formula and the example easier to read.

For example, if a product's list price is $89.99 and its net price is $62.99, then the discount rate is 100% – ($62.99 / $89.99), or 30 percent (see Figure 10-7).

B14		fx	=100% - (B13 / B12)	
	A		B	C
11	**Discount Rate**			
12	List Price		$89.99	
13	Net Price		$62.99	
14	Discount Rate		30%	
15				

FIGURE 10-7 This formula calculates the discount rate given the list price and the net price.

List price

The list price is the original price of a discounted item. Given the item's net price and a discount rate as a percentage, you calculate the list price using the following formula:

```
=Net Price / (100% - Discount Rate)
```

For example, if a product's net price is $62.99 and the discount rate is 30 percent, then the list price is $62.99 / (100% – 30%), or $89.99 (see Figure 10-8).

B19		fx	=B17 / (100% - B18)	
	A		B	C
16	**List Price**			
17	Net Price		$62.99	
18	Discount Rate		30%	
19	List Price		$89.99	
20				

FIGURE 10-8 This formula calculates the list price given the net price and a discount rate.

Break-even point

The *break-even point* for a product is the sales volume (in units) required so that total revenue matches the total costs. In other words, the break-even point specifies the minimum sales volume required for the total profit to be zero. Costs are divided into two categories:

- **Variable costs:** The expenses that incur with the sale of each product, such as materials or packaging.

- **Fixed costs:** The expenses that incur regardless of sales, such as equipment rentals, marketing costs, and employee salaries.

At the break-even point, the following equation is true:

```
Revenue = Variable Costs + Fixed Costs
```

A product's *contribution margin* is its selling price minus its variable costs:

```
=Selling Price - Variable Costs
```

For example, if a product sells for $10 and has variable costs of $6, the contribution margin is $10 – $6, or $4.

> **Note** In some cases, analysts break down variable costs into those associated with manufacturing the product and those associated with the product's operating expenses. Sales minus the variable manufacturing costs is sometimes called the *manufacturing contribution margin.*

Given the product's total fixed costs for the sales period, you can use the following formula to calculate the break-even point in units:

```
=Total Fixed Costs / Contribution Margin
```

For example, if a product has a contribution margin of $4, and its total fixed costs are $24,000, then the break-even point is $24,000 / $4, or 6,000 units (see Figure 10-9).

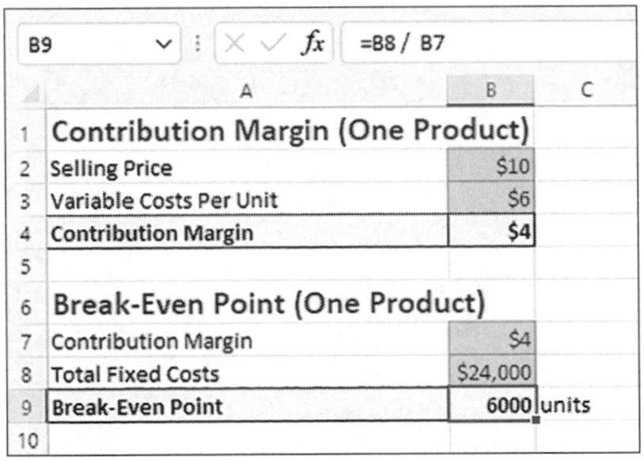
B9 =B8 / B7

	A	B	C
1	Contribution Margin (One Product)		
2	Selling Price	$10	
3	Variable Costs Per Unit	$6	
4	Contribution Margin	$4	
5			
6	Break-Even Point (One Product)		
7	Contribution Margin	$4	
8	Total Fixed Costs	$24,000	
9	Break-Even Point	6000	units
10			

FIGURE 10-9 This formula calculates the break-even point for a single product given the contribution margin and total fixed costs.

If you want to determine the break-even point for multiple products, you need to determine what percentage of overall unit sales applies to each product. This is called the *sales mix,* and you use it to calculate a weighted-average contribution margin for all the products. Here's the formula for two products (A and B). Again, I've added parentheses for clarity, but they're not required:

```
=(Product A CM * Product A Sales Mix) + (Product B CM * Product B Sales Mix)
```

For example, suppose Product A has a contribution margin (CM) of $4 and a sales mix of 62 percent, while Product B has a contribution margin of $8 and a sales mix of 38 percent. The weighted-average contribution margin is ($4 * .62) + ($8 * .38), or $5.52.

With the weighted-average contribution margin in hand, you can then calculate the overall break-even point:

```
=Total Fixed Costs / Weighted-Average Contribution Margin
```

For example, if the company's total fixed costs are $44,000, then the break-even point is $44,000 / $5.52, or 7,971 units (see Figure 10-10). Finally, you can then determine the break-even point for each product:

```
=Overall Break-Even Point / Product Sales Mix
```

Product A has a sales mix of 62 percent, so its break-even point is 7,971 * .62, or 4,942 units. Similarly, Product B has a sales mix of 38 percent, so its break-even point is 7,971 * .38, or 3,029 units.

B31	⌄ : ✕ ✓ *fx*	=B30 / B29		
◢	A	B	C
11	**Product A**		
12	Sales Mix	62%	
13	Selling Price	$10	
14	Variable Costs Per Unit	$6	
15	Contribution Margin	$4	
16			
17	**Product B**		
18	Sales Mix	38%	
19	Selling Price	$25	
20	Variable Costs Per Unit	$17	
21	Contribution Margin	$8	
22			
23	**Weighted-Average CM (A & B)**		
24	Product A CM	$4	
25	Product B CM	$8	
26	Weighted-Average CM	$5.52	
27			
28	**Break-Even Point (A & B)**		
29	Weighted-Average CM	$5.52	
30	Total Fixed Costs	$44,000	
31	Overall Break-Even Point	7971	units
32	Product A Break-Even Point	4942	units
33	Product B Break-Even Point	3029	units
34			

FIGURE 10-10 This formula calculates the break-even point for two products given the products' weighted-average contribution margin and total fixed costs.

Financial formulas

If you're a manager, an investor (or a would-be investor), or a creditor associated with a particular company, then it's important to analyze and monitor the financial health and performance of that company. As you see in the sections that follow, this goes way beyond simply comparing sales and expenses and includes vital measures, such as sales ratios, cost of goods sold, gross and net margins, and fixed-asset ratios.

Sales ratios

Sales are the lifeblood of any business, but the analysis of sales by a manager, investor, or creditor shouldn't stop at the total revenue generated in a given period. It's important to get a sense of how efficiently the company is generating its sales, and that efficiency can be seen through the lens of several sales-related ratios:

Sales to current assets

This ratio compares a company's sales with its current assets, such as cash and accounts receivable (see "Working capital," later in this chapter, for more on current assets). In other words, this ratio indicates how well the company generates revenue from its current assets, with higher values implying greater efficiency. Here's the formula:

```
=Sales / Current Assets
```

For example, if a company reports $897,000 in sales and has current assets of $315,000, then its sales to current assets ratio is $897,000 / $315,000, or 2.85 (see Figure 10-11).

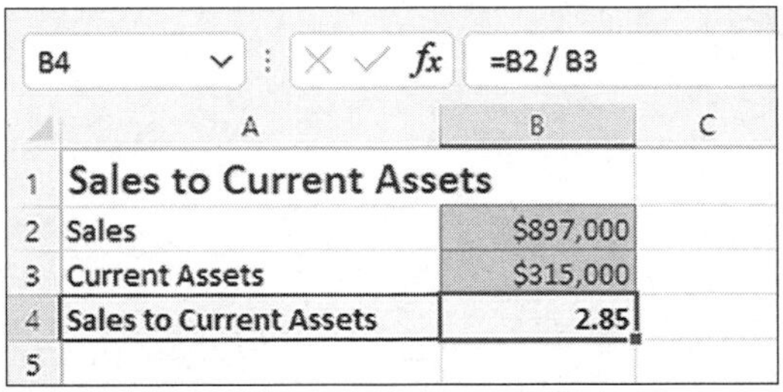

B4	✓ : ✕ ✓ fx	=B2 / B3	
◢	A	B	C
1	**Sales to Current Assets**		
2	Sales	$897,000	
3	Current Assets	$315,000	
4	Sales to Current Assets	2.85	
5			

FIGURE 10-11 This formula calculates the sales to current assets ratio.

Sales to short-term debt

This ratio compares a company's sales with its current short-term debts, particularly accounts payable. This value shows the extent to which the company's short-term debt finances its revenue growth, with higher values implying greater efficiency of short-term debt usage. Here's the formula:

```
=Sales / Short-Term Debt
```

For example, if a company reports $897,000 in sales and has short-term debt of $255,000, then its sales to short-term debt ratio is $897,000 / $255,000, or 3.52 (see Figure 10-12).

B9	⌄ : ✕ ✓ *fx*	=B7 / B8	
▲	A	B	C
6	Sales to Short-Term Debt		
7	Sales	$897,000	
8	Current Assets	$255,000	
9	Sales to Short-Term Debt	3.52	
10			

FIGURE 10-12 This formula calculates the sales to short-term debt ratio.

Sales per employee

This ratio divides a company's sales by the number of employees. This ratio shows the revenue generated per employee, which gives a rough measure of employee productivity. Here's the formula:

```
=Sales / Number of Employees
```

For example, if a company reports $897,000 in sales and has ten employees, then its sales per employee ratio is $897,000 / 10, or $89,700 (see Figure 10-13).

B14	⌄ : ✕ ✓ *fx*	=B12 / B13	
▲	A	B	C
11	Sales Per Employee		
12	Sales	$897,000	
13	Number of Employees	10	
14	Sales Per Employee	$89,700	
15			

FIGURE 10-13 This formula calculates the sales per employee ratio.

Cost of goods sold

The *cost of goods sold* (COGS) is the sum of the expenses incurred to manufacture, assemble, or purchase the goods or services that a company sells over a given period. The COGS is also known as the *direct costs*, because it includes only those costs that are directly related to the production or acquisition of the goods that a company sells.

To calculate COGS for a given period, use the following formula:

```
=Starting Inventory + Direct Costs Incurred - Ending Inventory
```

Here, Direct Costs Incurred refers to the costs incurred to manufacture, assemble, or acquire new inventory during that period. For example, if a company had $1,200,000 in inventory at the start of the year, incurred $3,800,000 in direct costs during the year, and has $1,300,000 in inventory at the end of the year, its COGS is $1,200,000 + $3,800,000 – $1,300,000, or $3,700,000 (see Figure 10-14).

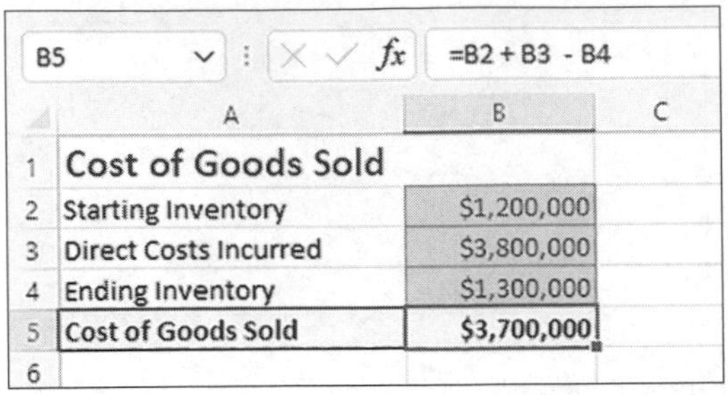
B5 =B2 + B3 - B4

	A	B	C
1	Cost of Goods Sold		
2	Starting Inventory	$1,200,000	
3	Direct Costs Incurred	$3,800,000	
4	Ending Inventory	$1,300,000	
5	Cost of Goods Sold	$3,700,000	
6			

FIGURE 10-14 This formula calculates the cost of goods sold.

Gross margin

The *gross margin* (or *gross profit margin*) is the percentage of revenue that a company retains after taking into account the direct costs associated with producing a particular good or service (or the company's entire portfolio of goods or services). The higher the gross margin, the more money the company retains from each dollar of revenue and the more money the company can direct elsewhere, such as debt repayment, indirect expenses, or shareholder dividends. Here's the formula:

```
=(Revenue - Direct Costs) / Revenue
```

For example, if a product's revenue is $145,000 and its direct costs are $62,000, then the product's gross margin is ($145,000 – $62,000) / $145,000, or 57.2 percent (see Figure 10-15).

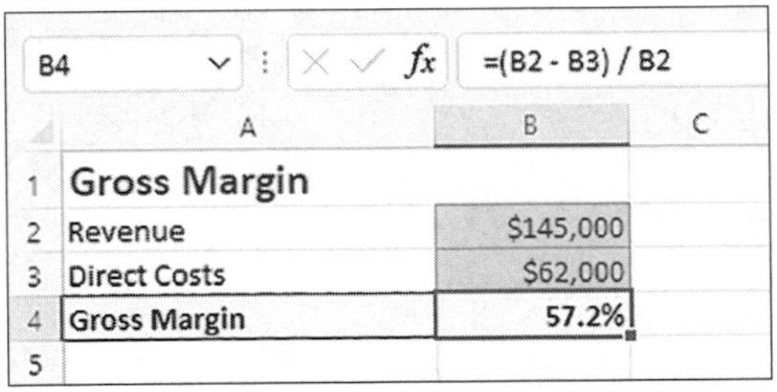
B4 =(B2 - B3) / B2

	A	B	C
1	Gross Margin		
2	Revenue	$145,000	
3	Direct Costs	$62,000	
4	Gross Margin	57.2%	
5			

FIGURE 10-15 This formula calculates gross margin.

Net margin

The *net margin* (or *net profit margin*) is the percentage of revenue that a company retains after taking into account not only the direct costs associated with producing its goods or services, but also the company's overall operating expenses and tax liabilities. The higher the net margin, the better the company is at generating revenue from its operations. Here's the formula:

```
=(Revenue - Direct Costs - Operating Expenses - Tax Liabilities) / Revenue
```

For example, if a product's revenue is $145,000, its direct costs are $62,000, its operating expenses are $45,000, and its tax liabilities are $20,000, then the company's net margin is ($145,000 – $62,000 – $45,000 – $20,000) / $145,000, or 12.4 percent (see Figure 10-16).

	B11	fx	=(B7 - B8 - B9 - B10) / B7		
	A	B	C	D	
6	Net Margin				
7	Revenue	$145,000			
8	Direct Costs	$62,000			
9	Operating Expenses	$45,000			
10	Tax Liabilites	$20,000			
11	Net Margin	12.4%			
12					

FIGURE 10-16 This formula calculates net margin.

Fixed-asset ratios

A company's *fixed assets* are those assets that can't be readily turned into cash. They're generally referred to as *property, plant, and equipment* (PP&E), and they represent the company's major capital investments. There are several ratios related to fixed assets that analysts, investors, creditors, and managers find useful.

Fixed-asset turnover

The fixed-asset turnover is the ratio of sales over a given period to the average fixed-assets value during that period. This ratio shows how efficiently the company is able to use its property, plant, and equipment to generate revenue. Here's the formula:

```
=Sales / Average Fixed Assets
```

Note that the average fixed-assets value is often calculated by adding the fixed-asset value from the beginning and the end of the period and dividing that sum by 2. For example, if a company has $9.5 million in sales and an average fixed-assets value of $15.1 million over the same period, then the fixed-asset turnover ratio is $9,500,000 / $15,100,000, or 0.63 (see Figure 10-17).

	B4	fx	=B2 / B3	
	A	B	C	
1	Fixed-Asset Turnover			
2	Sales	$9,500,000		
3	Average Fixed Assets	$15,100,000		
4	Fixed-Asset Turnover	0.63		
5				

FIGURE 10-17 This formula calculates the fixed-asset turnover ratio.

Return on fixed assets

The return on fixed assets is the ratio of net income over a given period to the average fixed-assets value during that period. This ratio shows how efficiently the company is able to use its property, plant, and equipment to generate profit. Here's the formula:

```
=Net Income / Average Fixed Assets
```

Note that the average fixed-assets value is often calculated by adding the fixed-asset value from the beginning and the end of the period and dividing that sum by 2. For example, if a company has $3.1 million in sales and an average fixed-assets value of $15.1 million over the same period, then the fixed-asset turnover ratio is $3,100,000 / $15,100,000, or 0.21 (see Figure 10-18).

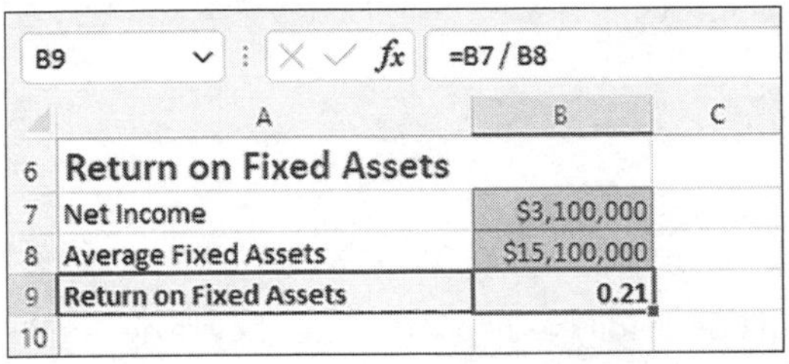

FIGURE 10-18 This formula calculates the return on fixed assets.

Fixed assets to short-term debt

The fixed assets to short-term debt is the ratio of a company's current fixed-assets value to its current short-term debt obligations. This ratio shows how readily the company can pay its short-term debts, given how much money it has tied up in long-term fixed assets. A higher value indicates the company's short-term debt is manageable relative to its fixed assets. Here's the formula:

```
=Fixed Assets / Short-Term Debt
```

For example, if a company has a fixed-assets value of $15.1 million and a short-term debt value of $7.3 million, then the fixed-asset to short-term debt ratio is $15,100,000 / $7,300,000, or 2.07 (see Figure 10-19).

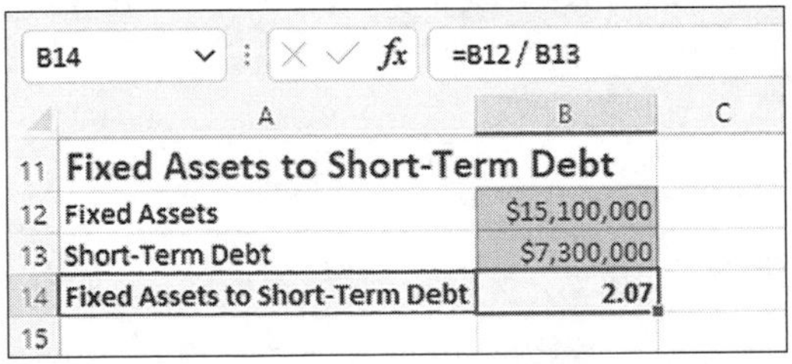

FIGURE 10-19 This formula calculates the fixed assets to short-term debt ratio.

Inventory formulas

Inventory refers to raw materials, works-in-progress (that is, goods in the process of being manufactured or assembled), and finished goods that a company has on hand. Investors, creditors, and managers need to analyze inventory because having too much on hand implies a number of negatives, including slow sales, improper forecasting, and high carrying costs, while having too little inventory on hand could mean forgoing sales due to lack of stock.

Inventory ratios

The following three ratios are most often used to assess a company's inventory.

Inventory turnover

The inventory turnover is the ratio of the cost of goods sold (COGS) over a given period to the average inventory during that period. This ratio shows how often the company replaces its inventory during the specified period. The higher the value, the better the company is at turning over its inventory, which implies strong sales. Here's the formula:

```
=Cost of Goods Sold / Average Inventory
```

Note that the average inventory value is often calculated by adding the inventory on hand from the beginning and the end of the period and dividing that sum by 2. For example, if a company's COGS over a given period is $678,000 and has an average inventory of $71,000 over the same period, then the inventory turnover ratio is $678,000 / $71,000, or 9.5 (see Figure 10-20).

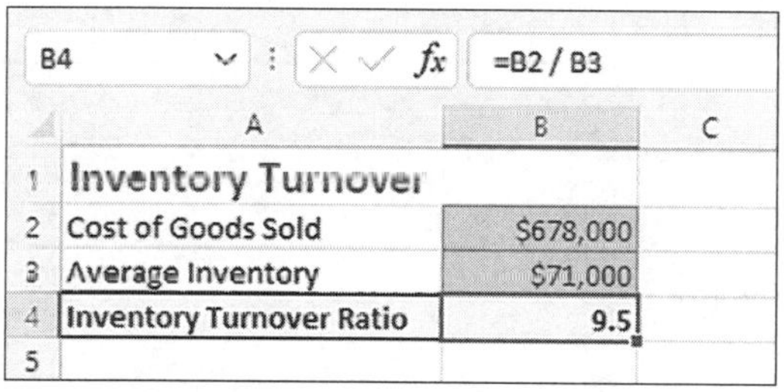

FIGURE 10-20 This formula calculates the inventory turnover ratio.

Inventory turnover rate

The inventory turnover rate is the ratio of the number of days in a given period and the inventory turnover ratio (see the previous section) for that period. This ratio tells you the average number of days it takes a company to turn over its inventory. A falling inventory turnover rate might indicate poor marketing, high prices, excess inventory, product problems, or product obsolescence. Here's the formula:

```
=Days in Period / Inventory Turnover
```

For example, if the period is one year (365 days) and the inventory turnover ratio for that year is 9.5, then the inventory turnover rate is 365 / 9.5, or 38.2 days (see Figure 10-21).

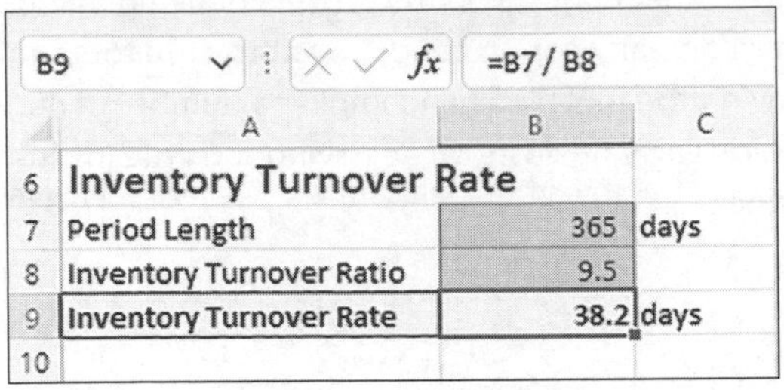

FIGURE 10-21 This formula calculates the inventory turnover rate.

Sales to inventory ratio

The sales to inventory ratio is the ratio of a company's sales in a given period to the total inventory for that period. An increasing sales to inventory ratio shows that the company is becoming better at inventory management and more efficient at utilizing inventory to generate sales. Here's the formula:

```
=Total Sales / Total Inventory
```

For example, if a company has annual sales of $2 million and a total inventory of $140,000 for the year, the sales to inventory ratio is $2,000,000 / $140,000, or 14.3 (see Figure 10-22).

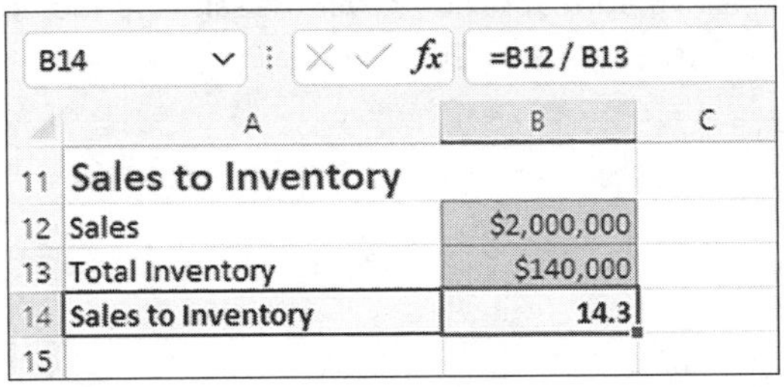

FIGURE 10-22 This formula calculates the sales to inventory ratio.

Inventory management formulas

When managing inventory, you need to make sure you have enough on hand to meet demand, but not too much that your costs for storing that inventory become excessive. Here are two formulas that can help with inventory management.

Inventory safety stock

The inventory *safety stock* is the number of extra units of a product you should keep in inventory as protection against a rapid increase in demand or a sudden decrease in supply. In general, you want to keep enough safety stock to handle most unforeseen changes in supply or demand, but not so much that your carrying costs get too high. Here's the formula. Again, the parentheses are optional but are included here for clarity:

```
=(Maximum Daily Demand * Maximum Lead Time) - (Average Daily Demand * Average
Lead Time)
```

Here, *lead time* is the time it takes for the reorder to arrive from the company's supplier. For example, suppose the maximum daily demand is 100 units, the maximum lead time is 21 days, the average daily demand is 75 units, and the average lead time is 14 days. The safety stock is (100 * 21) – (75 * 14), or 1050 units (see Figure 10-23).

	A	B	C
	B6 ⌄ ⋮ ✕ ✓ *fx*	=(B2 * B3) - (B4 * B5)	
1	Inventory Safety Stock		
2	Maximum Daily Demand	100	units
3	Maximum Lead Time	21	days
4	Average Daily Demand	75	units
5	Average Lead Time	14	days
6	Inventory Safety Stock	1050	units
7			

FIGURE 10-23 This formula calculates the inventory safety stock.

Inventory reorder level

The inventory reorder level is the inventory stock level at which it's time to reorder the product. To avoid selling out of a product, you need to reorder when you're down to enough units to cover demand over the amount of time it will take for the reorder to arrive—the lead time for the reorder—plus your safety stock (see the previous section). Here's the formula; you don't need to include the parentheses in this formula, but I've added them here and in the example for clarity:

```
=(Average Daily Demand * Average Lead Time) + Safety Stock
```

For example, suppose the average daily demand is 75 units, the average lead time is 14 days, and the safety stock is 1050 units. The inventory reorder level is (75 * 14) + 1050, or 2100 units (see Figure 10-24).

	A	B	C
	B12 ⌄ ⋮ ✕ ✓ *fx*	=(B9 * B10) + B11	
8	Inventory Reorder Level		
9	Average Daily Demand	75	units
10	Average Lead Time	14	days
11	Safety Stock	1050	units
12	Inventory Reorder Level	2100	units
13			

FIGURE 10-24 This formula calculates the inventory reorder level.

Liquidity formulas

From an accounting perspective, *liquidity* is a measure of how readily a company can meet its financial obligations in the short term. A company's *liquid assets* are those that can be quickly and easily turned into cash without substantially affecting the assets' market value. Cash is, by definition, a liquid asset, as are commercial papers, money market funds, short-term investments, Treasury bills, and accounts receivable.

All companies require some liquidity to meet unforeseen circumstances, so investors, creditors, and managers turn to a number of liquidity-related formulas to assess the financial health of companies.

Accounts receivable ratios

A company's *accounts receivable* (also: *AR* or *receivables*) balance is the amount of money owed by customers for services or products used or delivered. Investors and managers use a couple of AR ratios to evaluate and monitor a company's financial strength.

Accounts receivable turnover

The accounts receivable turnover is the ratio of total credit sales over a given period to the average receivables balance during that period. This ratio shows how often the company collects its receivables during the specified period. The higher the value, the better the company is at collecting on its customer credit. Here's the formula:

```
=Credit Sales / Average Accounts Receivable
```

Note that the average AR value is often calculated by adding the AR balances from the beginning and the end of the period and dividing that sum by 2. For example, if a company has $575,000 in credit sales and an average AR balance of $45,000 over the same period, then the AR turnover ratio is $575,000 / $45,000, or 12.8 (see Figure 10-25).

B4		⌄	⋮	✕ ✓	*fx*	=B2 / B3	
◢		A			B		C
1	**Accounts Receivable Turnover**						
2	Credit Sales				$575,000		
3	Average Accounts Receivable				$45,000		
4	AR Turnover Ratio				12.8		
5							

FIGURE 10-25 This formula calculates the accounts receivable turnover ratio.

Average AR duration

The average AR duration is the ratio of the number of days in a given period and the AR turnover ratio (see the previous section) for that period. This ratio tells you average number of days it takes customers to pay their invoices. If, for example, the company has a 30-day payment policy for receivables, and the average AR duration is greater than 30, it's a sign that the company is having trouble getting customers to pay their invoices on time. Here's the formula:

```
=Days in Period / AR Turnover
```

For example, if the period is one year (365 days) and the AR turnover ratio for that year is 12.8, then the average AR duration is 365 / 12.8, or 28.6 days (see Figure 10-26).

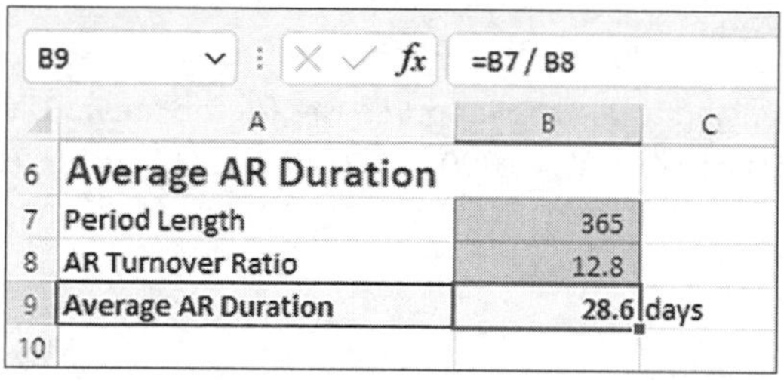

FIGURE 10-26 This formula calculates the average accounts receivable duration.

Accounts payable ratios

Accounts payable (also: *AP* or *payables*) are short-term debts owed by a company to its suppliers. Creditors and managers often look at three payables-related ratios to get a sense of a company's financial health.

Accounts payable turnover

The accounts payable turnover is the ratio of supplier purchases to average accounts payable over a given period. This ratio shows how many times the company paid its payables over the period. If this ratio decreases over time, it means the company is taking longer to pay its debts to suppliers, which is possibly a sign of financial problems. Here's the formula:

```
=Supplier Purchases / Average Accounts Payable
```

Note that the average AP value is often calculated by adding the AP balances from the beginning and the end of the period and dividing that sum by 2. For example, if annual supplier purchases are $172 million and the average payables amount over the year is $37 million, then the accounts payable turnover ratio is $172,000,000 / $37,000,000, or 4.6 (see Figure 10-27).

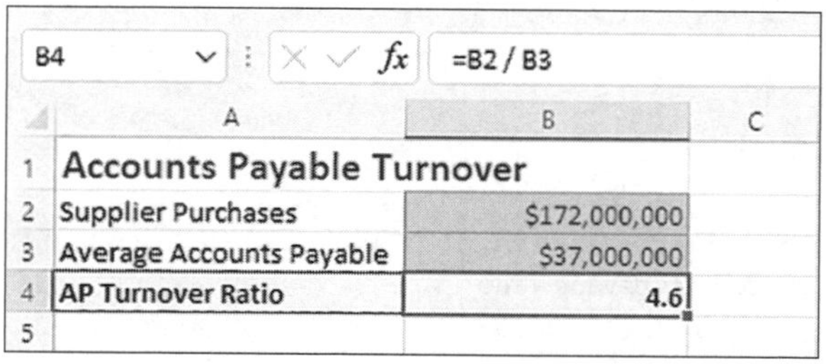

FIGURE 10-27 This formula calculates the accounts payable turnover ratio.

Days purchases in accounts payable

The days purchases in accounts payable is the ratio of the current accounts payables balance to the average daily supplier purchases over a given period. This ratio shows the average number of days it takes the company to pay off its suppliers. If this ratio decreases over time—or if the value remains below the company's average payment terms—it's a possible sign of good financial health because it means the company is repaying creditors at a faster rate. Here's the formula:

```
=Accounts Payable / (Supplier Purchases / 360)
```

For example, if the payables balance is $40,000 and total supplier purchases for the previous year are $775,000, then the days purchases in accounts payable is $40,000 / ($775,000 / 360), or 18.6 (see Figure 10-28).

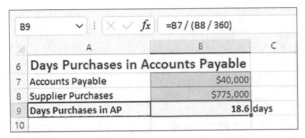

FIGURE 10-28 This formula calculates the days purchases in accounts payable.

Sales to accounts payable

The sales to accounts payable is the ratio of a company's sales over a given period to its current accounts payable balance. Since payables are essentially interest-free loans from suppliers, a declining sales to AP ratio—that is, payables are increasing relative to sales—is considered a positive sign of financial health. Here's the formula:

```
=Sales / Accounts Payable
```

For example, if a company had $2 million in sales last year and has a payables balance of $85,000, the sales to AP ratio is $2,000,000 / $85,000, or 23.5 (see Figure 10-29).

B14	fx	=B12 / B13
	A	B	C
11	Sales to Accounts Payable		
12	Sales	$2,000,000	
13	Accounts Payable	$85,000	
14	Sales to AP Ratio	23.5	
15			

FIGURE 10-29 This formula calculates the sales to accounts payable ratio.

Working capital

A company's *working capital* compares two financial metrics:

- **Current assets:** Those assets that can be turned into cash within one year. Besides cash itself, examples include cash equivalents, short-term investments, and accounts receivable.

- **Current liabilities:** Those debts or obligations (such as accounts payable) that are due within one year.

There are two main formulas to consider.

Working capital

Working capital is the difference between current assets and current liabilities. Having current assets greater than current liabilities is an indicator of financial health because it means the company is in position not only to meet its short-term obligations but also to handle any negative or unforeseen events. Here's the formula:

```
=Current Assets - Current Liabilities
```

For example, if a company has $185,000 in current assets and $95,000 in current liabilities, then its working capital is $185,000 – $95,000, or $90,000 (see Figure 10-30).

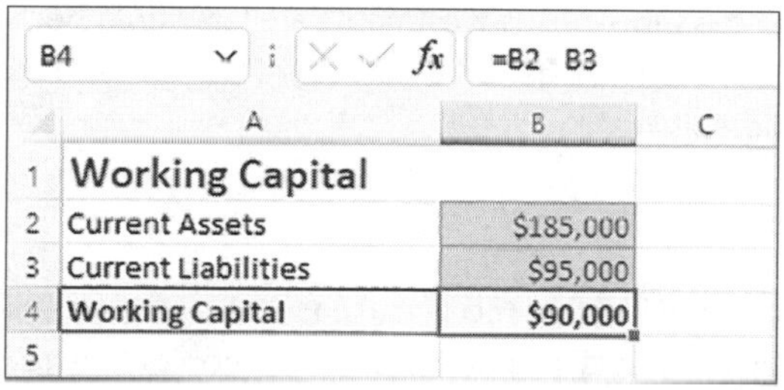

FIGURE 10-30 This formula calculates the working capital.

Working capital turnover

The working capital turnover is the ratio of sales to the average working capital over a given period. This ratio shows how efficiently a company is using its operational funds to generate revenue. Here's the formula:

```
=Sales / Average Working Capital
```

Note that the average working capital value is often calculated by adding the working capital from the period's beginning and end and dividing that sum by 2. For example, if annual sales are $438,000 and the average working capital amount over the year is $90,000, then the working capital turnover ratio is $438,000 / $90,000, or 4.9 (see Figure 10-31).

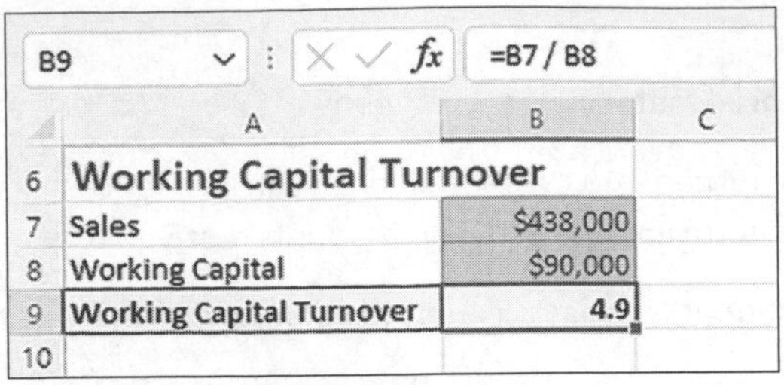

FIGURE 10-31 This formula calculates the working capital turnover.

> **Note** Some analysts reverse the working capital turnover formula:
>
> `=Average Working Capital / Sales`
>
> In that case, a *lower* ratio is a signal that the company is using its working capital efficiently.

Liquidity ratios

When you examine the liquidity of an asset based on the amount of time it would take to turn it into cash, you quickly see that the so-called liquid assets are not equally liquid. Cash is perfectly liquid; that is, it takes no time to turn it into cash. However, some short-term investments are less liquid because they can take days to become cash. Given these different liquidation timetables, investors and managers use different ratios to measure a company's liquidity.

Current ratio

Current ratio is also called the *working capital ratio*, and it's the ratio of current assets to current liabilities. Because current liabilities are settled with current assets, this ratio is an indication of how readily a company can meet its financial obligations. Current ratios between 1.25 and 2 are considered ideal. Here's the formula:

`=Current Assets / Current Liabilities`

For example, if a company has $185,000 in current assets and $95,000 in current liabilities, then the current ratio is $185,000 / $95,000, or 1.9 (see Figure 10-32).

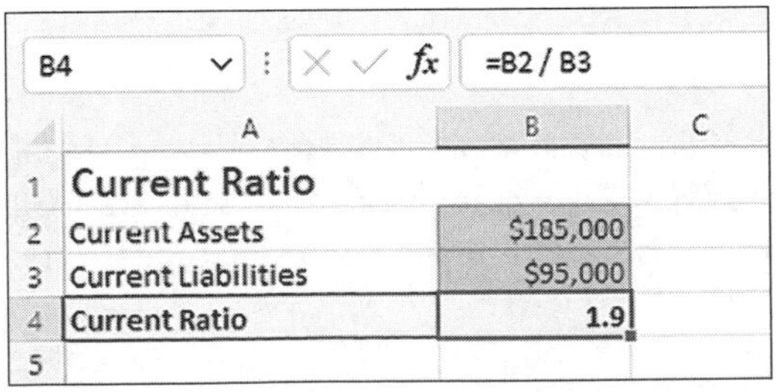

FIGURE 10-32 This formula calculates the current ratio.

Acid-test ratio

The acid-test ratio is also called the *quick ratio*, and it's the ratio of a company's most liquid assets—cash (and cash equivalents, such as commercial paper), short-term investments, and accounts receivable—to its current liabilities. This is a stricter measure of company liquidity than the current ratio because it doesn't include certain less-liquid assets, particularly inventory. Ideally, a company's acid-test ratio should be 1 or higher. Here's the formula:

```
=(Cash + Short-Term Investments + Accounts Receivable) / Current Liabilities
```

For example, if a company has $51,000 in cash, $40,000 in short-term investments, an accounts receivable balance of $21,000, and current liabilities of $89,000, then the acid-test ratio is ($51,000 + $40,000 + $21,000) / $89,000, or 1.3 (see Figure 10-33).

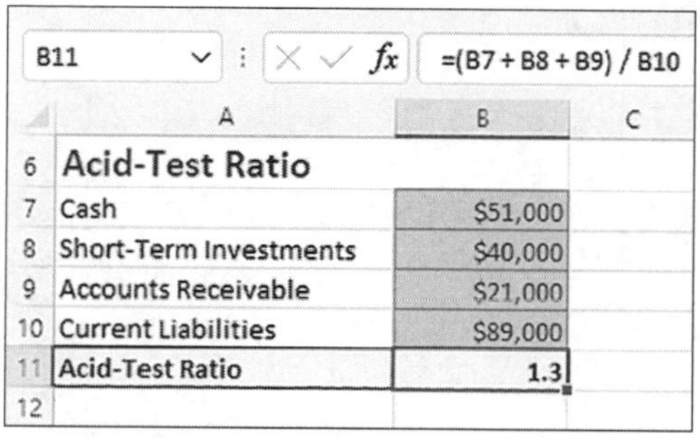

FIGURE 10-33 This formula calculates the acid-test ratio.

Cash ratio

The cash ratio is the same as the acid-test ratio, except that it excludes the accounts receivable balance (sensibly, to some, because customer debts aren't necessarily liquid). That is, it's the ratio of a company's cash (and cash equivalents) plus short-term investments to its current liabilities. This is the strictest of the liquidity measures because it indicates how readily a company will stay solvent given an emergency or other immediate negative event. A cash ratio of less than 1 is a red flag. Here's the formula:

```
=(Cash + Short-Term Investments) / Current Liabilities
```

For example, if a company has $51,000 in cash and $40,000 in short-term investments, and current liabilities of $89,000, then the cash ratio is ($51,000 + $40,000) / $89,000, or 1.02 (see Figure 10-34).

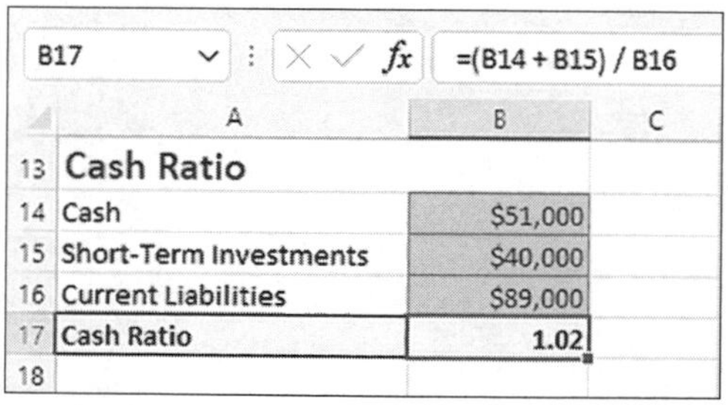

FIGURE 10-34 This formula calculates the cash ratio.

Liquidity index

The *liquidity index* approximates the number of days it would take a company to turn its receivables and inventory into cash. Therefore, the liquidity index is a measure of a company's ability to meet its current liabilities. Here's the formula:

```
=((Accounts Receivable * Average AR Duration) + (Inventory * Days to Liquidate))
/ (Accounts Receivable + Inventory)
```

For example, if a company has an AR balance of $21,000, an average AR duration of 29 days, inventory of $40,000, and an average inventory liquidation of 82 days, then the liquidity index is (($21,000 * 29) + ($40,000 * 82)) / ($21,000 + $40,000), or 63.8 days (see Figure 10-35).

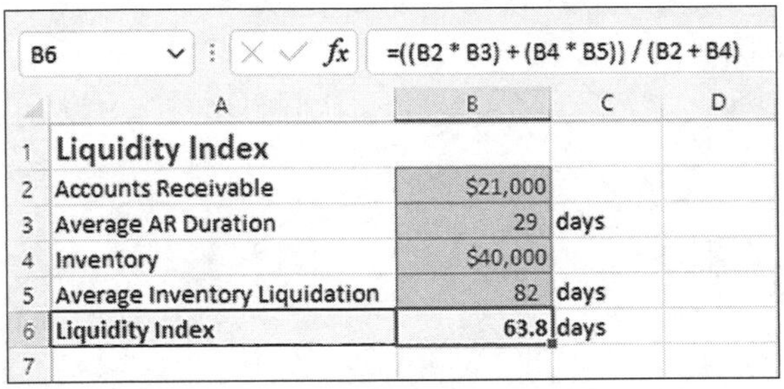

	A	B	C	D
1	**Liquidity Index**			
2	Accounts Receivable	$21,000		
3	Average AR Duration	29	days	
4	Inventory	$40,000		
5	Average Inventory Liquidation	82	days	
6	Liquidity Index	63.8	days	
7				

B6 fx =((B2 * B3) + (B4 * B5)) / (B2 + B4)

FIGURE 10-35 A formula to calculate the liquidity index.

CHAPTER 11

Building descriptive statistical formulas

In this chapter, you will:

- Understand descriptive statistics

- Learn how to count items and calculate permutations and combinations

- Calculate the mean, median, mode, and other averages

- Work with maximums, minimums, and other extreme values

- Calculate measures of variation such as the range, variance, and standard deviation

In Excel's list of worksheet functions, the Statistical category boasts well over 100 functions. That's a massive number, and it inevitably means that many of those functions are obscure and highly specialized. That's great if you're a specialist, but for general business uses, it's highly unlikely you'll ever need the Fisher transformation (via the **FISHER** function), the Pearson product moment coefficient correlation (via the **PEARSON** function), or the value of the density function for a standard normal distribution (via the **PHI** function).

That's not to say there aren't useful statistical functions for business. Quite the opposite: Excel is chock-full of statistical functions that are both powerful and useful in a business context. When building your Excel worksheet models, you'll need to count things, calculate averages, look for extreme values, calculate measures of variation, and more. You learn how to do all that and more in this chapter, and you explore even more statistical functions in Chapter 12, "Building inferential statistical formulas," and 13, "Applying regression to track trends and make forecasts."

Understanding descriptive statistics

One of the goals of this book is to show you how to use formulas and functions to turn a jumble of numbers and values into results and summaries that give you useful information about the data. Excel's statistical functions are particularly useful for extracting analytical sense out of data nonsense. Many of these functions might seem strange and obscure, but they reward a bit of patience and effort with striking new views of your data.

This is particularly true of the branch of statistics known casually as *descriptive statistics* (or *summary statistics*). As the name implies, you use descriptive statistics to describe various aspects of a data set, so you get a better overall picture of the phenomenon underlying the numbers. In Excel's statistical repertoire, the following measures make up its descriptive statistics package: sum, count, mean, median, mode, maximum, minimum, kth largest, kth smallest, rank, percentile, range, standard deviation, variance, covariance, frequency distribution, kurtosis, and skewness.

In this chapter, you learn how to wield all these statistical measures (except sum, which I cover earlier in this book in Chapter 9, "Working with math functions"). The context is the worksheet database of product inventory shown in Figure 11-1.

> **Note** You can work with all the examples in this chapter by downloading Chapter11.xslx from either of the companion content sites mentioned in the Introduction.

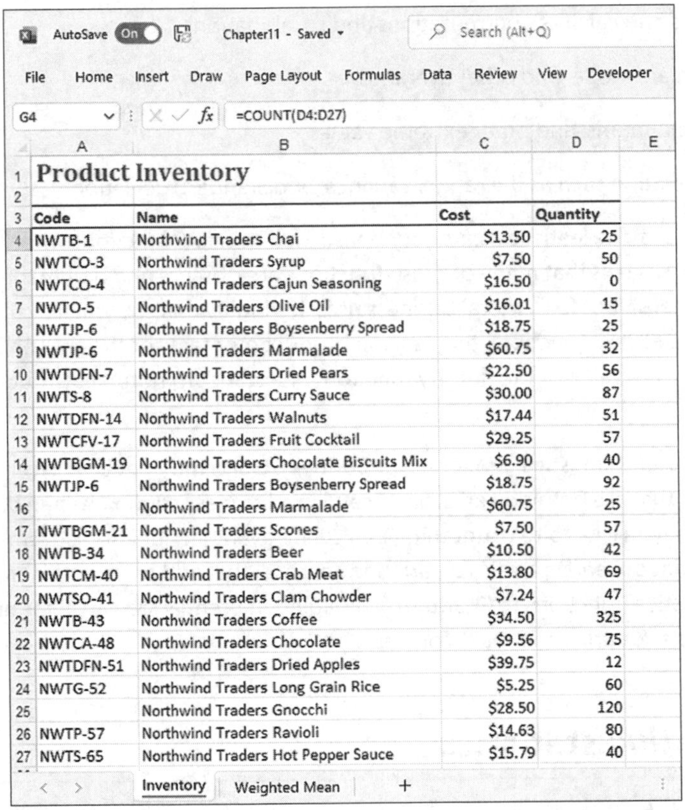

FIGURE 11-1 To demonstrate Excel's descriptive statistics capabilities, this chapter uses the data from a table of product inventory.

Counting items

The simplest of the descriptive statistics is the total number of values in a data set. However, that simplicity isn't reflected in Excel's worksheet functions, which offer no less than five count-related functions. The next five sections take a quick look at each of Excel's counting functions.

The **COUNT** function

To count only the numeric values in a data set (that is, to ignore text values, dates, logical values, and errors), use the **COUNT** function:

COUNT(*value1*[,*value2*,...])

value1, *value2*, ...	One or more ranges, arrays, function results, expressions, or literal values of which you want the count

In the table shown in Figure 11-1, you can count the number of products in the table by using the following formula to count the numeric values in the Quantity column:

=COUNT(D4:D27)

> **Tip** To get a quick look at the count, select the range or, if you're working with data in a table, select a single column in the table. Excel displays the count in the status bar. If you want to know how many numeric values are in the selection, right-click the status bar and then select the Numerical Count value.

The **COUNTA** function

To count not only the numeric values that appear in a data set but also the text values, dates, logical values, and errors, use the **COUNTA** function:

COUNTA(*value1*[,*value2*,...])

value1, *value2*, ...	One or more ranges, arrays, function results, expressions, or literal values of which you want the count

In the table shown in Figure 11-1, you can count the total number of rows in the table by using the following formula to count the values in the Quantity column, including the column header (cell D3):

=COUNTA(D3:D27)

The **COUNTBLANK** function

To count the empty cells in a data set, use the **COUNTBLANK** function:

```
COUNTBLANK(value1[,value2,...])
```

value1, *value2*, ...	One or more ranges, arrays, function results, expressions, or literal values of which you want the count

In the table shown in Figure 11-1, you can use the following formula to count the number of blank cells in the Code column:

```
=COUNTBLANK(A4:A27)
```

The **COUNTIF** function

The **COUNTIF** function counts the number of cells in a range that meet a single criteria:

```
COUNTIF(range, criteria)
```

range	The range of cells to use for the count.
criteria	The criteria, entered as text, that determines which cells to count. Excel applies the criteria to *range*.

For example, in the table shown in Figure 11-1, you can use the following formula to count the number of products for which the Quantity is greater than or equal to 100:

```
=COUNTIF(D4:D27, ">= 100")
```

The **COUNTIFS** function

The **COUNTIFS** function counts the number of cells in one or more ranges that meet one or more criteria:

```
COUNTIFS(range1, criteria1[, range2, criteria2, ...])
```

range1	The first range of cells to use for the count.
criteria1	The first criteria, entered as text, that determines which cells to count. Excel applies the criteria to *range1*.
range2	The second range of cells to use for the count.
criteria2	The second criteria, entered as text, that determines which cells to count. Excel applies the criteria to *range2*.

You can enter up to 127 range/criteria pairs, and Excel only counts those cells that match all the criteria. For example, in the table shown in Figure 11-1, you can use the following formula to count the number of products where the Cost is greater than $30, and the Quantity is less than 50:

```
=COUNTIF(C4:C27, "> 30", D4:D27, "< 50")
```

Calculating averages

The most basic statistical analysis worthy of the name is probably the average, although you always need to ask yourself *which* average you need: mean, median, or mode. The next few sections show you the worksheet functions that calculate them.

The AVERAGE function

The *mean* is what you probably think of when someone uses the term *average*. That is, it's the arithmetic average of a set of numbers. In Excel, you calculate the mean by using the AVERAGE function:

```
AVERAGE(number1[,number2,...])
```

number1, number2, ...	A range, an array, or a list of values of which you want the mean

For example, to calculate the mean of the values in the Quantity field of the table shown earlier in Figure 11-1, use the following formula:

```
=AVERAGE(D4:D27)
```

Tip If you need just a quick glance at the mean value, select the range. Excel displays the average in the status bar.

Caution The AVERAGE function (as well as the MEDIAN and MODE functions discussed in the next two sections) ignores text and logical values. It also ignores blank cells, but it does *not* ignore cells that contain the value 0. If you want to include non-numeric values, use the AVERAGEA function, which treats text values as 0 and the Boolean values TRUE and FALSE as 1 and 0, respectively.

The AVERAGEIF function

The AVERAGEIF function calculates the average of a data set for those items that meet a specified condition:

```
AVERAGEIF(range, criteria[, average_range])
```

Range	The range of cells to use for the criteria.
Criteria	The criteria, entered as text, that determines which cells to average. Excel applies the criteria to *range*.
average_range	The range from which the average values are taken. Excel averages only those cells in *average_range* that correspond to the cells in *range* and meet the criteria. If you omit *average_range*, Excel uses *range* for the average.

For example, in the table shown earlier in Figure 11-1, you can use the following formula to calculate the average Quantity value for those products where the Cost field is greater than $25:

```
=AVERAGEIF(C4:C27, "> 25", D4:D27)
```

The AVERAGEIFS function

The **AVERAGEIFS** function averages cells in one or more ranges that meet one or more criteria:

```
AVERAGEIFS(average_range, range1, criteria1[, range2, criteria2, ...])
```

average_range	The range from which the average values are taken. Excel averages only those cells in *average_range* that correspond to the cells that meet the criteria.
range1	The first range of cells to use for the average criteria.
criteria1	The first criteria, entered as text, that determines which cells to average. Excel applies the criteria to *range1*.
range2	The second range of cells to use for the average criteria.
criteria2	The second criteria, entered as text, that determines which cells to average. Excel applies the criteria to *range2*.

You can enter up to 127 range/criteria pairs, and Excel only averages those cells that match all the criteria. For example, in the table shown earlier in Figure 11-1, you can use the following formula to calculate the average Quantity value where the Cost is greater than $30 and less than $50:

```
=AVERAGEIFS(D4:D27, C4:C27, "> 30", C4:C27, "< 50")
```

The MEDIAN function

The *median* is the value in a data set that would fall in the middle if you sorted the values in numeric order. That is, 50 percent of the values fall below the median, and 50 percent fall above it. The median is useful in data sets that have one or two extreme values that can throw off the mean result because the median isn't affected by extremes.

You calculate the median by using the **MEDIAN** function:

```
MEDIAN(number1[,number2,...])
```

number1, *number2*, ...	A range, an array, or a list of values of which you want the median

For example, to calculate the median of the Quantity values in the Product Inventory table (refer to Figure 11-1), you use the following formula:

```
=MEDIAN(D4:D27)
```

The MODE function

The *mode* is the value in a data set that occurs most frequently. The mode is useful when you're dealing with data that doesn't lend itself to being either added (necessary for calculating the mean) or sorted (necessary for calculating the median). For example, you might be tabulating the result of a poll that included a question about the respondent's favorite color. The mean and median don't make sense with such a question, but the mode will tell you which color was chosen the most.

You calculate the mode using one of the following functions:

```
MODE.MULT(number1[,number2,...])
MODE.SNGL(number1[,number2,...])
```

number1, number2, ...	A range, an array, or a list of values for which you want the mode

The `MODE.SNGL` function returns the most common value in the list, so it's the function you'll use most often. If your list has multiple common values, use `MODE.MULT` to return those values as an array.

For example, to calculate the mode of the Quantity values in the Product Inventory table (refer to Figure 11-1), you use the following formula:

```
=MODE.SNGL(D4:D27)
```

Calculating the weighted mean

In some data sets, one value might be more important than another. For example, suppose that your company has several divisions, the biggest of which generates $100 million in annual sales and the smallest of which generates only $1 million in sales. If you want to calculate the average profit margin for the divisions, treating the divisions equally doesn't make sense because the largest is two orders of magnitude bigger than the smallest. You need some way of factoring the size of each division into your average profit margin calculation.

You can do this by calculating the *weighted mean*. This is an arithmetic mean in which each value is weighted according to its importance in the data set. Here's the general procedure to follow to calculate the weighted mean:

1. For each value, multiply the value by its weight.

2. Sum the results from step 1.

3. Sum the weights.

4. Divide the sum from step 2 by the sum from step 3.

This procedure works, but it requires building three extra calculations into your worksheet model: the products of the value-weight pairs, the sum of those products, and the sum of the weights. You can avoid all that extra work by using Excel's **SUMPRODUCT** function:

SUMPRODUCT(*array1*[,*array2*,...])

array1, *array2*, ...	The ranges or arrays you want to work with, each of which must have the same number of elements

SUMPRODUCT works by multiplying the corresponding items in each range or array (that is, the first items are multiplied, then the second items are multiplied, and so on) and then summing those products.

For example, Figure 11-2 shows a worksheet that lists the profit margin (B2:B5) and sales (C2:C5) for four divisions. Cell C7 uses the following formula to calculate the weighted mean profit margin:

=SUMPRODUCT(B2:B5, C2:C5) / SUM(C2:C5)

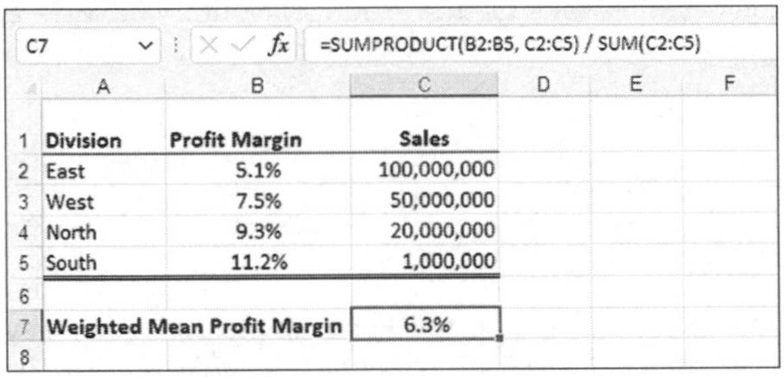

FIGURE 11-2 You use the SUMPRODUCT function to calculate the weighted mean.

Calculating extreme values

The average calculations tell you things about the "middle" of the data, but it can also be useful to know something about the "edges" of the data. For example, what's the biggest value, and what's the smallest? The next two sections take you through the worksheet functions that return the extreme values of a data set.

The MAX and MIN functions

If you want to know the largest value in a data set, use the MAX function:

MAX(*number1*[,*number2*,...])

number1, *number2*, ...	A range, an array, or a list of values of which you want the maximum

For example, to calculate the maximum Quantity value in the Product Inventory table (refer to Figure 11-1), you use the following formula:

```
=MAX(D4:D27)
```

To get the smallest value in a data set, use the MIN function:

```
MIN(number1[,number2,...])
```

number1, *number2*, ...	A range, an array, or a list of values of which you want the minimum

For example, to calculate the minimum value in the Product Inventory table (refer to Figure 11-1), you use the following formula:

```
=MIN(D4:D27)
```

Tip If you need just a quick glance at the maximum or minimum value, select the range, right-click the status bar, and then click the Maximum or Minimum value.

Note If you need to determine the maximum or minimum over a range or an array that includes text values or logical values, use the MAXA or MINA functions instead. These functions ignore text values and treat logical values as either 1 (for TRUE) or 0 (for FALSE).

The LARGE and SMALL functions

Instead of knowing just the largest value, you might need to know the kth largest value, where k is some integer. You can calculate this by using Excel's LARGE function:

```
LARGE(array, k)
```

array	A range, an array, or a list of values.
k	The position (beginning at the largest) within *array* that you want to return. (When k equals 1, this function returns the same value as MAX.)

For example, the following formula returns 120, the second-largest Quantity value in the Product Inventory table (refer to Figure 11-1):

```
=LARGE(D4:D27, 2)
```

Similarly, instead of knowing just the smallest value, you might need to know the kth smallest value, where k is some integer. You can determine this value by using the SMALL function:

```
SMALL(array, k)
```

array	A range, an array, or a list of values.
k	The position (beginning at the smallest) within *array* that you want to return. (When *k* equals **1**, this function returns the same value as **MIN**.)

For example, the following formula returns **15**, the third-smallest Quantity value in the Product Inventory table (refer to Figure 11-1):

```
=SMALL(D4:D27, 3)
```

Performing calculations on the top *k* values

Sometimes, you might need to sum only the top three values in a data set or take the average of the top 10 values. You can do this by combining the **LARGE** function and the appropriate arithmetic function (such as **SUM**) in an array formula. Here's the general formula:

```
=FUNCTION(LARGE(range, {1,2,3,...,k}))
```

Here, *FUNCTION* is the arithmetic function, *range* is the array or range containing the data, and *k* is the number of values you want to work with. In other words, **LARGE** applies the top *k* values from *range* to the **FUNCTION**.

For example, suppose you want to find the mean of the top five Quantity values in the Product Inventory table (refer to Figure 11-1). Here's an array formula that does this:

```
=AVERAGE(LARGE(D4:D27,{1,2,3,4,5}))
```

Performing calculations on the bottom *k* values

You can probably guess that performing calculations on the smallest *k* values is similar to performing calculations on the top *k* values. In fact, the only difference is that you substitute the **SMALL** function for **LARGE** in the array formula:

```
=FUNCTION(SMALL(range, {1,2,3,...,k}))
```

For example, the following array formula sums the smallest three Quantity values in the Product Inventory table (refer to Figure 11-1):

```
=SUM(SMALL(D4:D27,{1,2,3}))
```

Working with rank and percentile

The **MAX**, **MIN**, **LARGE**, and **SMALL** functions examine a range and return the maximum, minimum, *k*th largest, and *k*th smallest value, respectively, in that range. These functions examine the forest and return a tree. The opposite technique, in a sense, is the trees-instead-of-forest approach: Given a cell within a range, you want to know where that cell's value stands with respect to all the other values in that range. There are two measures you can use to examine a cell's value in relation to the range values:

- **Rank:** This is the position of the cell's value if you were to sort the range in descending order. The largest value gets rank 1, the second-largest value gets rank 2, and so on.

- **Percentile:** This is the percentage of items in the range that are at the same level or a lower level than the cell's value.

Calculating rank

To calculate the rank, you can use one of the following functions:

```
RANK.AVG(number, ref[, order])
RANK.EQ(number, ref[, order])
```

number	The number for which you want to find the rank.
ref	A reference, a range name, or an array that corresponds to the set of values in which *number* will be ranked. (Note that *ref* must include *number*.)
order	An integer that specifies how *number* is ranked within the set. If *order* is **0** (this is the default), Excel treats the set as though it were ranked in descending order; if *order* is any nonzero value, Excel treats the set as though it were ranked in ascending order.

For example, the following formula returns the rank of cell D14 in the Product Inventory table (see Figure 11-1):

```
=RANK.AVG(D14, D4:D27)
```

With **RANK.AVG**, if two or more cells in the range have the same value, Excel returns the average of their ranks. For example, given the values 50, 42, 37, 37, 25, 10, **RANK.AVG** ranks both instances of 37 as 3.5, which is the average of 3 and 4. By contrast, **RANK.EQ** would give both instances of 37 the rank 3. With both **RANK.AVG** and **RANK.EQ**, if two or more numbers have the same rank, subsequent ranks are affected. For example, in the preceding list, the number 25 ranks fifth.

Calculating percentile

To calculate the percentile, you can use one of the following functions:

```
PERCENTILE.EXC(array, k)
PERCENTILE.INC(array, k)
```

array	A reference, a range name, or an array of values for the set of data.
k	The percentile, expressed as a decimal value between 0 and 1. This value can be 0 or 1 if you use PERCENTILE.INC but not if you use PERCENTILE.EXC.

For example, the following formula returns the Quantity value in the Product Inventory table (refer to Figure 11-1) that represents the 90th percentile:

```
=PERCENTILE.EXC(D4:D27, 0.9)
```

Calculating measures of variation

Descriptive statistics such as the mean, median, and mode fall under what statisticians call *measures of central tendency* (or sometimes *measures of location*). These numbers are designed to give you some idea of what constitutes a "typical" value in a data set.

Contrast this with the so-called *measures of variation* (or sometimes *measures of dispersion*), which are designed to give you some idea of how the values in a data set vary with respect to one another. That is, are the values spread out, bunched together, or something in between those extremes? For example, a data set in which all the values are the same would have no variability; in contrast, a data set with wildly different values would have high variability. Just what is meant by "wildly different" is what the statistical techniques in this section are designed to help you calculate.

Calculating the range

The simplest measure of variability is the *range* (also sometimes called the *spread*), which is defined as the difference between a data set's maximum and minimum values. Excel doesn't have a function that calculates the range directly. Instead, you first apply the **MAX** and **MIN** functions to the data set. Then, when you have these extreme values, you calculate the range by subtracting the minimum from the maximum.

For example, here's a formula that calculates the range for the Quantity column of the Product Inventory table (refer to Figure 11-1):

```
=MAX(D4:D27) - MIN(D4:D27)
```

In general, the range is a useful measure of variation only for small sample sizes. The larger the sample is, the more likely it becomes that an extreme maximum or minimum (or both) will occur, and the range will be skewed accordingly.

Calculating the variance

When computing the variability of a set of values, one straightforward approach is to calculate how much each value deviates from the mean. You can then add those differences and divide by the number of values in the sample to get what might be called the *average difference*. However, the problem is that, by definition of the arithmetic mean, adding the differences (some of which are positive and some of which are negative) gives the result **0**. To solve this problem, you need to add the *absolute values* of the deviations and then divide by the sample size. This is what statisticians call the *average deviation*.

Unfortunately, this simple state of affairs is still problematic because (for highly technical reasons) mathematicians tend to shudder at equations that require absolute values. To get around this, they instead use the *square* of each deviation from the mean, which always results in a positive number. They sum these squares and divide by the number of values, and the result is then called the *variance*. This is a common measure of variation, although interpreting it is difficult because the result isn't in the units of the sample: It's in those units squared. What does it mean to speak of "quantity squared," for example? This doesn't matter that much for our purposes because, as I explain in the next section, the variance is used chiefly to get to the standard deviation.

> **Note** Keep in mind that this explanation of variance is simplified considerably. If you'd like to know more about this topic, you can consult an intermediate statistics book.

In any case, variance is usually a standard part of a descriptive statistics package, so that's why I'm covering it. Excel calculates the variance by using the **VAR.P** and **VAR.S** functions:

```
VAR.P(number1[,number2,...])
VAR.S(number1[,number2,...])
```

number1, number2, ...	A range, an array, or a list of values of which you want the variance

You use the **VAR.P** function if your data set represents the entire population (as it does, for example, in the Product Inventory table; refer to Figure 11-1); you use the **VAR.S** function if your data set represents only a sample from the entire population.

For example, to calculate the variance of the Quantity values in the Product Inventory table, you use the following formula:

```
=VAR.P(D4:D27)
```

> **Note** If you need to determine the variance over a range or an array that includes text values or logical values, use the **VARPA** (for a population) or **VARA** (for a sample) function instead. These functions ignore text values and treat logical values as either **1** (for **TRUE**) or **0** (for **FALSE**).

Calculating the standard deviation

As I mentioned in the previous section, in real-world scenarios, the variance is really used only as an intermediate step for calculating the most important of the measures of variation: the *standard deviation*. This measure tells you how much the values in the data set vary with respect to the average (the arithmetic mean). What exactly this means won't become clear until you learn about frequency distributions in the next section. For now, however, it's enough to know that a low standard deviation means that the data values are clustered near the mean, and a high standard deviation means that the values are spread out from the mean.

The standard deviation is defined as the square root of the variance. This means that the resulting units will be the same as those used by the data. For example, the variance of the product quantity is expressed as the meaningless *units squared* value, but the standard deviation is expressed in *units*.

You could calculate the standard deviation by taking the square root of the VAR.P or VAR.S result, but Excel offers a more direct route:

```
STDEV.P(number1[,number2,...])
STDEV.S(number1[,number2,...])
```

number1, number2, . . .	A range, an array, or a list of values of which you want the standard deviation

You use the STDEV.P function if your data set represents the entire population (as in the Product Inventory table; see Figure 11-1); you use the STDEV.S function if your data set represents only a sample from the entire population.

For example, to calculate the standard deviation of the Quantity values in the Product Inventory table, you use the following formula:

```
=STDEV.P(D4:D27)
```

> **Note** If you need to determine the standard deviation over a range or an array that includes text values or logical values, use the STDEVPA (for a population) or STDEVA (for a sample) function instead. These functions ignore text values and treat logical values as either **1** (for TRUE) or **0** (for FALSE).

Working with frequency distributions

A *frequency distribution* is a data table that groups data values into *bins*—ranges of values—and shows how many values fall into each bin. For example, here's a possible frequency distribution for the Product Inventory data (refer to Figure 11-1):

Bin (Quantity)	Count
0–75	19
76–150	4
151–225	0
225–300	0
301–375	1

The size of each bin is called the *bin interval*. How many bins should you use? The answer usually depends on the data. If you want to calculate the frequency distribution for a set of student grades, for example, you'd probably set up six bins: 0–49, 50–59, 60–69, 70–79, 80–89, and 90–100. For poll results, you might group the data by age into four bins: 18–34, 35–49, 50–64, and 65+.

If your data has no obvious bin intervals, you can use the following rule:

If n is the number of values in the data set, enclose n between two successive powers of 2 and take the higher exponent to be the number of bins.

For example, if n is 100, you'd use 7 bins because 100 lies between 2^6 (64) and 2^7 (128). For the Product Inventory table, n is 24, so the number of bins should be 5 because 24 falls between 2^4 (16) and 2^5 (32).

> **Tip**   Here's a worksheet formula that implements the bin-calculation rule:
>
> `=CEILING(LOG(COUNT(input_range), 2), 1)`

To help you construct a frequency distribution, Excel offers the **FREQUENCY** function:

FREQUENCY(*data_array*, *bins_array*)

data_array	A range or an array of data values
bins_array	A range or an array of numbers representing the upper bounds of each bin

Here are some things you need to know about this function:

- For the *bins_array*, you enter only the upper limit of each bin. If the last bin is open ended (such as 16+), you don't include it in the *bins_array*. For example, here's the *bins_array* for the Product Inventory table's frequency distribution shown earlier: {75, 150, 225, 300, 375}.

> **Caution**   Make sure you enter your bin values in ascending order.

- The **FREQUENCY** function returns an array, where each item in the array is the number of values that fall within each bin.

- Because **FREQUENCY** returns an array, you must enter it as an array formula. For a dynamic array, enter the formula and press Enter. For a regular array, select the range in which you want the function results to appear, type the formula, and press Ctrl+Shift+Enter.

Figure 11-3 shows the Product Inventory table with a frequency distribution added. The *bins_array* is the range I5:I9, and the **FREQUENCY** results appear in the range J5:J10, with the following formula spilled (see Chapter 2) as a dynamic array in that range:

`=FREQUENCY(D4:D27, I5:I9)`

| J5 | =FREQUENCY(D4:D27, I5:I9) |

	A	B	C	D	H	I	J
1	**Product Inventory**						
2							
3	Code	Name	Cost	Quantity		**Frequency Distribution**	
4	NWTB-1	Northwind Traders Chai	$13.50	25		Bins	FREQUENCY()
5	NWTCO-3	Northwind Traders Syrup	$7.50	50		75	19
6	NWTCO-4	Northwind Traders Cajun Seasoning	$16.50	0		150	4
7	NWTO-5	Northwind Traders Olive Oil	$16.01	15		225	0
8	NWTJP-6	Northwind Traders Boysenberry Spread	$18.75	25		300	0
9	NWTJP-6	Northwind Traders Marmalade	$60.75	32		375	1
10	NWTDFN-7	Northwind Traders Dried Pears	$22.50	56			0
11	NWTS-8	Northwind Traders Curry Sauce	$30.00	87			
12	NWTDFN-14	Northwind Traders Walnuts	$17.44	51			
13	NWTCFV-17	Northwind Traders Fruit Cocktail	$29.25	57			
14	NWTBGM-19	Northwind Traders Chocolate Biscuits Mix	$6.90	40			
15	NWTJP-6	Northwind Traders Boysenberry Spread	$18.75	92			
16		Northwind Traders Marmalade	$60.75	25			
17	NWTBGM-21	Northwind Traders Scones	$7.50	57			
18	NWTB-34	Northwind Traders Beer	$10.50	42			
19	NWTCM-40	Northwind Traders Crab Meat	$13.80	69			
20	NWTSO-41	Northwind Traders Clam Chowder	$7.24	47			
21	NWTB-43	Northwind Traders Coffee	$34.50	325			
22	NWTCA-48	Northwind Traders Chocolate	$9.56	75			
23	NWTDFN-51	Northwind Traders Dried Apples	$39.75	12			
24	NWTG-52	Northwind Traders Long Grain Rice	$5.25	60			
25		Northwind Traders Gnocchi	$28.50	120			
26	NWTP-57	Northwind Traders Ravioli	$14.63	80			
27	NWTS-65	Northwind Traders Hot Pepper Sauce	$15.79	40			

FIGURE 11-3 The range J5:J10 shows the frequency distribution for the Product Inventory table.

Figure 11-4 shows the final Product Inventory worksheet, including all the descriptive statistical values I discussed in this chapter.

| G4 | =COUNT(D4:D27) |

	A	B	C	D	E	F	G
1	**Product Inventory**						
2							
3	Code	Name	Cost	Quantity		**Descriptive Statistics**	
4	NWTB-1	Northwind Traders Chai	$13.50	25		COUNT()	24
5	NWTCO-3	Northwind Traders Syrup	$7.50	50		COUNTA()	25
6	NWTCO-4	Northwind Traders Cajun Seasoning	$16.50	0		COUNTBLANK()	2
7	NWTO-5	Northwind Traders Olive Oil	$16.01	15		COUNTIF()	2
8	NWTJP-6	Northwind Traders Boysenberry Spread	$18.75	25		COUNTIFS()	3
9	NWTJP-6	Northwind Traders Marmalade	$60.75	32		AVERAGE()	61.75
10	NWTDFN-7	Northwind Traders Dried Pears	$22.50	56		AVERAGEIF()	94
11	NWTS-8	Northwind Traders Curry Sauce	$30.00	87		AVERAGEIFS()	168.5
12	NWTDFN-14	Northwind Traders Walnuts	$17.44	51		MEDIAN()	50.5
13	NWTCFV-17	Northwind Traders Fruit Cocktail	$29.25	57		MODE.SNGL()	25
14	NWTBGM-19	Northwind Traders Chocolate Biscuits Mix	$6.90	40		MAX()	325
15	NWTJP-6	Northwind Traders Boysenberry Spread	$18.75	92		MIN()	0
16		Northwind Traders Marmalade	$60.75	25		LARGE()	120
17	NWTBGM-21	Northwind Traders Scones	$7.50	57		SMALL()	15
18	NWTB-34	Northwind Traders Beer	$10.50	42		Top 5 Average	140.8
19	NWTCM-40	Northwind Traders Crab Meat	$13.80	69		Bottom 3 Sum	27
20	NWTSO-41	Northwind Traders Clam Chowder	$7.24	47		RANK.AVG()	16.5
21	NWTB-43	Northwind Traders Coffee	$34.50	325		PERCENTILE.EXC()	106
22	NWTCA-48	Northwind Traders Chocolate	$9.56	75		Range	325
23	NWTDFN-51	Northwind Traders Dried Apples	$39.75	12		VAR.P()	3764.44
24	NWTG-52	Northwind Traders Long Grain Rice	$5.25	60		STDEV.P()	61.27
25		Northwind Traders Gnocchi	$28.50	120		SKEW()	3.4
26	NWTP-57	Northwind Traders Ravioli	$14.63	80		KURTOSIS()	14.4
27	NWTS-65	Northwind Traders Hot Pepper Sauce	$15.79	40			

FIGURE 11-4 This final Product Inventory worksheet shows the descriptive statistical results.

CHAPTER 12

Building inferential statistical formulas

In this chapter, you will:

- Learn about inferential statistics and how they apply to business

- Build formulas to show the relationship between two sets of data

- Extract sample data from a larger population

- Use probabilities to make decisions under uncertainty

- Infer characteristics of a population using confidence intervals and hypothesis testing

In Chapter 11, "Building descriptive statistical formulas," you learned how to measure useful statistical values such as the count, mean, maximum, minimum, rank, and standard deviation. These so-called *descriptive* statistics tell you a great deal about your data, but business analysis and decision-making require more than just descriptions. As an analyst or manager, you also need to draw conclusions about your data. Fortunately, Excel is up to that challenge by offering many worksheet functions that enable you to construct formulas that help you make inferences, such as whether two sets of data are related, the probability of an observation occurring, or whether there's enough evidence to reject a hypothesis about some data. This chapter introduces you to these worksheet functions, and you learn even more in Chapter 13, "Applying regression to track trends and make forecasts."

Understanding inferential statistics

Descriptive statistics consists of count, sum, mean, rank, and standard deviation measures that tell you something about a data set. The assumption underlying descriptive statistics is that you're working with a subset of a larger collection of data. In the language of statisticians, descriptive statistics operates on a *sample* of some larger *population*.

Inferential statistics is a set of techniques that enables you to derive conclusions—that is, make *inferences*—about the entire population based on a sample. It's important to understand that inferring population characteristics based on a sample is inherently uncertain. Certainty only comes when you measure the population as a whole, such as when the government performs a census. These sorts of large-scale experiments are almost always impractical (too time-consuming and expensive), so samples of the population are observed. That injects uncertainty into the process, but one of the key characteristics of inferential statistics is that it gives you multiple ways to measure that uncertainty.

In statistics, a *variable* is an aspect of a data set that can be measured in some way (counted, averaged, and so on). The following are all statistical variables:

- In company financial data, the revenues generated over a fiscal year

- In a database of historical economic data, the annual interest rate

- In a series of coin tosses, the collection of flips that turn up "tails"

Much of inferential statistics involves interrogating the relationship between variables such as these. Note, however, that not all variables are inherently interesting, at least from a statistical point of view. For example, a table of invoices might include a Units Ordered column, a Unit Price column, and a Total Price column that's calculated by multiplying the units ordered by the unit price. In this example, there's no point analyzing the "relationship" between the units ordered and total price variables because that relationship is purely arithmetic (and hence trivial).

Of more interest to us are three other types of variables:

- **Independent variable:** These are values that are generated without reference to or reliance upon another process. For example, if you're analyzing revenues per month, the months represent the independent variable.

- **Dependent variable:** These are values that are generated due to some other process. In the revenues per month example, the revenues represent the dependent variable.

- **Random variable:** These are values that are generated by a chance process. For example, the results of a coin toss represent a random variable. Random variables can be either *discrete*, which means the variable only has a finite number of possible values, or *continuous*, which means the variable has an infinite number of possible values.

Sampling data

If you have a population data set, you might find that it's too large or too slow to work with directly. To speed up your work, you can generate a sample from that population and then use the rest of this chapter's inferential statistics functions and formulas to draw conclusions about the entire population based on your sample. There are two main types of samples you can generate:

- **Periodic:** A sample that consists of every *n*th observation from the population. If *n* is 10, for example, the sample would consist of data points 10, 20, 30, and so on.

- **Random:** A sample that consists of *n* values chosen randomly from the population.

If you have the Analysis ToolPak add-in installed (see Chapter 4's "Loading the Analysis ToolPak" section), the Data Analysis command (on the Data tab, select Data Analysis) comes with a Sampling tool that can generate either a periodic or a random sample.

The Sampling tool gets the job done, but you can also generate custom samples using formulas. One way to do this is to use Excel's **OFFSET** function, which returns a reference to a cell or range that's a specified number of rows and columns from a given reference:

OFFSET(*reference*, *rows*, *cols*[, *height*, *width*])

reference	The cell or range that acts as the starting point for the offset.
rows	The number of rows up or down that you want the result offset from the upper-left cell of *reference*.
cols	The number of columns left or right that you want the result offset from the upper-left cell of *reference*.
height	The number of rows in the result; if omitted, the height is the number of rows in *reference*.
width	The number of columns in the result; if omitted, the width is the number of columns in *reference*.

The next two sections show you how to use **OFFSET** to extract a sample from a population.

Extracting a periodic sample

If you want to extract every *n*th data point from the population for your sample, use Excel's **OFFSET** function as follows:

- The *reference* argument is the first data cell in the population range.

- The *rows* argument is the period—that is, *n*—multiplied by the sample data point's position in the resulting range. For example, if *n* is 10, then the first *rows* value is 10 * 1, the second is 10 * 2, and so on. To generate the sample data positions (1, 2, and so on) automatically, use the **ROW** function, which returns the row value of the current cell. For example, if the formula for your first sample data point is in cell A1, **ROW** returns 1, so you can use ROW as is. If, instead, the formula for the first sample point is in A2, **ROW** returns 2, so you'd need to use ROW - 1.

- The *cols* argument is 0.

- The *height* and *width* arguments are omitted.

For example, check out the Invoices worksheet shown in Figure 12-1.

> **Note**   You can work with all the examples in this chapter by downloading Chapter12.xslx from either of the companion content sites mentioned in the Introduction.

Here's an **OFFSET** formula that extracts every 10th value from the Quantity column—column Q—of the Invoices table, assuming the first formula is in cell A5 (hence the need for **ROW** – 4):

```
=OFFSET(Invoices!$Q$2, 10 * (ROW() - 4), 0)
```

Assuming you store the value for *n* in cell A3, here's a more general formula that works for any sample size:

```
=OFFSET(Invoices!$Q$2, $A$3 * (ROW() - 4), 0)
```

	O	P	Q	R	S
1	ProductName	UnitPrice	Quantity	Discount	ExtendedPrice
2	Thüringer Rostbratwurst	$99.00	21	0%	$2,079.00
3	Steeleye Stout	$14.40	35	0%	$504.00
4	Maxilaku	$16.00	30	0%	$480.00
5	Nord-Ost Matjeshering	$20.70	18	0%	$372.60
6	Gnocchi di nonna Alice	$30.40	70	0%	$2,128.00
7	Louisiana Fiery Hot Pepper Sauce	$16.80	20	0%	$336.00
8	Fløtemysost	$17.20	60	0%	$1,032.00
9	Tunnbröd	$7.20	60	0%	$432.00
10	Vegie-spread	$35.10	65	0%	$2,281.50
11	Pavlova	$13.90	21	15%	$248.11
12	Chocolade	$10.20	70	15%	$606.90
13	Gumbär Gummibärchen	$24.90	30	5%	$709.65
14	Singaporean Hokkien Fried Mee	$11.20	40	5%	$425.60
15	Maxilaku	$16.00	30	5%	$456.00
16	Aniseed Syrup	$8.00	50	0%	$400.00
17	Chai	$14.40	10	0%	$144.00
18	Sir Rodney's Scones	$8.00	30	10%	$216.00
19	Rössle Sauerkraut	$36.40	42	10%	$1,375.92
20	Inlagd Sill	$15.20	5	10%	$68.40
21	Boston Crab Meat	$14.70	2	10%	$26.46
22	Queso Cabrales	$16.80	30	0%	$504.00
23	Gudbrandsdalsost	$28.80	15	0%	$432.00
24	Fløtemysost	$17.20	15	0%	$258.00
25	Gravad lax	$20.80	10	0%	$208.00
26	Tourtière	$5.90	6	0%	$35.40
27	Tarte au sucre	$39.40	35	0%	$1,379.00

FIGURE 12-1 An Invoices worksheet containing a table of invoices, with the quantity ordered for each product in column Q.

Note the use of the absolute cell addresses, which means you can fill this formula down to create as many data points as you need for your sample. Ideally, your sample should include every *n*th item from the population. If you fill this formula past that number, Excel generates a **#VALUE!** error (or just the value 0). That's no big deal, but if you prefer to avoid the error, use an **IF** test to check whether the sample number—that is, $A$3 * **ROW()** – 4—is greater than the number of items in the population, as given by the **COUNT** function (or **COUNTA**, if your population data includes non-numeric items). Here's the full formula:

```
=IF($A$3 * (ROW() - 4) <= COUNT(Invoices!Q:Q), OFFSET(Invoices!$Q$2,
$A$3 * (ROW() - 4), 0), "Out of range!")
```

If the condition returns **TRUE**, the formula runs the **OFFSET** function to extract the sample data point; otherwise, it displays "Out of range!". Figure 12-2 shows this formula in action.

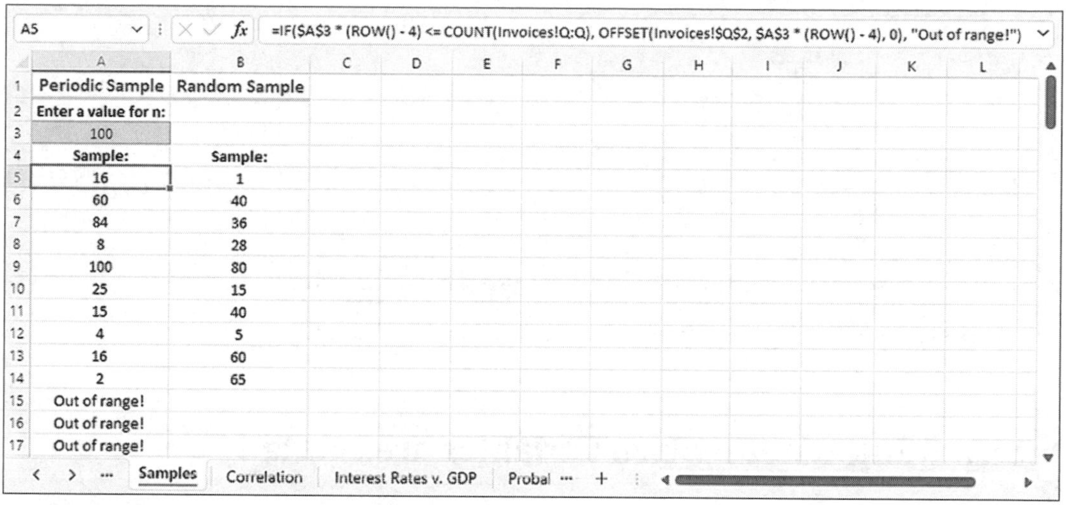

FIGURE 12-2 This formula extracts periodic sample data from the Invoices table.

Extracting a random sample

To extract random data points from the population for your sample, use the **OFFSET** function as follows:

- The *reference* argument is the first data cell in the population range.

- The *rows* argument is a random number between 1 and the number of items in the population. This is a job for the **RANDBETWEEN** function:

  RANDBETWEEN(0, COUNT(*population_range*) - 1)

- The *cols* argument is 0.

- The *height* and *width* arguments are omitted.

Given the Invoices worksheet shown earlier in Figure 12-1, here's an **OFFSET** formula that extracts a random value from the Quantity column—column Q—of the Invoices table:

=OFFSET(Invoices!$Q$2, RANDBETWEEN(0, COUNT(Invoices!Q:Q - 1), 0)

Figure 12-3 shows this formula at work.

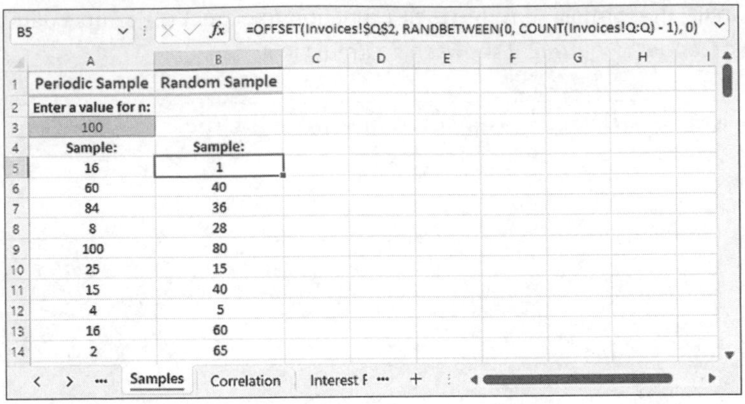

FIGURE 12-3 This formula extracts random sample data from the Invoices table.

Determining whether two variables are related

One of the fundamental statistical questions you can ask is: Are two variables related? That is, do the two variables tend to move in the same direction (when one goes up or down, so does the other) or in the opposite direction (when one goes up, the other goes down, or vice versa)? For example, when advertising expenses increase, do sales also rise? When interest rates fall, does gross domestic product tend to rise?

To answer these types of questions, statisticians turn to *measures of association*, each of which provides a numerical result that tells you whether two variables are related. If the variables tend to move in the same direction, they're said to have a *direct* relationship; if the two variables tend to move in the opposite direction, they're said to have an *inverse* relationship. Some measures of association can also tell you the relative strength of that relationship.

The next two sections cover two measures of association that you can calculate in your Excel statistical models: covariance and correlation.

Calculating covariance

Covariance is a measure of association that tells you whether two variables "move" together: that is, have either a direct or an inverse relationship. In Excel, you measure covariance using the following worksheet functions:

```
COVARIANCE.S(array1, array2)
COVARIANCE.P(array1, array2)
```

array1	The range or array that contains the values of the first variable.
array2	The range or array that contains the values of the second variable.

Use **COVARIANCE.S** when your variables represent a sample of a population; use **COVARIANCE.P** when your variables represent the entire population. For example, Figure 12-4 shows advertising and sales numbers over 12 fiscal quarters. Are these two variables related? To find out, you can use the following formula:

```
=COVARIANCE.S(C3:C14, D3:D14)
```

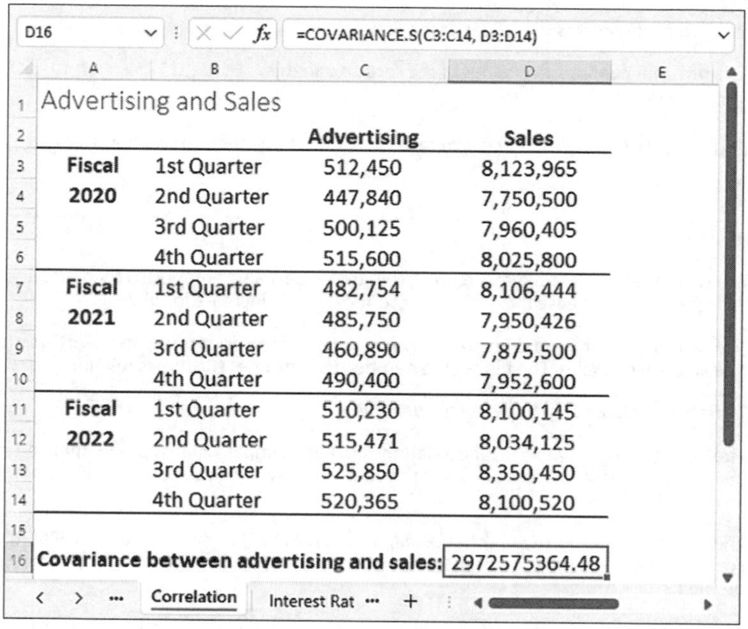

Advertising and Sales

		Advertising	Sales
Fiscal	1st Quarter	512,450	8,123,965
2020	2nd Quarter	447,840	7,750,500
	3rd Quarter	500,125	7,960,405
	4th Quarter	515,600	8,025,800
Fiscal	1st Quarter	482,754	8,106,444
2021	2nd Quarter	485,750	7,950,426
	3rd Quarter	460,890	7,875,500
	4th Quarter	490,400	7,952,600
Fiscal	1st Quarter	510,230	8,100,145
2022	2nd Quarter	515,471	8,034,125
	3rd Quarter	525,850	8,350,450
	4th Quarter	520,365	8,100,520

Covariance between advertising and sales: 2972575364.48

FIGURE 12-4 This worksheet calculates the covariance between advertising and sales.

The result, as you can see in cell D16 in Figure 12-4, is a large positive number. What does that mean? Strangely, the number itself isn't all that meaningful. Here's how to interpret the covariance result:

- If the covariance value is a positive number, it means the two variables have a direct relationship.
- If the covariance value is a negative number, it means the two variables have an inverse relationship.
- If the covariance value is 0 (or close to it), it means the two variables are not related.

Therefore, you can say that advertising and sales have a direct relationship with each other. What you *can't* say is how strong or weak that relationship might be. To get that, you have to turn to a different measure of association.

Calculating correlation

Correlation is a measure of association that tells you not only whether two variables have either a direct or an inverse relationship, but also the relative strength of that relationship. In Excel, you measure correlation using the following worksheet function:

CORREL(*array1*, *array2*)

array1	The range or array that contains the values of the first variable.
array2	The range or array that contains the values of the second variable.

The **CORREL** function calculates the *correlation coefficient*. The coefficient is a number between –1 and 1 that has the following properties:

Correlation Coefficient	Interpretation
1	The two variables have a direct relationship that is perfectly and positively correlated. For example, a 10% increase in advertising produces a 10% increase in sales.
Between 0 and 1	The two variables have a direct relationship. For example, an increase in advertising leads to an increase in sales. The higher the number, the stronger the direct relationship.
0	There is no relationship between the variables.
Between 0 and –1	The two variables have an inverse relationship. For example, an increase in interest rates leads to a decrease in gross domestic product. The lower the number, the stronger the inverse relationship.
–1	The variables have an inverse relationship that is perfectly and negatively correlated. For example, a 10% increase in interest rates leads to a 10% decrease in gross domestic product.

For example, consider again the advertising and sales numbers shown earlier in Figure 12-4. To calculate the correlation between these variables, use the following formula:

=CORREL(C3:C14, D3:D14)

The result, as you can see in cell D17 in Figure 12-5, is 0.81, which tells you not only that advertising and sales have a direct relationship, but also that this relationship is relatively strong.

> **Warning** There's an old saying in statistical circles: Correlation doesn't imply causation. That is, just because two variables have a strong (direct or indirect) relationship, it doesn't follow that one variable is the cause of the other. The most you can say is that the two variables tend to vary together.

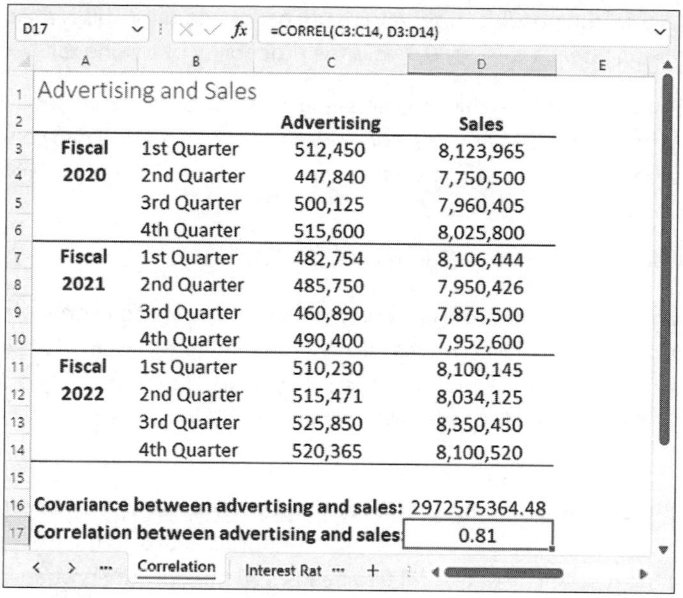

D17 =CORREL(C3:C14, D3:D14)

Advertising and Sales

		Advertising	Sales
Fiscal 2020	1st Quarter	512,450	8,123,965
	2nd Quarter	447,840	7,750,500
	3rd Quarter	500,125	7,960,405
	4th Quarter	515,600	8,025,800
Fiscal 2021	1st Quarter	482,754	8,106,444
	2nd Quarter	485,750	7,950,426
	3rd Quarter	460,890	7,875,500
	4th Quarter	490,400	7,952,600
Fiscal 2022	1st Quarter	510,230	8,100,145
	2nd Quarter	515,471	8,034,125
	3rd Quarter	525,850	8,350,450
	4th Quarter	520,365	8,100,520

Covariance between advertising and sales: 2972575364.48

Correlation between advertising and sales: 0.81

FIGURE 12-5 This worksheet calculates the correlation between advertising and sales.

Working with probability distributions

When you're working with a variable, you're dealing with a collection of observations, such as sales or coin tosses. However, before looking at the values of a variable's actual observations, much statistical analysis begins by looking at all the *possible* values that the variable can have:

- For a coin toss, the possible values are heads or tails.
- For a die roll, the possible values are one through six.
- For student grades, the possible values are 0 through 100.
- For a playing card selection, the 52 possible values are two through ten, jack, queen, king, and ace, with each of these available in four suits: clubs, diamonds, hearts, and spades.

If you then assign a probability to each of these values, the resulting set of probabilities is known as the variable's *probability distribution*. This could be a table that lists each possible value and its probability, or it could be a function that returns the probability for each possible value. One key point for a probability distribution is that the sum of all the probabilities must add up to 1.

Calculating probability

To determine the probability of a single variable value, you divide the number of observations for that value by the total size of the sample:

```
=observations / sample size
```

For example, if you're tossing a coin, the possible observations are heads and tails. This is a sample size of two, so the probability of tossing heads is 1/2, or 0.5, as is the probability of tossing tails.

If your variable consists of multiple, mutually exclusive events—such as multiple coin tosses—then you need some way of calculating combined probabilities. For example, if you're tossing two coins—call them Coin A and Coin B—the possible observations are two heads, heads on Coin A and tails on Coin B, tails on Coin A and heads on Coin B, and two tails.

There are two possibilities for calculating combined probabilities:

- **The probability of one observation *or* another occurring:** Use the *rule of addition*, which means that you add the probabilities of the possible observations. In the two-coin toss example, to calculate the probability of tossing one heads and one tails, you add the probability of heads on Coin A and tails on Coin B (0.25) and the probability of tails on Coin A and heads on Coin B (0.25): 0.25 + 0.25 = 0.5.

- **The probability of one observation *and* another occurring:** Use the *rule of multiplication*, which means that you multiply the probabilities of the possible observations. In the two-coin toss example, to calculate the probability of tossing two heads, you multiply the probability of getting a single heads (0.5) by itself: 0.5 * 0.5 = 0.25.

For more complex observations, one useful approach is to use the **FREQUENCY** function to create a frequency distribution, as I describe in Chapter 11, then calculate the probability for each bin. Figure 12-6 shows such a probability distribution for a set of student grades.

| G3 | | fx | =F3 / $F$9 | | | | |

Student Grades

Student ID	Grade		Bin	Frequency	Probability
64947	82		50	2	0.04
69630	66		60	4	0.09
18324	52		70	19	0.41
89826	94		80	15	0.33
63600	40		90	5	0.11
25089	62		100	1	0.02
89923	88		Total	46	1
13000	75				
16895	67				

FIGURE 12-6 This probability distribution is created from a frequency distribution for student grades.

The probability of getting a grade less than 50 is 0.04, while the probability of getting a grade between 50 and 59 is 0.09. Therefore, using the rule of addition, the probability of getting a grade less than 60 is 0.04 + 0.09 = 0.13.

That works, but what if you want to answer more specific questions, such as what is the probability of getting a grade between 70 and 75 or between 66 and 82? You could fiddle with the bins on your frequency distribution, but let me show you a more flexible method.

First, list all the possible grades. You could start at 0, but it's probably more practical to start with the smallest grade. Now calculate the frequency of each grade in the sample. The COUNTIF function works nicely for this. For example, suppose you have the grade 50 in cell I13 and the grades sample is in the range C3:C48. Then the following formula returns the number of times the grade 50 appears in the sample:

```
=COUNTIF($C$3:$C$48, I13)
```

Once you've filled this calculation to cover all the grades, create a new column that calculates the probability for each grade. Figure 12-7 shows how I've set this up.

J3		fx	=COUNTIF($C$3:$C$48, I3)		
	A	B	C	D	I	J	K	L
1		Student Grades						
2		Student ID	Grade		Grade	Frequency	Probability	
3		64947	82		40	1	0.02	
4		69630	66		41	0	0.00	
5		18324	52		42	0	0.00	
6		89826	94		43	0	0.00	
7		63600	40		44	0	0.00	
8		25089	62		45	0	0.00	
9		89923	88		46	0	0.00	
10		13000	75		47	0	0.00	
11		16895	67		48	1	0.02	
12		24918	62		49	0	0.00	
13		45107	71		50	0	0.00	
14		64090	53		51	0	0.00	
15		94395	74		52	1	0.02	
16		58749	65		53	1	0.02	
17		26916	66		54	0	0.00	
18		59033	67		55	0	0.00	
19		15450	68		56	0	0.00	
20		56415	69		57	0	0.00	
21		88069	69		58	2	0.04	
22		75784	68		59	0	0.00	
23		51262	71		60	0	0.00	
24		96452	72		61	0	0.00	
25		87415	75		62	2	0.04	
26		56961	58		63	1	0.02	

< > ··· Probability   Inte ··· +

FIGURE 12-7 This worksheet shows a probability distribution for every possible grade.

To calculate the probability of a grade falling within any range, you could add up the probabilities yourself. However, it's almost always easier and more flexible to let Excel's PROB worksheet function do the heavy lifting here:

```
PROB(x range, prob_range, lower_limit[, upper_limit])
```

x_range	A range or array containing the possible observations.
prob_range	A range or array containing the probability values for each observation in x_range.
lower_limit	The lower bound on the range of values for which you want to know the probability.
upper_limit	The upper bound on the range of values for which you want to know the probability; if omitted, the returned value is the probability that an observation equals the lower_limit.

For example, here's a formula that uses **PROB** to calculate the probability that a student grade falls between 66 and 82:

```
=PROB(I3:I63, K3:K63, 66, 82)
```

Figure 12-8 shows this formula in action.

A	B	C	D	I	J	K	L	M	N
	Student Grades								
	Student ID	Grade		Grade	Frequency	Probability		Custom Probability Range	
	64947	82		40	1	0.02		Lower limit:	66
	69630	66		41	0	0.00		Upper limit:	82
	18324	52		42	0	0.00		Probability	0.61
	89826	94		43	0	0.00			
	63600	40		44	0	0.00			
	25089	62		45	0	0.00			
	89923	88		46	0	0.00			
	13000	75		47	0	0.00			
	16895	67		48	1	0.02			
	24918	62		49	0	0.00			
	45107	71		50	0	0.00			
	64090	53		51	0	0.00			
	94395	74		52	1	0.02			
	58749	65		53	1	0.02			
	26916	66		54	0	0.00			
	59033	67		55	0	0.00			
	15450	68		56	0	0.00			
	56415	69		57	0	0.00			
	88069	69		58	2	0.04			
	75784	68		59	0	0.00			
	51262	71		60	0	0.00			
	96452	72		61	0	0.00			
	87415	75		62	2	0.04			
	56961	58		63	1	0.02			

FIGURE 12-8 Using the **PROB** function to determine the probability that a grade falls between 66 and 82.

Discrete probability distributions

If you're working with discrete variables, there are some probability distributions that you can take advantage of to quickly calculate probabilities. These are the binomial, hypergeometric, and Poisson distributions, and I cover them in the next three sections.

The binomial distribution

The *binomial distribution* is a probability distribution for samples that have the following characteristics:

- **There are only two possible observations, and these are mutually exclusive.** Examples include coin tosses (heads and tails), die rolls (for example, even numbers and odd numbers), and sales calls (the sale is made or not). By convention, these observations are labeled *success* and *failure*.

- **Each observation is independent of the others**. That is, the outcome of a given trial doesn't affect the outcome of any subsequent trial. For example, coming up heads on a coin toss has no effect on whether you turn up heads or tails on the next coin toss.

- **The probability of the *success* observation is constant from one trial to the next.** For example, the probability of turning up heads on a coin toss remains 0.5 no matter how many trials you perform.

If your variable conforms to this so-called *Bernoulli* sampling process, then you've got yourself a binomial distribution, and you can calculate probabilities based on this distribution using Excel's `BINOM.DIST` function. Specifically, given the number of trials in a sample and the probability of getting a successful observation in each trial, you use `BINOM.DIST` to calculate the probability of generating a particular number of success observations. Here's the syntax:

BINOM.DIST(*number_s, trials, probability_s, cumulative*]

number_s	The number of success observations for which you want to calculate the probability.
Trials	A total number of trials in the sample.
probability_s	The probability of getting a success observation in each trial.
Cumulative	A logical value that determines how Excel calculates the result. Use **FALSE** to calculate the probability that the sample has *number_s* successes; use **TRUE** to return the cumulative probability that the sample contains at most *number_s* successes.

For example, suppose you know that the probability of a salesperson making a sale is 0.1. What is the probability of that salesperson making 3 sales in 10 sales calls? The following formula answers this question (with a result of 0.057):

=BINOM.DIST(3, 10, 0.1, FALSE)

The hypergeometric distribution

A common variation on the Bernoulli sampling process that I described in the previous section is to extract a sample from a population by taking items out and not replacing them for the next trial. This takes us out of the binomial distribution because the probability of success does not remain constant with each trial (because we're removing items and not putting them back). This variation is saddled with the unlovely name *hypergeometric distribution* (so-called because of the form of its mathematical equation).

For example, suppose you have two political parties: the Circumlocutionists and the Platitudinists. In a population of 10,000, you know that 5,200 are Circumlocutionists and 4,800 are Platitudinists. Given a sample size of 10, what is the probability that six will be Circumlocutionists? To find out, use the **HYPGEOM.DIST** function:

```
HYPGEOM.DIST(sample_s, number_sample, population_s, number_pop, cumulative)
```

sample_s	The number of sample success observations for which you want to calculate the probability.
number_sample	The size of the sample.
population_s	The number of success observations in the population.
number_pop	The size of the population.
cumulative	A logical value that determines how Excel calculates the result. Use **FALSE** to calculate the probability that the sample has *sample_s* successes; use **TRUE** to return the cumulative probability that the sample contains at most *sample_s* successes.

Here's the formula that answers the example question (which returns the probability 0.22):

```
=HYPGEOM.DIST(6, 10, 5200, 10000, FALSE)
```

The Poisson distribution

Another variation on the Bernoulli process is to assume that the sampling occurs during a time interval instead of via separate trials. The observations are still independent of each other. This is known in the stats trade as a *Poisson distribution*. How is it useful? If you know the mean number of observations that occur in a specified interval, then the Poisson distribution calculates the probability that a specified number of observations will occur in a randomly selected interval of the same duration.

For example, suppose a manager knows that her store receives an average of 50 customers per hour. What is the probability that her store will receive just 40 customers in the next hour? To calculate this, you use the **POISSON.DIST** function:

```
POISSON.DIST(x, mean, cumulative)
```

X	The number of observations for which you want to calculate the probability.
Mean	The average number of observations.
cumulative	A logical value that determines how Excel calculates the result. Use **FALSE** to calculate the probability of *x* observations; use **TRUE** to return the cumulative probability that at most *x* observations will occur.

Here's the formula that answers the example question (which returns the probability of 0.021):

```
=POISSON.DIST(40, 50, FALSE)
```

Understanding the normal distribution and the NORM.DIST function

The next few sections require some knowledge of perhaps the most famous object in the statistical world: the *normal distribution* (also called the *normal frequency curve*). This distribution refers to a set of values that have the following characteristics:

- The mean occurs in the middle of the distribution at the topmost point of the curve.

- The curve is symmetric around the central mean, meaning that the shape of the curve to the left of the mean is a mirror of the shape of the curve to the right of the mean.

- The frequencies of each value are highest at the mean, fall off slowly on either side of the mean, and stretch out into long tails on either end.

- The middle part of the curve to the left and right of the mean has a concave shape, whereas the parts further left and further right have a convex shape. These changes from concave to convex occur at one standard deviation to the left and to the right of the mean and are known as *saddle points*.

- Approximately 68 percent of all the values fall within one standard deviation of the mean (that is, either one standard deviation above or one standard deviation below).

- Approximately 95 percent of all the values fall within two standard deviations of the mean.

- Approximately 99.7 percent of all the values fall within three standard deviations of the mean.

Figure 12-9 shows a chart that displays a typical normal distribution. In fact, this particular example is called the *standard normal distribution*, and it's defined as having mean **0** and standard deviation **1**. The distinctive bell shape of this distribution is why it's often called the *bell curve*.

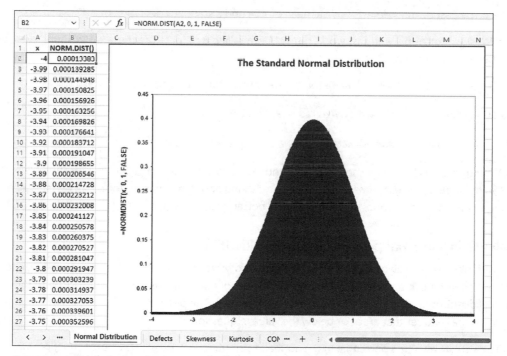

FIGURE 12-9 This is the standard normal distribution (mean 0 and standard deviation 1) generated by the NORM. DIST function.

Calculating standard scores

All normal distributions are bell curves, meaning they all have a shape similar to the one shown in Figure 12-9, but its mean and standard deviation uniquely defines each. How do you analyze or interpret a value from one of these other normal distributions? The answer is to convert the value to a *standard score*—also called a *Z-score*—which tells you where the value would appear in the standard normal distribution. By doing this with values from different normal distributions, you can compare those values apples-to-apples.

To convert a value from a normal distribution to a standard score, use the following formula:

```
=(value - mean) / standard deviation
```

Here, *value* is the value you want to convert, whereas *mean* and *standard deviation* are, respectively, the arithmetic mean and standard deviation of *value*'s normal distribution.

For example, suppose you have two manufacturing groups named East and West, each of which is subdivided into multiple workgroups. Suppose you're tracking defects in these groups, and these defects have normal distributions as follows:

- The West group's defects have a mean of 9.0 and a standard deviation of 2.97.

- The East group's defects have a mean of 7.54 and a standard deviation of 2.47.

If West workgroup A and East workgroup M both tallied 8 defects, are these workgroups even, or is one better than the other?

To answer that question, calculate the standard score for both workgroups:

```
West Workgroup A standard score: (8 - 9) / 2.97 = -0.34
```

```
East Workgroup M standard score: (8 - 7.54) / 2.47 = 0.19
```

Workgroup A is below the mean on the standard normal distribution, while workgroup M is a bit above the mean. Because these are defects we're talking about, fewer is better, so we can say, all else being equal, that workgroup A's defects total is "better" than workgroup M's.

Calculating normal percentiles with NORM.DIST

As I describe in the previous section, figuring standard scores enables you to interpret a value in terms of the standard normal distribution. Another useful bit of data analysis you can perform with the normal distribution is to calculate the percentile of a value. The percentile refers to the percentage of values in the data set that are at or below the value in question.

To calculate a value's percentile in the normal distribution, use Excel's NORM.DIST function, which returns the probability that a given value exists within a population:

```
NORM.DIST(x, mean, standard_dev, cumulative)
```

x	The value you want to work with.
mean	The arithmetic mean of the distribution.
standard_dev	The standard deviation of the distribution.
cumulative	A logical value that determines how the function results are calculated. If *cumulative* is **TRUE**, the function returns the cumulative probabilities of the observations that occur at or below x; if *cumulative* is **FALSE**, the function returns the probability associated with x.

Returning the defects example from the previous section, what is the percentile for West workgroup A? Recall that this workgroup had 8 defects, and the West group has a mean of 9 and a standard deviation of 2.97. The answer is 0.368 as generated by the following formula:

```
=NORM.DIST(8, 9, 2.97, TRUE)
```

To generate the values in the standard normal distribution shown earlier in Figure 12-9, I used a series of **NORM.DIST** functions with mean **0** and standard deviation **1**. For example, here's the formula for the value **0**:

```
=NORM.DIST(0, 0, 1, TRUE)
```

With the *cumulative* argument set to **TRUE**, this formula returns **0.5**, which makes intuitive sense because, in the standard normal distribution, half of the values fall below 0. In other words, the probabilities of all the values below 0 add up to 0.5.

Now consider the same function, but this time with the *cumulative* argument set to **FALSE**:

```
=NORM.DIST(0, 0, 1, FALSE)
```

This time, the result is **0.39894228**. In other words, in this distribution, about 39.9% of all the values in the population are 0.

The shape of the curve I: The SKEW function

How do you know if your data set's frequency distribution is at or close to a normal distribution? In other words, does the shape of your data's frequency curve mirror that of the normal distribution's bell curve?

One way to find out is to consider how the values cluster around the mean. For a normal distribution, the values cluster symmetrically about the mean. Other distributions are asymmetric in one of two ways:

- **Negatively skewed:** The values are bunched above the mean and drop off quickly in a "tail" below the mean.

- **Positively skewed:** The values are bunched below the mean and drop off quickly in a "tail" above the mean.

Figure 12-10 shows two charts that display examples of negative and positive skewness.

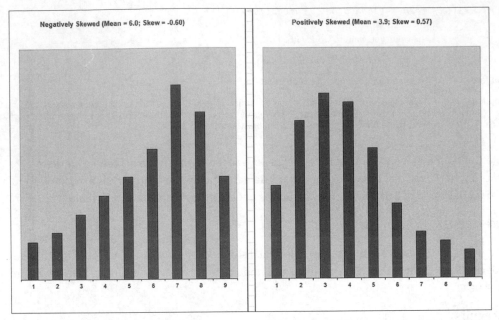

FIGURE 12-10 The distribution on the left is negatively skewed; the distribution on the right is positively skewed.

In Excel, you calculate the skewness of a data set by using the **SKEW** function:

`SKEW(number1[,number2,...])`

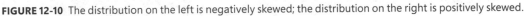

| *number1, number2, ...* | A range, an array, or a list of values for which you want the skewness |

The closer the **SKEW** result is to 0, the more symmetric the distribution is, so the more like the normal distribution it is.

The shape of the curve II: The KURT function

Another way to find out how close your frequency distribution is to a normal distribution is to consider the flatness of the curve:

- **Flat:** The values are distributed evenly across all or most of the bins.

- **Peaked:** The values are clustered around a narrow range of values.

Statisticians call the flatness of the frequency curve the *kurtosis*. A flat curve has a negative kurtosis, and a peaked curve has a positive kurtosis. The further these values are from 0, the less the frequency is like the normal distribution. Figure 12-11 shows two charts that display examples of negative and positive kurtosis.

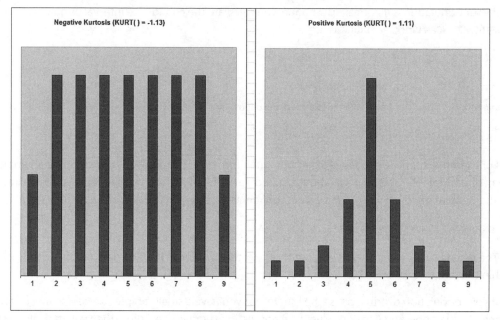

FIGURE 12-11 The distribution on the left has a negative kurtosis; the distribution on the right has a positive kurtosis.

In Excel, you calculate the kurtosis of a data set by using the **KURT** function:

KURT(*number1*[,*number2*,...])

number1, *number2*, ...	A range, an array, or a list of values for which you want the kurtosis

Determining confidence intervals

A *confidence interval* for a population mean is a measure of the probability that the population mean falls within a specified range of values. The confidence interval calculation typically requires four things:

- A mean value calculated from a sample of the population.

- A standard deviation value for the population.

- A range of values, which is determined on the low end by subtracting the confidence interval from the sample mean, and on the high end by adding the confidence interval to the sample mean.

- A *confidence level*, which is a percentage that specifies the probability that the actual population mean lies within the range (it is within the sample mean plus or minus the confidence interval). The calculation itself uses the *significance level*, which is 100 percent minus the confidence level.

If your population is a normal distribution, you calculate the confidence interval using the **CONFIDENCE.NORM** worksheet function:

CONFIDENCE.NORM(*alpha, standard_dev, size*)

alpha	The significance level
standard_dev	The standard deviation of the population
size	The sample size

For example, suppose you sample the commute times for 250 employees and calculate a sample mean of 44.7 minutes, with a population standard deviation of 8. To determine the confidence interval for the population mean using a 95 percent confidence level, you'd use the following formula:

=CONFIDENCE.NORM(0.05, 8, 250)

The result is 0.99, which means you can be 95 percent confident that the population mean falls within the range 43.71 and 45.69.

If your population distribution is a bell curve, but you have a small sample size (say, at most a few dozen observations) and you don't know the population standard deviation, then you're dealing with a t-distribution. In this case, you calculate the confidence interval by using the **CONFIDENCE.T** function:

CONFIDENCE.T(*alpha, standard_dev, size*)

alpha	The significance level
standard_dev	The standard deviation of the sample
size	The sample size

For the employee commute times example, suppose you only have a sample of size of 25, and you don't know the population standard deviation, but you calculate the sample standard deviation to be 8.91. To determine the confidence interval for the population mean using a 95 percent confidence level, you'd use the following formula:

=CONFIDENCE.T(0.05, 8.91, 25)

The resulting confidence interval is 3.68. Assuming the sample mean is 44.7, you can be 95 percent confident that the population mean falls within the range 40.99 and 48.35.

Hypothesis testing

One common technique in inferential statistics is *hypothesis testing*, where you posit a hypothesis about a population parameter (such as its mean value) and then test that so-called *null hypothesis* to find out whether it should be rejected.

If you know the standard deviation of the population, then given a sample data set you can perform such a test in Excel by using the **Z.TEST** function:

```
Z.TEST(array,x[,sigma])
```

array	A reference, a range name, or an array of sample values for the data against which you want to test x.
x	The null hypothesis value you want to test.
sigma	The population standard deviation. If you omit this argument, Excel uses the sample standard deviation.

Z.TEST returns the *p-value*, which is the probability that, if the null hypothesis is true, the value of x will be greater than its hypothesized value. Note that the probability that the value of x is *less* than its hypothesized value is given by the formula `1 - p-value`.

For example, suppose you have a pizza business, and your company goal is to average 30 minutes for delivery. If delivery times exceed that duration, then an automatic (and expensive) review procedure kicks in. So, you take a sample of delivery times, and your sample shows an average of 30.7 minutes. Your null hypothesis, then, is that overall delivery times are greater than the desired 30 minutes. Does it follow from the data that you should accept the null hypothesis?

To find out, first, you need to set up the test as follows:

- Assume you know the standard deviation for delivery times is 3.

- Decide on the significance level you want to use. A probability above this level means you can't reject the null hypothesis. In this example, I'm going with a 10 percent level of significance.

- Assume your sample delivery times reside in the range A3:A27 (see this chapter's example workbook).

Given all that, here's the formula that returns the p-value for the z-test:

```
=Z.TEST(A3:A27, 30, 3)
```

The result is 0.129, or 12.9%. Because this is greater than the significance level of 10 percent, I can't reject the null hypothesis.

I should also mention the t-test, which is similar to the z-test but is handy when you don't know the population's standard deviation (which is commonly the case). There are two types of t-test you can run:

- **Two-sample:** Determines the probability that, given two samples from the same population, the population mean inferred from those samples is the same. There are two variations on this scenario: one where sample variances are equal and one where the variances are unequal.

- **Paired two-sample:** Determines the probability that, given two samples, one each from a different population, those populations have the same mean.

For both scenarios, use Excel's **T.TEST** function:

```
T.TEST(array1, array2, tails, type)
```

array1	A reference, a range name, or an array of values for the first set of data.
array2	A reference, a range name, or an array of values for the second set of data.
tails	The number of distribution tails: Use **1** for a one-tailed distribution (that is, one mean is either less than or greater than the other); use **2** for a two-tailed distribution (that is, one mean is not equal to the other).
type	The type of t-test you want to run: Use **1** for a paired two-sample t-test; use **2** for a two-sample t-test where the samples have equal variances; use **3** for a two-sample t-test where the samples have unequal variances.

For example, if you have two samples from the same population in ranges A3:A27 and B3:B27, what is the probability that the population means inferred by the samples aren't equal? Here's a formula that calculates the p-value:

```
=T.TEST(A3:A27, B3:B27, 2, 3)
```

Again, you compare the result with a significance level (such as 5 percent for a one-tailed distribution or 10 percent for a two-tailed distribution). If the calculated p-value is less than your significance level, you must infer that the population means are different.

CHAPTER 13

Applying regression to track trends and make forecasts

In this chapter, you will:

- Understand regression analysis

- Learn how to use simple regression on linear data

- Plot and calculate best-fit trendlines

- Plot and calculate forecasted values

- Learn how to use simple regression on nonlinear data

- Understand and use multiple regression analysis

In these complex and uncertain times, forecasting business performance is increasingly important. Today, more than ever before, managers at all levels need to make intelligent predictions of future sales and profit trends as part of their overall business strategy. By forecasting sales six months, a year, or even three years down the road, managers can anticipate related needs such as employee acquisitions, warehouse space, and raw material requirements. Similarly, a profit forecast enables a company to plan for its future expansion.

Business forecasting has been around for many years, and various methods have been developed—some of them more successful than others. The most common forecasting method is the qualitative "seat of the pants" approach, in which a manager (or a group of managers) estimates future trends based on experience and knowledge of the market. This method, however, suffers from an inherent subjectivity and a short-term focus because many managers tend to extrapolate from recent experience and ignore the long-term trend. Other methods (such as averaging past results) are more objective but generally are useful for forecasting only a few months in advance.

This chapter presents a technique called *regression analysis*. Regression is a powerful statistical procedure that has become a popular business tool. In its general form, you use regression analysis to determine the relationship between one phenomenon and another. For example, car sales might be dependent on interest rates, and units sold might be dependent on the amount spent on advertising. The dependent phenomenon is called the *dependent variable*, or the *y-value*, and the phenomenon upon which it's dependent is called the *independent variable*, or the *x-value*. (Think of a chart or graph on which the independent variable is plotted along the horizontal [x] axis, and the dependent variable is plotted along the vertical [y] axis.)

Given these variables, you can do two things with regression analysis:

- Determine the relationship between the known x- and y-values and use the results to calculate and visualize the overall trend of the data.

- Use the existing trend to forecast new y-values.

As you'll see in this chapter, Excel is well stocked with tools that enable you to both calculate the current trend and make forecasts no matter what type of data you're dealing with.

Choosing a regression method

Three methods of regression analysis are used most often in business:

- **Simple regression:** Use this type of regression when you're dealing with only one independent variable. For example, if the dependent variable is car sales, the independent variable might be interest rates. You also need to decide whether your data is linear or nonlinear:

  - *Linear* means that if you plot the data on a chart, the resulting data points resemble (roughly) a line.

  - *Nonlinear* means that if you plot the data on a chart, the resulting data points form a curve.

- **Polynomial regression:** Use this type of regression when you're dealing with only one independent variable, but the data fluctuates in such a way that the pattern in the data doesn't resemble either a straight line or a simple curve.

- **Multiple regression:** Use this type of regression when you're dealing with more than one independent variable. For example, if the dependent variable is car sales, the independent variables might be interest rates and disposable income.

You'll learn about all three methods in this chapter.

Using simple regression on linear data

With linear data, the dependent variable is related to the independent variable by some constant factor. For example, you might find that car sales (the dependent variable) increase by 1 million units whenever interest rates (the independent variable) decrease by 1 percent. Similarly, you might find that division revenue (the dependent variable) increases by $100,000 for every $10,000 you spend on advertising (the independent variable).

Analyzing trends using best-fit lines

You make these sorts of determinations by examining the trend underlying the current data you have for the dependent variable. In linear regression, you analyze the current trend by calculating the *line of best fit*, or the *trendline*. This is a line through the data points for which the differences between the points above and below the line cancel each other out (more or less).

> **Note** Excel includes a tool called Forecast Sheet that simplifies many of the tasks and calculations that I present in this chapter. To use it, select your data, select the Data tab, and then select Forecast Sheet. This opens the Create Forecast Worksheet dialog box, which shows a basic best-fit trendline. You can select Options and change the default settings to gain a bit more control over the result. Select Create to add the new forecasting worksheet.

Plotting a best-fit trendline

The easiest way to see the best-fit line is to use a chart. Note, however, that this works only if your data is plotted using an XY (scatter) chart. For example, Figure 13-1 shows a worksheet with quarterly sales figures plotted on an XY chart. Here, the quarterly sales data is the dependent variable, and the period is the independent variable. (In this example, the independent variable is just time, represented, in this case, by fiscal quarters.) You can add a trendline through the plotted points.

> **Note** You can work with all the examples in this chapter by downloading Chapter13.xslx from either of the companion content sites mentioned in the Introduction.

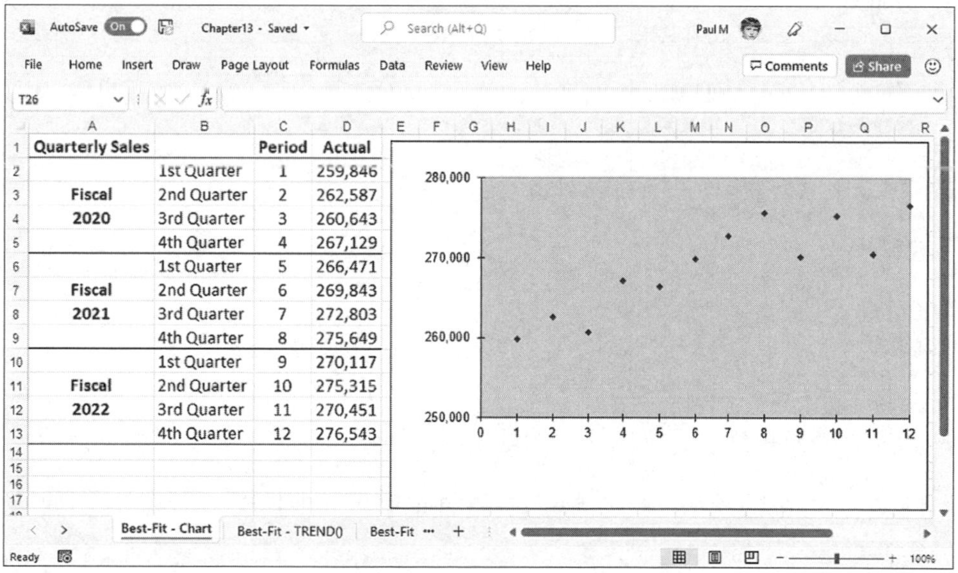

FIGURE 13-1 To see a trendline through your data, first make sure the data is plotted using an XY chart.

The following steps show you how to add a trendline to a chart:

1. Select the chart and, if more than one data series is plotted, select the series you want to work with.

2. Select **Chart Design** > **Add Chart Element** > **Trendline** > **More Trendline Options**. Excel displays the **Format Trendline** task pane, shown in Figure 13-2.

3. On the **Trendline Options** tab, select **Linear**.

4. Select the **Display Equation On Chart** check box. (See the next section, "Understanding the regression equation.")

5. Select the **Display R-Squared Value On Chart** check box. (See "Understanding R^2," later in this chapter.)

6. Select **Close** (X). Excel inserts the trendline. Note that you might need to drag the regression equation text box away from the trendline to read the values.

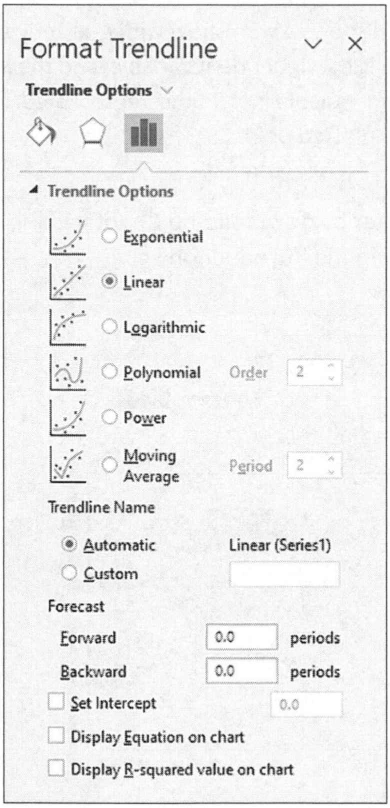

FIGURE 13-2 In the Format Trendline task pane, use the Trendline Options tab to select the type of trendline you want to see.

Figure 13-3 shows the best-fit trendline added to the chart.

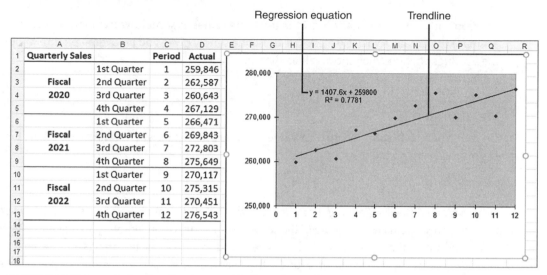

FIGURE 13-3 This quarterly sales chart has an added best-fit trendline.

Understanding the regression equation

In the steps outlined in the previous section, I instructed you to select the **Display Equation On Chart** check box. Doing this displays the *regression equation* on the chart, as pointed out in Figure 13-3. This equation is crucial to regression analysis because it gives you a specific formula for the relationship between the dependent and independent variables.

For linear regression, the best-fit trendline is a straight line with an equation that takes the following form:

$$y = mx + b$$

Here's how you can interpret this equation with respect to the quarterly sales data:

y	This is the dependent variable, so it represents the trendline value (quarterly sales) for a specific period.
x	This is the independent variable, which, in this example, is the period (quarter) you're working with.
m	This is the slope of the trendline. In other words, it's the amount by which the sales increase per period, according to the trendline.
b	This is the y-intercept, which means that it's the starting value for the trend.

Here's the regression equation for the example (refer to Figure 13-3):

$$y = 1407.6x + 259800$$

To determine the first point on the trendline, substitute 1 for *x*:

$$y = 1407.6 * 1 + 259800$$

The result is 261,207.6.

> **Caution** It's important not to view the trendline values as somehow trying to predict or estimate the actual y-values (sales). The trendline simply gives you an overall picture of how the y-values change when the x-values change.

Understanding R^2

When you select the **Display R-Squared Value On Chart** check box when adding a trendline, Excel places the following on the chart:

$R^2 = n$

Here, n is called the *coefficient of determination* (which statisticians abbreviate as r^2, and Excel abbreviates as R^2). This is actually the square of the correlation; as I discuss in Chapter 12, "Building inferential statistical formulas," the correlation tells you something about how well two things are related to each other. In this context, R^2 gives you some idea of how well the trendline fits the data. Roughly, it tells you the proportion of the variance in the dependent variable that is associated with the independent variable. Generally, the closer the result is to 1, the better the fit. Values below about 0.7 mean that the trendline is not a very good fit for the data.

> **Tip** If you don't get a good fit with a linear trendline, your data might not be linear. Try using a different trendline type to see if you can increase the value of R^2.

You'll see in the next section that it's possible to calculate values for the best-fit trendline. Having those values enables you to calculate the correlation between the known y-values and the generated trend values by using the CORREL function, which I describe in Chapter 12. Note that squaring the CORREL result gives you the value of R^2.

Calculating best-fit values using TREND

The problem with using a chart best-fit trendline is that you don't get actual values to work with. If you want to get some values on the worksheet, you can calculate individual trendline values using the regression equation. However, what if the underlying data changes? For example, those values might be estimates, or they might change as more accurate data comes in. In that case, you need to delete the existing trendline, add a new one, and then recalculate the trend values based on the new equation.

If you need to work with worksheet trend values, you can avoid having to perform repeated trendline analyses by calculating the values using Excel's TREND function:

```
TREND(known_y's[, known_x's][, new_x's][, const])
```

known_y's	A range reference or an array of the known y-values—such as the historical values—from which you want to calculate the trend.
known_x's	A range reference or an array of the x-values associated with the known y-values. If you omit this argument, the known_x's are assumed to be the array {1,2,3,...,n}, where n is the number of known_y's.
new_x's	A range reference or an array of the new x-values for which you want corresponding y-values.
const	A logical value that determines where Excel places the y-intercept. If you use **FALSE**, the y-intercept is placed at 0; if you use **TRUE** (this is the default), Excel calculates the y-intercept based on the known_y's.

To generate the best-fit trend values, you need to specify the known_y's argument and, optionally, the known_x's argument. In the quarterly sales example, the known y-values are the actual sales numbers, which lie in the range D2:D13. The known x-values are the period numbers in the range C2:C13. Therefore, to calculate the best-fit trend values, you enter the following formula to create a dynamic array:

```
=TREND(D2:D13, C2:C13)
```

(Remember that dynamic arrays only work in Excel 2019 and later. If you need your formula to be compatible with earlier versions of Excel, create an old-style array by first selecting a range that's the same size as the known values, entering the above formula, and then pressing Ctrl+Shift+Enter. For compatibility, the examples shown in this chapter use this method.)

Figure 13-4 shows the results of this **TREND** array formula in column F. For comparison purposes, the sheet also includes the trend values (in column E) generated using the regression equation from the chart trendline shown in Figure 13-3. (Note that some of the values are slightly off. That's because the values for the slope and intercept shown in the regression equation have been rounded off for display in the chart.)

F2			fx	{=TREND(D2:D13, C2:C13)}	
	A	B	C	D	E	F

	A	B	C	D	E	F
1	Quarterly Sales		Period	Actual	Trend (Equation)	TREND
2		1st Quarter	1	259,846	261,208	261,208
3	Fiscal	2nd Quarter	2	262,587	262,615	262,615
4	2020	3rd Quarter	3	260,643	264,023	264,023
5		4th Quarter	4	267,129	265,430	265,431
6		1st Quarter	5	266,471	266,838	266,838
7	Fiscal	2nd Quarter	6	269,843	268,246	268,246
8	2021	3rd Quarter	7	272,803	269,653	269,654
9		4th Quarter	8	275,649	271,061	271,061
10		1st Quarter	9	270,117	272,468	272,469
11	Fiscal	2nd Quarter	10	275,315	273,876	273,876
12	2022	3rd Quarter	11	270,451	275,284	275,284
13		4th Quarter	12	276,543	276,691	276,692
14						

< > ... Best-Fit - TREND | Best-Fit - LINEST | Sales v. A ... +

FIGURE 13-4 Best-fit trend values (F2:F13) created with the TREND function.

> **Tip** In the previous section, I mentioned that you can determine the correlation between the known dependent values and the calculated trend values by using the **CORREL** function. Here's an array formula that provides a shorthand method for returning the correlation:
>
> ```
> =CORREL(array1, TREND(known_y's, known_x's))
> ```

Calculating best-fit values using LINEST

Using **TREND** is the most direct way to calculate trend values, but Excel offers a second method that calculates the trendline's slope and y-intercept. You can then plug these values into the general linear regression equation—$y = mx + b$—as m and b, respectively. You calculate the slope and y-intercept by using the **LINEST** function:

```
LINEST(known_y's[, known_x's][, const][, stats])
```

known_y's	A range reference or an array of the known y-values from which you want to calculate the trend.
known_x's	A range reference or an array of the x-values associated with the known y-values. If you omit this argument, the *known_x's* are assumed to be the array {1,2,3,...,n}, where *n* is the number of *known_y's*.
const	A logical value that determines where Excel places the y-intercept. If you use **FALSE**, the y-intercept is placed at 0; if you use **TRUE** (this is the default), Excel calculates the y-intercept based on the *known_y's*.
stats	A logical value that determines whether **LINEST** returns additional regression statistics besides the slope and intercept. The default is **FALSE**.

When you use **LINEST** without the *stats* argument, the function returns a 1×2 array, where the value in the first column is the slope of the trendline and the value in the second column is the intercept. For example, the following formula, entered as a 1×2 array, returns the slope and intercept of the quarterly sales trendline:

```
=LINEST(D2:D13, C2:C13)
```

In Figure 13-5, the returned array values are shown in cells H2 and I2. This worksheet also uses these values to compute the trendline values by substituting $H$2 for m and $I$2 for b in the linear regression equation. For example, the following formula calculates the trend value for period 1:

```
=$H$2 * C2 + $I$2
```

If you set the *stats* argument to **TRUE**, the **LINEST** function returns 10 regression statistics in a 5×2 array. The returned statistics are listed in Table 13-1, and Figure 13-6 shows an example of the returned array.

TABLE 13-1 Regression statistics returned by **LINEST** when the *stats* argument is set to **TRUE**

Array Location	Statistic	Description
Row 1, column 1	m	The slope of the trendline
Row 1, column 2	b	The y-intercept of the trendline
Row 2, column 1	Se	The standard error value for m
Row 2, column 2	seb	The standard error value for b
Row 3, column 1	R^2	The coefficient of determination
Row 3, column 2	sey	The standard error value for the y estimate
Row 4, column 1	F	The F statistic
Row 4, column 2	df	The degrees of freedom
Row 5, column 1	ssreg	The regression sum of squares
Row 5, column 2	Ssresid	The residual sum of squares

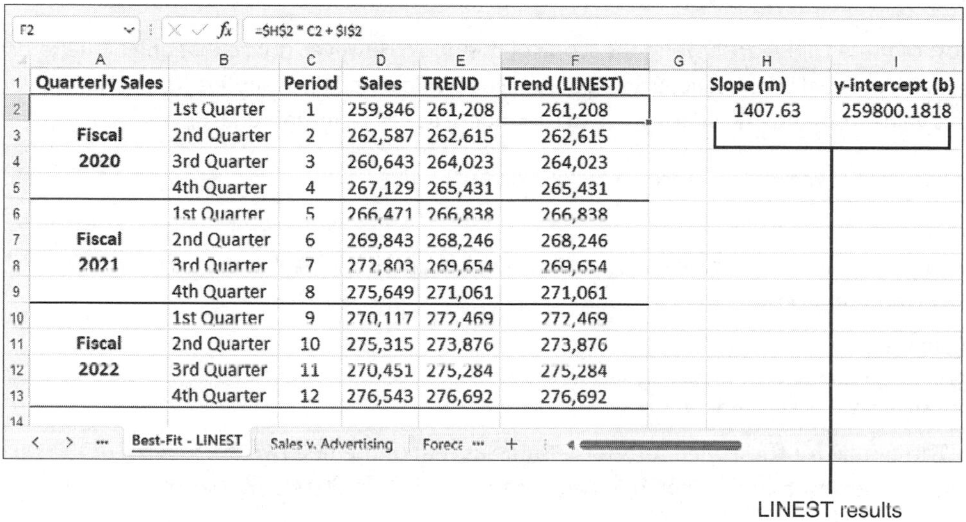

LINEST results

FIGURE 13-5 This worksheet shows the best-fit trend values (F2:F13) created with the results of the LINEST function (H2:I2) plugged into the linear regression equation.

Note These and other regression statistics are available via the Analysis ToolPak's Regression tool. Assuming that the Analysis ToolPak add-in is installed (see "Loading the Analysis ToolPak" in Chapter 4, "Understanding functions"), select **Data** > **Data Analysis**, select **Regression**, and then select **OK**. Use the Regression dialog box to specify the ranges for the y-values and x-values and to select which statistics you want to see in the output.

	A	B	C	D	E	F	G	H	I	J
						=INDEX(LINEST(D2:D13, C2:C13, , TRUE), 3, 1)				
1	Quarterly Sales		Period	Sales	TREND	Trend (LINEST)		Slope (m)	y-intercept (b)	
2		1st Quarter	1	259,846	261,208	261,208		1407.63	259800.1818	
3	Fiscal	2nd Quarter	2	262,587	262,615	262,615				
4	2020	3rd Quarter	3	260,643	264,023	264,023		LINEST( ) Statistics		
5		4th Quarter	4	267,129	265,431	265,431	m	1407.625874	259800.1818	b
6		1st Quarter	5	266,471	266,838	266,838	se	237.7017321	1749.43738	seb
7	Fiscal	2nd Quarter	6	269,843	268,246	268,246	R^2	0.778112593	2842.499292	sey
8	2021	3rd Quarter	7	272,803	269,654	269,654	F	35.06790243	10	df
9		4th Quarter	8	275,649	271,061	271,061	ssreg	283341716	80798022.23	ssresid
10		1st Quarter	9	270,117	272,469	272,469				
11	Fiscal	2nd Quarter	10	275,315	273,876	273,876		R^2	0.778112593	
12	2022	3rd Quarter	11	270,451	275,284	275,284				
13		4th Quarter	12	276,543	276,692	276,692				

Best-Fit - LINEST   Sales v. Advertising   Forec⋯ +

FIGURE 13-6 The range H5:I9 contains the array of regression statistics returned by LINEST when its stats argument is set to TRUE.

Most of these values are beyond the scope of this book. However, notice that one of the returned values is R^2, the coefficient of determination, which tells how well the trendline fits the data. If you want just this value from the **LINEST** array, use this formula (see cell I11 in Figure 13-6):

```
=INDEX(LINEST(known_y's, known_x's, , TRUE), 3, 1)
```

> **Note** You can also calculate the slope, intercept, and R^2 value directly by using the following functions:
>
> ```
> SLOPE(known_y's, known_x's)
> INTERCEPT(known_y's, known_x's)
> RSQ(known_y's, known_x's)
> ```
>
> The syntax for these functions is the same as that of the first two arguments of the **TREND** function, except that the known_x's argument is required. Here's an example:
>
> ```
> =RSQ(D2:D13, C2:C13)
> ```

Analyzing the sales versus advertising trend

We tend to think of trend analysis as having a time component. That is, when we think about looking for a trend, we usually think about finding a pattern over a period of time. But regression analysis is more versatile than that. You can use it to compare any two phenomena, as long as one is dependent on the other in some way.

For example, it's reasonable to assume that there is some relationship between how much you spend on advertising and how much you sell. In this case, the advertising costs are the independent variable, and the sales revenues are the dependent variable. You can apply regression analysis to investigate the exact nature of the relationship.

Figure 13-7 shows a worksheet that does this. The advertising costs are in A2:A13, and the sales revenues over the same period (these could be monthly numbers, quarterly numbers, and so on—the time period doesn't matter) are in B2:B13. The rest of the worksheet applies the same trend-analysis techniques that you've learned in the past few sections.

	A	B	C	D	E	F	G	H	I
	H2		f_x {=LINEST(B2:B13, A2:A13)}						
1	Advertising	Sales	Trend (Equation)	TREND( )	Trend (LINEST( ))		Slope (m)	y-intercept (b)	
2	$15,173	$262,587	$259,744	$259,745	$259,745		7.96	139037.0755	
3	$15,810	$266,471	$264,816	$264,817	$264,817				
4	$18,312	$280,219	$284,718	$284,719	$284,719		LINEST( ) Statistics		
5	$20,382	$300,010	$301,186	$301,187	$301,187	m	7.955541232	139037.0755	b
6	$16,487	$269,843	$270,197	$270,198	$270,198	se	0.35665636	6503.01033	seb
7	$16,584	$270,643	$270,968	$270,969	$270,969	R^2	0.980297632	2572.828923	sey
8	$18,099	$285,030	$283,024	$283,024	$283,024	F	497.5531911	10	df
9	$21,294	$308,012	$308,441	$308,442	$308,442	ssreg	3293527808	66194486.68	ssresid
10	$17,031	$270,451	$274,527	$274,528	$274,528				
11	$17,204	$277,129	$275,903	$275,904	$275,904		R^2	0.980297632	
12	$19,005	$290,032	$290,231	$290,232	$290,232				
13	$21,987	$317,294	$313,955	$313,956	$313,956				

FIGURE 13-7 This figure shows a trend analysis for advertising costs versus sales revenues.

Making forecasts

Knowing the overall trend exhibited by a data set is useful because it tells you the broad direction that sales or costs or employee acquisitions is going, and it gives you a good idea of how related the dependent variable is to the independent variable. But a trend is also useful in a couple of other ways:

- Making forecasts in which you extend the trendline into the future. For example, what will sales be in the first quarter of next year?

- Calculating the trend value given some new independent value. For example, if we spend $25,000 on advertising, what will the corresponding sales be?

How accurate is such a prediction? A projection based on historical data assumes that the factors influencing the data over the historical period will remain constant. If this is a reasonable assumption in your case, the projection will be a reasonable one. Of course, the longer you extend the line, the more likely it is that some factors will change or new ones will arise. As a result, best-fit extensions should be used only for short-term projections.

Plotting forecasted values

If you want just a visual idea of a forecasted trend, you can extend the chart trendline that you created earlier. The following steps show you how to add a forecasting trendline to a chart:

1. Select the chart and, if more than one data series is plotted, click the series you want to work with.

2. Select **Chart Design** > **Add Chart Element** > **Trendline** > **More Trendline Options** to display the **Format Trendline** task pane.

3. On the **Trendline Options** tab, select **Linear**.

4. Select the **Display Equation On Chart** check box. (See "Understanding the regression equation," earlier in this chapter.)

5. Select the **Display R-Squared Value On Chart** check box. (See "Understanding R^2," earlier in this chapter.)

6. Use the **Forward** text box to select the number of units you want to project the trendline into the future. (For example, to extend the quarterly sales number into the next year, set **Forward** to **4** to extend the trendline by four quarters.)

7. Select **Close** (**X**). Excel inserts the trendline and extends it into the future.

Figure 13-8 shows the quarterly sales trendline extended by four quarters.

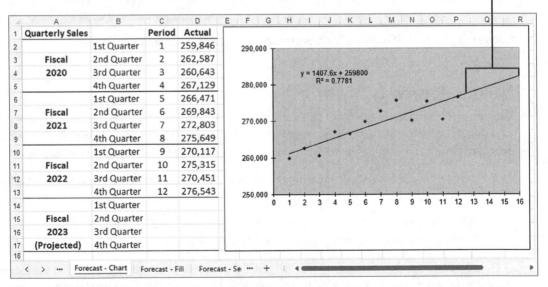

FIGURE 13-8 The trendline has been extended four quarters into the future.

Extending a linear trend with the fill handle

If you prefer to see exact data points in your forecast, you can use the fill handle to project a best-fit line into the future. Here are the steps to follow:

1. Select the historical data on the worksheet.

2. Click and drag the fill handle to extend the selection. Excel calculates the best-fit line from the existing data, projects this line into the new data, and calculates the appropriate values.

Figure 13-9 shows an example. Here, I've used the fill handle to project the period numbers and quarterly sales figures over the next fiscal year. The accompanying chart clearly shows the extended best-fit values.

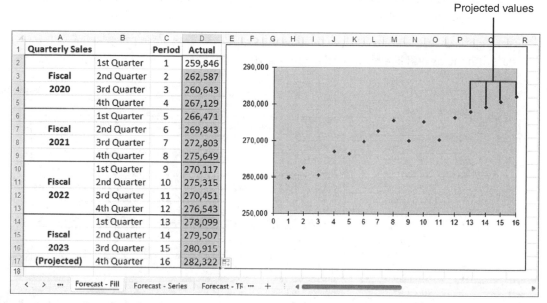

FIGURE 13-9 When you use the fill handle to extend historical data into the future, Excel uses a linear projection to calculate the new values.

Extending a linear trend using the Series command

You also can use the Series command to project a best-fit line. The following steps show you how it's done:

1. Select the range that includes both the historical data and the cells that will contain the projections (and ensure that the projection cells are blank).

2. Select **Home** > **Fill** > **Series**. Excel displays the Series dialog box.

3. Select the **AutoFill** option.

4. Select **OK**. Excel fills in the blank cells with the best-fit projection.

The Series command is also useful for producing the data that defines the full best-fit line so that you can see the actual trendline values. The following steps show you how it's done:

1. Copy the historical data into an adjacent row or column.

2. Select the range that includes both the copied historical data and the cells that will contain the projections. (Again, ensure that the projection cells are blank).

3. Select **Home > Fill > Series**. Excel displays the **Series** dialog box.

4. Select the **Trend** check box.

5. Select the **Linear** option.

6. Select **OK**. Excel replaces the copied historical data with the best-fit numbers and projects the trend onto the blank cells.

In Figure 13-10, the trend values created by the Series command are in E2:E17 and are plotted on the chart with the best-fit line on top of the historical data.

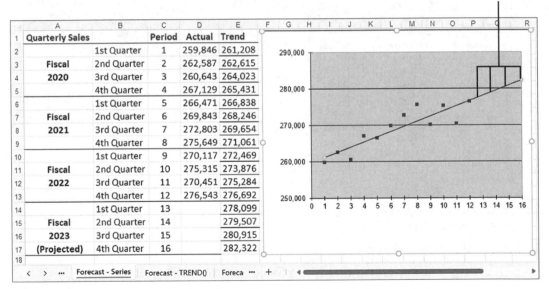

FIGURE 13-10 This worksheet shows a best-fit trendline created with the Series command.

Forecasting with the regression equation

You can also forecast individual dependent values by using the regression equation that is returned when you add the chart trendline. (Remember that you must click the **Display Equation On Chart** check box when adding the trendline.) Recall the general regression equation for a linear model:

$$y = mx + b$$

The regression equation displayed by the trendline feature gives you the *m* and *b* values, so to determine a new value for *y*, just plug in a new value for *x*.

For example, in the quarterly sales model, Excel calculated the following regression equation:

$$y = 1407.6x + 259800$$

To find the trend value for the thirteenth period, you substitute 13 for *x*:

$$y = 1407.6 * 13 + 259800$$

The result is 278,099, the projected sales for the thirteenth period (first quarter 2023).

Forecasting with TREND

The **TREND** function is also capable of forecasting new values. To extend a trend and generate new values, you need to add the *new_x's* argument to the **TREND** function. Here's the basic procedure for setting this up on the worksheet:

1. Add the new x-values to the worksheet. For example, to extend the quarterly sales trend into the next fiscal year, you'd add the values 13 through 16 to the Period column.

2. If you're creating an old-style array formula, select a range large enough to hold all the new values. For example, if you're adding four new values, select four cells in a column or row, depending on the structure of your data.

3. Enter the **TREND** function as an array formula, specifying the range of new x-values as the *new_x's* argument. Here's the array formula for the quarterly sales example:

   ```
   =TREND(D2:D13, C2:C13, C14:C17)
   ```

Figure 13-11 shows the forecasted values in F14:F17. The values in column E were derived using the regression equation and are included for comparison.

Forecasting with LINEST

Recall that the **LINEST** function returns the slope and y-intercept of the trendline. When you know these numbers, forecasting new values is a straightforward matter of plugging them into the linear regression equation along with a new value of *x*. For example, if the slope is in cell H2, the intercept is in I2, and the new x-value is in C14, the following formula will return the forecasted value:

```
=$H$2 * C14 + $I$2
```

Figure 13-12 shows a worksheet that uses this method to forecast the Fiscal 2023 sales figures.

		Period	Actual	Trend (Equation)	TREND( )
1 Quarterly Sales					
2	1st Quarter	1	259,846	261,208	261,208
3 Fiscal	2nd Quarter	2	262,587	262,615	262,615
4 2020	3rd Quarter	3	260,643	264,023	264,023
5	4th Quarter	4	267,129	265,430	265,431
6	1st Quarter	5	266,471	266,838	266,838
7 Fiscal	2nd Quarter	6	269,843	268,246	268,246
8 2021	3rd Quarter	7	272,803	269,653	269,654
9	4th Quarter	8	275,649	271,061	271,061
10	1st Quarter	9	270,117	272,468	272,469
11 Fiscal	2nd Quarter	10	275,315	273,876	273,876
12 2022	3rd Quarter	11	270,451	275,284	275,284
13	4th Quarter	12	276,543	276,691	276,692
14	1st Quarter	13		278,099	278,099
15 Fiscal	2nd Quarter	14		279,506	279,507
16 2023	3rd Quarter	15		280,914	280,915
17 (Projected)	4th Quarter	16		282,322	282,322

Forecasted values

FIGURE 13-11 The range F14:F17 contains the forecasted values calculated by the TREND function.

F14 fx =$H$2 * C14 + $I$2

		Period	Sales	TREND( )	Trend (LINEST( ))		Slope (m)	y-intercept (b)
1 Quarterly Sales								
2	1st Quarter	1	259,846	261,208	261,208		1407.63	259800.1818
3 Fiscal	2nd Quarter	2	262,587	262,615	262,615			
4 2020	3rd Quarter	3	260,643	264,023	264,023			
5	4th Quarter	4	267,129	265,431	265,431			
6	1st Quarter	5	266,471	266,838	266,838			
7 Fiscal	2nd Quarter	6	269,843	268,246	268,246			
8 2021	3rd Quarter	7	272,803	269,654	269,654			
9	4th Quarter	8	275,649	271,061	271,061			
10	1st Quarter	9	270,117	272,469	272,469			
11 Fiscal	2nd Quarter	10	275,315	273,876	273,876			
12 2022	3rd Quarter	11	270,451	275,284	275,284			
13	4th Quarter	12	276,543	276,692	276,692			
14	1st Quarter	13		278,099	278,099			
15 Fiscal	2nd Quarter	14		279,507	279,507			
16 2023	3rd Quarter	15		280,915	280,915			
17 (Projected)	4th Quarter	16		282,322	282,322			

Forecasted values

FIGURE 13-12 The range F14:F17 contains the forecasted values calculated by the regression equation, using the slope (H2) and intercept (I2) returned by the LINEST function.

Note You also can calculate a forecasted value for *x* by using the **FORECAST** function:

```
FORECAST(x, known_y's, known_x's)
```

Here, *x* is the new x-value that you want to work with, and *known_y's* and *known_x's* are the same as with the **TREND** function (except that the *known_x's* argument is required). Here's an example:

```
=FORECAST(13, D2:D13, C2:C13)
```

Case study: Trend analysis and forecasting for a seasonal sales model

This case study applies some of the forecasting techniques from the previous sections to a more sophisticated sales model. The worksheets explore two different cases:

- **Sales as a function of time:** Essentially, this case determines the trend over time of past sales and extrapolates the trend in a straight line to determine future sales.

- **Sales as a function of the season (in a business sense):** Many businesses are seasonal; that is, their sales are traditionally higher or lower during certain periods of the fiscal year. Retailers, for example, usually have higher sales in the fall, leading up to Christmas. If the sales for your business are a function of the season, you need to remove these seasonal biases to calculate the true underlying trend.

About the forecast workbook

The Forecast workbook includes the following worksheets:

- **Monthly Data:** Use this worksheet to enter up to 10 years of monthly historical data. This worksheet also calculates the 12-month moving averages used by the Monthly Seasonal Index worksheet. Note that the data in column C—specifically, the range C2:C121—is a range named Actual.

- **Monthly Seasonal Index:** Calculates the seasonal adjustment factors (the seasonal indexes) for the monthly data.

- **Monthly Trend:** Calculates the trend of the monthly historical data. Both a normal trend and a seasonally adjusted trend are computed.

- **Monthly Forecast:** Derives a three-year monthly forecast based on both the normal trend and the seasonally adjusted trend.

- **Quarterly Data:** Consolidates the monthly actuals into quarterly data and calculates the four-quarter moving average (used by the Quarterly Seasonal Index worksheet).

- **Quarterly Seasonal Index:** Calculates the seasonal indexes for the quarterly data.

- **Quarterly Trend:** Calculates the trend of the quarterly historical data. Both a normal trend and a seasonally adjusted trend are computed.
- **Quarterly Forecast:** Derives a three-year quarterly forecast based on both the normal trend and the seasonally adjusted trend.

> **Tip** The Forecast workbook contains dozens of formulas. You'll probably want to switch to manual calculation mode when working with this file.

The sales forecast workbook is driven entirely by the historical data entered into the Monthly Data worksheet, shown in Figure 13-13.

		Actual	12-Month Moving Avg
Monthly Sales - Data			
	January, 2013	90.0	-
	February, 2013	95.0	-
	March, 2013	110.0	-
	April, 2013	105.0	-
	May, 2013	100.0	-
2013	June, 2013	100.0	-
	July, 2013	105.0	-
	August, 2013	105.0	-
	September, 2013	110.0	-
	October, 2013	120.0	-
	November, 2013	130.0	-
	December, 2013	140.0	109.2
	January, 2014	90.0	109.2
	February, 2014	95.0	109.2
	March, 2014	115.0	109.6
	April, 2014	110.0	110.0
	May, 2014	105.0	110.4
2014	June, 2014	105.0	110.8
	July, 2014	110.0	111.3
	August, 2014	115.0	112.1
	September, 2014	115.0	112.5
	October, 2014	125.0	112.9

FIGURE 13-13 The Monthly Data worksheet contains the historical sales data.

Calculating a normal trend

As I mentioned earlier, you can calculate either a normal trend that treats all sales as a simple function of time or a deseasoned trend that takes seasonal factors into account. This section covers the normal trend.

All the trend calculations in the workbook use a variation of the TREND function. Recall that the TREND function's *known_x's* argument is optional; if you omit it, Excel uses the array {1,2,3,...,n}, where n is the number of values in the *known_y's* argument. When the independent variable is time-related, you can usually get away with omitting the *known_x's* argument because the values are just the period numbers.

In this case study, the independent variable is in terms of months, so you can leave out the *known_x's* argument. The *known_y's* argument is the data in the Actual column, which, as I pointed out earlier, has been given the range name Actual. Therefore, the following array formula generates the best-fit trend values for the existing data:

```
=TREND(Actual)
```

This formula generates the values in the Normal Trend column of the Monthly Trend worksheet, shown in Figure 13-14.

	A	B	C	D	E	F
C5			{=TREND(Actual)}			
1				Correlation to Actual Sales:		
2	Monthly Sales - Historical Trend			Normal Trend --> 0.42		
3				Reseasoned Trend --> 0.96		
4		Actual	Normal Trend	Deseasoned Actual	Deseasoned Trend	Reseasoned Trend
5	January, 2013	90.0	108.3	108.7	111.4	92.2
6	February, 2013	95.0	108.6	112.9	111.6	93.9
7	March, 2013	110.0	108.8	118.0	111.8	104.2
8	April, 2013	105.0	109.1	114.9	112.0	102.3
9	May, 2013	100.0	109.3	110.9	112.2	101.2
10	June, 2013	100.0	109.6	109.0	112.4	103.2
11	July, 2013	105.0	109.8	108.9	112.6	108.6
12	August, 2013	105.0	110.1	103.6	112.8	114.3
13	September, 2013	110.0	110.3	105.9	113.0	117.4
14	October, 2013	120.0	110.6	106.3	113.2	127.8
15	November, 2013	130.0	110.8	107.9	113.4	136.7
16	December, 2013	140.0	111.1	106.5	113.6	149.3
17	January, 2014	90.0	111.3	108.7	113.8	94.2
18	February, 2014	95.0	111.6	112.9	114.0	95.9
19	March, 2014	115.0	111.8	123.4	114.2	106.4
20	April, 2014	110.0	112.0	120.4	114.4	104.5
21	May, 2014	105.0	112.3	116.4	114.6	103.3
22	June, 2014	105.0	112.5	114.4	114.7	105.3

Monthly Trend | Monthly Forecast | Sales Char ... +

FIGURE 13-14 The Normal Trend column uses the TREND function to return the best-fit trend values for the data in the Actual range.

Note The values in column B of the Monthly Trend sheet are linked to the values in the Actual column of the Monthly Data worksheet. You use the values in the Monthly Data worksheet to calculate the trend, so technically, you don't need the figures in column B. I included them, however, to make it easier to compare the trend and the actuals. It's also handy to include the Actual values if you want to create a chart that includes these values.

To get some idea of whether the trend is close to your data, cell F2 uses the following array formula to calculate the correlation between the trend values and the actual sales figures:

```
=CORREL(Actual, TREND(Actual))
```

The correlation value of 0.42—and its corresponding value for R^2 of about 0.17—shows that the normal trend doesn't fit this data very well. You'll fix that later by taking into account the seasonal nature of the historical data.

Calculating the forecast trend

As you saw earlier in this chapter, to get a sales forecast, you extend the historical trendline into the future. This is the job of the Monthly Forecast worksheet, shown in Figure 13-15.

Calculating a forecast trend requires that you specify the *new_x's* argument for the **TREND** function. In this case, the *new_x's* are the sales periods in the forecast interval. For example, suppose that you have a 10-year period of monthly data from January 2013 to December 2022. This involves 120 periods of data. Therefore, to calculate the trend for January 2023 (the 121st period), you use the following formula:

```
=TREND(Actual, , 121)
```

C2		fx	=TREND(Actual, , ROWS(Actual) + ROW() - 1)		
	A	B	C	D	E
1		**Monthly Sales - Forecast**	**Normal Trend**	**Deseasoned Trend**	**Reseasoned Trend**
2		January, 2023	138.2	134.8	111.6
3		February, 2023	138.4	135.0	113.6
4		March, 2023	138.7	135.2	126.0
5		April, 2023	138.9	135.4	123.7
6		May, 2023	139.2	135.6	122.3
7	2023	June, 2023	139.4	135.8	124.6
8		July, 2023	139.7	136.0	131.1
9		August, 2023	139.9	136.2	138.0
10		September, 2023	140.2	136.4	141.7
11		October, 2023	140.4	136.6	154.2
12		November, 2023	140.7	136.8	164.8
13		December, 2023	140.9	136.9	180.1
14		January, 2024	141.2	137.1	113.5
15		February, 2024	141.4	137.3	115.6
16		March, 2024	141.7	137.5	128.2
17		April, 2024	141.9	137.7	125.8
18		May, 2024	142.2	137.9	124.4
19	2024	June, 2024	142.4	138.1	126.8
20		July, 2024	142.7	138.3	133.4
21		August, 2024	142.9	138.5	140.4
22		September, 2024	143.2	138.7	144.1

< > ... Monthly Forecast   Sales Chart   Sales Chart +   ...   +

FIGURE 13-15 The Monthly Forecast worksheet calculates a sales forecast by extending the historical trend data.

You use **122** as the *new_x's* argument for February 2023, **123** for March 2023, and so on.

The Monthly Forecast worksheet uses the following formula to calculate these *new_x's* values:

```
ROWS(Actual) + ROW() - 1
```

`ROWS(Actual)` returns the number of sales periods in the Actual range in the Monthly Data worksheet. `ROW() - 1` is a trick that returns the number you need to add to get the forecast sales period. For example, the January 2023 forecast is in cell C2; therefore, `ROW() - 1` returns 1.

Calculating the seasonal trend

Many businesses experience predictable fluctuations in sales throughout their fiscal year. Beach resort operators see most of their sales during the summer months; retailers look forward to the Christmas season for the revenue that will carry them through the rest of the year. Figure 13-16 shows a sales chart for a company that experiences a large increase in sales during the fall.

Because of the nature of the sales in companies that see seasonal fluctuations, the normal trend calculation doesn't give an accurate forecast. You need to include seasonal variations in your analysis, which involves four steps:

1. For each month (or quarter), calculate a *seasonal index* that identifies seasonal influences.

2. Use these indexes to calculate seasonally adjusted (or *deseasoned*) values for each month.

3. Calculate the trend based on these deseasoned values.

4. Compute the true trend by adding the seasonal indexes to the calculated trend (from step 3).

The next few sections show how the Forecast workbook implements each step.

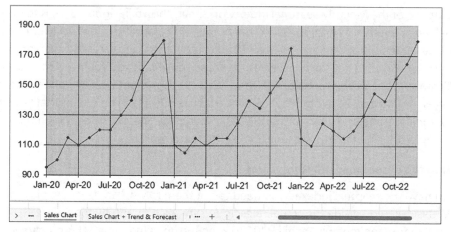

FIGURE 13-16 This figure shows a chart for a company showing seasonal sales variations.

Computing the monthly seasonal indexes

A *seasonal index* is a measure of how the average sales in a given month compare to a "normal" value. For example, if January has an index of 90, January's sales are (on average) only 90 percent of what they are in a normal month.

Therefore, you first must define what "normal" signifies. Because you're dealing with monthly data, you define normal as the 12-month moving average. (An *n*-month moving average is the average taken over the past *n* months.) The 12-Month Moving Avg column in the Monthly Data sheet (refer to column D in Figure 13-13) uses a formula named TwelveMonthMovingAvg to handle this calculation. This is a relative range name, so its definition changes with each cell in the column.

For example, here's the formula that's used in cell D13:

`=AVERAGE(C2:C13)`

In other words, this formula calculates the average for the range C2:C13, which is the preceding 12 months.

This moving average defines the "normal" value for any given month. The next step is to compare each month to the moving average. This is done by dividing each monthly sales figure by its corresponding moving-average calculation and multiplying by 100, which equals the sales *ratio* for the month. For example, the sales in December 2013 (cell C13) totaled 140.0, with a moving average of 109.2 (D13). Dividing C13 by D13 and multiplying by 100 returns a ratio of about 128. You can loosely interpret this to mean that sales in December were 28% higher than sales in a normal month.

To get an accurate seasonal index for December (or any other month), however, you must calculate ratios for every December for which you have historical data. Take an average of all these ratios to reach a true seasonal index (except for a slight adjustment, as you'll see).

The purpose of the Monthly Seasonal Index worksheet, shown in Figure 13-17, is to derive a seasonal index for each month. The worksheet's table calculates the ratios for every month over the span of the historical data. The Avg. Ratio column then calculates the average for each month. However, to get the final values for the seasonal indexes, you need to make a small adjustment. The indexes should add up to 1,200 (100 per month, on average) to be true percentages. As you can see in cell B15, however, the sum is 1,214.0. This means that you have to reduce each average by a factor of 1.0116 (1,214/1,200). The Seasonal Index column does that, thereby producing the true seasonal indexes for each month.

Calculating the deseasoned monthly values

When you have the seasonal indexes, you need to put them to work to "level the playing field." Basically, you divide the actual sales figures for each month by the appropriate monthly index (and multiply them by 100 to keep the units the same). This effectively removes the seasonal factors from the data. (This process is called *deseasoning*, or *seasonally adjusting*, the data.)

D14 =IF('Monthly Data'!D13 <> 0, 100 * 'Monthly Data'!C13 / 'Monthly Data'!D13, "")

Monthly Seasonal Index Calculations

	Avg. Ratio	Seasonal Index	2013 Ratios*	2014 Ratios	2015 Ratios	2016 Ratios	2017 Ratios	2018 Ratios	2019 Ratios	2020 Ratios	2021 Ratios	2022 Ratios
Jan	83.7	82.8	-	82.4	83.2	84.8	85.1	88.3	78.4	78.1	84.1	89.0
Feb	85.1	84.2	-	87.0	87.3	88.7	88.9	84.6	82.4	82.5	80.0	84.9
Mar	94.3	93.2	-	104.9	104.3	93.6	92.6	88.9	86.3	94.5	87.6	95.8
Apr	92.4	91.4	-	100.0	107.5	98.6	85.1	92.3	82.9	90.1	83.8	91.4
May	91.2	90.2	-	95.1	94.3	94.3	85.4	95.4	87.4	93.9	87.6	87.6
Jun	92.8	91.8	-	94.7	90.0	97.9	89.8	91.1	95.0	98.0	87.9	91.1
Jul	97.6	96.4	-	98.9	94.3	97.5	97.6	98.7	99.0	98.3	95.2	98.4
Aug	102.5	101.4	-	102.6	94.6	101.1	101.4	102.3	99.3	106.1	106.0	109.4
Sep	105.1	103.9	-	102.2	98.9	108.3	105.4	105.9	103.7	113.5	102.5	105.3
Oct	114.2	112.9	-	110.7	111.4	115.9	113.5	113.4	108.4	127.6	111.2	115.9
Nov	121.9	120.5	-	119.1	119.6	123.3	125.3	121.2	113.5	132.9	120.0	122.6
Dec	133.0	131.5	128.2	127.5	127.7	134.2	136.9	136.4	131.1	138.9	135.9	133.3
Total	1214.0	1200.0										
Adj	1.0116											

***Each Ratio = Monthly Actual ÷ 12-Month Moving Average**

Monthly Seasonal Index | Sales Chart + Trend & ...

FIGURE 13-17 The Monthly Seasonal Index worksheet calculates the seasonal index for each month, based on monthly historical data.

The Deseasoned Actual column in the Monthly Trend worksheet performs these calculations (see Figure 13-18). Following is a typical formula (from cell D5):

```
=100 * B5 / INDEX(MonthlyIndexTable, MONTH(A5), 3)
```

B5 refers to the sales figure in the Actual column, and **`MonthlyIndexTable`** is the range A3:C14 in the Monthly Seasonal Index worksheet. The **`INDEX`** function finds the appropriate seasonal index for the month (given by the **`MONTH(A5)`** function).

D5 =100 * B5 / INDEX(MonthlyIndexTable, MONTH(A5), 3)

Monthly Sales - Historical Trend

Correlation to Actual Sales:

Normal Trend --> 0.42

Reseasoned Trend --> 0.96

	Actual	Normal Trend	Deseasoned Actual	Deseasoned Trend	Reseasoned Trend
January, 2013	90.0	108.3	108.7	111.4	92.2
February, 2013	95.0	108.6	112.9	111.6	93.9
March, 2013	110.0	108.8	118.0	111.8	104.2
April, 2013	105.0	109.1	114.9	112.0	102.3
May, 2013	100.0	109.3	110.9	112.2	101.2
June, 2013	100.0	109.6	109.0	112.4	103.2
July, 2013	105.0	109.8	108.9	112.6	108.6
August, 2013	105.0	110.1	103.6	112.8	114.3
September, 2013	110.0	110.3	105.9	113.0	117.4
October, 2013	120.0	110.6	106.3	113.2	127.8
November, 2013	130.0	110.8	107.9	113.4	136.7
December, 2013	140.0	111.1	106.5	113.6	149.3
January, 2014	90.0	111.3	108.7	113.8	94.2
February, 2014	95.0	111.6	112.9	114.0	95.9
March, 2014	115.0	111.8	123.4	114.2	106.4

Monthly Trend | Monthly Forecast | Sales Char ...

FIGURE 13-18 The Deseasoned Actual column calculates seasonally adjusted values for the actual data.

Calculating the deseasoned trend

The next step is to calculate the historical trend based on the new deseasoned values. The Deseasoned Trend column uses the following array formula to accomplish this task:

```
=TREND(DeseasonedActual)
```

The name **DeseasonedActual** refers to the values in the Deseasoned Actual column (D5:D124).

Calculating the reseasoned trend

By itself, the deseasoned trend doesn't amount to much. To get the true historical trend, you need to add the seasonal factor back into the deseasoned trend. (This process is called *reseasoning* the data.) The Reseasoned Trend column does the job with a formula similar to the one used in the Deseasoned Actual column:

```
=E5 * INDEX(MonthlyIndexTable, MONTH(A5), 3) /100
```

Cell F3 uses **CORREL** to determine the correlation between the Actual data and the Reseasoned Trend data:

```
=CORREL(Actual, ReseasonedTrend)
```

Here, **ReseasonedTrend** is the name applied to the data in the Reseasoned Trend column (F5:F124). As you can see, the correlation of 0.96 is extremely high, indicating that the new trend "line" is an excellent match for the historical data.

Calculating the seasonal forecast

To derive a forecast based on seasonal factors, combine the techniques you used to calculate a normal trend forecast and a reseasoned historical trend. In the Monthly Forecast worksheet (see Figure 13-15), the Deseasoned Trend Forecast column computes the forecast for the deseasoned trend:

```
=TREND(DeseasonedTrend, , ROWS(DeseasonedTrend) + ROW() - 1)
```

The Reseasoned Trend Forecast column adds the seasonal factors back into the deseasoned trend forecast:

```
=D2 * Index(MonthlyIndexTable, MONTH(B2), 3) / 100
```

D2 is the value from the Deseasoned Trend Forecast column, and B2 is the forecast month.

Figure 13-19 shows a chart comparing the actual sales and the reseasoned trend for the past three years of the sample data. The chart also shows two years of the reseasoned forecast.

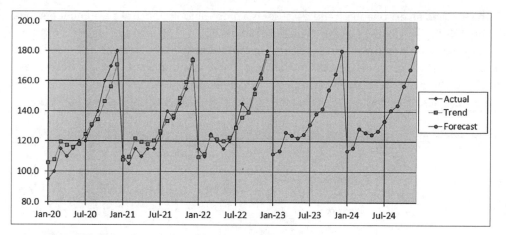

FIGURE 13-19 This figure shows a chart of the sample data, which compares actual sales, the reseasoned trend, and the reseasoned forecast.

Working with quarterly data

If you prefer to work with quarterly data, the Quarterly Data, Quarterly Seasonal Index, Quarterly Trend, and Quarterly Forecast worksheets perform the same functions as their monthly counterparts. You don't have to reenter the data because the Quarterly Data worksheet consolidates the monthly numbers by quarter.

Using simple regression on nonlinear data

As you saw in the case study, the data you work with doesn't always fit a linear pattern. If the data shows seasonal variations, you can compute the trend and forecast values by working with seasonally adjusted numbers, which you also saw in the case study. But many business scenarios aren't either linear or seasonal. The data might look more like a curve, or it might fluctuate without any apparent pattern.

These nonlinear patterns might seem more complex, but Excel offers a number of useful tools for performing regression analysis on this type of data.

Working with an exponential trend

An *exponential* trend is a trend that rises or falls at an increasingly higher rate. Fads often exhibit this kind of behavior. A product might sell steadily and unspectacularly for a while, but then word starts getting around—perhaps because of a mention in the newspaper or on television—and sales start to rise. If these new customers enjoy the product, they tell their friends about it, and those people purchase the product, too. They tell *their* friends, the media notice that everyone's talking about this product, and a bona fide fad ensues.

This is called an exponential trend because, as a graph, it looks much like a number being raised to successively higher values of an exponent (for example, 10^1, 10^2, 10^3, and so on). This is often modeled using the constant *e* (approximately 2.71828), which is the base of the natural logarithm. Figure 13-20 shows a worksheet that uses the **EXP** function in column B to return *e* raised to the successive powers in column A. The chart shows the results as a classic exponential curve.

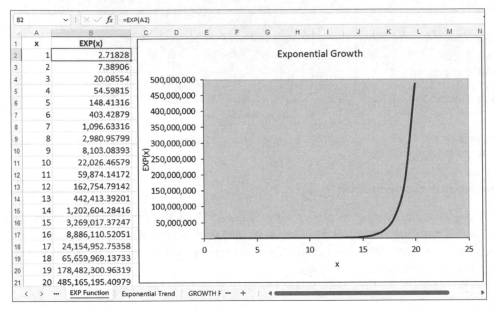

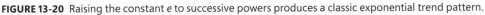

FIGURE 13-20 Raising the constant *e* to successive powers produces a classic exponential trend pattern.

Figure 13-21 shows a worksheet that contains weekly data for the number of units sold of a product. As you can see, the unit sales hold steady for the first eight or nine weeks and then climb rapidly. As this chart illustrates, the sales curve is very much like an exponential growth curve. The next couple of sections show you how to track the trend and make forecasts based on such a model.

Plotting an exponential trendline

The easiest way to see the trend and forecast is to add a trendline—specifically, an exponential trendline—to the chart. Here are the steps to follow:

1. Select the chart and, if more than one data series are plotted, click the series you want to work with.

2. Select **Chart Design > Add Chart Element > Trendline > More Trendline Options** to display the Format Trendline task pane.

3. On the **Trendline Options** tab, select the **Exponential** option.

4. Select the **Display Equation on Chart** and **Display R-Squared Value on Chart** check boxes.

5. Select **Close** (**X**). Excel inserts the trendline.

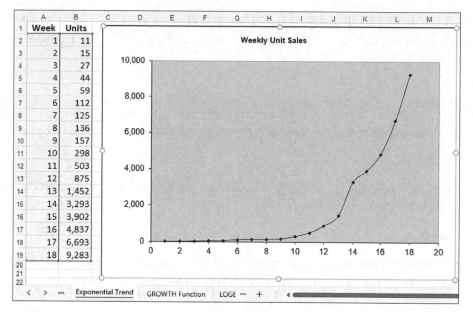

FIGURE 13-21 This chart of weekly unit sales shows a definite exponential pattern.

Figure 13-22 shows the exponential trendline added to the chart.

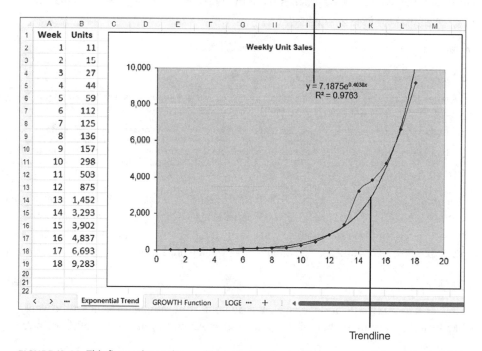

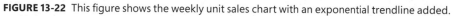

FIGURE 13-22 This figure shows the weekly unit sales chart with an exponential trendline added.

Calculating exponential trend and forecast values

In Figure 13-22, notice that the regression equation for an exponential trendline takes the following general form:

$$y = be^{mx}$$

Here, b and m are constants. So, knowing these values, given an independent value x, you can compute its corresponding point on the trendline using the following formula:

```
=b * EXP(m * x)
```

In the trendline of Figure 13-22, these constant values are **7.1875** and **0.4038**, respectively. So, the formula for trend values becomes this:

```
=7.1875 * EXP(0.4038 * x)
```

If x is a value between 1 and 18, you get a trend point for the existing data. To get a forecast, you use a value higher than 18. For example, using x equal to **19** gives a forecast value of 15,437 units:

```
=7.1875 * EXP(0.4038 * 19)
```

Exponential trending and forecasting using the GROWTH function

As you learned with linear regression, it's often useful to work with actual trend values instead of just visualizing the trendline. With a linear model, you use the **TREND** function to generate actual values. The exponential equivalent is the **GROWTH** function:

```
GROWTH(known_y's[, known_x's][, new_x's][, const])
```

known_y's	A range reference or an array of the known y-values.
known_x's	A range reference or an array of the x-values associated with the known y-values. If you omit this argument, the *known_x's* are assumed to be the array {1,2,3,...,n}, where *n* is the number of *known_y's*.
new_x's	A range reference or an array of the new x-values for which you want corresponding y-values.
const	A logical value that determines the value of the *b* constant in the exponential regression equation. If you use **FALSE**, *b* is set to **1**; if you use **TRUE** (which is the default), Excel calculates *b* based on the *known_y's*.

With the exception of a small difference in the *const* argument, the **GROWTH** function syntax is identical to that of **TREND**. You use the two functions in the same way as well. For example, to return the exponential trend values for the known values, you specify the *known_y's* argument and, optionally, the *known_x's* argument. Here's the array formula for the weekly units example:

```
=GROWTH(B2:B19, A2:A19)
```

To forecast values using **GROWTH**, add the *new_x's* argument. For example, to forecast the weekly sales for weeks 19 and 20, assuming that these x-values are in A20:A21, you use the following array formula:

```
=GROWTH(B2:B19, A2:A19, A20:A21)
```

Figure 13-23 shows the **GROWTH** formulas at work. The numbers in C2:C19 are the existing trend values, and the numbers in C20 and C21 are the forecast values.

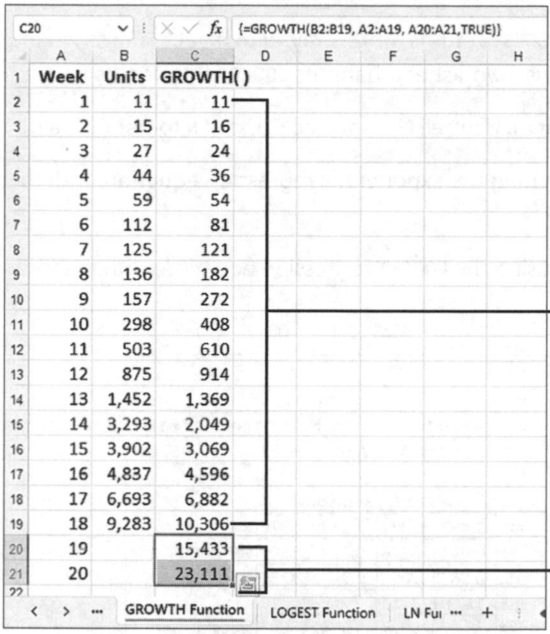

FIGURE 13-23 This worksheet shows the weekly unit sales with existing trend and forecast values calculated by the GROWTH function.

What if you want to calculate the constants **b** and **m**? You can do that by using the exponential equivalent of **LINEST**, which is **LOGEST**:

LOGEST(*known_y's*[, *known_x's*][, *const*][, *stats*])

known_y's	A range reference or an array of the known y-values from which you want to calculate the trend.
known x's	A range reference or an array of the x-values associated with the known y-values. If you omit this argument, the *known_x's* are assumed to be the array {1,2,3,...,n}, where *n* is the number of *known_y's*.
const	A logical value that determines the value of the **b** constant in the exponential regression equation. If you use **FALSE**, **b** is set to **1**; if you use **TRUE** (this is the default), Excel calculates **b** based on the *known_y's*.
stats	A logical value that determines whether **LOGEST** returns additional regression statistics besides *b* and *m*. The default is **FALSE**. If you use **TRUE**, **LOGEST** returns the extra *stats*, which are (except for *b* and *m*) the same as those returned by **LINEST**.

Actually, **LOGEST** doesn't return the value for *m* directly. That's because **LOGEST** is designed for the following regression formula:

$$y = bm_1{}^x$$

However, this is equivalent to the following:

$$y = b * EXP(LN(m_1) * x)$$

This is the same as our exponential regression equation, except that we have $LN(m_1)$ instead of just m. Therefore, to derive m, you need to use $LN(m_1)$ to take the natural logarithm of the m_1 value returned by **LOGEST**.

As with **LINEST**, if you set **stats** to **FALSE**, **LOGEST** returns a 1×2 array, with m (actually m_1) in the first cell and b in the second cell. Figure 13-24 shows a worksheet that puts **LOGEST** through its paces:

- The value of b is in cell H2. The value of m_1 is in cell G2, and cell I2 uses **LN** to get the value of m.

- The values in column D are calculated using the exponential regression equation, with the values for b and m plugged in.

- The values in column E are calculated using the **LOGEST** regression equation, with the values for b and m_1 plugged in.

I2			f_x	=LN(G2)					
	A	B	C	D	E	F	G	H	I
1	Week	Units	GROWTH	y = b * EXP(m * x)	y = b * m1x		m1	b	m = LN(m1)
2	1	11	11	11	11		1.497483	7.187455976	0.403785747
3	2	15	16	16	16				
4	3	27	24	24	24		LOGEST( ) Statistics		
5	4	44	36	36	36	m1	1.497483072	7.187455976	b
6	5	59	54	54	54	se	0.011325276	0.122588809	seb
7	6	112	81	81	81	R2	0.987569651	0.249284732	sey
8	7	125	121	121	121	F	1271.172211	16	df
9	8	136	182	182	182	ssreg	78.99429927	0.994286043	ssresid
10	9	157	272	272	272				
11	10	298	408	408	408				
12	11	503	610	610	610				
13	12	875	914	914	914				
14	13	1,452	1,369	1,369	1,369				
15	14	3,293	2,049	2,049	2,049				
16	15	3,902	3,069	3,069	3,069				
17	16	4,837	4,596	4,596	4,596				
18	17	6,693	6,882	6,882	6,882				
19	18	9,283	10,306	10,306	10,306				
20	19		15,433	15,433	15,433				
21	20		23,111	23,111	23,111				

< > ··· | LOGEST Function | LN Function | Loga ··· +

FIGURE 13-24 This worksheet shows the weekly unit sales with data generated by the LOGEST function.

Working with a logarithmic trend

A *logarithmic* trend is a trend that is the inverse of an exponential trend: The values rise (or fall) quickly in the beginning and then level off. This is a common pattern in business. For example, a new company hires many people up front, and then hiring slows over time. A new product often sells many units soon after it's launched, and then sales level off.

This pattern is described as logarithmic because it's typified by the shape of the curve made by the natural logarithm. Figure 13-25 shows a chart that plots the $LN(x)$ function for various values of x.

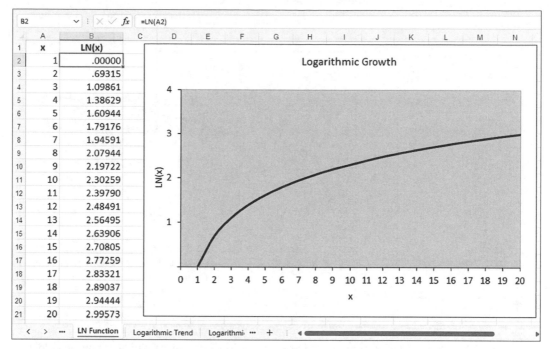

	A	B
1	x	LN(x)
2	1	.00000
3	2	.69315
4	3	1.09861
5	4	1.38629
6	5	1.60944
7	6	1.79176
8	7	1.94591
9	8	2.07944
10	9	2.19722
11	10	2.30259
12	11	2.39790
13	12	2.48491
14	13	2.56495
15	14	2.63906
16	15	2.70805
17	16	2.77259
18	17	2.83321
19	18	2.89037
20	19	2.94444
21	20	2.99573

FIGURE 13-25 The natural logarithm produces a classic logarithmic trend pattern.

Plotting a logarithmic trendline

The easiest way to see the trend and forecast is to add a trendline—specifically, a logarithmic trendline—to the chart. Here are the steps to follow:

1. Select the chart and, if more than one data series is plotted, click the series you want to work with.

2. Select **Chart Design** > **Add Chart Element** > **Trendline** > **More Trendline Options** to display the Format Trendline task pane.

3. On the **Trendline Options** tab, select the **Logarithmic** option.

4. In the **Forecast** section, use the **Forward** text box to enter the number of periods into the future you want the trendline extended.

5. Select the **Display Equation on Chart** and **Display R-Squared Value on Chart** check boxes.

6. Select **Close** (**X**). Excel inserts the trendline.

Figure 13-26 shows a worksheet that tracks the total number of employees at a new company. The chart shows the employee growth and a logarithmic trendline fitted to the data and extended eight periods into the future.

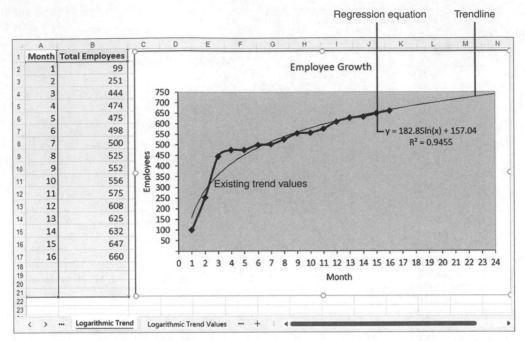

FIGURE 13-26 This worksheet shows a chart of total employee growth, with a logarithmic trendline added.

Calculating logarithmic trend and forecast values

The regression equation for a logarithmic trendline takes the following general form:

$y = m * LN(x) + b$

As usual, *b* and *m* are constants. So, knowing these values, given an independent value *x*, you can use this formula to compute its corresponding point on the trendline. In the trendline in Figure 13-26, these constant values are **182.85** and **157.04**, respectively. So the formula for trend values becomes this:

```
=182.85 * LN(x) + 157.04
```

If *x* is a value between 1 and 16, you get a trend point for the existing data. To get a forecast, you use a value higher than 16. For example, using *x* equal to **17** gives a forecast value of 675 employees:

```
=182.85 * LN(17) + 157.04
```

Excel doesn't have a function that enables you to calculate the values of *b* and *m* yourself. However, it's possible to use the **LINEST** function if you transform the pattern so that it becomes linear. When you have a logarithmic curve, you "straighten it out" by changing the scale of the x-axis to a logarithmic scale. Therefore, you can turn your logarithmic regression into a linear one by applying the **LN** function to the *known_x's* argument:

```
=LINEST(known_y's, LN(known_x's))
```

For example, the following array formula returns the values of *m* and *b* for the Total Employees data:

```
=LINEST(B2:B17, LN(A2:A17))
```

Figure 13-27 shows a worksheet that calculates *m* (cell E2) and *b* (cell F2) and that uses the results to derive values for the current trend and the forecasts (column C).

C18	⌄	:	× ✓ *fx*	=$E$2 * LN(A18) + $F$2				
	A	B	C	D	E	F	G
1	Month	Total Employees	y = m * LN(x) + b		m	b	
2	1	99	157		182.8527069	157.0355	
3	2	251	284				
4	3	444	358				
5	4	474	411				
6	5	475	451				
7	6	498	485				
8	7	500	513				
9	8	525	537				
10	9	552	559				Existing trend values
11	10	556	578				
12	11	575	595				
13	12	608	611				
14	13	625	626				
15	14	632	640				
16	15	647	652				
17	16	660	664				
18	17		675				
19	18		686				
20	19		695				Forecast values
21	20		705				
22	21		714				
23	22		722				

< > ··· | Logarithmic Trend Values | y = x^b | Power Tr ··· | +

FIGURE 13-27 This figure shows the Total Employees worksheet, with existing trend and forecast values calculated by the logarithmic regression equation and values returned by the LINEST function.

Working with a power trend

The exponential and logarithmic trendlines are both "extreme" in the sense that they have radically different velocities at different parts of the curve. The exponential trendline begins slowly and then takes off at an ever-increasing pace; the logarithmic trendline shoots off the mark and then levels off.

Most measurable business scenarios don't exhibit such extreme behavior. Revenues, profits, margins, and employee head count often tend to increase steadily over time (in successful companies, anyway). If you're analyzing a dependent variable that increases (or decreases) steadily with respect to some independent variable, but the linear trendline doesn't give a good fit, you should try a *power* trendline. This is a pattern that curves steadily in one direction. To give you a flavor of a power curve, consider the graphs of the equations $y = x^2$ and $y = x^{-0.25}$ in Figure 13-28. The $y = x^2$ curve shows a steady increase, whereas the $y = x^{-0.25}$ curve shows a steady decrease.

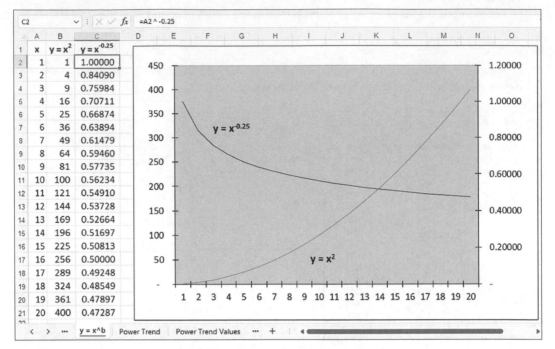

FIGURE 13-28 Power curves are generated by raising x-values to some power.

Plotting a power trendline

If you think that your data fits the power pattern, you can quickly check by adding a power trendline to the chart. Here are the steps to follow:

1. Select the chart and, if more than one data series is plotted, click the series you want to work with.

2. Select **Chart Design** > **Add Chart Element** > **Trendline** > **More Trendline Options** to display the Format Trendline task pane.

3. On the **Trendline Options** tab, select the **Power** option.

4. In the **Forecast** section, use the **Forward** text box to enter the number of periods into the future you want the trendline extended.

5. Select the **Display Equation On Chart** and **Display R-Squared Value On Chart** check boxes.

6. Select **Close** (**X**). Excel inserts the trendline.

Figure 13-29 shows a worksheet that compares the list price of a product (the independent variable) with the number of units sold (the dependent variable). As the chart shows, this relationship plots as a steadily declining curve, so a power trendline has been added. Note, too, that the trendline has been extended back to the $5.99 price point and forward to the $15.99 price point.

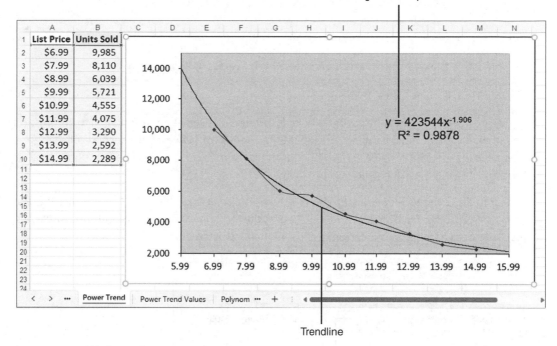

FIGURE 13-29 This figure shows a product's list price versus unit sales, with a power trendline added.

Calculating power trend and forecast values

The regression equation for a power trendline takes the following general form:

$$y = mx^b$$

As usual, b and m are constants. Given these values and an independent value x, you can use this formula to compute its corresponding point on the trendline. In the trendline in Figure 13-29, these constant values are **423544** and **-1.906**, respectively. Plugging these into the general equation for a power trend gives the following:

```
=423544 * x ^ -1.906
```

If x is a value between 6.99 and 14.99, you get a trend point for the existing data. To get a forecast, you use a value lower than 6.99 or higher than 14.99. For example, using x equal to **16.99** gives a forecast value of 1,915 units sold:

```
=423544 * 16.99 ^ -1.906
```

As with the logarithmic trend, Excel doesn't have functions that enable you to directly calculate the values of b and m. However, you can "straighten" a power curve by changing the scale of *both* the y-axis and the x-axis to a logarithmic scale. Therefore, you can transform the power regression into a linear regression by applying the natural logarithm—the **LN** function—to both the *known_y's* and *known_x's* arguments:

```
=LINEST(LN(known_y's), LN(known_x's))
```

Here's how the array formula looks for the list price versus units sold data:

```
=LINEST(LN(B2:B10, LN(A2:A10))
```

The first cell of the array holds the value of *b*. Because it's used as an exponent in the regression equation, you don't need to "undo" the logarithmic transform. However, the second cell in the array— let's call it m_1—holds the value of *m* in its logarithmic form. Therefore, you need to "undo" the transform by applying the **EXP** function to the result.

Figure 13-30 shows a worksheet performing these calculations. The **LINEST** array is in E2:F2, and E2 holds the value of *b* (cell E2). To get *m*, cell G2 uses the formula =**EXP(F2)**. The worksheet uses these results to derive values for the current trend and the forecasts (column C).

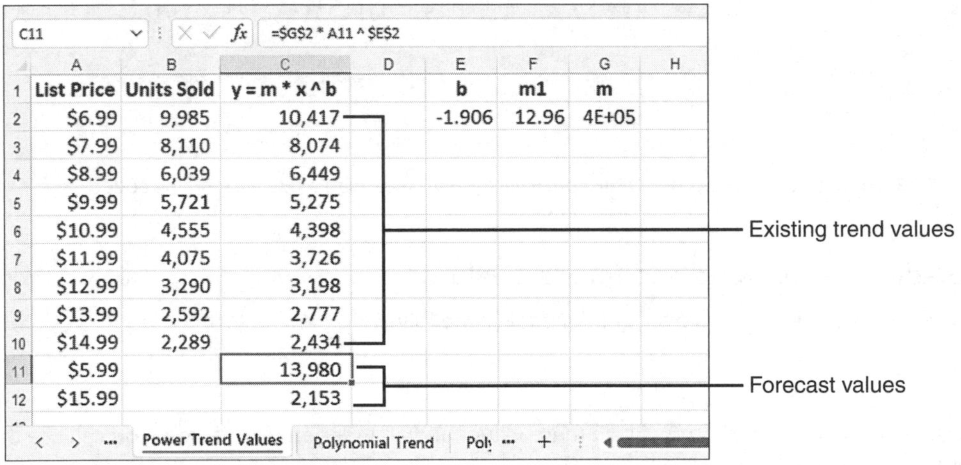

FIGURE 13-30 The worksheet of list price versus units sold, with existing trend and forecast values calculated by the power regression equation and values returned by the LINEST function.

Using polynomial regression analysis

The trendlines you've seen so far have been unidirectional. That's fine if the curve formed by the dependent variable values is also unidirectional, but that's often not the case in a business environment. Sales fluctuate, profits rise and fall, and costs move up and down, thanks to varying factors such as inflation, interest rates, exchange rates, and commodity prices. The trendlines covered so far might not provide either a good fit or good forecasts for these more complex curves.

If that's the case, you might need to turn to a *polynomial* trendline, which is a curve constructed out of an equation that uses multiple powers of x. For example, a *second-order* polynomial regression equation takes the following general form:

$$y = m_2x^2 + m_1x + b$$

The values m_2, m_1, and b are constants. Similarly, a *third-order* polynomial regression equation takes the following form:

$$y = m_2x^3 + m_2x^2 + m_1x + b$$

These equations can go as high as a sixth-order polynomial.

Plotting a polynomial trendline

Here are the steps to follow to add a polynomial trendline to a chart:

1. Select the chart and, if more than one data series is plotted, click the series you want to work with.

2. Select **Chart Design** > **Add Chart Element** > **Trendline** > **More Trendline Options** to display the Format Trendline task pane.

3. On the **Trendline Options** tab, select the **Polynomial** option.

4. Use the **Order** spin box to select the order of the polynomial equation you want.

5. In the **Forecast** section, use the **Forward** text box to enter the number of periods into the future you want the trendline extended.

6. Select the **Display Equation On Chart** and **Display R-Squared Value On Chart** check boxes.

7. Select **Close** (**X**). Excel inserts the trendline.

Figure 13-31 displays a simple worksheet that shows annual profits over 10 years, with accompanying charts showing two different polynomial trendlines.

Generally, the higher the order you use, the tighter the curve will fit your existing data, but the more unpredictable will be your forecasted values. In Figure 13-31, the top chart shows a third-order polynomial trendline, and the bottom chart shows a fifth-order polynomial trendline. The fifth-order curve ($R^2 = 0.6236$) gives a better fit than the third-order curve ($R^2 = 0.3048$).

However, the forecasted profit for the 11th year seems more realistic in the third-order case (about 17) than in the fifth-order case (about 26).

In other words, you'll often have to try different polynomial orders to get a fit that you are comfortable with and forecasted values that seem realistic.

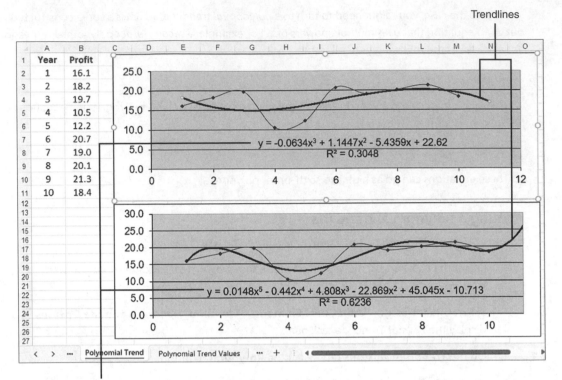

Trendlines

Regression equations

FIGURE 13-31 This figure shows the annual profits with two charts showing different polynomial trendlines.

Calculating polynomial trend and forecast values

You've seen that the regression equation for an nth-order polynomial curve takes the following general form:

$$y = m_n x^n + \ldots + m_2 x^2 + m_1 x + b$$

So, as with the other regression equations, if you know the value of the constants, for any independent value x, you can use this formula to compute its corresponding point on the trendline. For example, the top trendline in Figure 13-31 is a third-order polynomial, so we need the values of m_3, m_2, and m_1, as well as b. From the regression equation displayed on the chart, we know that these values are, respectively, **-0.0634**, **1.1447**, **-5.4359**, and **22.62**. Plugging these into the general equation for a third-order polynomial trend gives the following:

```
=-0.0634 * x ^ 3 + 1.1447 * x ^ 2 + -5.4359 * x + 22.62
```

If *x* is a value between 1 and 10, you get a trend point for the existing data. To get a forecast, you use a value higher than 10. For example, using *x* equal to **11** gives a forecast profit value of 16.9:

```
=-0.0634 * 11 ^ 3 + 1.1447 * 11 ^ 2 + -5.4359 * 11 + 22.62
```

However, you don't need to put yourself through these intense calculations because the **TREND** function can do it for you. The trick here is to raise each of the *known_x's* values to the powers from 1 to *n* for an *n*th-order polynomial:

```
=TREND(known_y's, known_x's ^ {1,2,...,n})
```

For example, here's the array formula to use to get the existing trend values for a third-order polynomial using the year and profit ranges from the worksheet in Figure 13-31:

```
=TREND(B2:B11, A2:A11 ^ {1,2,3})
```

To get a forecast value, you raise each of the *new_x's* values to the powers from 1 to *n* for an *n*th-order polynomial:

```
=TREND(known_y's, known_x's ^ {1,2,...,n}, new_x's ^ {1,2,...,n})
```

For the profits forecast, if A12 contains 11, the following array formula returns the predicted value:

```
=TREND(B2:B11, A2:A11 ^ {1,2,3}, A12 ^ {1,2,3})
```

Figure 13-32 shows a worksheet that uses this **TREND** technique to compute both the trend values for years 1 through 10 and a forecast value for year 11 for all the second-order through sixth-order polynomials.

Also, note that Figure 13-32 calculates the m_n values and *b* for each order of polynomial. This is done using **LINEST** by again raising each of the *known_x's* values to the powers from 1 to *n*, for an *n*th-order polynomial:

```
=LINEST(known_y's, known_x's ^ {1,2,...,n})
```

The formula returns an *n* + 1×1 array in which the first *n* cells contain the constants m_n through m_1, and then the *n*+1st cell contains *b*. For example, the following array formula returns a 3×1 array of the constant values for a third-order polynomial using the year and profit ranges:

```
=LINEST(B2:B11, A2:A11 ^ {1,2,3})
```

Existing trend values

D12	⌄ : × ✓ fx	=TREND(B2:B11, A2:A11 ^ {1,2,3}, A12 ^ {1,2,3})						

	A	B	C	D	E	F	G	H
1	Year	Profit	TREND Order 2	TREND Order 3	TREND Order 4	TREND Order 5	TREND Order 6	
2	1	16.1	16.7	18.3	16.7	15.8	15.8	
3	2	18.2	16.4	15.8	17.7	19.8	20.1	
4	3	19.7	16.2	14.9	16.4	16.2	15.9	
5	4	10.5	16.3	15.1	14.9	13.3	13.1	
6	5	12.2	16.6	16.1	14.6	13.7	13.9	
7	6	20.7	17.1	17.5	16.0	16.9	17.1	
8	7	19.0	17.7	18.9	18.7	20.3	20.1	
9	8	20.1	18.6	19.9	21.4	21.5	21.2	
10	9	21.3	19.7	20.2	22.1	20.0	20.3	
11	10	18.4	20.9	19.3	17.8	18.7	18.6	
12	11		22.4	17.0	4.8	25.9	17.6	
13								
14	Order	m6	m5	m4	m3	m2	m1	b
15	2					0.098863636	-0.612348485	17.18166667
16	3				-0.063383838	1.14469697	-5.435858586	22.62
17	4			-0.035533217	0.718346931	-4.576150932	10.1987568	10.425
18	5		0.014782051	-0.442039627	4.808047786	-22.86893939	45.04497902	-10.71333333
19	6	-0.001333333	0.058782051	-1.006282051	8.348047786	-34.07063636	61.46097902	-19.03333333

< > ⋯ Polynomial Trend Values   Multiple Independen ⋯   +

Forecast values

FIGURE 13-32 This figure shows the profits worksheet, with existing trend and forecast values calculated by the TREND function.

Using multiple regression analysis

Focusing on a single independent variable is a useful exercise because it can tell you a great deal about the relationship between the independent variable and the dependent variable. However, in the real world of business, the variation that you see in most phenomena is a product of multiple influences. The movement of car sales isn't solely a function of interest rates; it's also affected by internal factors such as price, advertising, warranties, and factory-dealer incentives, as well as external factors such as total consumer disposable income and the employment rate.

The good news is that the linear regression techniques you learned earlier in this chapter are easily adapted to multiple independent variables.

As a simple example, let's consider a sales model in which the units sold—the dependent variable—is a function of two independent variables: advertising costs and list price. The worksheet in Figure 13-33 shows data for 10 products, each with its own advertising costs (column A) and list price (column B), as well as the corresponding unit sales (column C). The upper chart shows the relationship between units sold and list price, whereas the lower chart shows the relationship between units sold and advertising costs. As you can see, the individual trends look about right: Units sold goes down as the list price goes up; units sold goes up as the advertising costs go up.

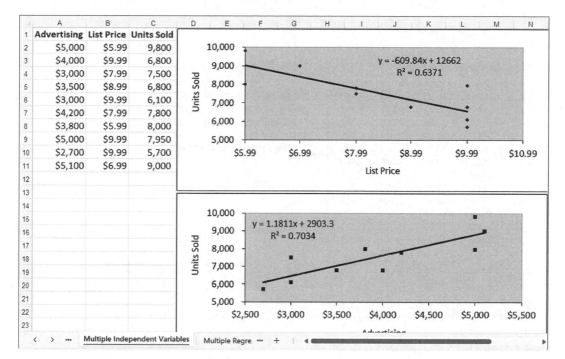

	A	B	C
1	Advertising	List Price	Units Sold
2	$5,000	$5.99	9,800
3	$4,000	$9.99	6,800
4	$3,000	$7.99	7,500
5	$3,500	$8.99	6,800
6	$3,000	$9.99	6,100
7	$4,200	$7.99	7,800
8	$3,800	$5.99	8,000
9	$5,000	$9.99	7,950
10	$2,700	$9.99	5,700
11	$5,100	$6.99	9,000

FIGURE 13-33 This worksheet shows raw data and trendlines for units sold versus advertising costs and list price.

However, the individual trends don't tell us much about how advertising and price *together* affect sales. Clearly, a low advertising budget combined with a high price will result in lower sales; conversely, a high advertising budget combined with a low price should increase sales. What we really want, of course, is to attach some hard numbers to these seat-of-the-pants speculations. You can get those numbers using that linear regression workhorse, the **TREND** function.

To use **TREND** when you have multiple independent variables, you expand the *known_x's* argument so that it includes the entire range of independent data. In Figure 13-33, for example, the independent data resides in the range A2:B11, so that's the reference you plug into the **TREND** function. Here's the array formula for computing the existing trend values:

```
=TREND(C2:C11, A2:B11)
```

In multiple regression analysis, you're most often interested in what-if scenarios. What if you spend $6,000 in advertising on a $5.99 product? What if you spend $1,000 on a $9.99 product?

To answer these questions, you plug the values into the *new_x's* argument as an array. For example, the following array formula returns the predicted number of units that will sell if you spend $6,000 in advertising on a $5.99 product:

```
=TREND(C2:C11, A2:B11, {6000, 5.99)
```

Figure 13-34 shows a worksheet that puts the multiple regression form of **TREND** to work. The values in D2:D11 are for the existing trend, and values in D12:D13 are forecasts.

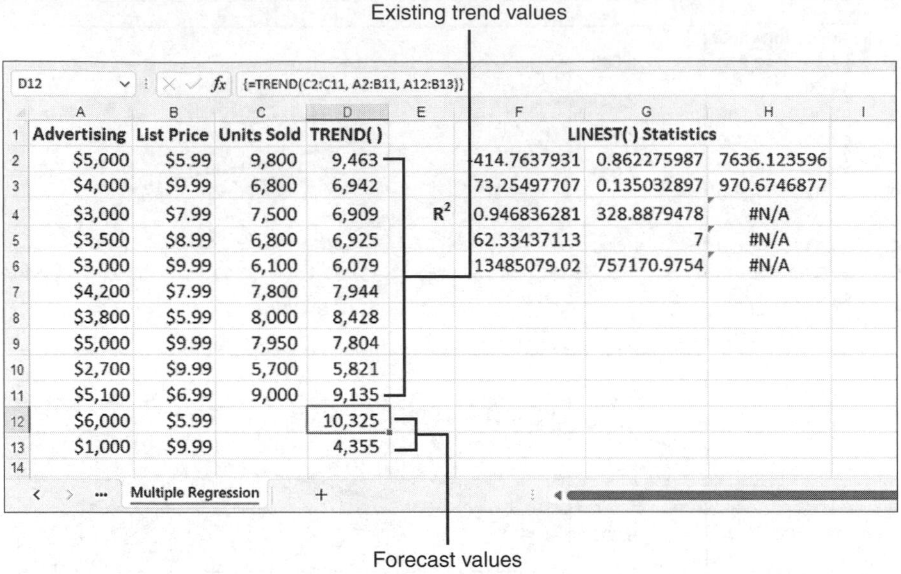

Existing trend values

D12		fx	{=TREND(C2:C11, A2:B11, A12:B13)}					
	A	B	C	D	E	F	G	H	I
1	Advertising	List Price	Units Sold	TREND( )		LINEST( ) Statistics		
2	$5,000	$5.99	9,800	9,463		414.7637931	0.862275987	7636.123596
3	$4,000	$9.99	6,800	6,942		73.25497707	0.135032897	970.6746877
4	$3,000	$7.99	7,500	6,909	R^2	0.946836281	328.8879478	#N/A
5	$3,500	$8.99	6,800	6,925		62.33437113	7	#N/A
6	$3,000	$9.99	6,100	6,079		13485079.02	757170.9754	#N/A
7	$4,200	$7.99	7,800	7,944				
8	$3,800	$5.99	8,000	8,428				
9	$5,000	$9.99	7,950	7,804				
10	$2,700	$9.99	5,700	5,821				
11	$5,100	$6.99	9,000	9,135				
12	$6,000	$5.99		10,325				
13	$1,000	$9.99		4,355				
14								

Multiple Regression   +

Forecast values

FIGURE 13-34 This worksheet shows the trend and forecast values calculated by the multiple regression form of the TREND function.

Notice, too, that the worksheet in Figure 13-34 includes the statistics generated by the **LINEST** function. The returned array is *three* columns wide because you're dealing with three variables (two independent and one dependent). Of particular interest is the value for R^2 (cell F4)—0.946836. It tells us that the fit between unit sales and the combination of advertising and price is an excellent one, which gives us some confidence about the validity of the predicted values.

CHAPTER 14

Building loan formulas

In this chapter, you will:

- Understand the concept of the time value of money

- Calculate loan payments, interest costs, and cumulative principal and interest payments

- Build fixed-rate and dynamic loan amortization schedules

- Determine the term of a loan given the interest rate, the regular payment, and the principal loan amount

- Calculate the interest rate required for a loan given the loan term, the loan payment, and the loan principal

- Figure out how much you can borrow given the interest rate, loan payment, and loan term

Excel is loaded with financial features that give you powerful tools for building worksheets that manage both business and personal finances. You can use these functions to calculate such things as the monthly payment on a loan, the future value of an annuity, the internal rate of return of an investment, or the yearly depreciation of an asset. This chapter and the next two chapters cover these functions and many other uses for Excel's financial formulas.

This chapter covers formulas and functions related to loans and mortgages. You'll learn about the time value of money; how to calculate loan payments, loan periods, the principal and interest components of a payment, and the interest rate; and how to build an amortization schedule.

Understanding the time value of money

The time value of money means that a dollar in hand now is worth more than a dollar promised at some future date. This seemingly simple idea underlies not only the concepts and techniques you learn in this chapter but also the investment formulas in Chapter 15, "Working with investment formulas," and the discount formulas in Chapter 16, "Building discount formulas." A dollar now is worth more than a dollar promised in the future for two reasons:

- You can invest a dollar now. If you earn a positive return, the sum of the dollar and interest earned will be worth more than the future dollar.

- You might never see the future dollar. Due to bankruptcy, cash-flow problems, or any number of other reasons, there's a risk that the company or person promising you the future dollar might not be able to deliver it.

These two factors—interest and risk—are at the heart of most financial formulas and models. More realistically, these factors mean that you're mostly comparing the benefits of investing a dollar now versus getting a dollar in the future *plus* some *risk premium*—an amount that compensates for the risk you're taking in waiting for the dollar to be delivered.

You compare these by looking at the *present value* (the amount something is worth now) and the *future value* (the amount something is worth in the future). They're related as follows:

- Future value = Present value + Interest

- Present value = Future value – discount

Much financial analysis boils down to comparing these formulas. If the present value in A is greater than the present value in B, A is the better investment; conversely, if the future value in B is greater than the future value in A, B is the better investment.

Most of the formulas you'll work with over the next three chapters involve these three factors—the present value, the future value, and the interest rate (or the discount rate)—plus two related factors: the *periods*, which are the number of payments or deposits over the term of the loan or investment and the *payment*, which is the amount of money paid out or invested in each period.

When building your financial formulas, you need to ask yourself the following questions:

- **Who or what is the subject of the formula?** In a mortgage analysis, for example, are you performing the analysis on behalf of yourself or the bank?

- **Which way is the money flowing with respect to the subject?** For the present value, future value, and payment, enter money that the subject receives as a positive quantity and enter money that the subject pays out as a negative quantity. For example, if you're the subject of a mortgage analysis, the loan principal (the present value) is a positive number because it's money that you receive from the bank; the payment and the remaining principal (the future value) are negative because they're amounts that you pay to the bank.

- **What is the time unit?** The underlying unit of both the interest rate and the period must be the same. For example, if you're working with the annual interest rate, you must express the period in years. Similarly, if you're working with monthly periods, you must use a monthly interest rate.

- **When are the payments made?** Excel differentiates between payments made at the end of each period and those made at the beginning.

Calculating a loan payment

When negotiating a loan to purchase equipment or a mortgage for your house, the first concern that comes up is almost always the size of the payment you'll need to make each period. This is just basic cash-flow management because the monthly (or whatever) payment must fit within your budget.

To return the periodic payment for a loan, use the **PMT** function:

```
PMT(rate, nper, pv[, fv][, type])
```

rate	The fixed rate of interest over the term of the loan.
nper	The number of payments over the term of the loan.
pv	The loan principal.
fv	The future value of the loan.
type	The type of payment. Use **0** (the default) for end-of-period payments; use **1** for beginning-of-period payments.

For example, the following formula returns the monthly payment of a $10,000 loan with an annual interest rate of 6 percent (0.5 percent per month) over five years (60 months):

```
=PMT(0.005, 60, 10000)
```

Loan payment analysis

Financial formulas rarely use hard-coded function arguments. Instead, you almost always are better off placing the argument values in separate cells and then referencing those cells in the formula. This enables you to do a rudimentary form of loan analysis by plugging in different argument values and seeing their effects on the formula result.

Figure 14-1 shows an example of a worksheet set up to perform such an analysis. The **PMT** formula is in cell B7, and the function arguments are stored in B4 (*rate*), B5 (*nper*), and B6 (*pv*).

> **Note** You can work with all the examples in this chapter by downloading Chapter14.xslx from either of the companion content sites mentioned in the Introduction.

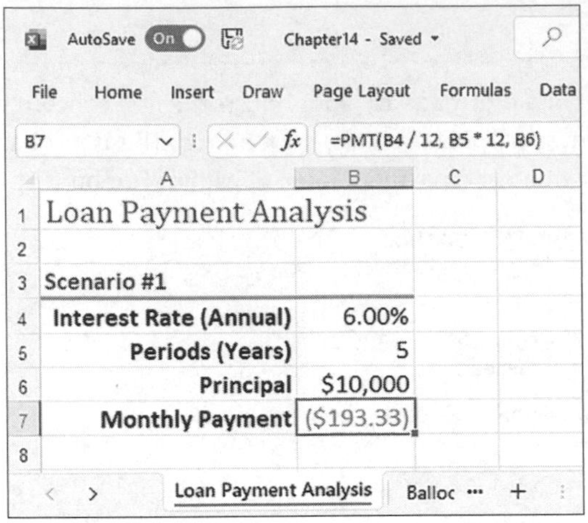

FIGURE 14-1 To perform a simple loan analysis, place the PMT function arguments in separate cells and then change those cell values to see the effect on the formula.

Note two things about the formula and result in cell B7:

- The interest rate is an annual value, and the periods are expressed in years, so to get a monthly payment, you must convert these values to their monthly equivalents. This means that the interest rate is divided by 12 and the number of periods is multiplied by 12:

```
=PMT(B4 / 12, B5 * 12, B6)
```

- The **PMT** function returns a negative value, which is correct because this worksheet is set up from the point of view of the person receiving the loan, and the payment is money that flows away from that person.

Working with a balloon loan

Many loans are set up so that the payments take care of only a portion of the principal, with the remainder due as an end-of-loan balloon payment. This balloon payment is the future value of the loan, so you need to factor it into the **PMT** function as the *fv* argument.

You might think that the *pv* argument should be the partial principal—that is, the original loan principal minus the balloon amount. This seems right because the loan term is designed to pay off the partial principal. That's not the case, however. In a balloon loan, you also pay interest on the balloon part of the principal. That is, each payment in a balloon loan has three components:

- A paydown of the partial principal
- Interest on the partial principal
- Interest on the balloon portion of the principal

Therefore, the **PMT** function's *pv* argument must be the entire principal, with the balloon portion as the (negative) *fv* argument.

For example, suppose that the loan from the previous section has a $3,000 balloon payment. Figure 14-2 shows a new worksheet that adds the balloon payment to the model and then calculates the payment using the following revised formula:

```
=PMT(B2 / 12, B3 * 12, B4, -B5)
```

	A	B	C	D
1	Loan Payment Analysis			
2	Interest Rate (Annual)	6.00%		
3	Periods (Years)	5		
4	Principal	$10,000		
5	Balloon Payment	$3,000		
6	Monthly Payment	($150.33)		
7				

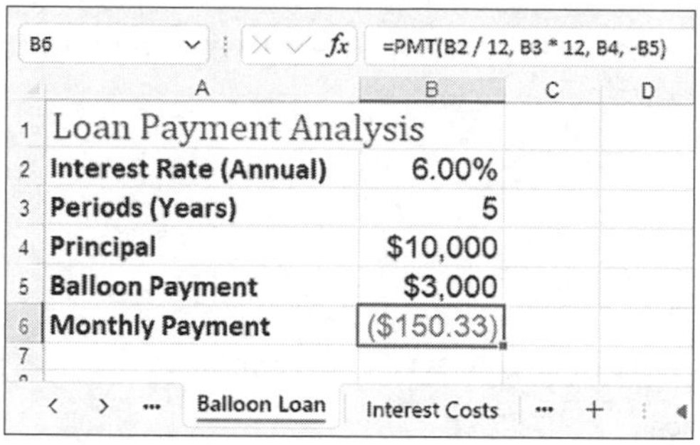

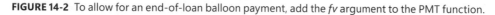

FIGURE 14-2 To allow for an end-of-loan balloon payment, add the *fv* argument to the PMT function.

Note that the balloon payment is entered into the worksheet (in cell B5) as a positive value. However, the balloon payment represents, in this model, money going out, so the negation operator (–) is used in the formula (**-B5**) to convert the balloon payment to a negative value.

Calculating interest costs, part I

When you know the payment, you can calculate the total interest costs of a loan by first figuring the total of all the payments and then subtracting the principal. The remainder is the total interest paid over the life of the loan.

Figure 14-3 shows a worksheet that performs this calculation. In column B, cell B7 contains the total amount paid (the monthly payment multiplied by the number of months), and cell B8 takes the difference. Column C performs the same calculations on the loan with a balloon payment. As you can see, in the balloon payment scenario, the payment total is about $2,600 smaller, but the total interest is about $400 higher.

	A	B	C
1	Loan Payment Analysis		
2	Interest Rate (Annual)	6.00%	6.00%
3	Periods (Years)	5	5
4	Principal	$10,000	$10,000
5	Balloon Payment	$0	$3,000
6	Monthly Payment	($193.33)	($150.33)
7	Total Payments	($11,599.68)	($9,019.78)
8	Total Interest Costs	($1,599.68)	($2,019.78)
9			

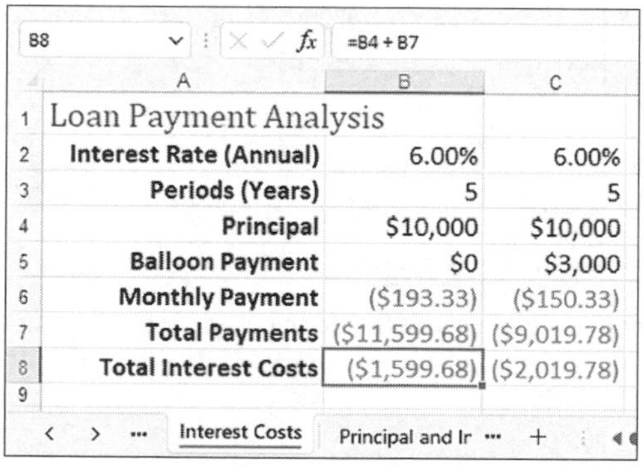

FIGURE 14-3 The total interest paid out over the life of a loan is the difference between the total of all the loan payments and the loan principal.

Calculating the principal and interest

Any loan payment has two components: principal repayment and interest charges. Interest charges are almost always *front loaded*, which means that the interest component is highest at the beginning of the loan and gradually decreases with each payment. This means, conversely, that the principal component increases gradually with each payment.

To calculate the principal and interest components of a loan payment, use the **PPMT** and **IPMT** functions, respectively:

```
PPMT(rate, per, nper, pv[, fv][, type])
IPMT(rate, per, nper, pv[, fv][, type])
```

Rate	The fixed rate of interest over the term of the loan.
Per	The number of the payment period (where the first payment is **1** and the last payment is the same as *nper*).
Nper	The number of payments over the term of the loan.
Pv	The loan principal.
Fv	The future value of the loan. (The default is **0**.)
Type	The type of payment. Use **0** (the default) for end-of-period payments; use **1** for beginning-of-period payments.

Figure 14-4 shows a worksheet that applies these functions to the loan. The table shows the principal (column F) and interest (column G) components of the loan for the first 10 periods and for the final period. Note that with each period, the principal portion increases and the interest portion decreases. However, the total remains the same (as confirmed by the Total column), which is as it should be because the payment remains constant throughout the life of the loan.

F2			fx	=PPMT($B$2 / 12, E2, $B$3 * 12, $B$4)			
	A	B	C	D	E	F	G	H

	A	B	E	F	G	H
1	Loan Payment Analysis		Period	Principal	Interest	Total
2	Interest Rate (Annual)	6.00%	1	($143.33)	($50.00)	($193.33)
3	Periods (Years)	5	2	($144.04)	($49.28)	($193.33)
4	Principal	$10,000	3	($144.76)	($48.56)	($193.33)
5	Monthly Payment	($193.33)	4	($145.49)	($47.84)	($193.33)
6	Total Loan Costs	($1,599.68)	5	($146.22)	($47.11)	($193.33)
7			6	($146.95)	($46.38)	($193.33)
8			7	($147.68)	($45.65)	($193.33)
9			8	($148.42)	($44.91)	($193.33)
10			9	($149.16)	($44.17)	($193.33)
11			10	($149.91)	($43.42)	($193.33)
12			60	($192.37)	($0.96)	($193.33)
13						

Principal and Interest   Cumul...   +

FIGURE 14-4 This worksheet uses the PPMT and IPMT functions to break out the principal and interest components of a loan payment.

Calculating interest costs, part II

Another way to calculate the total interest paid on a loan is to sum the various **IPMT** values over the life of the loan. You can do this by using an array formula that generates the values of the **IPMT** function's *per* argument. Here's the general array formula:

```
=IPMT(rate, ROW(INDIRECT("A1:A" & nper)), nper, pv[, fv][, type])
```

The array of *per* values is generated by the following expression:

```
ROW(INDIRECT("A1:A" & nper))
```

The **INDIRECT** function converts a string range reference into an actual range reference, and then the **ROW** function returns the row numbers from that range. By starting the range at A1, this expression generates integer values from **1** to *nper*, which covers the life of the loan.

For example, here's an array formula that calculates the total interest cost of the loan model shown in Figure 14-4:

```
=SUM(IPMT(B2 / 12, ROW(INDIRECT("A1:A" & B3 * 12)), B3 * 12, B4))
```

> **Caution**   The array formula doesn't work if the loan includes a balloon payment.

Calculating cumulative principal and interest

Knowing how much principal and interest you pay each period is useful, but it's usually handier to know how much principal or interest you've paid in total up to a given period. For example, if you sign up for a mortgage with a five-year term, how much principal will you have paid off by the end of the term? Similarly, a business might need to know the total interest payments a loan requires in the first year so that it can factor the result into its expense budgeting.

You could solve these kinds of problems by building a model that uses the **PPMT** and **IPMT** functions over the time frame you're dealing with and then summing the results. However, Excel has two functions that offer a more direct route:

```
CUMPRINC(rate, nper, pv, start_period, end_period, type)
CUMIPMT(rate, nper, pv, start_period, end_period, type)
```

rate	The fixed rate of interest over the term of the loan.
nper	The number of payments over the term of the loan.
pv	The loan principal.
start_period	The first period to include in the calculation.
end_period	The last period to include in the calculation.
type	The type of payment. Use **0** for end-of-period payments; use **1** for beginning-of-period payments.

> **!** **Caution** In both **CUMPRINC** and **CUMIPMT**, *all* of the arguments are required. If you omit the *type* argument (which is optional in most other financial functions), Excel returns the #N/A error.

The main difference between **CUMPRINC** and **CUMIPMT** and **PPMT** and **IPMT** is the *start_period* and *end_period* arguments. For example, to find the cumulative principal or interest in the first year of a loan, you set *start_period* to **1** and *end_period* to **12**; for the second year, you set *start_period* to **13** and *end_period* to **24**. Here are a couple of formulas that calculate these values for any year, assuming that the year value (**1**, **2**, and so on) is in cell D2:

```
start_period: (D2 - 1) * 12 + 1
end_period: D2 * 12
```

Figure 14-5 shows a worksheet that returns the cumulative principal and interest paid in each year of a loan, as well as the total principal and interest for all five years.

E2			*fx*	=CUMPRINC($B$2 / 12, $B$3 * 12, $B$4, (D2 - 1) * 12 + 1, D2 * 12, 0)		
	A	B	C	D	E	F	G
1	Loan Payment Analysis			Year	Cumulative Principal	Cumulative Interest	Total
2	Interest Rate (Annual)	6.00%		1	($1,768.03)	($551.90)	($2,319.94)
3	Periods (Years)	5		2	($1,877.08)	($442.86)	($2,319.94)
4	Principal	$10,000		3	($1,992.85)	($327.08)	($2,319.94)
5	Monthly Payment	($193.33)		4	($2,115.77)	($204.17)	($2,319.94)
6				5	($2,246.27)	($73.67)	($2,319.94)
7				1 - 5	($10,000.00)	($1,599.68)	($11,599.68)
8							

FIGURE 14-5 This worksheet uses the CUMPRINC and CUMIPMT functions to return the cumulative principal and interest for each year of a loan.

> **≡** **Note** The **CUMIPMT** function gives you an easier way to calculate the total interest costs for a loan. Just set *start_period* to **1** and *end_period* to the number of periods (the value of *nper*).

> **!** **Caution** Although the **CUMPRINC** function works as advertised if the loan includes a balloon payment, the **CUMIPMT** function does not.

Building a loan amortization schedule

A loan *amortization schedule* is a table that shows a sequence of calculations over the life of a loan. For each period, the schedule shows figures such as the payment, the principal and interest components of the payment, the cumulative principal and interest, and the remaining principal. The next few sections take you through various amortization schedules designed for different scenarios.

Building a fixed-rate amortization schedule

The simplest amortization schedule is just a straightforward application of three of the payment functions you've seen so far: **PMT**, **PPMT**, and **IPMT**. Figure 14-6 shows the result, which has the following features:

- The values for the four main arguments of the payment functions are stored in the range B2:B5.

- The amortization schedule is shown in A9:G18. Column A contains the period, and subsequent columns calculate the payment (B), principal component (C), interest component (D), cumulative principal (E), and cumulative interest (F). The Remaining Principal column (G) shows the original principal amount (B4) minus the cumulative principal for each period.

- The cumulative principal and interest values are calculated by adding the running totals of the principal and interest components. You need to do this because the **CUMPRINC** and **CUMIPMT** functions don't work with balloon payments. If you never use balloon payments, you can convert the worksheet to use these functions.

- This schedule uses a yearly time frame, so no adjustments are applied to the *rate* and *nper* arguments.

G9		f_x	=$B$4 + E9				
	A	B	C	D	E	F	G
1	Loan Data						
2	Interest Rate	6.00%					
3	Amortization	10					
4	Principal	$500,000					
5	Payment Type	0					
6							
7	Amortization Schedule						
8	Period	Payment	Principal	Interest	Cumulative Principal	Cumulative Interest	Remaining Principal
9	1	($67,933.98)	($37,933.98)	($30,000.00)	($37,933.98)	($30,000.00)	$462,066.02
10	2	($67,933.98)	($40,210.02)	($27,723.96)	($78,144.00)	($57,723.96)	$421,856.00
11	3	($67,933.98)	($42,622.62)	($25,311.36)	($120,766.62)	($83,035.32)	$379,233.38
12	4	($67,933.98)	($45,179.98)	($22,754.00)	($165,946.59)	($105,789.32)	$334,053.41
13	5	($67,933.98)	($47,890.77)	($20,043.20)	($213,837.37)	($125,832.53)	$286,162.63
14	6	($67,933.98)	($50,764.22)	($17,169.76)	($264,601.59)	($143,002.29)	$235,398.41
15	7	($67,933.98)	($53,810.07)	($14,123.90)	($318,411.66)	($157,126.19)	$181,588.34
16	8	($67,933.98)	($57,038.68)	($10,895.30)	($375,450.34)	($168,021.49)	$124,549.66
17	9	($67,933.98)	($60,461.00)	($7,472.98)	($435,911.34)	($175,494.47)	$64,088.66
18	10	($67,933.98)	($64,088.66)	($3,845.32)	($500,000.00)	($179,339.79)	$0.00

Amortization Schedule   Dyna ...   +

FIGURE 14-6 This worksheet shows a basic amortization schedule for a fixed-rate loan.

The amortization schedule in Figure 14-6 assumes that the interest rate remains fixed throughout the life of the loan. To learn how to build an amortization schedule for a variable-rate loan, see "Building a variable-rate mortgage amortization schedule," later in this chapter.

Building a dynamic amortization schedule

The problem with the amortization schedule in Figure 14-6 is that it's static. It works well if you change the interest rate or the principal, but it doesn't handle other types of changes very well:

- If you want to use a different time basis—for example, monthly instead of annual—you need to edit the initial formulas for payment, principal, interest, cumulative principal, and cumulative interest, and then refill the schedule.

- If you want to use a different number of periods, you need to either extend the schedule (for a longer term) or shorten the schedule and delete the extraneous periods (for a shorter term).

Both operations are tedious and time-consuming enough that they greatly reduce the value of the amortization schedule. To make the schedule truly useful, you need to reconfigure it so that the schedule formulas and the schedule itself adjust automatically to any change in the time basis or the length of the term.

Figure 14-7 shows a worksheet that implements such a dynamic amortization schedule.

A11		f_x	=IF(A10 < $E$5, A10 + 1, "")			
	A	B	C	D	E	F	G
1	Loan Data						
2		Interest Rate	6.00%	Time Basis	Monthly ▼		4 Time Basis
3		Amortization	15	Time Factor	12		Annual
4		Principal	$500,000	Adjusted Rate	0.5%		Semi-Annual
5		Balloon Payment	$0	Total Periods	180		Quarterly
6		Payment Type	0				Monthly
7							
8	Amortization Schedule						
9	Period	Payment	Principal	Interest	Cumulative Principal	Cumulative Interest	Remaining Principal
10	1	($4,219.28)	($1,719.28)	($2,500.00)	($1,719.28)	($2,491.40)	$498,280.72
11	2	($4,219.28)	($1,727.88)	($2,491.40)	($3,447.16)	($4,991.40)	$496,552.84
12	3	($4,219.28)	($1,736.52)	($2,482.76)	($5,183.68)	($7,474.17)	$494,816.32
13	4	($4,219.28)	($1,745.20)	($2,474.08)	($6,928.89)	($9,948.25)	$493,071.11
14	5	($4,219.28)	($1,753.93)	($2,465.36)	($8,682.82)	($12,413.60)	$491,317.18
15	6	($4,219.28)	($1,762.70)	($2,456.59)	($10,445.51)	($14,870.19)	$489,554.49
16	7	($4,219.28)	($1,771.51)	($2,447.77)	($12,217.03)	($17,317.96)	$487,782.97
17	8	($4,219.28)	($1,780.37)	($2,438.91)	($13,997.40)	($19,756.88)	$486,002.60
18	9	($4,219.28)	($1,789.27)	($2,430.01)	($15,786.67)	($22,186.89)	$484,213.33
19	10	($4,219.28)	($1,798.22)	($2,421.07)	($17,584.88)	($24,607.96)	$482,415.12

‹ › ⋯ Dynamic Amortization Schedule ⋯ +

FIGURE 14-7 This worksheet uses a dynamic amortization schedule that adjusts automatically to changing the time basis or the length of the term.

Here's a summary of the changes you make to create this schedule's dynamic behavior:

- To change the time basis, select a value—**Annual**, **Semi-Annual**, **Quarterly**, or **Monthly**—in the **Time Basis** drop-down menu. These values come from the text literals in the range G3:G6. The number of the selected list item is stored in cell F2.

- The time basis determines the *time factor*, the amount by which you have to adjust the rate and the term. For example, if the time basis is **Monthly**, the time factor is 12. This means that you divide the annual interest rate (C2) by 12, and you multiply the term (C3) by 12. These new values are stored in the Adjusted Rate (E4) and Total Periods (E5) cells. The Time Factor cell (E3) uses the following formula:

  `=CHOOSE(F2, 1, 2, 4, 12)`

- Given the adjusted rate (E4) and the total periods (E5), the schedule formulas can reference these cells directly and always return the correct value for any selected time basis. For example, here's the formula that calculates the payment:

  `=PMT(E4, E5, C4, C5, C6)`

- The schedule adjusts its size automatically, depending on the Total Periods value (E5). If Total Periods is 15, the schedule contains 15 rows (not including the headers); if Total Periods is 180, the schedule contains 180 rows.

- Dynamically adjusting the size of the schedule is a function of the Total Periods value (E5). The first period (A10) is always 1; each subsequent period checks the previous value to see if it's less than Total Periods. Here's the formula in cell A11:

  `=IF(A10 < $E$5, A10 + 1, "")`

  If the period value of the cell above the current cell is less than Total Periods, the current cell is still within the schedule, so calculate the current period (the value from the cell above plus 1) and display the result; otherwise, you've gone past the end of the schedule, so display a blank.

- The various payment columns check the period value. If It's not blank, calculate and display the result; otherwise, display a blank. Here's the formula for the Payment value in B11:

  `=IF(A11 <> "", PMT($E$4, $E$5, $C$4, $C$5, $C$6), "")`

These changes result in a totally dynamic schedule that adjusts automatically as you change the time basis or the term.

> **Note** The formulas in the amortization schedule have been filled down to row 500, which should be enough room for just about any schedule (up to about 40 years, using the monthly basis). If you require a longer schedule, you have to fill in the schedule formulas past the last row that will appear in your schedule.

Calculating the term of a loan

In some loan scenarios, you need to borrow a certain amount at the current interest rates, but you can spend only so much on each payment. If the other loan factors are fixed, the only way to adjust the payment is to adjust the term of the loan: A longer term means smaller payments; a shorter term means larger payments.

You could figure out the term by adjusting the *nper* argument of the PMT function until you get the payment you want. However, Excel offers a more direct solution in the form of the NPER function, which returns the number of periods of a loan:

NPER(*rate*, *pmt*, *pv*[, *fv*][, *type*])

rate	The fixed rate of interest over the term of the loan.
pmt	The periodic payment.
pv	The loan principal.
fv	The future value of the loan. (The default is **0**.)
type	The type of payment. Use **0** (the default) for end-of-period payments; use **1** for beginning-of-period payments.

For example, suppose that you want to borrow $10,000 at 6 percent interest with no balloon payment, and the most you can spend is $750 per month. What term should you get? Figure 14-8 shows a worksheet that uses NPER to calculate the answer: 13.8 months. Here are some things to note about this model:

- The interest rate is an annual value, so the NPER function's *rate* argument divides the rate by 12.

- The payment is already a monthly number, so no adjustment is necessary for the *pmt* attribute.

- The payment is negative because it's money that you pay to the lender.

B7	⌄ ⠇ ✕ ✓ *fx*	=NPER(B2 / 12, B3, B4, B5, B6)					
	A	B	C	D	E	F	G
1	Loan Term Analysis						
2	Interest Rate (Annual)	6.00%					
3	Payment (Monthly)	($750)					
4	Principal	$10,000					
5	Balloon Payment	$0					
6	Type	0					
7	Term (Months)	13.8					
9	Ending the Loan After 13 Months				Ending the Loan After 14 Months		
10	Period	Principal	Cumulative Principal		Period	Principal	Cumulative Principal
11	1	($700.00)	($700.00)		1	($700.00)	($700.00)
12	2	($703.50)	($1,403.50)		2	($703.50)	($1,403.50)
13	3	($707.02)	($2,110.52)		3	($707.02)	($2,110.52)
14	4	($710.55)	($2,821.07)		4	($710.55)	($2,821.07)
15	5	($714.11)	($3,535.18)		5	($714.11)	($3,535.18)
16	6	($717.68)	($4,252.85)		6	($717.68)	($4,252.85)
17	7	($721.26)	($4,974.12)		7	($721.26)	($4,974.12)
18	8	($724.87)	($5,698.99)		8	($724.87)	($5,698.99)
19	9	($728.49)	($6,427.48)		9	($728.49)	($6,427.48)
20	10	($732.14)	($7,159.62)		10	($732.14)	($7,159.62)
21	11	($735.80)	($7,895.42)		11	($735.80)	($7,895.42)
22	12	($739.48)	($8,634.89)		12	($739.48)	($8,634.89)
23	13	($743.17)	($9,378.07)		13	($743.17)	($9,378.07)
24	Remaining Principal After 13 Months		($621.93)		14	($746.89)	($10,124.96)
25	Future Value After 13 Months		($621.93)	Overpayment Principal After 14 Months			$124.96
26				Future Value After 14 Months			$124.96
	‹ › ⋯ Loan Term Analysis Loan Rate ⋯ +						

FIGURE 14-8 This worksheet uses NPER to determine the number of months that a $10,000 loan should be taken out at 6 percent interest to ensure a monthly payment of $750.

Of course, in the real world, although it's not unusual to have a noninteger term, the last payment must occur at the beginning or end of the last loan period. In the example, the bank uses the term 13.8 months to calculate the payment, principal, and interest, but it rightly insists that the last payment be made at either the 13th or 14th period. The tables after the NPER formula in Figure 14-8 investigate both scenarios.

If you elect to end the loan after the 13th period, you'll still have a bit of principal left over. To see why, the amortization table shows the period (column A) as well as the principal paid each period (column B), as returned by the PPMT function. The Cumulative Principal column (column C) shows a running total of the principal. As you can see, after 13 months, the total principal paid is only $9,378.07, which leaves $621.93 remaining (cell C24). Therefore, the 13th payment will be $1,371.93 (the usual $750 payment, plus the remaining $621.93 principal).

> **Note** The cumulative principal values are calculated using the SUM function. You can't use the CUMPRINC function in this case because CUMPRINC truncates the *nper* argument to an integer value.

If you elect to end the loan after the 14th period instead, you'll end up overpaying the principal. To see why, the second amortization table shows the Period (column E), Principal (column F), and Cumulative Principal (column G) columns. After 14 months, the total principal paid is $10,124.96, which is $124.96 more than the original $10,000 principal. Therefore, the 14th payment will be $625.04 (the usual $750 payment minus the $124.96 principal overpayment).

> **Note** Another way to calculate the principal that is left over or overpaid is to use the FV function, which returns the future value of a series of payments. For the 13-month scenario, you run FV with the *nper* argument set to 13 (see cell C25 in Figure 14-8); for the 14-month scenario, you run FV with the *nper* argument set to 14 (see cell G26). You'll learn about FV in detail in Chapter 15.

Calculating the interest rate required for a loan

A slightly less common loan scenario arises when you know the loan term, payment, and principal, and you need to know what interest rate will satisfy these parameters. This is useful in a number of circumstances:

- You might want to wait until interest rates fall to the value you want.

- You might regard the calculated interest rate as a maximum rate that you can pay, knowing that anything less will enable you to reduce either the payment or the term.

- You could use the calculated interest rate as a negotiating tool with your lender by asking for that rate and walking away from the deal if you don't get it.

To determine the interest rate given the other loan factors, use the **RATE** function:

```
RATE(nper, pmt, pv[, fv][, type][, guess])
```

Nper	The number of payments over the term of the loan.
Pmt	The periodic payment.
Pv	The loan principal.
Fv	The future value of the loan. (The default is **0**.)
Type	The type of payment. Use **0** (the default) for end-of-period payments; use **1** for beginning-of-period payments.
Guess	A percentage value that Excel uses as a starting point for calculating the interest rate. (The default is 10 percent.)

The **RATE** function's *guess* argument indicates that this function uses iteration to determine the answer. To learn more about iteration, see "Using iteration and circular references," in Chapter 2, "Creating advanced formulas."

For example, suppose you want to borrow $10,000 over five years with no balloon payment and a monthly payout of $200. What rate will satisfy these criteria? The worksheet in Figure 14-9 uses **RATE** to derive the result: 7.4 percent. Here are some notes about this model:

- The term is in years, so the **RATE** function's *nper* argument multiplies the term by 12.

- The payment is already a monthly number, so no adjustment is necessary for the *pmt* attribute.

- The payment is negative because it's money that you pay to the lender.

- The result of the **RATE** function is multiplied by 12 to get the annual interest rate.

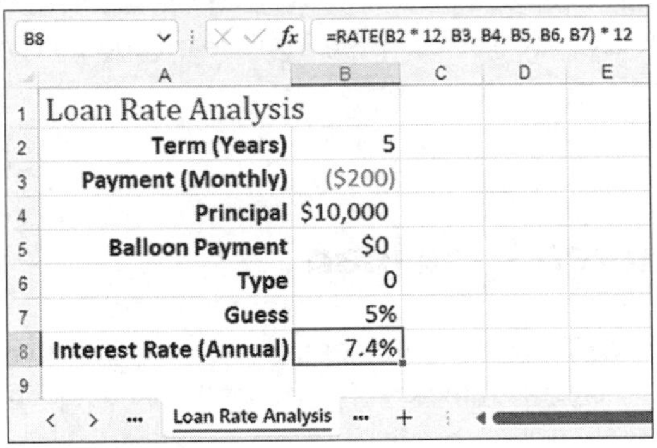

FIGURE 14-9 This worksheet uses RATE to determine the interest rate required to pay a $10,000 loan over five years at $200 per month.

Calculating how much you can borrow

If you know the current interest rate your bank is offering for loans, when you want to have the loan paid off, and how much you can afford each month for the payments, you might then wonder what is the maximum amount you can borrow under those terms. To figure this out, you need to solve for the principal—that is, present value. You do this in Excel by using the **PV** function:

```
PV(rate, nper, pmt[, fv][, type])
```

rate	The fixed rate of interest over the term of the loan.
nper	The number of payments over the term of the loan.
pmt	The periodic payment.
fv	The future value of the loan. (The default is **0**.)
type	The type of payment. Use **0** (the default) for end-of-period payments; use **1** for beginning-of-period payments.

For example, suppose the current loan rate is 6 percent, you want the loan paid off in five years, and you can afford payments of $500 per month. Figure 14-10 shows a worksheet that calculates the maximum amount you can borrow—$25,862.78—using the following formula:

```
=PV(B2 / 12, B3 * 12, B4, B5, B6)
```

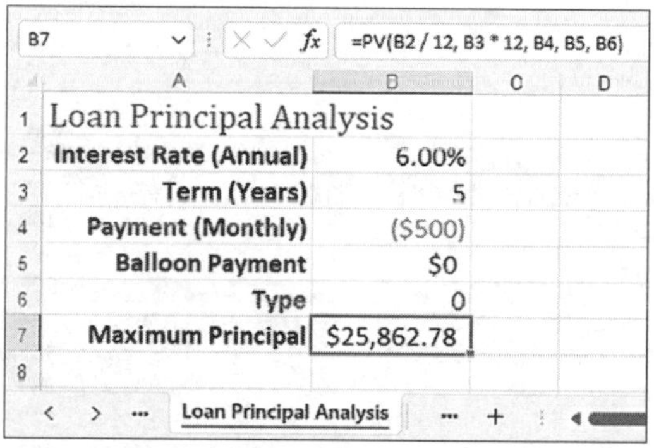

FIGURE 14-10 This worksheet uses PV to calculate the maximum principal you can borrow, given a fixed interest rate, term, and monthly payment.

Case study: Working with mortgages

For both businesses and people, a mortgage is almost always the largest financial transaction. Whether it's millions of dollars for a new building or hundreds of thousands of dollars for a house, a mortgage is serious business. It pays to know exactly what you're getting into, both in terms of long-term cash flow and in terms of making good decisions up front about the type of mortgage so that you minimize your interest costs. This case study looks at mortgages from both points of view.

Building a variable-rate mortgage amortization schedule

For simplicity's sake, it's possible to build a mortgage amortization schedule like the ones shown earlier in this chapter. However, these are not always realistic because a mortgage rarely uses the same interest rate over the full amortization period. Instead, you usually have a fixed rate over a specific *term* (usually one to five years), and you then renegotiate the mortgage for a new term. This renegotiation involves changing three things:

- The interest rate over the coming term, which will reflect current market rates.

- The amortization period, which will now be shorter by the length of the previous term. For example, a 25-year amortization will drop to a 20-year amortization after a 5-year term.

- The present value of the mortgage, which will be the remaining principal at the end of the term.

Figure 14-11 shows an amortization schedule that takes these mortgage realities into account.

E11			f_x	=PMT(C11, D11, OFFSET(E11, -B11, 5), 0, $B$6)						
A	B	C	D	E	F	G	H	I		J

Initial Mortgage Data

Interest Rate	6.00%	per annum
Amortization	25	years
Term	5	years
Principal	$100,000	
Payment Type	0	

Amortization Schedule

Amortization Year	Term Period	Interest Rate	NPER	Payment	Principal	Interest	Cumulative Principal	Cumulative Interest	Remaining Principal
0	0								$100,000.00
1	1	6.0%	25	($7,822.67)	($1,822.67)	($6,000.00)	($1,822.67)	($6,000.00)	$98,177.33
2	2	6.0%	25	($7,822.67)	($1,932.03)	($5,890.64)	($3,754.70)	($11,890.64)	$96,245.30
3	3	6.0%	25	($7,822.67)	($2,047.95)	($5,774.72)	($5,802.66)	($17,665.36)	$94,197.34
4	4	6.0%	25	($7,822.67)	($2,170.83)	($5,651.84)	($7,973.49)	($23,317.20)	$92,026.51
5	5	6.0%	25	($7,822.67)	($2,301.08)	($5,521.59)	($10,274.57)	($28,838.79)	$89,725.43
6	1	7.0%	20	($8,469.45)	($2,188.67)	($6,280.78)	($12,463.24)	($35,119.57)	$87,536.76
7	2	7.0%	20	($8,469.45)	($2,341.87)	($6,127.57)	($14,805.11)	($41,247.14)	$85,194.89
8	3	7.0%	20	($8,469.45)	($2,505.80)	($5,963.64)	($17,310.91)	($47,210.78)	$82,689.09
9	4	7.0%	20	($8,469.45)	($2,681.21)	($5,788.24)	($19,992.12)	($52,999.02)	$80,007.88
10	5	7.0%	20	($8,469.45)	($2,868.89)	($5,600.55)	($22,861.02)	($58,599.57)	$77,138.98
11	1	8.0%	15	($9,012.11)	($2,840.99)	($6,171.12)	($25,702.01)	($64,770.69)	$74,297.99
12	2	8.0%	15	($9,012.11)	($3,068.27)	($5,943.84)	($28,770.28)	($70,714.53)	$71,229.72

‹ › ⋯ Mortgage Amortization Schedule Mortgage Paydow ⋯ +

FIGURE 14-11 This mortgage amortization schedule reflects the changing interest rates, amortization periods, and present value at each new term.

Here's a summary of what's happening with each column in the amortization:

- **Amortization Year:** This column gives the year of the overall amortization. This is mainly used to help calculate the Term Period values. Note that the values in this column are generated automatically based on the value in the Amortization (Years) cell (B3).

- **Term Period:** This column gives the year of the current term. This is a calculated value (it uses the MOD function) based on the value in the Amortization Year column and the value in the Term (Years) cell (B4).

- **Interest Rate:** This is the interest rate applied to each term. You enter these rates by hand.

- **NPER:** This is the amortization period applied to each term. It's used as the *nper* argument for the PMT, PPMT, and IPMT functions. You enter these values by hand.

- **Payment:** This is the monthly payment for the current term. The PMT function uses the Interest Rate column value for the *rate* argument and the NPER column value for the *nper* argument. For the *pv* argument, the function grabs the remaining balance at the end of the previous term by using the OFFSET function in the following general form:

```
OFFSET(current_cell, -Term_Period, 5)
```

In this formula, *current_cell* is a reference to the cell containing the formula, and *Term_Period* is a reference to the corresponding cell in the Term Period column. For example, here's the formula in E11:

```
OFFSET(E11, -B11, 5)
```

Because the value in B11 is **1**, the function goes up one row and right five columns, which returns the value in J10 (in this case, the original principal).

- **Principal and Interest:** These columns calculate the principal and interest components of the payment, and they use the same techniques as the Payment column.

- **Cumulative Principal and Cumulative Interest:** These columns calculate the total principal and interest paid through the end of each year. Because the interest rate isn't constant over the life of the loan, you can't use CUMPRINC and CUMIPMT. Instead, these columns use running SUM functions.

- **Remaining Principal:** This column calculates the principal left on the loan by subtracting the value in the Principal column for each year. At the end of each term, the Remaining Principal value is used as the *pv* argument in the PMT, PPMT, and IPMT functions over the next term. In Figure 14-11, for example, at the end of the first five-year term, the remaining principal is $89,725.43, so that's the present value used throughout the second five-year term.

Allowing for mortgage principal paydowns

Many mortgages today allow you to include in each payment an extra amount that goes directly to paying down the mortgage principal. Before you decide to take on the financial burden of these extra paydowns, you probably want two questions answered:

- How much more quickly will I pay off the mortgage?

- How much money will I save over the amortization period?

Both questions are easily answered using Excel's financial functions. Consider the mortgage-analysis model I've set up in Figure 14-12. The Initial Mortgage Data area shows the basic numbers needed for the calculations: the annual interest rate (cell B2), the amortization period (B3), the principal (B4), and the paydown that is to be added to each payment (B5; notice that this is a negative number because it represents a monetary outflow).

F10			f_x	=NPER(E4, F9, B4)			
	A	B	C	D	E	F	G
1	Initial Mortgage Data			Payment Adjustments			
2	Interest Rate (Annual)	6.00%		Payment Frequency	Monthly ▼	2	Annual
3	Amortization (Years)	25		Payments Per Year	12		Monthly
4	Principal	$100,000		Rate Per Payment	0.50%		Semi-Monthly
5	Paydown	($100.00)		Total Payments	300		Bi-Weekly
6							Weekly
7				Mortgage Analysis			
8					Regular Mortgage	With Extra Payment	
9				Monthly Payment	($644.30)	($744.30)	
10				Total Payments	300	223.4	
11				Total Paid	($193,290)	($166,251)	
12				Savings	-	$27,039	
13							
	< > ... Mortgage Paydown Analysis			+			

FIGURE 14-12 This mortgage-analysis worksheet calculates the effect of making extra monthly paydowns toward the principal.

The Payment Adjustments area contains four values:

- **Payment Frequency:** Use this drop-down menu to specify how often you make your mortgage payments. The available values—Annual, Monthly, Semi-Monthly, Bi-Weekly, and Weekly—come from the range G2:G6; the number of the selected list item is stored in cell F2.

- **Payments Per Year (E3):** This is the number of payments per year, as given by the following formula:

=CHOOSE(F2, 1, 12, 24, 26, 52)

- **Rate Per Payment:** This is the annual rate divided by the number of payments per year.

- **Total Payments:** This is the amortization value multiplied by the number of payments per year.

The Mortgage Analysis area shows the results of various calculations:

- **Frequency Payment (*Frequency* is the selected item in the drop-down menu):** The Regular Mortgage payment (E9) is calculated using the PMT function, where the *rate* argument is the Rate Per Payment value (E4) and the *nper* argument is the Total Payments value (E5):

=PMT(E4, E5, B4, 0, 0)

The With Extra Payment value (F9) is the sum of the Paydown (B5) and the Regular Mortgage payment (E9).

- **Total Payments:** For the Regular Mortgage (E10), this is the same as the Total Payments value (E5). It's copied here to make it easy for you to compare this value with the With Extra Payment value (F10), which calculates the revised term with the extra paydown included. It does this with the **NPER** function, where the *rate* argument is the Rate Per Payment value (E4) and the *pmt* argument is the payment in the With Extra Payment column (F9).

- **Total Paid:** These values multiply the Payment value by the Total Payments value for each column.

- **Savings:** This value (cell F12) takes the difference between the Total Paid values to show how much money you save by including the paydown in each payment.

In the example shown in Figure 14-12, paying an extra $100 per month toward the mortgage principal reduces the term on a $100,000 mortgage from 300 months (25 years) to 223.4 months (about 18.5 years) and reduces the total amount paid from $193,290 to $166,251, a savings of $27,039.

CHAPTER 15

Working with investment formulas

In this chapter, you will:

- Understand concepts such as compound, nominal, and effective interest rates

- Calculate the future value of an investment

- Learn formulas that enable you to work toward an investment goal

The time value of money concept introduced in Chapter 14, "Building loan formulas," applies equally well to investments. The only difference is that you need to reverse the signs of the cash values. That's because loans generally involve receiving a principal amount (positive cash flow) and paying it back over time (negative cash flow). An investment, on the other hand, involves depositing money into the investment (negative cash flow) and then receiving interest payments (or whatever) in return (positive cash flow).

With this sign change in mind, this chapter takes you through some Excel tools for building investment formulas. You'll learn about the wonders of compound interest; how to convert between nominal and effective interest rates; how to calculate the future value of an investment; ways to work toward an investment goal by calculating the required interest rate, term, and deposits; and how to build an investment schedule.

Working with interest rates

As I mentioned in Chapter 14, the interest rate is the mechanism that transforms a present value into a future value. (Or, operating as a discount rate, it's what transforms a future value into a present value.) Therefore, when working with financial formulas, it's important to know how to work with interest rates and to be comfortable with certain terminology. You've already seen (again, in Chapter 14) that it's crucial for the interest rate, term, and payment to use the same time basis. The next sections show you a few other interest rate techniques you should know.

Understanding compound interest

An interest rate is described as *simple* if it pays the same amount each period. For example, if you have $1,000 in an investment that pays a simple interest rate of 10 percent per year, you'll receive $100 each year.

Suppose, however, that you were able to add the interest payments to the investment. At the end of the first year, you would have $1,100 in the account, which means you would earn $110 in interest (10 percent of $1,100) the second year. Being able to add interest earned to an investment is called *compounding*, and the total interest earned (the normal interest plus the extra interest on the reinvested interest—the extra $10, in the example) is called *compound interest*.

Nominal versus effective interest

Interest can also be compounded within the year. For example, suppose that your $1,000 investment earns 10 percent compounded semiannually. At the end of the first six months, you receive $50 in interest (5 percent of the original investment). This $50 is reinvested, and for the second half of the year, you earn 5 percent of $1,050, or $52.50. Therefore, the total interest earned in the first year is $102.50. In other words, the interest rate appears to actually be 10.25 percent. So which is the correct interest rate, 10 percent or 10.25 percent?

To answer that question, you need to know about the two ways that most interest rates are most often quoted:

- **The nominal rate:** This is the annual rate before compounding (the 10 percent rate, in the example). The nominal rate is always quoted along with the compounding frequency—for example, 10 percent compounded semiannually.

> **Note** The nominal annual interest rate is often shortened to APR, or the annual percentage rate.

- **The effective rate:** This is the annual rate that an investment actually earns in the year after the compounding is applied (the 10.25 percent, in the example).

In other words, both rates are "correct," except that, with the nominal rate, you also need to know the compounding frequency.

If you know the nominal rate and the number of compounding periods per year (for example, semi-annually means 2 compounding periods per year, and monthly means 12 compounding periods per year), you get the effective rate per period by dividing the nominal rate by the number of periods:

```
=nominal_rate / npery
```

Here, *npery* is the number of compounding periods per year. To convert the nominal annual rate into the effective annual rate, you use the following formula:

```
=(1 + nominal_rate / npery) ^ npery - 1
```

Conversely, if you know the effective rate per period, you can derive the nominal rate by multiplying the effective rate by the number of periods:

```
=effective_rate * npery
```

To convert the effective annual rate to the nominal annual rate, you use the following formula:

```
=npery * (effective_rate + 1) ^ (1 / npery) - npery
```

Fortunately, the next section shows you two functions that can handle the conversion between the nominal and effective annual rates for you.

Converting between the nominal rate and the effective rate

To convert a nominal annual interest rate to the effective annual rate, use the **EFFECT** function:

EFFECT(*nominal_rate*, *npery*)

nominal_rate	The nominal annual interest rate
npery	The number of compounding periods in the year

For example, the following formula returns the effective annual interest rate for an investment with a nominal annual rate of 10 percent that compounds semiannually:

```
=EFFECT(0.1, 2)
```

Figure 15-1 shows a worksheet that applies the **EFFECT** function to a 10 percent nominal annual rate using various compounding frequencies.

> **Note**   You can work with all the examples in this chapter by downloading Chapter15.xslx from either of the companion content sites mentioned in the Introduction.

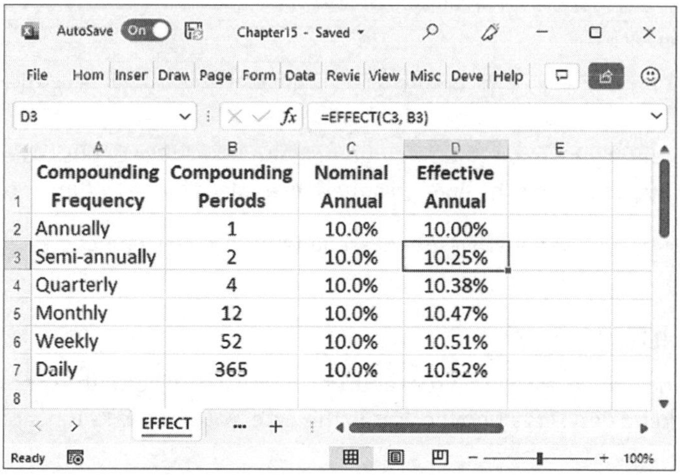

FIGURE 15-1 The formulas in column D use the EFFECT function to convert the nominal rates in column C to effective rates based on the compounding periods in column B.

If you already know the effective annual interest rate and the number of compounding periods, you can convert the rate to the nominal annual interest rate by using the **NOMINAL** function:

```
NOMINAL(effect_rate, npery)
```

effect_rate	The effective annual interest rate
npery	The number of compounding periods in the year

For example, the following formula returns the nominal annual interest rate for an investment with an effective annual rate of 10.52 percent that compounds daily:

```
=NOMINAL(0.1052, 365)
```

Calculating the future value

Just as the payment is usually the most important value for a loan calculation, the future value is usually the most important value for an investment calculation. After all, the purpose of an investment is to place a sum of money (the present value) in some instrument for a time, after which you end up with some new (and hopefully greater) amount: the future value.

To calculate the future value of an investment, Excel offers the **FV** function:

```
FV(rate, nper[, pmt][, pv][, type])
```

rate	The fixed rate of interest over the term of the investment.
nper	The number of periods in the term of the investment.
pmt	The amount deposited in the investment each period. (The default is **0**.)
pv	The initial deposit. (The default is **0**.)
type	The type of deposit. Use **0** (the default) for end-of-period deposits; use **1** for beginning-of-period deposits.

Because both the amount deposited per period (the *pmt* argument) and the initial deposit (the *pv* argument) are sums that you pay out, these must be entered as negative values in the **FV** function.

The next few sections take you through various investment scenarios using the **FV** function.

The future value of a lump sum

In the simplest future value scenario, you invest a lump sum and let it grow according to the specified interest rate and term, without adding deposits along the way. In this case, you use the **FV** function with the *pmt* argument set to **0**:

```
FV(rate, nper, 0, pv, type)
```

For example, Figure 15-2 shows the future value of $10,000 invested at 5 percent over 10 years.

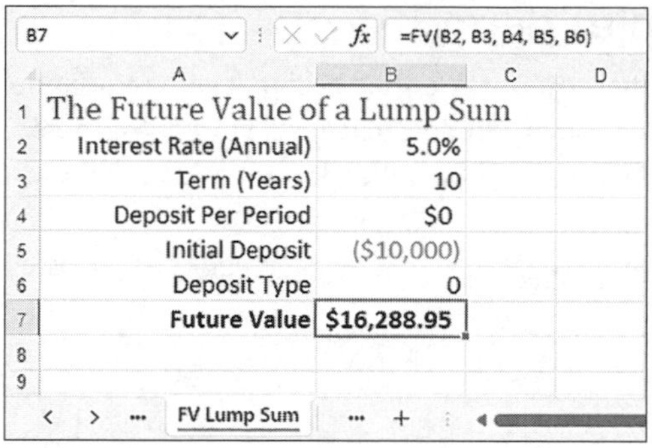

FIGURE 15-2 When calculating the future value of an initial lump sum deposit, set the FV function's *pmt* argument to 0.

> **Tip** Excel's **FV** function doesn't work with continuous compounding. Instead, you need to use a worksheet formula that takes the following general form (where **e** is the mathematical constant *e*):
>
> ```
> =pv * e ^ (rate * nper)
> ```
>
> For example, the following formula calculates the future value of $10,000 invested at 5 percent over 10 years compounded continuously (and it returns a value of $16,487.21):
>
> ```
> =10000 * EXP(0.05 * 10)
> ```

The future value of a series of deposits

Another common investment scenario is to make a series of deposits over the investment term without depositing an initial sum. In this case, you use the **FV** function with the *pv* argument set to **0**:

```
FV(rate, nper, pmt, 0, type)
```

For example, Figure 15-3 shows the future value of $100 invested each month at 5 percent over 10 years. Notice that the interest rate and term are both converted to monthly amounts because the deposit occurs monthly.

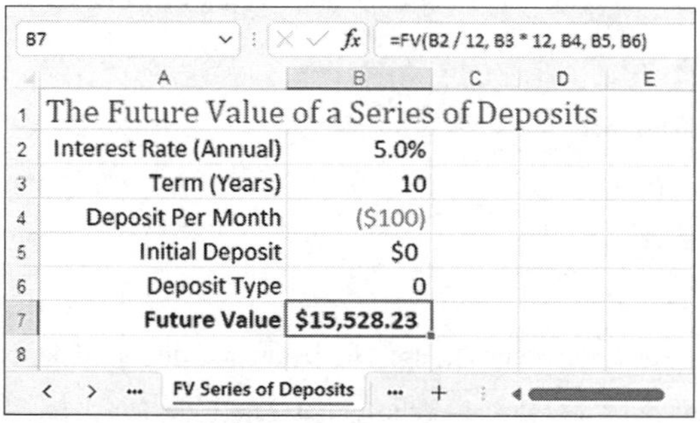

FIGURE 15-3 When calculating the future value of a series of deposits, set the FV function's *pv* argument to 0.

The future value of a lump sum plus deposits

For best investment results, you should invest an initial amount and then add to it with regular deposits. In this scenario, you need to specify all the FV function arguments (except *type*). For example, Figure 15-4 shows the future value of an investment with a $10,000 initial deposit and $100 monthly deposits at 5 percent over 10 years.

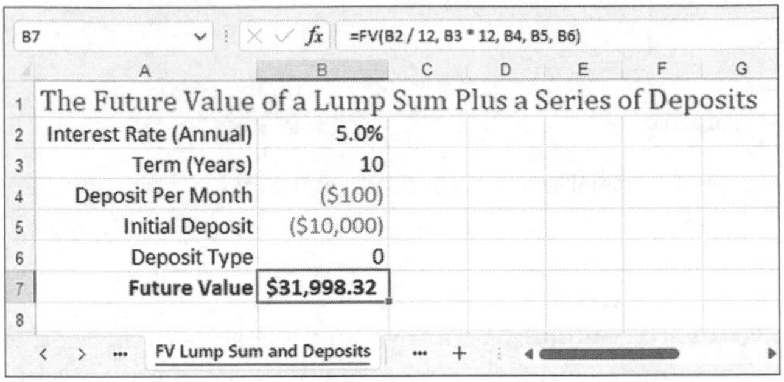

FIGURE 15-4 This worksheet uses the full FV function syntax to calculate the future value of a lump sum plus a series of deposits.

Working toward an investment goal

Instead of just seeing where an investment will end up, it's often desirable to have a specific monetary goal in mind and then ask yourself, "What will it take to get me there?"

Answering this question means solving for one of the four main future value parameters—interest rate, number of periods, regular deposit, and initial deposit—while holding the other parameters (and, of course, your future value goal) constant. The next four sections take you through this process.

Calculating the required interest rate

Say that you know the future value you want, when you want it, and the initial and periodic deposits you can afford. What interest rate do you require to meet your goal? You answer this question by using the RATE function, which you first encountered in Chapter 14. Here's the syntax for that function from the point of view of an investment:

RATE(*nper*, *pmt*, *pv*, *fv*[, *type*][, *guess*])

nper	The number of deposits over the term of the investment.
pmt	The amount invested with each deposit.
pv	The initial investment.
fv	The future value of the investment.
type	The type of deposit. Use **0** (the default) for end-of-period deposits; use **1** for beginning-of-period deposits.
guess	A percentage value that Excel uses as a starting point for calculating the interest rate. (The default is 10 percent.)

For example, if you need $100,000 10 years from now, you are starting with $10,000, and you can deposit $500 per month. What interest rate is required to meet your goal? Figure 15-5 shows a worksheet that comes up with the answer: 6 percent.

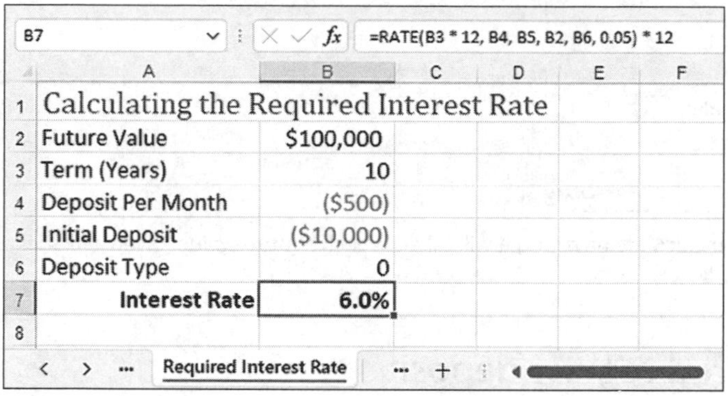

B7		fx	=RATE(B3 * 12, B4, B5, B2, B6, 0.05) * 12		
	A	B	C	D	E	F
1	Calculating the Required Interest Rate					
2	Future Value	$100,000				
3	Term (Years)	10				
4	Deposit Per Month	($500)				
5	Initial Deposit	($10,000)				
6	Deposit Type	0				
7	Interest Rate	6.0%				
8						

‹ › ⋯ Required Interest Rate ⋯ + ⋮ ◀

FIGURE 15-5 Use the RATE function to work out the interest rate required to reach a future value, given a fixed term, a periodic deposit, and an initial deposit.

Calculating the required number of periods

Given your investment goal, if you have an initial deposit and an amount that you can afford to deposit periodically, how long will it take to reach your goal at the prevailing market interest rate? You answer this question by using the **NPER** function (which was introduced in Chapter 14). Here's the **NPER** syntax from the point of view of an investment:

NPER(*rate*, *pmt*, *pv*, *fv*[, *type*])

rate	The fixed rate of interest over the term of the investment.
pmt	The amount invested with each deposit.
pv	The initial investment.
fv	The future value of the investment.
type	The type of deposit. Use **0** (the default) for end-of-period deposits; use **1** for beginning-of-period deposits.

For example, suppose that you want to retire with $1,000,000. You have $50,000 to invest, you can afford to deposit $1,000 per month, and you expect to earn 5 percent interest. How long will it take to reach your goal? The worksheet in Figure 15-6 answers this question: 349.4 months, or 29.1 years.

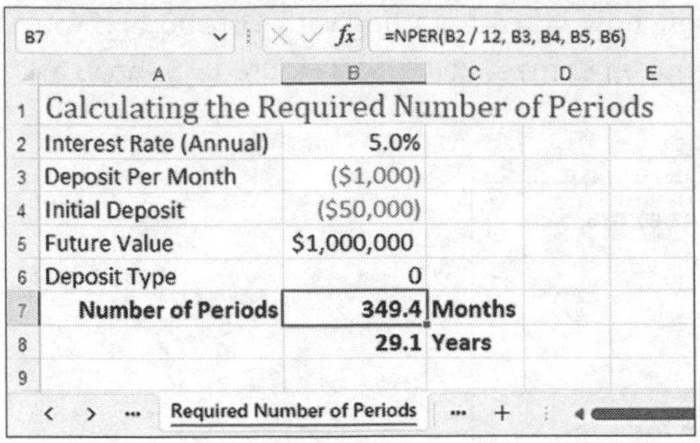

FIGURE 15-6 Use the NPER function to calculate how long it will take to reach a future value, given a fixed interest rate, a periodic deposit, and an initial deposit.

Calculating the required regular deposit

Suppose that you want to reach your future value goal by a certain date and that you have an initial amount to invest. Given current interest rates, how much extra do you have to periodically deposit into the investment to achieve your goal? The answer here lies in the **PMT** function from Chapter 14. Here are the **PMT** function details from the point of view of an investment:

PMT(*rate*, *nper*, *pv*, *fv*[, *type*])

rate	The fixed rate of interest over the term of the investment.
nper	The number of deposits over the term of the investment.
pv	The initial investment.
fv	The future value of the investment.
type	The type of deposit. Use **0** (the default) for end-of-period deposits; use **1** for beginning-of-period deposits.

For example, suppose you want to end up with $50,000 in 15 years to finance your child's college education. If you have no initial deposit and you expect to get 4 percent interest over the term of the investment, how much do you need to deposit each month to reach your target? Figure 15-7 shows a worksheet that calculates the result using **PMT**: $203.18 per month.

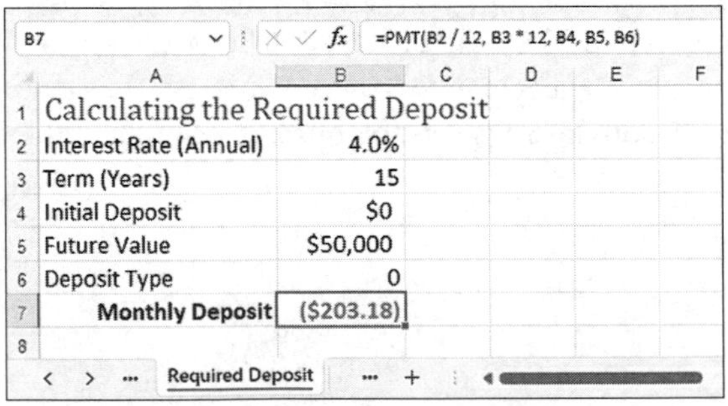

FIGURE 15-7 Use the PMT function to derive how much you need to deposit periodically to reach a future value, given a fixed interest rate, a number of deposits, and an initial deposit.

Calculating the required initial deposit

For the final standard future value calculation, suppose that you know when you want to reach your goal, how much you can deposit each period, and how much the interest rate will be. What, then, do you need to deposit initially to achieve your future value target? To find the answer, you use the **PV** function. Here are the **PV** function details from the point of view of an investment:

PV(*rate, nper, pmt, fv[, type]*)

rate	The fixed rate of interest over the term of the investment.
nper	The number of deposits over the term of the investment.
pmt	The amount invested with each deposit.
fv	The future value of the investment.
type	The type of deposit. Use **0** (the default) for end-of-period deposits; use **1** for beginning-of-period deposits.

For example, suppose your goal is to end up with $100,000 in three years to purchase new equipment. If you expect to earn 6 percent interest and can deposit $2,000 monthly, what does your initial deposit have to be to make your goal? The worksheet in Figure 15-8 uses **PV** to calculate the answer: $17,822.46.

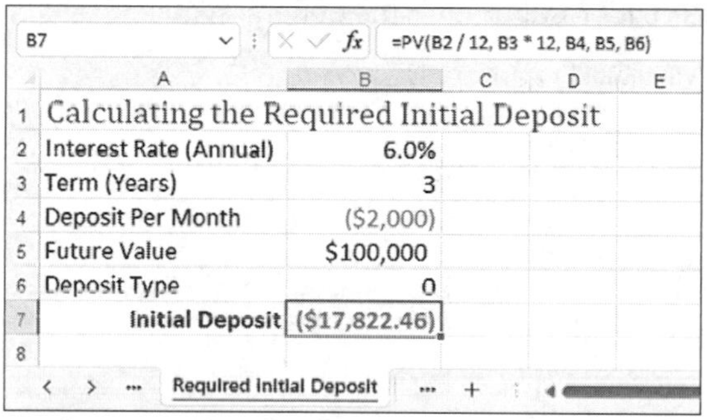

FIGURE 15-8 Use the PV function to find out how much you need to deposit initially to reach a future value, given a fixed interest rate, number of deposits, and periodic deposit.

Calculating the future value with varying interest rates

All the future value examples that you've worked with so far have assumed that the interest rate remained constant over the term of the investment. This will always be true for fixed-rate investments, but for other investments, such as mutual funds, stocks, and bonds, using a fixed rate of interest is, at best, a guess about what the average rate will be over the term.

For investments that offer a variable rate over the term, or when the rate fluctuates over the term, Excel offers the **FVSCHEDULE** function, which returns the future value of some initial amount, given a schedule of interest rates:

FVSCHEDULE(*principal*, *schedule*)

principal	The initial investment
schedule	A range or an array containing the interest rates

For example, the following formula returns the future value of an initial $10,000 deposit that makes 5 percent, 6 percent, and 7 percent over three years:

=FVSCHEDULE(10000, {0.05, 0.06, 0.07})

Similarly, Figure 15-9 shows a worksheet that calculates the future value of an initial deposit of $100,000 into an investment that earns 5 percent, 5.5 percent, 6 percent, 7 percent, and 6 percent over five years.

> **Note** If you want to know the average rate earned on the investment, use the **RATE** function, where *nper* is the number of values in the interest rate schedule, *pmt* is **0**, *pv* is the initial deposit, and *fv* is the negative of the **FVSCHEDULE** result. Here's the general syntax:
>
> RATE(ROWS(*schedule*), 0, *principal*, -FVSCHEDULE(*principal*, *schedule*))

B9			*fx*	=FVSCHEDULE(B2, B4:B8)				
	A	B	C	D	E	F	G	H
1	Calculating the Future Value with Varying Interest Rates							
2	**Principal**	$100,000						
3	**Rates:**							
4	2021	5.0%						
5	2022	5.5%						
6	2023	6.0%						
7	2024	7.0%						
8	2025	6.0%						
9	**Future Value**	$133,179.47						
10	**Average Rate**	5.9%						
11								

FIGURE 15-9 Use the FVSCHEDULE function to return the future value of an initial deposit in an investment that earns varying rates of interest.

Case study: Building an investment schedule

If you're planning future cash-flow requirements or future retirement needs, it's often not enough just to know how much money you'll have at the end of an investment. You also might need to know how much money is in the investment account or fund at each period throughout the life of the investment.

To do this, you need to build an *investment schedule.* This is similar to an amortization schedule, except it shows the future value of an investment at each period in the term of the investment. (To learn about amortization schedules, see "Building a loan amortization schedule," in Chapter 14.)

In a typical investment schedule, you need to take two things into account:

- The periodic deposits put into the investment, particularly the amount deposited and the frequency of the deposits. The frequency of the deposits determines the total number of periods in the investment. For example, a 10-year investment with semiannual deposits has 20 periods.

- The compounding frequency of the investment (annually, semiannually, and so on). Assuming that you know the APR (that is, nominal annual interest rate), you can use the compounding frequency to determine the effective rate.

Note, however, that you can't simply use the EFFECT function to convert the known nominal rate into the effective rate. That's because you're going to calculate the future value at the end of each period, which might or might not correspond to the compounding frequency. (For example, if the investment compounds monthly and you deposit semiannually, there will be six months of compounding to factor into the future value at the end of each period.)

Getting the proper effective rate for each period requires three steps:

1. Use the EFFECT function to convert the nominal annual rate into the effective annual rate, based on the compounding frequency.

2. Use the NOMINAL function to convert the effective rate from step 1 into the nominal rate based on the deposit frequency.

3. Divide the nominal rate from step 2 by the deposit frequency to get the effective rate per period. This is the value that you'll plug in to the FV function.

Figure 15-10 shows a worksheet that implements an investment schedule using this technique.

	A	B	C	D	E	F
			fx	=FV($D$6, A11, $B$5, $B$4, $B$6)		
1	Investment Data					
2	Nominal Rate (APR)	6.00%	Deposit Frequency	Annually ▾	1	Annually
3	Term (Years)	10	Deposits Per Year	1		Semi-Annually
4	Initial Deposit	($100,000)	Compounding Frequency	Semi-Annually ▾	2	Quarterly
5	Periodic Deposit	($5,000)	Compounds Per Year	2		Monthly
6	Deposit Type	0	Effective Rate Per Period	6.09%		Weekly
7			Total Periods	10		Daily
8						
9	Investment Schedule					
10	Period	Interest Earned	Cumulative Interest	Cumulative Deposits	Total Increase	Future Value
11	1	$6,090.00	$6,090.00	$5,000.00	$11,090.00	$111,090.00
12	2	$6,765.38	$12,855.38	$10,000.00	$22,855.38	$122,855.38
13	3	$7,481.89	$20,337.27	$15,000.00	$35,337.27	$135,337.27
14	4	$8,242.04	$28,579.31	$20,000.00	$48,579.31	$148,579.31
15	5	$9,048.48	$37,627.79	$25,000.00	$62,627.79	$162,627.79
16	6	$9,904.03	$47,531.83	$30,000.00	$77,531.83	$177,531.83
17	7	$10,811.69	$58,343.51	$35,000.00	$93,343.51	$193,343.51
18	8	$11,774.62	$70,118.13	$40,000.00	$110,118.13	$210,118.13
19	9	$12,796.19	$82,914.33	$45,000.00	$127,914.33	$227,914.33
20	10	$13,879.98	$96,794.31	$50,000.00	$146,794.31	$246,794.31
21						

< > ⋯ Investment Schedule +

FIGURE 15-10 An investment schedule that takes into account deposit frequency and compounding frequency to return the future value of an investment at the end of each deposit period.

Here's a summary of the items in the Investment Data portion of the worksheet:

- **Nominal Rate (APR) (B2):** This is the nominal annual rate of interest for the investment.

- **Term (Years) (B3):** This is the length of the investment in years.

- **Initial Deposit (B4):** This is the amount deposited at the start of the investment. Enter this as a negative number (because it's money that you're paying out).

- **Periodic Deposit (B5):** This is the amount deposited at each period of the investment. (Again, this number must be negative.)

- **Deposit Type (B6):** This is the *type* argument of the FV function.

- **Deposit Frequency:** Use this drop-down menu to specify how often the periodic deposits are made. The available values—**Annually**, **Semi-Annually**, **Quarterly**, **Monthly**, **Weekly**, and **Daily**—come from the range F2:F7; the number of the selected list item is stored in cell E2.

- **Deposits Per Year (D3):** This is the number of periods per year, as given by the following formula:

```
=CHOOSE(E2, 1, 2, 4, 12, 52, 365)
```

- **Compounding Frequency:** Use this drop-down menu to specify how often the investment compounds. You get the same options as in the **Deposit Frequency** menu. The number of the selected list item is stored in cell E4.

- **Compounds Per Year (D5):** This is the number of compounding periods per year, as given by the following formula:

  ```
  =CHOOSE(E4, 1, 2, 4, 12, 52, 365)
  ```

- **Effective Rate Per Period (D6):** This is the effective interest rate per period, as calculated using the three-step algorithm outlined earlier in this section. Here's the formula:

  ```
  =NOMINAL(EFFECT(B2, D5), D3) / D3
  ```

- **Total Periods (D7):** This is the total number of deposit periods in the loan, which is just the term multiplied by the number of deposits per year.

Here's a summary of the columns in the Investment Schedule portion of the worksheet:

- **Period (column A):** This is the period number of the investment. The Period values are generated automatically based on the Total Periods value (D7).

  The dynamic features used in the investment schedule are similar to those used in the dynamic amortization schedule that I talked about in Chapter 14. (See "Building a dynamic amortization schedule.")

- **Interest Earned (column B):** This is the interest earned during the period. It's calculated by multiplying the future value from the previous period by the Effective Rate Per Period (D6).

- **Cumulative Interest (column C):** This is the total interest earned in the investment at the end of each period. It's calculated by using a running sum of the values in the Interest Earned column.

- **Cumulative Deposits (column D):** This is the total amount of the deposits added to the investment at the end of each period. It's calculated by multiplying the Periodic Deposit (B5) by the current period number (column A).

- **Total Increase (column E):** This is the total amount by which the investment has increased over the Initial Deposit at the end of each period. It's calculated by adding the Cumulative Interest and the Cumulative Deposits.

- **Future Value (column F):** This is the value of the investment at the end of each period. Here's the FV formula for cell F11:

  ```
  =FV($D$6, A11, $B$5, $B$4, $B$6)
  ```

CHAPTER 16

Building discount formulas

In this chapter, you will:

- Learn how to calculate the present value

- See various ways to discount cash flows, including calculating the net present value

- Determine the payback period where you recoup an initial outlay

- Calculate the internal rate of return for an investment

Chapter 15, "Working with investment formulas," explains that investment calculations largely use the same time-value-of-money concepts as the loan calculations in Chapter 14, "Building loan formulas." The difference is the direction of the cash flows. For example, the present value of a loan is a positive cash flow because the money comes to you; the present value of an investment is a negative cash flow because the money goes out to the investment.

Discounting also fits into the time-value-of-money scheme and you can see its relation to present value, future value, and interest earned in the following equations:

Future value = Present value + Interest

Present value = Future value − Discount

Chapter 14's "Calculating how much you can borrow" section explains a form of discounting when you determined how much money you could borrow (the present value) when you know the current interest rate that your bank offers for loans, when you want to have the loan paid off, and how much you can afford each month for the payments.

Similarly, Chapter 15's "Calculating the required initial deposit" section discusses another application of discounting when you calculated the initial deposit required (the present value) to reach a future goal, knowing how much you can deposit each period and how much the interest rate will be.

This chapter takes a closer look at Excel's discounting tools, including present value and profitability as well as cash-flow analysis measures such as net present value and internal rate of return.

Calculating the present value

The time-value-of-money concept tells you that a dollar now is not the same as a dollar in the future. You can't compare them directly because it's like comparing the temporal equivalent of the proverbial apples and oranges. From a discounting perspective, the present value is important because it turns those future oranges into present apples. That is, it enables you to make a true comparison by restating the future value of an asset or investment in today's terms.

You know from Chapter 15 (see "Understanding compound interest") that calculating a future value relies on compounding. That is, a dollar today grows by applying interest on interest, like this:

Year 1: $1.00 × (1 + *rate*)

Year 2: $1.00 × (1 + *rate*) × (1 + *rate*)

Year 3: $1.00 × (1 + *rate*) × (1 + *rate*) × (1 + *rate*)

More generally, given an interest *rate* and a period *nper*, the future value of a dollar today is calculated as follows:

```
=$1.00 * (1 + rate) ^ nper
```

Calculating the present value uses the reverse process. That is, given some discount *rate*, a future dollar is expressed in today's dollars by dividing instead of multiplying:

Year 1: $1.00 / (1 + *rate*)

Year 2: $1.00 / (1 + *rate*) / (1 + *rate*)

Year 3: $1.00 / (1 + *rate*) / (1 + *rate*) / (1 + *rate*)

In general, given a discount *rate* and a period *nper*, the present value of a future dollar is calculated as follows:

```
=$1.00 / (1 + rate) ^ nper
```

The result of this formula is called the *discount factor*, and multiplying it by any future value restates that value in today's dollars.

Taking inflation into account

The future value tells you how much money you'll end up with, but it doesn't tell you how much that money is *worth*. In other words, if an object costs $10,000 now and your investment's future value is $10,000, it's unlikely that you'll be able to use that future value to purchase the object because it will probably have gone up in price. That is, inflation erodes the purchasing power of any future value; to know what a future value is worth, you need to express it in today's dollars.

For example, suppose that you put $10,000 initially and $100 per month into an investment that pays 5 percent annual interest. After 10 years, the future value of that investment will be $31,998.32.

Assuming that the inflation rate stays constant at 2 percent per year, what is the investment's future value worth in today's dollars?

Here, the discount rate is the inflation rate, so the discount factor is calculated as follows:

```
=1 / (1.02) ^ 10
```

This returns 0.82. Multiplying the future value by this discount factor gives the present value: $26,249.77.

Calculating present value using PV

You're probably wondering what happened to Excel's **PV** function. I've held off on introducing it so that you could see how to calculate the present value from the first principles. Now that you know what's going on behind the scenes, you can make your life easier by calculating present values directly using the **PV** function:

```
PV(rate, nper, pmt[, fv][, type])
```

rate	The fixed rate over the term of the asset or investment.
nper	The number of periods in the term of the asset or investment.
pmt	The amount earned by the asset or deposited into the investment with each deposit.
fv	The future value of the asset or investment.
type	When the *pmt* occurs. Use **0** (the default) for the end of each period; use **1** for the beginning of each period.

For example, to calculate the effect of inflation on a future value, you apply the **PV** function to the future value, where the *rate* argument is the inflation rate:

```
PV(inflation rate, nper, 0, fv)
```

> **Note** When you set the **PV** function's *pmt* argument to **0**, you can ignore the *type* argument because it's meaningless without payments.

Figure 16-1 shows a worksheet that uses **PV** to derive the answer of $26,249.77 using the following formula:

```
=PV(B9, B3, 0, -B7)
```

Note that this is the same result you derived using the discount factor, which is shown in Figure 16-1 in cell B10. (The table in D2:E13 shows the various discount factors for each year.)

> **Note** You can work with all the examples in this chapter by downloading Chapter16.xslx from either of the companion content sites mentioned in the Introduction.

The next few sections take you through some examples of using **PV** in discounting scenarios.

B11		fx	=PV(B9, B3, 0, -B7)		
	A	B	C	D	E
1	Taking Inflation Into Account				
2	Interest Rate (Annual)	5.0%		Year	Discount Factor
3	Term (Years)	10		0	1.00
4	Deposit Per Month	($100)		1	0.98
5	Initial Deposit	($10,000)		2	0.96
6	Deposit Type	0		3	0.94
7	Future Value	$31,998.32		4	0.92
8				5	0.91
9	Inflation Rate	2%		6	0.89
10	Present Value (Discount Factor)	$26,249.77		7	0.87
11	Present Value (PV() Function)	$26,249.77		8	0.85
12				9	0.84
13				10	0.82
14					

FIGURE 16-1 Use the PV function to calculate the effects of inflation on a future value.

Income investing versus purchasing a rental property

If you have some cash to invest, one common scenario is to wonder whether the cash is better invested in a straight income-producing security (such as a bond or certificate) or in a rental property.

One way to analyze this is to gather the following data:

- On the fixed-income security side, find your best deal in the time frame you're looking at. For example, you might find that you can get a bond that matures in 10 years with a 5 percent yield.

- On the rental property side, find out what the property produces in annual rental income. Also, estimate what the rental property will be worth at the same future date that the fixed-income security matures. For example, you might be looking at a rental property that generates $24,000 a year and is estimated to be worth $1 million in 10 years.

Given this data (and ignoring complicating factors such as rental property expenses), you want to know the maximum that you should pay for the property to realize a better yield than with the fixed-income security.

To solve this problem, use the **PV** function as follows:

```
=PV(fixed income yield, nper, rental income, future property value)
```

Figure 16-2 shows a worksheet model that uses this formula. The result of the **PV** function is $799,235. You interpret this to mean that if you pay less than that amount for the property, the property is a better deal than the fixed-income security; if you pay more, you're better off going the fixed-income route.

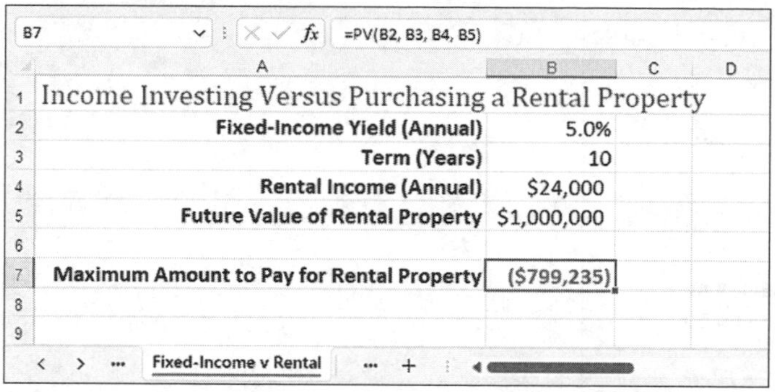

B7		✓	:	× ✓ *fx*	=PV(B2, B3, B4, B5)		

	A	B	C	D
1	Income Investing Versus Purchasing a Rental Property			
2	Fixed-Income Yield (Annual)	5.0%		
3	Term (Years)	10		
4	Rental Income (Annual)	$24,000		
5	Future Value of Rental Property	$1,000,000		
6				
7	Maximum Amount to Pay for Rental Property	($799,235)		
8				
9				

⟨ ⟩ ⋯   Fixed-Income v Rental   ⋯ +

FIGURE 16-2 Use the PV function to compare investing in a fixed-income security versus purchasing a rental property.

Buying versus leasing

Another common business conundrum is whether to purchase equipment outright or to lease it. Again, you figure the present value of both sides to compare them, with the preferable option being the one that provides the lower present value. (This ignores complicating factors such as depreciation and taxes.)

Assume (for now) that the purchased equipment has no market value at the end of the term and that the leased equipment has no residual value at the end of the lease. In this case, the present value of the purchase option is simply the purchase price. For the lease option, you determine the present value using the following form of the **PV** function.

```
=PV(discount rate, lease term, lease payment)
```

For the *discount rate*, you plug in a value that represents either a current investment rate or a current loan rate. For example, if you could invest the lease payment and get 6 percent per year, you would plug 6 percent into the function as the *rate* argument.

Suppose you can either purchase a piece of equipment for $5,000 now or lease the equipment for $240 a month over two years. Assuming a discount rate of 6 percent, what's the present value of the leasing option? Figure 16-3 shows a worksheet that calculates the answer: $5,415.09. This means that purchasing the equipment is the less costly choice.

What if the equipment has a future market value (on the purchase side) or a residual value (on the lease side)? This won't make much difference in terms of which option is better because the future value of the equipment raises the two present values by about the same amount. However, note how you calculate the present value for the purchase option:

```
=purchase price + PV(discount rate, term, 0, future value)
```

That is, the present value of the purchase option is the price plus the present value of the equipment's future market value. (For the lease option, you include the residual value as the **PV** function's *fv* argument.) Figure 16-4 shows the worksheet with a future value added.

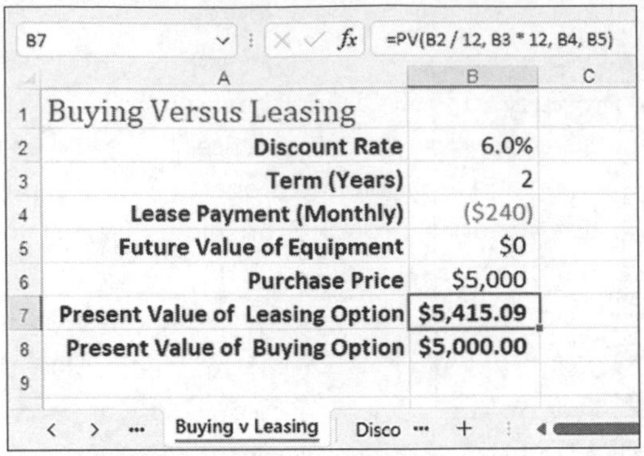

FIGURE 16-3 Use the PV function to compare buying versus leasing equipment.

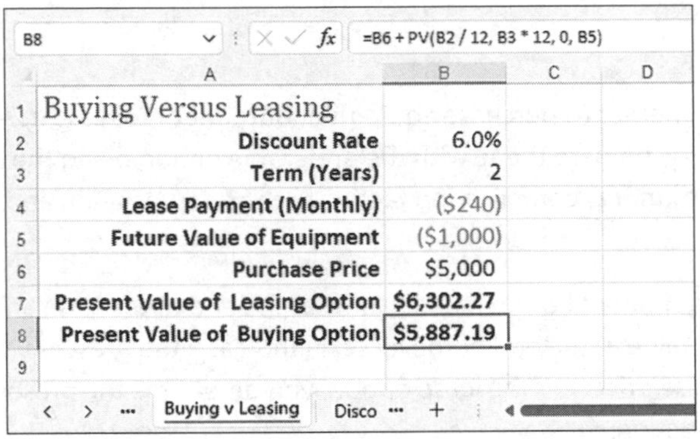

FIGURE 16-4 Use the PV function to compare buying versus leasing equipment that has a future market or residual value.

Discounting cash flows

One very common business scenario is to put some money into an asset or investment that generates income. By examining the cash flows—the negative cash flows for the original investment and any subsequent outlays required by the asset, and the positive cash flows for the income generated by the asset—you can figure out whether you've made a good investment.

For example, consider the situation discussed earlier in this chapter: You invest in a property that generates a regular cash flow of rental income. When analyzing this investment, you have three types of cash flow to consider:

- The initial purchase price (negative cash flow)

- The annual rental income (positive cash flow)

- The price you get by selling the property (positive cash flow)

Earlier you used the **PV** function to calculate that an initial purchase price of $799,235 and an assumed sale price of $1 million gives you the same return as a 5 percent fixed-income security over 10 years. Let's verify this using a cash-flow analysis. Figure 16-5 shows a worksheet set up to show the cash flows for this investment. Row 3 shows the net cash flow each year. (In practice, this would be the rental income minus the costs incurred while maintaining and repairing the property.) Row 4 shows the cumulative net cash flows. Note that columns F through I (years 4 through 7) are hidden so that you can see the final cash flow: the rent in year 10 plus the property's sale price.

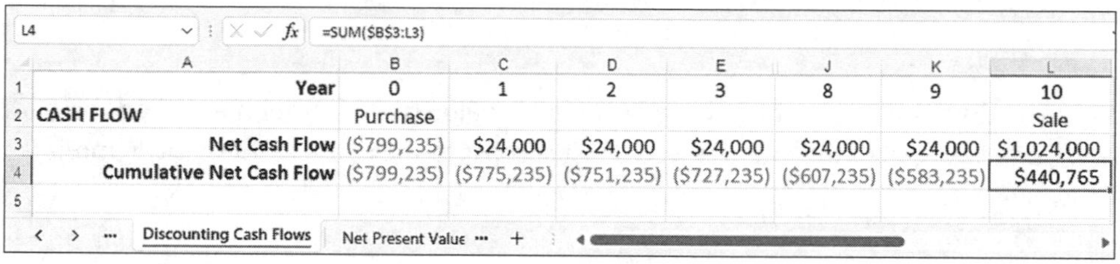
L4 =SUM($B$3:L3)

	A	B	C	D	E	J	K	L
1	Year	0	1	2	3	8	9	10
2	CASH FLOW	Purchase						Sale
3	Net Cash Flow	($799,235)	$24,000	$24,000	$24,000	$24,000	$24,000	$1,024,000
4	Cumulative Net Cash Flow	($799,235)	($775,235)	($751,235)	($727,235)	($607,235)	($583,235)	$440,765
5								

FIGURE 16-5 This worksheet shows the yearly and cumulative cash flows for a rental property.

Calculating the net present value

The *net present value* is the sum of a series of net cash flows, each of which has been discounted to the present using a fixed discount rate. If all the cash flows are the same, you can use the **PV** function to calculate the present value. But when you have a series of varying cash flows, as in the rental property example, you can't apply the **PV** function directly.

Excel has a direct route to calculating net present value, but let's take a second to examine a method that calculates this value from first principles. This will help you understand exactly what's happening in this kind of cash-flow analysis.

To get the net present value, you first have to discount each cash flow. You do that by multiplying the cash flow by the discount factor, which you calculate as described earlier in this chapter.

Figure 16-6 shows the rental property cash-flow worksheet with the discount factors (row 8) and the discounted cash flows (rows 9 and 10).

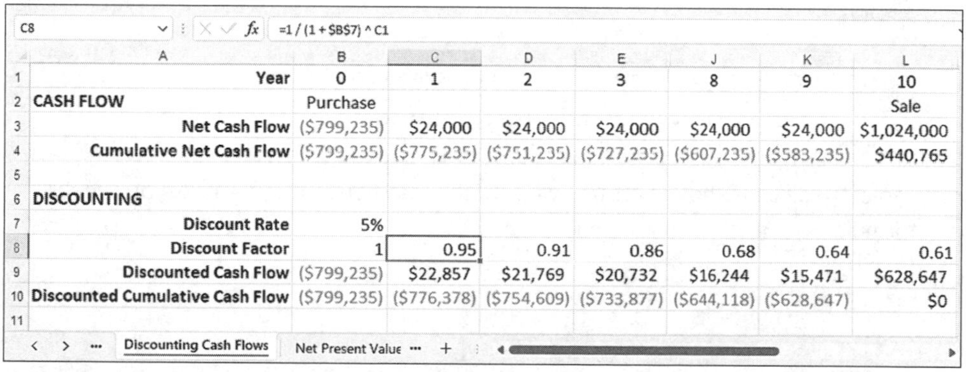
C8 =1 / (1 + $B$7) ^ C1

	A	B	C	D	E	J	K	L
1	Year	0	1	2	3	8	9	10
2	CASH FLOW	Purchase						Sale
3	Net Cash Flow	($799,235)	$24,000	$24,000	$24,000	$24,000	$24,000	$1,024,000
4	Cumulative Net Cash Flow	($799,235)	($775,235)	($751,235)	($727,235)	($607,235)	($583,235)	$440,765
5								
6	DISCOUNTING							
7	Discount Rate	5%						
8	Discount Factor	1	0.95	0.91	0.86	0.68	0.64	0.61
9	Discounted Cash Flow	($799,235)	$22,857	$21,769	$20,732	$16,244	$15,471	$628,647
10	Discounted Cumulative Cash Flow	($799,235)	($776,378)	($754,609)	($733,877)	($644,118)	($628,647)	$0
11								

FIGURE 16-6 This worksheet shows the discounted yearly and cumulative cash flows for a rental property.

The key number to notice in Figure 16-6 is the final Discounted Cumulative Cash Flow value in cell L10, which is $0. This is the net present value, the sum of the cumulative discounted cash flows at the end of year 10. This result makes sense because you already know that the initial cash flow—the purchase price of $799,235—was the present value of the rental income with a discount rate of 5 percent and a sale price of $1 million.

In other words, purchasing the property for $799,235 enables you to break even—that is, the net present value is 0—when all the cash flows are discounted into today's dollars using the specified discount rate.

> **Note** The discount rate that returns a net present value of 0 is sometimes called the *hurdle rate*. In other words, it's the rate that you must surpass to make the asset or investment worthwhile.

The net present value can also tell you whether an investment is positive or negative:

- If the net present value is negative, this can generally be interpreted in two ways: Either you paid too much for the asset or the income from the asset is too low. For example, if you plug –$900,000 into the rental property model as the initial cash flow (that is, the purchase price), the net present value works out to –$100,765, which is the loss on the property in today's dollars.

- If the net present value is positive, this can generally be interpreted in two ways: Either you got a good deal for the asset, or the income makes the asset profitable. For example, if you plug –$700,000 into the rental property model as the initial cash flow (that is, the purchase price), the net present value works out to $99,235, which is the profit on the property in today's dollars.

Calculating net present value using NPV

The model built in the previous section was designed to show you the relationship between the present value and the net present value. Fortunately, you don't have to jump through all those worksheet hoops every time you need to calculate the net present value. Excel offers a much quicker method with the **NPV** function:

NPV(*rate*, *values*)

rate	The discount rate over the term of the asset or investment
values	The cash flows over the term of the asset or investment

For example, to calculate the net present value of the cash flows in Figure 16-6, you use the following formula:

=NPV(B7, B3:L3)

That's markedly easier than figuring out discount factors and discounted cash flows. However, the NPV function has one quirk that can seriously affect its results. NPV assumes that the initial cash flow occurs at the end of the first period. However, in most cases, the initial cash flow—usually a negative cash flow, indicating the purchase of an asset or a deposit into an investment—occurs at the beginning of the term. This is usually designated as period 0. The first cash flow resulting from the asset or investment is designated as period 1.

The upshot of this NPV quirk is that the function result is usually understated by a factor of the discount rate. For example, if the discount rate is 5 percent, the NPV result must be increased by 5 percent to factor in the first period and get the true net present value. Here's the general formula:

```
net present value = NPV * (1 + discount rate)
```

Figure 16-7 shows a new worksheet that contains the rental property's net cash flows (B3:L3) as well as the discount rate (B5). The net present value is calculated using the following formula:

```
=NPV(B5, B3:L3) * (1 + B5)
```

B6		fx	=NPV(B5, B3:L3) * (1 + B5)									
	A	B	C	D	E	F	G	H	I	J	K	L
1	Year	0	1	2	3	4	5	6	7	8	9	10
2	CASH FLOW	Purchase										Sale
3	Net Cash Flow	($799,235)	$24,000	$24,000	$24,000	$24,000	$24,000	$24,000	$24,000	$24,000	$24,000	$1,024,000
4	DISCOUNTING											
5	Discount Rate	5%										
6	Net Present Value	$0.00										
7												

‹ › ⋯ Net Present Value with NPV | NPV Varying ⋯ +

FIGURE 16-7 This worksheet shows the net present value calculated using the NPV function plus an adjustment.

Caution   Make sure that you adjust the discount rate to reflect the frequency of the discounting periods. If the periods are annual, the discount rate must be an annual rate. If the periods are monthly, you need to divide the discount rate by 12 to get the monthly rate.

Net present value with varying cash flows

The major advantage of using NPV over PV is that NPV can easily accommodate varying cash flows. You can use PV directly to calculate the break-even purchase price, assuming that the asset or investment generates a constant cash flow each period. Alternatively, you can use PV to help calculate the net present value for different cash flows if you build a complicated discounted cash-flow model such as the one shown for the rental property in Figure 16-6.

You don't need to worry about either of these scenarios if you use NPV. That's because you can simply enter the cash flows as the NPV function's *values* argument.

For example, suppose that you're thinking of investing in a new piece of equipment that will generate income, but you don't want to make the investment unless the machine will generate a return of at least 10 percent in today's dollars over the first five years. Your cash-flow projection looks like this:

Year 0: –$50,000 (purchase price)

Year 1: –$5,000

Year 2: $15,000

Year 3: $20,000

Year 4: $21,000

Year 5: $22,000

Figure 16-8 shows a worksheet that models this scenario with the cash flows in B4:G4. Using the target return of 10 percent as the discount rate (B6), the **NPV** function returns $881 (B7). This amount is positive, which means that the machine will make at least a 10 percent return in today's dollars over the first five years.

B7			fx	=NPV(B6, B4:G4) * (1 + B6)			
	A	B	C	D	E	F	G
1							
2	Year	0	1	2	3	4	5
3	**CASH FLOW**						
4	Net Cash Flow	($50,000)	($5,000)	$15,000	$20,000	$21,000	$22,000
5	**DISCOUNTING**						
6	Discount Rate	10%					
7	**Net Present Value**	$881					
8							

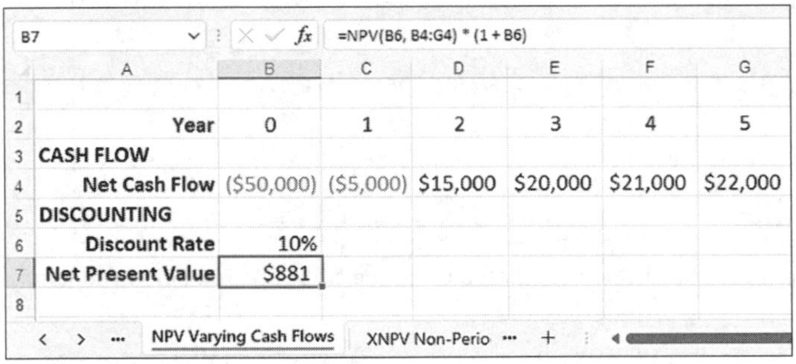

< > ⋯ NPV Varying Cash Flows   XNPV Non-Perio ⋯ +

FIGURE 16-8 To see whether a series of cash flows meets a desired rate of return, use that rate as the discount rate in the NPV function.

Net present value with nonperiodic cash flows

The examples you've seen so far have assumed that the cash flows were periodic, meaning that they occur with the same frequency throughout the term (such as yearly or monthly). In some investments, however, the cash flows occur sporadically. In such a case, you can't use the **NPV** function, which works only with periodic cash flows.

Happily, Excel offers the **XNPV** function, which can handle nonperiodic cash flows:

XNPV(*rate*, *values*, *dates*)

rate	The annual discount rate over the term of the asset or investment.
values	The cash flows over the term of the asset or investment.
dates	The dates on which each of the cash flows occurs. Make sure the first value in *dates* is the date of the initial cash flow. All the other dates must be later than this initial date, but they can be listed in any order.

For example, Figure 16-9 shows a worksheet with a series of cash flows (B4:G4) and the dates on which they occur (B5:G5). Assuming a 10 percent discount rate (B7), the **XNPV** function returns a value of $845, using the following formula (B8):

```
=XNPV(B7, B4:G5, B5:G5)
```

> **Note** The **XNPV** function doesn't have the missing-first-period quirk of the **NPV** function. Therefore, you can use **XNPV** straight up without adding a first-period factor.

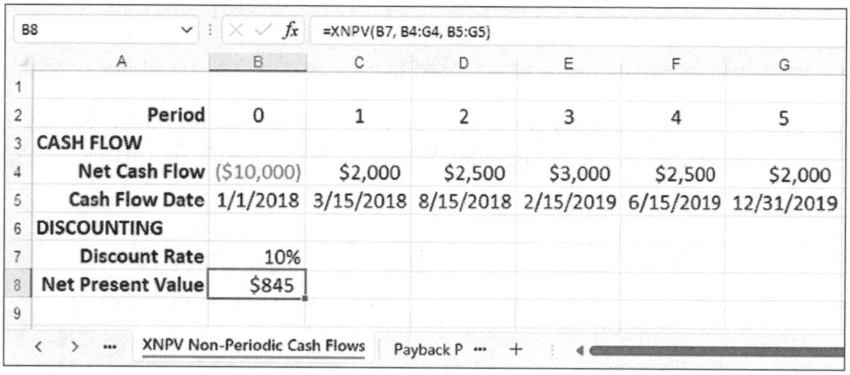

B8			f_x	=XNPV(B7, B4:G4, B5:G5)			
	A	B	C	D	E	F	G
1							
2	Period	0	1	2	3	4	5
3	CASH FLOW						
4	Net Cash Flow	($10,000)	$2,000	$2,500	$3,000	$2,500	$2,000
5	Cash Flow Date	1/1/2018	3/15/2018	8/15/2018	2/15/2019	6/15/2019	12/31/2019
6	DISCOUNTING						
7	Discount Rate	10%					
8	Net Present Value	$845					
9							

FIGURE 16-9 Use the XNPV function to calculate the net present value for a series of nonperiodic cash flows.

Calculating the payback period

If you purchase a store, a piece of equipment, or an investment, your hope always is to at least recoup your initial outlay through the positive cash flows generated by the asset. The point at which you recoup the initial outlay is called the *payback period*. When analyzing a business case, one of the most common concerns is when the payback period occurs: A short payback period is better than a long one.

Simple undiscounted payback period

Finding the undiscounted payback period is a matter of calculating the cumulative cash flows and watching when they turn from negative to positive. The period that shows the first positive cumulative cash flow is the payback period.

For example, suppose you purchase a store for $500,000 and project the following cash flows:

Year	Net Cash Flow	Cumulative Net Cash Flow
0	–$500,000	–$500,000
1	$55,000	–$445,000
2	$75,000	–$370,000
3	$80,000	–$290,000
4	$95,000	–$195,000
5	$105,000	–$90,000
6	$120,000	$30,000

As you can see, the cumulative cash flow turns positive in year 6, so that's the payback period.

Instead of simply eyeballing the payback period, you can use a formula to calculate it. Figure 16-10 shows a worksheet that lists the cash flows and uses the following array formula to calculate the payback period (see cell B5):

```
=SUM(IF(SIGN(C4:I4) <> SIGN(OFFSET(C4:I4, 0, -1)), C1:I1, 0))
```

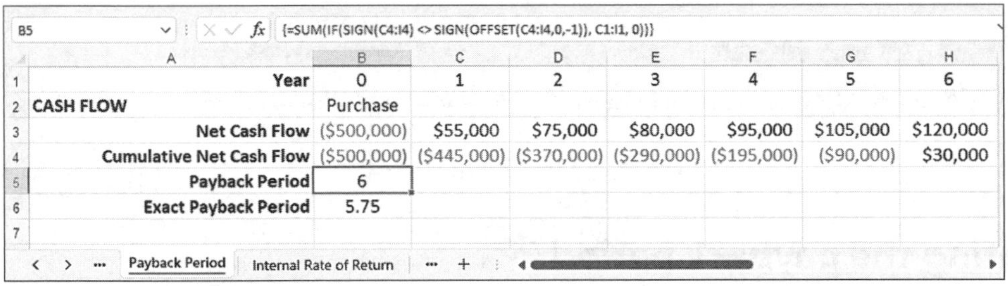

FIGURE 16-10 This worksheet shows how to use a formula to calculate the payback period.

The payback period occurs when the sign of the cumulative cash flows turns from negative to positive. Therefore, this formula uses IF to compare each cumulative cash flow (C4:I4; you can ignore the first cash flow for this) with the cumulative cash flow from the previous period, as given by OFFSET(C4:I4, 0, -1). IF returns 0 for all cases in which the signs are the same, and it returns the year value from row 1 (C1:I1) for the case in which the sign changes. Summing these values returns the year in which the sign changed, which is the payback period.

Exact undiscounted payback point

If the income generated by the asset is always received at the end of the period, your analysis of the payback period is done. However, many assets generate income throughout the period. In this case, the payback period tells you that sometime within the period, the cumulative cash flow reaches 0. It might be useful to calculate exactly when during the period the payback occurs. Assuming that the income is received at regular intervals throughout the period, you can find the exact payback point by comparing how much is required to reach the payback with how much was earned during the payback period.

For example, suppose that the cumulative cash flow value was –$50,000 at the end of the previous period and that the asset generates $100,000 during the payback period. Assuming regular cash flow throughout the period, this means that the first $50,000 brought the cumulative cash flow to **0**. Because this is half the amount earned in the payback period, you can say that the exact payback point occurred halfway through the period.

More generally, you can use the following formula to calculate the exact payback point:

```
=Payback Period - Cumulative Cash Flow at Payback / Cash Flow at Payback
```

For example, suppose you know that the store's payback period occurs in year 6, that the cumulative cash flow after year 6 is $30,000, and that the cash flow for year 6 was $120,000. Here's the formula:

```
=6 - 30,000 / 120,000
```

The answer is 5.75, meaning that the exact payback point occurs three-quarters of the way through the sixth year.

To derive this in a worksheet, you first calculate the payback period and then use this number in the **INDEX** function to return the payback period's cumulative cash flow and net cash flow values. Here's the formula used in Figure 16-11:

```
=B5 - INDEX(B4:H4, B5 + 1) / INDEX(B3:H3, B5 + 1)
```

B6		fx	=B5 -@ INDEX(B4:H4, B5 + 1) /@ INDEX(B3:H3, B5 + 1)					
	A	B	C	D	E	F	G	H
1	Year	0	1	2	3	4	5	6
2	CASH FLOW	Purchase						
3	Net Cash Flow	($500,000)	$55,000	$75,000	$80,000	$95,000	$105,000	$120,000
4	Cumulative Net Cash Flow	($500,000)	($445,000)	($370,000)	($290,000)	($195,000)	($90,000)	$30,000
5	Payback Period	6						
6	Exact Payback Period	5.75						
7								

‹ › ⋯ Payback Period Internal Rate of Return ⋯ +

FIGURE 16-11 This worksheet shows how to use a formula to calculate the exact payback point.

Discounted payback period

Of course, the undiscounted payback period tells you only so much. To get a true measure of the payback, you need to apply these payback methods to the discounted cash flows. This tells you when the investment is paid back in today's dollars.

To do this, you need to set up a schedule of discounted net cash flow and cumulative cash flow for each period and extend the periods until the cumulative discounted cash flow becomes positive. You can then use the formulas presented in the previous two sections (adjusted for the extra periods) to calculate the payback period and exact payback point (if applicable). Figure 16-12 shows the discounted payback values for the store's cash flows.

B13		✓ : ✗ ✓ f_x	{=SUM(IF(SIGN(C12:K12) <> SIGN(OFFSET(C12:K12,0,-1)), C1:K1, 0))}						
	A	B	C	D	E	F	G	H
1	Year	0	1	2	3	4	5	6
2	**CASH FLOW**	Purchase						
3	Net Cash Flow	($500,000)	$55,000	$75,000	$80,000	$95,000	$105,000	$120,000
4	Cumulative Net Cash Flow	($500,000)	($445,000)	($370,000)	($290,000)	($195,000)	($90,000)	$30,000
5	Payback Period	6						
6	Exact Payback Period	5.75						
7								
8	**DISCOUNTING**							
9	Discount Rate	10%						
10	Discount Factor	1	0.91	0.83	0.75	0.68	0.62	0.56
11	Discounted Cash Flow	($500,000)	$50,000	$61,983	$60,105	$64,886	$65,197	$67,737
12	Discounted Cumulative Cash Flow	($500,000)	($450,000)	($388,017)	($327,911)	($263,025)	($197,828)	($130,091)
13	Payback Period	9						
14	Exact Payback Period	8.25						
15								
	‹ › ⋯ Payback Period	Internal Rate of Return	⋯ + ⋮					

FIGURE 16-12 To derive the discounted payback values, create a schedule of discounted cash flows, extend the periods until the cumulative discounted cash flow turns positive, and then apply the payback formulas.

Calculating the internal rate of return

In the earlier example with varying cash flows, the discount rate was set to 10 percent because that was the minimum return required in today's dollars over the first five years after purchasing the equipment. This rate of return of an investment based on today's dollars is called the *internal rate of return*. It's actually defined as the discount rate required to get a net present value of $0.

In the equipment example, using a discount rate of 10 percent produced a net present value of $881. This is a positive amount, which means that the equipment actually produced an internal rate of return higher than 10 percent. What, then, was the actual internal rate of return?

Using the IRR function

You could figure this out by adjusting the discount rate up (in this case) until the NPV calculation returns 0. However, Excel offers an easier method in the form of the IRR function:

IRR(*values*[, *guess*])

Values	The cash flows over the term of the asset or investment.
Guess	An initial estimate of the internal rate of return. If you omit this argument, Excel uses the default value of 0.1.

> **Caution** The **IRR** function's *values* argument must contain at least one positive value and one negative value. If all the values have the same sign, the function returns the #NUM! error.

Figure 16-13 shows the cash flows generated by the equipment purchase and the resulting internal rate of return (cell B7) calculated by the **IRR** function:

```
=IRR(B3:G3)
```

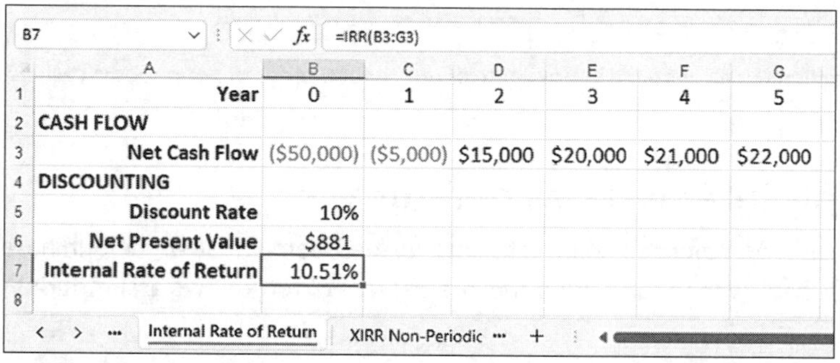

FIGURE 16-13 Use the IRR function to calculate the internal rate of return for a series of periodic cash flows.

The calculated value of 10.51 percent means that plugging this value into the **NPV** function as the discount rate would return a net present value of **0**.

> **Note** The **IRR** function uses iteration to find a solution that is accurate to within 0.00001 percent. If it can't find a solution within 20 iterations, it returns the #NUM! error. If this happens, try using a different value for the **guess** argument.

Calculating the internal rate of return for nonperiodic cash flows

As with **NPV**, the **IRR** function works only with periodic cash flows. If your cash flows are nonperiodic, use the **XIRR** function instead:

```
XIRR(values, dates[, guess])
```

values	The cash flows over the term of the asset or investment.
dates	The dates on which each of the cash flows occurs. Make sure that the first value in *dates* is the date of the initial cash flow. All the other dates must be later than this initial date, but they can be listed in any order.
guess	An initial estimate of the internal rate of return. If you omit this argument, Excel uses the default value of 0.1.

Figure 16-14 shows a worksheet with nonperiodic cash flows and the resulting internal rate of return (cell B8) calculated using the **XIRR** function:

```
=XIRR(B3:G3, B4:G4)
```

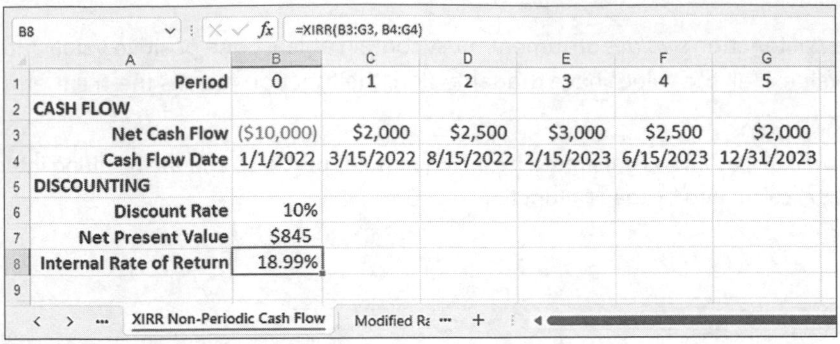

B8 =XIRR(B3:G3, B4:G4)

	A	B	C	D	E	F	G
1	Period	0	1	2	3	4	5
2	CASH FLOW						
3	Net Cash Flow	($10,000)	$2,000	$2,500	$3,000	$2,500	$2,000
4	Cash Flow Date	1/1/2022	3/15/2022	8/15/2022	2/15/2023	6/15/2023	12/31/2023
5	DISCOUNTING						
6	Discount Rate	10%					
7	Net Present Value	$845					
8	Internal Rate of Return	18.99%					
9							

FIGURE 16-14 Use the XIRR function to calculate the internal rate of return for a series of nonperiodic cash flows.

Calculating multiple internal rates of return

Rarely does a business pay cash for major capital investments. Instead, some or all of the purchase price is usually borrowed from the bank. When calculating the internal rate of return, two assumptions are made:

- The discount for negative cash flows is money paid to the bank to service borrowed money.
- The discount for positive cash flows is money reinvested.

However, a third assumption also is at work when you use the **IRR** function: The finance rate for negative cash flows and the reinvestment rate for positive cash flows are the same. In the real world, this is rarely true: Most banks charge interest for a loan that is 2 to 4 points higher than what you can usually get for an investment.

To handle the difference between the finance rate and the reinvestment rate, Excel enables you to calculate the *modified internal rate of return* using the **MIRR** function:

```
MIRR(values, finance_rate, reinvest_rate)
```

Values	The cash flows over the term of the asset or investment
finance_rate	The interest rate you pay for negative cash flows
reinvest_rate	The interest rate you get for positive cash flows that are reinvested

For example, suppose you're charged 8 percent for loans, and you can get 6 percent for investments. Figure 16-15 shows a worksheet that calculates the modified internal rate of return based on the cash flows in B3:G3 and these rates:

```
=MIRR(B3:G3, B5, B6)
```

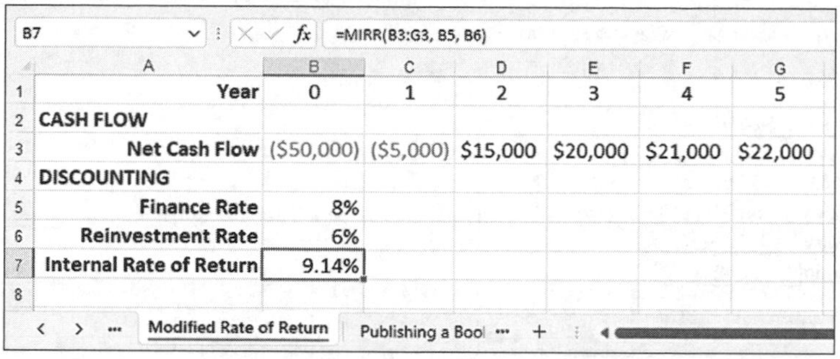

B7			f_x	=MIRR(B3:G3, B5, B6)			
	A	B	C	D	E	F	G
1	Year	0	1	2	3	4	5
2	**CASH FLOW**						
3	Net Cash Flow	($50,000)	($5,000)	$15,000	$20,000	$21,000	$22,000
4	**DISCOUNTING**						
5	Finance Rate	8%					
6	Reinvestment Rate	6%					
7	Internal Rate of Return	9.14%					
8							

⟨ ⟩ ⋯ Modified Rate of Return   Publishing a Book ⋯ +

FIGURE 16-15 Use the MIRR function to calculate the modified internal rate of return when you're charged one rate for negative cash flows and a different rate for positive cash flows.

Case study: Publishing a book

Let's put some of this cash-flow analysis to work in an example that, although still simplified, is more realistically detailed than the ones you've seen so far in this chapter. Specifically, this case study looks at the business case of publishing a book, taking into account the costs involved (both up front and ongoing) and the positive cash flow generated by the book. The cash-flow analysis will calculate the book's payback period (undiscounted and discounted), as well as the yearly values for the net present value and the internal rate of return.

Per-Unit Constants

In publishing, many calculations involving operating costs and sales are performed using per-unit (that is, per-book) constants. This case study uses the following six constants, as shown in Figure 16-16:

- **List Price:** The suggested retail price of the book
- **Average Customer Discount:** The amount taken off the retail price when selling the book to bookstores
- **PP&B:** The per-unit costs for paper, printing, and binding
- **Cost of Sales:** The per-unit costs of selling the book, including commissions, distribution, and so on
- **Author Royalty:** The percentage of the list price that the author receives
- **Margin:** The per-unit margin, which is the list price minus the customer discount, PP&B, cost of sales, and author royalty, divided by the list price

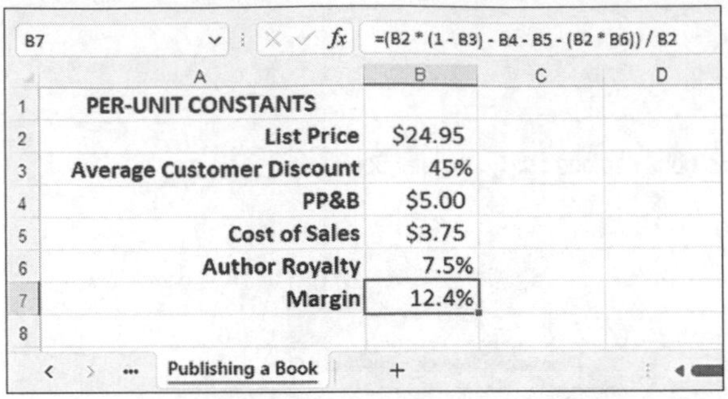

B7 | =(B2 * (1 - B3) - B4 - B5 - (B2 * B6)) / B2

	A	B	C	D
1	PER-UNIT CONSTANTS			
2	List Price	$24.95		
3	Average Customer Discount	45%		
4	PP&B	$5.00		
5	Cost of Sales	$3.75		
6	Author Royalty	7.5%		
7	Margin	12.4%		
8				

Publishing a Book

FIGURE 16-16 This worksheet shows the per-unit constants used in the operating cost and sales calculations.

Operating costs and sales

Figure 16-17 shows the annual operating costs and sales for the book over 10 years. For the references to cells B2 through B7 in the following list of costs and sales, see Figure 16-16:

- **Units Printed:** The number of books printed during the year.
- **Units Sold:** The number of units sold during the year.
- **New Title Costs:** Costs associated with producing the book, including acquiring, editing, indexing, and so on.
- **Total PP&B:** The total paper, printing, and binding costs during the year. This is the year's Units Printed value (from row 10) multiplied by the PP&B value (B4).
- **Marketing:** The marketing and publicity costs during the year.
- **Total Cost of Sales:** The total cost of sales during the year. This is the year's Units Sold value (from row 11) multiplied by the Cost of Sales value (B5).
- **Author Advance:** The advance on royalties paid to the author. The assumption is that this value is paid at the beginning of the project, so it's placed in year 0.
- **Author Royalties:** The royalties paid to the author during the year. This is generally the year's Units Sold value (from row 11) multiplied by the List Price (B2) and the Author Royalty (B6). However, the formula also takes into account the Author Advance, and it doesn't pay royalties until the advance has earned out.
- **$ Sales:** The total sales, in dollars, during the year. This is the year's Unit Sold value (from row 11) multiplied by the List Price (B2) minus the Average Customer Discount (B3).
- **Translation Rights:** Payments for translation rights sold during the year.
- **Book Club Rights:** Payments for book club rights sold during the year.

C15   =C10 * $B$4

		B	C	D	E	F	G	H	I
9	Year	0	1	2	3	4	5	6	7
10	Units Printed	0	50,000	0	0	0	0	0	0
11	Units Sold	0	17,000	10,500	4,000	3,500	3,000	2,500	2,000
12									
13	OPERATING COSTS								
14	New Title Costs	$0	$2,500	$0	$0	$0	$0	$0	$0
15	Total PP&B	0	$250,000	$0	$0	$0	$0	$0	$0
16	Marketing	0	$15,000	$5,000	$2,000	$2,000	$1,000	$1,000	$1,000
17	Total Cost of Sales	$0	$63,750	$39,375	$15,000	$13,125	$11,250	$9,375	$7,500
18	Author Advance	$25,000	$0	$0	$0	$0	$0	$0	$0
19	Author Royalties	$0	$6,811	$19,648	$7,485	$6,549	$5,614	$4,678	$3,743
20									
21	SALES								
22	$ Sales	$0	$233,283	$144,086	$54,890	$48,029	$41,168	$34,306	$27,445
23	Translation Rights	$0	$5,000	$0	$0	$2,500	$0	$0	$0
24	Book Club Rights	$0	$0	$1,000	$0	$0	$0	$1,000	$0
25									
26	CASH FLOW								
27	Net	($25,000)	($99,779)	$81,063	$30,405	$28,854	$23,304	$20,253	$15,203
28	Cumulative	($25,000)	($124,779)	($43,716)	($13,311)	$15,544	$38,848	$59,101	$74,303

Publishing a Book   +

FIGURE 16-17 This worksheet shows the operating costs and sales for each year.

Cash Flow

With the operating costs and sales available, you can calculate the net cash flow for each year by subtracting the sum of the operating costs from the sum of the sales. Figure 16-18 shows the book's net cash flows in row 27, as well as its cumulative net cash flows (row 28). You also get the discounted net and cumulative cash flows using a discount rate of 12.4 percent. This is the same as the per-unit Margin value (B7 from Figure 16-16), and it is the target rate of return for the book.

B27   =SUM(B22:B24) - SUM(B14:B19)

		B	C	D	E	F	G	H	I
13	OPERATING COSTS								
14	New Title Costs	$0	$2,500	$0	$0	$0	$0	$0	$0
15	Total PP&B	0	$250,000	$0	$0	$0	$0	$0	$0
16	Marketing	0	$15,000	$5,000	$2,000	$2,000	$1,000	$1,000	$1,000
17	Total Cost of Sales	$0	$63,750	$39,375	$15,000	$13,125	$11,250	$9,375	$7,500
18	Author Advance	$25,000	$0	$0	$0	$0	$0	$0	$0
19	Author Royalties	$0	$6,811	$19,648	$7,485	$6,549	$5,614	$4,678	$3,743
20									
21	SALES								
22	$ Sales	$0	$233,283	$144,086	$54,890	$48,029	$41,168	$34,306	$27,445
23	Translation Rights	$0	$5,000	$0	$0	$2,500	$0	$0	$0
24	Book Club Rights	$0	$0	$1,000	$0	$0	$0	$1,000	$0
25									
26	CASH FLOW								
27	Net	($25,000)	($99,779)	$81,063	$30,405	$28,854	$23,304	$20,253	$15,203
28	Cumulative	($25,000)	($124,779)	($43,716)	($13,311)	$15,544	$38,848	$59,101	$74,303
29	Discount Rate	12.4%							
30	Discount Factor	1.00	0.89	0.79	0.70	0.63	0.56	0.50	0.44
31	Discounted Net	($25,000)	($88,748)	$64,130	$21,394	$18,059	$12,972	$10,028	$6,695
32	Discounted Cumulative	($25,000)	($113,748)	($49,618)	($28,223)	($10,165)	$2,808	$12,835	$19,530

Publishing a Book   +

FIGURE 16-18 This worksheet shows the yearly net and cumulative cash flows and their discounted versions.

Cash-Flow Analysis

Finally, you're ready to analyze the cash flow, as shown in Figure 16-19. There are six values:

- **Undiscounted Payback Period:** The year in which the book's undiscounted cumulative cash flows turn positive.

- **Undiscounted Payback Point:** The exact point in the payback period at which the book's undiscounted cumulative cash flows turn positive.

- **Discounted Payback Period:** The year in which the book's discounted cumulative cash flows turn positive.

- **Discounted Payback Point:** The exact point in the payback period at which the book's discounted cumulative cash flows turn positive.

- **Net Present Value:** The net present value calculation at the end of each year, as returned by the NPV function (with the fudge factor added, as explained earlier; see "Calculating net present value using NPV").

- **Internal Rate of Return:** The internal rate of return calculation at the end of each year, as returned by the IRR function. Note that we don't start this calculation until year 2 because in year 1, there are nothing but negative cash flows.

G39   fx   =NPV($B$29, $B$27:G27) * (1 + $B$29)

	A	B	C	D	E	F	G	H	I
26	**CASH FLOW**								
27	Net	($25,000)	($99,779)	$81,063	$30,405	$28,854	$23,304	$20,253	$15,203
28	Cumulative	($25,000)	($124,779)	($43,716)	($13,311)	$15,544	$38,848	$59,101	$74,303
29	Discount Rate	12.4%							
30	Discount Factor	1.00	0.89	0.79	0.70	0.63	0.56	0.50	0.44
31	Discounted Net	($25,000)	($88,748)	$64,130	$21,394	$18,059	$12,972	$10,028	$6,695
32	Discounted Cumulative	($25,000)	($113,748)	($49,618)	($28,223)	($10,165)	$2,808	$12,835	$19,530
33									
34	**CASH FLOW ANALYSIS**								
35	Undiscounted Payback Period	4							
36	Undiscounted Payback Point	3.5							
37	Discounted Payback Period	5							
38	Discounted Payback Point	4.8							
39	Net Present Value		($113,748)	($49,618)	($28,223)	($10,165)	$2,808	$12,835	$19,530
40	Internal Rate of Return			-30.77%	-7.36%	6.69%	13.78%	17.87%	20.02%
41									

< > ... Publishing a Book   +

FIGURE 16-19 This worksheet shows the cash-flow analysis for the book example.

> **Note** To get the internal rate of return for year 2 (cell D40), I had to use –0.1 as the *guess* argument for the IRR function:
>
> ```
> =IRR($B$27:D27, -0.1)
> ```
>
> Without this initial estimate, Excel can't complete the iteration, and it returns the #NUM! error.

PART 4

Building Business Models

CHAPTER 17

Analyzing data with tables

In this chapter, you will:

- Use formulas to perform advanced table sorting

- Use formulas to create advanced table filters

- Learn how to reference table data in your formulas

- Investigate Excel's powerful database functions for analyzing table data

Excel's forte is spreadsheet work, of course, but its row-and-column layout also makes it a natural database manager. In Excel, a table is a collection of related information with an organizational structure that makes it easy to find or extract data from its contents. Specifically, a table is a worksheet range that has the following properties:

- **Field:** A single type of information, such as a name, an address, or a phone number. In Excel tables, each column is a field.

- **Field name:** A unique name you assign to every table field. These names are always found in the first row of the table.

- **Field value:** A single item in a field. In an Excel table, the field values are the individual cells.

- **Record:** A collection of associated field values. In Excel tables, each row is a record.

- **Table range:** The worksheet range that includes all the records, fields, and field names of a table.

In this chapter, I assume you know how to create, edit, and format tables and how to perform basic table maintenance, so I don't cover any of those things. Instead, I concentrate on using Excel formulas to help you analyze your table data.

Sorting a table

One of the advantages of a table is that you can rearrange its records so that they're sorted alphabetically or numerically. This feature enables you to view the data in order by customer name, account number, part number, or any other field. You even can sort on multiple fields, which would enable you, for example, to sort a client table by state and then by name within each state.

For quick sorts on a single field, you have two choices to get started:

- Select a cell anywhere inside the field and then select the **Data** tab.

- Select the field's **Sort & Filter** drop-down menu.

For an ascending sort, select **Sort A to Z** (or **Sort Smallest To Largest** for a numeric field or **Sort Oldest To Newest** for a date field); for a descending sort, select **Sort Z To A** (or **Sort Largest To Smallest** for a numeric field or **Sort Newest To Oldest** for a date field).

> ⚠ **Caution** Be careful when you sort table records that contain formulas. If the formulas use relative addresses that refer to cells outside their own record, the new sort order might change the references and produce erroneous results. If your table formulas must refer to cells outside the table, be sure to use absolute addresses.

Sorting on part of a field

Excel performs its sorting chores based on the entire contents of each cell in a field. This method is fine for most sorting tasks, but occasionally you need to sort on only part of a field. For example, your table might have a ContactName field that contains a first name and then a last name. Sorting on this field orders the table by each person's first name, which is probably not what you want. To sort on the last name, you need to create a new column that extracts the last name from the ContactName field. You can then use this new column for the sort.

Excel's text functions make it easy to extract substrings from a cell. In this case, assume that each cell in the ContactName field has a first name, followed by a space, followed by a last name. Your task is to extract everything after the space, and the following formula does the job (assuming that the name is in cell D4):

```
=RIGHT(D4, LEN(D4) - FIND(" ", D4))
```

For an explanation of how this formula works, see "Extracting a first name or last name," in Chapter 5, "Working with text functions."

Figure 17-1 shows this formula in action. Column D contains the names, and column A contains the formula to extract the last name. I sorted on column A to order the table by last name.

> 💡 **Tip** If you'd rather not have the extra sort field (column A in Figure 17-1) cluttering the table, you can hide it by selecting a cell in the field and selecting **Home** >**Format** > **Hide & Unhide** > **Hide Columns**. Fortunately, you don't have to unhide the field to sort on it because Excel still includes the field in the **Sort** dialog box (select **Data** > **Sort**).

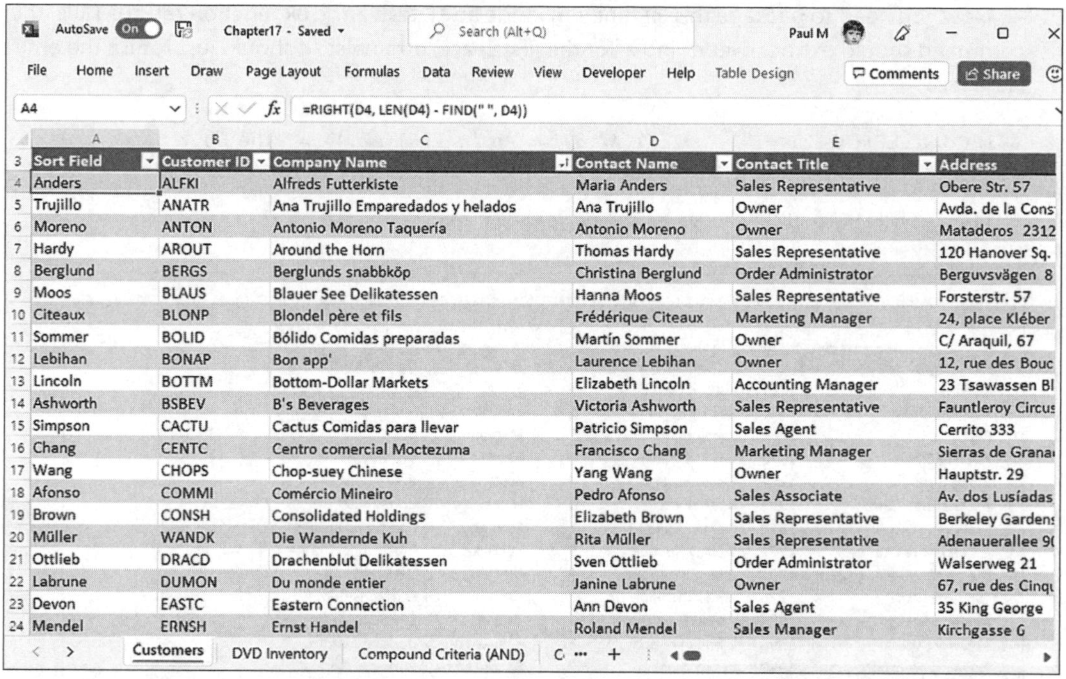

	A	B	C	D	E	
3	Sort Field	Customer ID	Company Name	Contact Name	Contact Title	Address
4	Anders	ALFKI	Alfreds Futterkiste	Maria Anders	Sales Representative	Obere Str. 57
5	Trujillo	ANATR	Ana Trujillo Emparedados y helados	Ana Trujillo	Owner	Avda. de la Cons
6	Moreno	ANTON	Antonio Moreno Taquería	Antonio Moreno	Owner	Mataderos 2312
7	Hardy	AROUT	Around the Horn	Thomas Hardy	Sales Representative	120 Hanover Sq.
8	Berglund	BERGS	Berglunds snabbköp	Christina Berglund	Order Administrator	Berguvsvägen 8
9	Moos	BLAUS	Blauer See Delikatessen	Hanna Moos	Sales Representative	Forsterstr. 57
10	Citeaux	BLONP	Blondel père et fils	Frédérique Citeaux	Marketing Manager	24, place Kléber
11	Sommer	BOLID	Bólido Comidas preparadas	Martín Sommer	Owner	C/ Araquil, 67
12	Lebihan	BONAP	Bon app'	Laurence Lebihan	Owner	12, rue des Bouc
13	Lincoln	BOTTM	Bottom-Dollar Markets	Elizabeth Lincoln	Accounting Manager	23 Tsawassen Bl
14	Ashworth	BSBEV	B's Beverages	Victoria Ashworth	Sales Representative	Fauntleroy Circus
15	Simpson	CACTU	Cactus Comidas para llevar	Patricio Simpson	Sales Agent	Cerrito 333
16	Chang	CENTC	Centro comercial Moctezuma	Francisco Chang	Marketing Manager	Sierras de Grana
17	Wang	CHOPS	Chop-suey Chinese	Yang Wang	Owner	Hauptstr. 29
18	Afonso	COMMI	Comércio Mineiro	Pedro Afonso	Sales Associate	Av. dos Lusíadas
19	Brown	CONSH	Consolidated Holdings	Elizabeth Brown	Sales Representative	Berkeley Gardens
20	Müller	WANDK	Die Wandernde Kuh	Rita Müller	Sales Representative	Adenauerallee 9(
21	Ottlieb	DRACD	Drachenblut Delikatessen	Sven Ottlieb	Order Administrator	Walserweg 21
22	Labrune	DUMON	Du monde entier	Janine Labrune	Owner	67, rue des Cinqu
23	Devon	EASTC	Eastern Connection	Ann Devon	Sales Agent	35 King George
24	Mendel	ERNSH	Ernst Handel	Roland Mendel	Sales Manager	Kirchgasse 6

FIGURE 17-1 To sort on part of a field, use Excel's text functions to extract the string you need for the sort.

> **Note** You can work with all the examples in this chapter by downloading Chapter17.xslx from either of the companion content sites mentioned in the Introduction.

Sorting without articles

Tables that contain field values starting with articles (*A*, *An*, and *The*) can throw off your sorting. To fix this problem, you can borrow the technique from the preceding section and sort on a new field in which the leading articles have been removed. As before, you want to extract everything after the first space, but you can't just use the same formula because not all the titles have a leading article. You need to test for a leading article by using the following **OR** function:

```
OR(LEFT(A2,2) = "A ", LEFT(A2,3) = "An ", LEFT(A2,4) = "The ")
```

Here, I'm assuming that the text being tested is in cell A2. This function returns **TRUE** if the left two characters are *A* followed by a space, or the left three characters are *An* followed by a space, or the left four characters are *The* followed by a space. (That is, you're dealing with a title that has a leading article.)

Now you need to package this **OR** function inside an **IF** test. If the **OR** function returns **TRUE**, the command should extract everything after the first space; otherwise, it should just return the entire title. Here it is:

```
=IF( OR(LEFT(A2,2) = "A ", LEFT(A2,3) = "An ", LEFT(A2,4) = "The "),
RIGHT(A2, LEN(A2) - FIND(" ", A2, 1)), A2)
```

Figure 17-2 shows this formula in action using cell A3.

F3 | =IF(OR(LEFT(A3,2) = "A ", LEFT(A3,3) = "An ", LEFT(A3,4) = "The "), RIGHT(A3, LEN(A3) - FIND(" ", A3, 1)), A3)

	A	B	C	D	E	F
1	Title	Year	Director	In Stock	Sort Field	Sort Field2
2	Alien	1979	Ridley Scott	3	Scott	Alien
3	An Angel from Texas	1940	Ray Enright	1	Enright	Angel from Texas
4	Big	1988	Penny Marshall	5	Marshall	Big
5	The Big Sleep	1946	Howard Hawks	2	Hawks	Big Sleep
6	Blade Runner	1982	Ridley Scott	4	Scott	Blade Runner
7	A Christmas Carol	1951	Brian Hurst	0	Hurst	Christmas Carol
8	Christmas In July	1940	Preston Sturges	1	Sturges	Christmas In July
9	A Clockwork Orange	1971	Stanley Kubrick	3	Kubrick	Clockwork Orange
10	Die Hard	1991	John McTiernan	6	McTiernan	Die Hard
11	Old Ironsides	1926	James Cruze	1	Cruze	Old Ironsides
12	An Old Spanish Custom	1936	Adrian Brunel	1	Brunel	Old Spanish Custom
13	A Perfect World	1993	Clint Eastwood	3	Eastwood	Perfect World
14	Perfectly Normal	1990	Yves Simoneau	2	Simoneau	Perfectly Normal
15	The Shining	1980	Stanley Kubrick	5	Kubrick	Shining
16	The Terminator	1984	James Cameron	7	Cameron	Terminator
17						

DVD Inventory | Compound Criteria (AND) | Compound Crite ...

FIGURE 17-2 This worksheet shows a formula that removes leading articles for proper sorting.

Sorting table data into an array, part I: The SORT function

Rather than sorting a table in place, you might prefer to extract a sorted subset of a table and store that subset in a dynamic array. You can do that with ease using Excel's **SORT** function:

```
SORT(array [, sort_index][, sort_order][, by_col])
```

array	The range, array, or table data to extract into the dynamic array.
sort_index	The column to use for the sort. If *by_col* is **TRUE**, then this is the row to use for the sort. If you omit *sort_index*, the default value is **1**.
sort_order	A number that specifies the sort order: **1** for ascending (this is the default) or **-1** for descending.
by_col	A Boolean value that specifies the sort direction: **FALSE** to sort by row (this is the default) or **TRUE** to sort by column.

For example, suppose you want to extract the first two columns in the table shown in Figure 17-2, and you want to sort the resulting array by the values in the Year column. Here's a **SORT** formula that will get the job done:

```
=SORT(A2:B16, 2)
```

Sorting table data into an array, part II: The SORTBY function

One possible annoyance with the **SORT** function introduced in the previous section is that it requires the sort field to be part of the resulting dynamic array. If you don't mind seeing the sort field in the results, then there's no problem. However, if you don't want the sort field in the results, then you need to turn to yet another Excel sorting function called **SORTBY**:

SORTBY(*array*, *by_array1* [, *sort_order1*][, *by_array2*][, *sort_order2*],…)

array	The range, array, or table data to extract into the dynamic array.
by_array1	The first range, array, or table data on which to sort *array*.
sort_order1	A number that specifies the sort order for *by_array1*: **1** for ascending (this is the default) or **-1** for descending.
by_array2	The second range, array, or table data on which to sort *array*.
sort_order2	A number that specifies the sort order for *by_array2*: **1** for ascending (this is the default) or **-1** for descending.

The key difference here is that *by_array1* can be outside of *array*. For example, suppose you want to extract the first four columns in the table shown in Figure 17-2, and you want to sort the resulting array by the values in the Sort Field2 column. Here's a **SORTBY** formula that will do it:

=SORTBY(A2:E16, F2:F16)

Filtering table data

One of the biggest problems with large tables is that it's often hard to find and extract the data you need. Sorting can help, but in the end, you're still working with the entire table. You need a way to define the data you want to work with and then have Excel display only those records onscreen. This is called *filtering* your data, and Excel's Filter command makes filtering out subsets of your data as easy as selecting an option from a drop-down list. In fact, that's literally what happens. When you convert a range to a table, Excel automatically turns on the Filter feature, which is why you see drop-down arrows in the cells containing the table's column labels. (You can toggle the Filter buttons off and on by choosing **Data** > **Filter**.) Selecting one of these arrows displays a table of all the unique entries in the column. Figure 17-3 shows the drop-down menu for the **Account Name** field in the accounts receivable table.

There are two basic techniques you can use in a **Filter** list:

- Deselect an item's check box to hide that item in the table.

- Deselect the **Select All** item, which deselects all the check boxes, and then select the check box for each item you want to see in the table.

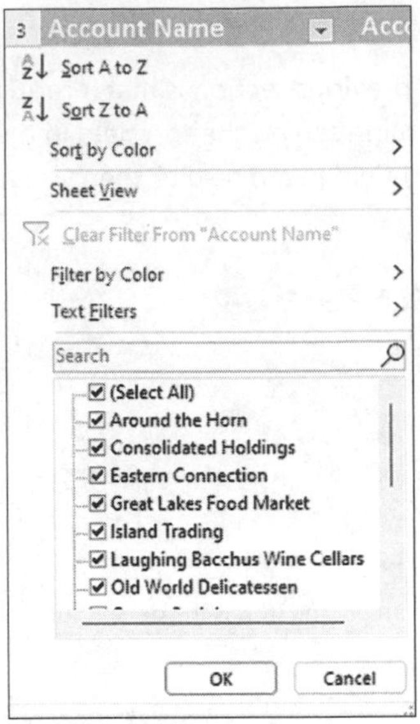

FIGURE 17-3 For each table field, Filter adds drop-down menus that contain only the unique entries in the column.

Using complex criteria to filter a table

The Filter command should take care of most of your filtering needs, but it's not designed for heavy-duty work. For example, it can't handle the following accounts receivable criteria:

- Invoice amounts greater than $100, less than $1,000, or greater than $10,000

- Account numbers that begin with 01, 05, or 12

- Days overdue greater than the value in cell J1

To work with these more sophisticated requests, you need to use *complex criteria*.

Setting up a criteria range

Before you can work with complex criteria, you must set up a *criteria range*. A criteria range has some or all of the table field names in the top row, with at least one blank row directly underneath. You enter your criteria in the blank row below the appropriate field name, and Excel searches the table for records with field values that satisfy the criteria. This setup gives you two major advantages over the Filter command:

- By using either multiple rows or multiple columns for a single field, you can create compound criteria with as many terms as you like.

- Because you're entering your criteria in cells, you can use formulas to create *computed criteria*.

You can place the criteria range anywhere on the worksheet outside the table range. The most common position, however, is a couple of rows above the table range. Figure 17-4 shows the accounts receivable table with a criteria range (A3:G4). As you can see, the criteria are entered in the cell below the field name. In this case, the displayed criteria will find all Around the Horn invoices that are greater than or equal to $1,000 and that are overdue (that is, invoices that have a value greater than 0 in the Days Overdue field).

	A	B	C	D	E	F	G
3	Account Name	Account Number	Invoice Number	Invoice Amount	Due Date	Date Paid	Days Overdue
4	Around the Horn			>= 1000		>0	
5							
6	Account Name	Account Number	Invoice Number	Invoice Amount	Due Date	Date Paid	Days Overdue
7	Around the Horn	10-0009	117321	$2,144.55	19-Jan-22		32
8	Around the Horn	10-0009	117327	$1,847.25	1-Feb-22		19
9	Around the Horn	10-0009	117339	$1,234.69	19-Feb-22	17-Feb-22	
10	Around the Horn	10-0009	117344	$875.50	5-Mar-22	28-Feb-22	
11	Around the Horn	10-0009	117353	$898.54	20-Mar-22	15-Mar-22	
12	Consolidated Holdings	02-0200	117318	$3,005.14	14-Jan-22	19-Jan-22	
13	Consolidated Holdings	02-0200	117334	$303.65	12-Feb-22	16-Feb-22	
14	Consolidated Holdings	02-0200	117345	$588.88	6-Mar-22	6-Mar-22	
15	Consolidated Holdings	02-0200	117350	$456.21	15-Mar-22	11-Mar-22	
16	Eastern Connection	01-0045	117319	$78.85	16-Jan-22	16-Jan-22	
17	Eastern Connection	01-0045	117324	$101.01	26-Jan-22		25
18	Eastern Connection	01-0045	117328	$58.50	2-Feb-22		18
19	Eastern Connection	01-0045	117333	$1,685.74	11-Feb-22	9-Feb-22	
20	Great Lakes Food Mark	08-2255	117316	$1,584.20	12-Jan-22		39

< > ... Compound Criteria (AND) Compound Criteria (OR) Compu ... + :

FIGURE 17-4 Set up a separate criteria range (A3:G4, in this case) to enter complex criteria.

Filtering a table with a criteria range

After you've set up your criteria range, you can use it to filter the table. The following steps take you through the basic procedure:

1. Copy the table field names that you want to use for the criteria, and paste them into the first row of the criteria range. If you'll be using different fields for different criteria, consider copying all your field names into the first row of the criteria range.

> **Tip** The only problem with copying the field names to the criteria range is that if you change a field name, you must change it in two places (that is, in the table and in the criteria). So, instead of just copying the names, you can make the field names in the criteria range dynamic by using a formula to set each criteria field name equal to its corresponding table field name. For example, you could enter =A6 in cell A3 of Figure 17-4.

2. Below each field name in the criteria range, enter the criteria you want to use.

3. Select a cell in the table and then select **Data** > **Advanced**. Excel displays the **Advanced Filter** dialog box, shown in Figure 17-5.

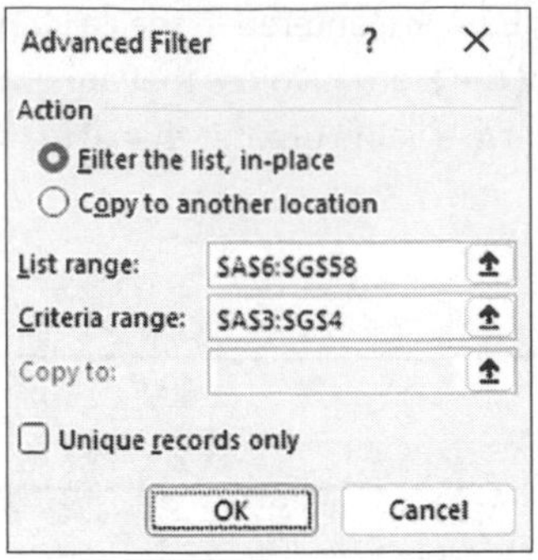

FIGURE 17-5 Use the Advanced Filter dialog box to select your table and criteria ranges.

4. Ensure that the **List Range** text box contains the table range (which it should if you selected a cell in the table beforehand). If it doesn't, select the text box and select the table (including the field names).

5. In the **Criteria Range** text box, select the criteria range (again, including the field names you copied).

6. To avoid including duplicate records in the filter, select the **Unique Records Only** check box.

7. Select **OK**. Excel filters the table to show only those records that match your criteria (see Figure 17-6).

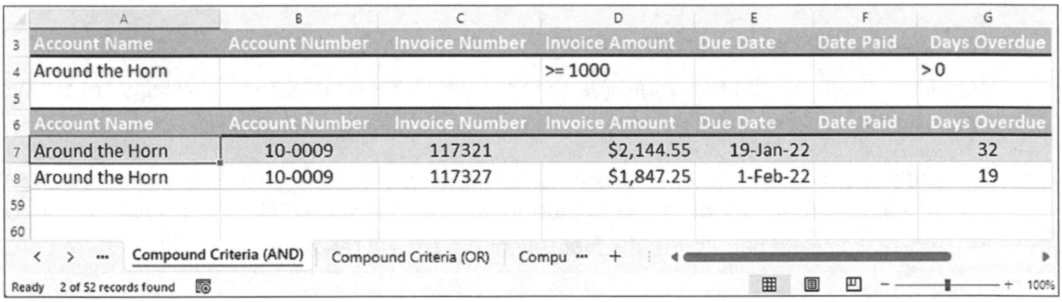

	A	B	C	D	E	F	G
3	Account Name	Account Number	Invoice Number	Invoice Amount	Due Date	Date Paid	Days Overdue
4	Around the Horn			>= 1000			> 0
5							
6	Account Name	Account Number	Invoice Number	Invoice Amount	Due Date	Date Paid	Days Overdue
7	Around the Horn	10-0009	117321	$2,144.55	19-Jan-22		32
8	Around the Horn	10-0009	117327	$1,847.25	1-Feb-22		19
59							
60							

Compound Criteria (AND)   Compound Criteria (OR)   Compu ··· +

Ready   2 of 52 records found

FIGURE 17-6 This worksheet shows the accounts receivable table filtered using the complex criteria specified in the criteria range.

Entering compound criteria

To enter compound criteria in a criteria range, use the following guidelines:

- To find records that match all the criteria, enter the criteria on a single row.

- To find records that match one or more of the criteria, enter the criteria on separate rows.

Finding records that match all the criteria is equivalent to activating the **And** button in the **Custom AutoFilter** dialog box. The sample criteria shown in Figure 17-6 match records with the account name Around the Horn *and* an invoice amount greater than $1,000 *and* a positive number in the **Days Overdue** field. To narrow the displayed records, you can enter criteria for as many fields as you like.

> **Tip** You can use the same field name more than once in compound criteria. To do this, you include the appropriate field multiple times in the criteria range and enter the appropriate criteria below each label.

Finding records that match at least one of several criteria is equivalent to activating the **Or** button in the **Custom AutoFilter** dialog box. In this case, you need to enter each criterion on a separate row. For example, to display all invoices with amounts greater than or equal to $10,000 or that are more than 30 days overdue, you would set up your criteria as shown in Figure 17-7.

	A	B	C	D	E	F	G
3	Account Name	Account Number	Invoice Number	Invoice Amount	Due Date	Date Paid	Days Overdue
4				>= 10000			
5							> 30
6							
7	Account Name	Account Number	Invoice Number	Invoice Amount	Due Date	Date Paid	Days Overdue
8	Around the Horn	10-0009	117321	$2,144.55	19-Jan-22		32
21	Great Lakes Food Marke	08-2255	117316	$1,584.20	12-Jan-22		39
24	Island Trading	12-1212	117322	$234.69	20-Jan-22		31
26	Island Trading	12-1212	117351	$12,474.25	17-Mar-22		
31	Old World Delicatessen	12-3456	117341	$11,585.23	25-Feb-22		
37	Rattlesnake Canyon Gro	14-5741	117317	$303.65	13-Jan-22		38
60							
61							

< > ⋯ **Compound Criteria (OR)** Computed Criteria Table Formulas ⋯ +

Ready   6 of 52 records found

FIGURE 17-7 To display records that match one or more of the criteria, enter the criteria in separate rows.

> **Caution** Don't include any blank rows in your criteria range because blank rows throw off Excel when it tries to match the criteria.

Entering computed criteria

The fields in your criteria range aren't restricted to the table fields. You can create *computed criteria* that use a calculation to match records in the table. The calculation can refer to one or more table fields—or even to cells outside the table—and must return either TRUE or FALSE. Excel selects records that return TRUE.

To use computed criteria, add a column to the criteria range and enter the formula in the new field. Make sure that the name you give the criteria field is different from any field name in the table (or leave the name blank). When referencing the table cells in the formula, use the first data row of the table.

For example, to select all records in which Date Paid is equal to Due Date in the accounts receivable table, enter the following formula:

```
=F6 = E6
```

Note the use of relative addressing. If you want to reference cells outside the table, use absolute addressing.

> **Tip** Use Excel's **AND**, **OR**, and **NOT** functions to create compound computed criteria. For example, to select all records in which the Days Overdue value is less than 90 and greater than 31, type this:
>
> ```
> =AND(G7 < 90, G7 > 31)
> ```

Figure 17-8 shows a more complex example. The goal is to select all records whose invoices were paid after the due date. The new criterion—named Late Payers—contains the following formula:

```
=IF(ISBLANK(F7), FALSE, F7 > E7)
```

A4	▾ : × ✓ *fx*	=IF(ISBLANK(F7), FALSE(), F7 > E7)					
	A	B	C	D	E	F	G
3	Late Payers						
4	FALSE						
5							
6	Account Name	Account Number	Invoice Number	Invoice Amount	Due Date	Date Paid	Days Overdue
12	Consolidated Holdings	02-0200	117318	$3,005.14	14-Jan-22	19-Jan-22	
13	Consolidated Holdings	02-0200	117334	$303.65	12-Feb-22	16-Feb-22	
35	QUICK-Stop	14-1882	117342	$2,567.12	28-Feb-22	15-Mar-22	
39	Rattlesnake Canyon Gro	14-5741	117361	$854.50	21-Apr-22	6-May-22	
40	Rattlesnake Canyon Gro	14-5741	117363	$3,210.98	5-May-22	20-May-22	
46	Simon's Bistro	07-4441	117357	$2,144.55	30-Mar-22	14-Apr-22	
47	Split Rail Beer & Ale	07-4441	117336	$78.85	15-Feb-22	2-Mar-22	
48	Split Rail Beer & Ale	16-9734	117348	$157.25	13-Mar-22	28-Mar-22	
49	Split Rail Beer & Ale	16-9734	117348	$157.25	13-Mar-22	28-Mar-22	
59							
60							

< > ⋯ **Computed Criteria** Table Formulas Inventory DAVERAG ⋯ +
Ready 9 of 52 records found

FIGURE 17-8 Use a separate criteria range column for calculated criteria.

If the Date Paid field (column F) is blank, the invoice hasn't been paid, so the formula returns **FALSE**. Otherwise, the logical expression **F7 > E7** is evaluated. If the Date Paid field (column F) is greater than the Due Date field (column E), the expression returns **TRUE**, and Excel selects the record. In Figure 17-8, the Late Payers cell (A4) displays **FALSE** because the formula evaluates to **FALSE** for the first row in the table.

Filtering table data with the FILTER function

Rather than filtering a table in-place, you might prefer to extract a filtered subset of a table and store that subset in a dynamic array. You can do that using Excel's **FILTER** function:

FILTER(*array*, *include*[, *if_empty*])

array	The range, array, or table data to extract into the dynamic array.
include	A comparison array that determines which elements of *array* are included in the filtered results.
if_empty	The value you want Excel to return if the filter matches no values (that is, returns an empty result).

For example, suppose you want to extract the first four columns in the table shown in Figure 17-2, and you want to filter the resulting array to include only those DVDs where the Year value is greater than or equal to 1980. Here's a **FILTER** formula that does this:

=FILTER(A2:E16, B2:B16 >= 1980)

UNIQUE

To filter a table to return only its unique values into a dynamic array, give Excel's **UNIQUE** function a whirl:

UNIQUE(*array* [, *by_col*][, *occurs_once*])

array	The range, array, or table data to extract into the dynamic array.
by_col	A Boolean value that specifies the filter direction: **FALSE** to filter by row (this is the default) or **TRUE** to filter by column.
occurs_once	A Boolean value that determines how Excel returns unique values. The default is **FALSE**, which means that Excel includes all unique values; to include unique values only if they occur once, use **TRUE**.

For example, suppose you want to extract the unique director names in the table shown in Figure 17-2. Here's a **UNIQUE** formula that does this:

=UNIQUE(C2:C16)

Referencing tables in formulas

Excel supports a feature called *structured referencing* of tables. This means that Excel offers a set of defined names—or *specifiers*, as Microsoft calls them—for various table elements (such as the data, the headers, and the entire table), as well as the automatic creation of names for the table fields. You can include these names in your table formulas to make your calculations much easier to read and maintain.

Using table specifiers

First, let's look at the predefined specifiers that Excel offers for tables. Table 17-1 lists the names you can use.

TABLE 17-1 Excel's predefined table specifiers

Specifier	Refers To
#All	The entire table, including the column headers and total row.
#Data	The table data (that is, the entire table, not including the column headers and total row).
#Headers	The table's column headers.
#Totals	The table's total row.
@	The table row in which the formula appears. (This was #This Row in Excel 2007.)

Most table references start with the table name (as given by the Design, Table Name property). In the simplest case, you can use the table name by itself. For example, the following formula counts the numeric values in a table named Table1:

```
=COUNT(Table1)
```

If you want to reference a specific part of the table, you must enclose that reference in square brackets after the table name. For example, the following formula calculates the maximum data value in a table named Sales:

```
=MAX(Sales[#Data])
```

> **Tip** You can also reference tables in other workbooks by using the following syntax:
>
> ```
> 'Workbook'!Table
> ```
>
> Here, replace *Workbook* with the workbook file name, and replace *Table* with the table name.

> **Note** Using just the table name by itself is equivalent to using the **#Data** specifier. So, for example, the following two formulas produce the same result:
>
> ```
> =MAX(Sales[#Data])
> =MAX(Sales)
> ```

Excel also generates column specifiers based on the text in the column headers. Each column specifier references the data in the column, so it doesn't include the column's header or total. For example, suppose you have a table named Inventory, and you want to calculate the sum of the values in the field named Qty On Hand. The following formula does the trick:

```
=SUM(Inventory[Qty On Hand])
```

If you want to refer to a single value in a table field, you need to specify the row you want to work with. Here's the general syntax for this:

```
Table[[Row],[Field]]
```

Here, replace *Table* with the table name, *Row* with a row specifier, and *Field* with a field specifier. For the row specifier, you have only two choices: the current row and the totals row. The current row is the row in which the formula resides, and in Excel 2010 and later, you use the @ specifier to designate the current row (in Excel 2007, this specifier was `#This Row`). In this case, however, you use @ followed by the name of the field in square brackets, like so:

```
@[Standard Cost]
```

For example, in a table named Inventory with a field named Standard Cost, the following formula multiplies the Standard Cost value in the current row by 1.25:

```
=Inventory[@[Standard Cost]] * 1.25
```

> **Note** If your formula needs to reference a cell in a row other than the current row or the totals row, you need to use a regular cell reference such as A3 or D6.

For a cell in the totals row, use the `#Totals` specifier, as in this example, which references the totals row for both the Qty On Hand field and the Qty On Hold field:

```
=Inventory[[#Totals],[Qty On Hand]] - Inventory[[#Totals],[Qty On Hold]]
```

Finally, you can also create ranges by using structured table referencing. As with regular cell references, you create a range by inserting a colon between two specifiers. For example, the following reference includes all the data cells in the Inventory table's Qty On Hold and Qty On Hand fields:

```
Inventory[[Qty On Hold]:[Qty On Hand]]
```

Entering table formulas

When you build a formula using structured referencing, Excel offers several tools that make it easy and accurate. First, note that table names are part of Excel's Formula AutoComplete feature. This means that after you type the first few letters of the table name, you'll see the formula name in the AutoComplete list, so you can then select the name and press Tab to add it to your formula. When you then type the opening square bracket ([), Excel displays a list of the table's available specifiers, as shown in Figure 17-9. The first few items are the field names, and the bottom four are the built-in specifiers. Select the specifier and press Tab to add it to your formula. Each time you type an opening square bracket—([)—Excel displays the specifier list.

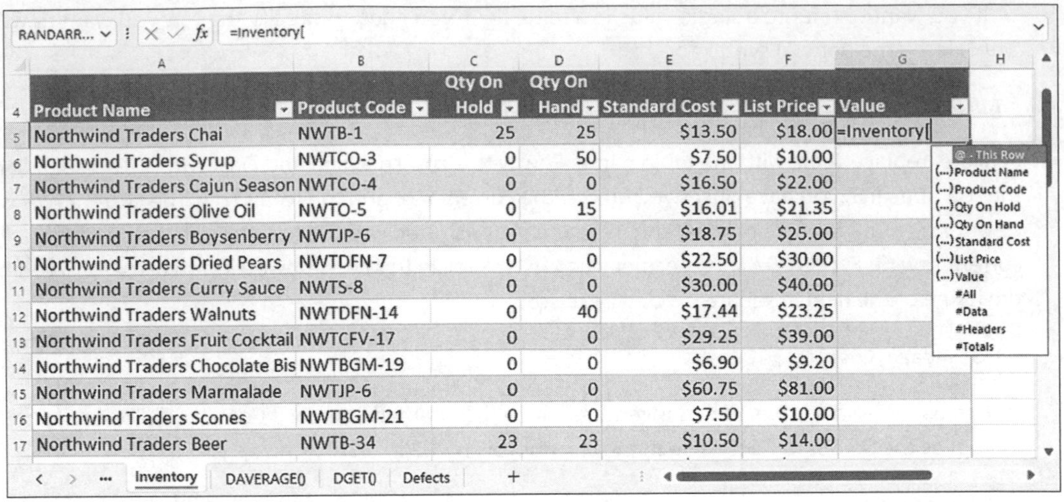

FIGURE 17-9 Type a table name and the opening square bracket ([), and Excel displays a list of the table's specifiers.

One of my favorite Excel features is its support for automatic calculated columns. To demonstrate how this works, Figure 17-10 shows a full formula that I've typed into a table cell but haven't yet completed (by, say, pressing Enter). When I press Enter, Excel automatically fills the same formula into the rest of the table's rows, as you can see in Figure 17-11. Excel also displays an **AutoCorrect Options** button, which enables you to reverse the calculated column, if desired.

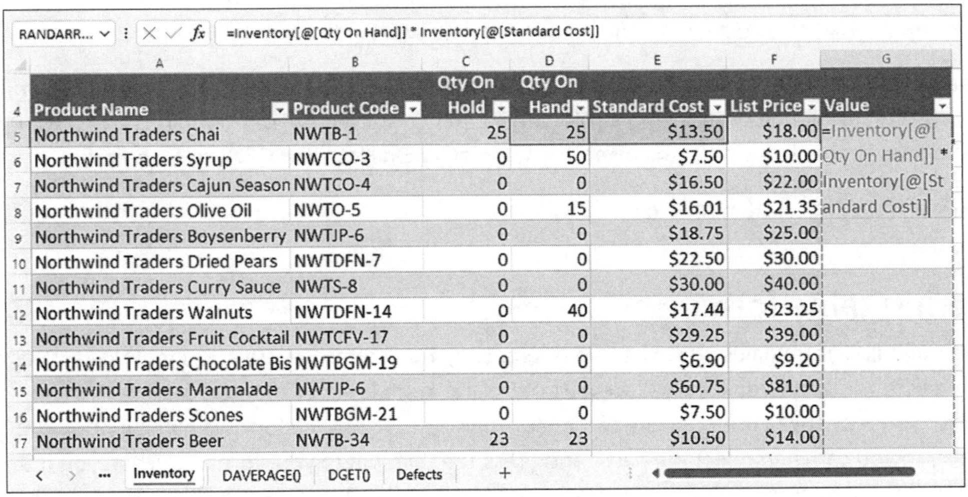

FIGURE 17-10 This worksheet shows a new table formula, ready to be confirmed.

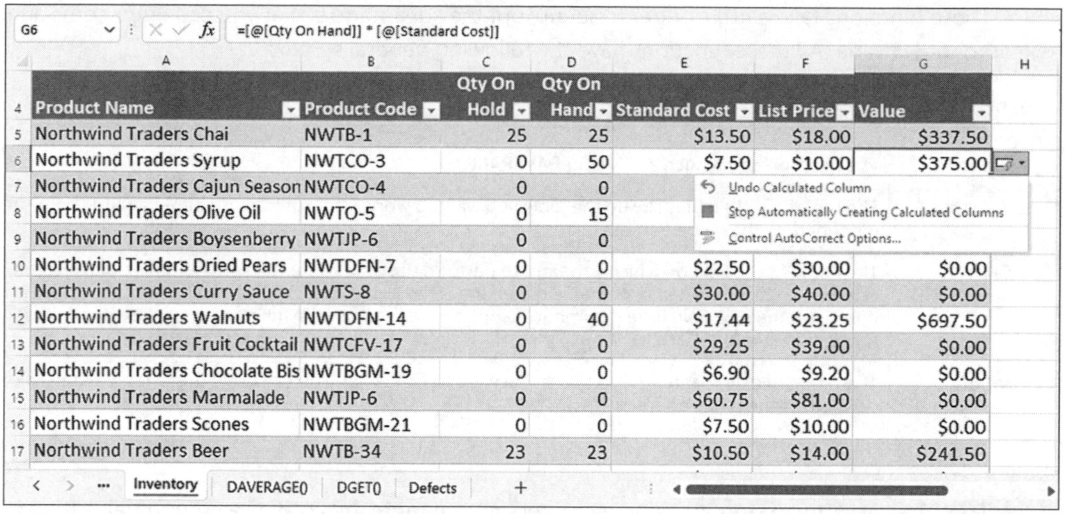

	Product Name	Product Code	Qty On Hold	Qty On Hand	Standard Cost	List Price	Value
5	Northwind Traders Chai	NWTB-1	25	25	$13.50	$18.00	$337.50
6	Northwind Traders Syrup	NWTCO-3	0	50	$7.50	$10.00	$375.00
7	Northwind Traders Cajun Season	NWTCO-4	0	0			
8	Northwind Traders Olive Oil	NWTO-5	0	15			
9	Northwind Traders Boysenberry	NWTJP-6	0	0			
10	Northwind Traders Dried Pears	NWTDFN-7	0	0	$22.50	$30.00	$0.00
11	Northwind Traders Curry Sauce	NWTS-8	0	0	$30.00	$40.00	$0.00
12	Northwind Traders Walnuts	NWTDFN-14	0	40	$17.44	$23.25	$697.50
13	Northwind Traders Fruit Cocktail	NWTCFV-17	0	0	$29.25	$39.00	$0.00
14	Northwind Traders Chocolate Bis	NWTBGM-19	0	0	$6.90	$9.20	$0.00
15	Northwind Traders Marmalade	NWTJP-6	0	0	$60.75	$81.00	$0.00
16	Northwind Traders Scones	NWTBGM-21	0	0	$7.50	$10.00	$0.00
17	Northwind Traders Beer	NWTB-34	23	23	$10.50	$14.00	$241.50

FIGURE 17-11 When you confirm a new table formula, Excel automatically fills the formula into the rest of the table.

> **Note** In Figure 17-11, also notice that Excel simplified the table formula by removing the table names, which it considers redundant.

Excel's table functions

To take your table analysis to a higher level, you can use Excel's *table functions*, which give you the following advantages:

- You can enter the functions into any cell in the worksheet.
- You can specify the range the function uses to perform its calculations.
- You can reference a criteria range to perform calculations on subsets of the table.

About table functions

To illustrate the table functions, consider an example: If you want to calculate the sum of a table field, you can enter **`SUM(range)`**, and Excel produces the result. If you want to sum only a subset of the field, you must specify as arguments the particular cells to use. For tables containing hundreds of records, however, this process is impractical.

The solution is to use **`DSUM`**, which is the table equivalent of the **`SUM`** function. The **`DSUM`** function takes three arguments: a table range, field name, and criteria range. **`DSUM`** looks at the specified field in the table and sums only records that match the criteria in the criteria range.

These functions take a little longer to set up, but the advantage is that you can enter compound and computed criteria. All these functions have the following general syntax:

```
Dfunction(database, field, criteria)
```

Dfunction	The function name, such as **DSUM** or **DAVERAGE**.
database	The range of cells that make up the table you want to work with. You can use either a range name, if one is defined, or the range address.
field	The name of the field on which you want to perform the operation. You can use the field name, the cell reference of the field name, or the field number as the argument (in which the leftmost field is field number 1, the next field is field number 2, and so on). If you use the field name, enclose it in quotation marks (for example, **"Total Cost"**).
criteria	The range of cells that hold the criteria you want to work with. You can use either a range name, if one is defined, or the range address.

> **Tip** To perform an operation on every record in a table, leave all the *criteria* fields blank. This causes Excel to select every record in the table.

> **Note** If you don't want to set up a separate criteria range, you can still analyze your tables with calculations such as counts, averages, and sums using Excel's criteria-based worksheet functions, including COUNTIF, AVERAGEIF, and SUMIF. See Chapter 11, "Building descriptive statistical formulas."

Table 17-2 summarizes the table functions.

TABLE 17-2 Excel's table functions

Function	Description
DAVERAGE	Returns the average of the matching records in a specified field
DCOUNT	Returns the count of the matching records
DCOUNTA	Returns the count of the nonblank matching records
DGET	Returns the value of a specified field for a single matching record
DMAX	Returns the maximum value of a specified field for the matching records
DMIN	Returns the minimum value of a specified field for the matching records
DPRODUCT	Returns the product of the values of a specified field for the matching records
DSTDEV	Returns the estimated standard deviation of the values in a specified field if the matching records are a sample of the population
DSTDEVP	Returns the standard deviation of the values of a specified field if the matching records are the entire population
DSUM	Returns the sum of the values of a specified field for the matching records

Function	Description
DVAR	Returns the estimated variance of the values of a specified field if the matching records are a sample of the population
DVARP	Returns the variance of the values of a specified field if the matching records are the entire population

(To learn about statistical operations such as standard deviation and variance, see Chapter 11.)

You enter table functions the same way you enter any other Excel function. You type an equal sign (=) and then enter the function—either by itself or combined with other Excel operators in a formula. The following examples show valid table functions:

```
=DSUM(A6:H14, "Total Cost", A1:H3)
=DSUM(Table, "Total Cost", Criteria)
=DSUM(AR_Table, 3, Criteria)
=DSUM(2022_Sales, "Sales", A1:H13)
```

The next two sections provide examples of the **DAVERAGE** and **DGET** table functions.

Using DAVERAGE

The **DAVERAGE** function calculates the average *field* value in the *database* records that match the *criteria*. In the Parts database, for example, suppose that you want to calculate the average gross margin for all parts assigned to Division 2. You set up a criteria range for the Division field and enter **2**, as shown in Figure 17-12. You then enter the following **DAVERAGE** function (see cell H3):

```
=DAVERAGE(Parts[#All], "Gross Margin", A2:A3)
```

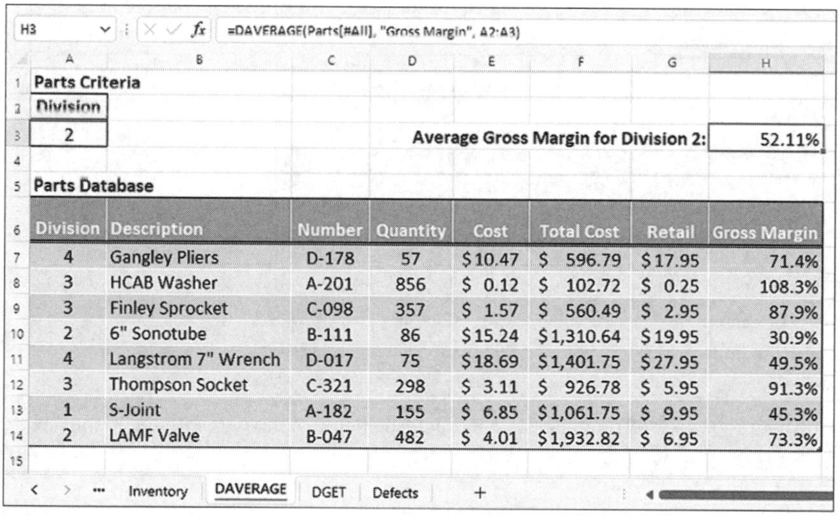

FIGURE 17-12 Use DAVERAGE to calculate the field average in the matching records.

Using DGET

The **DGET** function extracts the value of a single *field* in the *database* records that match the *criteria*. If there are no matching records, **DGET** returns **#VALUE!**. If there's more than one matching record, **DGET** returns **#NUM!**.

DGET typically is used to query the table for a specific piece of information. For example, in the Parts table, you might want to know the cost of the Finley Sprocket. To extract this information, you would first set up a criteria range with the Description field and enter **Finley Sprocket**. You would then extract the information with the following formula (assuming that the table and criteria ranges are named Parts and Criteria, respectively):

```
=DGET(Parts[#All], "Cost", Criteria)
```

A more interesting application of this function would be to extract the name of a part that satisfies a certain condition. For example, you might want to know the name of the part that has the highest gross margin. Creating this model requires two steps:

1. Set up the criteria to match the highest value in the Gross Margin field.

2. Add a **DGET** function to extract the description of the matching record.

Figure 17-13 shows how this is done. For the criteria, a new field called Highest Margin is created. As the text box shows, this field uses the following computed criteria:

```
=H7 = MAX(Parts2[Gross Margin])
```

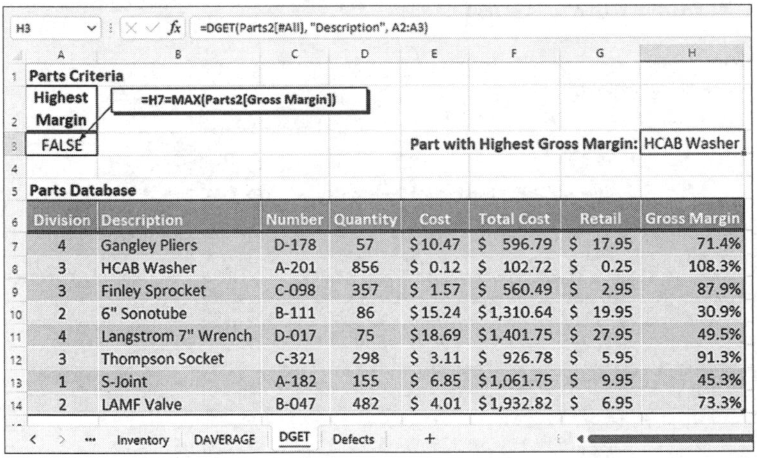

FIGURE 17-13 This worksheet shows a DGET function that extracts the name of the part with the highest margin.

Excel matches only the record that has the highest gross margin. The **DGET** function in cell H3 is straightforward:

```
=DGET(Parts2[#All], "Description", A2:A3)
```

This formula returns the description of the part that has the highest gross margin.

Case study: Applying statistical table functions to a defects database

Many table functions are most often used to analyze statistical populations. Figure 17-14 shows a table of defects found among 12 work groups in a manufacturing process. In this example, the table (B3:D15) is named Defects, and two criteria ranges are used—one for each of the group leaders, Johnson (G3:G4 is `Criteria1`) and Perkins (H3:H4 is `Criteria2`).

| G10 | ⌄ : ✕ ✓ *fx* | =(DSUM(Defects[#All], "Defects", Criteria1) - G6 - G7) / (DCOUNT(Defects[#All], , Criteria1) - 2) |

	A	B	C	D	E	F	G	H	I	J
1		**Defects Database**						**Criteria**		
2								**1**	**2**	
3								Group Leader	Group Leader	
4		**Workgroup**	**Group Leader**	**Defects**				Johnson	Perkins	
4		A	Johnson	8						
5		B	Perkins	10						
6		C	Perkins	0			Maximum	26	14	
7		D	Johnson	11			Minimum	6	0	
8		E	Johnson	9			Range	20	14	
9		F	Johnson	6			Average	11.67	8.67	
10		G	Perkins	11			Adjusted Avg	10	10	
11		H	Perkins	10			Std Deviation (sample)	7.23	4.80	
12		I	Perkins	7			Std. Deviation (pop.)	6.60	4.38	
13		J	Perkins	14			Variance (sample)	52.27	23.07	
14		K	Johnson	10			Variance (pop.)	43.56	19.22	
15		L	Johnson	26						
16										

| < > ⋯ | Inventory | DAVERAGE() | DGET() | Defects | + |

FIGURE 17-14 You can use statistical table functions to analyze a database of defects in a manufacturing process.

The table shows several calculations. First, **DMAX** and **DMIN** are calculated for each criterion. The **range** (a statistic that represents the difference between the largest and smallest numbers in the sample; it's a crude measure of the sample's variance) is then calculated using the following formula (Johnson's groups):

```
=DMAX(Defects[#All], "Defects", Criteria1) - DMIN(Defects[#All],
"Defects", Criteria1)
```

Of course, instead of using **DMAX** and **DMIN** explicitly, you can simply refer to the cells containing the **DMAX** and **DMIN** results.

The next line uses **DAVERAGE** to find the average number of defects for each group leader. Notice that the average for Johnson's groups (11.67) is significantly higher than that for Perkins's groups (8.67). However, Johnson's average is skewed higher by one anomalously large number (26), and Perkins's average is skewed lower by one anomalously small number (0).

To allow for this situation, the Adjusted Avg line uses **DSUM**, **DCOUNT**, and the **DMAX** and **DMIN** results to compute a new average without the largest and smallest number for each sample. As you can see, without the anomalies, the two leaders have the same average.

> **Note** As shown in cell G10 of Figure 17-14, if you don't include a `field` argument in the **DCOUNT** function, it returns the total number of records in the table.

The rest of the calculations use the **DSTDEV**, **DSTDEVP**, **DVAR**, and **DVARP** functions.

CHAPTER 18

Analyzing data with PivotTables

In this chapter, you will:

- Hide and customize PivotTable subtotals

- Change the value field summary calculation

- Create custom PivotTable calculations, including calculated fields and calculated items

- Learn how to use PivotTable results in worksheet formulas

Tables and external databases can contain hundreds or even thousands of records. Analyzing that much data can be a nightmare without the right kinds of tools. To help you, Excel offers a powerful data analysis tool called a *PivotTable*. This tool enables you to summarize hundreds—or even hundreds of thousands—of records in a concise tabular format. You can then manipulate the layout of the table to see different views of your data. Because this is a book about Excel formulas and functions, I don't provide instructions on building and customizing PivotTables. Instead, I focus on the extensive work you can do with built-in and custom PivotTable calculations.

Working with PivotTable subtotals

When you build a PivotTable, Excel adds grand totals for the row field and the column field. However, Excel also displays subtotals for the outer field of a PivotTable with multiple fields in the row or column area. For example, in Figure 18-1, you see two fields in the row area: Product (Mouse pad, HDMI cable, and so on) and Promotion (1 Free with 10 and Extra Discount). Product is the outer field, so Excel displays subtotals for that field.

The next few sections show you how to manipulate both the grand totals and the subtotals.

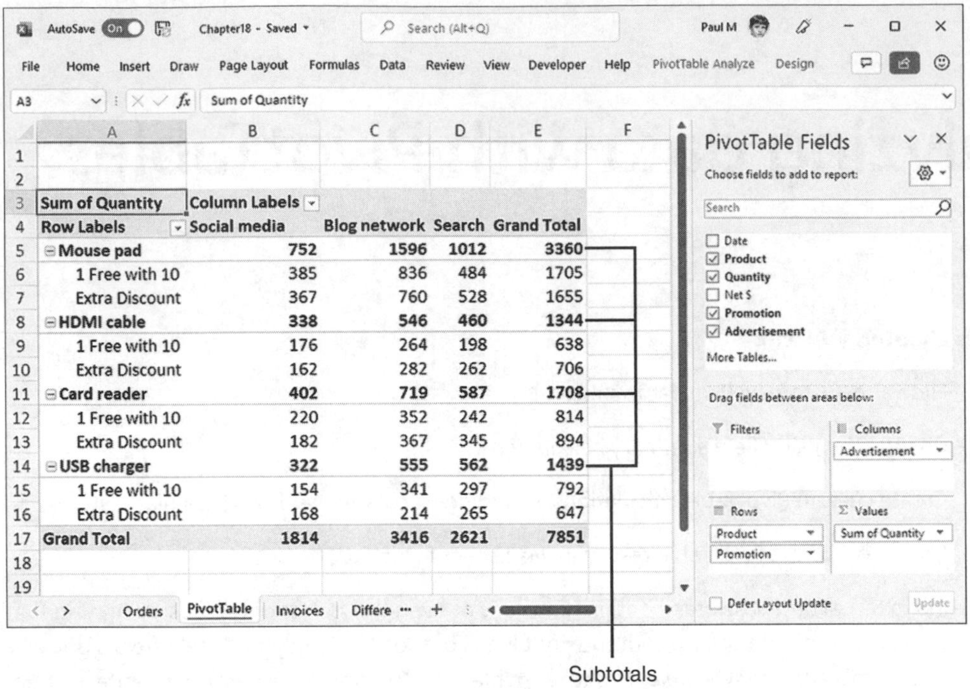

FIGURE 18-1 When you add multiple fields to the row or column area, Excel displays subtotals for the outer field.

Hiding PivotTable grand totals

To remove grand totals from a PivotTable, follow these steps:

1. Select a cell inside the PivotTable.

2. Select the **Design** tab.

3. Select **Grand Totals** > **Off For Rows And Columns**. Excel removes the grand totals from the PivotTable.

Hiding PivotTable subtotals

PivotTables with multiple row or column fields display subtotals for all fields except the innermost field (that is, the field closest to the data area). To remove these subtotals, follow these steps:

1. Select a cell in the field.

2. Select the **Design** tab.

3. Select **Subtotals** > **Do Not Show Subtotals**. Excel removes the subtotals from the PivotTable.

Customizing the subtotal calculation

The subtotal calculation that Excel applies to a field is the same calculation it uses for the data area. (See the next section for details on how to change the value field summary calculation.) You can, however, change this calculation, add extra calculations, and even add a subtotal for the innermost field. Select the field you want to work with, select **PivotTable Analyze** > **Field Settings**, and then use either of these methods:

- To change the subtotal calculation, select **Custom** in the **Subtotals** group, select one of the calculation functions (**Sum**, **Count**, **Average**, and so on) in the **Select One Or More Functions** list, and then select **OK**.

- To add extra subtotal calculations, select **Custom** in the **Subtotals** group, use the **Select One Or More Functions** list to select each calculation function you want to add, and then select **OK**.

Changing the value field summary calculation

By default, Excel uses a Sum function for calculating the value field summaries. Although **Sum** is the most common summary function used in PivotTables, it's by no means the only one. In fact, Excel offers 11 summary functions, as outlined in Table 18-1.

TABLE 18-1 Excel's value field summary calculations

Function	Description
Sum	Adds the values for the underlying data
Count	Displays the total number of values in the underlying data
Average	Calculates the average of the values for the underlying data
Max	Returns the largest value for the underlying data
Min	Returns the smallest value for the underlying data
Product	Calculates the product of the values for the underlying data
Count Numbers	Displays the total number of numeric values in the underlying data
StdDev	Calculates the standard deviation of the values for the underlying data, treated as a sample
StdDevp	Calculates the standard deviation of the values for the underlying data, treated as a population
Var	Calculates the variance of the values for the underlying data, treated as a sample
Varp	Calculates the variance of the values for the underlying data, treated as a population

Follow these steps to change the value field summary calculation:

1. Right-click any cell inside the value field.

2. Select **Summarize Values By**. Excel displays a partial list of the available summary calculations.

3. If you see the calculation you want, select it and skip the rest of these steps; otherwise, select **More Options** to open the **Value Field Settings** dialog box.

4. Select the summary calculation you want to use.

5. Select **OK**. Excel changes the value field calculation.

Using a difference summary calculation

When you analyze business data, it's almost always useful to summarize the data as a whole: the sum of the units sold, the total number of orders, the average margin, and so on. For example, the PivotTable report shown in Figure 18-2 summarizes invoice data from a two-year period. For each customer in the row field, we see the total of all invoices broken down by the invoice date, which, in this case, has been grouped by year (2021 and 2022).

	A	B	C	D
1	Country	USA		
2				
3	**Sum of Extended Price**	Column Labels		
4	**Row Labels**	2021	2022	Grand Total
5	Great Lakes Food Market	$8,565.30	$9,942.14	$18,507.44
6	Hungry Coyote Import Store	$2,283.20	$780.00	$3,063.20
7	Lazy K Kountry Store	$357.00		$357.00
8	Let's Stop N Shop	$1,698.40	$1,378.07	$3,076.47
9	Lonesome Pine Restaurant	$1,837.20	$2,421.40	$4,258.60
10	Old World Delicatessen	$5,475.38	$9,795.74	$15,271.12
11	Rattlesnake Canyon Grocery	$19,383.75	$31,714.05	$51,097.80
12	Save-a-lot Markets	$57,716.57	$46,648.37	$104,364.94
13	Split Rail Beer & Ale	$2,475.00	$8,966.63	$11,441.63
14	The Big Cheese	$2,955.40	$405.60	$3,361.00
15	The Cracker Box	$1,621.24	$326.00	$1,947.24
16	Trail's Head Gourmet Provisioners	$1,333.30	$237.90	$1,571.20
17	White Clover Markets	$9,146.50	$18,217.10	$27,363.60
18	**Grand Total**	$114,848.24	$130,833.00	$245,681.24
19				

FIGURE 18-2 This worksheet displays a PivotTable report showing customer invoice totals by year.

However, it's also useful to compare one part of the data with another. In the PivotTable shown in Figure 18-2, for example, it would be valuable to compare each customer's invoice totals in 2022 with those in 2021.

In Excel, you can perform this kind of analysis by using PivotTable *difference calculations*:

- **Difference From:** This difference calculation compares two numeric items and calculates the difference between them.

- **% Difference From:** This difference calculation compares two numeric items and calculates the percentage difference between them.

In each case, you must specify both a *base field* (the field in which you want Excel to perform the difference calculation) and the *base item* (the item in the base field that you want to use as the basis of the difference calculation). In the PivotTable shown in Figure 18-2, for example, Order Date would be the base field, and 2021 would be the base item.

Here are the steps to follow to set up a difference calculation:

1. Right-click any cell inside the value field.

2. Select **Show Values As** and then select either **Difference From** or **% Difference From**. Excel displays the **Show Values As** dialog box.

3. In the **Base Field** list, select the field you want to use as the base field.

4. In the **Base Item** list, select the item you want to use as the base item.

5. Select **OK**. Excel updates the PivotTable with the difference calculation.

Figure 18-3 shows both the completed **Show Values As** dialog box and the updated PivotTable with the **Difference From** calculation applied to the report from Figure 18-2.

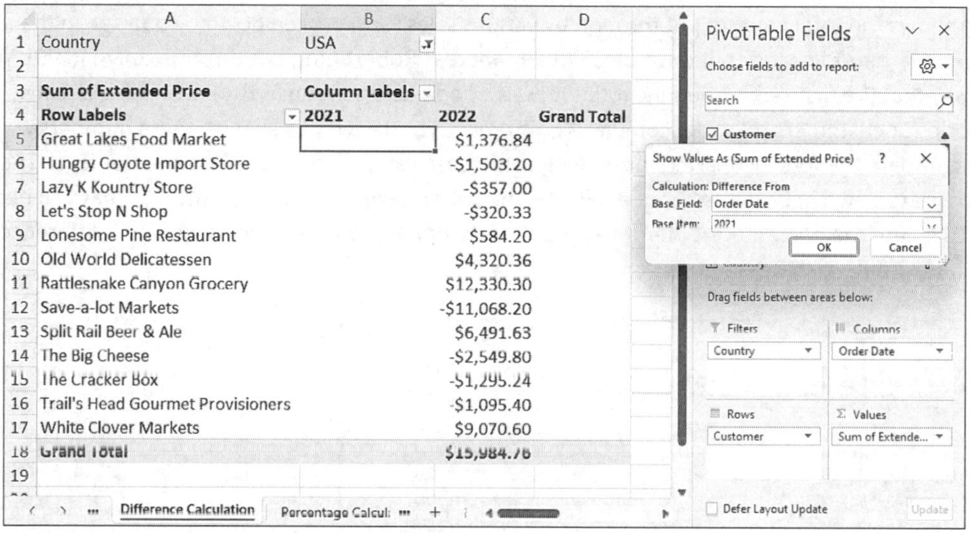

FIGURE 18-3 This worksheet shows the PivotTable report from Figure 18-2 with a Difference From calculation applied.

Toggling the difference calculation with VBA

Here's a VBA macro that toggles the PivotTable report in Figure 18-3 between a **Difference From** calculation and a **% Difference From** calculation:

```
Sub ToggleDifferenceCalculations
    ' Work with the first value field
    With Selection.PivotTable.DataFields(1)
        ' Is the calculation currently Difference From?
        If .Calculation = xlDifferenceFrom Then
            ' If so, change it to % Difference From
```

```
        .Calculation = xlPercentDifferenceFrom
        .BaseField = "Order Date"
        .BaseItem = "2021"
        .NumberFormat = "0.00%"
    Else
        ' If not, change it to Difference From
        .Calculation = xlDifferenceFrom
        .BaseField = "Order Date"
        .BaseItem = "2021"
        .NumberFormat = "$#,##0.00"
    End If
End With
End Sub
```

Using a percentage summary calculation

When you need to compare the results that appear in a PivotTable report, just looking at the basic summary calculations isn't always useful. For example, consider the PivotTable report in Figure 18-4, which shows the total invoices put through by various sales reps, broken down by quarter. In the fourth quarter, Margaret Peacock put through $64,429, whereas Robert King put through only $16,951. You can't say that the first rep is (roughly) four times as good a salesperson as the second rep because their territories or customers might be completely different. A better way to analyze these numbers would be to compare the fourth-quarter figures with some base value, such as the first-quarter total. The numbers are down in both cases, but again, the raw differences won't tell you much. What you need to do is calculate the percentage differences and then compare them with the percentage difference in the Grand Total.

Row Labels	Qtr1	Qtr2	Qtr3	Qtr4
Andrew Fuller	$48,905	$57,294	$23,250	$37,088
Anne Dodsworth	$34,074	$13,689	$14,610	$14,936
Janet Leverling	$92,398	$46,859	$18,647	$44,908
Laura Callahan	$50,782	$23,958	$25,582	$26,541
Margaret Peacock	$79,279	$40,423	$48,763	$64,429
Michael Suyama	$12,797	$19,053	$14,564	$27,499
Nancy Davolio	$58,492	$33,929	$45,899	$53,787
Robert King	$38,054	$42,357	$27,206	$16,951
Steven Buchanan	$22,002	$7,748	$14,705	$24,338
Grand Total	$436,783	$285,309	$233,226	$310,477

FIGURE 18-4 This worksheet displays a PivotTable report showing sales rep invoice totals by quarter.

Similarly, knowing the raw invoice totals for each rep in a given quarter gives you only the most general idea of how the reps did with respect to each other. If you really want to compare them, you need to convert those totals into percentages of the quarterly grand total.

When you want to use percentages in your data analysis, you can use Excel's *percentage calculations* to view data items as a percentage of some other item or as a percentage of the total in the current row, column, or the entire PivotTable. Excel offers the following percentage calculations:

■ **% Of:** This calculation returns the percentage of each value with respect to a selected base item. If you use this calculation, you must also select a base field and a base item upon which Excel will calculate the percentages.

■ **% of Row Total:** This calculation returns the percentage that each value in a row represents with respect to the Grand Total for that row.

■ **% of Column Total:** This calculation returns the percentage that each value in a column represents with respect to the Grand Total for that column.

■ **% of Parent Row Total:** If you have multiple fields in the row area, this calculation returns the percentage that each value in an inner row represents with respect to the total of the parent item in the outer row. (This calculation also returns the percentage that each value in the outer row represents with respect to the Grand Total.)

■ **% of Parent Column Total:** If you have multiple fields in the column area, this calculation returns the percentage that each value in an inner column represents with respect to the total of the parent item in the outer column. (This calculation also returns the percentage that each value in the outer column represents with respect to the Grand Total.)

■ **% of Parent Total:** If you have multiple fields in the row or column area, this calculation returns the percentage of each value with respect to a selected base field in the outer row or column. If you use this calculation, you must also select a base field upon which Excel will calculate the percentages.

■ **% of Grand Total:** This calculation returns the percentage that each value in the PivotTable represents with respect to the Grand Total of the entire PivotTable.

Here are the steps to follow to set up a difference calculation:

1. Right-click any cell inside the value field.

2. Select **Show Values As** and then select the percentage calculation you want to use. Excel displays the **Show Values As** dialog box.

3. If you selected either **% Of** or **% Of Parent Total**, use the **Base Field** list to select the field you want to use as the base field.

4. If you selected **% Of**, use the **Base Item** list to select the item you want to use as the base item.

5. Select **OK**. Excel updates the PivotTable with the percentage calculation.

Figure 18-5 shows both the completed **Show Values As** dialog box and the updated PivotTable with the **% Of** calculation applied to the report from Figure 18-4.

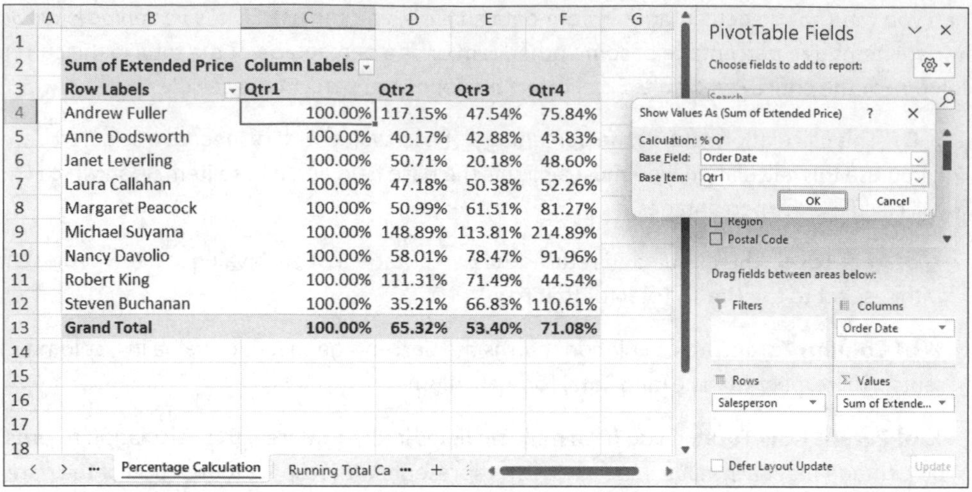

FIGURE 18-5 This worksheet shows the PivotTable report from Figure 18-4 with a % Of calculation applied.

> **Tip** If you want to use a VBA macro to set the percentage calculation for a value field, set the `PivotField` object's `Calculation` property to one of the following constants: `xlPercentOf`, `xlPercentOfRow`, `xlPercentOfColumn`, or `xlPercentOfTotal`.

When you switch back to **Normal** in the **Show Values As** list, Excel formats the value field as General, so you lose any numeric formatting you had applied. You can restore the numeric format by selecting inside the value field, choosing **PivotTable Analyze** > **Field Settings**, selecting **Number Format**, and then choosing the format in the **Format Cells** dialog box. Alternatively, you can use a macro that resets the `NumberFormat` property. Here's an example:

```
Sub ReapplyCurrencyFormat
    With Selection.PivotTable.DataFields(1)
        .NumberFormat = "$#,##0.00"
    End With
End Sub
```

Using a running total summary calculation

When you set up a budget, it's common to have sales targets not only for each month but also cumulative targets as the fiscal year progresses. For example, you might have sales targets for the first month and the second month and also for the two-month total. You'd also have cumulative targets for three months, four months, and so on. Cumulative sums such as these are known as *running totals*, and they can be valuable in analysis. For example, if you find that you're running behind budget cumulatively at the six-month mark, you can make adjustments to process, marketing plans, customer incentives, and so on.

Excel PivotTable reports come with a Running Total summary calculation that you can use for this kind of analysis. Note that the running total is always applied to a base field, which is the field on which you want to base the accumulation. This is almost always a date field, but you can use other field types, as appropriate.

Here are the steps to follow to set up a running total calculation:

1. Right-click any cell inside the value field.

2. Select **Show Values As** > **Running Total In**. Excel displays the **Show Values As** dialog box.

3. Use the **Base Field** list to select the field you want to use as the base field.

4. Select **OK**. Excel updates the PivotTable with the running total calculation.

Figure 18-6 shows both the completed **Show Values As** dialog box and a PivotTable with the **Running Total In** calculation applied to the **Order Date** field (grouped by month).

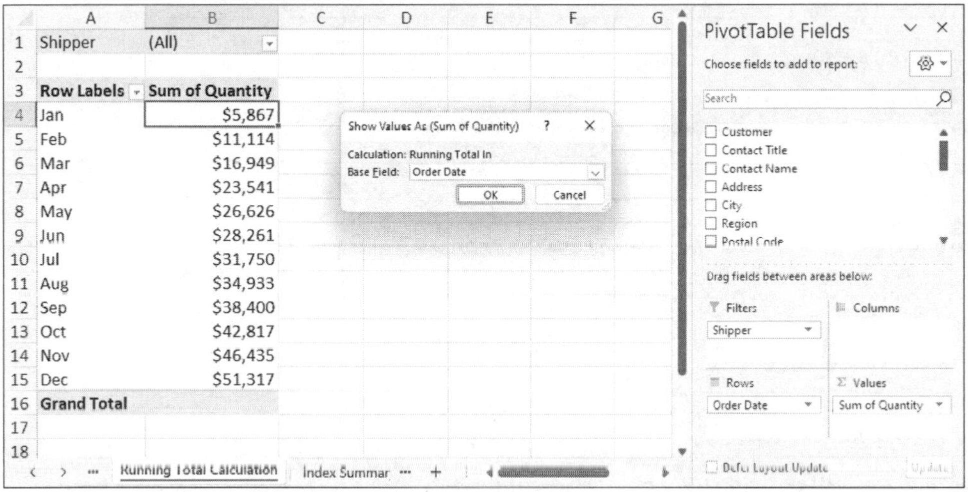

FIGURE 18-6 This worksheet shows the PivotTable report with a running total calculation.

> **Tip** If you use many of these extra summary calculations, you might find yourself con-stantly returning the **No Calculation** value in the **Show Values As** menu. That requires a few mouse clicks, so it can be a hassle to repeat the procedure frequently. You can save time by creating a VBA macro that resets the PivotTable to Normal by setting the `Calculation` property to `xlNoAdditionalCalculation`. Here's an example:

```
Sub ResetCalculationToNormal
    With Selection.PivotTable.DataFields(1)
        .Calculation = xlNoAdditionalCalculation
    End With
End Sub
```

Using an index summary calculation

A PivotTable is great for reducing a large amount of relatively incomprehensible data into a compact, more easily grasped summary report. As you've seen in the past few sections, however, a standard summary calculation doesn't always provide you with the best analysis of the data.

Another good example of this is trying to determine the relative importance of the results in the value field. For example, consider the PivotTable report shown in Figure 18-7. This report shows the unit sales of four items (mouse pad, HDMI cable, card reader, and USB charger), broken down by the type of advertisement the customer responded to (social media, blog network, and search).

You can see, for example, that 1,012 mouse pads were sold via the search ad (the second-highest number in the report), but only 562 USB chargers were sold through the search ad (one of the lower numbers in the report). Does this mean that you should only sell mouse pads in search ads? That is, is the mouse pad/search combination somehow more "important" than the USB charger/search combination?

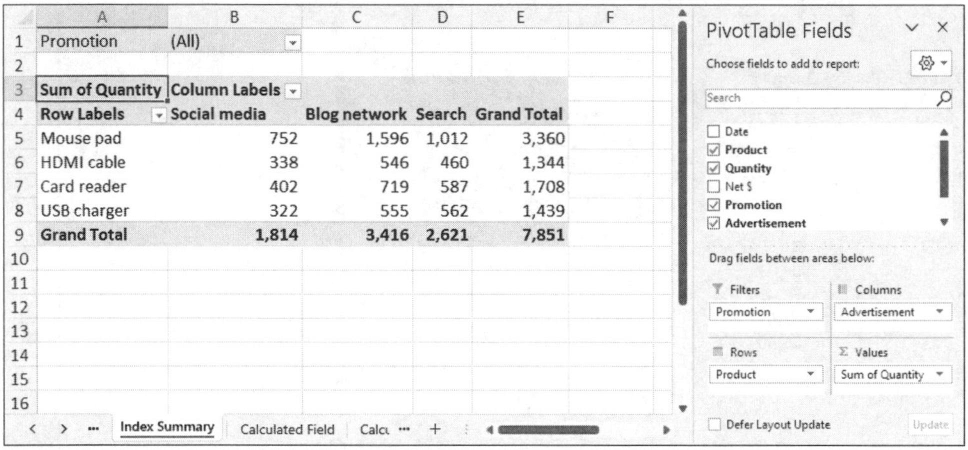

FIGURE 18-7 This worksheet displays a PivotTable report showing unit sales of products broken down by advertisement.

You might think the answer is yes to both questions in the previous paragraph, but that's not necessarily the case. To get an accurate answer, you'd need to take into account the total number of mouse pads sold, the total number of USB chargers sold, the total number of units sold through the search ad, and the number of units overall. This is a complicated bit of business, to be sure, but each PivotTable report has an Index calculation that handles it for you automatically. The Index calculation returns the *weighted average* of each cell in the PivotTable value field, using the following formula:

```
(Cell Value * Grand Total) / (Row Total * Column Total)
```

In the Index calculation results, the higher the value, the more important the cell is in the overall results. Here are the steps to follow to set up an Index calculation:

1. Right-click any cell inside the value field.

2. Select **Summarize Values By** and then select the summary calculation you want to use.

3. Right-click any cell inside the value field.

4. Select **Show Values As** > **Index**. Excel updates the PivotTable with the index summary calculation.

Figure 18-8 shows the updated PivotTable with the Index applied to the report from Figure 18-7. As you can see, the mouse pad/search combination scored an index of only 0.90 (the second-lowest value), whereas the USB charger/search combination scored 1.17 (the highest value). (Note that to get the index values to display with just two decimal places for easier reading, right-click a cell in the value field, click **Value Field Settings** > **Number Format** and select **Number**. Set the **Decimal Places** spin box to 2.)

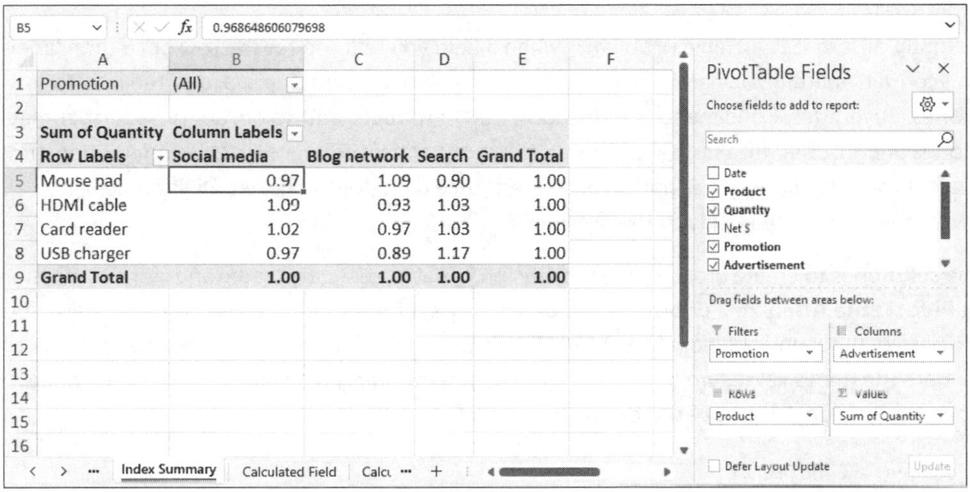

FIGURE 18-8 This worksheet shows the PivotTable report from Figure 18-7 with an Index calculation applied.

Creating custom PivotTable calculations

Excel's 11 built-in summary functions enable you to create powerful and useful PivotTable reports, but they don't cover every data analysis possibility. For example, suppose you have a PivotTable report that summarizes invoice totals by sales rep using the Sum function. That's useful, but you might also want to pay out a bonus to those reps whose total sales exceed some threshold. You could use the GETPIVOTDATA function to create regular worksheet formulas to calculate whether bonuses should be paid and how much they should be (assuming each bonus is a percentage of the total sales). (For the details on the GETPIVOTDATA function, see "Using PivotTable results in a worksheet formula," later in this chapter.)

However, this isn't very convenient. If you add sales reps, you need to add formulas; if you remove sales reps, existing formulas generate errors. And, in any case, one of the points of generating a Pivot-Table report is to perform *fewer* worksheet calculations, not more.

The solution, in this case, is to take advantage of Excel's *calculated field* feature. A calculated field is a new value field based on a custom formula. For example, if your invoice's PivotTable has an Extended Price field and you want to award a 5% bonus to those reps who did at least $75,000 worth of business, you'd create a calculated field based on the following formula:

```
=IF('Extended Price' >= 75000, 'Extended Price' * 0.05, 0)
```

> **Note** When you reference a field in your formula, Excel interprets this reference as the *sum* of that field's values. For example, if you include the logical expression `'Extended Price'` `>= 75000` in a calculated field formula, Excel interprets this as `Sum of 'Extended Price'` `>= 75000`. That is, it adds the Extended Price field and *then* compares it with 75000.

A slightly different PivotTable problem is when a field you're using for the row or column labels doesn't contain an item you need. For example, suppose your products are organized into various categories: Beverages, Condiments, Confections, Dairy Products, and so on. Suppose further that these categories are grouped into several divisions: Beverages and Condiments in Division A, Confections and Dairy Products in Division B, and so on. If the source data doesn't have a Division field, how do you see PivotTable results that apply to the divisions?

One solution is to create groups for each division. (That is, select the categories for one division, select **PivotTable Analyze** > **Group Selection** and repeat for the other divisions.) That works, but Excel gives you a second solution: Use calculated items. A *calculated item* is a new item in a row or column where the item's values are generated by a custom formula. For example, you could create a new item named Division A that is based on the following formula:

```
=Beverages + Condiments
```

Before getting to the details of creating calculated fields and items, you should know that Excel imposes a few restrictions on them. Here's a summary:

- You can't use a cell reference, range address, or range name as an operand in a custom calculation formula.

- You can't use the PivotTable's subtotals, row totals, column totals, or Grand Total as an operand in a custom calculation formula.

- In a calculated field, Excel defaults to a Sum calculation when you reference another field in your custom formula. However, this can cause problems. For example, suppose your invoice table has Unit Price and Quantity fields. You might think that you can create a calculated field that returns the invoice totals with the following formula:

    ```
    =Unit Price * Quantity
    ```

However, this won't work because Excel treats the Unit Price operand as Sum of Unit Price, and it doesn't make sense to "add" the prices together.

- For a calculated item, the custom formula can't reference items from any field except the one in which the calculated item resides.

- You can't create a calculated item in a PivotTable that has at least one grouped field. You must ungroup all the PivotTable fields before you can create a calculated item.

- You can't use a calculated item as a filter.

- You can't insert a calculated item into a PivotTable in which a field has been used more than once.

- You can't insert a calculated item into a PivotTable that uses the **Average**, **StdDev**, **StdDevp**, **Var**, or **Varp** summary calculations.

Creating a calculated field

Here are the steps to follow to insert a calculated field into a PivotTable data area:

1. Select any cell in the PivotTable's value field.

2. Select PivotTable **Analyze** > **Fields, Items, & Sets** > **Calculated Field**. Excel displays the **Insert Calculated Field** dialog box.

3. Use the **Name** text box to enter a name for the calculated field.

4. Use the **Formula** text box to enter the formula you want to use for the calculated field.

> **Note** If you need to use a field name in the formula, position the cursor where you want the field name to appear, select the field name in the **Fields** list, and then select **Insert Field**.

5. Select **Add**.

6. Select **OK**. Excel inserts the calculated field into the PivotTable.

Figure 18-9 shows a completed version of the **Insert Calculated Field** dialog box, as well as the resulting **Bonus** field in the PivotTable. Here's the full formula that appears in the Formula text box:

```
=IF('Extended Price' >= 75000, 'Extended Price' * 0.05, 0)
```

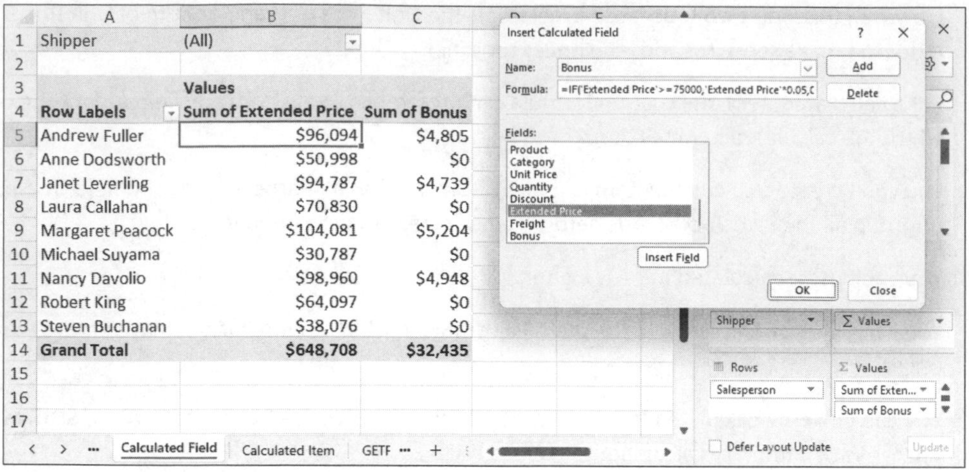

FIGURE 18-9 This worksheet shows a PivotTable report with a Bonus calculated field.

Note If you need to make changes to a calculated field, select any cell in the PivotTable's value field, select **PivotTable Analyze > Fields, Items, & Sets > Calculated Field**, and then use the **Name** list to select the calculated field you want to work with. Make your changes to the formula, select **Modify**, and then select **OK**.

Caution In Figure 18-9, notice that the Grand Total row also includes a total for the Bonus field. Notice, too, that the total displayed is incorrect! This is almost always the case with calculated fields. The problem is that Excel doesn't derive the calculated field's Grand Total by adding up the field's values. Instead, Excel applies the calculated field's formula to the Grand Total of whatever field you reference in the formula. For example, in the logical expression `'Extended Price' >= 75000`, Excel uses the Grand Total of the Extended Price field. Because this is definitely more than 75,000, Excel calculates the "bonus" of 5 percent, which is the value that appears in the Bonus field's Grand Total.

Creating a calculated item

Here are the steps to follow to insert a calculated item into a PivotTable's row or column area:

1. Select any cell in the row or column field to which you want to add the item.

2. Select **PivotTable Analyze > Fields, Items, & Sets > Calculated Item**. Excel displays the Insert Calculated Item in *"Field"* dialog box (where *Field* is the name of the field you're working with).

3. Use the **Name** text box to enter a name for the calculated item.

4. Use the **Formula** text box to enter the formula you want to use for the calculated item.

> **Note** To add a field name to the formula, position the cursor where you want the field name to appear, select the field name in the **Fields** list, and then select **Insert Field**. To add a field item to the formula, position the cursor where you want the item name to appear, select the field in the **Fields** list, select the item in the Items list, and then select **Insert Item**.

5. Select **Add**.

6. Repeat steps 3–5 to add other calculated items to the field.

7. Select **OK**. Excel inserts the calculated item or items into the row or column field.

Figure 18-10 shows a completed version of the **Insert Calculated Item in "*Field*"** dialog box (where *Field* is the name of the field you selected in Step 1), as well as three items added to the Category row field:

```
Division A: =Beverage + Condiments
Division B: =Confections + 'Dairy Products'
Division C: ='Grains/Cereals' + 'Meat/Poultry' + Produce + Seafood
```

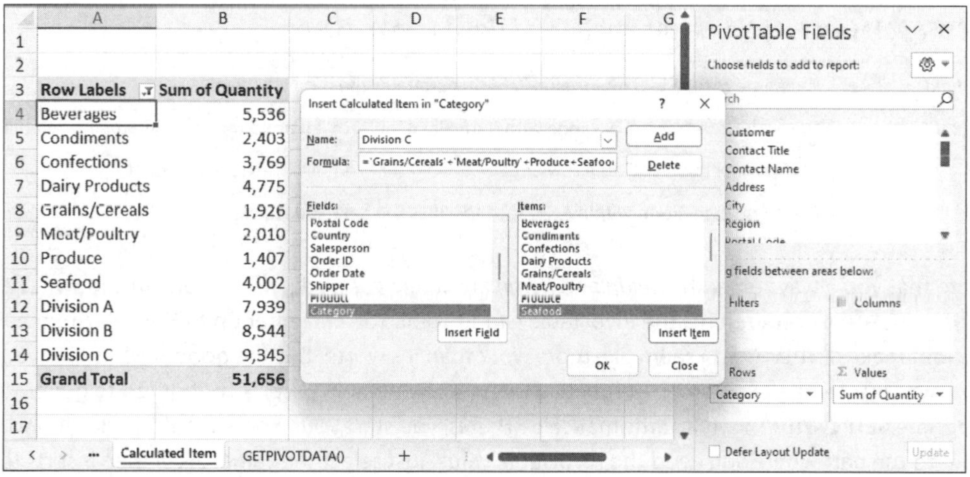

FIGURE 18-10 This worksheet shows a PivotTable report with three calculated items added to the Category row field.

> **Note** To make changes to a calculated item, select any cell in the field that contains the item, select **PivotTable Analyze** > **Fields, Items, & Sets** > **Calculated Item**, and then use the **Name** list to select the calculated item you want to work with. Make your changes to the formula, select **Modify**, and then select **OK**.

> **Caution** When you insert an item into a field, Excel remembers that item. (Technically, it becomes part of the data source's pivot cache.) If you then insert the same field into another PivotTable based on the same data source, Excel also includes the calculated items in the new PivotTable. If you don't want the calculated items to appear in the new PivotTable report, open the field's drop-down menu and deselect the check box beside each calculated item.

Using PivotTable results in a worksheet formula

What do you do when you need to include a PivotTable result in a regular worksheet formula? At first, you might be tempted just to include a reference to the appropriate cell in the PivotTable's data area. However, that works only if your PivotTable is static and never changes. In the vast majority of cases, the reference won't work because the addresses of the report values change as you pivot, filter, group, and refresh the PivotTable.

If you want to include a PivotTable result in a formula and you want that result to remain accurate even as you manipulate the PivotTable, use Excel's **GETPIVOTDATA** function. This function uses the value field, PivotTable location, and one or more (row or column) field/item pairs that specify the exact value you want to use. Here's the syntax:

GETPIVOTDATA(*data_field*, *pivot_table*[, *field1*, *item1*...])

data_field	The name of the PivotTable value field that contains the data you want
pivot_table	The address of any cell or range within the PivotTable, or a named range within the PivotTable
field1	The name of the PivotTable row or column field that contains the data you want
item1	The name of the item within *field1* that specifies the data you want

Note that you always enter the *fieldn* and *itemn* arguments as a pair. If you don't include any field/item pairs, **GETPIVOTDATA** returns the PivotTable Grand Total. You can enter up to 126 field/item pairs. This might make **GETPIVOTDATA** seem like more work than it's worth, but the good news is that you'll rarely have to enter the **GETPIVOTDATA** function by hand. By default, Excel is configured to generate the appropriate **GETPIVOTDATA** syntax automatically. That is, you start your worksheet formula, and when you get to the part where you need the PivotTable value, just select the value. Excel then inserts the **GETPIVOTDATA** function with the syntax that returns the value you want.

For example, in Figure 18-11, you can see that I started a worksheet formula in cell F5 by typing an equal sign (=), and then I selected cell B5 in the PivotTable. Excel generated the **GETPIVOTDATA** function shown.

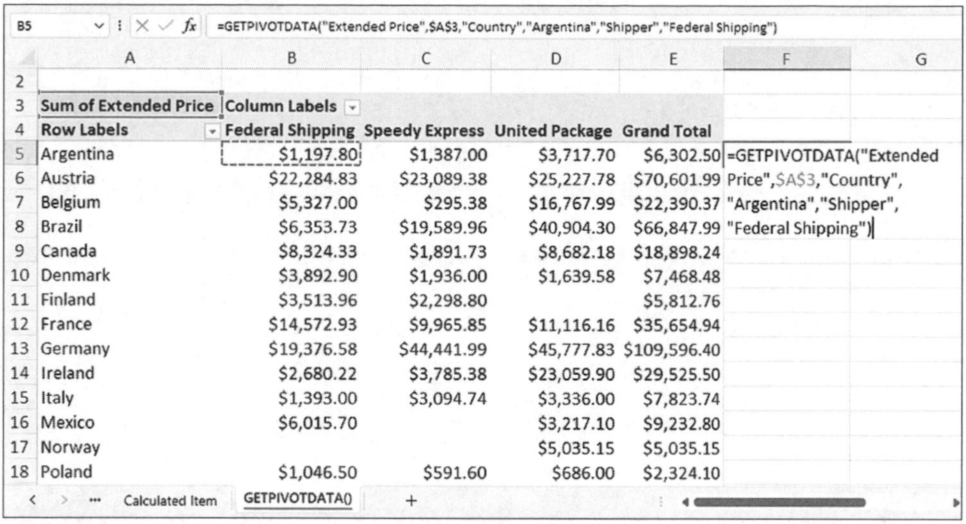

B5 =GETPIVOTDATA("Extended Price",$A$3,"Country","Argentina","Shipper","Federal Shipping")

	A	B	C	D	E	F
2						
3	Sum of Extended Price	Column Labels				
4	Row Labels	Federal Shipping	Speedy Express	United Package	Grand Total	
5	Argentina	$1,197.80	$1,387.00	$3,717.70	$6,302.50	=GETPIVOTDATA("Extended
6	Austria	$22,284.83	$23,089.38	$25,227.78	$70,601.99	Price",$A$3,"Country",
7	Belgium	$5,327.00	$295.38	$16,767.99	$22,390.37	"Argentina","Shipper",
8	Brazil	$6,353.73	$19,589.96	$40,904.30	$66,847.99	"Federal Shipping")
9	Canada	$8,324.33	$1,891.73	$8,682.18	$18,898.24	
10	Denmark	$3,892.90	$1,936.00	$1,639.58	$7,468.48	
11	Finland	$3,513.96	$2,298.80		$5,812.76	
12	France	$14,572.93	$9,965.85	$11,116.16	$35,654.94	
13	Germany	$19,376.58	$44,441.99	$45,777.83	$109,596.40	
14	Ireland	$2,680.22	$3,785.38	$23,059.90	$29,525.50	
15	Italy	$1,393.00	$3,094.74	$3,336.00	$7,823.74	
16	Mexico	$6,015.70		$3,217.10	$9,232.80	
17	Norway			$5,035.15	$5,035.15	
18	Poland	$1,046.50	$591.60	$686.00	$2,324.10	

Calculated Item | GETPIVOTDATA()

FIGURE 18-11 When you're entering a worksheet formula, select a cell in a PivotTable's data area, and Excel automatically generates the corresponding GETPIVOTDATA function.

If Excel doesn't generate the **GETPIVOTDATA** function automatically, that feature may be turned off. Follow these steps to turn it back on:

1. Select **File** > **Options** to open the **Excel Options** dialog box.
2. Select **Formulas**.
3. Select the **Use GetPivotData Functions For PivotTable References** check box.
4. Select **OK**.

Tip You can also use a VBA procedure to toggle automatic **GETPIVOTDATA** functions on and off. Set the **Application.GenerateGetPivotData** property to **True** or **False**, as in the following macro:

```
Sub ToggleGenerateGetPivotData
    With Application
        .GenerateGetPivotData = Not .GenerateGetPivotData
    End With
End Sub
```

CHAPTER 19

Using Excel's business modeling tools

In this chapter, you will:

- Understand and build formulas for performing what-if analysis

- Learn the details of Excel's powerful Goal Seek tool

- Understand, create, and work with scenarios

At times, it's not enough to simply enter data into a worksheet, build a few formulas, and add a little formatting to make things presentable. In the business world, you're often called on to divine some inner meaning from the jumble of numbers and formula results that litter your workbooks. In other words, you need to *analyze* your data to see what nuggets of understanding you can unearth. In Excel, analyzing business data means using the program's business modeling tools. This chapter looks at a few of those tools and some analytic techniques that have many uses. You'll find out how to use Excel's numerous methods for what-if analysis, how to wield Excel's useful Goal Seek tool, and how to create scenarios.

Using what-if analysis

What-if analysis is perhaps the most basic method for interrogating your worksheet data. With what-if analysis, you first calculate a formula, D, based on the input from variables A, B, and C. You then say, "What if I change variable A? Or B or C? What happens to the result?"

For example, Figure 19-1 shows a worksheet that calculates the future value of an investment based on five variables: the interest rate, period, annual deposit, initial deposit, and deposit type. Cell C9 shows the result of the FV function (which I covered in Chapter 15, "Working with investment formulas"; see the section "Calculating the future value"). Now the questions begin:

- What if the interest rate is 7 percent?

- What if you deposit $8,000 per year? Or $12,000?

- What if you reduce the initial deposit?

Answering these questions is a straightforward matter of changing the appropriate variables and watching the effect on the result.

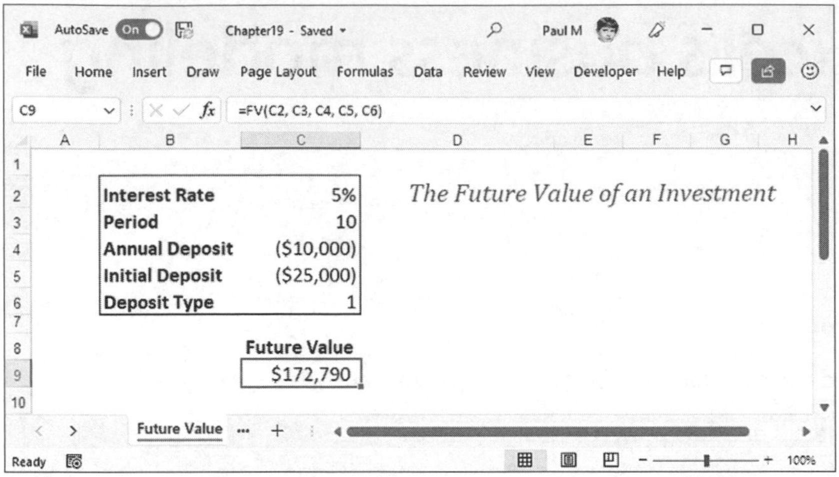

FIGURE 19-1 The simplest what-if analysis involves changing worksheet variables and watching the result.

Setting up a one-input data table

The problem with modifying formula variables is that you see only a single result at one time. If you're interested in studying the effect a range of values has on a formula, you need to set up a *data table*. In the investment analysis worksheet, for example, suppose you want to see the future value of the investment with the annual deposit varying between $7,000 and $13,000. You could enter these values in a row or column and then create the appropriate formulas. Setting up a data table, however, is much easier, as the following procedure shows:

1. Add to the worksheet the values you want to input into the formula. You have two choices for the placement of these values:

   - If you want to enter the values in a row, start the row one cell up and one cell to the right of the formula.

   - If you want to enter the values in a column, start the column one cell down and one cell to the left of the cell containing the formula, as shown in Figure 19-2.

2. Select the range that includes the input values and the formula. (In Figure 19-2, this is B9:C16.)

3. Select **Data** > **What-If Analysis** > **Data Table**. Excel displays the **Data Table** dialog box.

4. Fill in this dialog box based on how you set up your data table:

   - If you entered the input values in a row, use the **Row Input Cell** text box to enter the cell address of the input cell.

   - If the input values are in a column, enter the input cell's address in the **Column Input Cell** text box. In the investment analysis example, you select cell **C4**, and then $C$4 appears in the **Column Input Cell** text box, as shown in Figure 19-3.

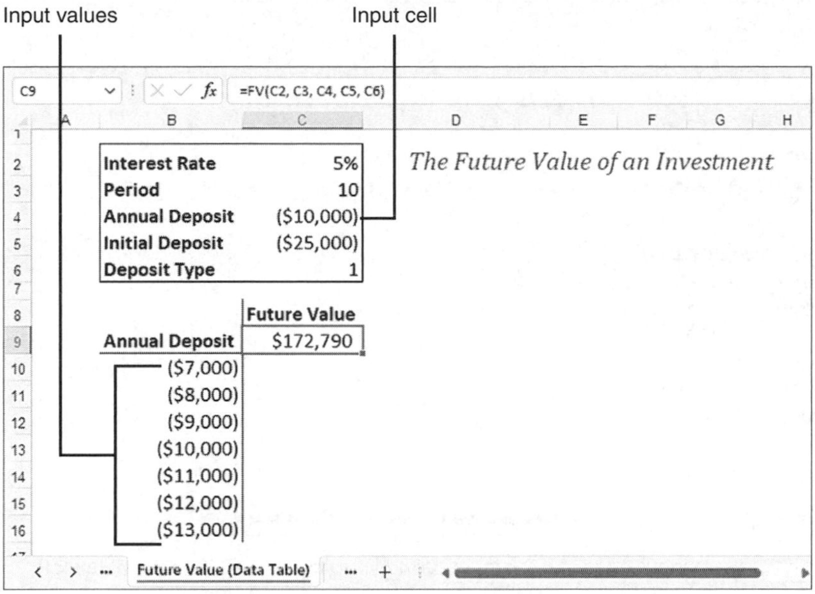

Input values   Input cell

FIGURE 19-2 Enter the values you want to input into the formula.

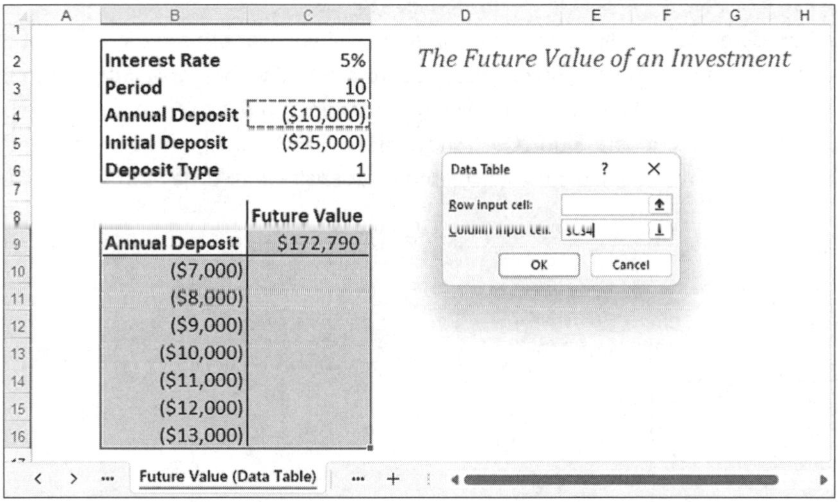

FIGURE 19-3 In the Data Table dialog box, enter the input cell where you want Excel to substitute the input values.

5. Select **OK**. Excel places each of the input values in the input cell; Excel then displays the results in the data table. Format the cells as necessary (see Figure 19-4).

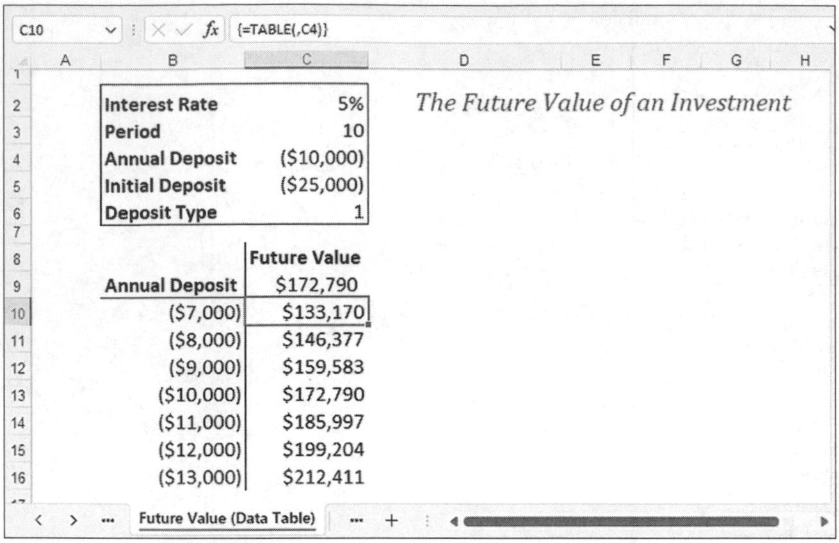

FIGURE 19-4 Excel substitutes each input value into the input cell and displays the results in the data table.

Adding more formulas to the input table

You're not restricted to using just a single formula in a data table. If you want to see the effect of the various input values on different formulas, you can easily add them to the data table. For example, in the future value worksheet, it would be interesting to factor inflation into the calculations to see how the investment appears in today's dollars. Figure 19-5 shows the revised worksheet with a new Inflation variable (cell C7) and a formula that converts the calculated future value into today's dollars (cell D9).

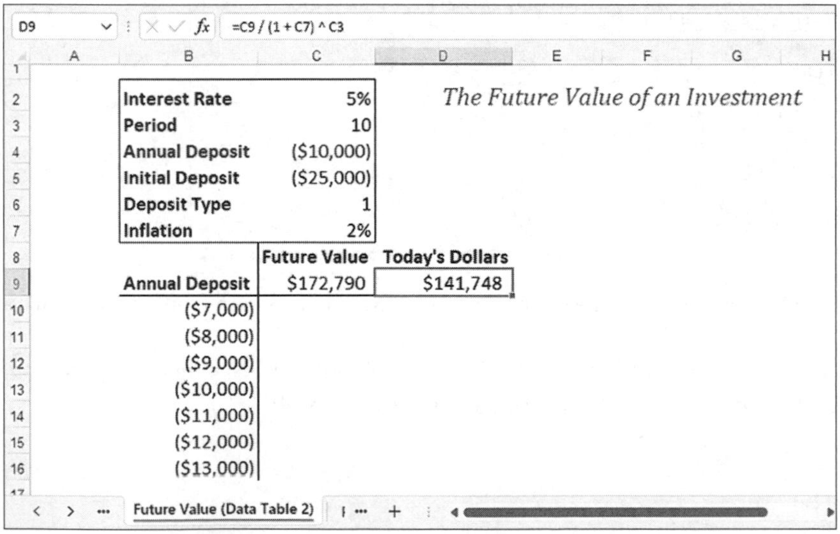

FIGURE 19-5 To add a formula to a data table, enter the new formula next to the existing one.

> **Note** This is the formula for converting a future value into today's dollars:
>
> `Future Value / (1 + Inflation Rate) ^ Period`
>
> Here, *Period* is the number of years from now that the future value exists.

To create the new data table, follow the steps outlined previously. However, make sure that the range you select in step 2 includes the input values and *both* formulas (that is, the range B9:D16 in Figure 19-5). Figure 19-6 shows the results.

		Future Value	Today's Dollars
Interest Rate	5%	*The Future Value of an Investment*	
Period	10		
Annual Deposit	($10,000)		
Initial Deposit	($25,000)		
Deposit Type	1		
Inflation	2%		
		Future Value	Today's Dollars
Annual Deposit		$172,790	$141,748
	($7,000)	$133,170	$109,246
	($8,000)	$146,377	$120,080
	($9,000)	$159,583	$130,914
	($10,000)	$172,790	$141,748
	($11,000)	$185,997	$152,582
	($12,000)	$199,204	$163,417
	($13,000)	$212,411	$174,251

FIGURE 19-6 The figure shows the results of using multiple formulas in the data table.

> **Note** After you have a data table set up, you can do regular what-if analysis by adjusting the other worksheet variables. Each time you make a change, Excel recalculates every formula in the table.

Setting up a two-input data table

You also can set up data tables that take two input variables. This option enables you to see the effect on an investment's future value when you enter different values—for example, the annual deposit and the interest rate. The following steps show you how to set up a two-input data table:

1. Enter one set of values in a column below the formula and the second set of values to the right of the formula in the same row, as shown in Figure 19-7.

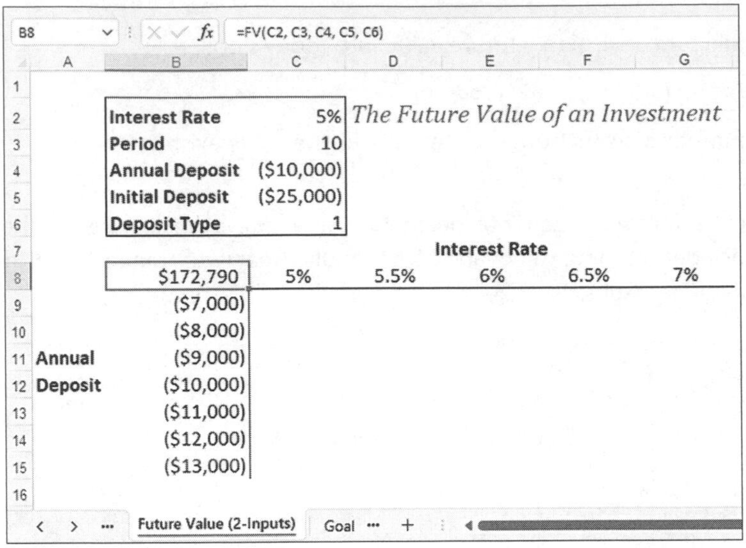

FIGURE 19-7 Enter the two sets of values that you want to input into the formula.

2. Select the range that includes the input values and the formula (B8:G15 in Figure 19-7).

3. Select **Data** > **What-If Analysis** > **Data Table** to display the **Data Table** dialog box.

4. In the **Row Input Cell** text box, enter the cell address of the input cell that corresponds to the row values you entered (C2 in Figure 19-7—the Interest Rate variable).

5. In the **Column Input Cell** text box, enter the cell address of the input cell you want to use for the column values (C4 in Figure 19-7—the Annual Deposit variable).

6. Select **OK**. Excel runs through the various input combinations and then displays the results in the data table. Format the cells as necessary (see Figure 19-8).

> **Tip** As mentioned earlier, if you make changes to any of the variables in a table formula, Excel recalculates the entire table. This isn't a problem in small tables, but large ones can take a very long time to calculate. If you prefer to control the table recalculation, select **Formulas** > **Calculation** > **Calculation Options** > **Automatic Except for Data Tables**. This tells Excel not to include data tables when it recalculates a worksheet. To recalculate your data tables, select **Formulas** > **Calculation** > **Calculate Now** (or press F9); to recalculate just the data tables in the current worksheet, select **Formulas** > **Calculation** > **Calculate Sheet** (or press Shift+F9).

C9		:	× ✓	fx	{=TABLE(C2,C4)}		

	A	B	C	D	E	F	G
1							
2		Interest Rate	5%	*The Future Value of an Investment*			
3		Period	10				
4		Annual Deposit	($10,000)				
5		Initial Deposit	($25,000)				
6		Deposit Type	1				
7					Interest Rate		
8		$172,790	5%	5.5%	6%	6.5%	7%
9		($7,000)	$133,170	$137,788	$142,573	$147,529	$152,664
10		($8,000)	$146,377	$151,372	$156,544	$161,901	$167,448
11	Annual	($9,000)	$159,583	$164,955	$170,516	$176,272	$182,231
12	Deposit	($10,000)	$172,790	$178,539	$184,488	$190,644	$197,015
13		($11,000)	$185,997	$192,122	$198,459	$205,016	$211,798
14		($12,000)	$199,204	$205,706	$212,431	$219,387	$226,582
15		($13,000)	$212,411	$219,289	$226,403	$233,759	$241,366
16							

< > ··· Future Value (2-Inputs) Goal ··· + ◀ ▄▄▄▄▄▄▄▄

FIGURE 19-8 Excel substitutes each input value into the input cell and displays the results in the two-input data table.

Editing a data table

If you want to make changes to a data table, you can edit the formula (or formulas) as well as the input value. However, the data table results are a different matter. When you run the **Data Table** command, Excel enters an array formula in the interior of the data table. This formula is a **TABLE** function (a special function available only by using the **Data Table** command) with the following syntax:

{=TABLE(row_input_ref, column_input_ref)}

Here, *row_input_ref* and *column_input_ref* are the cell references you entered in the **Data Table** dialog box. The braces ({ }) indicate that this is an array, which means that you can't change or delete individual elements of the array. If you want to change the results, you need to select the entire data table and then run the **Data Table** command again. If you just want to delete the results, you must first select the entire array and then delete it. (To learn more about arrays, see "Working with arrays," in Chapter 2, "Creating advanced formulas.")

Working with Goal Seek

Here's a what-if question for you: What if you already know the result you want? For example, you might know that you want to have $50,000 saved to purchase new equipment five years from now or that you have to achieve a 30 percent gross margin in your next budget. If you need to manipulate only a single variable to achieve these results, you can use Excel's Goal Seek feature. You tell Goal Seek the final value you need and which variable to change, and it finds a solution for you (if one exists). (For more complicated scenarios with multiple variables and constraints, you need to use Excel's Solver feature. See Chapter 20, "Solving complex problems with Solver.")

How does Goal Seek work?

When you set up a worksheet to use Goal Seek, you usually have a formula in one cell and the formula's variable—with an initial value—in another. (Your formula can have multiple variables, but Goal Seek enables you to manipulate only one variable at a time.) Goal Seek operates by using an *iterative method* to find a solution. That is, Goal Seek first tries the variable's initial value to see whether that produces the result you want. If it doesn't, Goal Seek tries different values until it converges on a solution. (To learn more about iterative methods, see "Using iteration and circular references" in Chapter 2.)

Running Goal Seek

Before you run Goal Seek, you need to set up your worksheet in a particular way. This means doing three things:

1. Set up one cell as the *changing cell*. This is the value that Goal Seek will iteratively manipulate to attempt to reach the goal. Enter an initial value (such as **0**) into the cell.

2. Set up the other input values for the formula and make them proper initial values.

3. Create a formula for Goal Seek to use to try to reach the goal.

For example, suppose you're a small-business owner looking to purchase new equipment worth $50,000 five years from now. Assuming your investments earn 5% annual interest, how much do you need to set aside every year to reach this goal? Figure 19-9 shows a worksheet set up to use Goal Seek:

■ Cell C5 is the changing cell: the annual deposit into the fund (with an initial value of **0**).

■ The other cells (C3 and C4) are used as constants for the **FV** function.

■ Cell C7 contains the **FV** function that calculates the future value of the equipment fund. When Goal Seek is done, this cell's value should be $50,000.

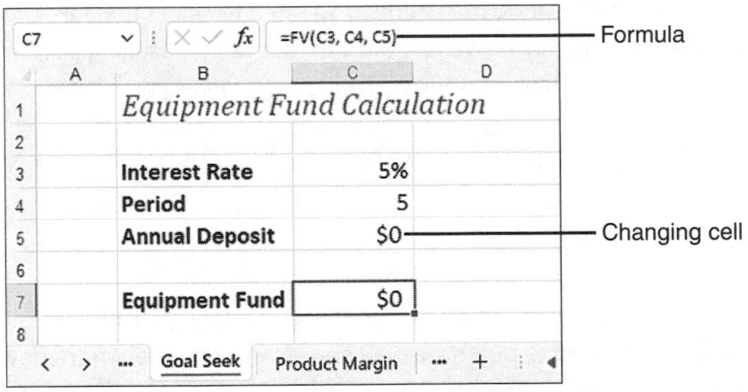

FIGURE 19-9 A worksheet set up to use Goal Seek to find out how much to set aside each year to end up with a $50,000 equipment fund in five years.

With your worksheet ready to go, follow these steps to use Goal Seek:

1. Select **Data**, **What-If Analysis**, **Goal Seek**. Excel displays the **Goal Seek** dialog box.

2. Use the **Set Cell** text box to enter a reference to the cell that contains the formula you want Goal Seek to manipulate (cell C7 in Figure 19-9).

3. Use the **To Value** text box to enter the final value you want for the goal cell (such as **50000**).

4. Use the **By Changing Cell** text box to enter a reference to the changing cell. (This is cell C5 in Figure 19-9.) Figure 19-10 shows the completed **Goal Seek** dialog box.

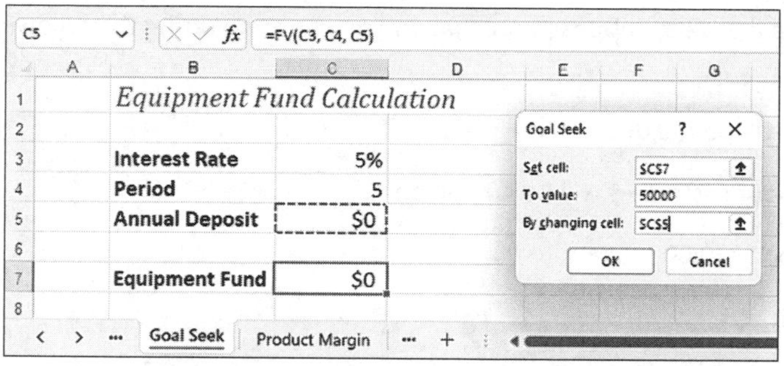

FIGURE 19-10 This is the completed Goal Seek dialog box.

5. Select **OK**. Excel begins the iteration and displays the **Goal Seek Status** dialog box. When you are finished, the dialog box tells you whether Goal Seek found a solution (see Figure 19-11).

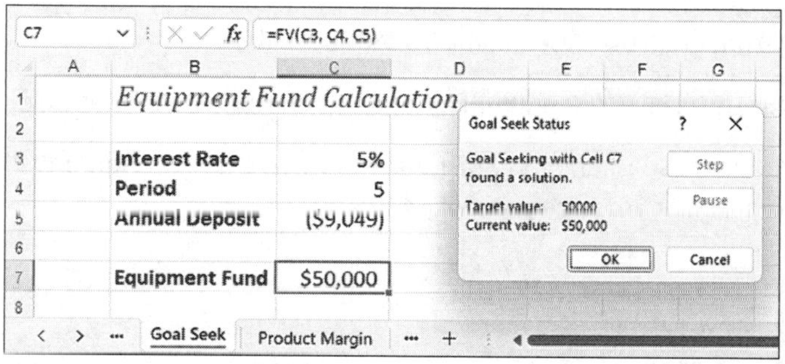

FIGURE 19-11 The Goal Seek Status dialog box shows you the solution (if one was found).

Note Most of the time, Goal Seek finds a solution relatively quickly, and the **Goal Seek Status** dialog box displays the solution within a second or two. For longer operations, you can select **Pause** in the **Goal Seek Status** dialog box to stop Goal Seek. To walk through the process one iteration at a time, select **Step**. To resume Goal Seek, select **Continue**.

6. If Goal Seek found a solution, you can accept the solution by selecting **OK**. To ignore the solution, select **Cancel**.

Optimizing product margin

Many businesses use product margin as a measure of fiscal health. A strong margin usually means that expenses are under control and that the market is satisfied with your price points. Product margin depends on many factors, of course, but you can use Goal Seek to find the optimum margin based on a single variable.

For example, suppose you want to introduce a new product line, and you want the product to return a margin of 30 percent during the first year. Suppose, too, that you're operating under the following assumptions:

- The sales during the year will be 100,000 units.

- The average discount to your customers will be 40 percent.

- The total fixed costs will be $750,000.

- The cost per unit will be $12.63.

Given all this information, you want to know what price point will produce the 30 percent margin.

Figure 19-12 shows a worksheet set up to handle this situation. An initial value of $1.00 is entered into the Price per Unit cell (C4), and Goal Seek is set up in the following way:

- The **Set Cell** reference is C14, the **Margin** calculation.

- A value of 0.3 (the 30% **Margin** goal) is entered in the **To Value** text box.

- A reference to the **Price Per Unit** cell (C4) is entered into the **By Changing Cell** text box.

When you run Goal Seek, it produces a solution of $47.87 for the price, as shown in Figure 19-13. This solution can be rounded up to a more standard price point of $47.95.

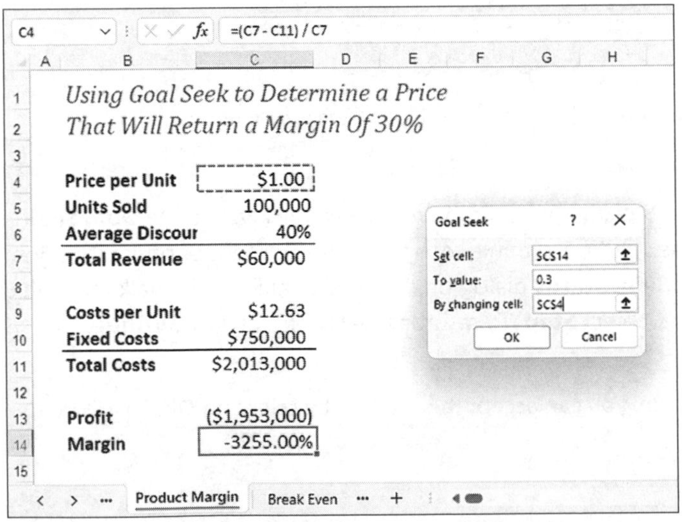

FIGURE 19-12 This worksheet is set up to calculate a price point that will optimize gross margin.

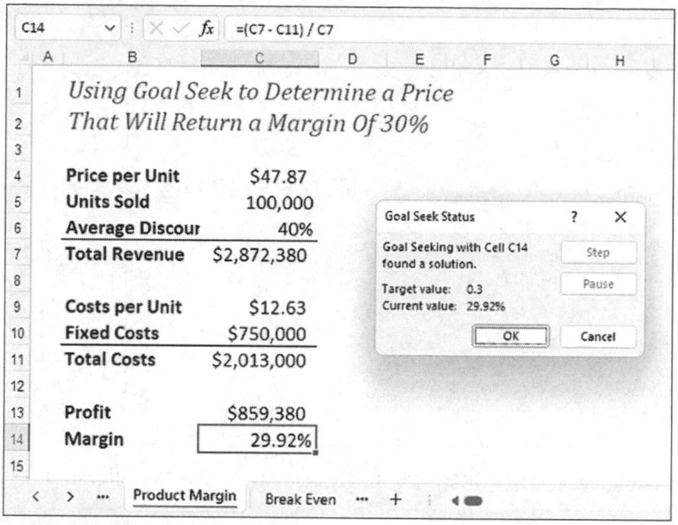

FIGURE 19-13 This figure shows the result of Goal Seek's labors.

A note about Goal Seek's approximations

Notice that the solution in Figure 19-13 is an approximate figure. That is, the margin value is 29.92 percent, not the 30 percent you were looking for. It's pretty close (it's off by only 0.0008), but it's not exact. Why didn't Goal Seek find the exact solution?

The answer lies in one of the options Excel uses to control iterative calculations. Some iterations can take an extremely long time to find an exact solution, so Excel compromises by setting certain limits on iterative processes. To see these limits, select **File** > **Options** and then select **Formulas** in the **Excel Options** dialog box that appears (see Figure 19-14). Two options control iterative processes:

- **Maximum Iterations:** The value in this text box controls the maximum number of iterations. In Goal Seek, this represents the maximum number of values that Excel plugs into the changing cell.

- **Maximum Change:** The value in this text box is the threshold that Excel uses to determine whether it has converged on a solution. If the difference between the current solution and the desired goal is less than or equal to this value, Excel stops iterating.

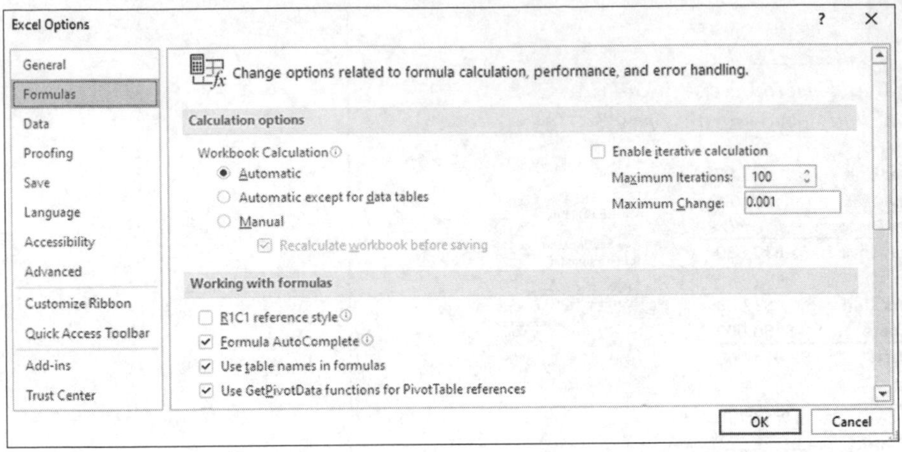

FIGURE 19-14 The Maximum Iterations and Maximum Change options place limits on iterative calculations.

The **Maximum Change** value prevented me from getting an exact solution for the profit margin calculation. On a particular iteration, Goal Seek found the solution .2992, which put me within 0.0008 of the goal of 0.3. However, 0.0008 is less than the default value of 0.001 in the **Maximum Change** text box, so Excel called a halt to the procedure.

To get an exact solution, you would need to adjust the **Maximum Change** value to 0.0001.

Performing a break-even analysis

In a *break-even analysis*, you determine the number of units you have to sell of a product so that your total profits are 0 (that is, the product revenue equals the product costs). Setting up a profit equation with a goal of 0 and varying the units sold is perfect for Goal Seek.

To try this, extend the example used in the "Optimizing product margin" section. In this case, assume a unit price of $47.95 (the solution found to optimize product margin, rounded up to the nearest 95¢). Figure 19-15 shows the **Goal Seek** dialog box filled out as detailed here:

■   The **Set Cell** reference is set to C12, the profit calculation.

■   A value of 0 (the profit goal) is entered in the **To Value** text box.

■   A reference to the **Units Sold** cell (C4) is entered into the **By Changing Cell** text box.

Figure 19-16 shows the solution: A total of 46,468 units must be sold to break even.

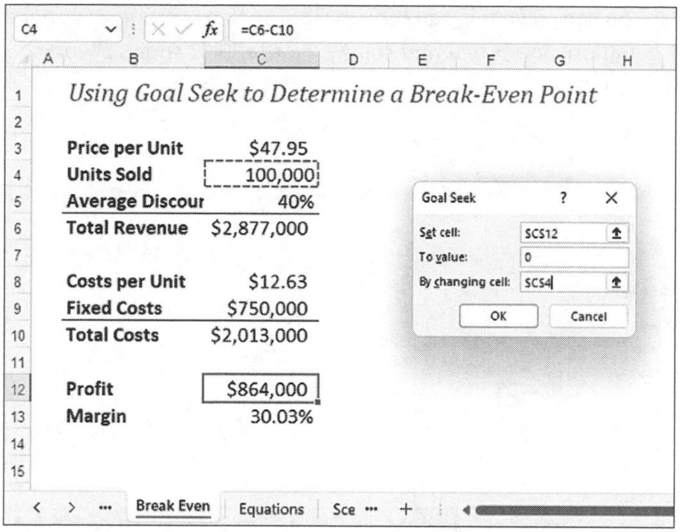

FIGURE 19-15 This worksheet is set up to calculate a price point that optimizes gross margin.

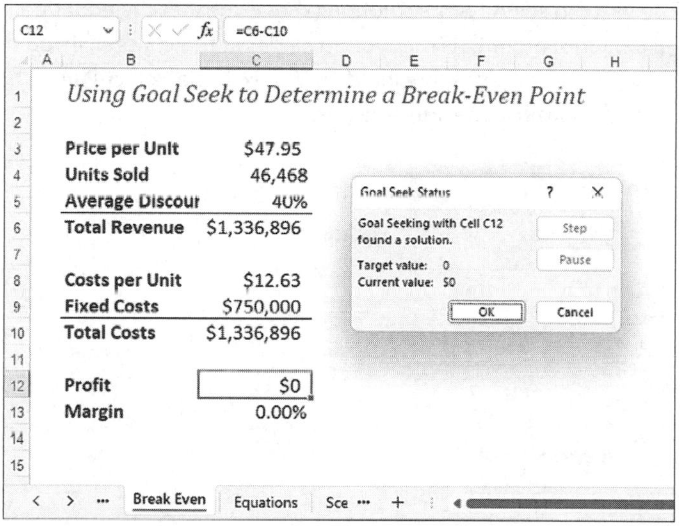

FIGURE 19-16 This is the break-even solution.

Solving algebraic equations

Algebraic equations don't come up all that often in a business context, but they do appear occasionally in complex models. Fortunately, Goal Seek also is useful for solving complex algebraic equations of one variable. For example, suppose you need to find the value of *x* to solve the rather nasty equation displayed in Figure 19-17. Although this equation is too complex for the quadratic formula, it can be easily rendered in Excel. The left side of the equation can be represented with the following formula:

```
=(((3 * A2 - 8) ^ 2) * (A2 - 1)) / (4 * A2 ^ 2 - 5)
```

Cell A2 represents the variable *x*. You can solve this equation in Goal Seek by setting the goal for this equation to 1 (the right side of the equation) and by varying cell A2. Figure 19-17 shows a worksheet and the **Goal Seek** dialog box.

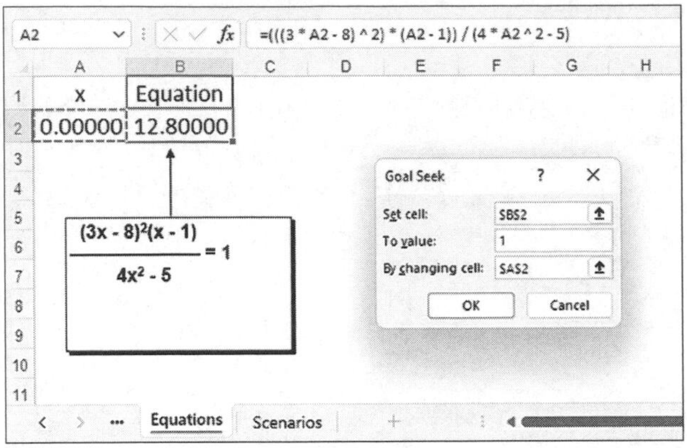

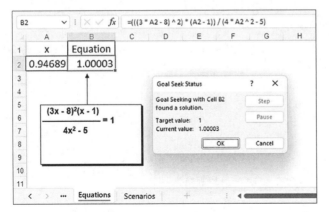

FIGURE 19-17 You can solve an algebraic equation with Goal Seek.

Figure 19-18 shows the result. The value in cell A2 is the solution (*x*) that satisfies the equation. Notice that the equation result (cell B2) is not quite 1. As mentioned earlier in this chapter, if you need higher accuracy, you must change Excel's convergence threshold. In this example, select **File** > **Options** > **Formulas** and type **0.000001** in the **Maximum Change** text box.

FIGURE 19-18 Cell A2 holds the solution for the equation in cell B2.

Working with scenarios

By definition, what-if analysis is not an exact science. All what-if models make guesses and assumptions based on history, expected events, or some sort of magic. A particular set of guesses and assumptions that you plug into a model is called a *scenario*. Because most what-if worksheets can take a wide range of input values, you usually end up with a large number of scenarios to examine. Instead of going through the tedious chore of inserting all these values into the appropriate cells, Excel has a Scenario Manager feature that can handle the process for you. This section shows you how to wield this useful tool.

Understanding scenarios

As you've seen in this chapter, Excel has powerful features that enable you to build sophisticated models that can answer complex questions. The problem, though, isn't in *answering* questions but in *asking* them. For example, Figure 19-19 shows a worksheet model that analyzes a mortgage. You use this model to decide how much of a down payment to make, how long the term should be, and whether to include an extra principal paydown every month. The Results section compares the monthly payment and total paid for the regular mortgage and for the mortgage with a paydown. It also shows the savings and reduced term that result from the paydown.

The formula shown in Figure 19-19 uses the **PMT** function, which is covered earlier in the book; see "Calculating a loan payment," in Chapter 14, "Building loan formulas."

Regular_P... ∨	:	× ✓ *fx*	=PMT(Interest_Rate / 12, Term * 12, House_Price - Down_Payment)

	A	B	C	D	E	F	G
1		Mortgage Analysis					
2	Fixed Cells:						
3	House Price	$100,000					
4	Interest Rate	4.00%					
5							
6	Changing Cells:						
7	Down Payment	$20,000					
8	Term	20					
9	Paydown	($100)					
10							
11	Results:	Regular Mortgage	With Paydown				
12	Monthly Payment	($484.78)	($584.78)				
13	Total Paid	($116,348.22)	($106,986.75)				
14	Total Savings	#N/A	$9,361.47				
15	Revised Term	#N/A	15.2				
16							

‹ › ···	Equations	Scenarios	+

FIGURE 19-19 This is a mortgage analysis worksheet.

Here are some possible questions to ask this model:

- How much will I save over the term of the mortgage if I use a shorter term, make a larger down payment, and include a monthly paydown?

- How much more will I end up paying if I extend the term, reduce the down payment, and forgo the paydown?

These are examples of *scenarios* that you would plug into the appropriate cells in the model. Excel's Scenario Manager helps by letting you define a scenario separately from the worksheet. You can save specific values for any or all of the model's input cells, give the scenario a name, and then recall the name (and all the input values it contains) from a list.

Setting up your worksheet for scenarios

Before creating a scenario, you need to decide which cells will be the input cells in your model. These will be the worksheet variables—the cells that, when you change them, change the results of the model. (Not surprisingly, Excel calls these the *changing cells*.) You can have as many as 32 changing cells in a scenario. For best results, follow these guidelines when setting up your worksheet for scenarios:

- The changing cells should be constants. Formulas can be affected by other cells, and that can throw off the entire scenario.

- To make it easier to set up each scenario and to make your worksheet easier to understand, group the changing cells and label them (refer to Figure 19-19).

- For even greater clarity, assign a range name to each changing cell.

Adding a scenario

To work with scenarios, you use Excel's Scenario Manager tool. This feature enables you to add, edit, display, and delete scenarios as well as create summary scenario reports.

When your worksheet is set up the way you want it, you can add a scenario to the sheet by following these steps:

1. Select **Data** > **What-If Analysis** > **Scenario Manager**. Excel displays the Scenario Manager dialog box.

2. Select **Add**. The **Add Scenario** dialog box appears. Figure 19-20 shows a completed version of this dialog box.

3. Use the **Scenario Name** text box to enter a name for the scenario.

4. Use the **Changing Cells** box to enter references to your worksheet's changing cells. You can type in the references (be sure to separate noncontiguous cells with commas) or select the cells directly on the worksheet.

5. Use the **Comment** box to enter a description for the scenario. This description appears in the **Comment** section of the **Scenario Manager** dialog box.

6. Select **OK**. Excel displays the **Scenario Values** dialog box, shown in Figure 19-21.

7. Use the text boxes to enter values for the changing cells.

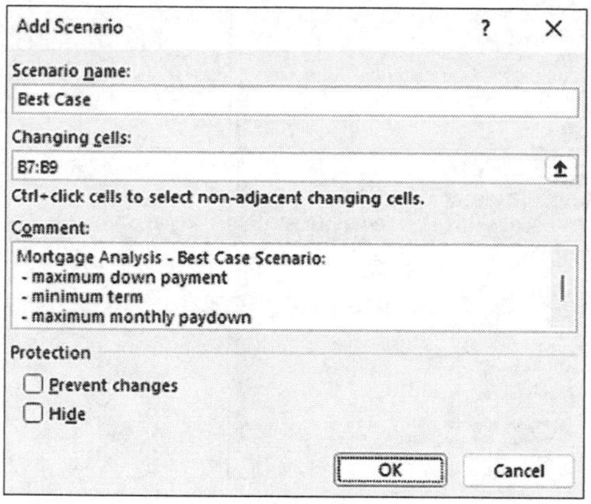

FIGURE 19-20 Use the Add Scenario dialog box to define a scenario.

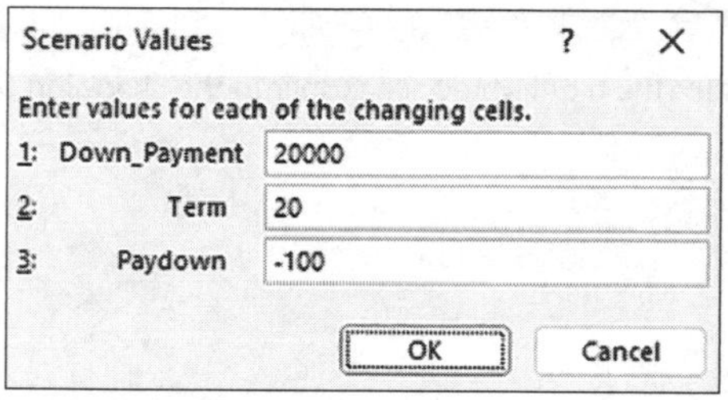

FIGURE 19-21 Use the Scenario Values dialog box to enter the values you want to use for the scenario's changing cells.

> **Note** Notice in Figure 19-21 that Excel displays the range name for each changing cell, which makes it easier to enter your numbers correctly. If your changing cells aren't named, Excel just displays the cell addresses instead.

8. To add more scenarios, select **Add** to return to the **Add Scenario** dialog box and repeat steps 3 through 7. Otherwise, select **OK** to return to the **Scenario Manager** dialog box.

9. Select **Close** to return to the worksheet.

Displaying a scenario

After you define a scenario, you can enter its values into the changing cells by displaying the scenario from the **Scenario Manager** dialog box. The following steps give you the details:

1. Select **Data** > **What-If Analysis** > **Scenario Manager**.

2. In the **Scenarios** list, select the scenario you want to display.

3. Select **Show**. Excel enters the scenario values into the changing cells. Figure 19-22 shows an example.

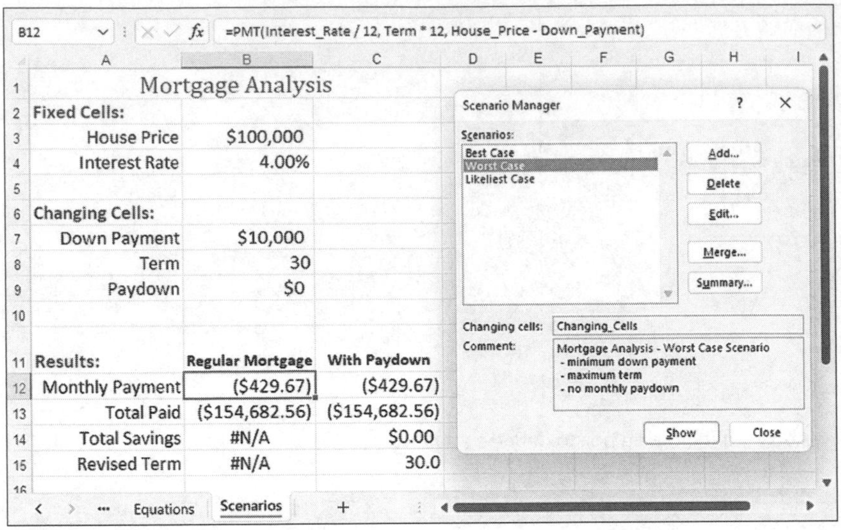

FIGURE 19-22 When you select Show, Excel enters the values for the highlighted scenario into the changing cells.

4. Repeat steps 2 and 3 to display other scenarios.

5. Select **Close** to return to the worksheet.

> **Tip** Displaying a scenario isn't hard, but it does require having the Scenario Manager onscreen. You can bypass the Scenario Manager by adding the Scenario list to the Quick Access Toolbar. Pull down the **Customize Quick Access Toolbar** menu and then select **More Commands**. In the **Choose Commands From** list, select **All Commands**. In the list of commands, select **Scenario**, select **Add**, and then select **OK**. (One caveat, though: If you select the same scenario twice in succession, Excel asks whether you want to redefine the scenario. Be sure to select **No** to keep the current scenario definition.)

Editing a scenario

If you need to make changes to a scenario—whether to change the scenario's name, select different changing cells, or enter new values—follow these steps:

1. Select **Data** > **What-If Analysis** > **Scenario Manager**.

2. In the **Scenarios** list, select the scenario you want to edit.

3. Select **Edit**. Excel displays the **Edit Scenario** dialog box (which is identical to the **Add Scenario** dialog box, shown in Figure 19-20).

4. Make your changes, if necessary, and select **OK**. The **Scenario Values** dialog box appears (refer to Figure 19-21).

5. Enter the new values, if necessary, and then select **OK** to return to the **Scenario Manager** dialog box.

6. Repeat steps 2 through 5 to edit other scenarios.

7. Select **Close** to return to the worksheet.

Merging scenarios

The scenarios you create are stored with each worksheet in a workbook. If you have similar models in different sheets (for example, budget models for different divisions), you can create separate scenarios for each sheet and then merge them later. Here are the steps to follow:

1. Select the worksheet in which you want to store the merged scenarios.

2. Select **Data** > **What-If Analysis** > **Scenario Manager**.

3. Select **Merge**. Excel displays the **Merge Scenarios** dialog box.

4. Use the **Book** drop-down menu to select the workbook that contains the scenario sheet.

5. Use the **Sheet** list to select the worksheet that contains the scenario.

6. Select **OK** to return to the **Scenario Manager**.

7. Select **Close** to return to the worksheet.

Generating a summary report

You can create a summary report that shows the changing cells in each of your scenarios along with selected result cells. This is a handy way to compare different scenarios. You can try it by following these steps:

> **Note**   When Excel sets up the scenario summary, it uses either the cell addresses or defined names of the individual changing cells and results cells, as well as the entire range of changing cells. Your reports will be more readable if you name the cells you'll be using before generating the summary.

1. Select **Data** > **What-If Analysis** > **Scenario Manager**.

2. Select **Summary**. Excel displays the **Scenario Summary** dialog box.

3. In the **Report Type** group, select either **Scenario Summary** or **Scenario PivotTable Report**.

4. In the **Result Cells** box, enter references to the result cells that you want to appear in the report (see Figure 19-23). You can select the cells directly on the sheet or type in the references. (Remember to separate noncontiguous cells with commas.)

Regular_P... ∨	:	× ✓	ƒx	=PMT(Interest_Rate / 12, Term * 12, House_Price - Down_Payment)

	A	B	C	D	E	F	G	H
1		Mortgage Analysis						
2	**Fixed Cells:**							
3	House Price	$100,000						
4	Interest Rate	4.00%						
5								
6	**Changing Cells:**							
7	Down Payment	$10,000						
8	Term	30						
9	Paydown	$0						
10								
11	**Results:**	**Regular Mortgage**	**With Paydown**					
12	Monthly Payment	($429.67)	($429.67)					
13	Total Paid	($154,682.56)	($154,682.56)					
14	Total Savings	#N/A	$0.00					
15	Revised Term	#N/A	30.0					
16								

Scenario Summary dialog box:

Scenario Summary ? ×

Report type
- ◉ Scenario summary
- ○ Scenario PivotTable report

Result cells:
B12:C13,C14,C15 ⬆

OK   Cancel

‹ › ⋯ Equations | Scenarios | +

FIGURE 19-23 Use the Scenario Summary dialog box to select the report type and result cells.

5. Select **OK**. Excel displays the report.

Figure 19-24 shows the **Scenario Summary** report for the Mortgage Analysis worksheet. The names shown in column C (Down_Payment, Term, and so on) are the names I assigned to each of the changing cells and result cells.

	Current Values:	Best Case	Worst Case	Likeliest Case
Scenario Summary				
Changing Cells:				
Down_Payment	$10,000	$20,000	$10,000	$15,000
Term	30	20	30	25
Paydown	$0	($100)	$0	($50)
Result Cells:				
Regular_Payment	($429.67)	($484.78)	($429.67)	($448.66)
Paydown_Payment	($429.67)	($584.78)	($429.67)	($498.66)
Regular_Total	($154,682.56)	($116,348.22)	($154,682.56)	($134,598.39)
Paydown_Total	($154,682.56)	($106,986.75)	($154,682.56)	($125,836.73)
Total_Savings	$0.00	$9,361.47	$0.00	$8,761.67
Revised_Term	30.0	15.2	30.0	21.0

Notes: Current Values column represents values of changing cells at time Scenario Summary Report was created. Changing cells for each scenario are highlighted in gray.

‹ › ⋯ Equations | Scenario Summary | ⋯ + :

FIGURE 19-24 This is the Scenario Summary report for the Mortgage Analysis worksheet.

Figure 19-25 shows the Scenario PivotTable report for the Mortgage Analysis worksheet.

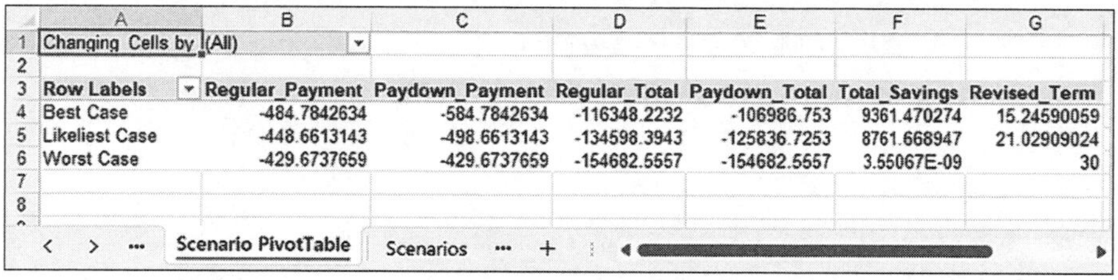

	A	B	C	D	E	F	G
1	Changing Cells by	(All)					
2							
3	Row Labels	Regular_Payment	Paydown_Payment	Regular_Total	Paydown_Total	Total_Savings	Revised_Term
4	Best Case	-484.7842634	-584.7842634	-116348.2232	-106986.753	9361.470274	15.24590059
5	Likeliest Case	-448.6613143	-498.6613143	-134598.3943	-125836.7253	8761.668947	21.02909024
6	Worst Case	-429.6737659	-429.6737659	-154682.5557	-154682.5557	3.55067E-09	30
7							
8							

FIGURE 19-25 This is the Scenario PivotTable report for the Mortgage Analysis worksheet.

Note The PivotTable's page field—labeled Changing Cells By—enables you to switch between scenarios created by different users. If no other users have access to this workbook, you'll see only your name in this field's list.

Deleting a scenario

If you have scenarios you no longer need, you can delete them by following these steps:

1. Select **Data** > **What-If Analysis** > **Scenario Manager**.
2. Use the **Scenarios** list to select the scenario you want to delete.

Caution Excel doesn't ask you to confirm the deletion, and there's no way to retrieve a scenario that you've deleted accidentally (other than closing the workbook without saving changes or opening a previous version of the workbook), so be sure the scenario you highlighted is one you can live without.

3. Select **Delete**. Excel deletes the scenario.
4. Select **Close** to return to the worksheet.

CHAPTER 20

Solving complex problems with Solver

In this chapter, you will:

- Learn some crucial background on what Solver can do for you

- Learn how to load Solver and use it to run basic optimizations

- Improve Solver results by adding one or more constraints

- Learn how to save a Solver solution as a scenario

- Work with Solver's options, understand Solver's messages, and display Solver's reports

In Chapter 19, "Using Excel's business modeling tools," you learned how to use Goal Seek to find solutions to formulas by changing a single variable. Unfortunately, most problems in business aren't so easy. You'll usually face formulas with at least two and sometimes dozens of variables. Often, a problem will have more than one solution, and your challenge will be to find the *optimal* solution (that is, the one that maximizes profit, minimizes costs, or matches other criteria). For these bigger challenges, you need a more muscular tool. Excel has just the answer: Solver. Solver is a sophisticated optimization program that enables you to find solutions to complex problems that would otherwise require high-level mathematical analysis. This chapter introduces you to Solver (a complete discussion would require a book in itself) and takes you through a few examples.

Some background on Solver

Problems such as "What product mix will maximize profit?" and "What transportation routes will minimize shipping costs while meeting demand?" traditionally have been solved by using numerical methods such as *linear programming* and *nonlinear programming*. An entire mathematical field known as *operations research* has been developed to handle such problems, which are found in all kinds of disciplines. The drawback to linear and nonlinear programming is that solving even the simplest problem by hand is a complicated, arcane, and time-consuming business. In other words, it's a perfect job to hand off to a computer.

This is where Solver comes in. Solver incorporates many of the algorithms from operations research, but it keeps the sordid details in the background. All you do is fill out a dialog box or two, and Solver does the rest.

The advantages of Solver

Solver, like Goal Seek, uses an iterative method to perform its magic. This means that Solver tries a solution, analyzes the results, tries another solution, and so on. However, this cyclic iteration isn't just guesswork on Solver's part. The program looks at how the results change with each new iteration and, through some sophisticated mathematical trickery, can tell (usually) in what direction it should head for the solution.

However, the fact that Goal Seek and Solver are both iterative doesn't make them equal. In fact, Solver brings a number of advantages to the table:

- Solver enables you to specify multiple adjustable cells. You can use up to 200 adjustable cells in all.

- Solver enables you to set up constraints on the adjustable cells. For example, you can tell Solver to find a solution that not only maximizes profit but also satisfies certain conditions, such as achieving a gross margin between 20 and 30 percent or keeping expenses less than $100,000. These conditions are said to be *constraints* on the solution.

- Solver seeks not only a desired result (the "goal" in Goal Seek) but also the optimal one. This means you can find a solution that is the maximum or minimum possible.

- For complex problems, Solver can generate multiple solutions. You then can save these different solutions under different scenarios, as described later in this chapter.

When do you use Solver?

Solver is a powerful tool that most Excel users don't need. It would be overkill, for example, to use Solver to compute net profit given fixed revenue and cost figures. Many problems, however, require nothing less than the Solver approach. These problems cover many different fields and situations, but they all have the following characteristics in common:

- They have a single *objective cell* (also called the *target cell*) that contains a formula you want to maximize, minimize, or set to a specific value. This formula could be a calculation, such as total transportation expenses or net profit.

- The objective cell formula contains references to one or more *variable cells* (also called *unknowns* or *changing cells*). Solver adjusts these cells to find the optimal solution for the objective cell formula. These variable cells might include items such as units sold, shipping costs, or advertising expenses.

- Optionally, there are one or more *constraint cells* that must satisfy certain criteria. For example, you might require that advertising be less than 10 percent of total expenses, or that the discount to customers be a number between 40 and 60 percent.

What types of problems exhibit these kinds of characteristics? A surprisingly broad range, as the following list shows:

- **The transportation problem:** This problem involves minimizing shipping costs from multiple manufacturing plants to multiple warehouses while meeting demand.

- **The allocation problem:** This problem requires minimizing employee costs while maintaining appropriate staffing requirements.

- **The product mix problem:** This problem requires generating the maximum profit with a mix of products while still meeting customer requirements. You solve this problem when you sell multiple products with different cost structures, profit margins, and demand curves.

- **The blending problem:** This problem involves manipulating the materials used for one or more products to minimize production costs, meet consumer demand, and maintain a minimum level of quality.

- **Linear algebra:** This problem involves solving sets of linear equations.

Loading Solver

Solver is an add-in to Microsoft Excel, so you need to load Solver before you can use it. Follow these steps to load Solver:

1. Select **File** > **Options** to open the Excel Options dialog box.

2. Select **Add-Ins**.

3. Use the **Manage** list to select **Excel Add-Ins** (although it should be selected by default), and then select **Go**. Excel displays the **Add-Ins** dialog box.

> **Tip**   If you have the ribbon's Developer tab displayed, an easier way to open the Add-Ins dialog box is to select **Developer** and then select **Excel Add-Ins**.

4. In the **Add-Ins Available** list, select the **Solver Add-In** check box.

5. Select **OK**. Excel installs the add-in and adds a **Solver** button to the **Data** tab's **Analyze** group.

Using Solver

To help you get a feel for how Solver works, let's look at an example. In Chapter 19, you used Goal Seek to compute the break-even point for a new product. (Recall that the break-even point is the number of units that need to be sold to produce a profit of 0.) I'll extend this analysis by computing the break-even point for two products: a Finley sprocket and a Langstrom wrench. The goal is to compute the number of units to sell for both products so that the total profit is 0.

The most obvious way to proceed is to run Goal Seek twice to determine the break-even points for each product separately. Figure 20-1 shows the results.

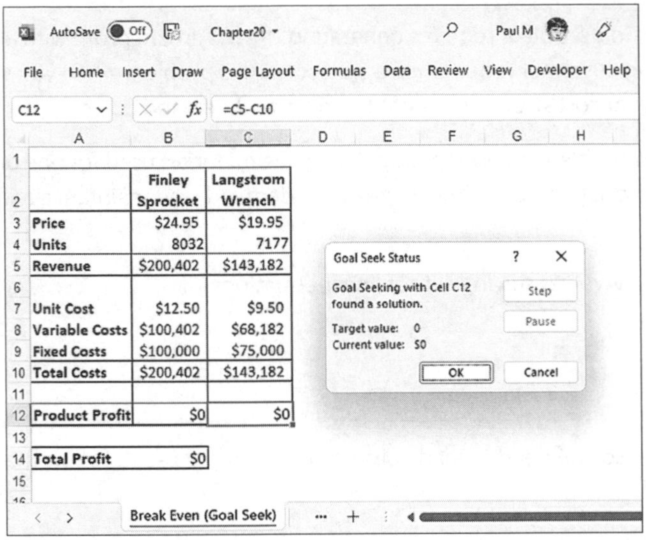

FIGURE 20-1 The figure shows the break-even points for two products (using separate Goal Seek calculations on the Product Profit cells).

This method works, but the problem is that the two products don't exist in a vacuum. For example, there will be cost savings associated with each product because of joint advertising campaigns, combined shipments to customers (larger shipments usually mean better freight rates), and so on. To allow for this, you need to reduce the cost for each product by a factor related to the number of units sold of the other product. In practice, this would be difficult to estimate, but to keep things simple, I'll use the following assumption: The costs for each product are reduced by $1 for every unit sold of the other product. For instance, if the Langstrom wrench sells 10,000 units, the costs for the Finley sprocket are reduced by $10,000. I'll make this adjustment in the Variable Costs formula. For example, the formula that calculates variable costs for the Finley sprocket (cell B8) becomes the following:

```
=B4 * B7 - C4
```

Similarly, the formula that calculates variable costs for the Langstrom wrench (cell C8) becomes the following:

```
=C4 * C7 - B4
```

By making this change, you move out of Goal Seek's territory. The Variable Costs formulas now have two variables: the units sold for the Finley sprocket and the units sold for the Langstrom wrench. I've changed the problem from one of two single-variable formulas, which Goal Seek can easily handle (individually), to a single formula with two variables, which is the terrain of Solver.

To see how Solver handles such a problem, follow these steps:

1. Select **Data** > **Solver**. Excel displays the **Solver Parameters** dialog box.

2. In the **Set Objective** range box, enter a reference to the objective cell—that is, the cell with the formula you want to optimize. In the example, you enter **B14**. (Note that Solver converts your relative references to absolute references.)

3. In the **To** section, select the appropriate option button: Select **Max** to maximize the objective cell, select **Min** to minimize it, or select **Value Of** to solve for a particular value (in which case you also need to enter the value in the text box provided). In the example, you select **Value Of** and enter **0** in the text box.

4. Use the **By Changing Variable Cells** box to enter the cells you want Solver to change while it looks for a solution. In the example, you enter **B4,C4**. Figure 20-2 shows the completed **Solver Parameters** dialog box for this example. (Again, note that Solver changes all cell addresses to the absolute reference format.)

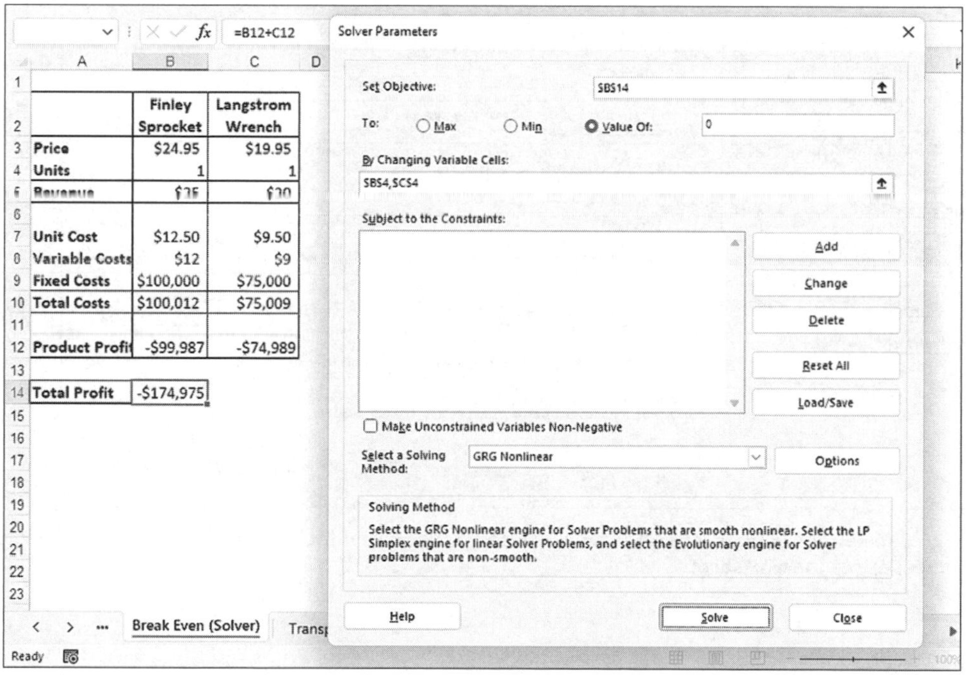

FIGURE 20-2 Use the Solver Parameters dialog box to set up the problem for Solver.

Note You can enter a maximum of 200 cells in the **By Changing Variable Cells** text box.

5. Select **Solve**. (I discuss constraints and other Solver options in the next few sections.) As Solver works on the problem, you might see one or more **Show Trial Solution** dialog boxes. If so, select **Continue** in each one. Finally, Solver displays the **Solver Results** dialog box, which tells you whether it found a solution. (See the section "Making sense of Solver's messages," later in this chapter.)

6. If Solver found a solution you want to use, select the **Keep Solver Solution** option and then select **OK**. If you don't want to accept the new numbers, either select **Restore Original Values** and then select **OK**, or just select **Cancel**. (To learn how to save a solution as a scenario, see the section "Saving a solution as a scenario," later in this chapter.)

Figure 20-3 shows the results for this example. As you can see, Solver has produced a total profit of 0 by running one product (the Langstrom wrench) at a slight loss and the other at a slight profit. Although this is certainly a solution, it's not really the one you want. Ideally, for a true break-even analysis, both products should end up with a product profit of 0. The problem is that you didn't tell Solver that was the way you wanted the problem solved. In other words, you didn't set up *constraints*.

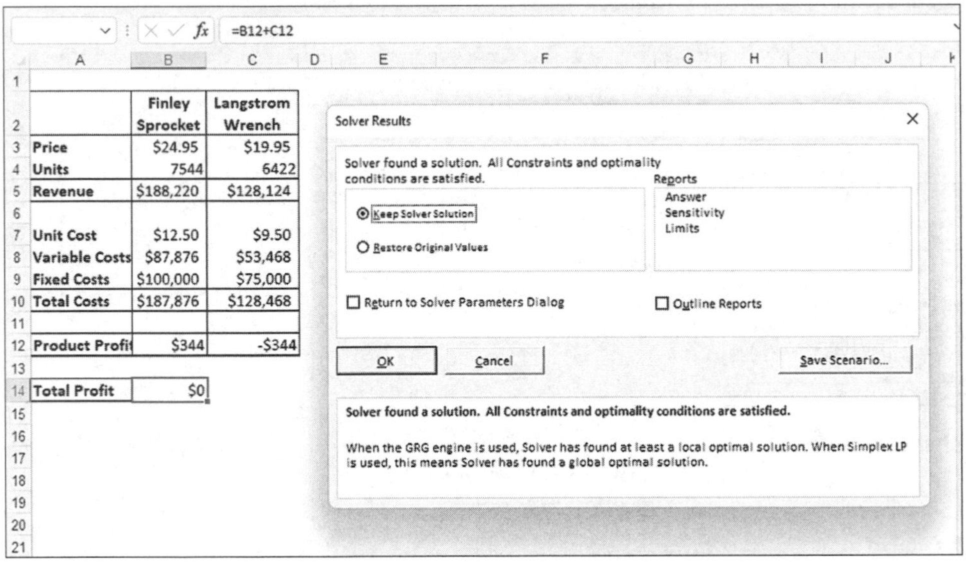

FIGURE 20-3 When Solver finishes its calculations, it displays the Solver Results dialog box and enters the solution (if it found one) into the worksheet cells.

Adding constraints

The real world puts restrictions and conditions on formulas. A factory might have a maximum capacity of 10,000 units a day, the number of employees in a company has to be a number greater than or equal to zero (negative employees would really reduce staff costs, but nobody has been able to figure out how to do it yet), and your advertising costs might be restricted to 10 percent of total expenses. These are examples of what Solver calls *constraints*. Adding constraints tells Solver to find a solution so that these conditions are not violated.

To find the best solution for the break-even analysis, you need to tell Solver to optimize both Product Profit formulas to 0. The following steps show you how to do this:

> **Note** If Solver's completion message is still onscreen from the previous section, select **Cancel** to return to the worksheet without saving the solution.

1. Select **Data** > **Solver** to display the **Solver Parameters** dialog box. Solver reinstates the options you entered the last time you used Solver.

2. To add a constraint, select **Add**. Excel displays the **Add Constraint** dialog box.

3. In the **Cell Reference** box, enter the cell you want to constrain. In this case, enter cell **B12** (the Product Profit formula for the Finley sprocket).

4. Use the drop-down menu in the middle of the dialog box to select the operator you want to use. The list contains several comparison operators for the constraint—less than or equal to (<=), equal to (=), and greater than or equal to (>=)—as well as two other data type operators—integer (int) and binary (bin). In this case, select the equal to operator (=).

> **Note** Use the int (integer) operator when you need a constraint, such as total employees, to be an integer value instead of a real number. Use the bin (binary) operator when you have a constraint that must be either TRUE or FALSE (or 1 or 0).

5. If you chose a comparison operator in step 4, use the **Constraint** box to enter the value by which you want to restrict the cell. In this case, enter **0**. Figure 20-4 shows the completed dialog box for this example.

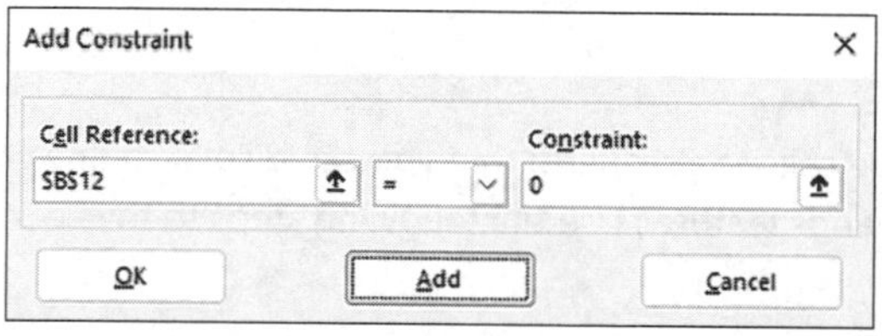

FIGURE 20-4 Use the Add Constraint dialog box to specify the constraints you want to place on the solution.

6. If you want to enter more constraints, select **Add** and repeat steps 3 through 5. For the example, you also need to constrain cell C12 (the Product Profit formula for the Langstrom wrench) so that it, too, equals 0.

7. When you're done, select **OK** to return to the **Solver Parameters** dialog box. Excel displays your constraints in the **Subject To The Constraints** list box.

> **Note** You can add a maximum of 100 constraints. Also, if you need to make a change to a constraint before you begin solving, select the constraint in the **Subject To The Constraints** list box, select **Change**, and then make your adjustments in the **Change Constraint** dialog box that appears. If you want to delete a constraint that you no longer need, select it and then select **Delete**.

8. Select **Solve**. Solver again tries to find a solution, but this time it uses your constraints as guidelines. Note that you might need to select **Continue** one or more times while Solver works on the solution.

Figure 20-5 shows the results of the break-even analysis after the constraints have been added. As you can see, Solver was able to find a solution in which both product margins are 0.

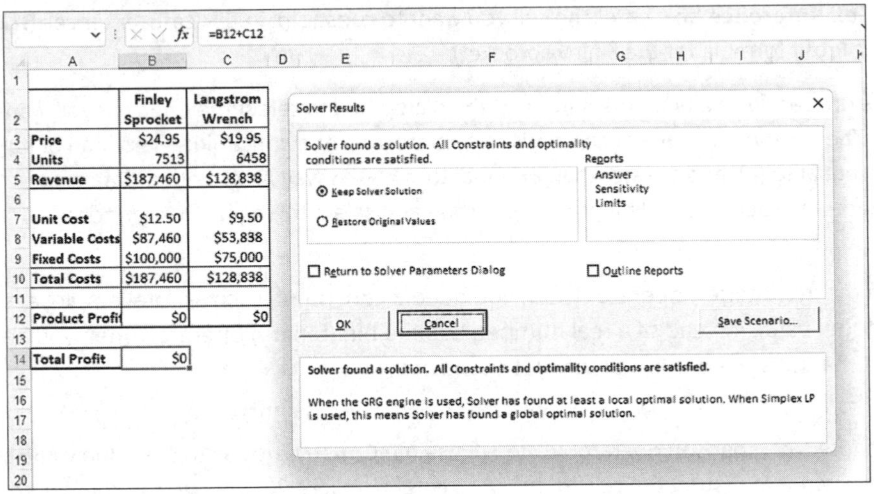

FIGURE 20-5 The worksheet shows the solution to the break-even analysis after the constraints have been added.

Saving a solution as a scenario

If Solver finds a solution, you can save the variable cells as a scenario that you can display at any time. (See Chapter 19 to learn more about Excel's Scenarios feature.) Use the following steps to save a solution as a scenario:

1. Select **Data** > **Solver** to display the **Solver Parameters** dialog box.

2. Enter the appropriate objective cell, variable cells, and constraints, if necessary.

3. Select **Solve** to begin solving.

4. If Solver finds a solution, select **Save Scenario** in the **Solver Results** dialog box. Excel displays the **Save Scenario** dialog box.

5. Use the **Scenario Name** text box to enter a name for the scenario.

6. Select **OK**. Excel returns you to the **Solver Results** dialog box.

7. Keep or discard the solution, as appropriate.

Setting other Solver options

Most Solver problems should respond to the basic objective-cell/variable-cell/constraint-cell model you've looked at so far. However, for times when you're having trouble getting a solution for a particular model, Solver has a number of options that might help. Select **Data** > **Solver** and, in the **Solver Parameters** dialog box, first note the check box named **Make Unconstrained Variables Non-Negative**. Select this check box to force Solver to assume that the cells listed in the **By Changing Variable Cells** list must have values greater than or equal to 0. This is the same as adding >=0 constraints for each of those cells, so it operates as a kind of implicit constraint on them. This is handy in models that use quite a few variable cells, none of which should have negative values.

Selecting the method Solver uses

Solver can use one of several solving methods—called *engines*—to perform its calculations. In the **Solver Parameters** dialog box, use the **Select A Solving Method** list to select one of the following engines:

- **Simplex LP:** Select this engine (where LP is short for linear programming) if your worksheet model is linear. In the simplest possible terms, a *linear* model is one in which the variables are not raised to any powers, and none of the so-called transcendent functions—such as SIN and COS—is used. A linear model is so named because it can be charted as straight lines. If your formulas are linear, be sure to select Simplex LP because this will greatly speed up the solution process.

- **GRG Nonlinear:** Select this engine (where GRG is short for generalized reduced gradient) if your worksheet model is nonlinear and smooth. In general terms, a *smooth* model is one in which a graph of the equation used would show no sharp edges or breaks (called *discontinuities*).

- **Evolutionary:** Select this engine if your worksheet model is nonlinear and nonsmooth. In practical terms, this usually means your worksheet model uses functions such as XLOOKUP, VLOOKUP, HLOOKUP, CHOOSE, and IF to calculate the values of the variable cells or constraint cells.

> **Note** If you're not sure which engine to use, start with Simplex LP. If it turns out that your model is nonlinear, Solver will recognize this and let you know. You can then try the GRG Nonlinear engine; if Solver can't seem to converge on a solution, you should try the Evolutionary engine.

Controlling how Solver works

Solver has several options that you can set to determine how the tool performs its tasks. To see these options, open the **Solver Parameters** dialog box and select **Options** to display the **Options** dialog box, shown in Figure 20-6.

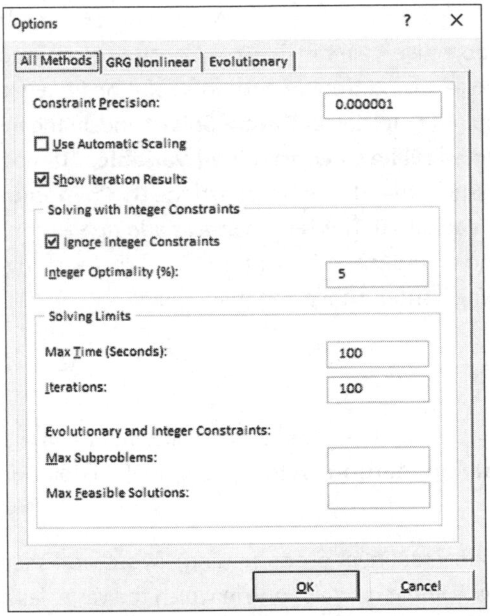

FIGURE 20-6 The Options dialog box controls how Solver solves a problem.

The following options in the **All Methods** tab control how Solver works no matter which method you use:

- **Constraint Precision:** This number determines how close a constraint cell must be to the constraint value you entered before Solver declares the constraint satisfied. The higher the precision (that is, the lower the number), the more accurate the solution, but the longer it takes Solver to find it.

- **Use Automatic Scaling:** Select this check box if your model has variable cells that are significantly different in magnitude. For example, you might have a variable cell that controls customer discount (a number between 0 and 1) and sales (a number that might be in the millions).

- **Show Iteration Results:** Leave this check box selected to have Solver pause and show you its trial solutions, as demonstrated in Figure 20-7. To resume, select **Continue** in the **Show Trial Solution** dialog box. If you find these intermediate results annoying, deselect the **Show Iteration Results** check box.

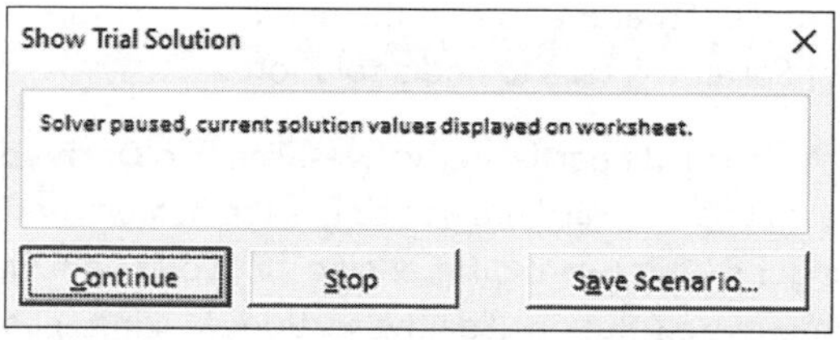

FIGURE 20-7 When the Show Iteration Results check box is selected, Solver displays the Show Trial Solution dialog box so that you can view each intermediate solution.

- **Ignore Integer Constraints:** Integer programming (in which you have integer constraints) can take a long time because of the complexity involved in finding solutions that satisfy exact integer constraints. If you find your models taking an abnormally long time to solve, select this check box. (Alternatively, increase the value in the **Integer Optimality** box, discussed next, to get an approximate solution.)

- **Integer Optimality:** If you have integer constraints, this box determines what percentage of the integer Solver has to be within before declaring the constraint satisfied. For example, if the integer tolerance is set to 5 (that is, 0.05 percent), Solver will declare a cell with the value 99.95 to be close enough to 100 to declare it an integer.

- **Max Time:** The amount of time Solver takes is a function of the size and complexity of the model, the number of variable cells and constraint cells, and the other Solver options you've chosen. If you find that Solver runs out of time before finding a solution, increase the number in this text box.

- **Iterations:** This box controls the number of iterations Solver tries before giving up on a problem. Increasing this number gives Solver more of a chance to solve the problem, but it takes correspondingly longer.

- **Max Subproblems:** If you use the Evolutionary engine or if you deselect the **Ignore Integer Constraints** check box, the value in the **Max Subproblems** box tells Solver the maximum number of subproblems it can investigate before it asks if you want to continue. A *subproblem* is an intermediate step that Solver uses to get closer to the final solution.

- **Max Feasible Solutions:** If you use the Evolutionary engine or if you deselect the **Ignore Integer Constraints** check box, the value in the **Max Feasible Solutions** box tells Solver the maximum number of feasible solutions that it can generate before it asks if you want to continue. A *feasible solution* is any solution (even a nonoptimal one) that satisfies all the constraints.

If you want to use the GRG Nonlinear engine, consider the following options in the **GRG Nonlinear** tab:

- **Convergence:** This number determines when Solver decides that it has reached (converged on) a solution. If the objective cell value changes by less than the **Convergence** value for five straight iterations, then Solver decides that a solution has been found, and it stops iterating. Enter a number between 0 and 1, keeping in mind that the smaller the number, the more accurate the solution will be but also the longer Solver will take to find a solution.

- **Derivatives:** Some models require Solver to calculate partial derivatives. The two **Derivatives** options specify the method Solver uses to do this. Forward differencing is the default method. The Central differencing method takes longer than forward differencing, but you might want to try it when Solver reports that it can't improve a solution. (See the section "Making sense of Solver's messages," later in this chapter.)

- **Use Multistart:** Select this check box to run the GRG Nonlinear engine using its Multistart feature. This means that Solver automatically runs the GRG Nonlinear engine from a number of different starting points, which Solver selects at random (although see the **Require Bounds On Variables** item, later in the list, for more information on this). Solver then gathers the points that produced locally optimal solutions and compares them to come up with a globally optimal solution. Use Multistart if the GRG Nonlinear engine is having trouble finding a solution to your model.

- **Population Size:** If you select the **Use Multistart** check box, use this text box to set the number of starting points that Solver uses. If Solver has trouble finding a globally optimal solution, try increasing the population size; if Solver takes a long time to find a globally optimal solution, try reducing the population size.

- **Random Seed:** If you select the **Use Multistart** check box, Solver generates random starting points for the GRG Nonlinear engine, and the random number generator is seeded with the current system clock value. This is almost always the best way to go. However, if you want to ensure that the GRG Nonlinear engine always uses the same starting points for consecutive runs, enter an integer (nonzero) value in the **Random Seed** text box.

- **Require Bounds On Variables:** Leave this check box selected to improve the likelihood that the GRG Nonlinear engine finds a solution when you use the Multistart method. This means that you must add constraints that specify both a lower bound and an upper bound for each cell in the **By Changing Variable Cells** range box. When Solver generates the random starting points for the GRG Nonlinear engine, it generates values that are within these lower and upper bounds, so it's more likely to find a solution (assuming that you enter realistic bounds for the variable cells). It's possible to use the GRG Nonlinear engine if you deselect the **Require Bounds On Variables** check box, but it means that Solver must select its random starting points from, essentially, an infinite supply of values, so it's less likely to find a globally optimal solution.

If you want to use the Evolutionary engine, you can configure the engine using the options in the **Evolutionary** tab. The **Convergence**, **Population Size**, **Random Seed**, and **Require Bounds On Variables** options are the same as those in the **GRG Nonlinear** tab, discussed earlier. The **Evolutionary** tab has the following unique options:

- **Mutation Rate:** The Evolutionary engine operates by randomly trying out certain values, usually within upper and lower bounds of the variable cells (assuming that you leave the **Require Bounds On Variables** check box selected), and if a trial solution is found to be "fit," that result becomes part of the *solution population*. It then mutates members of this population to see if it can find better solutions. The **Mutation Rate** value is the probability that a member of the solution population will be mutated. If you're having trouble getting good results from the Evolutionary engine, try increasing the mutation rate.

- **Maximum Time Without Improvement:** This is the maximum number of seconds the Evolutionary engine will take without finding a better solution before it asks if you want to stop the iteration. If you find that the Evolutionary engine runs out of time before finding a solution, increase the number in this text box.

Working with Solver models

Excel attaches your most recent Solver parameters to the worksheet when you save it. If you want to save different sets of parameters, you can do so by following these steps:

1. Select **Data** > **Solver** to display the Solver Parameters dialog box.

2. Enter the parameters you want to save.

3. Select **Options** to display the Options dialog box.

4. Enter the options you want to save and then select **OK** to return to the **Solver Parameters** dialog box.

5. Select **Load/Save**. Solver displays the **Load/Save Model** dialog box to prompt you to enter a range in which to store the model.

6. Enter the range in the **Range** box. Note that you don't need to specify the entire area—just the first cell. Keep in mind that Solver displays the data in a column, so pick a cell with enough empty space below it to hold all the data. You'll need one cell for the objective cell reference, one for the variable cells, one for each constraint, and one to hold the array of Solver options.

7. Select **Save**. Solver gathers the data, enters it into your selected range, and then returns you to the **Solver Parameters** dialog box.

Figure 20-8 shows an example of a saved model (the range F4:F9). I've changed the worksheet view to show formulas, and I've added some explanatory text so you can see exactly how Solver saves the model. Notice that the formula for the objective cell (F4) includes both the target (B14) and the target value (=0).

> **Note** To toggle formulas on and off in Excel, select **Formulas**, **Show Formulas** or press Ctrl+` (backtick).

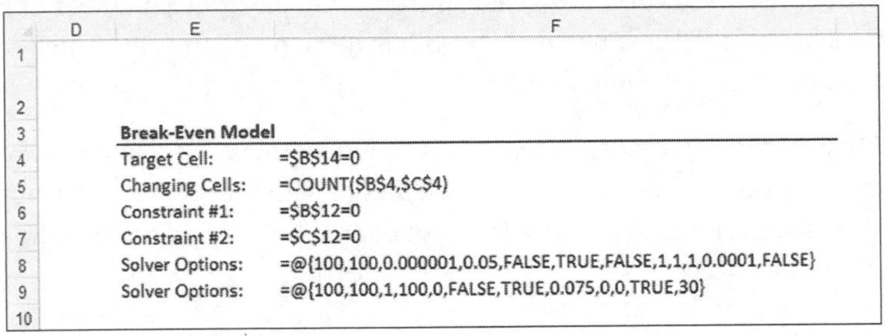

FIGURE 20-8 This saved Solver model has the formulas turned on so you can see what Solver saves to the sheet.

To use your saved settings, follow these steps:

1. Select **Data** > **Solver** to display the **Solver Parameters** dialog box.

2. Select **Load/Save**. Solver displays the **Load/Save Model** dialog box.

3. Select the entire range that contains the saved model.

4. Select **Load**. Excel asks if you want to replace the current model or merge the saved model with the current model.

5. Select **Replace** to use the saved model cells or select **Merge** to add the saved model to the current Solver model. Excel returns you to the **Solver Parameters** dialog box.

Making sense of Solver's messages

When Solver finishes its calculations, it displays the **Solver Results** dialog box and a message that tells you what happened. Some of these messages are straightforward, but others are more than a little cryptic. This section looks at the most common messages and gives their translations.

If Solver finds a solution successfully, you see one of the following messages:

- **Solver found a solution. All constraints and optimality conditions are satisfied.** This is the message you hope to see. It means that the value you wanted for the objective cell has been found, and Solver was able to find the solution while meeting your constraints within the precision and integer tolerance levels you set.

- **Solver has converged to the current solution. All constraints are satisfied.** Solver normally assumes that it has a solution if the value of the objective cell formula remains virtually unchanged during a few iterations. This is called *converging to a solution*. Such is the case with this message, but it doesn't necessarily mean that Solver has found a solution. The iterative process might just be taking a long time, or the initial values in the variable cells might have been set too far from the solution. You should try rerunning Solver with different values. You also can try using a higher precision setting (that is, entering a smaller number in the **Constraint Precision** text box).

- **Solver cannot improve the current solution. All constraints are satisfied.** This message tells you that Solver has found a solution, but it might not be the optimal one. Try setting the precision to a smaller number or, if you're using the GRG Nonlinear engine, try using the central differencing method for partial derivatives.

If Solver doesn't find a solution, you see one of the following messages telling you why:

- **The Set Cell values do not converge.** This means that the value of the objective cell formula has no finite limit. For example, if you're trying to maximize profit based on product price and unit costs, Solver won't find a solution; the reason is that continually higher prices and lower costs lead to higher profit. You need to add (or change) constraints in your model, such as setting a maximum price or minimum cost level (for example, the amount of fixed costs).

- **Solver could not find a feasible solution.** Solver couldn't find a solution that satisfied all your constraints. Check your constraints to make sure they're realistic and consistent.

- **Stop chosen when the maximum x limit was reached.** This message appears when Solver bumps up against either the maximum time limit or the maximum iteration limit. If it appears that Solver is heading toward a solution, select **Keep Solver Solution** and try again.

- **The conditions for Assume Linear Model are not satisfied.** Solver based its iterative process on a linear model, but when the results are put into the worksheet, they don't conform to the linear model. You need to select the GRG Nonlinear engine and try again.

Case study: Solving the transportation problem

The best way to learn how to use a complex tool such as Solver is to get your hands dirty with some examples. Excel thoughtfully comes with several sample worksheets that use simplified models to demonstrate the various problems Solver can handle. This case study looks at one of these worksheets in detail.

The *transportation problem* is the classic model for solving linear programming problems. The basic goal is to minimize the costs of shipping goods from several production plants to various warehouses scattered around the country. Your constraints are as follows:

- The amount shipped to each warehouse must meet the warehouse's demand for goods.
- The amount shipped from each plant must be greater than or equal to 0.
- The amount shipped from each plant can't exceed the plant's supply of goods.

Figure 20-9 shows the model for solving the transportation problem.

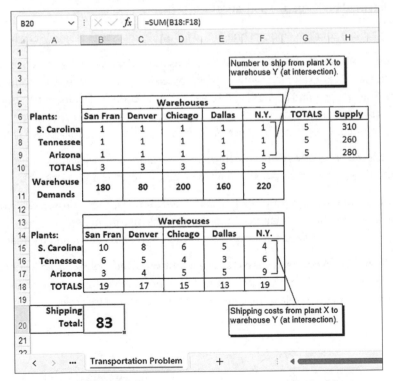

FIGURE 20-9 This is a worksheet for solving the transportation problem.

The top table (A6:F10) lists the three plants (A7:A9) and the five warehouses (B6:F6). This table holds the number of units shipped from each plant to each warehouse. In the Solver model, these are the variable cells. The total shipped to each warehouse (B10:F10) must match the warehouse demands (B11:F11) to satisfy constraint number 1. The amount shipped from each plant (B7:F9) must be greater than or equal to 0 to satisfy constraint number 2. The total shipped from each plant (G7:G9) must be less than or equal to the available supply for each plant (H7:H9) to satisfy constraint number 3.

> **Note** When you need to use a range of values in a constraint, you don't need to set up a separate constraint for each cell. Instead, you can compare entire ranges. For example, the constraint that the total shipped from each plant must be less than or equal to the plant supply can be entered as follows:
>
> `G7:G9 <= H7:H9`

The bottom table (A14:F18) holds the corresponding shipping costs from each plant to each warehouse. The total shipping cost (cell B20) is the objective cell you want to minimize.

Figure 20-10 shows the final **Solver Parameters** dialog box that you'll use to solve this problem. (Note also that I selected the Simplex LP engine in the **Select A Solver Method** list.) Figure 20-11 shows the solution that Solver found.

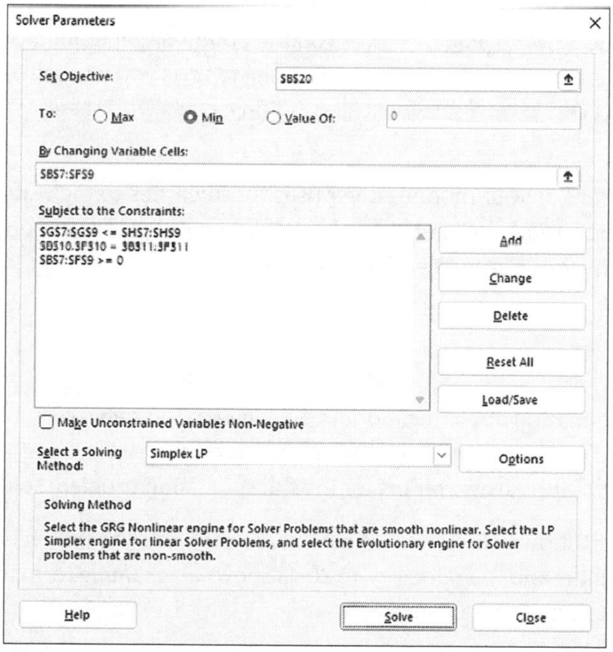

FIGURE 20-10 The Solver Parameters dialog box is filled in for the transportation problem.

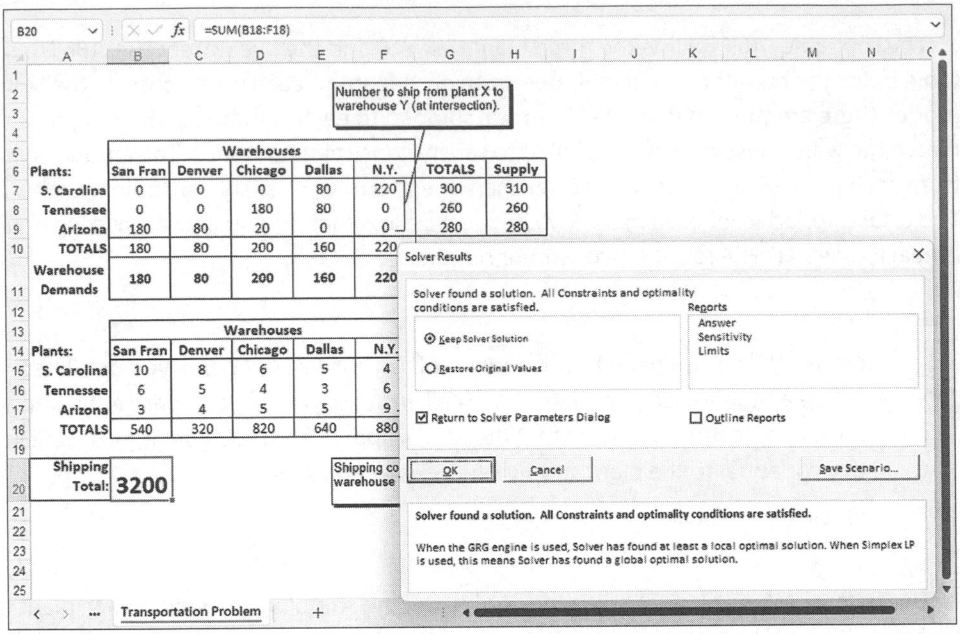

FIGURE 20-11 This is the optimal solution for the transportation problem.

Displaying Solver's reports

When Solver finds a solution, the Solver dialog box gives you the option of generating three reports: the Answer report, Sensitivity report, and Limits report. Select the reports you want to see in the **Reports** list box and then select **OK**. Excel displays each report on its own worksheet.

> **Tip** If you've named the cells in your model, Solver uses these names to make its reports easier to read. If you haven't already done so, you should define names for the objective cell, variable cells, and constraint cells before creating a report.

The Answer report

The Answer report displays information about the model's objective cell, variable cells, and constraints. For the objective cell and variable cells, Solver shows the original and final values. For example, Figure 20-12 shows this portion of the Answer report for the transportation problem solution.

For the constraints, the report shows the address and name for each cell, the final value, the formulas, and two values called the *status* and the *slack*. Figure 20-13 shows an example from the transportation problem. The status can be one of three values:

- **Binding:** The final value in the constraint cell equals the constraint value (or the constraint boundary, if the constraint is an inequality).

- **Not Binding:** The constraint cell value satisfied the constraint, but it doesn't equal the constraint boundary.
- **Not Satisfied:** The constraint was not satisfied.

Microsoft Excel 16.0 Answer Report
Worksheet: [Chapter20.xlsx]Transportation Problem
Report Created: 10/25/2021 3:20:31 PM
Result: Solver found a solution. All Constraints and optimality conditions are satisfied.
Solver Engine
Engine: Simplex LP
Solution Time: 0.078 Seconds.
Iterations: 17 Subproblems: 0
Solver Options
Max Time 100 sec, Iterations 100, Precision 0.000001
Max Subproblems Unlimited, Max Integer Sols Unlimited, Integer Tolerance 5%, Solve Without Integer Constraints

Objective Cell (Min)

Cell	Name	Original Value	Final Value
$B$20	Shipping Total: San Fran	83	3200

Variable Cells

Cell	Name	Original Value	Final Value	Integer
$B$7	S. Carolina San Fran	1	0	Contin
$C$7	S. Carolina Denver	1	0	Contin
$D$7	S. Carolina Chicago	1	0	Contin
$E$7	S. Carolina Dallas	1	80	Contin
$F$7	S. Carolina N.Y.	1	220	Contin
$B$8	Tennessee San Fran	1	0	Contin
$C$8	Tennessee Denver	1	0	Contin
$D$8	Tennessee Chicago	1	180	Contin
$E$8	Tennessee Dallas	1	80	Contin
$F$8	Tennessee N.Y.	1	0	Contin
$B$9	Arizona San Fran	1	180	Contin
$C$9	Arizona Denver	1	80	Contin
$D$9	Arizona Chicago	1	20	Contin
$E$9	Arizona Dallas	1	0	Contin

< > ... Answer Report 1 | Sensitivity Report 1 | ... +

FIGURE 20-12 This figure shows the Objective Cell and Variable Cells sections of Solver's Answer report.

The slack is the difference between the final constraint cell value and the value of the original constraint (or its boundary). In the optimal solution for the transportation problem, for example, the total shipped from the South Carolina plant is 300, but the constraint on this total was 310 (the total supply). Therefore, the slack value is 10 (or close enough to it). If the status is binding, the slack value is always 0.

	A	B	C	D	E	F	G
37							
38	Constraints						
39		Cell	Name	Cell Value	Formula	Status	Slack
40		$G$7	S. Carolina TOTALS	300	$G$7<=$H$7	Not Binding	10
41		$G$8	Tennessee TOTALS	260	$G$8<=$H$8	Binding	0
42		$G$9	Arizona TOTALS	280	$G$9<=$H$9	Binding	0
43		$B$10	TOTALS San Fran	180	$B$10=$B$11	Binding	0
44		$C$10	TOTALS Denver	80	$C$10=$C$11	Binding	0
45		$D$10	TOTALS Chicago	200	$D$10=$D$11	Binding	0
46		$E$10	TOTALS Dallas	160	$E$10=$E$11	Binding	0
47		$F$10	TOTALS N.Y.	220	$F$10=$F$11	Binding	0
48		$B$7	S. Carolina San Fran	0	$B$7>=0	Binding	0
49		$C$7	S. Carolina Denver	0	$C$7>=0	Binding	0
50		$D$7	S. Carolina Chicago	0	$D$7>=0	Binding	0
51		$E$7	S. Carolina Dallas	80	$E$7>=0	Not Binding	80
52		$F$7	S. Carolina N.Y.	220	$F$7>=0	Not Binding	220
53		$B$8	Tennessee San Fran	0	$B$8>=0	Binding	0
54		$C$8	Tennessee Denver	0	$C$8>=0	Binding	0
55		$D$8	Tennessee Chicago	180	$D$8>=0	Not Binding	180
56		$E$8	Tennessee Dallas	80	$E$8>=0	Not Binding	80
57		$F$8	Tennessee N.Y.	0	$F$8>=0	Binding	0
58		$B$9	Arizona San Fran	180	$B$9>=0	Not Binding	180
59		$C$9	Arizona Denver	80	$C$9>=0	Not Binding	80
60		$D$9	Arizona Chicago	20	$D$9>=0	Not Binding	20
61		$E$9	Arizona Dallas	0	$E$9>=0	Binding	0
62		$F$9	Arizona N.Y.	0	$F$9>=0	Binding	0
63							

FIGURE 20-13 This figure shows the Constraints section of Solver's Answer report.

The Sensitivity report

The Sensitivity report attempts to show how sensitive a solution is to changes in the model's formulas. The layout of the Sensitivity report depends on the type of model you're using. For a linear model (that is, a model in which you selected the Simplex LP engine), you see a report similar to the one shown in Figure 20-14.

Microsoft Excel 16.0 Sensitivity Report
Worksheet: [Chapter20.xlsx]Transportation Problem
Report Created: 10/25/2021 3:20:31 PM

Variable Cells

Cell	Name	Final Value	Reduced Cost	Objective Coefficient	Allowable Increase	Allowable Decrease
$B$7	S. Carolina San Fran	0	6	10	1E+30	6
$C$7	S. Carolina Denver	0	3	8	1E+30	3
$D$7	S. Carolina Chicago	0	0	6	1E+30	0
$E$7	S. Carolina Dallas	80	0	5	0	1
$F$7	S. Carolina N.Y.	220	0	4	4	1E+30
$B$8	Tennessee San Fran	0	4	6	1E+30	4
$C$8	Tennessee Denver	0	2	5	1E+30	2
$D$8	Tennessee Chicago	180	0	4	0	1
$E$8	Tennessee Dallas	80	0	3	1	0
$F$8	Tennessee N.Y.	0	4	6	1E+30	4
$B$9	Arizona San Fran	180	0	3	4	1E+30
$C$9	Arizona Denver	80	0	4	2	1E+30
$D$9	Arizona Chicago	20	0	5	1	2
$E$9	Arizona Dallas	0	1	5	1E+30	1
$F$9	Arizona N.Y.	0	6	9	1E+30	6

Constraints

Cell	Name	Final Value	Shadow Price	Constraint R.H. Side	Allowable Increase	Allowable Decrease
$G$7	S. Carolina TOTALS	300	0	310	1E+30	10
$G$8	Tennessee TOTALS	260	-2	260	80	10
$G$9	Arizona TOTALS	280	-1	280	80	10
$B$10	TOTALS San Fran	180	4	180	10	80
$C$10	TOTALS Denver	80	5	80	10	80
$D$10	TOTALS Chicago	200	6	200	10	80
$E$10	TOTALS Dallas	160	5	160	10	80

< > ⋯ Answer Report 1 **Sensitivity Report 1** ⋯ +

FIGURE 20-14 This figure shows the Variable Cells section of Solver's Sensitivity report.

This report is divided into two sections. The top section, called Variable Cells, shows for each cell the address and name of the cell, its final value, and the following measures:

- **Reduced Cost:** The corresponding increase in the objective cell, given a one-unit increase in the variable cell

- **Objective Coefficient:** The relative relationship between the variable cell and the objective cell

- **Allowable Increase:** The change in the objective coefficient before there would be an increase in the optimal value of the variable cell

- **Allowable Decrease:** The change in the objective coefficient before there would be a decrease in the optimal value of the variable cell

The bottom section of the Sensitivity report, called Constraints (see Figure 20-15), shows for each constraint cell the address and name of the cell, its final value, and the following values:

- **Shadow Price:** The corresponding increase in the objective cell, given a one-unit increase in the constraint value

- **Constraint R.H. Side:** The constraint value that you specified (that is, the right-hand side of the constraint equation)

- **Allowable Increase:** The change in the constraint value before there would be an increase in the optimal value of the variable cell

- **Allowable Decrease:** The change in the constraint value before there would be a decrease in the optimal value of the variable cell

Cell	Name	Final Value	Shadow Price	Constraint R.H. Side	Allowable Increase	Allowable Decrease
$G$7	S. Carolina TOTALS	300	0	310	1E+30	10
$G$8	Tennessee TOTALS	260	-2	260	80	10
$G$9	Arizona TOTALS	280	-1	280	80	10
$B$10	TOTALS San Fran	180	4	180	10	80
$C$10	TOTALS Denver	80	5	80	10	80
$D$10	TOTALS Chicago	200	6	200	10	80
$E$10	TOTALS Dallas	160	5	160	10	80
$F$10	TOTALS N.Y.	220	4	220	10	220

FIGURE 20-15 This figure shows the Constraints section of Solver's Sensitivity report.

The Sensitivity report for a nonlinear model shows the variable cells and the constraint cells. For each cell, the report displays the address, name, and final value. The Variable Cells section also shows the Reduced Gradient value, which measures the corresponding increase in the objective cell, given a one-unit increase in the variable cell (similar to the Reduced Cost measure for a linear model). The Constraints section also shows the Lagrange Multiplier value, which measures the corresponding increase in the objective cell, given a one-unit increase in the constraint value (similar to the Shadow Price in the linear report).

The Limits report

The Limits report, shown in Figure 20-16, displays the objective cell and its value, as well as the variable cells and their addresses, names, values, and the following measures:

- **Lower Limit:** The minimum value that the variable cell can assume while keeping the other variable cells fixed and still satisfying the constraints

- **Upper Limit:** The maximum value that the variable cell can assume while keeping the other variable cells fixed and still satisfying the constraints

- **Objective Result:** The objective cell's value when the variable cell is at the lower limit or upper limit

1	Microsoft Excel 16.0 Limits Report								
2	Worksheet: [Chapter20.xlsx]Transportation Problem								
3	Report Created: 10/25/2021 3:20:32 PM								

		Objective							
	Cell	Name	Value						
	$B$20	Shipping Total: San Fran	3200						

Cell	Variable Name	Value	Lower Limit	Objective Result	Upper Limit	Objective Result
$B$7	S. Carolina San Fran	0	0	3200	0	3200
$C$7	S. Carolina Denver	0	0	3200	0	3200
$D$7	S. Carolina Chicago	0	0	3200	0	3200
$E$7	S. Carolina Dallas	80	80	3200	80	3200
$F$7	S. Carolina N.Y.	220	220	3200	220	3200
$B$8	Tennessee San Fran	0	0	3200	0	3200
$C$8	Tennessee Denver	0	0	3200	0	3200
$D$8	Tennessee Chicago	180	180	3200	180	3200
$E$8	Tennessee Dallas	80	80	3200	80	3200
$F$8	Tennessee N.Y.	0	0	3200	0	3200
$B$9	Arizona San Fran	180	180	3200	180	3200
$C$9	Arizona Denver	80	80	3200	80	3200
$D$9	Arizona Chicago	20	20	3200	20	3200
$E$9	Arizona Dallas	0	0	3200	0	3200
$F$9	Arizona N.Y.	0	0	3200	0	3200

Sensitivity Report 1   **Limits Report 1**

FIGURE 20-16 This figure shows Solver's Limits report.

Index

Symbols

W

X

Y-Z

Plug into learning at

MicrosoftPressStore.com

The Microsoft Press Store by Pearson offers:

- Free U.S. shipping

- Buy an eBook, get three formats – Includes PDF, EPUB, and MOBI to use with your computer, tablet, and mobile devices

- Print & eBook Best Value Packs

- eBook Deal of the Week – Save up to 50% on featured title

- Newsletter – Be the first to hear about new releases, announcements, special offers, and more

- Register your book – Find companion files, errata, and product updates, plus receive a special coupon* to save on your next purchase